THE MAKING OF CONSTITUTIONAL DEMOCRACY

This book addresses a palpable, yet widely neglected, tension in legal discourse. In our everyday legal practices – whether taking place in a courtroom, classroom, law firm or elsewhere – we routinely and unproblematically talk of the activities of creating and applying law. However, when legal scholars have analysed this distinction in their theories (rather than simply assuming it), many have undermined it, if not dismissed it as untenable.

The author shows that the relevance of distinguishing between law-creation and law-application transcends the boundaries of jurisprudential enquiry and is a crucial component of political theory. For if there is no possibility of applying a legal rule that was created by a different institution at a previous moment in time, then our current constitutional-democratic frameworks are effectively empty vessels which conceal a power relationship between public authorities and citizens which is very different from the one on which constitutional democracy is grounded.

After problematising the most relevant objections in the literature, the book presents a comprehensive defence of the distinction between creation and application of law within the structure of constitutional democracy. It does so through an integrated jurisprudential methodology, which combines insights from different disciplines (including history, anthropology, political science, philosophy of language and philosophy of action) while also casting new light on long-standing issues in public law, such as the role of legal discretion in the law-making process and the scope of the separation of powers doctrine.

Volume 13 in the series Law and Practical Reason

Law and Practical Reason

The intention of this series is that it should encompass monographs and collections of essays that address the fundamental issues in legal philosophy. The foci are conceptual and normative in character, not empirical. Studies addressing the idea of law as a species of practical reason are especially welcome. Recognising that there is no occasion sharply to distinguish analytic and systematic work in the field from historico-critical research, the editors also welcome studies in the history of legal philosophy. Contributions to the series, inevitably crossing disciplinary lines, will be of interest to students and professionals in moral, political, and legal philosophy.

General Editor

Prof George Pavlakos (Glasgow)

Advisory Board

Prof Robert Alexy (Kiel)
Prof Samantha Besson (Collége de France and Fribourg, CH)
Prof Emilios Christodoulidis (Glasgow)
Prof Sean Coyle (Birmingham)
Prof Mattias Kumm (New York and Berlin)
Prof Stanley Paulson (St Louis and Kiel)
Prof Joseph Raz (Columbia Law School and King's College London)†
Prof Arthur Ripstein (Toronto)
Prof Scott Shapiro (Yale Law School)
Prof Victor Tadros (Warwick)

Recent titles in the series

Volume 7: Shared Authority
Dimitrios Kyritsis

Volume 8: Private Law and the Value of Choice
Emmanuel Voyiakis

Volume 9: Freedom and Force: Essays on Kant's Legal Philosophy
Edited by *Sari Kisilevsky and Martin J Stone*

Volume 10: The Nature and Value of Vagueness in the Law
Hrafn Asgeirsson

Volume 11: Law's Humility: Enlarging the Scope of Jurisprudential Disagreement
Triantafyllos Gkouvas

Volume 12: Rightful Relations with Distant Strangers: Kant, the EU, and the Wider World
Aravind Ganesh

Volume 13: The Making of Constitutional Democracy: From Creation to Application of Law
Paolo Sandro

The Making of
Constitutional Democracy

From Creation to Application of Law

Paolo Sandro

·HART·
OXFORD · LONDON · NEW YORK · NEW DELHI · SYDNEY

HART PUBLISHING

Bloomsbury Publishing Plc

Kemp House, Chawley Park, Cumnor Hill, Oxford, OX2 9PH, UK

1385 Broadway, New York, NY 10018, USA

29 Earlsfort Terrace, Dublin 2, Ireland

HART PUBLISHING, the Hart/Stag logo, BLOOMSBURY and the Diana logo are
trademarks of Bloomsbury Publishing Plc

First published in Great Britain 2022

First published in hardback, 2022

Paperback edition, 2024

Copyright © Paolo Sandro, 2022

Paolo Sandro has asserted his right under the Copyright, Designs and
Patents Act 1988 to be identified as Author of this work.

All rights reserved. No part of this publication may be reproduced or transmitted in any form or by any
means, electronic or mechanical, including photocopying, recording, or any information storage
or retrieval system, without prior permission in writing from the publishers.

While every care has been taken to ensure the accuracy of this work, no responsibility for loss or
damage occasioned to any person acting or refraining from action as a result of any statement in it can
be accepted by the authors, editors or publishers.

All UK Government legislation and other public sector information used in the work is Crown Copyright ©.
All House of Lords and House of Commons information used in the work is Parliamentary Copyright ©.
This information is reused under the terms of the Open Government Licence v3.0 (http://www.
nationalarchives.gov.uk/doc/open-government-licence/version/3) except where otherwise stated.

All Eur-lex material used in the work is © European Union,
http://eur-lex.europa.eu/, 1998–2024.

A catalogue record for this book is available from the British Library.

Library of Congress Cataloging-in-Publication data

Names: Sandro, Paolo, author.

Title: The making of constitutional democracy : from creation to application of law / Paolo Sandro.

Description: Oxford ; New York : Hart, 2022. | Series: Law and practical reason ; volume 13 |
Based on author's thesis (doctoral – University of Edinburgh, 2014) issued under title: Creation and
application of law : a neglected distinction. | Includes bibliographical references and index.

Identifiers: LCCN 2021042195 (print) | LCCN 2021042196 (ebook) | ISBN 9781509905225
(hardback) | ISBN 9781509955213 (paperback) | ISBN 9781509905218 (pdf) |
ISBN 9781509905232 (Epub)

Subjects: LCSH: Effectiveness and validity of law. | Law—Methodology. | Law—Political
aspects. | Democracy.

Classification: LCC K260 .S26 2021 (print) | LCC K260 (ebook) | DDC 340/.11—dc23/eng/20211005

LC record available at https://lccn.loc.gov/2021042195

LC ebook record available at https://lccn.loc.gov/2021042196

ISBN:	PB:	978-1-50995-521-3
	ePDF:	978-1-50990-521-8
	ePub:	978-1-50990-523-2

Typeset by Compuscript Ltd, Shannon

To find out more about our authors and books visit www.hartpublishing.co.uk.
Here you will find extracts, author information, details of forthcoming events
and the option to sign up for our newsletters.

To my parents, Carolina Pandolfi and Mauro Sandro. Grazie

Acknowledgements

THIS BOOK WOULD not have been possible without the support, over the years, of a number of good people. Therefore, the lines that follow are, for me, the most important lines in the book. The usual disclaimer applies, to wit: I am of course responsible for whatever mistakes and omissions are there in the book.

Most of the arguments developed here originated as a part of my PhD project at the University of Edinburgh under the supervision of Claudio Michelon and Neil Walker. Their support, both during the work on the Ph.D. and thereafter, has lent to me an unwavering source of resilience in the face of the usual rejections and setbacks that, I reckon, take place in most academic careers. I also want to thank my examiners, Timothy Endicott and Euan MacDonald, for their generous engagement with my PhD thesis, which prompted me to reconsider and improve many of the underlying assumptions of the work in the years following the viva.

George Pavlakos, the General Editor of the Law and Practical Reason Series, believed in the potential of this work from very early on, prompting Hart to offer me a contract already at the point of my PhD thesis. This was a dream come true; I had met Richard Hart in Edinburgh in 2013 and was mesmerised by his passion and pride in publishing work in legal theory.

Since then, I am afraid that I have tested George Pavlakos' patience with me, for what were supposed to have been minor revisions of the thesis became a part of a substantial rewriting and expansion of the manuscript. All of this took a good bit longer than I had expected. I hope that the final product repays, at least in part, George's trust in me. I also wish to thank the team at Hart/ Bloomsbury: in particular Bill Asquith for initial support, and Kate Whetter and Rosemarie Mearns who have accompanied me in bringing the manuscript to completion.

At the University of Salford, I want to thank Nicolas Kang-Riou and David Rossati for providing vital intellectual stimulation and camaraderie during what I can only describe as challenging professional years, and Phil Scarf for substantive research support, particularly in the form of a trimester of research leave in the fall of 2018, which made possible the concentration I needed for the rewriting of the first part of the manuscript.

Martin Kelly, Alex Latham, and Felipe Oliveira de Sousa (who make up my own Fellowship of the Ring) not only have each read and commented on various parts of the work, but also continued to provide me with the support to navigate the Misty Mountains of academic life. Many more friends and colleagues have generously read and commented on drafts, encouraging me to clarify my ideas

viii *Acknowledgements*

and, at the same time, saving me from many mistakes: Zenon Bankowski, Donald Bello Hutt, Stefano Bertea, Eoin Carolan, Mathieu Carpentier, Pablo Castillo-Ortiz, Pierluigi Chiassoni, Robert Craig, David Duarte, Marco Goldoni, Riccardo Guastini, Andrew Halpin, Bernard Jackson, Marcin Matczak, Thomas McSweeney, José Juan Moreso, Georgios Papanicolaou, Giorgio Pino, Francesca Poggi, Torben Spaak, Vito Velluzzi, and Peter Verovšek. I could not be more grateful for their contributions. I also want to thank an anonymous reviewer for Hart, whose comments prompted me to add what is now the last chapter of the book (on the separation of powers), and George Dick, who agreed to proofread the entire manuscript and help me prepare it for publication. His help has been invaluable.

I presented earlier drafts of chapter three in Girona and Belgrade: my thanks go to Andrej Kristan, Miodrag Jovanović, and Bojan Spaic for inviting me, and to members of the audiences there for fruitful debate. The ideas in chapter seven were refined through discussion on two separate occasions: first at a special workshop on the separation of powers during the 2018 IACL Inaugural Younger Scholars Forum in Comparative Law, held in Fukuoka and organised by Daniel Wunder Hachem and Ren Yatsunami. The second occasion, in 2019, was the Inaugural Constitutional works-in-progress Workshop at the University College Dublin Centre for Constitutional Studies, organised by Eoin Carolan. To all of these good people as well as the participants at these events, go my heartfelt thanks.

I also benefitted immensely from the discussion of some of the themes underlying this book at the special workshop that I organised as part of the IVR 2019 World Congress in Lucerne. My gratitude go to all the participants on that occasion for their generous engagement: Mathieu Carpentier, Sebastián Figueroa Rubio, Paula Gaido, Mathias Klatt, Andrej Kristan, Marcin Matczak, Lorena Ramírez-Ludeña, Francesca Poggi, Brian Slocum, and Pauline Westerman.

I would not be writing this – or anything else, for that matter – without the love and support of my family and friends scattered around the world. I hope they are proud of me. Last but not least, the fact that Anastasia Shesterinina still plans on marrying me – notwithstanding how long it took to finish this book – is a testament to her patience and endurance as well as to my good fortune when our paths crossed. Since then, she has been partner, friend, driving force, discussant, editor, and so much more. Only Dante's words (*'L'amor che move il sole e l'altre stelle'*) can capture what she is to me.

PS
Salford
05/05/2021

Contents

Acknowledgements ....*vii*

Introduction 1
    I. Aims and Structure of the Work...9

1. **Law, Power, and Political Authority. On the Scope and**
    Limitations of the Work 17
        I.   Introduction...17
        II. Brief Methodological Remarks 19
        III. The Province of the Problem Determined: What is Law?.............23
        IV. Politics, Political Power, Political Authority....................26
        V. From Powers to Power. The Familiar Tale of the Ineluctability
          of the State..30
          A. And its Two-pronged Critique: Isonomia and 'Early' States 32
        VI. The Conditions of Existence of Political Authority: Insights
          from the Theory of Normative Orders 36

2. **The Dependence of Constitutional Democracy on the Distinction**
    between Creation and Application of Law 43
        I.   Introduction...43
        II. The Contested Relationship between Law and Politics....................47
        III. Law as *lex* and as *ius*: The Duality that Makes
          Constitutionalism Possible..50
        IV. From Constitutions to Constitutionalism: Narrowing
          the Focus of Constitutional Theory....................................55
        V. The (Proverbial) Tension between Democracy and
          Constitutionalism...60
        VI. Modern Constitutionalism as 'Legal Otherness'.......................64
        VII. The Two-fold Justificatory Dependence of Constitutional
          Democracy on the Idea of Application of Law 71

3. **A Critical Evaluation of Moderate Legal Realism**....................80
        I.   Introduction...80
        II. Realism vs Formalism 82

x   *Contents*

	III.	Let Us be Realist about Adjudication. What do Judges Eat for Breakfast?	85

III. Let Us be Realist about Adjudication. What do Judges Eat
for Breakfast? 85
IV. Realism and Realisms in Law: Meta-theory 87
V. The Lowest Common Denominator of Legal Realism 90
VI. The Two Axes of Rule-scepticism 93
    A. Radical-immanent Indeterminacy Thesis 94
    B. Radical-transcendental Indeterminacy Thesis 95
    C. Moderate-immanent Indeterminacy Thesis.........................97
    D. Moderate-transcendental Indeterminacy Thesis 99
VII. The Unbearable Lightness of Moderate Scepticism...................100
VIII. On the Normativity of Law, and On the Digestion of Judges......110

4. Towards a Unified Account of Discretion in Law.................................116
I. Introduction..116
II. HLA Hart and the Concept of Discretion. Back to the
Future?..119
III. Dworkin and the (Normative) No-Strong-Discretion Thesis 128
IV. Discretion as a Pervasive Feature of Kelsen's *Stufenbaulehre* 131
V. Discretion as Balancing in Klatt (and Alexy) 136
VI. The History of Discretion in the Administrative Domain 142
VII. Administrative Discretion in Germany 145
VIII. Discretion in the French-Italian Administrative Tradition...........149
IX. The Concept of Discretion in English Administrative Law 152
X. Towards a Unified Account of Discretion in Law 158
    A. Normative Discretion 162
    B. Interpretive Discretion 165
XI. Conclusion 168

**5. Law *and* Language and *as* Language. An Alternative Picture
of a Multifaceted Relationship...169**
I. Introduction..169
II. The Communicative Model of Law. A Two-way Affair?.............172
III. Beyond 'What is Said'. Speech-act Theory and the Rise
of Pragmatics in Legal Interpretation 178
IV. First Objection: Law as Language, Law and Language(s) 184
V. Second Objection: Speech-act vs Text-act Theory......................190
VI. Legal Texts as 'Autonomous' Text-acts 195
VII. An Alternative Theory of Legal Meaning: Semantic
Minimalism..200
VIII. Prolegomena to a Theory of Legal Interpretation......................205
IX. Conclusion 209

Contents xi

6. **Creation and Application of Law. An Analytical Distinction**.................211
   - I. Introduction 211
   - II. The Two Extremes: Rejecting vs Assuming the Distinction 213
   - III. Kelsen on the Relativity of the Distinction between Creation
     and Application of Law 216
   - IV. Creation of Law: Of the Typicality of Legal Rules 219
   - V. The Principle of Legality as a (Semantic) Meta-norm
     on Law-creation and Law-application 222
   - VI. Unpacking the Idea of 'Application of Law' 227
   - VII. The Potential Asymmetry between Norm-following and
     Norm-application..231
   - VIII. On the (Different) Normativity of Power-conferring Norms 234
   - IX. Can only Officials Apply the Law? 237
   - X. Form and Substance. Towards an Analytical Account of
     Law-application 240
   - XI. Conclusion..244
   - XII. PS One Final Objection: Interpretation, Interpretation,
     Interpretation! 245

7. **The Separation of Powers. A Meta-theoretical Reassessment**...............260
   - I. Introduction 260
   - II. Genealogical Issues. When was the Separation of Powers
     'Invented'?...262
   - III. A Twofold Meta-theoretical Ambiguity Plaguing the
     Discussion...265
   - IV. The Justificatory Debate. Monism vs Pluralism 271
   - V. Critical Approaches...274
   - VI. The Separation of Powers as a Formal Theory and as a
     Normative Doctrine. On the Advantages of Maintaining
     a Strict Distinction 277
     - A. The Formal Theory of the Separation or Division
       of Powers 278
     - B. A Normative Doctrine of the Organisation of Political
       Power Based on the Distinction between Law-creation
       and Law-application...281
   - VII. Conclusion 287

Bibliography 288
Index 309

Introduction

THIS BOOK SEEKS to address a palpable, yet widely neglected,[1] tension in legal discourse. In our everyday legal practices – whether taking place in a courtroom, a classroom, a law firm, or elsewhere – we routinely talk of the activities of *creating* and *applying* the law. We say that some institutions or bodies are tasked with creating legal rules for our societies, and that other institutions are instead chiefly tasked with applying those rules when particular sets of facts occur. For HLA Hart, this is 'common knowledge'.[2]

The clearest example here, even more than that of courts of law, is perhaps that of police forces. Police officers' main job is that of seeing to the application of certain criminal and administrative rules created by Parliament (or, via delegated legislation, by the government). A police officer in the UK applies a certain legislative and administrative provision, for instance, when she directs members of the public away from an area subject to a Public Spaces Protection Order.

This kind of parlance – in terms of law-creation and law-application – is unproblematic in everyday legal discourse. Judges declare they are *applying* the law (or, more precisely, a specific legal rule or principle) when rendering judgment between the two parties before them. Members of Parliament inform their constituents about the latest legislation they have *made* in Parliament. Law professors teach students using the language of law-creation and law-application in all legal subjects. Lawyers, when advising a client, let them know that a certain legal norm *applies* to their business or renovation project, and what the consequences (in financial or legal terms) of such *applicability* are. Therefore, the distinction between the activities of *creating* and *applying* the law can be reasonably assumed to be one the foundations of our existing legal practices.

Yet, when legal theorists have examined (rather than assumed) the distinction between creation and application of law, most of them have undermined it or dismissed it altogether as untenable. Be it legal realists (from the North American, Scandinavian, or Italian schools),[3] critical legal scholars (CLS),[4]

---

[1] A notable exception – albeit adopting a very different philosophical strategy to address this tension, namely Robert Brandom's normative pragmatics – is M Klatt, *Making the Law Explicit: The Normativity of Legal Argumentation* (Oxford, Hart Publishing, 2008).

[2] HLA Hart, *The Concept of Law*, 3rd edn (Oxford, Oxford University Press, 2012) 3.

[3] Consider, eg, Oliver Wendell Holmes' famous dictum that '[g]eneral propositions do not decide concrete cases' in *Lochner v New York*, 198 U.S. 45, 76; J Frank, *Law and the Modern Mind* (first published 1930, Gloucester, P. Smith, 1970). The different legal realist 'schools' (and their various sceptical claims) are the subject of ch 3 of this book.

[4] See the discussion in D Kennedy, *A Critique of Adjudication: Fin de Siecle* (Cambridge, Harvard University Press, 1997) chs 2–3; M Kelman, *A Guide to Critical Legal Studies* (Cambridge, Harvard University Press, 1987) ch 1.

2 Introduction

or legal constructivists,[5] the objection is that there is no such thing as 'application of law', properly speaking. Or that – in any event – what judges do is not really objectively *constrained* or *determined* by legal rules previously created by another institution. As a result, the law-making process that is thought to constitute the framework of our current constitutional-democratic systems turns out to be indeterminate.[6]

This conclusion is highly problematic on two levels. First, from a legal-theoretical perspective, if law is a practice that is always (or even just mostly) indeterminate, it is unclear how it can provide reasons for action that can help solve coordination problems and ultimately foster cooperation among members of social groups. In other words, it is unclear how law can have any action-guiding function (or capacity) at all. Second, if law is indeterminate, the basic idea that democratically-elected legislatures make the law, and judges (among other officials) apply it, is to be rejected[7] – or at least significantly reconsidered. This in turn undermines the legitimacy of our political practices – what would the point be in electing representatives to make laws, if then what courts decide in individual cases is not, to a significant extent, determined by those laws?[8]

On this second level, the possibility of distinguishing between creation and application of law transcends the boundaries of legal theory and becomes a crucial component of political theory. For if there is indeed no possibility of *applying* a legal rule created by a different institution at a previous moment in time, then our current constitutional-democratic frameworks are effectively empty vessels which conceal a power relationship between public authorities and citizens that is very different from the one upon which constitutional democracy is grounded.

As I show in chapter two, this is true regardless of whether one holds a more (or chiefly) procedural or substantive conception of democracy. Even in purely procedural conceptions, the intersubjective application of certain (procedural) rules governing the political process is clearly a pre-condition of the attainability of democracy. Perhaps more importantly, if there is no such thing as application of law, it is not clear in what sense the people can be said to be self-governing. For this to occur, the rules applied by officials in individual cases must *correspond to* – or at least be substantively *determined by* – the rules created by the people themselves (either directly through popular referenda or indirectly through elected representatives). Political autonomy requires, in a nutshell, at least the *possibility* of law-application.

---

[5] A Somek, *The Legal Relation: Legal Theory After Legal Positivism* (Cambridge, Cambridge University Press, 2017) 27–32.

[6] This is captured, from another angle, by the claim that legal interpretation is a *pervasively* creative activity: see, eg, HM Hart and AM Sacks, *The Legal Process: Basic Problems in the Making and Application of Law* (Westbury, Foundation Press, 1994) 1415; P Chiassoni, *Interpretation without Truth: A Realistic Enquiry* (Cham, Springer International Publishing, 2019) 6.

[7] This is the explicit thesis recently defended, from a Dworkinian perspective, in D Kyritsis, *Shared Authority: Courts and Legislatures in Legal Theory* (Oxford, Hart Publishing, 2017).

[8] *cf* K Günther, 'Legal Adjudication and Democracy: Some Remarks on Dworkin and Habermas' (1995) 3(1) *European Journal of Philosophy* 36; Kennedy, *A Critique of Adjudication* (n 4) 27–28.

Introduction   3

Things would be even worse for substantive conceptions of democracy, where the ideal of self-government by the people is qualified by a set of basic freedoms and rights that are protected within a constitutional framework. Here, the relevance of the possibility of distinguishing between creation and application of law is even greater, given that law plays a double role vis-à-vis political power: that of its code and of its limitation. But how can the legal norms contained in a codified and entrenched constitution limit anything, if they cannot be applied? What would be the point of having a constitution – and, in the same vein, a constitutional or supreme court – in the first place?

In short, if we were to accept that there is no such thing as application of law, we would also have to admit that we are living in some sort of collective delusion, given that our modern political practices would turn out to be essentially meaningless. And while some – particularly some CLS writers – who deny the distinction might not be particularly worried by the implications of their arguments, others do not seem to realise the far-reaching disruptive potential of their scepticism.

In this book I offer an argument – the first of its kind – to resist such scepticism. I put forward (in chapter six) a comprehensive analytical defence of the distinction between the activities of creating and applying the law in the context of our modern constitutional democracies. My argument consists of four crucial theoretical moves, which I will now summarise.

The first move is to delimit the scope of law-creation. In this respect, and contrary to what Kelsen famously claimed, I argue that it makes little sense (if any) to consider the individual prescriptions contained in judicial decisions – such as 'John Gray must pay £100 compensation to Alicia Black' – as instances of creation of law. Instead, acts of law-creation are only those that result in a new *general* and *abstract* legal norm. While this excludes the idea that every judicial decision necessarily creates new law (as Kelsen holds, barring two exceptions),[9] it does not exclude the possibility that some judicial decisions *might* do so. In this sense, it is only with this account of law-creation, as I argue in chapter six, that it is conceptually possible to distinguish between those judicial decisions that apply pre-existing law, and those instead that apply law created by the decision itself (and thus are, properly speaking, *law-creating*). This means that the 'narrow' conception of law-creation defended in this work has far greater explanatory potential vis-à-vis our current legal practices than Kelsen's.

The second theoretical move (which takes place in chapter four) concerns one of the most contentious concepts in legal theory, that of discretion. My innovative approach is to juxtapose the jurisprudential discussion of the concept (which, in Anglo-American jurisprudence, is still centred around the Hart-Dworkin debate) with that in continental administrative law scholarship. These two discussions have evolved in parallel for many decades, but have rarely

---

[9] H Kelsen, *General Theory of Law and State* (first published 1945, with a new introduction by A Javier Treviño, New Brunswick, Transaction Publishers, 2005) 134.

4   *Introduction*

intersected. However, it is only by combining the insights from both of these traditions, I argue, that we can clarify the role that discretion must play in our theories of law.

I reject both the functional distinction between administrative and judicial discretion, as well as the Dworkinian distinction between weak and strong discretion. Both of these distinctions confuse rather than illuminate matters. Instead, I distinguish between what I term, respectively, 'normative' and 'interpretive' discretion. The former indicates the (usually intentional) delegation of decision-making power across the different levels of the legal system (the Kelsenian *Stufenbaulehre*). The latter instead captures the intrinsic – and therefore unintended – degree of choice that every legal decision-maker, to a greater or lesser extent, finds herself faced with. This is because there might be, for any given legal decision, three different sources of interpretive discretion: a semantic, a factual, and a systemic source. And it is only when the amount of discretion deriving from these three sources is negligible that we can consider that a legal decision is *determinate*.

The third theoretical move deals with a significant objection to the idea that we can draw a clear analytical distinction between the activities of creation and application of law. This objection is borne out of the use of Gricean and Neo-Gricean pragmatic theories in philosophy of language to explain legal interpretation. The gist of the objection is that legal communication is pragmatic in the same way ordinary communication is: ie, the meaning of an utterance is constituted by the intention of the speaker. Therefore, the meaning of a legal norm can only and always be retrieved through an inferential process of interpretation that requires access to wide contextual resources. Or, to put it more clearly, the objection is that there is not even such a thing as the *literal* meaning of a legal utterance (a legislative provision, for instance) before the interpreter can draw on the wide context of the utterance to *retrieve* the intention of the speaker (in the legal case, typically the legislature). But if the meaning of a legislative legal utterance is always pragmatic (rather than chiefly conventional because of semantic and syntactic rules), then we can never know what the law prescribes or establishes before a necessarily inferential process of interpretation. And if (knowledge of) the meaning of a legislative utterance does not pre-exist the pragmatic interpretation of judges, it simply cannot be *applied* by them – or by anyone else, for that matter – in the relevant sense we are after here.[10]

In chapter five, I reject this objection by questioning the very assumption on which it is based, namely, the idea that legal communication is akin to ordinary communication, and that as a result it can be analysed through the lenses of speech-act theory. My strategy here is two-fold. First, I show why we should resist the idea that legal language is merely a sub-set of natural languages.

---

[10] F Poggi, 'The Myth of Literal Meaning in Legal Interpretation' (2013) 13 *Analisi e Diritto* 313.

Introduction 5

This becomes apparent once we take the perspective of macro-pragmatics – that is, of the functional analysis of languages as a whole (*qua* semiotic systems). In this respect, legal language has a different pragmatic function from natural languages, since many legal norms are nothing but semantic rules to qualify certain sets of facts in the world in particular ways (as a contract, as a tort, etc). Thus, legal language should be considered as belonging to the category of 'administered' languages[11] – that is, languages whose formation rules do not evolve spontaneously according to the use by its speakers. This also implies that the relationship between legal language and the natural languages through which the former is expressed is more complex than is commonly appreciated.

The second limb of my strategy is to explain why the application of speech-act theory to legal communication is unsatisfactory and should be replaced by what I instead call 'text-act' theory. The point here is straightforward: speech-act theory is modelled after face-to-face – or conversational – communicative exchanges, that is, those taking place (at the same place and moment in time) between a speaker and a hearer. But this is clearly not what happens with legal communication.

First of all, the widespread assumption that legal communication is a two-way affair between lawmakers (usually a legislature) and courts runs against the equally widespread understanding of 'law' as the enterprise of subjecting human conducts to the guidance of rules. For how can law guide the conduct of laypeople, if it is not directed first and foremost at them? And how are we to make sense of all those instances where laypeople achieve a cooperative outcome on the basis of legal directives without having to invoke the intervention of a judge? As I have argued elsewhere,[12] putting laypeople back at the centre of law's interpretive field greatly undermines the explanatory capacity of many existing theories of legal interpretation (particularly those favoured by legal realists).

Second, legal communication, unlike ordinary communication, takes place mostly via (complex) written texts. The relevance of this difference is vastly under-appreciated not just in legal theory,[13] but in philosophy of language more generally. This is surprising, as communication that happens via complex text-acts (or a combination of text-acts and visual signs, as with traffic codes) clearly misses many of the potential features of its face-to-face counterpart. Among these are the possibility of paralinguistic cues (like pointing when asking for something) and prosody (those changes in the intonation, rhythm or other features of the speech-act that might constitute evidential cues to the intention

---

[11] M Jori, 'Legal Pragmatics' in A Capone and F Poggi (eds), *Pragmatics and Law: Philosophical Perspectives* (Cham, Springer International Publishing, 2016).

[12] P Sandro, 'To whom does the law speak? Canvassing a neglected picture of law's interpretive field' in M Araszkiewicz, P Banas, T Gizbert-Studnicki and K Pleszka (eds), *Problems of Normativity, Rules and Rule-Following* (Cham, Springer International Publishing, 2015).

[13] Some notable exceptions include PM Tiersma, 'A Message in a Bottle: Text, Autonomy, and Statutory Interpretation' (2001) 76(2) *Tulane Law Review* 431; BG Slocum, *Ordinary Meaning: A Theory of the Most Fundamental Principle of Legal Interpretation* (Chicago, University of Chicago Press, 2015).

6 Introduction

of the speaker). On this negative basis alone, the relevance for pragmatic interpretation of complex text-acts appears greatly reduced.

The differences between speech- and text-acts do not stop here. In fact, besides the lack of conversational features that can supplement or qualify semantic meaning, we ought to understand writing as an altogether different communicative technique from oral conversation. As noted by Slocum, writing allows for far greater degrees of precision and objectivity (in the sense of intersubjectivity) in expressing one's thoughts than ordinary conversational exchanges.[14] But its most important feature, as a social tool, is that it allows for successful communicative exchanges across time and space.[15]

A written text can be successfully understood by readers who do not know the identity of the author and the precise features of the context surrounding her. This in turn is only possible if the meaning expressed by text-acts is chiefly a conventional rather than a pragmatic meaning. This is where I adopt, with some minor integrations, the semantic minimalism developed by Emma Borg over the course of more than a decade in a number of important contributions to philosophy of language.[16] Semantic minimalism is, in a nutshell, a theory of (truth-evaluable) meaning that reduces the scope for pragmatic enrichment of semantic and syntactic 'vehicles'. It is without a doubt a contentious position in philosophy of language. While many contextualists accept that there might be a level of meaning that is indeed conventional (or a-contextual), the objection is that semantic minimalism lacks an explanatory role in ordinary communication – that is, that it cannot account for the type of (pragmatic) meaning that governs our linguistic exchanges. My contention is that we can concede this point while affirming the crucial explanatory role that semantic minimalism has when it comes to communication via text-acts, and legal communication in particular. The upshot of this move, for our purposes, is that we can then identify a level of meaning in legal communication that is essentially conventional (what legal interpreters already call 'literal' meaning), and as such pre-exists the (pragmatic) interpretation by courts.

The fourth and final move that grounds my account of the distinction between creation and application of law is to highlight one crucial difference, in our modern legal systems, between formal and substantive requirements in the law-making process. By formal (or procedural) requirements, I mean all those demands of legal norms that pertain to either the procedure or to the form in which a certain legal act must be adopted if it is to be valid (eg the written form of a contract, a relevant signature on a will, the publication in the official gazette of a legislative act). By substantive (or material) requirements I refer instead to all those demands, established by the norms that govern the exercise

---

[14] Slocum, *Ordinary Meaning* (n 12) 51.

[15] ibid.

[16] See, eg E Borg, *Minimal Semantics* (Oxford, Oxford University Press, 2004); E Borg, *Pursuing Meaning* (Oxford, Oxford University Press, 2012).

Introduction 7

of a certain legal power, that have to do with the contents (rather than with the form or the procedure) of the decision to be adopted.[17] Examples are: whether a certain establishment should be authorised to operate between certain hours in a residential street; how much distance there should be between a manufacturing plant and a river; or what should be the punishment for a certain type of criminal behaviour.

The crucial difference is the following: while formal requirements always demand conformity – so that any given formal requirement is either satisfied or not – substantive requirements can regulate the exercise of legal decision-making powers in two alternative ways. They can either demand conformity like formal requirements – so that the contents of the decision are pre-determined by the norms on its production – or they can demand *mere* non-contradiction. That is to say, the decision-maker can establish some (or all) of the contents of the decision to be taken – for instance, how many metres a given manufacturing plant must be distant from a river – provided that those contents are not prohibited by the same or other relevant legal norms in the system.

This difference has been captured for a long time in continental administrative law theory with the distinction between *bound* and *discretionary* law-application.[18] Thus, if all of the contents of the decision to be taken have already been pre-determined by higher norms in the system, we say that the decision-*maker* (or better, the decision-*taker*) is bound to take such decision if a certain set of facts obtains. For instance, if a learner driver has passed all the relevant exams satisfactorily, and 'ticks' all the other necessary eligibility boxes, the Driver and Vehicle Licensing Agency (DVLA) will have to issue her with a full driving licence. The DVLA does not have a discretionary power in this case: they cannot issue the driving licence but (say) limit it to a restricted part of Great Britain; or issue it but only for one month. Where the DVLA may instead have a discretionary power is when a driver reports a new medical condition that has emerged and which could affect her driving: here the DVLA can decide, upon an evaluation of the severity of the condition and of the likelihood that it will affect the driving, not only whether to subject the licence to certain conditions, but what precisely such conditions should be (for instance, how often there should be a reassessment of the medical problem).

My overall claim is that the distinction between *bound* and *discretionary* law-application should become part of legal theoretical discourse in general. Whether an act of law-application is bound does not only depend on the deontic modality established by the norms governing the exercise of the decision-making power (ie obligatory or permissive). It is also a function of the amount of interpretive discretion available to the decision-maker. In other words, the fact that

---

[17] For details and further discussion see P Sandro, 'Unlocking Legal Validity: Some Remarks on the Artificial Ontology of Law' in P Westerman, J Hage, S Kirste and AR Mackor (eds), *Legal Validity and Soft Law* (Cham, Springer International Publishing, 2018).

[18] In Italian administrative law the distinction is between *attività vincolata* and *attività discrezionale*; in French administrative law between *compétence (povouir) liée* and *pouvoir discrétionnaire*.

8   Introduction

a decision is bound, as to its contents, by higher norms of the system does not necessarily mean that it is also determinate in that respect. To go back to one of the examples already mentioned, the relevant norm could establish that there should be 'adequate' distance between a manufacturing plant and a river, without specifying what counts as 'adequate'. Is two metres 'adequate'? What about 50?

As such, under my analytical model we can talk of *bound* law-application only when: i) the contents of the decision to be taken are pre-determined by the higher norms that govern the decision-making power;[19] and ii) the extent of interpretive discretion available to the decision-maker (in the three different types identified in chapter four: semantic, factual, and systemic) is *negligible*.[20] These are the cases that other philosophers of law have identified, within the model of the so-called legal syllogism, as cases of subsumption, but without spelling out the different sources of (interpretive) discretion or the different modalities of substantive requirements.

My model clarifies that (substantive) law-application still takes place even when the decision is not bound as to its contents, or when those contents are not (fully) determinate – although in these cases what we have is the *discretionary* application of law. Finally, in those cases where the contents of the decision to be taken are neither determinate nor bound (but merely *permitted*), we shall talk instead – adopting Luigi Ferrajoli's terminology[21] – of *autonomous* application of law. Most legislative acts in a constitutional democracy fall in this category: here, there is still a necessary degree of application vis-à-vis: i) the formal and procedural norms on the production of legislative acts; and ii) the non-contradiction of relevant constitutional norms and principles. But the contents of these decisions are effectively to be established by the *agents* tasked with making them (not just officials: private contracts fall in this category as well).

In concluding this summary of the core argument, a relevant consequence of the defence of the distinction between law-creation and law-application that is not explored fully in the book is worth mentioning. It lies in the clarification of the scope for judicial review of administrative action, and particularly of the role of discretion in it. For if we do not differentiate between normative and interpretive discretion, as I do in chapter four of this book, we risk conflating: (a) situations where the choice of the administrative decision-maker should be accorded a degree of deference by the reviewing courts; with (b) cases where no such deference, in principle, is due.

The cases where (a varying degree of) deference is due are those situations in which the decision-maker has been lawfully equipped with normative discretion

---

[19] The 'contents of the decision' are, in other words, its legal effects.

[20] The reason why I talk of 'negligible' extent of interpretive discretion, rather than of the absence of it, is due to the ultimate evaluative (and fallible) nature of all empirical knowledge, no matter how widely intersubjectively shared its findings are.

[21] L Ferrajoli, *Principia Iuris*, vol 1 (Bari, Laterza, 2007) 609.

by the system. Here, provided that the decision-maker stays within the legal boundaries of her power – that is, provided that she complies with the applicable *formal* norms and does not contradict the applicable *substantive* norms – the contents of her decision should not be second-guessed by the reviewing courts.[22] For the legitimacy underpinning the exercise of normative discretion as part of a democratic law-making process is, in this respect, different from the authority exercised by (usually non-elected) courts in reviewing administrative action.

Where instead only interpretive discretion (of the semantic and factual type) is at play, nothing should prevent (in principle) the reviewing courts from questioning the decision taken by the original decision-maker. Different jurisdictions have different approaches in this regard, particularly when it comes to reviewing *factual interpretive* discretion; and even within the same jurisdiction there might be different standards depending on the type of facts at play (ie mere historical facts versus scientific or medical facts). But the point is to highlight that the legitimacy underlying the judgement involved with these types of discretion does not change depending on whether it is exercised by administrative officials or judges.

The issue, as discussed at the end of chapter four, remains that of the identification and evaluation of systemic discretion in a legal system. For systemic discretion – particularly when caused by the contradiction and fragmentation of the established legal sources – blurs the distinction between normative and interpretive discretion, and as a result makes the evaluation of the legitimacy of judicial review of administrative action more uncertain. In this respect, the argument of this book prompts us to rediscover a neglected lesson of the European Legal Enlightenment and to advocate a shift in the focus of current general jurisprudence: away from ever more complex theories of interpretation, and instead towards a more rigorous 'science of legislation'.[23] This would buttress the legitimacy of our constitutional democracies, by increasing the determinacy (and objectivity) of their law-making and law-applying practices in the vast majority of cases.

I. AIMS AND STRUCTURE OF THE WORK

While completing two different doctorates in Rome and Edinburgh, I became acutely aware of a lack of engagement of Anglo-American jurisprudential scholarship with Romance languages-speaking legal philosophers. The lack of English translation from Italian, Spanish, French, or Portuguese of many important works in legal and political theory might contribute to explaining

---

[22] As I show in ch 4, different legal systems make the conferral of this type of normative discretion upon public officials more or less salient, and this in turn affects also the presence (or lack thereof) of what I call systemic interpretive discretion. Both of these factors affect the degree of clarity about the scope of judicial review of administrative action in each respective system.

[23] G Filangieri, *La scienza della legislazione* (first published 1780–1785, Naples, Grimaldi, 2003).

10 Introduction

this, as well as the perceived differences between common and civil law systems. However, as I argue throughout the book, modern constitutional democracies share a common fundamental structure, regardless of the 'legal family' they belong to. Therefore, one of the overall key aims of this work is to contribute bridging this gap between the two jurisprudential scholarships, and this explains in part the extensive citation apparatus of the book.

At the same time, this book has not been written only for professional legal philosophers and public lawyers. My hope is that it will be of interest to scholars from a variety of different disciplines (from political theory to philosophy of language, to name but two), to legal practitioners, and advanced law and politics students – who should hopefully also benefit from the citation apparatus of the work. In order to keep the text accessible to non-specialists, I sought to establish a (difficult) balance between the use of technical language and concepts and a deeper engagement with the existing scholarship in the respective fields. In this regard, the only chapter that requires some background knowledge in a specific discipline (philosophy of language and linguistics) is chapter five, although I have tried my very best to make the 'border wars'[24] between semantic and pragmatics theories accessible to the non-initiated.

This book consists of seven chapters. While the core argument of the work develops linearly across them, most chapters can also be read as self-contained contributions. This is a consequence of the efforts made to contextualise each discrete argumentative move within the wider body of scholarship in that field – be it constitutional law, political theory, or philosophy of language.

In chapter one, after presenting the two main claims of the book about the distinction between law-creation and law-application and its relevance for political theory, I address some methodological concerns. First, I engage with those arguments in legal scholarship (particularly from the legal pluralism and anthropology approaches) that criticise general jurisprudence as 'parochial'. That criticism cuts deeper than most authors realise. For the exclusive attention that jurisprudence has given to the structure of the paradigmatic western nation-state would make it ultimately irrelevant as a method of investigation of law 'in general' – a glaring contradiction, given its avowed *universal* explanatory aims. This is true, I submit, only if 'law' and 'state-law' are assumed to be equivalent – and this might have been the case for some jurisprudential works of the past. But while this book does focus on the constitutional-democratic model that has become widespread especially after the Second World War, the concept of law that underpins my argument is not tied at all to the nation-state. Rather, the idea of law as the enterprise of subjecting human conduct to the guidance of rules (and rulings)[25] is broad enough to accommodate a number of normative phenomena beyond that of 'state-law'.

---

[24] I Skoczeń, *Implicatures within Legal Language* (Cham, Springer International Publishing, 2019) ch 4.

[25] J Gardner, 'The Supposed Formality of the Rule of Law' in J Gardner, *Law as a Leap of Faith: Essays on Law in General* (Oxford, Oxford University Press, 2012) 206–211.

Aims and Structure of the Work   11

I also make clear, in this respect, that the argument of this book does not presuppose an understanding of the state as an unqualified good. On the one hand, I build on insights from legal history and anthropology to show why we should reject once and for all the Hobbesian tale of the ineluctability of the state. Not only does the creation of a state not automatically imply the amelioration of the living conditions of all its subjects, but also there have existed historical legal orders that prescinded from a state-like structure altogether. In this sense, I offer a critical reconstruction of the form of government that the Greeks called ἰσονομία (isonomia), and that for far too long has been confused with democracy.

On the other hand, I clarify the conceptual relationship between natural powers and political power (or authority). While the latter can be reasonably conceived of as an institutional device to address the dangers of social settings where only natural powers exist, it carries potentially a far greater danger for members of social groups. In this respect, two problems with regard to political power manifest themselves after its emergence: that of its legitimation and that of its limitation. This part of my argument addresses the worries of many critical legal scholars that general jurisprudence, with its emphasis on legal forms and process, conceals true power relations that govern our modern societies. I argue instead, following Norberto Bobbio,[26] that a theory of power constitutes the core of any legal and political theory which understands its object of study correctly.

The problems of legitimation and limitation of political authority constitute the starting point of chapter two. The first step of the argument is to investigate and clarify the relationship between political authority and law: as several authors deny that there is a stable relationship to begin with. This, I submit, is a consequence of the failure to appreciate that with the English term 'law' we refer to two very different types of law that have materialised in the history of western legal theory and practice. The crucial distinction between law as *lex* and law as *ius* allows us to identify a more stable connection, throughout western history, between the exercise of political power and law as the code (and product) of that exercise. This latter is law as *lex*. But since the late Roman Republic,[27] a different type of law – with a source independent from the will of the political authority – has appeared: namely, law that is grounded in the customary traditions of a society, as interpreted by a specialised group of agents with a unique kind of technical knowledge. This is law as *ius*. Does this second kind of law sound familiar? Indeed, the common law of the land that has developed in England since the twelfth century represents – or so it can be argued – a direct evolution of the Roman *ius* model.[28]

---

[26] N Bobbio, *Democracy and Dictatorship: The Nature and Limits of State Power* (Oxford, Polity Press, 1989) 70.

[27] A Schiavone, *The Invention of Law in the West* (J Carden and A Shugaar trans, Cambridge, Harvard University Press, 2012) (translation of the original Italian: A Schiavone, *Ius. L'invenzione del Diritto in Occidente* (Turin, Einaudi, 2005)).

[28] TJ McSweeney, *Priests of the Law. Roman Law and the Making of the Common Law's First Professionals* (Oxford, Oxford University Press, 2019).

12 *Introduction*

This distinction is crucial in showing that the fundamental structure of modern constitutional democracies does not change between civil and common law systems. In this respect, I demonstrate how the defining feature of modern constitutionalism is that of providing a political system with *legal otherness*. This means that a second source of law exists in the system, independent (at least in its fundamental elements) from the political lawmaker, which limits what the lawmaker can *lawfully* decide, from an institutional (and not just normative) point of view.

As such, a constitutionalist framework can be achieved in two ways: by entrenching a set of norms in a constitutional document that sits above ordinary politics and is enforced by an institution different from the legislature, or by the systemic acceptance of the existence of a second type of law that embodies the (inner and outer) limits of legislative power. And while in the latter model this dualism of law is premised on an even more delicate institutional equilibrium, the point is that in both cases *ius* acts as a constraint to *lex*.

In this regard, the account of constitutionalism defended in this book has three major explanatory upshots. First, it detaches the realisation of the doctrine in a given political system from the presence of *a* constitution (of any kind). Second, and relatedly, it undermines political constitutionalism theories insofar as these identify the 'constitutional' of the British model of constitutionalism in an ephemeral 'political constitution', rather than in the body of law developed over centuries by the common law courts of the land. Finally, the model of constitutionalism put forward allows me to clarify, in the last part of chapter two, the two-fold dependence of constitutional democracy on the distinction between creation and application of law. This dependence is two-fold because both democracy and constitutionalism, taken individually, rely on the distinction being possible.

In concluding the chapter, I discuss the implications of this relation of dependence in general, and in particular again for political constitutionalist theories. I show how these theories implicitly postulate the possibility of application of law in both their accounts of democracy and of the rule of law, but effectively deny it when it comes to the application of constitutional provisions as constraints on the legislature. I then evaluate the conundrum political constitutionalists end up in, and how it supports – from a different viewpoint – the relevance of the distinction between creation and application of law for political and legal theory alike.

Chapters three to five are dedicated to analysing, and addressing, the three most significant objections in the literature that run against the idea of application of law.

Chapter three engages with legal realism, offering an overall taxonomy of the different realist approaches in the legal philosophical literature. After explaining how the legal realist movements – in their three main 'schools' (the North American, the Scandinavian, and the Italian) – have emerged as a reaction to the dominating 'formalist' paradigm in legal education, I seek to identify

Aims and Structure of the Work 13

what all these realist strands have in common (at a minimum). The answer lies in their rule-scepticism, which sustains – through different theoretical routes – their related claims about the indeterminacy of legal rules and about the need to find a different epistemology for legal science. I explore the rule-scepticism of realist scholars across two axes: that of its scope (radical or moderate) and that of its source (whether internal or external to law).

After this reconstruction effort, in the second and final part of chapter three I address the realist objections to the possibility of application of law. I focus, in particular, on moderate legal realism, given that radical sceptic positions have been rejected as untenable by moderate realists themselves. I engage with the theories of two of the most prominent moderate legal realists in the literature: Brian Leiter and Riccardo Guastini. Leiter's 'naturalized jurisprudence' project is grounded directly in the work of the historical American Legal Realist School, while Guastini has developed his legal realism – as one of the most prominent members of the Genoa School founded by Giovanni Tarello in Italy – over a number of decades. I show how, in both cases and for different reasons, a truly moderate realist position is unfeasible, as it eventually collapses and becomes radical scepticism. We are then left with a dichotomy: either embrace the (moderate) cognitivism adopted by most modern legal positivists (following Hart), or maintain a radical rule-sceptic position. This choice, I conclude, is primarily an ontological one (which arguably tracks wider philosophical commitments), and legal scholars cannot simply remain agnostic towards it – given that law's epistemic status as an object of study depends on it.

Chapter four deals with the concept of legal discretion. At least since the Hart-Dworkin debate, the idea that judges in our legal systems might possess and exercise what Dworkin calls 'strong' discretion constitutes a reason to reject legal positivism (both descriptively and normatively) and embrace his theory of 'law as integrity'. For Dworkin believes that judges should apply the law, not make it, for both democratic and fairness reasons.[29] Is the exercise of discretion then incompatible with the idea of law-application?

To answer this question, I critically analyse four key accounts of legal discretion in jurisprudential scholarship. The recent re-discovery of Hart's 'lost essay' on discretion sheds a different light on Hart's thinking on the matter (and makes it more explanatorily fruitful). I then critically engage with the theories of discretion in Dworkin and Kelsen. In the end, I show why Matthias Klatt's sophisticated analysis of the concept provides the most helpful departure point for my own considerations on it. But my account is at the same time based on the administrative law scholarship on the concept of discretion. In this regard, after presenting the crucial role that the idea of discretion has played for a long time in the administrative domain, I offer concise statements of the main theoretical features of the concept of discretion in the German, French-Italian, and English administrative law traditions, highlighting commonalities and differences.

---

[29] WJ Waluchow, 'Strong Discretion' (1983) 33(133) *The Philosophical Quarterly* 321, 321–2.

14   *Introduction*

The account I propose in the last part of chapter four is *unified* because it merges jurisprudential and administrative law insights while departing from two commonly held distinctions: the Dworkinian one between weak and strong discretion, and the functional one between administrative and judicial discretion. These distinctions are unhelpful and confuse matters rather than illuminate them. Instead, my account – which also bridges the gap between common and civil law systems – is based on the identification of two fundamental types of discretion in our modern legal systems: normative and interpretive. The chapter concludes with the illustration of how this understanding of discretion contributes to clarifying the idea of law-application.

The final main objection against the possibility of law-application is considered in chapter five. The objection stems from the use of speech-act theory in legal interpretation and undermines the idea that the meaning of legal utterances (and particularly legislative utterances) pre-exists the pragmatic interpretations of judges. If that is the case, the norms created by the legislature cannot simply be *applied* by courts. I begin the chapter by criticising the 'two-way affair' model of legal communication, which is predominant in the literature.[30] I show that law is a communicative enterprise, but not just between legislatures and courts. This discussion serves also as an introduction to the rise of pragmatics in legal interpretation, following the work of Paul Grice (and those 'Neo-Griceans' whose work is based on his insights) in the philosophy of language.

I then illustrate the two objections that are raised against the pragmatic turn in jurisprudence: that of the relationship between law and natural language, and that of the inability of mainstream speech-act theory to account for the features of written communication. Legal texts are conceived of as autonomous 'text-acts', that is, complex acts of communication which require a different theory of meaning. This theory of meaning – semantic minimalism – is illustrated in the following section. Lastly, I discuss (in broad strokes) how a theory of legal interpretation based on this text-act theory looks like, and how it can ground the idea of application of law.

In chapter six I draw all the relevant threads of the argument together to put forward the analytical defence of the distinction between law-creation and law-application. After surveying two extreme attitudes in the literature (that of assuming and of denying the distinction), I start from Kelsen's influential, and yet obfuscating, idea that all legal acts – besides two 'borderline' cases[31] – are at the same time law-creating and law-applying acts. On the one hand, that all law-creating acts are also law-applying – with the exception of the act that expresses the original constituent power in a system – is a consequence of the principle of legality, understood as a meta-norm on the production of law. On the other hand, all law-applying facts are also law-creating only if 'creation of law' is deemed to include individual prescriptions (like those included in the ruling of

---

[30] Sandro, 'To whom does the law speak? (n 11).
[31] Kelsen, *General Theory of Law and State* (n 8) 133.

Aims and Structure of the Work   15

a judicial decision). I argue against this idea (based on its limited explanatory fruitfulness) and stipulate that 'law-creation' should be reserved only for those legal acts that create a new *general* and *abstract* norm (or innovate, as to its generality and/or abstractness, an already existing one).

I then turn to unpacking the concept of law-application. After disambiguating different uses of the expression, I focus on the application of norms (and not of provisions) to forms of behaviour. In this regard, I illustrate that it is norms – and not provisions (despite colloquial usage) – that 'require things of agents'.[32] I continue by distinguishing norm-application from norm-following, given not only that the former appears to involve something more than merely following a norm, but also because following most legal norms does not seem to require an intentional state by the agent. Here the different normative character of duty-imposing vis-à-vis power-conferring norms assumes centre stage, and it allows me to clarify why it is unnecessary to think (as many in the literature do) that only legal officials can apply the law. Law-application pertains to the exercise of all legal powers, no matter whether held by public officials or private individuals.

This series of clarifications allows me to flesh out in full the analytical account of law-application. This revolves around two axes – that of determinacy and that of the deontic modality of the power-conferring norms – which are discussed in the preceding chapters. The resulting distinction between *bound, discretionary,* and *autonomous* types of law-application is explained and contextualised in relation to some of the existing classifications in the literature. Finally, the objection to the possibility of rule-following which is based on the sceptical reading of Wittgenstein's argument in the *Philosophical Investigations* is considered and addressed.

The final chapter of the book, which serves also as its conclusion, explores a first significant consequence of the account of law-application defended in this work. This consequence lies in the possibility of reconsidering the scope and explanatory fruitfulness of the separation of powers doctrine in the context of modern constitutional democracies. For the separation of powers, in its traditional tripartite version, has been recently the subject of widespread criticism in the literature (both from a descriptive and normative point of view).

My contention instead is that the doctrine, once reconceptualised, can still play a crucial role in our political and legal theories. To this end, in the first part of chapter seven I review current critical approaches, particularly in constitutional theory. I highlight how many of these criticisms are based on two types of confusion about the doctrine. The first confusion is caused by the inconsistent use in the literature of two ideas that should be kept distinct: the separation of powers and the division of power. The second confusion pertains to the equivocal use of the doctrine as an explanatory device or as normative principle.

---

[32] G Brennan, L Eriksson, R Goodin, and N Southwood, *Explaining Norms* (Oxford, Oxford University Press, 2013) 3.

16 Introduction

Dispelling these confusions allows us to explain away most of the criticisms levied against the separation of powers. It also paves the way for a more robust reconceptualisation of the doctrine, one that can prove useful in the context of our current constitutional democracies. The first reconceptualisation regards the formal theory of the separation of powers, which is based on the distinction between two opposing techniques to organise and limit public power: separation (as independence) and division (as sharing or distribution). A formal theory of the doctrine based on this basic dichotomy has far greater explanatory potential vis-à-vis our current practices than the tripartite structure of legislative, executive, and judiciary.

The second reconceptualisation is of the separation of powers as a normative doctrine, that is, as a blueprint of how powers in a constitutional democracy should be separated or divided. Again, we should abandon the tripartite version of the separation even from a normative point of view and adopt instead a model that is based on the different legitimation of law-creating and law-applying functions proposed in this book. This is particularly true when it comes to the executive or administrative function, which is nothing but a variable combination of law-creating and law-applying functions. In this respect, the model proposed has the merit – among others – of dispelling the common objection that substantive judicial review of administrative action is generally incompatible with the separation of powers. I conclude the book by sketching how the reconceptualised separation of powers doctrine may be relevant, beyond the nation-state, at the supra-national level.

1

Law, Power, and Political Authority. On the Scope and Limitations of the Work

I. INTRODUCTION

I N THIS BOOK I do two main things. First, I propose an analytical distinction between the activities of creation and application of law and defend it from several important objections. Second, I argue that modern constitutional democracies are premised on such distinction to the extent that, if we deny the latter, we delegitimise the former, perhaps fatally. This relationship of dependency of our current political frameworks on the distinction between law-creation and law-application, as I will show in chapter two, obtains independently of whether one holds a purely procedural or more substantive conception of democracy. This dependency is, instead, due to the nature of the more general relationship between political power and law, which comes distinctively to the fore when analysed through the lenses of the theory of power and authority. This is the subject of chapter one.

How does the distinction between creation and application of law bear on the legitimacy of our constitutional democracies? Anticipating the gist of the argument developed in the next chapter, if there is no possibility of such a thing as applying the law (because the legal process is one of constant creation of meaning by the different actors involved), it is doubtful whether law could ever achieve the function of guiding conduct in large and complex societies. This 'action-guiding' requirement is not just traditionally associated in constitutional theory with the normative and institutional principle of the rule of law, but it is more fundamentally considered to be (in general jurisprudence) an essential feature of the nature of law, that is, of what it takes for a social practice to belong to the type of 'thing' law is.

As a result, it is unclear how our current political systems could be deemed to be 'constitutional' – or even simply 'juridical' – if there was no such thing as law-application. I will discuss this at length in chapter two. In addition, I will show also how purely procedural conceptions of democracy (mostly defended

18   Law, Power, and Political Authority

in public law scholarship by political constitutionalists like Griffith, Waldron, or Bellamy) would be affected as well. For how could people be considered to be ruling themselves – even indirectly, that is, through their elected representatives – if the output of their deliberation could not determine the outcome of individual cases? In other words, what happens to the core democratic principle of 'collective autonomy' if we take at face value the legal realist thesis that legal norms do not determine the outcome of judicial decisions?

What I have just said should suffice to indicate, for now at least, why defending the possibility of distinguishing between creation and application of law is crucial not just for legal and constitutional theory, but for political theory too. As I shall argue in this chapter, given that law has come to constitute the predominant 'mode of expression' of political power, it does matter for our political theories whether it can in turn constitute something more than the mere medium in which political power is encoded. But even when considered exclusively as the code through which political power is expressed, law cannot perform such a role in a democratic system unless it is possible to distinguish acts of law-application from acts of law-creation. Therefore, I will argue that one cannot reject the possibility of the application of law (even constitutional law) in our juridical practices and at the same time hold our political frameworks legitimate without incurring into a glaring contradiction.

Following some general methodological remarks, in the remainder of this chapter I introduce my analytical approach and the more specific scope and limitations of the work. After a conceptual genealogy of the inception of law and political power, I explain how, with this transformative change in human civilisation, a whole new set of issues arise, which require to be dealt with. In particular, two problems about political power *qua* centralised normative power constitute to this day persistent open questions for democratic theory: that of its limitation and that of its legitimation. This will lead me, in chapter two, to discuss how modern constitutionalism seeks to provide democratic theory with (contingent) answers to these open questions, and to show how both these fundamental political doctrines are ultimately dependent on the possibility of distinction between the activities of creating and applying the law. If successful, the overall argument presented in these two chapters will point to the unavoidable degree of interconnectedness between political and legal theory, something that it is still too seldom properly accounted for on both sides of the disciplinary divide.[1]

---

[1] Wade and Forsyth talk, for instance, of a lasting and extensive 'legal antipathy' in English public law scholarship towards political theory, which is even stronger in administrative law, as this field has been traditionally even more insulated from political and moral considerations than constitutional law: W Wade and CF Forsyth, *Administrative Law*, 10th edn (Oxford, Oxford University Press, 2009) 7–8. Conversely, Sartori stressed (back in the 1960s) the tendency of political doctrine to underplay legal constitutionalism: G Sartori, 'Constitutionalism: A Preliminary Discussion' (1962) 56(4) *American Political Science Review* 853, 863.

II. BRIEF METHODOLOGICAL REMARKS

There is at least one theoretical risk in aspiring to write a book in legal theory (that is, general jurisprudence) nowadays. It is the possibility of putting forward some claims regarding 'the nature' of law – claims that seem necessarily rooted, at least to some extent, in a given spatio-temporal context – as universal claims about law.[2] Brian Tamanaha, for one, has not spared Anglo-American analytical jurisprudence harsh criticism for its assumption that the modern 'state' or 'municipal' law amounts to the paradigmatic case of law, and for the effects that this assumption has had on mainstream legal scholarship over the last century or so.[3] The vast field known as 'legal pluralism' can be considered a forceful reaction to that assumption and to its epistemological and methodological premises, among which conceptual analysis – understood as the identification and explanation of the nature of things picked out by our concepts[4] – stands tall. And as with many reactions to intellectual or philosophical 'dogmas', after an initial phase of rejection of the dogma and calls for 'revolution', it seems now that we have entered a phase in which what is sought is 'methodological balance'.[5]

On the one hand, while conceptual analysis should not be rejected a-priori as a misguided method of investigation into law,[6] it should always be conducted while being mindful of its unavoidable empirical premises – our shared linguistic and social practices[7] – and ensuing contextual scope.[8] On the other hand, the wanting character of purely empirical approaches that cannot yield further understanding of the phenomenon of law without deeper philosophical analysis of the

---

[2] *cf*, for the claim that the task of analytical jurisprudence is to 'search and explain' those properties 'which law, at any time, and in any place, must exhibit', J Dickson, *Evaluation and Legal Theory* (Oxford, Hart Publishing, 2001) 17–18; L Green, 'Gender and the Analytical Jurisprudential Mind' (2020) 83(4) *Modern Law Review* 893, 894, for whom general jurisprudence 'addresses the nature of law ... anywhere and everywhere'.

[3] See most recently B Tamanaha, *A Realistic Theory of Law* (Cambridge, Cambridge University Press, 2017). For a comprehensive assessment of the different criticisms levelled against legal theory from the pluralist camp, see C Mac Amhlaigh, 'Does Legal Theory Have a Pluralism Problem?', in S Berman (ed), *The Oxford Handbook of Legal Pluralism* (Oxford, Oxford University Press 2020).

[4] KE Himma, 'Conceptual Jurisprudence. An Introduction to Conceptual Analysis and Methodology in Legal Theory' (2015) 26 *Revus* 65, 69–71.

[5] M Del Mar, 'Beyond the State in and of Legal Theory', in SP Dolan and L Heckendorn Urscheler (eds), *Concepts of Law: Comparative, Jurisprudential, and Social Science Perspectives* (Burlington, Ashgate, 2012) 20. See also, M Croce, '*Self-sufficiency of Law: A Critical-Institutional Theory of Social Order* (Dordrecht, Springer, 2012) 195; N Roughan and A Halpin (eds), *In Pursuit of Pluralist Jurisprudence*, (Cambridge, Cambridge University Press, 2017).

[6] For an example of this extreme position, see R Posner, *Law and Legal Theory in England and America* (Oxford, Clarendon Press, 1996) 3; Tamanaha, *A Realistic Theory of Law* (n 3) ch 3.

[7] Himma, 'Conceptual Jurisprudence' (n 4) 75; J Raz, *Ethics in the Public Domain* (Oxford, Oxford University Press 1994) 216–17.

[8] As opposed to an 'immodest' version of it, according to which the analysis of our concepts would allow us to explore the nature of things as they 'really' are, that is, independently of 'our linguistic and conceptual frameworks': Himma, 'Conceptual Jurisprudence' (n 4) 73, quoting F Jackson, *From Metaphysics to Ethics: A Defence of Conceptual Analysis* (Oxford, Oxford University Press, 1998) 43–44.

20   Law, Power, and Political Authority

concepts deployed is being underscored within the legal pluralism camp itself.[9] Perhaps the best illustration of this is Tamanaha's non-essentialist 'concept' of law as 'whatever people identify and treat through their social practices as "law"'[10] and its critique from within the pluralist camp. William Twining, for instance, has stressed how accepting Tamanaha's proposal would amount to giving up the very purposes for which a concept of law *should* be sought – among others, comparative and historical analysis would hardly be possible (or meaningful).[11] And upon closer inspection, I am not sure whether Tamanaha's method can be considered 'mere minimalism' to begin with: for some concept of law would have to be present in order to translate whatever term is used by the society taken into consideration to describe its normative practices.[12]

The main outcome of this intellectual debate seems to be a two-pronged 'methodological checklist' against which every work in legal theory must be assessed. First, it is necessary for legal theorists to make explicit from the outset not only the methodology applied, but also the scope and limitations of their analysis, depending on their empirical references and the associated contextual background. Second, general jurisprudence should not consist exclusively of so-called 'armchair' conceptual analysis, but should rather adopt a more integrated approach which is actively informed by the methods and/or results from empirical disciplines. Let me say a bit more about each of these points.

As to the first, if we take analytical jurisprudence as a discipline over the course of the last century or so, a certain tendency to 'parochialism' can be identified.[13] While the charge to individual legal theorists of neglecting empirical analysis and aiming at building universally applicable theories of law might be overstated,[14] on the whole it is sensible to expect legal theorists to do a better job of clearly putting forward their aims (explanatory, normative, etc), underlying methodology, and resulting limitations, at the outset of their inquiries. One logical reason should suffice: the extension of concepts, and particularly of concepts related to social or artifactual kinds,[15] is partly determined by their intension, and this in turn affects the theoretical framework in which those concepts are used.

---

[9] See F Pirie, *The Anthropology of Law* (Oxford, Oxford University Press, 2013) introduction and ch 1.

[10] B Tamanaha, *A General Jurisprudence of Law and Society* (Oxford, Oxford University Press, 2001) 166.

[11] W Twining, 'A Post-Westphalian Concept of Law' (2003) 37(1) *Law and Society Review* 199; see also F Oliveira de Sousa, 'A Realistic Theory of Law' (2018) 9(2) *Jurisprudence* 438, 445 (quoting Gardner and Green who both make a similar point).

[12] KE Himma, 'Do Philosophy and Sociology Mix? A Non-Essentialist Socio-Legal Positivist Analysis of the Concept of Law' (2004) 24(4) *Oxford Journal of Legal Studies* 717, 736–738; K Ehrenberg, *The Functions of Law* (Oxford, Oxford University Press, 2016) 143.

[13] For a recent acknowledgement, see J Raz, 'Why the State?' in N Roughan and A Halpin (eds), *In Pursuit of Pluralist Jurisprudence* (Cambridge, Cambridge University Press, 2017).

[14] Certainly vis-à-vis Hart's 'descriptive sociology': F Schauer, '(Re)taking Hart' (2006) 119(3) *Harvard Law Review* 852, 860–861. For discussion, see Ehrenberg, *The Functions of Law* (n 12) 140–47; Green, 'Gender and the Analytical Jurisprudential Mind' (n 2) 894, fn 4.

[15] *cf* Himma, 'Conceptual Jurisprudence' (n 4) 74–75.

Brief Methodological Remarks 21

In other words, the empirical or normative scope of one's theory of law – viz the capability of that theory to explain or justify a set of legal phenomena across time and space – depends on one's definition of basic concepts like 'norm', 'obligation', 'right', and so forth. For example, the more a theory attempts to provide an account of legal validity in the context of our modern constitutional democratic legal systems, the less probable it is for such an account to be fruitfully applicable to legal systems developed at other moments in time and in other cultural and social contexts.[16]

The second methodological requirement, that legal theory should be informed by methods and/or results of empirical disciplines, can be conceived of in a weak or strong sense. In a weak sense, what seems to be required of legal theory is to take into account, consistently with the specific characteristics of its subject matter – and in particular its institutional-normative nature – the empirical findings reached in other fields of knowledge. To put it differently, an explanation of the nature of law that turned out to be incompatible with all plausible existing empirical theories that bear on the study of law would have to be discarded, at least prima facie. But this is a most sensible methodological claim, and one that few (if any) legal theorists are willing to deny.[17] What it does seem to exclude though is the possibility for theorists to base their analyses of law and legal concepts exclusively on their 'intuitions' as competent members of the relevant linguistic community.[18] Instead, general jurisprudence should be based on a more integrated methodology whereby the philosophical reflection on legal concepts and on the concept of law itself is actively informed by the results yielded by other disciplines like history, anthropology, sociology, and so forth.

But this requirement of continuity between legal theory and empirical sciences can also be understood in a much stronger sense: as the claim that the scope and methods of the former ought to be fully determined by the scope and methods of the latter. This is the meta-theoretical position behind not only some versions of legal pluralism, but also the vast majority of approaches that we group under the headings of legal realism.[19] In this respect, the project of a 'naturalised jurisprudence' as famously defended by Brian Leiter[20] can also be considered the intellectual outcome of an innate reaction[21] within legal scholarship to the

---

[16] L Ferrajoli, *Principia Iuris*, vol I (Bari, Laterza, 2007) 5–6. As Ferrajoli argues, this does not exclude that a theory of law might be built via progressive intensifications, with the result that different stages of the theory might have different explanatory capacities depending on the empirical references chosen.

[17] A notable exception might be S Shapiro, *Legality* (Cambridge, Harvard University Press, 2011) 406–07 (and see on this Ehrenberg, *The Functions of Law* (n 12) 141–42).

[18] Himma, 'Conceptual Jurisprudence' (n 4) 75.

[19] On a rather unexplored connection between American legal realism and legal pluralism, see JL Halperin, 'Law in Books and Law in Action: The Problem of Legal Change' (2011) 64(4) *Maine Law Review* 45.

[20] B Leiter, *Naturalising Jurisprudence* (Oxford, Oxford University Press, 2007).

[21] In some case even anticipating Quine's naturalism in epistemology, to the point that Leiter calls the American legal realists 'prescient naturalists': ibid 58.

22   *Law, Power, and Political Authority*

predominance of analytical jurisprudence, in particular following the work of Austin. What is immediately noticeable about legal realism is that it developed almost simultaneously in three different schools across the western world: the American, the Scandinavian, and the Italian school (in Genoa). As Leiter's project (and legal realism more generally) will be considered in chapter three, I only want to emphasise for now the strong reservations (expressed even by scholars intellectually contiguous with legal realism) about Leiter's claim that legal scholars should give up conceptual analysis altogether and merely adopt the concepts already in use by successful empirical theories of law.[22]

One of the biggest obstacles for any project that purports to displace conceptual analysis from the toolkit of the legal scholar, as we shall argue more at length in chapter three, is the inability of any empirical approach on its own to account for what is considered to be one of the central features of law, its normativity. To be sure, one should certainly not take normativity as everything there is to the study of law:[23] at best, norms are always only one aspect of the legal phenomena, which must also be investigated from the point of view of those forms of human behaviour that are regulated by those norms.[24] Conceptual and empirical analyses should be seen then as complementary rather than in opposition to one another: the former holds as its references primarily those entities that we intuitively call legal norms, while the latter looks at the legal phenomena by considering the forms of behaviour of those agents to which legal norms assign a meaning that goes beyond the physical act itself. For instance, when we click a particular area on our smartphones' touchscreens and *by doing that* we enter into a commercial contract (that produces rights and obligations) with an online retailer. Analysing a form of behaviour without reference to the norms that give legal meaning to it would yield no understanding of the way in which law is a *normative* practice, that is of the way in which law purports to coordinate or generally organise conduct. At the same time, analysing the normative language of the law without reference to those regulated forms of behaviour that are involved in the creation and application of legal norms would contribute little to our understanding of law as a normative *practice*, that is, as a human-made system of signs and meanings that is to some degree efficacious (a social fact).

Indeed, this ambivalence of legal theory has been accounted for in different ways by different scholars: while HLA Hart distinguished the internal point of view of norm-users from the external one of the mere observer of a legal practice,[25] Roscoe Pound brought to fame the distinction between 'law in books' – as the text of legal documents as laid down by legislatures and officials – and

---

[22] See T Spaak, 'Book Review: Brian Leiter, Naturalizing Jurisprudence' (2008) 74(4) *Theoria* 352.

[23] Nor should one take accounting for the normativity of law as the only justification for conceptual analysis as a method in general jurisprudence: see Green, 'Gender and the Analytical Jurisprudential Mind' (n 2) 900, for whom the 'fruitfulness of conceptual analysis can depend on how anthropocentric and mind-dependent a thing is' (law being 'thoroughly' both).

[24] Ferrajoli, *Principia Iuris* (n 16) 8–11.

[25] HLA Hart, *The Concept of Law*, 3rd edn (Oxford, Oxford University Press, 2012).

The Province of the Problem Determined: What is Law? 23

'law in action' as the actual decision-making practices of courts and officials more generally.[26] What makes the epistemic status of conceptual analysis within legal theory so relevant though is not just this gap between human behaviour and norms which purport to regulate those forms of behaviour, but the fact that its subject matter – the purposive organisation of human conduct through the guidance of rules – is directly responsive to (if not partially constituted by)[27] its theoretical elaboration. To wit, legal science bears an inherent reflexive quality, in the sense that it can performatively impact and ultimately modify its very object of study.

This is perhaps most clearly shown by the example of a court in a modern legal system that adopts a certain definition of a legal institution (or solution to a given legal issue) as presented in a scholarly contribution, thus making it into law for that legal system. But already for hundreds of years one can see the reflexive status of legal science at work in the great systematisations and codifications of law operated by jurists across Europe (at least since the redaction of the *Corpus Iuris Civilis*) and in the writing of many thousands of textbooks in individual legal disciplines, like criminal or commercial law (what is called 'legal dogmatics' in Europe and 'legal doctrine' in Anglo-American parlance).

Overall, this shows why general jurisprudence should be understood as a pluralistic enterprise: an overarching discourse in which different and complementary viewpoints on the legal phenomenon – the theoretical, the empirical, and the doctrinal (at least) – are to be considered together in an overarching explanatory project.[28] And while the study of law can never be reduced to any of its components without a significant loss of explanatory capacity, one should also always be aware at the same time of its potential pragmatic effects vis-à-vis its object of study. *Pace* Kelsen, there can never be a pure theory of law and, as such, the legal theorist should make every effort to make explicit the methodological and axiological premises undergirding her approach as much as possible.[29] A 'modest' theory of law seems all we can, and should, hope to achieve.[30]

III. THE PROVINCE OF THE PROBLEM DETERMINED: WHAT IS LAW?

What has just been said was not aimed, just to be sure, at offering a comprehensive methodology for legal theory. That would require a book in itself. My intention instead was merely to pave the way for articulating the scope and

---

[26] R Pound, 'Law in Books and Law in Action' (1910) 44(1) *American Law Review* 12.

[27] Especially if we understand law as an 'artefactual kind': see the contributions in L Burazin, KE Himma, and C Roversi (eds), *Law as an Artifact* (Oxford, Oxford University Press, 2018).

[28] See L Ferrajoli, 'The General Theory of Law: on Its Subject, Its Method and Its Function' (2012) 1(2) *Rivista di Filosofia del Diritto – Journal of Legal Philosophy* 229.

[29] *cf* Dickson, *Evaluation and Legal Theory* (n 2) ch 1.

[30] Ehrenberg, *The Functions of Law* (n 12) ch 6.

24 *Law, Power, and Political Authority*

limits of this work. In relation to the scope, there is no better way to illustrate it than to point at the undisputed contention that the problem of political obligation is the problem of why one should obey the law.[31] To be sure, in this book I will not be addressing this problem – that is, I will not discuss whether or not there exists a moral obligation to obey the law, or under which conditions such obligation might obtain. Rather, I am interested in the relationship between law and politics that seems to be commonly implied by political and legal philosophers. In fact, taken at face value, the statement in question seems to presuppose some relation of identity between law and politics, at least in terms of their outputs. As we shall see shortly, this might not be necessarily true of all (systems of) law and of all frameworks of organisation of communities all the time, everywhere around the world. Or at least there is no scholarly consensus on this.

And yet, it seems historically hard to deny that if we are referring to our late modernity and to the systems of politics developed in or around that time, the hallmark of any type of political authority is precisely the capacity to rule over a certain population via the creation and application of standards of conduct and other types of norms which are also usually backed by threat of sanctions or coercive enforcement.[32] It is this connection between law and political power, in both its conceptual and contingent elements, that I am interested in here, and in particular in the context of our constitutional democratic frameworks. This also should clarify the boundaries of my enquiry: my ultimate intention is to show how the very possibility of distinguishing between the activities of law-creation and law-application represents a necessary (but not sufficient) condition of legitimacy of modern constitutional democracies. But before we begin to analyse the relation between law and politics, we have to clarify the way in which the two limbs of this relation will be understood in this work.

In this regard, I understand 'law' as a specific social technique for subjecting human conduct to the guidance of rules (and rulings).[33] What are the main explanatory benefits of this definition? While it is clearly able to refer empirically to the complex institutional normative practice that we are most familiar with, it also seems to constitute a good starting point for comparative analysis of different legal phenomena through time and space. For it is conceptually thin enough to accommodate a wider variety of law practices than (for instance) an

---

[31] D Miller, *Political Philosophy: A Very Short Introduction* (Oxford, Oxford University Press, 2003) 31; J Wolff, *An Introduction to Political Philosophy*, 3rd edn (Oxford, Oxford University Press, 2015) 38.

[32] For a discussion of the role that the connection between law and political power might have in marking law's distinctiveness vis-à-vis other normative systems, see A Halpin, 'The Search for Law' (2014) 5(2) *Jurisprudence* 410.

[33] J Gardner, 'The Supposed Formality of the Rule of Law' in J Gardner, *Law as a Leap of Faith: Essays on Law in General* (Oxford, Oxford University Press, 2012) 206–211, who underscores the importance of adding 'and rulings' to Fuller's famous definition of law (L Fuller, *The Morality of Law*, rev. edn (New Haven, Yale University Press, 1977)). See also, at least, H Kelsen, 'The Law as a Specific Social Technique' (1941) 9(1) *University of Chicago Law Review* 75; J Rawls, *A Theory of Justice*, rev edn (Cambridge, Belknap Press, 1999) 206–13.

The Province of the Problem Determined: What is Law? 25

exclusive understanding of law as 'state law'.[34] And yet it has the advantage of doing so without losing completely analytical purchase, as it would happen if we were to follow Tamanaha's 'non-essentialism'.[35] In other words, despite its apparent 'thinness', this is a definition of law that tells us a good deal about its characteristics and that as such allows us to distinguish law from at least some other social phenomena that are nonetheless related to it. In addition, at this level of generality, this definition is compatible with both positivism and non-positivism, as it does not necessarily imply any particular thesis on the (ultimate) source of the validity of the rules that are supposed to guide behaviour. Finally, despite its conciseness, this definition points already to several features that, if not essential, must be at least considered as central or 'focal' to our subject of enquiry:[36]

1. law is a human activity, which for some entails the further thesis of the artifactual nature of law;[37]
2. law is a purposeful activity, which yields the importance of a functional analysis of law;[38]
3. law is a normative activity, as it involves mainly (but not only) the provision and manipulation of standards of behaviour;[39]
4. law is a linguistic, and more generally expressive, activity, in that it is based on (abstract) entities such as rules (and norms) created through speech-acts;
5. law is a communicative activity, for its addressees must be generally capable of taking rules into account in their practical reasoning;
6. for rules to be able to guide conduct, law must be generally capable of being applied by the rule-users themselves (*ad impossibilia nemo tenetur*);[40]
7. law is an activity that involves mainly (but not only) rules, and as such is premised on certain formal characteristics such as generality and abstractness (in other words, the idea of formal equality is embedded in the concept of law).

In the rest of the book I will engage at several points with one or more of the features above, either individually or jointly. For the moment I will just limit

---

[34] *cf* Del Mar, 'Beyond the State in and of Legal Theory' (n 5).

[35] SP Dolan and L Heckendorn Urscheler, 'Concepts of Law: An Introduction', in SP Dolan and L Heckendorn Urscheler (eds), *Concepts of Law: Comparative, Jurisprudential, and Social Science Perspectives*, (Surrey, Ashgate, 2012) 9–10.

[36] *cf* J Finnis, *Natural Law and Natural Rights*, 2nd edn (Oxford, Oxford University Press, 2011) ch 1. For a recent discussion on the scope of the philosophical debate on the nature of law, see F Schauer, *The Force of Law* (Cambridge, Harvard University Press, 2015) 3–5.

[37] See, eg: Burazin, Himma and Roversi (eds), *Law as an Artifact* (n 27).

[38] See Ehrenberg, *The Functions of Law* (n 12) 121–22 for the claim of the relevance of a functional analysis of law even if law is not a functional kind.

[39] On the normativity of law, see, eg: S Bertea, *The Normative Claim of Law* (Oxford, Hart Publishing, 2009); S Bertea, *A Theory of Legal Obligation* (Cambridge, Cambridge University Press, 2019).

[40] This feature can be understood in two senses, as 'clarity' and as 'compliability': B Celano, 'Law as Power: Two Rule of Law Requirements', in W Waluchow and S Sciaraffa (eds), *Philosophical Foundations of the Nature of Law* (Oxford, Oxford University Press, 2013) 129–51.

26 *Law, Power, and Political Authority*

myself to pre-empting the objection of those who might think that (especially with the sixth and seventh feature) I may be conflating a definition of law with that of the ideal of the rule of law. In one sense, this is indeed the case, for the ideal of the rule of law – in its formal conception – is usually understood as the list of attributes that a system of government must possess to avoid being considered a system of arbitrary or purely discretionary rule.[41] And while I shall say more on the rule of law (and its institutional dimension) in chapter two, the point is that we can only establish what it takes for political power to be exercised according to 'law' if we know what 'law' is in the first place. There is an internal relation between the two, and in putting forward any definition of law we are already determining (in part at least) what it will take for a political system to conform to the ideal of the rule of law (in its institutional and normative senses).

IV. POLITICS, POLITICAL POWER, POLITICAL AUTHORITY

A different difficulty in approaching the relation between law and politics is that, if we embrace the conceptual fragmentation in legal and political literature, we might actually be referring to at least three different phenomena at the same time:

a. the relationship between law and *politics*, that is the vast array of practices, activities, and structures that make up the exercise of governmental power over a certain community;

b. the relationship between law and *political authority*, that is the legitimate normative power held by those in office vis-à-vis the other members of the social group; and

c. the relationship between law and *political power*, which instead amounts, at least prima facie, to the sheer capacity of some institutions to elicit behaviour through non-normative mechanisms.

If terminological usages were to be consistent across authors and disciplines, there would be little or no problem. For there is clearly a sense in which one thing is the relationship between law and politics – for instance, in the legal structure of political parties, or in the influence that prosecutorial and judicial activities can have on any political system (as seen more than two decades ago in Italy with the 'Clean Hands' operation, and more recently in Brazil with *Lava Jato*) – and another is the more specific relationship between law and political authority, as expressed by the problem of political obligation. But, alas, such terminological consistency is nowhere to be found, as is readily shown by

---

[41] See J Waldron, 'The Rule of Law', in EN Zalta (ed), *The Stanford Encyclopedia of Philosophy* (Summer 2020 Edition) plato.stanford.edu/archives/sum2020/entries/rule-of-law/. See also Rawls, *A Theory of Justice* (n 33) 206–13.

the different (and sometimes contradictory) uses of the concept of 'political power' in the existing literature:[42]

i. in some cases, and probably following Locke, 'political power' is taken to be equivalent to 'political authority' (as the normative power that rulers legitimately or merely de facto exercise over the governed);[43]

ii. for other scholars 'political authority' (as normative) and 'political power' stand in stark contrast to each other, the latter being the type of power that 'operates completely in the realm of threats and offers';[44]

iii. yet, in another influential strand of the literature, 'political power' is institutional and relational – as the 'power to act in concert'[45] – and thus contrasted with coercive power that equates to domination (exemplified by power exercised in non-democratic regimes).

What is to be made of this variance, and how can we move forward in considering the relationship between law and political power? Let me start by specifying that, in the rest of this work, I will use political power and political authority interchangeably to signify the 'right to rule' (either legitimate or de facto).[46] This will be distinguished from (collective) coercive power (non-normative 'power over', in the terminology below) on the one hand, and politics (as the wider understanding of practices and processes that determine the output of the exercise of political power) on the other.[47] By way of illustration, I take coercive power to be the type of power exercised exclusively through the use of threats and force by a belligerent army invading a foreign territory. While this type of power might be effective in the same way that a de facto political authority is – members of the group which are subject to the military rule will comply more often than not with it – their compliance will not be grounded in any set of normative attitudes towards the exercise of power itself. For any type of even minimal acceptance or acquiescence towards the military rule by the population – which would suffice to constitute it as a de facto political authority – seems

---

[42] See for discussion, K Dowding, 'Why should we care about the definition of power?' (2012) 5(1) *Journal of Political Power* 119; a very useful collection of different accounts of power can be found in M Haugaard (ed), *Power: A Reader* (Manchester, Manchester University Press, 2012).

[43] See, eg: Wolff, *Introduction to Political Philosophy* (n 31) 1–2; M Loughlin, *Sword and Scales: An Examination of the Relationship between Law and Politics* (Oxford, Hart Publishing, 2000); F Peter, 'Political Legitimacy' in EN Zalta (ed), *The Stanford Encyclopedia of Philosophy* (Summer 2017 Edition) http://plato.stanford.edu/archives/sum2017/entries/legitimacy/.

[44] T Christiano, 'Authority' in EN Zalta (ed) *The Stanford Encyclopedia of Philosophy* (Summer 2020 Edition) http://plato.stanford.edu/archives/sum2020/entries/authority.

[45] H Arendt, *On Violence* (New York, Harcourt, 1970) 44; Loughlin, *Sword and Scales* (n 43) 16.

[46] On how different accounts of political legitimacy differ in this respect, see, eg: Peter, 'Political Legitimacy' (n 43).

[47] In making this distinction I do not wish to take position in the debate between scholars who take political legitimacy to be geared towards the justification of authority (see, eg: L Green, *The Authority of the State* (Oxford, Oxford University Press, 1988) 75), and those who instead see the justification of coercive political power as the main object of political theory (for this latter position, see A Ripstein, 'Authority and Coercion' (2004) 32(1) *Philosophy & Public Affairs* 2; and R Dworkin, *Law's Empire* (Cambridge, Harvard University Press, 1986).

28   Law, Power, and Political Authority

excluded a-priori by the use of force and threats to elicit such compliance.[48] This also points to the centrality of the distinction between the conditions of existence and those of legitimacy of political authority.[49]

According to Bobbio, 'power' is one (if not *the*) main concern of political theory, to the extent that the latter should 'be considered as part of the theory of power'.[50] In general, one could say that the concept of power in political discourse is used to characterise the ability of some entity to control itself, its environment, and the beings within it. But at the same time, 'power' is routinely deployed in several fields of knowledge with different meanings: the CPU power of calculus, a power cord, a car's powertrain, etc. Is it then, perhaps, what Wittgenstein would call a 'family resemblance' concept?[51]

Notably, the polysemy of 'power' seems variably dependent on language. For instance, in English the same word 'power' is used to express at least two different concepts that are, in other languages, expressed with different words. Here I refer to the difference between the Italian *potere* – the ability to do something – and *potenza* – the potentiality, or also the strength (or its measurement) of an entity. These two concepts are clearly different, and this distinction can be found in other Romance languages too: in French *pouvoir* and *puissance*, in Spanish *poder* and *potencia*.[52]

This polysemy in the English language, while it can be arguably clarified in everyday linguistic usage by the context of specific utterances,[53] remains more problematic for philosophical and political enquiry. This has been the case, for instance, in translating and discussing Spinoza's works in the English-speaking world.[54] In this regard, the *Tractatus politicus* is based prominently upon the distinction between *potentia* and *potestas*, respectively 'power-to-create' and 'power-to-command'[55] – where the latter is also translated

---

[48] See Hart, *Concept of Law* (n 25) ch 2.

[49] Stressing the importance of this distinction is A Marmor, 'An Institutional Conception of Authority' (2011) 39(3) *Philosophy & Public Affairs* 238.

[50] N Bobbio, *Democracy and Dictatorship: The Nature and Limits of State Power* (Oxford, Polity Press, 1989), 70.

[51] M Haugaard, 'Introduction', in Haugaard, *Power: A Reader* (n 42) 1.

[52] As I argue below, the distinction derives from the Latin '*potestas*' and '*potentia*'. While both 'potency' and 'might' exist in the English vocabulary, they are not routinely used to differentiate power as *potestas* and power as *potentia*.

[53] Haugaard, 'Introduction' (n 51) 2.

[54] *cf* M Walther, 'Natural Law, Civil Law, and International Law in Spinoza' (2003) 25(2) *Cardozo Law Review* 657, who translates *potentia* with potency; see also M Hardt, 'Translator's Forward: The Anatomy of Power' in A Negri, *The Savage Anomaly: The Power of Spinoza's Metaphysics and Politics*, 3rd edn, (M Hardt tr, Minneapolis, University of Minnesota Press, 2003) (originally published in Italian as *L'anomalia selvaggia. Saggio su potere e Potenza in Baruch Spinoza* (Milan, Feltrinelli, 1981)); J Steinberg, 'Spinoza's Political Philosophy' in EN Zalta (ed), *The Stanford Encyclopedia of Philosophy* (Summer 2019 Edition) http://plato.stanford.edu/archives/sum2019/entries/spinoza-political/.

[55] M Henninger and A Negri, 'From Sociological to Ontological Inquiry: An Interview with Antonio Negri' (2005) 23(1) *Italian Culture* 153, 156. While *potestas* is always relational (you have *potestas* over somebody or something), *potentia* is more of a relationship with the universe surrounding a certain being. For a different reading of Spinoza's *potestas* and *potentia* and relative

with 'authority'.[56] The lack of agreement in the literature has prompted Dowding to suggest that power might not been just polysemic and polythetic, but perhaps ultimately an essentially contested concept.[57]

A trend has emerged however in the literature that recognises at least two distinct understandings (that is, two different concepts) of power loosely traceable back to Spinoza's.[58] In the first one, 'power to', power expresses the immanent or original ability of most living beings to affect reality, that is, to shape and change the structure of the sensorial world: from the insignificant and temporary fact of leaving traces of one's passage on untouched soil, to the much more meaningful fact of mastering the world's features for one's own purposes (such as the transformation of a piece of wood into an artifact).[59]

On the other hand, power can be conceived of as the capacity to influence and cause behaviour (through persuasion or coercion, for instance) on the parts of others: 'power over'. While in the first sense power is dispositional, in the latter sense power is always, and by definition, a relational matter, for it presupposes a relation between its exercise and some subjects, towards whom it is directed, in a certain situation. Also, 'power over' can be possessed by human artifacts (ie institutions) and not just by individuals and groups. What is relevant for our purposes is that there are two very different types of 'power over' that can be exercised: a non-normative and a normative one. The former amounts to influence, persuasion, or (brute) force or strength: the natural fact that one animal is stronger than others and can influence and/or control their behaviour. The latter instead can be conceived of as the meaning of practical authority – the 'normative power to change another's normative relations'[60] – that has been so prominently at the centre of philosophical debate.[61] It is a normative

---

critical discussion, see M Loughlin, *Foundations of Public Law* (Oxford, Oxford University Press, 2010) 164–171.

[56] Although this is not considered entirely satisfactory in the context of Spinoza's work: Hardt, 'The Anatomy of Power' (n 54) xi. For a general overview of the interconnections between power, influence and authority in law, see E Pattaro, *The Law and The Right: A Reappraisal of the Reality that Ought to Be, A Treatise of Legal Philosophy and General Jurisprudence*, vol 1 (Dordrecht, Springer, 2007) 202.

[57] Dowding, 'Why should we care about the definition of power?' (n 42).

[58] *cf* for a critical analysis of the distinction, P Pansardi, 'Power to and power over: two distinct concepts of power?' (2012) 5(1) *Journal of Political Power* 73.

[59] Anthony Giddens in his influential theory of structuration defines power as a 'transformative capacity', that is, 'the capability to intervene in a given set of events so as in some way to alter them'. For him it constitutes an 'elementary concept' for social sciences, along with 'agency' and 'structure'. In this regard, 'to be a human being is to be an agent – although not all agents are human beings – and to be an agent is to have power': A Giddens, *A Contemporary Critique of Historical Materialism*, vol 2 (Berkeley, University of California Press, 1985) 7.

[60] See S Shapiro, 'Authority', in J Coleman, KE Himma and S Shapiro (eds), *The Oxford Handbook of Jurisprudence and Philosophy of Law* (Oxford, Oxford University Press, 2004), 398; Loughlin, *Foundations of Public Law* (n 55) 164. Marmor notes that a power to change normative relations between two or more parties implies those relations exist before the power is exercised: Marmor, 'An Institutional Conception of Authority' (n 49) 241.

[61] For one of the most helpful discussions of the complex debate in the literature on the concept of authority, see N Roughan, *Authorities: Conflicts, Cooperation, and Transnational Legal Theory* (Oxford, Oxford University Press, 2013) ch 2.

30 Law, Power, and Political Authority

relation between two or more subjects (which Raz has rendered simply as the 'right to rule')[62] of which political authority is a species.[63] Importantly, only some people or institutional entities, such as chiefs, monarchs, or governments, can claim or possess it. How is this so?

V. FROM POWERS TO POWER. THE FAMILIAR TALE OF THE INELUCTABILITY OF THE STATE

I submit that the difference between the non-normative and the normative senses of 'power over' sits prominently at the core of political and legal theory. It is such difference – and in particular the transition from the unavoidability of the former to the possibility of the latter – that Hobbes for instance tried to capture, within the specific historical context of his writing,[64] with the metaphor of the state of nature. In the most familiar and influential interpretation of Hobbes' thought, people free themselves from the fear of succumbing to (the powers of) others, by means of the constituted political sovereign and its authority.[65] This enables them to radically improve their prospects of survival and to pursue better conditions of life and more forward-looking endeavours. But this passage from the pre-political to the political is not without cost. Rather, it comes at the price of creating and enabling another kind of power, much bigger both in qualitative and quantitative terms and on the whole perhaps even more dangerous than pre-political 'power(s) over': the political power of the 'state'.[66] Seen from this perspective, there seems to be a circular problem of limitation of power: in order to limit 'power(s) over' in the pre-political condition, men create a different and more dangerous type of power, political power, which needs in turn to be limited.

There are clearly echoes of this familiar tale – from the short and 'brutish' state of nature to the security and prosperity allowed by the existence of a political authority – in Hannah Arendt's idea of power within the 'political condition'. Through her reading of the Greek civilisation, she defines political power as formed of action (*praxis*) and speech (*lexis*), with a special weight on the latter.[67] These are the two components, at least at the outset, of the *bios politikos* (the political life), which stood in contrast to the private life in the household, and which marked for her the distinctiveness of the Greek *polis*

---

[62] J Raz, 'Introduction', in J Raz (ed), *Authority* (New York, New York University Press, 1990) 2–3.

[63] See, for discussion, Roughan, *Authorities* (n 61) 19–20.

[64] On the relevance of Hobbes' historical context to his political philosophy, see J Sommerville, *Thomas Hobbes: Political Ideas in Historical Context* (New York, St Martin's Press, 1992).

[65] *cf* H Arendt, *The Human Condition*, 2nd edn (Chicago, University of Chicago Press, 1998) 32.

[66] Here 'state' stands for any kind of (centralised) political institution. For discussion, see, eg: Bobbio, *Democracy and Dictatorship* (n 50) 125–132; Del Mar, Beyond the State in and of Legal Theory (n 5).

[67] Arendt, *Human Condition* (n 65) 25.

From Powers to Power. The Familiar Tale of the Ineluctability of the State 31

from the institutional forms of organisation of the primitive empires of Asia.[68] As such,

> [t]o be political, to live in a *polis*, meant that everything was decided through words and persuasion and not through force and violence.[69]

From Arendt's considerations it emerges that collective decision-making, *qua* political power, acquires its distinctiveness from its pre-political antecedent. It is power (*potestas*) *qua* 'ability not just to act but to act in concert'.[70] Violence, to the extent that amounts to a manifestation of strength, is excluded by the 'communicative togetherness' of the political life.[71] In the pre-political condition (or the state of nature) there is no such togetherness, for animals are driven by necessity and conceive of each other as pure objects of material action, rather than subjects of rational *inter*-action. Hence communicative togetherness can only take place in the public space of the *polis*, where free and equal agents recognise each other as belonging to the same space,[72] and also to a shared destiny. This marks a new beginning for human history, namely the passage from sheer strength and violence – which is always and significantly 'mute'[73]– to speech *qua* 'rational *inter*-action' with other beings.[74] In Arendt's words,

> [i]n Greek self-understanding, to force people by violence, to command rather than persuade, were prepolitical ways to deal with people characteristic of life outside the polis, of home and family life, where the household head ruled with uncontested, despotic powers, or of life in the barbarian empires of Asia, whose despotism was frequently likened to the organization of the household.[75]

In her account, the naturalistic notion of 'power over', in order to be reconciled with the rational and reflexive understanding of men as 'social animals',[76] departs from its meaning as 'brute force' and is normatively reconceived of as a limited (*qua* positive) capacity to 'act in concert' as part of the political community:[77] a normative place which people access by deciding to leave the animal condition – the 'non-state' of Bobbio[78] – and the laws of nature. And within this teleological view of history, one that sees a linear evolution from the

---

[68] ibid 27.

[69] ibid 26.

[70] See Arendt, *On Violence* (n 45). For the claim that the evolution of politics is an 'achievement of considerable human significance': Loughlin, *Sword and Scales* (n 43) 7.

[71] The relevance of this 'communicative togetherness' for law will be highlighted in ch 5.

[72] H Arendt, *On Revolution* (London, Penguin Books, 1963) 31.

[73] Arendt, *Human Condition* (n 65) 26.

[74] *cf* ibid 27. This implies a conception of the *other* as capable of recognising and understanding speech precisely as the distinctive decision-making process on and of the public space. Yet this change must not be understood in universalising scope, since equality and freedom do not belong to everyone within the polis.

[75] ibid 26–27.

[76] ibid 23.

[77] In this regard 'political power' stands for both the power of the political institution – polis, state, etc – and for the power of individuals that can be legitimately exercised within that political institution: Bobbio, *Democracy and Dictatorship* (n 50) 89.

[78] ibid 126ff.

32 Law, Power, and Political Authority

state of nature to the *polis*, political theory can be understood as the enterprise of supplementing the exercise of normative 'power over' with a set of (necessary) conditions for its acceptance *qua* political (and nourishment as such).[79]

What is wrong with this familiar, and still very influential, tale of the genesis of political power? In short, there is growing archaeological evidence on which anthropologists and political scientists ground quite a different picture of the passage from the pre-political to the political condition. Two assumptions are contested in particular: first, that coordination and (some level of) stability and prosperity are not possible in the absence of centralised rule or authority, as Hobbes and many following him clearly presuppose; second, that the passage from the acephalous societies of hunter-gatherers of the Mesolithic to the emergence of centralised settlements which appeared around the world (for instance in Mesopotamia, in Egypt, and in ancient China) some 8,500 years ago is to be understood as a linear and evolutionary process, one that necessarily brings about the amelioration of the living conditions of those who experienced it.

A. And its Two-pronged Critique: Isonomia and 'Early' States

As to the first assumption, the historical significance and political relevance of what the Greeks had originally called 'ἰσονομία' ('isonomia', subsequently translated in English as 'isonomy') was progressively lost, until recently.[80] For especially in political literature the term came for centuries to be taken simply as a synonym for 'democracy', until Arendt and Friedrich von Hayek (writing at around the same period) questioned the received view.[81] In this regard, far from being a synonym of democracy, isonomia was instead consistently juxtaposed with it, as a

> form of political organization in which the citizens lived together under conditions of no-rule, without a division between rulers and ruled [and] whose outstanding characteristic among the forms of government ... was that the notion of rule ... was entirely absent from it.[82]

Interestingly, both Arendt and Hayek, after having correctly debunked the identification of isonomia with democracy, end up conceiving of it as equality before (or under) the law, which could only thrive if protected by the institution of the *polis*. But this seems to amount to an even bigger misconception of the ideal, one that is particularly surprising in the context of Arendt's accurate understanding of isonomia as 'no-rule'.[83] As she correctly stresses, in fact, isonomia

---

[79] See, eg: N Machiavelli, *Il Principe* (first published 1532, Milan, Garzanti, 2008).

[80] K Katarani, *Isonomia and the Origins of Philosophy* (J Murphy tr, Durham, Duke University Press, 2017) 13.

[81] Arendt, *Human Condition* (n 65) 32, and Arendt, *On Revolution* (n 72) 30–31; FA Hayek, *The Constitution of Liberty* (Chicago, University of Chicago Press, 1978) 165.

[82] Arendt, *On Revolution* (n 72) 30.

[83] For a discussion of the role of isonomia in Arendt's concept of law, see MA Wilkinson, 'Between Freedom and Law: Hannah Arendt on the Promise of Modern Revolution and the Burden of

From Powers to Power. The Familiar Tale of the Ineluctability of the State 33

appears to be rather different already at the terminological level from the other forms of government 'as the ancients had enumerated them': that is, monarchy, aristocracy and democracy. For in all of them the notion of 'authority' or 'power' is present – *ἀρχή* in monarchy and oligarchy, and *κράτος* in democracy[84] – while it is completely absent in that of isonomia. Perhaps this is due to the fact that Arendt might have understood isonomia as being present throughout mainland Greece, and rather as an ideal than as a historical reality.[85]

As Katarani has recently argued, instead, isonomia was not an ideal but a 'living reality' in the city-states of Ionia, on the western coast of present-day Turkey, up until their demise somewhere during the mid-sixth century BCE.[86] It was a particular type of 'covenant community (*schwurgemeinschaft*)' that arose because of the particular conditions of the *poleis* of Ionia, which were made up by migrants from mainland Greece who renounced whatever type of 'clan and tribal traditions' (and kinship ties) while 'constraints and privileges' were 'set aside'.[87] This meant that 'In Ionia, people were free from traditional ruling relations', while also being 'economically equal in their lives.'[88] Such economic equality was practically guaranteed by a double kind of mobility that people living in the Ionian *poleis* (unlike people in the mainland) had: the freedom, on the one hand, to migrate to a new city in the Ionia region if they found themselves landless (thus preventing large landowners and slavery)[89] and, on the other, to freely pursue commerce and trade with the rest of the Asian region.[90]

In other words, the economic system of Ionia's cities was not based on slavery but on the free market of landowners and merchants, and in this sense it was intrinsically egalitarian. Karatani contends that it is precisely the absence of whatever type of political power or 'rule' in Ionian isonomia, in addition to the two freedoms just mentioned, that allowed its 'money economy' to flourish

---

"The Tradition"', in M Goldoni and C McCorkindale (eds), *Hannah Arendt and the Law* (Oxford, Hart Publishing, 2012) 54–60.

[84] Arendt, *On Revolution* (n 72) 30.

[85] Katarani, *Isonomia and the Origins of Philosophy* (n 80) 14–15. Herodotus himself, raised in Ionia, eventually equates isonomia with Athenian democracy: ibid 32.

[86] ibid, ch 1.

[87] ibid 15.

[88] ibid.

[89] This implies that a constant surplus of available land is a necessary pre-requisite for an isonomic order to develop: ibid 29. As such, the likelihood of isonomia progressively decreases as the population of the given community grows and reaches close to nil with the institutionalisation of (land) property.

[90] ibid 13–26. This reconstruction of the system of isonomia gives weight to the philological hypothesis that among three possible meanings of the second part of the word (νόμος) – goods, pastures (for flocks), or law – the second one should be privileged. In this sense isonomia would refer – at least initially, in the Ionian context – to the equal distribution of lands in customary practices; and only later – perhaps when idealised in the writing of Herodotus and other historians and political philosophers – as 'equality before the law': see, eg: G Vlastos, 'Isonomia' (1953) 74(4) *The American Journal of Philology* 337; M Ostwald, *Nomos and the Beginnings of the Athenian Democracy* (Oxford, Clarendon Press, 1969); V Costa, 'Osservazioni sul Concetto di Isonomia' in A D'Atena and E Lanzilotta (eds), *Da Omero alla Costituzione Europea. Costituzionalismo Antico e Moderno* (Tivoli, Tored, 2003).

34 *Law, Power, and Political Authority*

without any immediate and 'serious' creation of 'class disparities'.[91] In Arendt's consequential definition of isonomia,

> [to] be free meant both not to be subject to the necessity of life or to the command of another *and* not to be in command oneself. It meant neither to rule nor to be ruled.[92]

But it is only under the system of isonomia that freedom and equality are truly reconciled, because equality is realised through freedom.[93] Democracy, even Athenian direct democracy, does not escape the conflict between the two values, because the inequality in wealth (and practical conditions) between the many and the few requires that for equality to be achieved, the freedom of the wealthy few must be limited.[94] But this limitation could only obtain through the exercise of a centralised law-making power which,[95] as such, is revealed as a necessary 'prerequisite' of any type of democratic regime.[96]

For our purposes, what is important to note is that the historical presence of at least a peaceful and prosperous system of organisation of a community (a normative order) that was not based on centralised rule invalidates the Hobbesian thesis that such centralised power was necessary to overcome the 'state of nature'. 'Isonomic' communities have likely appeared at different times in different parts of the world, when a certain set of very specific conditions – new communities formed by immigrants in a new land who were thus able and willing to break free of traditional ties and customs and form a new fundamentally egalitarian covenant – occurred.[97] In these 'acephalous' communities we could find *rules* but no *rule*: no individual within them had higher normative power than anyone else, and thus no one – not even a majority of the members of the community – could legitimately impose requirements on someone else against their will. If that were to happen, the individual would be able to leave the community and go somewhere else, and the state of isonomia of the community would likely dissolve into something else. This is also the sense, I submit, in which we should more specifically understand isonomia in its modern rendition: not as 'equality before the law' given by a centralised political power, but rather as the state of equality in a normative order – equality in the *nomos*. This is a condition which cannot by definition obtain in a democratic system: for, like oligarchy and monarchy, democracy presupposes the presence of political rule

---

[91] Katarani, *Isonomia and the Origins of Philosophy* (n 80) 25–6

[92] Arendt, *Human Condition* (n 65) 32. See also Arendt, *On Revolution* (n 72) 30.

[93] Katarani, *Isonomia and the Origins of Philosophy* (n 80) 25.

[94] ibid 15–16, (recalling Aristotle on the point).

[95] Albeit not necessarily through a centralised system of enforcement: A Lanni, *Law and Order in Ancient Athens* (Cambridge, Cambridge University Press, 2016).

[96] Katarani, *Isonomia and the Origins of Philosophy* (n 80) 19.

[97] Katarani (ibid 27–29) cites as examples of other isonomic communities around the world the Icelandic Commonwealth (930–1264) and the decentralisation and autonomy enjoyed by American townships in the 18th and 19th century. On the conflicting accounts of the decentralised institutional evolution of the Icelandic Commonwealth, see BTR Solvason, 'Institutional evolution in the Icelandic Commonwealth' (1993) 4(1) *Constitutional Political Economy* 97.

From Powers to Power. The Familiar Tale of the Ineluctability of the State   35

in the hands of someone (the majority), and thus a state of ultimate normative *inequality*.

If the first criticism of the mainstream Hobbesian narrative questions the assumption of the 'ineluctability' of the state – in the sense of centralised political authority – vis-à-vis the prosperity of any social group, the second line of criticism contends that even when a centralised authority emerged some 8,000 years ago, this did not necessarily ameliorate the living conditions of the populations involved. As recently argued, in the 'earlier' states formed around 6000 BCE in Ancient Mesopotamia (and elsewhere),

> [c]ontrol over the sources and distribution of subsistence and wealth, the segregation and maintenance of the symbols of social integration and incorporation, and the ability to impose obedience by force, both on the governmental level and also within local groups, together constitute the main dimensions of power ...[98]

As a result, the centralisation of power, at least at its inception, seems to have actually benefited only a very small part of the population – the rulers – while leaving the vast majority in the same, if not worse, conditions.[99] This was hinted at already in Arendt's juxtaposition of the Greek *poleis* – where freedom and equality for many (but still not for all) obtain through their laws – and the despotism of the 'barbarian empires of Asia';[100] but it can be seen more clearly and generally through the recent archaeological discoveries that fundamentally undermine the 'basic narrative of sedentism and agriculture'[101] as linear progressive stages on the path to civilisation on which so many different accounts of social evolution have converged.[102] For, as it has been recently argued,

> [t]he shift from hunting and foraging to agriculture – a shift that was slow, halting, reversible, and sometimes incomplete – carried at least as many costs as benefits.[103]

I do not mean to deny that in any large society, and particularly in complex modern societies, centralised political structures are necessary to coordinate behaviour and thus facilitate cooperation, by way of, among other things, reassuring norm-followers of the enforcement of norms when these are breached by some members of the group. What matters for my purposes is to highlight the nature of any political structure as a contingent and artificial tool that always needs legitimation in light of its aims, and this comes to the fore when considering the first centralised normative orders we might identify as 'pre-states' or

---

[98] N Yoffee, *Myths of the Archaic State: Evolution of the Earliest Cities, States, and Civilizations* (Cambridge, Cambridge University Press, 2005) 34, and see more generally the discussion in ch 2.

[99] JC Scott, *Against the Grain: A Deep History of the Earliest States* (New Haven, Yale University Press, 2017).

[100] Arendt, *Human Condition* (n 65) 26–27.

[101] Scott, *Against the Grain* (n 99) 8.

[102] ibid 9. One can find a famous linear account of social evolution that ends with our current liberal democratic frameworks in F Fukuyama, *The End of History and the Last Man* (New York, Free Press, 1992).

[103] Scott, *Against the Grain* (n 99) 10, and further discussion in ch 4.

36 Law, Power, and Political Authority

chiefdoms.[104] In these orders, centralised rule most likely occurred because of the initial capacity of some chiefs to concentrate existing physical and military forces into their hands, and to impose – progressively – new structures over the existing clan and kinship-based groups and hierarchies.[105] Arguably, this centralisation could not have happened without the invention and diffusion of writing. For, crucially,

> [w]riting is basically a technology, a way of committing things to memory and communicating them, enabling people to send orders and to carry out administration at a distance. Empires and organized societies extending over space are the children of writing, which appeared everywhere at the same time as these political units, and by a similar process.[106]

But it is only when the centralised rule by these leaders is legitimated by the 'cultic establishment',[107] thus not being anymore merely the exercise of non-normative 'power over', that we might be truly warranted in calling these organisations *states* and this newly legitimated normative 'power over' *political*.[108] And it is precisely when the legitimation provided by religious texts (and the priests interpreting them) to the ruling leaders[109] was firstly thoroughly challenged that, I would argue, political theory was born.[110]

VI. THE CONDITIONS OF EXISTENCE OF POLITICAL AUTHORITY: INSIGHTS FROM THE THEORY OF NORMATIVE ORDERS

The upshot of the discussion so far is that political institutions, rather than being an inherent characteristic of human social evolution, should be conceived of as contingent (and fallible) solutions that emerged to deal with fundamental social problems, such as the avoidance of competition for primary resources (like food) or the reduction of violence between members of the community. But as history has proved time and time again, these praiseworthy institutional aims might be replaced with vicious objectives by the individuals who wield political authority at any given moment in time. As a result, we should constantly bear

---

[104] For a discussion of the functional connection between the birth of centralised 'pre-states' in Mesopotamia, Egypt, India, and China between 3500 and 2000 BCE and the production of bronze, see R Sacco, *Antropologia Giuridica. Contributo ad una Macrostoria del Diritto* (Bologna, il Mulino, 2007) 104–109 and 136–39.

[105] See ibid 100–08.

[106] F Braudel, *The Mediterranean in the Ancient World* (S Reynolds tr, London, Penguin Books, 2002) 76. For a discussion of the relationship between language, politics and law throughout history, see MA Cameron, *Strong Constitutions: Social-Cognitive Origins of the Separation of Powers* (Oxford, Oxford University Press, 2013) ch 3.

[107] See Yoffee, *Myths of the Archaic State* (n 98) 38; Sacco, *Antropologia Giuridica* (n 104) 137.

[108] Sacco, *Antropologia Giuridica* (n 104) 137–39.

[109] If the king was not a priest himself: Braudel, *The Mediterranean in the Ancient World* (n 106) 88.

[110] This is arguably one of the most important contributions of Ancient Greek culture, as testified by the fact that 'even today, over two millennia later, much of the world has still to face up to the problems it outlined': Cameron, *Strong Constitutions* (n 106) 77.

in mind the difference between the conditions of existence – which, as I shall show below, are always the same as a matter of conceptual necessity – and the conditions of legitimacy of political authority, which instead are contingent and context-sensitive, and as such might change during the existence of the same institution.[111]

While the conditions of legitimacy of our existing political institutions will be discussed in the next chapter, we will conclude the current one by looking at the conditions of existence of political authority in general. In particular, I claim that a crucial condition of existence of political authority is that it is generated by certain kinds of rules. To establish this, I will chart the emergence of polities with formal systems of rules from groups and communities that merely exhibit a customary order. What I want to illustrate is the normative shift that is necessary in the passage from a condition in which only natural powers exist, to one in which political power can also emerge. Once again, this passage should not be understood in evaluative terms: political power is not a 'good' in itself, but should be considered as a necessary social device once the dimensions (and/or composition) of the relevant group have grown beyond what it feasibly manageable through a spontaneous – and tendentially egalitarian – normative order.

My fundamental contention is that, while 'power over' in a non-normative sense is a characteristic of certain beings that can, naturally or artificially, elicit behaviour coercively from others, normative 'power over' (the 'right to rule') must be necessarily generated by something. And this something, as it has been explicitly argued by Marmor, must be social rules of a particular type, namely power-conferring rules.[112] In other words, political (*qua* practical) authority – as opposed to the military rule of a despot (mere coercive power) – is always an institutional phenomenon.[113] But *how* is it generated? In order to answer this crucial question, we must look at the theory of the evolution of normative orders, in particular as centred on the distinction between primary and secondary norms.[114]

According to the most comprehensive study in the literature to date of the nature of norms, all social norms are constituted by clusters of normative attitudes that exemplify acceptance of a given normative principle, 'N', plus mutual knowledge of those normative attitudes between members of the relevant social group.[115] According to this account, the main function of norms is precisely

---

[111] *cf* Marmor, 'An Institutional Conception of Authority' (n 49) 250–55.

[112] ibid 241–46. Here 'social rules' must be taken to mean rules belonging to both non-formal and formal orders. In this regard, I find Marmor's rejection of what he calls 'the Abstract view of power' (the possibility that practical authority might be granted or constituted not by actual social norms, but by norms 'required by reasons') convincing: see ibid 246–47.

[113] For a rebuttal of some potential objections to the claim that all practical authorities (once distinguished from 'ad hoc powers', like the one constituted by promises) are institutional: ibid 241–246.

[114] See Hart, *Concept of Law* (n 25) ch 5; for a critical reading, M Kramer, *H.L.A. Hart* (Cambridge, Polity Press, 2018) 70–78.

[115] Normative attitudes are a wide range of behavioural dispositions vis-à-vis the relevant normative principle 'N': G Brennan, L Eriksson, R Goodin and N Southwood, *Explaining Norms* (Oxford,

38 Law, Power, and Political Authority

the creation of accountability, which involves 'others having a recognized right or entitlement to determine how one is to behave'.[116] Accountability, in turn, facilitates coordination of behaviour and ultimately cooperation. Importantly, it also enables the conferral of new social meanings upon forms of behaviour: that is, social norms can, and often do, perform an expressive function.[117] This is relevant because, once it has reached a minimal level, group-level cooperation allows social groups to avoid competition between members based on natural abilities (non-normative 'power over') and dominance, at first for food and sex.[118] And while cooperation in itself does not seem to be a necessary evolutionary trait (though it is certainly not unique to human beings in the animal world), it is reasonable to think that groups of early humans who were able to coordinate prevailed over, or out-survived, those groups who did not.[119]

I assume, in discussing these matters, the basic Hartian distinction between primary and secondary norms. While Hart himself was not a model of analytical rigour in illustrating the distinction,[120] one can conceive of it straightforwardly: secondary (but not primary) norms are parasitic upon other norms. In other words, while secondary norms – as rules of identification, change, and adjudication (to maintain, loosely, the Hartian terminology) – necessarily presuppose the existence of other norms, primary norms do not.[121] Again following Hart, I submit that the emergence of secondary norms in a given normative order – until then constituted only by primary norms – marks the passage from a non-formal or customary normative order to a formal order. Importantly, the property of 'formality' comes in degrees for normative orders, unlike for individual norms. Thus, a normative order will be more or less formalised depending on the number and/or type of secondary norms that are present in it, but still at least one secondary norm must be present in the system in order for the given system to be considered as 'formal' at all; while if we are referring to individual norms in a social system, they will be either non-formal (that is, customary) or formal (in the sense of produced, or ascertained, or enforced by an authorised body or person and/or according to an authorised procedure).[122] How is all of this relevant for the theory of political authority?

Oxford University Press, 2013), chs 1–4. Importantly, in what follows, 'acceptance' should be understood to include 'acquiescence', a weaker normative attitude than full-blooded acceptance, yet capable of imbuing social norms with obligatoriness: see KE Himma, 'A Comprehensive Hartian Theory of Legal Obligation: Social Pressure, Coercive Enforcement, and the Legal Obligations of Citizens' in W Waluchow and S Sciaraffa (eds), *Philosophical Foundations of the Nature of Law* (Oxford, Oxford University Press, 2013) 172–177; *cf* Kramer, *HLA Hart* (n 114) 46–50.

[116] Brennan et al, *Explaining Norms* (n 115) 36.

[117] ibid 37.

[118] M Tomasello, *A Natural History of Human Morality* (Cambridge, Harvard University Press, 2016) 98. Cooperation should not be confused with coordination, which is one of the ways in which cooperation can be achieved: Brennan et al, *Explaining Norms* (n 115) 35.

[119] See Sacco, *Antropologia Giuridica* (n 104) 104–09.

[120] See Kramer, *HLA Hart* (n 114) 71–72.

[121] *cf* ibid 73.

[122] These considerations motivate my departure from the use in Brennan et al, *Explaining Norms* (n 115) of 'formal' and 'non-formal' primarily as a property of individual norms rather than

The Conditions of Existence of Political Authority 39

First, a key feature of non-formal, or customary, rules lies in these rules being necessarily practice-dependent, unlike formal norms (and norms of objective morality). That is, a customary rule exists in (and for) a group only insofar as it is practiced – or at least presumed to be practiced[123] – by a large number of members of the group in question. Second, the mutual knowledge requirement necessarily involves some form of outward expression of the normative principle at stake. This expression might be more or less determinate, on the basis of the available communicative and linguistic tools and abilities, but it is at least partially constitutive of customary norms. Third, in a group that is organised purely through (primary) non-formal rules – what we have called a non-formal or customary normative order – one can hardly talk of the deliberate 'creation' of norms. For while there might be some more identifiable patterns of norm-emergence, ultimately no single member of the group will have the normative capacity (by herself) to deliberately create a new norm (or modify an existing one). Customary norms emerge informally and always gradually:[124] a non-formal norm exists only when a relevant part of the group accepts it and practices it (at least presumptively). As such, customary norms exist to the extent that they are at least to a certain degree effective, and cease to exist once they are not effective any longer.[125]

Lastly, and most importantly for our purposes, *pure* customary norms are inherently egalitarian, in that no single member of the group whose acceptance contributes to constituting the norm yields a larger share of normative power than any other member of the same group (or subgroup). That is, in the absence of secondary rules which confer the right to change the existing normative relations among members of the group, no member of the group has normative 'power over' any other: for even when one individual were to exercise accountability and criticise another for the violation of the relevant norm (and possibly demand some form of retribution or punishment), she could only refer to the existing customary norm and enforce it on the norm-breaker. In this regard, as we saw above in section V.A with the state of isonomia, we could say that in a non-formal or customary normative order there are rules but no *ruler*. And this is why it is correct to identify those groups and societies in which only primary customary norms govern the interactions between their members as acephalous.

For while 'group pressure' can manifest in a variety of ways and is generally enough to secure compliance – otherwise a customary norm would not be

---

normative orders. While there is clearly a sense in which formal norms (both primary and secondary) only belong to formal normative systems, such a system will see at least a non-formal norm – what Hart famously defined as 'rule of recognition' – at its base. The authors prefer to label non-formal customary norms as 'social' (vis-à-vis moral and formal norms), but acknowledge that this is 'slightly misleading' because in one sense 'all norms are social': ibid 6.

[123] ibid 72.

[124] Hart, *Concept of Law* (n 25) 48.

[125] Social norms, *qua* non-formal, have only one mode of existence, unlike formal norms which can not only exist but also be valid (or invalid): P Sandro, 'Unlocking Legal Validity: Some Remarks on the Artificial Ontology of Law' in P Westerman, J Hage, S Kirste and AR Mackor (eds), *Legal Validity and Soft Law* (Cham, Springer International Publishing, 2018).

40 Law, Power, and Political Authority

effective, and, thus, would not exist – the enforcement of norms is eminently a private matter, as there is no person or body which is formally authorised to do so on behalf of others.[126] This not only means that norm-users must bear the costs and risks of norm-enforcement, but also that ultimately norm-enforcement is dependent on the pre-existing non-normative power relations between the members of the group. This is the sense in which customary normative orders are *spontaneous*. First, because there cannot be deliberate creation and alteration of the existing norms but only gradual evolution that resists precise spatio-temporal attribution; and second, because norm-enforcement is necessarily a matter of prospective mechanisms based on group pressure, as retrospective enforcement is a private matter without any institutionalised 'fall-back' option.

This last point also explains the demise and/or evolution of customary normative orders into formal orders. Once again, 'demise' and 'evolution' are not used here with evaluative connotation, so that customary normative orders should be considered deficient in respect of, and eventually displaced by, formal orders.[127] It is one of the main contributions of the legal pluralism movement to have reclaimed the attention of legal theory towards the myriad of customary orders – also called 'negotiated'[128] – that have kept developing within (and sometimes beyond) the encompassing legality of the modern state, like smouldering embers underneath a grate. The point is rather that the capacity of customary rules to foster cooperation seems dependent on the dimensions, compositions, and conditions of the social group.

For once those dimensions become too large and the group's homogeneity dissolves (as it is no longer mainly comprised of members tied by kinship or affective relations),[129] non-formal social rules are more likely than not to break down vis-à-vis their object of securing cooperation: not just in terms of their capacity to adapt and evolve vis-à-vis the necessities of the group, but also in terms of their enforcement, as group pressure based on kinship ties and roles will gradually fade and given that retrospective enforcement, as highlighted above, is not institutionally backed up. In other words, customary rules become 'inefficient' vis-à-vis their main purpose when certain conditions – that resist precise theoretical identification – do not obtain any longer.[130]

---

[126] Brennan et al, *Explaining Norms* (n 115) 45.

[127] This should also be the sense in which we understand Hart's considerations in ch 5 of his *Concept of Law*: L Green, 'Introduction', in Hart, *Concept of Law* (n 25) xxix.

[128] *cf* S Roberts, 'After Government? On Representing Law Without the State' (2005) 68(1) *Modern Law Review* 1.

[129] Tomasello's evolutionary hypothesis is that the capacity for normative judgement in our ancestors developed as a device to reinforce (strategic) trust during cooperative activities (Tomasello, *A Natural History of Human Morality* (n 118) ch 3). On the trust-enhancing role played by the concept of validity in modern legal systems, see P Westerman, 'Validity: The Reputation of Rules' in P Westerman, J Hage, S Kirste and AR Mackor (eds), *Legal Validity and Soft Law* (Cham, Springer International Publishing, 2018).

[130] *cf* Rawls, *A Theory of Justice* (n 33) 211.

The Conditions of Existence of Political Authority   41

Obviously, the transitions described here are not discrete phenomena that happen at specific moments in the history of a certain group, but slow and gradual processes of evolution from spontaneous, non-formal orders to formal systems,[131] at the centre of which lies the 'division of normative labour' made possible by the institutionalisation of secondary norms.[132] The point is that such institutionalisation brings about a number of 'fixes' vis-à-vis the functional limits exhibited by customary norms once the contextual circumstances of their emergence have changed drastically. These 'fixes' include: the possibility of deliberate creation and change of rules; a higher degree of determinacy in the identification of the content of rules; the transition from a (mere) set to a unified system of rules; and the institutionalised retrospective enforcement of rules against rules-breakers.[133]

As a result of institutionalisation, two major changes occur vis-à-vis the normative paradigm of pure customary orders:

i. it becomes possible to have norms without corresponding social practices; and
ii. there is no longer the normative equality that characterises customary normative orders: that is, a distinction between ruler(s) and ruled emerges.

As to the first change, formal norms – norms that have been created according to an accepted procedure (which in the simplest case could amount to the utterance of a norm-giver) – can exist independently of a corresponding social practice.[134] This is intuitive, as legal (*qua* formal) norms can be, and most often are, created to shape social practice (also through their expressive function). The artifactual nature of these norms is even more evident at this point, and so is the intelligibility of a distinctive role for the validity of formal norms.[135] As to the second change, it is only in the transition from non-formal orders to formal systems that the possibility of existence for practical (as opposed to theoretical) authority arises.[136] In other words, it is the presence of secondary rules or institutions that grounds the possibility of existence of any type of practical authority – or 'right to rule' – within a social order. Political authority, as a consequence, cannot be but rule-generated authority.[137]

---

[131] See Sacco, *Antropologia del Diritto* (n 104) 139–41.

[132] See Green, 'Introduction' (n 127) xxix; *cf* F Pirie, 'Law Before Government: Ideology and Aspiration' (2010) 30(2) *Oxford Journal of Legal Studies* 207, who claims (at 222) that 'the disjunction between law and custom' is 'often confused by anthropologists'.

[133] See Hart, *Concept of Law* (n 25) ch 5.

[134] However, the normative system as a whole must be efficacious to some degree.

[135] On which see Sandro, 'Unlocking Legal Validity' (n 125).

[136] Marmor ('An Institutional Conception of Authority' (n 49) 248–49 and fn 15) affirms that practical authorities 'rarely' operate in social practices (what I have defined as non-formal orders) that are not institutionalised to some degree, but I do not see how this admission is consistent with the gist of the theory of authority he defends.

[137] *cf* Loughlin, *Foundations of Public Law* (n 55) 165.

42   *Law, Power, and Political Authority*

And yet, it bears repeating one last time, the creation of political authority (as part of a formal normative system) is not necessarily a good development all things considered. As Leslie Green has put it, in his comments on an often overlooked passage of Hart's theory, the division of labour that results from the institutionalisation of a normative order 'is a mixed blessing' which brings 'both gains and costs', so that 'law is *not* universally good or good without qualification.'[138] The most important of these costs, namely the creation of a new kind of normative 'power over' that is potentially more threatening that any non-normative power, and the ensuing new problems of its legitimation and limitation, are the subject of the next chapter.

---

[138] L Green, 'Introduction' (n 127) xxix, commenting on Hart's passage at Hart, *Concept of Law* (n 25) 202.

2

The Dependence of Constitutional Democracy on the Distinction between Creation and Application of Law

I. INTRODUCTION

THE AIM OF this chapter is to illustrate how constitutional democracy is premised on the distinction between law-creation and law-application. In doing so, I will illustrate what I take to be the core element of the doctrine of modern constitutionalism, that of 'legal otherness'. This approach not only makes it easier to see why the possibility of law-application is so crucial for the legitimacy of constitutional democracy, but it also clarifies the structure of our existing constitutional systems by encompassing the supposedly alternative legal and political constitutionalist models under a single explanatory framework.

The existence of the distinction between creation and application of law is clearly not an original claim. One just has to open any law textbook to find that in those political organisations we call 'states', some bodies – principally legislatures – are tasked chiefly with the power to create laws for our communities while other bodies, such as courts, are called to apply such laws in individual cases. The separation of these two functions in the legal process is traditionally conceived of as a freedom-preserving institutional design and as one of the hallmarks of modern constitutionalism.

More recently, this institutional division of normative labour has been cast in a different light as an 'organizational consequence of human cognition'.[1] In this sense, the use of written speech in the machinery of the state not only allows us to coordinate collective action on a scale much larger than was previously possible, but it also allows for 'adaptation and deliberate change in social institutions'.[2] At the same time, while some relevant coordination problems

---

[1] MA Cameron, *Strong Constitutions: Social-Cognitive Origins of the Separation of Powers* (Oxford, Oxford University Press, 2013) 14. For discussion, see, eg: A Kavanagh, 'The Constitutional Separation of Powers', in D Dyzenhaus and M Thorburn (eds), *Philosophical Foundations of Constitutional Law* (Oxford, Oxford University Press, 2016).

[2] Cameron, *Strong Constitutions* (n 1) 5.

44   *The Distinction between Creation and Application of Law*

for the social group are solved, some new problems are created.[3] According to Cameron, this is due in particular to the rigid and fixed nature of textual communication (which I analyse in chapter five) vis-à-vis the flexibility and immediacy of oral communication. Written words read outside their context of utterance might need 'recontextualisation',[4] and this in turns creates, in some individual cases, the space for conflicts over the meaning to be assigned to contested texts.[5] As Cameron puts it:

> Writing and reading leads to monopolies of power and centralization of authority, but as it spreads, it also fosters criticism and the development of theories that challenge power.[6]

As we discussed already in chapter one, it does not seem accidental that the 'state' – in its 'early' instantiations such as chiefdoms – and writing appeared together at a very critical juncture for the history of human civilisation, some 8,000 years ago. It is in this transition from spontaneous normative orders to formal orders – where one individual (or group) wields the 'right to rule', ie the authority to manipulate rules 'to achieve more or less *explicitly* articulated ends'[7] – that we can identify the first appearance of 'law' in the history of human civilisation.[8] As a result, there seems to be an inescapable 'internal relation'[9] between law and political power. Habermas built his influential discourse theory of law and politics around it; while for Ferrajoli, who speaks of an isomorphic relation between the law and political power,[10] legal theory constitutes a necessary premise of political theory.

It is to the evolution of this 'internal' or 'isomorphic' relation that we turn in the first half of this chapter, in what constitutes a necessary step towards illustrating the deep juridical structure of our modern constitutional democracies.[11] The understanding of the relation between law and politics has evolved throughout history and it is still a contentious issue (to say the least). Loughlin, for instance, has highlighted how for many centuries an idealised understanding of

---

[3] ibid.

[4] ibid.

[5] For an example of this process, see M Loughlin, *Foundations of Public Law* (Oxford, Oxford University Press, 2010) 51–53.

[6] Cameron, *Strong Constitutions* (n 1) 13.

[7] GJ Postema, *Legal Philosophy in the Twentieth Century: The Common Law World, A Treatise of Legal Philosophy and General Jurisprudence*, vol 11 (Dordrecht, Springer, 2011) 307.

[8] See, eg: J Habermas, *Between Facts and Norms: Contributions to a Discourse Theory of Law and Democracy* (W Rehg tr, Cambridge, MIT Press, 1996) 132–150; S Roberts, 'After Government? On Representing Law Without the State' (2005) 68(1) *Modern Law Review* 1, 13–17; M Del Mar, 'Beyond the State in and of Legal Theory' in SP Dolan and L Heckendorn Urscheler (eds), *Concepts of Law: Comparative, Jurisprudential, and Social Science Perspectives* (Burlington, Ashgate, 2012) 21–30.

[9] Habermas, *Between Facts and Norms* (n 8) 136–44.

[10] L Ferrajoli, 'Il pensiero innovatore di Giovanni Tarello' (2018) 18(1) *Diritto & Questioni Pubbliche* 205, 212.

[11] *cf* A Sajó and R Uitz, *The Constitution of Freedom: An introduction to Legal Constitutionalism* (Oxford, Oxford University Press, 2017) 13.

law as being synonymous with justice ('the scales') has been juxtaposed with a negative understanding of politics as the realm of compromise, bargaining, and (always lurking) injustice.[12] Particularly after the rise of totalitarianism in the last century and the devastation caused by the two World Wars, we have witnessed in most countries around the world a clear tendency to institutionalise the limitation of politics through legal means.[13] Entrenched constitutions have been laid down which seem to a greater or lesser extent insulated from the *agora* of ordinary politics. This rise in the political relevance of non-elected courts, both on the national and international levels, has been hailed as a fundamental step in securing a more stable foundation to our liberal democracies.[14] But it has also been accompanied by progressive worries – which in the US might have turned into 'obsession'[15] – that, in hailing 'juristocracy', we might have discounted too quickly the wider democratic implications of the progressive loss of relevance of ordinary politics.[16]

In this respect, I discuss, towards the end of the chapter, some of the institutional and contextual factors which affect the legitimacy of courts in performing judicial review of legislation.[17] One should note from the outset how some of the strongest criticisms of judicial review of legislation seem chiefly developed within political traditions in which either the jurisdiction of the courts to perform such review is not fully determined by the relevant constitutional document (as in the US), or where there is no codified constitution to begin with (as in the UK). In noting this, I do not purport to dismiss altogether worries relating to an unchecked rise of constitutional courts as fully fledged political actors, for I do think there is a danger in the insulation of too many contentious issues from the *agora* of parliamentary politics. My point is rather that the overall legitimacy of any form of judicial review seems necessarily context-bound, and one of the key factors to be taken into consideration is precisely the type of constitutional norms which are in force in a given political system.

---

[12] M Loughlin, *Sword and Scales: An Examination of the Relationship between Law and Politics* (Oxford, Hart Publishing, 2000) 13.

[13] For an estimate that over 80% of countries have now a supreme court with the power to strike down legislation, see T Ginsburg and M Versteeg, 'Why do Countries Adopt Constitutional Review?' (2014) 30(3) *Journal of Law, Economics and Organization* 587, 587; see also, T Ginsburg, 'The Global Spread of Constitutional Review' in GA Caldeira, RD Kelemen and KE Whittington (eds), *The Oxford Handbook of Law and Politics* (Oxford, Oxford University Press, 2008).

[14] See, eg: D Grimm, *Constitutionalism: Past, Present, and Future* (Oxford, Oxford University Press, 2016).

[15] B Friedman, 'The Birth of an Academic Obsession: The History of the Countermajoritarian Difficulty, Part Five' (2002) 112(2) *Yale Law Journal* 153, 155.

[16] On juristocracy, see, eg: C Guarneri and P Pederzoli, *The Power of Judges: A Comparative Study of Courts and Democracy* (Oxford, Oxford University Press, 2002); A Stone Sweet, *Governing with Judges: Constitutional Politics in Europe* (Oxford, Oxford University Press, 2000); R Hirschl, *Towards Juristocracy: The Origins and Consequences of the New Constitutionalism* (Cambridge, Harvard University Press, 2004).

[17] See recently: P Castillo-Ortiz, 'The Dilemmas of Constitutional Courts and the Case for a New Design of Kelsenian Institutions' (2020) 39(6) *Law and Philosophy* 617.

46 The Distinction between Creation and Application of Law

Indeed, if we were to focus only on our current constitutional democratic frameworks, the resulting understanding of the relationship between law and politics would be partial at best. Modern constitutionalism has not emerged in a vacuum,[18] while the democratic ideal has only (relatively) recently acquired a sense of indispensability in the justificatory discourse of our political systems.[19] Moreover, how the relation between law and politics has actually unfolded throughout history and how that relation has been portrayed by political and legal writers has, at times, diverged greatly. To mention just a couple of relevant examples, Montesquieu presented his famous doctrine of the separation of powers as a purported description of the English political system of the time;[20] while Dicey celebrated the superiority of the English constitutional system (in its refusal of a separate administrative law domain) vis-à-vis the French system by misrepresenting both the extent of the administrative framework existing at the time in England, and the 'speciality' of French administrative law.[21]

Nowadays, the danger of glaring misrepresentations of existing arrangements in legal and political analysis is greatly reduced thanks to a combination of various factors. These include the distinction and specialisation (especially in methodological terms) of academic disciplines, and particularly of political science and political theory. Another factor is the simultaneous rise of comparative constitutional law, made possible not only by the emergence of information technologies, but also by a new generation of 'global' researchers with English as their academic *lingua franca*. And yet, the issue of judicial review of legislation is the one aspect of the theory of constitutional democracy where different levels of discourse and analysis, especially across the ideal vs non-ideal theory divide,[22] are either conflated or 'segregated' depending on one's argumentative strategy (or lack thereof).[23]

The result of this lack of methodological clarity is two-fold. On the one hand, supporters of strong constitutional review might be normatively 'blind' to the risks (especially for liberalism itself)[24] of over-reliance on the judicialisation

---

[18] CH McIlwain, *Constitutionalism, Ancient and Modern* (Ithaca, Cornell University Press, 1940); Sajó and Uitz, *The Constitution of Freedom* (n 11) ch 1.

[19] See, eg: J Wolff, *An Introduction to Political Philosophy*, 3rd edn (Oxford, Oxford University Press, 2015) ch 3.

[20] L Claus, 'Montesquieu's Mistakes and the True Meaning of Separation' (2005) 25(3) *Oxford Journal of Legal Studies* 419.

[21] W Robson, *Justice and Administrative Law: A Study of the British Constitution* (London, Macmillan, 1928).

[22] This applies whether or not judicial review is strong (where courts have the final word on the interpretation of the constitutional text) or weak (where legislatures retain such last word). For a very useful 'conceptual cartography' of the distinction between ideal and non-ideal theory in general, see L Valentini, 'Ideal vs. Non-ideal Theory: A Conceptual Map' (2012) 7(9) *Philosophy Compass* 654.

[23] See S Issacharoff, 'Judicial Review in Troubled Times: Stabilizing Democracy in a Second-Best World' (2019) 98(1) *North Carolina Law Review* 1.

[24] In this sense, see the almost prophetic warning in the review of John Rawls' Political Liberalism by Sandel: MJ Sandel, 'Political Liberalism' (1994) 107(7) *Harvard Law Review* 1765, particularly 1793–94.

The Contested Relationship between Law and Politics   47

of politics.[25] On the other, contemporary political constitutionalists such as Waldron or Bellamy defend parliamentary supremacy in the interpretation of the constitutional text, often on the basis of a number of assumed 'pre-conditions' of the political system,[26] which are nowadays difficult to observe empirically in some established western democracies, let alone emerging ones.[27] The recent processes of democratic decay in European democracies like Hungary and Poland appear to be just the latest case in point. With this in mind, let us now turn to the scholarly debate on the relationship between law and politics.

II. THE CONTESTED RELATIONSHIP BETWEEN LAW AND POLITICS

Despite the fact that the internal relation between law and politics has been analysed (albeit in different ways) throughout the history of western political thought – joining together, through a hypothetical intellectual thread, Aristotle and Plato with Rawls and Habermas – it is only at the end of the nineteenth century that 'law and politics' becomes an autonomous field of study. It was in fact the 'narrow professionalism' of the law school that prompted Columbia University to create a separate School of Political Science, the 'progenitor of the discipline'.[28] Since then, 'law and politics' has grown into a vast and fast-paced sub-field of research within both political and legal science.[29] For the purposes of this book, we will eschew some wider issues and concentrate instead on one specific aspect of the relationship. My ultimate aim in this chapter is to illustrate the way in which constitutional democracies are premised on the distinction between law-creation and law-application. I will, therefore, focus on the roles that law, as an institutional-normative system, can play vis-à-vis political power, understood as the 'right to rule' that is held usually by legislatures and governments in our existing political frameworks.

---

[25] R Bellamy, *Political Constitutionalism: A Republican Defence of the Constitutionality of Democracy* (Cambridge, Cambridge University Press, 2007) ch 1.

[26] Like a well-functioning and truly pluralistic deliberative body with fair electoral and voting procedures. See J Waldron, 'The Core of the Case Against Judicial Review' (2006) 115(6) *Yale Law Journal* 1346 ('Core Case').

[27] See T Roux, 'In Defence of Empirical Entanglement: The Methodological Flaw in Waldron's Case against Judicial Review' in R Levy, H Kong, G Orr and J King (eds), *The Cambridge Handbook of Deliberative Constitutionalism* (Cambridge, Cambridge University Press, 2018); Issacharoff, 'Judicial Review in Troubled Times' (n 23).

[28] KE Whittington, RD Kelemen and GA Caldeira, 'The Study of Law and Politics' in GA Caldeira, RD Kelemen and KE Whittington (eds), *The Oxford Handbook of Law and Politics* (Oxford, Oxford University Press, 2008) 4–5.

[29] For an introduction to the field in the US, see, eg: GA Caldeira, RD Kelemen and KE Whittington (eds), *The Oxford Handbook of Law and Politics* (Oxford, Oxford University Press, 2008); for the UK context, see D Feldman (ed), *Law in Politics, Politics in Law* (Oxford, Hart Publishing, 2013); for the continental tradition, see the texts published in the Routledge Series 'Law and Politics: Continental Perspectives' edited by Mariano Croce and Marco Goldoni, available at www.routledge.com/Law-and-Politics/book-series/LPCP.

48 *The Distinction between Creation and Application of Law*

This particular focus has already been explicitly explored from two perspectives in legal scholarship: a diachronic and a meta-theoretical perspective. The former is famously employed by Martin Loughlin, who concludes that 'the relationship between law and politics has no fixed or settled form'.[30] His approach, Neil Walker has noted, has some broad similarities with that of German systems theory, with an 'emphasis upon law and politics as autonomous yet mutually aware linguistically coded sub-systems within a highly differentiated ... framework of social organisation'.[31] This leads Loughlin to identify, aptly but with an inescapable degree of simplification,[32] three 'conceptions' of law and their respective role vis-à-vis the exercise of political power, as illustrated in Table 1.[33]

Table 1 Three conceptions of law and political power in Loughlin's Sword and Scales

Conception of law	As custom	As command	As right
Relation to political power	Accommodation	Instrument	Constraint

In the first conception, law as custom, law is to be understood as a set of customary rules recognised by the judiciary 'acting as the guardians of the immanent values of the common law'[34] which is in a relation of 'accommodation' with political power. Here, political power and law constitute two different (but related) normative spheres – along the same lines as the *gubernaculum* and *iurisdictio* coupling of medieval times[35] – that coexist in regulating the public life of a community, on the basis of a largely informal (and constantly shifting) equilibrium ultimately grounded in institutional comity.[36]

In the second conception, law as command, law amounts to both the institutionalisation and the result of the political process. As Hobbes famously put it, it is authority, and no longer reason (or truth), that makes law.[37] Law therefore ceases to be the 'medium of the relationship between ruler and ruled' and becomes the 'instrument of rule' itself.[38] For Loughlin this shift in the conception of law is 'closely linked' with the 'emergence of representative democracy as the key legitimating principle of modern government'.[39] This also leads to a fundamental change in the proper way to conceive of the judiciary: from 'guardians' of the customs of the land to 'functionaries whose task it is to give precise effect to the edicts of an authoritative law-giver'.[40]

---

[30] Loughlin, *Sword and Scales* (n 12) 217.

[31] N Walker, 'Review: Sword and Scales: An Examination of the Relationship between Law and Politics' [2001] *Public Law* 644, 645.

[32] Loughlin, *Sword and Scales* (n 12) 218.

[33] ibid, ch 14.

[34] ibid 217.

[35] McIlwain, *Constitutionalism, Ancient and Modern* (n 18) ch 4.

[36] Loughlin, *Sword and Scales* (n 12) 218–20.

[37] T Hobbes, A dialogue between a philosopher and a student of the common laws of England (first published 1681, Chicago, J Cropsey ed, University of Chicago Press, 1971).

[38] Loughlin, *Sword and Scales* (n 12) 222.

[39] ibid.

[40] ibid.

The Contested Relationship between Law and Politics 49

Lastly, law as right(s) is the conception of law that is precipitated by modern liberal constitutionalism, when principles of political and institutional morality (that, until then, were significantly extra-legal) become juridical preconditions of the political process.[41] As such, law's position shifts once again vis-à-vis political power: from 'mere' mode of expression to being the 'rational foundation' of the exercise of legislative power itself.[42]

The upshot of Loughlin's analysis should be clear: if there are different conceptions of law which have manifested throughout history, and each of these 'manifestations' has assumed a different relation vis-à-vis political power, then it becomes not just difficult, but fundamentally misguided, to try and capture in univocal terms the relationship between these two systems. Therefore, whatever 'solution' to the problem of articulating their relation we might encounter, it would always be, at best, a context-sensitive one.[43]

The second perspective, which I have termed 'meta-theoretical', has been adopted by Mauro Zamboni. He reconstructs how the major strands of modern jurisprudential scholarship – positivism, natural law, realism, critical scholarship, and law and economics – 'see' the relation of law to politics using Weberian 'ideal-types'.[44] The classification of the different strands is organised around their respective approaches to three 'aspects' of the relation: the 'static', the 'dynamic', and the 'epistemological'. The first aspect deals with law seen as the 'carrier' of the output of the political process, and to the question of its relative flexibility or rigidity towards its content. The second 'concerns the processes and mechanisms of the creation of the law'[45] and thus whether law-making is 'open' or 'closed' to the political order. And the third and last aspect takes into account the modern specialisation of the study of politics vis-à-vis that of law, weighing to what extent the different strands allow for concepts and methodologies that are developed in other academic disciplines, and in particular in political science, to be used in legal scholarship.

The resulting classification sees, unsurprisingly perhaps, the 'autonomous' model of the relation between law and politics as embodied by legal positivism (and analytical jurisprudence more generally) juxtaposed with the 'embedded' models of natural law theory, critical legal scholarship, and law and economics, as well as the 'intersecting' model of legal realism. The autonomous model considers law as a separate and rigid enterprise from that of politics, both as to

---

[41] This was the most important contribution by American and French revolutionaries according to D Grimm, 'Types of Constitutions', in M Rosenfeld and A Sajó (eds), *The Oxford Handbook of Comparative Constitutional Law* (Oxford, Oxford University Press, 2012), 102. Ferrajoli calls it the passage from the 'legislative state' to the 'constitutional' state, which brings a paradigm shift not only for law itself, but for legal science too: L Ferrajoli, *Principia Iuris*, vol 1 (Bari, Laterza, 2007) 847.

[42] Loughlin, *Sword and Scales* (n 12) 223–24.

[43] Loughlin, *Sword and Scales* (n 12) 225–27.

[44] M Zamboni, *Law and Politics: A Dilemma for Contemporary Legal Theory* (Berlin/Heidelberg, Springer, 2007). Zamboni has built on this argument, exploring more specifically what he calls the 'policy of law', in M Zamboni, *The Policy of Law, A Legal Theoretical Framework* (London, Hart Publishing, 2007).

[45] Zamboni, *Law and Politics* (n 44) 8.

50 *The Distinction between Creation and Application of Law*

its forms and contents as well as to its epistemological paradigm. Law in this sense has its own rationality which necessarily modifies the political substratum (or input) once this enters the legal process.

The embedded model sits instead at the opposite end of the spectrum: here law is inherently flexible vis-à-vis politics, both in terms of content as well as procedure and values, and this requires a mixed paradigm of legal studies. 'In order to fully understand the legal phenomenon', Zamboni writes, it is necessary to 'integrate the legal discipline with categories and concepts belonging to sociology, psychology, political sciences and economics'.[46]

The third model, the intersecting one, sits between the other two: law is not fully autonomous in relation to the political process, nor openly permeated by it. As such there is only limited scope for the use of non-legal concepts and methods in legal discipline. Overall, while it is clear that all major current theories of law see law and politics as distinct phenomena, they vary considerably in their evaluation of the extent to which the two phenomena interact with each other and of how this interaction should be factored in the methodology of legal science (as we discussed in chapter one).[47]

III. LAW AS *LEX* AND AS *IUS*: THE DUALITY THAT MAKES CONSTITUTIONALISM POSSIBLE

Both frameworks just surveyed are insightful and deepen our understanding of the relation between law and politics, by problematising it from an historical and meta-theoretical perspective. Yet, as we fall short of establishing the exact form (or forms) of this relation,[48] we might be tempted to conclude that law and politics are distinct and (partially) independent social spheres which 'collide'[49] with each other in different ways at different moments in time, a bit like bumper cars at a fairground. Adam Tomkins (for one) bluntly affirms that, in the end, 'there is no such thing as the relationship between law and politics'.[50]

While there might be no such thing as 'the' relationship between law and politics (especially if the latter is broadly understood), in this work our focus is narrower, and precisely on the relationship between law and political power

---

[46] ibid 140. This approach will be analysed more closely in ch 3 when discussing legal realism.

[47] This is especially in the context of the modern welfare state, where the traditional functions of law (criminal, private, and tort) have expanded to cover progressively larger portions of social life, to the point that nowadays there is hardly any area of our lives which is not regulated by law: ibid 141.

[48] Tomkins identifies five different questions (and their combinations) that we could be asking when we inquire into the relationship between law and politics: we could be asking of the relationship between legal and political *institutions*, or between legal and political *actors*, or between *academic disciplines*, or between legal and political *theories*, or between legal and political *values*: A Tomkins, 'Review: In Defence of the Political Constitution' (2002) 22(1) *Oxford Journal of Legal Studies* 157, 166; *cf* Walker, 'Review: Sword and Scales' (n 31) 647.

[49] Tomkins, 'Review' (n 48) 169.

[50] ibid.

Law as lex *and as* ius: *The Duality that Makes Constitutionalism Possible* 51

(or authority). Here, things appear more promising, especially if we recall the discussion in chapter one about the emergence of what can be meaningfully described as 'law' with the inchoate expressions of centralised rule in pre-states some 8,000 years ago. For, if we understand law as the mode of expression of political authority (as *lex*), there seems to be at least one clear relationship between the two phenomena:[51] a relationship that, if we discount linguistic variation, appears to be stable throughout the history of western civilisation.

And yet, as underscored by Loughlin's diachronic analysis, we must immediately notice that not all law seems to be the product, historically, of political power.[52] That is, at some point in the history of western civilisation – that Aldo Schiavone identifies (persuasively) with the late period of the Roman Republic[53] – a second and distinct body of law emerged, alongside that of law as the expression of the will of the political authority. This second type of law, autonomous from the first, was to be found in the customs of a given community as interpreted through the rulings – progressively organised in a more structured system of rules – of a specially trained subset of individuals. This is law, not as *lex*, but instead as *ius*:[54] that is, positive law that does not have its source in the will of the sovereign, but rather 'as something given [by the traditional *mores*, i.e. Roman customary norms], waiting to be discovered and declared' (*jus-dicere*).[55]

According to Schiavone, the *invention* of this second type of law is one of the biggest contributions of Roman society to the intellectual achievements of western civilisation. For it is only in Republican Rome, rather than in classical Greece and other earlier civilisations linked to the Mediterranean, that a different and *reflexive* normative ordering of reality – which is not fully integrated with that of politics and legislation – develops.[56] Instead, this second body of law is formed and 'shaped' by specially trained experts on the basis of technical

---

[51] *cf* A Halpin, 'The Search for Law: A review of Mariano Croce, *Self-Sufficiency of Law: A Critical-Institutional Theory of Social Order*' (2014) 5(2) *Jurisprudence* 409.

[52] From an analytical point of view, there are two additional potential sources of positive law: customary law (not to be confused with custom itself) and the case law of courts: J Gardner, 'Some Types of Law' in J Gardner, *Law as a Leap of Faith: Essays on Law in General* (Oxford, Oxford University Press, 2012).

[53] A Schiavone, *The Invention of Law in the West* (J Carden and A Shugaar trans, Cambridge, Harvard University Press, 2012) (translation of the original Italian: A Schiavone, *Ius. L'invenzione del Diritto in Occidente* (Turin, Einaudi, 2005)).

[54] To be sure, there have been notable exceptions – Aquinas being perhaps the most famous one – to the otherwise fairly common understanding of the substantive differences between *lex* and *ius* in Roman legal culture. On Aquinas's substitution of *lex* for *ius*, see JB Murphy, *The Philosophy of Positive Law: Foundations of Jurisprudence* (New Haven, Yale University Press, 2005) 64; and see, for further discussion, MJ White, *Political Philosophy: An Historical Introduction*, 2nd edn (Oxford, Oxford University Press, 2012) 104–07.

[55] PG Stein, 'The Roman Jurists' Conception of Law', in A Padovani and PG Stein (eds), *The Jurists' Philosophy of Law from Rome to the Seventeenth Century, A Treatise of Legal Philosophy and General Jurisprudence*, vol 7 (Dordrecht, Springer, 2007) 6.

[56] *cf* Grimm, 'Types of Constitutions' (n 41) 102–3, who instead represents the mainstream position in the literature according to which law becomes 'reflexive' only with the American and French revolutionary constitutions of the late 18th century.

52   *The Distinction between Creation and Application of Law*

knowledge.[57] Notably, it is this technical knowledge that allowed classical jurists to then interpret and develop traditions – which constituted the normative source of their authority – autonomously from the concomitant political ordering of society.[58] But why is the invention of this second type of law – and the resulting distinction with *lex* – so important?

Notwithstanding those in the literature who warn against exaggerating the distinction between *ius* and *lex*,[59] the emergence and development in Rome of this second body of law and the relative specialised method cannot be overestimated, as it still shapes to this day our existing legal systems. This is clearer in the civil law tradition where, thanks to the critical rediscovery and progressive assimilation of Roman law by civil and canon law scholars in or around the twelfth century,[60] the distinction between these two types of law has been part of the juridical vocabulary for a long time.

This cannot be said of the English-speaking world, however, where the distinction is muddled by the use of the same word 'law' to express both *ius* and *lex*.[61] And yet, once we go past linguistic confusion, it is in the historical development and practice of the English common law that we find perhaps the closest approximation to the Roman concept of *ius* (as described by Schiavone). In this regard, the emergence of the common law as a body of decisions by courts that is based on the 'common custom of the realm' appears to be more than just a 'founding myth'.[62] For there is growing evidence of a clear link between the work (and reflexive understanding) of Roman jurists and the establishment of the common law in the thirteenth century.[63]

This link is particularly evident in the source of authority of the decisions of common law courts at their inception.[64] For, despite their formal royal establishment, there was a sense – from as early as the end of the twelfth and increasingly in the early thirteenth century – 'that the king's courts were, and should be, somewhat separate from the king'.[65] The validity of their decisions, in short, did not derive from the will of the monarch, but rather from *congruence* of their

---

[57] Schiavone, *The Invention of Law in the West* (n 53) 57. *cf* Stein, 'The Roman Jurists' Conception of Law' (n 55) 5, for the claim that the systematisation method used by the first Roman jurists was nonetheless Greek.

[58] Schiavone, 'The Invention of Law' (n 53) 285.

[59] See, eg: J Finnis, *Natural Law and Natural Rights*, 2nd edn (Oxford, Oxford University Press, 2011) 228. It is not unreasonable to presume that Finnis' understanding of the distinction (and of its relevance) has been heavily influenced by Aquinas' thinking.

[60] Schiavone, *The Invention of Law in the West* (n 53) ch 1.

[61] See, eg: Murphy, *The Philosophy of Positive Law* (n 54) 63, who correctly notes how the distinction also sees no clear translation in ancient Greek.

[62] Gardner, 'Some Types of Law' (n 52) 83.

[63] See TJ McSweeney, *Priests of the Law. Roman Law and the Making of the Common Law's First Professionals* (Oxford, Oxford University Press, 2019).

[64] See, GJ Postema, 'Philosophy of the Common Law', in J Coleman and S Shapiro (eds), *The Oxford Handbook of Jurisprudence and Philosophy of Law* (Oxford, Oxford University Press, 2002) 590–92.

[65] McSweeney, *Priests of the Law* (n 63) 19.

Law as lex *and as* ius: *The Duality that Makes Constitutionalism Possible* 53

decisions with the customs that were 'second nature' to the people of England, as interpreted and developed through that 'distinctive discipline of reasoning'[66] adapted from the Roman jurists.

Importantly, in both the Roman development of *ius* and in the English emergence of the common law, this normative connection to the customs of the people implied a different relationship between this type of law and justice than the relationship developed when law is the product of political power. What I mean is that, from a conceptual point of view, this particular relationship between law as *ius* and justice has been broadly retained in the common law, even after it became fully autonomous, in the sixteenth century, from the underlying customs.[67] In this respect, the significance of the distinction between law as *lex* and law as *ius* was not lost on Hart. But he thought of them as two different concepts of law (one being 'narrower' than the other) because of their different *intrinsic* connection to morality.[68] Rather, they should be understood as two independent types, or bodies, of law, whose constitutive difference lies in their distinct sources. What Hart failed to appreciate, then, is that the different connection of *lex* and *ius* to morality is a consequence of the difference in their respective sources.

This is the main reason, in line with Schiavone's account, to affirm that the invention of *ius* in Roman legal thinking was a paradigmatic shift in political as well as legal theory. For it is only with the emergence of a new type of positive law (besides law as the expression of political authority) that it becomes possible, conceptually, to limit law *by* law.[69] It is in the creation and differentiation of *ius* from *lex* in Roman legal culture, together with the deployment of *ius* to limit *lex* during the crisis of the late Roman Republic,[70] that we see the first inchoate – and yet distinctive – historical attempt at what we would today call substantive constitutional thinking.[71] According to Straumann, it is in the writings of

---

[66] Postema, 'Philosophy of the Common Law' (n 64) 592.

[67] ibid. This might explain Loughlin's point (*Sword and Scales* (n 12) 15) that the 'ideal of justice' cannot be easily discounted in understanding how people engage with law (as he understands the term broadly).

[68] See HLA Hart, *The Concept of Law*, 3rd edn (Oxford, Oxford University Press, 2012), 208–12. Gardner, while casting doubts on Hart's 'foreign-language lexicography', follows his steps in identifying the second sense of law (*ius*) as necessarily 'moralised' law: J Gardner, 'The Legality of Law' in J Gardner, *Law as a Leap of Faith: Essays on Law in General* (Oxford, Oxford University Press, 2012), 193–94.

[69] See Grimm, 'Types of Constitutions' (n 41) 102–03.

[70] B Straumann, *Crisis and Constitutionalism: Roman Political Thought from the Fall of the Republic to the Age of Revolution* (Oxford, Oxford University Press, 2016) ch 4. This has been identified as the 'bold' claim of Straumann's book, 'that constitutionalism was not born from the practice of framing or of living under a constitution, but rather from the experience of its demise during the late Roman Republic': D Edelstein, 'The ancient constitution and the Roman law: on Benjamin Straumann's *Crisis and Constitutionalism*' (2019) 4(3) *Global Intellectual History* 261, 261. Such a claim could be vindicated as a general remark about the 'experience' of constitutionalism: Sajó and Uitz, *The Constitution of Freedom* (n 11) 13.

[71] In ch 5 of his book *Crisis and Constitutionalism* (n 70), Straumann compares and distinguishes the substantive constitutionalism in the late Roman Republic from the 'positivist' or 'formal' Athenian constitutionalism. But see, for an illuminating discussion of whether Athenian constitutionalism

54 *The Distinction between Creation and Application of Law*

Cicero (among others) that we can appreciate the first explicit historical argument for the limitation of existing political authority and its normative product (*lex*) through the constraints of what is mandated by a different type of law – *ius* (and *Mos Maiorium*, the 'ancient customs') – that the legislature cannot simply dispose of.[72]

What is less convincing, in Straumann's account, is the pervasive search for a Roman 'constitution' – seemingly, a *conditio sine qua non* of constitutionalism as we understand it today – in the late Roman Republic.[73] The problem is that the term 'constitution' had originally 'the very opposite [meaning] of what is now understood by "constitution"'.[74] In fact, for the Romans *constitutio* was a general term indicating legislative enactments; and after the demise of the Roman empire, in the plural *constitutions*, it came to mean, generally, 'a collection of laws enacted by the Sovereign'.[75] In our terminology, a 'constitution' was a matter of *lex* and not of *ius*. But, then, is it not a contradiction to affirm the existence of Roman constitutionalism (understood in a modern sense) without there being anything resembling a modern constitution? More generally, can there ever be constitutionalism in a political system without the presence of a constitution in a formal sense?

Based on its mainstream usage in legal and political discourse, the term 'constitution' appears to be a Janus-faced term. For its modern understanding as 'a means for limited government' would derive from a loose and historically layered meaning as 'political order', whose origin can be traced all the way back to Aristotle's *Politics*.[76] Against this, Sartori famously argues that it is only in the eighteenth century that the term acquires – with the emergence of American and French revolutionary liberalism – its 'true' *garantiste* meaning[77] as a 'technique of liberty'.[78] Therefore, notwithstanding the 'intimate relation'[79]

---

was indeed 'merely' positivist (or formal), M Canevaro, 'Athenian Constitutionalism: Nomothesia and Graphe Nomon Me Epitedeion Theinai', in G Thür, U Yiftach and R Zelnick-Abramovitz (eds), *Symposion 2017. Vorträge zur griechischen und hellenistischen Rechtsgeschichte (Tel Aviv, 20–23. August 2017)* (Vienna, Australian Academy of Sciences Press, 2019).

[72] Straumann, *Crisis and Constitutionalism* (n 70) ch 1. For Straumann, the 'working definition' of constitutionality of norms in the late Roman Republic is about their entrenchment and their political importance (ibid 36).

[73] ibid 28.

[74] G Sartori, 'Constitutionalism: A Preliminary Discussion' (1962) 56(4) *The American Political Science Review* 853, 853; *cf* also Sajó and Uitz, *The Constitution of Freedom* (n 11) 19–23.

[75] Sartori, 'Constitutionalism: A Preliminary Discussion' (n 74) 853; see also Grimm, 'Types of Constitutions' (n 41) 100.

[76] Sartori, 'Constitutionalism: A Preliminary Discussion' (n 74) 860. In this meaning it would amount to 'any state form', thus being something of a 'meaningless (and deceiving) duplicate of terms such as organization, structure, form, pattern, political system, and the like' (ibid 863).

[77] It is worth stressing that the political ideal of *garantismo* is developed as a *legal* limitation of government by Ferrajoli: P Chiassoni, 'Constitutionalism Out of a Positivist Mind Cast: The Garantismo Way' (2011) 17(4) *Res Publica* 327.

[78] Sartori, 'Constitutionalism: A Preliminary Discussion' (n 74) 859. In this sense, there is a 're-conceptualisation' (ibid 862) of the term 'constitution' as brought forth in the 18th century, having no precedent in the ancient world, and being inherently connected to liberalism and to the revolutionary *époque*. See also Sajó and Uitz, *The Constitution of Freedom* (n 11) 13; Grimm, *Constitutionalism: Past, Present, and Future* (n 14) 6.

[79] Sajó and Uitz, *The Constitution of Freedom* (n 11) 23.

between constitutions and constitutionalism in modern times, there can be (and have been) constitutions that are not designed according to the principles of constitutionalism (rule of law, separation of powers, protection of fundamental rights, etc).[80] It is also possible, as the Italian experience of the *Statuto Albertino* tragically showed, that a codified but flexible constitution might be progressively hollowed out via ordinary legislation – that is, *democratically*.

These worries, in light of the very recent constitutional developments in constitutional democracies like Hungary and Poland, are far from mere theoretical quibbles. For the unwarranted confusion of: (a) the presence of a formal constitution; with (b) the existence and preservation of a constitutionalist framework in a given political system, might turn out to be a very powerful rhetorical device in the hands of an illiberal government seeking to boost its legitimacy.[81] This points to the necessity of separating, in constitutional theory, discourses about constitutions and discourses about constitutionalism. Only by 'uncoupling' the two, as I illustrate in the next section, we can understand fully the meaning of constitutionalism, both in legal and political terms.[82]

IV. FROM CONSTITUTIONS TO CONSTITUTIONALISM: NARROWING THE FOCUS OF CONSTITUTIONAL THEORY

'Constitution' is a term with a long-standing and stratified meaning which originates in physiology. For the longest part of its history, it was employed to denote 'in quasi-organic terms' the political existence of a community. Once fully abstracted from the underlying biological metaphor, it came to stand for the 'institutional form and complex of the political settlement'.[83] But it is not until the end of the eighteenth century, and the revolutionary constitutionalism in France and in the US, that the term acquires its 'doubly normative character', to the extent that

> [n]ot only had it begun to refer to the specifically legal mode of articulation and regulation of the body politic (as opposed to the institutional consequences of that articulation), but also, in a more transformative stage of juridification, through the medium of the early written constitutions that legal modality now came to be seen as constitutive or generative of that body politic.[84]

[80] See, for instance, HWO Okoth-Ogendo, 'Constitutions without Constitutionalism. Reflections on an African Political Paradox' in D Greenberg, SN Katz, MB Oliviero and SC Wheatley (eds), *Constitutionalism and Democracy. Transitions in the Contemporary World* (New York/Oxford, Oxford University Press, 1993); A Zimmerman, 'Constitutions Without Constitutionalism: The Failure of Constitutionalism in Brazil' in M Sellers (ed), *The Rule of Law in Comparative Perspective*, (Dordrecht, Springer, 2010).

[81] *cf* Castillo-Ortiz, 'The Dilemma of Constitutional Courts and the Case for a New Design of Kelsenian Constitutions' (n 17) 624–25.

[82] *cf* Grimm, *Constitutionalism: Past, Present, and Future* (n 14) ch 1.

[83] N Walker, 'Constitutionalism and the Incompleteness of Democracy' (2010) 39(3) *Rechtsfilosofie & Rechtstheorie* 206, 208; *cf* Grimm, 'Types of Constitutions' (n 41).

[84] Walker, 'Constitutionalism and the Incompleteness of Democracy' (n 83) 208–09; *cf* Grimm, *Constitutionalism: Past, Present, and Future* (n 14), 4.

56   *The Distinction between Creation and Application of Law*

One distinction to be kept in mind, therefore, is between those historical constitutions which could be termed 'photographic' – that 'merely' provide a snapshot of the institutional organisation of the polity – and those which more directly represent a 'blueprint' for the organisation of the state.[85] Even more precisely, if we narrow the focus on the relation of historical constitutions with the exercise of political authority, there seems to be at least three different meanings of 'constitution':

1.   as a 'mere' enactment, that is as the outcome of the exercise of political power: more recent examples are certain types of law (often criminal codes) in the sixteenth century;[86]
2.   as the formal institutionalisation of the 'political order', both in its static and dynamic dimensions, in line with the underlying biological metaphor;[87] and
3.   as a 'technique of liberty' that stands normatively against the exercise of political power, purporting to constrain it, as per the American and French revolutionary traditions of the eighteenth century.

The problem lies in the fact that the meaning of 'constitutionalism' in political and legal theory appears to be a function of the different meanings (particularly 2 and 3) that the term 'constitution' has had throughout the history of western thought. As a result, different scholars understand 'constitutionalism' in different and tendentially incompatible ways, causing theoretical confusion and a loss in the explanatory fruitfulness of the notion itself. A more promising approach is to consider then constitutionalism from the legal-theoretical perspective, and in particular the theory of sources. This move allows us to identify the specificity of the doctrine vis-à-vis the stratified history of the term 'constitution'.

Grey provides us with a useful starting point by considering the framework established by three common ways of distinguishing constitutions:[88] written and unwritten; rigid and flexible;[89] and the Diceyan distinction between constitutional 'conventions' and constitutional laws.[90] These distinctions are useful for pedagogical purposes; but they are ultimately too coarse, as 'the primary object of discourse in the study of constitutionalism should be constitutional norms, and not entire constitutions'.[91] He then classifies constitutional norms along

---

[85] Walker, 'Constitutionalism and the Incompleteness of Democracy' (n 83) 209; WG Werner, 'Democracy, Constitutionalism and the Question of Authority' (2010) 39(3) *Rechtsfilosofie & Rechtstheorie* 267, 268. This alternative can be understood in either descriptive or normative terms (that is, as to what constitutions are supposed to be).

[86] Grimm, 'Types of Constitutions' (n 41) 100.

[87] Walker, 'Constitutionalism and the Incompleteness of Democracy' (n 83) 209.

[88] TC Grey, 'Constitutionalism: An Analytical Framework' in JR Pennock and JW Chapman (eds), *Constitutionalism: Nomos XX* (New York, New York University Press, 1979).

[89] J Bryce, 'Flexible and Rigid Constitutions' in J Bryce, *Studies in History and Jurisprudence*, vol 1 (Oxford, Oxford University Press, 1901).

[90] *cf* the typology in Grimm, 'Types of Constitutions' (n 41) 105ff.

[91] Grey, 'Constitutionalism: An Analytical Framework' (n 88) 190.

three dimensions: first, their 'normative force or hierarchical status';[92] second, their mode of enforcement; and third, their source.

The first dimension concerns their hierarchical status among the other norms of the legal system. As such, a constitutional system can see any combination of the three types as shown below in Figure 1:

Figure 1 Grey's classification of constitutional norms

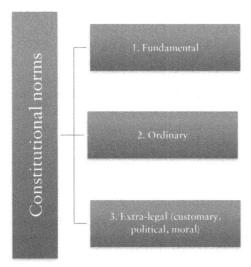

At the bottom, we find extra-legal norms: of which UK constitutional doctrine (or, at least, much of it) represents perhaps the best-known example.[93] These are what Dicey labelled 'conventions of the constitution':[94] that is, customary norms which are recognised as being 'constitutional' in terms of the forms of behaviour they govern but that, at least historically, have not been enforced by a court of law.[95] They are considered to be binding on institutional actors because of their moral weight and of the political consequences ensuing from their breach.

At the second level we find 'ordinary' legal norms, that is constitutional norms which can be modified any time through the ordinary legislative procedure. They are what Bryce has in mind when he defines some constitutions as 'flexible'[96] – the 1848 Italian *Statuto Albertino* being a historical example. These norms are constitutional in character (but not necessarily in status): they are deemed to belong to the constitution for the highly important subject matter

---

[92] ibid 191.
[93] ibid 192.
[94] AV Dicey, *Introduction to the Study of the Law of the Constitution*, 8th edn (London, Macmillan, 1915).
[95] Grey 'Constitutionalism: An Analytical Framework' (n 88) 194.
[96] Bryce, 'Flexible and Rigid Constitutions' (n 89).

58   *The Distinction between Creation and Application of Law*

they regulate. And yet, according to Grey, 'no useful purpose would be served by describing these provisions as not *truly* constitutional norms'.[97]

Lastly, the highest status is that of 'fundamental' or 'rigid' norms, to use Bryce's terminology once again.[98] Norms of this kind cannot be modified by ordinary legislative means (in other words, they are entrenched): either absolutely – through the adoption of so-called 'eternity clauses' – or just relatively, by requiring an extra-ordinary procedure to be amended. As to their force, these norms are considered hierarchically superior to ordinary law and thus prevailing in case of conflict with them. However, for Grey this is not by itself 'a sufficient condition for describing a legal rule as a constitutional norm'.[99]

This leads to the second dimension, that of enforcement. Grey distinguishes between 'political' and 'special' mechanisms of enforcement, the former being when the legislative branch has the final authority in resolving the conflict between constitutional and legislative norms. This is perhaps the most distinguishing feature of the 'political constitutionalism' model.[100] In such cases there is no strong judicial review administered by a separated supreme court that can strike down primary legislation, which amounts (in its different forms) to the paradigmatic 'special' mechanism of enforcement and is the hallmark of what is usually referred to as 'legal constitutionalism'.[101]

The third and last dimension refers to the source of constitutional norms.[102] The difference here is between codified and uncodified constitutional norms. The former are enacted by a body legitimated 'according to some established procedure' at a distinguishable moment in time;[103] while uncodified norms are not formally stated in a single document, but derive their 'constitutional' authority from their general acceptance by institutional actors or because they embody moral or political 'truths'.[104] Here we can find one of the clearest examples of the explanatory advantages in shifting focus away from the study of constitutions as a whole and focussing instead on constitutional norms. For, as Grey notes, if we apply the distinction between 'written' and 'unwritten' to constitutions, we might end up concluding that the two kinds are mutually exclusive.[105] Instead, most modern legal systems are a variable mix of 'written' and 'unwritten' constitutional norms.[106]

---

[97] Grey 'Constitutionalism: An Analytical Framework' (n 88) 194.

[98] Bryce, 'Flexible and Rigid Constitutions' (n 89).

[99] Grey 'Constitutionalism: An Analytical Framework' (n 88) 195.

[100] See, eg: Bellamy, *Political Constitutionalism* (n 25).

[101] See, eg: Sajó and Uitz, *The Constitution of Freedom* (n 11).

[102] Grey (n 88) 201.

[103] ibid 202.

[104] ibid.

[105] ibid 205–06.

[106] For an example of the relevance of constitutional conventions even in entrenched constitutional systems, see GU Rescigno, 'Ripensando le convenzioni costituzionali' (1997) 28(4) *Politica del Diritto* 499.

From Constitutions to Constitutionalism 59

What is the upshot of this discussion? Through the lenses of Grey's framework and its three 'dimensions' of analysis of constitutional norms, we should see even more clearly that if we conceive of the doctrine of modern constitutionalism as a function of the mainstream discussion about constitutions,[107] we overlook the deeper juridical core of the doctrine. For example, if we were to assume a purely static viewpoint, it would follow that 'Technically ... There is no British Constitution':[108] a seemingly paradoxical contention considering that, according to Sartori, the UK is understood by many as the 'mother country of modern constitutionalism'.[109] Instead, Grey's framework supports the observation that the presence of a formal constitution is only one among the possible normative-institutional designs through which the doctrine of constitutionalism can be implemented in a given political system.

To wit, the core of the doctrine of modern constitutionalism does not lie necessarily in the presence of an entrenched constitution which constrains the exercise of political power – although this is by far the most common model adopted around the world since the end of the global conflicts of the last century. Constitutionalism is realised whenever the exercise of political power through law is limited juridically – that is, by *another* type of law – in one of two ways.[110] First, by formally entrenching this other law in a codified constitution, thus making it normatively superior to ordinary legislation and, as such, at least in part out of the legislator's disposal. Second, by having another system of law alongside ordinary legislation whose source, administration, and ultimate foundations are institutionally beyond the reach of the political authority (even if not formally superior to legislation from a normative point of view).[111]

Thus, and in spite of the current terms of the debate between supporters of political and legal constitutionalism, it is only by going beyond the understanding of the doctrine as a function of the presence (or lack thereof) of a constitutional document that we can explore its meaning as 'government limited by law' at its fullest. This does not exclude the possibility that the doctrine might also play a 'positive' (and not just 'negative') function vis-à-vis government,[112]

---

[107] See W Waluchow, 'Constitutionalism' in EN Zalta (ed), *The Stanford Encyclopedia of Philosophy* (Spring 2018 Edition) http://plato.stanford.edu/entries/constitutionalism/: 'How, in the end, one answers these questions depends crucially on how one conceives the nature, identity and authority of constitutions.'

[108] Bryce, 'Flexible and Rigid Constitutions' (n 89) 156; see also KC Wheare, *Modern Constitutions*, 2nd edn (London, Oxford University Press, 1966) 21; A Tocqueville, *Democracy in America* (G Bevan trans, Penguin Classic, 2003) 118; and, significantly, Lord Neuberger (former president of the UK Supreme Court), 'The British and Europe' (Cambridge Freshfields Annual Law Lecture, Cambridge, 12 February 2014) http://resources.law.cam.ac.uk/privatelaw/Cambridge_Freshfields_Annual_Law_Lecture_2014_Lord_Neuberger_The_British_and_Europe.pdf.

[109] Sartori, 'Constitutionalism: A Preliminary Discussion' (n 74) 853.

[110] See, in this sense, Waluchow, 'Constitutionalism' (n 107): 'constitutionalism is the idea ... that government can and should be legally limited in its powers'.

[111] Because of an underlying constitutional convention.

[112] See, eg: NW Barber, *The Principles of Constitutionalism* (Oxford, Oxford University Press, 2018).

60   *The Distinction between Creation and Application of Law*

or even a democracy-enhancing function. But the point is that only when procedural and substantive legal constraints are placed (institutionally) upon the ordinary law-making power of the legislature can we then effectively conceive of a political system as 'constitutional'.[113]

V. THE (PROVERBIAL) TENSION BETWEEN DEMOCRACY AND CONSTITUTIONALISM

Let us take stock. In the first chapter I illustrated how, since the inception of a type of centralised rule for the community which can arguably be called 'political', two new and qualitatively different problems emerge that were not present in acephalous societies. The first issue is the potentially unlimited nature of the normative power of the ruler and the need for its limitation – as that power to rule could always be used against the very people who are ultimately responsible for its existence. The second problem lies in the constant need for legitimation of this formal power to change other people's normative positions.[114] In this chapter we have more specifically analysed the relationship between political power and law, starting from the internal relation at the outset (law as *lex*) and arriving at the 'invention' by Roman legal culture of a second and autonomous sense of law (as *ius*). It is *ius* that constitutes, conceptually, the space for the very possibility of constitutionalisation – that is, of *juridical limitation* – of political rule. But how is the problem of the limitation of political authority related to that of its legitimation?[115]

One intuitive way to frame the legitimation problem is by asking who should hold the power to rule within the political community. It could be one individual, a few individuals, or everyone; most historical political regimes fit one of these three categories. We have also already seen that the acceptance of democracy as the most legitimate form of government is a rather recent feature of political theory. In this respect, and without forgetting the distinction between isonomia and democracy, it is generally held that democracy blossomed in the sixth century BCE in Greece, precisely in Athens.

---

[113] L Ferrajoli, *La Democrazia Costituzionale* (Bologna, Il Mulino, 2016) 78. This is perhaps clearer with the 'entrenchment' model of constitutionalism, where there is a new dimension of (in)validity of legislation that leads to the possibility of 'unlawful law': P Sandro, 'Unlocking Legal Validity: Some Remarks on the Artificial Ontology of Law' in P Westerman, J Hage, S Kirste and AR Mackor (eds), *Legal Validity and Soft Law* (Cham, Springer International Publishing, 2018). This dimension of the potential invalidity of ordinary legislation was unknown to the first continental occurrences of the *Rechtsstaat* or *Stato di Diritto*, where law was still only the *form* of politics: Ferrajoli, *La Democrazia Costituzionale* (n 113 above) 20. As Pietro Calamandrei, prominent Italian scholar and one of the founders of the Italian Constitution, said: 'into the mould of legality one can pour gold or lead' ('*Nello stampo della legalità si può colare oro o piombo*'): P Calamandrei, 'Prefazione' in C Beccaria, *Dei Delitti e delle Pene*, 1st edn (P Calamandrei ed, Florence, Le Monnier, 1945) 92.

[114] See ch 1, s VI.

[115] *cf* the discussion in this section with the section in Grimm, 'Types of Constitutions' (n 41) 100–03.

The (Proverbial) Tension between Democracy and Constitutionalism   61

Democracy represents, if you will, the 'least bad'[116] form of government from the viewpoint of political equality, as it amounts to the 'rule of the people' or of 'the many' (from the union of *dêmos* and *kratos*), as opposed to the rule of one (tyranny) or to the rule of the few (oligarchy). At least initially then, the democratic paradigm is conceived of numerically,[117] in the sense that the participants in the decision-making process are the ones who bear the results of that decision. As a result, both political power and its outcomes are legitimated: the former because it is held directly by its own addressees; the latter because laws can be then considered as the expression of the autonomous will of the 'people'.[118] In direct democracy there is no separation between who exercises decision-making authority and who is subject to it; and, as such, this form of government embodies the essence of the principle of 'self-rule' (or political autonomy) in the public space.[119]

The problem with this initial understanding of democracy is not only that it seems theoretically impossible to reconcile majority rule with the autonomy of minorities, but also in the fact that direct democracy (as a form of legitimation of political rule) is always context-bound. When the dimensions of the political community become too large, and hence it becomes impossible for 'the people' to exercise political power directly, the democratic ideal of 'government of the people' dissolves into the different paradigms of representative democracy. Thus, the *demos* can be said to be governing only to a very narrow and qualified extent: as it has delegated the exercise of law-making authority to elected representatives (though it theoretically retains authority through the idea of popular sovereignty). But if the outcomes of the political process in a representative democracy are no longer the direct 'product' of the will of everyone (or even of the many), how can democracy still legitimate the exercise of political power?

These contradictions were apparent to Rousseau.[120] For him, the republican ideal[121] points towards a society through which 'each one, by uniting with all, obeys no one but himself, remaining free as before'.[122] For this reason

---

[116] As famously noted by Winston Churchill – 'No one pretends that democracy is perfect or all-wise. Indeed, it has been said that democracy is the worst form of Government except all those other forms that have been tried from time to time': *Hansard*, HC (Series 5) Vol 444, cols 206–207 (11 November 1947).

[117] *cf* N Bobbio, *Democracy and Dictatorship: The Nature and Limits of State Power* (Oxford, Polity Press, 1989) 135–36.

[118] Needless to say, who exactly made up 'the people' changed throughout history, as only in the 20th century did universal franchise become widespread.

[119] *cf* Ferrajoli, *La Democrazia Costituzionale* (n 113) 30.

[120] See S Freeman, 'Constitutional Democracy and the Legitimacy of Judicial Review' (1990) 9(4) *Law and Philosophy* 327, 341.

[121] Rousseau prefers the term 'republic' over 'democracy': Bobbio, *Democracy and Dictatorship* (n 117) 150.

[122] JJ Rousseau, *The Social Contract; and Discourses* (GDH Cole trans, London, Dent, 1973) book 1, ch 6.

62 *The Distinction between Creation and Application of Law*

he rejects, in the clearest possible terms, representative democracy, famously affirming that

> the moment a people allows itself to be represented, it is no longer free: it no longer exists. The day you elect representatives is the day you lose your freedom.[123]

Still, within a large (and pluralist) society in which majority rule is the only decision-making criterion that preserves equal weight for each individual's opinion – and thus the equal distribution of political power – unanimity on every issue is virtually unattainable, and so is it not clear how the autonomy of the minorities is preserved against that of the (ruling) majority. The way in which Rousseau escapes this conundrum[124] is with the idea of the social contract, and precisely by presupposing that

> [t]he rule of accepting the decision of the majority is itself established by agreement and presupposes unanimity on at least one occasion.[125]

This, significantly, is also Kant's position.[126] But then a second-order question arises: what is exactly in the social contract? Is the acceptance of majority rule enough to preserve the natural freedom of everyone, once the democratic association has been established? Or should we not rather assume that the very concept of autonomy – if it is the value upon which democracy is based – must be excluded from the possibility of disposal through the majority-minority dynamics? It is from this fundamental question, I think, that the distinction between purely procedural and more substantive conceptions of democracy emerges. For the latter, democracy does not just provide the rules of the game (majority rule), but it requires also the protection of a number of values (freedom of expression, to name but one) which are considered necessary for the majority-minority dynamics to be acceptable.

For our purposes what is relevant is that, if democracy is understood in a purely procedural fashion, there is an unwarranted consequence which plagues democratic theory, shaping the idea of majoritarian representative democracy as the process of expression of the autonomous will of the (sovereign) people.[127] This consequence is that, once the will of the majority becomes, unjustifiedly, the *general* will, individuals cease to be politically relevant. This is because 'the people' is an indivisible political subject – as Rousseau thinks and lay discourse often seems to assume – that legitimately acts in pursuit of its own well-being (and cannot fail to do so). Therefore, under this model, the decision of the

---

[123] ibid, book 3, ch 15.

[124] *cf* Ferrajoli, *La Democrazia Costituzionale* (n 113) 33.

[125] Rousseau, *The Social Contract* (n 122) book 1, ch 5.

[126] I Kant, 'Über den Gemeinspruch: Das mag in der Theorie richtig sein, taugt aber nicht für die Praxis' (originally published 1793) in I Kant, *Gesammelte Schriften, hrsg Konigliche Preussische Akademie der Wissenschaften*, vol 8 (H Maier, M Frischeisen-Köhler and P Menzer eds, Berlin and Leipzig, Walter de Gruyter, 1912) 297; English translation in I Kant, *Perpetual Peace and Other Essays*, (T Humphrey trans, Indianapolis, Hackett, 1983) 77–78.

[127] L Ferrajoli, *Principia Iuris: Teoria del Diritto e Della Democrazia*, vol 2 (Bari, Laterza, 2007) 9.

majority should have no limits, because it has been adopted by the (supposed) self-determination of 'the people' (that is, everyone).

Ultimately, this implies that the problem of limitation of political authority re-emerges from *within* the democratic process, given that both direct and representative forms of democracy seem normatively unable to provide for their own nourishment and survival. This remark is not prompted only by historical pragmatism,[128] but also by a theoretical issue which cannot be resolved by democratic theory alone: namely, that without limits (or pre-commitments) policed by an institution independent from the democratic process, a democratic regime can always be *democratically* terminated and turned into an authoritarian or autocratic one.[129]

Neil Walker has argued that the best way to understand the relationship between democracy and modern constitutionalism is to conceive of the former as an incomplete ideal and of the latter as contingently providing it with completeness.[130] For the relationship between the two cannot be captured in singular terms, in which one either 'defines up' democracy to meet a thick sense of constitutionalism or 'defines down' constitutionalism to match a procedural conception of democracy.[131] Their relationship must be conceived of as multi-levelled instead. Walker speaks in terms of a 'double-edged incompleteness', which refers

> both to the empirical incompleteness of democracy as a notion unable to supply its own terms and conditions of application – call this the internal dimension of incompleteness – as well as to the moral or normative incompleteness of democracy as a guide to good government – call this the external dimension of incompleteness.[132]

It follows that democratic theory cannot answer per se the 'who' and 'how' questions of collective decision-making[133] and it cannot account, from a normative point of view, for the possibility of its own institution (problem of legitimation).[134] It also cannot answer the 'what' (and 'what not') question, since it cannot provide the set of moral values and social aims that should separate what *can* from what *cannot* be decided through the democratic process (problem of limitation). As a result, modern constitutionalism supplies democracy with necessary – but contingently provided – completeness. Internalising in this

---

[128] See Sajó and Uitz, *The Constitution of Freedom* (n 11) 31–36.

[129] *cf* Dworkin's discussion of the majoritarian's premise in his introduction to R Dworkin, *Freedom's Law: The Moral Reading of the American Constitution* (Cambridge, Harvard University Press, 1996).

[130] Walker, 'Constitutionalism and the Incompleteness of Democracy' (n 83).

[131] ibid 211.

[132] ibid 206.

[133] *cf* ibid 214; and see also Bobbio, *Democracy and Dictatorship* (n 117), who identifies the formal meaning of democracy precisely with the answer to the questions of 'who governs' and 'how is government to be exercised'.

[134] See also, in this respect, C Mac Amhlaigh, 'Putting political constitutionalism in its place' (2016) 14(1) *International Journal of Constitutional Law* 175.

64 *The Distinction between Creation and Application of Law*

way the foundational paradox of democracy,[135] constitutionalism provides, in various degrees, overarching constraints on the power of the majority, so that democracy cannot be *democratically* terminated.[136]

And yet, crucially, the legitimacy of any constitutional system cannot be taken for granted: it is instead a function of the extent to which the procedures and values enshrined in the constitutional norms are actually shared by the polity as a whole.[137] In this sense, a legitimate constitutional system must reach and maintain a delicate balance between its aspirational character and the acceptance by a large part of society. For the less a constitution commands the support from a majority of members of the polity (both laypeople and officials) as to the rules and limits of the democratic process, the greater the risk that no amount of entrenchment will prevent a constitutional system from falling prey to authoritarian or autocratic turns.[138]

VI. MODERN CONSTITUTIONALISM AS 'LEGAL OTHERNESS'

Once an entrenched constitutional document is no longer a necessary condition for constitutionalism, one of the most paradoxical statements in constitutional theory – that the UK is the *motherland* of modern constitutionalism even though it has no constitution (in a formal sense) – becomes fully intelligible, but not because of the presence of a so-called 'political' constitution.[139] Rather, the point is that the *legitimating limitation* that constitutionalism provides democracy with has been pursued, and (contingently) achieved, through (at least) three models: the legal, the common law, and the Commonwealth.

In the so-called legal model of constitutionalism, historical pragmatism has been turned into an entrenched constitutional document policed by an institution – the courts – which is removed from the electoral competition.[140]

---

[135] See, eg: J Elster, 'Introduction' in J Elster and R Slagstad (eds), *Constitutionalism and Democracy* (Cambridge, Cambridge University Press, 1988) 2; S Holmes, 'Precommitment and the Paradox of Democracy' in J Elter and R Slagstad (eds), *Constitutionalism and Democracy* (Cambridge, Cambridge University Press, 1988) 195–240; S Holmes, 'Gag rules or the politics of ommision', in J Elter and R Slagstad (eds), *Constitutionalism and Democracy* (Cambridge, Cambridge University Press, 1988); J Habermas, 'Constitutional Democracy: a Paradoxical Union of Contradictory Principles' (2001) 29(6) *Political Theory* 766.

[136] This is exemplified, for instance, by Art 139 of the Italian Constitution (enacted 1947, last revised 2020): 'The form of Republic shall not be a matter for constitutional amendment'.

[137] *cf* L Ferrajoli, *Principia Iuris*, vol 1 (n 41) 9–15.

[138] See S Issacharoff, *Fragile Democracies: Contested Power in the Era of Constitutional Courts* (Cambridge, Cambridge University Press, 2015).

[139] On the political constitution, see at least: JAG Griffith, 'The Political Constitution' (1979) 42(1) *Modern Law Review* 1; A Tomkins, *Our Republican Constitution* (London, Hart Publishing, 2005); G Gee and GCN Webber, 'What is a Political Constitution' (2010) 30(2) *Oxford Journal of Legal Studies* 273.

[140] The extent of this 'removal' varies with each jurisdiction, and its importance for the independence of the court system should not be underestimated: see Castillo-Ortiz, 'The Dilemma of Constitutional Courts and the Case for a New Design of Kelsenian Constitutions' (n 17).

As such, the rights and procedures enshrined in the constitutional text are removed from the reach of the ordinary majority or, in the case of so-called 'eternity' clauses, of any majority. Entrenched constitutions become blueprints for the political community, merging fundamental rights and (aspirational) values that need protection precisely because they are not attained in reality. As such, they set negative limits upon, and broad objectives for, the political lawmaker. This also means that the formal entrenchment of the constitution removes the idea of *absolute* legislative sovereignty from the conceptual framework of the constitutional state,[141] and in this lies the most relevant difference from the other two models.[142]

What about the common law and the Commonwealth models of constitutionalism?[143] To begin with, the relationship between these two models is not of token to type: rather, the Commonwealth model is an evolution of the 'pure' common law model. This latter, best exemplified by the UK's constitutional arrangements prior to the accession to the European Communities and the enactment of the Human Rights Act 1998 (HRA 1998), is often considered as the clearest historical realisation of the doctrine of political constitutionalism.[144] In this model, parliamentary sovereignty retains its absolute character: there is, in principle, nothing that the legislature cannot decide in its legislative capacity, due to its perceived democratic legitimation. Thus, curbing its power would result in an unjustified limitation of the 'will of the people' that the legislature represents. As this doctrine of sovereignty gives the legislature the last word on the meaning of any norm of the 'political constitution', political constitutionalism is characterised by the absence of any higher law that could bind Parliament: limits and constraints on Parliament are only political in nature, and thus there is no judicial review of primary legislation.

'Commonwealth constitutionalism' refers to the mixed constitutional design which is found in several Commonwealth countries (Canada, New Zealand and Australia) in the last two decades or so, and in the UK after the enactment of the HRA 1998.[145] This model differentiates itself from the two models above as there is usually a Charter of Rights that is deemed superior, if not legally then at least politically, to ordinary legislation and whose respect is enforced by a supreme court with supervisory jurisdiction. However, the supreme court has

---

[141] See L Ferrajoli, *La sovranita' nel mondo moderno*, 2nd edn (Rome, Laterza, 2004); see also P Eleftheriadis, 'Law and Sovereignty' (2010) 29(5) *Law and Philosophy* 535.

[142] For the tension generated in the UK constitutional theory by the traditional concept of parliamentary sovereignty, see, eg: M Loughlin and S Tierney, 'The Shibboleth of Sovereignty' (2018) 81(6) *Modern Law Review* 989.

[143] S Gardbaum, *The New Commonwealth Model of Constitutionalism: Theory and Practice* (Cambridge, Cambridge University Press, 2013) chs 1–2.

[144] For an insightful critical discussion of the descriptive and/or normative character of the doctrine of political constitutionalism, see Gee and Webber, 'What is a Political Constitution?' (n 139).

[145] S Gardbaum, 'How Successful and Distinctive is the Human Rights Act? An Expatriate Comparatist's Assessment' (2011) 74(2) *Modern Law Review* 195.

66 The Distinction between Creation and Application of Law

only a weak power of review: it cannot strike down primary legislation, but only declare it as incompatible with the rights protected in the charter. The legislature, on the other hand, can theoretically at any moment repeal the Charter of Rights through ordinary legislative means.[146] Therefore, in keeping with the original common law 'pure' model, there is no formal entrenchment vis-à-vis the ordinary law-making power of the legislature, so it seems that the legislature retains the last word on the meaning of the political constitution. But how compelling is this mainstream understanding of these two models vis-à-vis the conception of constitutionalism put forward in this chapter?

My claim is that, in seeking the 'constitutional' in the common law (and, derivatively, in the Commonwealth) model of constitutionalism, we ought to focus on the rule of law, as developed through the common law by the courts. For it is indeed the common law, and not an ephemeral 'political' constitution, that provides the *legal otherness* required by constitutionalism as a bulwark against the political power wielded by Parliament.[147] This conclusion is possible because, as we have discussed already in the (inchoate) case of the late Roman republic, an institutional setting that is meaningfully *constitutional* can be identified without having to *force* the presence of a 'constitution' onto that system at all costs.

In other words, only when we understand constitutionalism as demanding not just a set of normative constraints on the law-making power of the legislature, but rather an institutional setting with two bodies of law that exist simultaneously, we can make sense of the common law model as truly *constitutional*. Here too, as with the 'legal' model of constitutionalism, historical trajectories play too important a role not to be factored in when elaborating our theoretical models.[148] In the UK case, it is apparent that the institutional need for entrenchment of a higher law in a formal constitutional document has not

---

[146] In this regard, the 'new model's great novelty – at least in theory or aspiration – is to decouple constitutional review from judicial supremacy or finality': ibid 197. The grouping under one heading of constitutional developments in Commonwealth countries (and the inclusion of Canada in particular) and post-HRA 1998 UK has been at the centre of a vigorous debate: see, eg: A Kavanagh, 'What's So Weak about "Weak-Form Review? The Case of the UK Human Rights Act 1998' (2015) 13(4) *International Journal of Constitutional Law* 1008, and the reply in S Gardbaum, 'What's so weak about "weak-form review"? A reply to Aileen Kavanagh' (2015) 13(4) *International Journal of Constitutional Law* 1040.

[147] *cf* the model of 'bi-polar sovereignty', which has been developed, in the context of English constitutional theory, by Trevor Allan: TRS Allan, *Law, Liberty, and Justice: The Legal Foundations of British Constitutionalism* (Oxford, Oxford University Press, 1993); TRS Allan, *Constitutional Justice: A Liberal Theory of the Rule of Law* (Oxford, Oxford University Press, 2001). See also S Lakin, 'Debunking the Idea of Parliamentary Sovereignty: The Controlling Factor of Legality in the British Constitution' (2008) 28(4) *Oxford Journal of Legal Studies* 709; CJS Knight, 'Bi-Polar Sovereignty Restated' (2009) 68(2) *Cambridge Law Journal* 361.

[148] See G Romeo, 'The Conceptualization of Constitutional Supremacy: Global Discourse and Legal Tradition' (2020) 21(5) *German Law Journal* 904. On the relationship between 'historical' and 'principled' accounts of public law, see TR Hickman, 'In Defence of the Legal Constitution: Review Article' (2005) 55(4) *University of Toronto Law Journal* 981, 1007–09.

Modern Constitutionalism as 'Legal Otherness' 67

been felt (at least not until very recently, and against the background of the 1998 devolution settlement)[149] because of two main factors.

On the one hand, there is the historical emergence of the rule of law, as developed by the common law courts (especially on the basis of the Magna Carta),[150] well before the liberal revolutions of the seventeenth and eighteenth centuries.[151] As noted by Palombella, the rule of law requires parts of positive law to 'be out of the disposal or "will", of the King, or of the sovereign power'.[152] As such, it internalises and 'entrenches' the separation of *jurisdiction* and *gubernaculum*, or of justice and sovereignty (of *ius* and *lex*),[153] thus providing for the protection of individual rights *inside* the political realm. In this regard,

> [j]urisdictio refers to law: but, in this domain, men have the duty to say it (*jus dicere*), and not to choose or decide. There is, then, some part of the law which remains at the disposal of the sovereign; but the other aspect of law is not at its disposal, and the sovereign is thus bound to be deferential.[154]

Therefore Sartori is correct, as we have seen, in identifying the UK as the 'motherland' of modern constitutionalism. For already from the thirteenth century, the common law was conceived of as an institutionally autonomous body of law that curbed the *sovereign* power held by the monarch (and later by Parliament).[155] Coke's famous dictum in *Bonham's case* evidences this,[156] as does – perhaps even more significantly, given the contested nature

---

[149] It does not seem a coincidence, in this respect, that Northern Ireland – the only nation of the UK which is governed by a document broadly comparable to a codified constitution (the Good Friday Agreement) – is the one in which a substantive part of the population has experienced something resembling authoritarian government. I owe this acute observation to Colm O'Cinneide. For a recent and sophisticated argument in favour of the codification of the UK constitutional arrangements see J King, 'The Democratic Case for a Written Constitution' (2019) 72(1) *Current Legal Problems* 1.

[150] Coke had already memorably declared in the 17th century that 'Magna Charta is such a Fellow, that he will have no sovereign' (Debate in the House of Commons, 17 May 1628, as recorded in J Rushworth, 'Historical Collections: 1628 (part 3 of 7)' in J Rushworth, *Historical Collections of Private Passages of State, Volume I 1618–29* (London, 1721) 549–588 (available at *British History Online* www.british-history.ac.uk/rushworth-papers/vol1/pp549-588 accessed 17 March 2021)).

[151] But *cf* RB Taylor, 'The Contested Constitution: An Analysis of the Competing Models of British Constitutionalism' [2018] *Public Law* 500, 505–11.

[152] G Palombella, 'The Rule of Law as an Institutional Ideal' in L Morlino and G Palombella (eds), *Rule of Law and Democracy: Inquiries into Internal and External Issues* (Leiden, Brill, 2010) 14.

[153] ibid.

[154] ibid 19. It is significant that Palombella here explicitly recalls Habermas: 'jurisdictio is associated with the preservation of the law, and not to the preservation of a sort of external morality' (ibid 16). *cf* also Gardner, 'Some Types of Law' (n 52) 85: '[w]hat seems most special about Common Law jurisdictions is that they have a great deal of case law that is not about the interpretation of legislation. It is only about the interpretation of other case law'.

[155] See Hickman, 'In Defence of the Legal Constitution: Review Article' (n 148) 987–88, underscoring how this conception is – despite widespread misconception – fundamentally Diceyan. *Contra*, see J Goldsworthy, *The Sovereignty of Parliament: History and Philosophy* (Oxford, Clarendon Press, 1999).

[156] *Thomas Bonham v College of Physicians ('Dr Bonham's Case')* (1610) 8 Co.Rep. 114a, 117b–118b: 'the common law will control acts of parliament, and sometimes adjudge them to be utterly void ... when ... against common right and reason'.

68   The Distinction between Creation and Application of Law

of Coke's remarks[157] – a seemingly little-known passage in Bracton's *On the Law and Customs of England* which discusses what happens when the king is deceived in a particular case.[158] Bracton said that if the king is alerted by his justices that his decision is unjust, and yet he still persists in ordering them to render it, they must issue the judgment, but 'it follows that the judgment is a matter of will rather than *jus*, if it can be called a judgment'.[159] In other words, according to Bracton that judgement is not *valid* (as law).

On the other hand, this institutional 'equilibrium' could have not been achieved if it was not for the dynamic adherence by all political actors to this dualist setting, which resulted in the slow emergence and consolidation of 'constitutional' conventions buttressed by '[t]rust in a shared ideal of fairness, accountability, and mutual respect'.[160] This stance is clearly exhibited in some (by now) very famous obiter dicta by the House of Lords that pledge continuous abidance by the 'inter-institutional comity'[161] between the British Parliament and the courts, provided that the former does not go beyond the 'outer limits' – as determined by the rule of law – of its law-making power.[162]

To summarise, the entrenchment of a constitutional document above the ordinary legislator is only one way in which constitutionalism can be implemented. At the core of modern constitutionalism there is the juridical limitation of political rule, which is realised by placing a different type of law (*ius*) alongside the law created by the political authority (*lex*).[163] This clarification allows us to identify a shared structure between the legal and the common law models. This shared structure consists of two complementary spheres: one that is available for the political decision-maker to fill, and one that is instead pre-determined either by a perennial tradition of judge-made law or by a crystallised and entrenched constitutional document.[164] The latter, as such, cannot be disposed of by the

---

[157] See for a critical discussion of the conflicting interpretations of Coke's words, D Edlin, *Judges and Unjust Law: Common Law Constitutionalism and the Foundations of Judicial Review*, (Ann Arbor, University of Michigan Press, 2008) 53–73; Goldsworthy, *The Sovereignty of Parliament* (n 155) 111–17.

[158] My utmost gratitude goes to Thomas McSweeney, who alerted me to the existence and significance of this passage for the argument defended here.

[159] H Bracton, *On the Law and Customs of England* (vol 4) (available at http://amesfoundation.law.harvard.edu/Bracton/Unframed/English/v4/159.htm), 159. For a contextual discussion of Bracton's concept of kingship and its relationship with *lex terrae* (the law of the land), see Loughlin, *Foundations of Public Law* (n 5) 39–41.

[160] Sajó and Uitz, *The Constitution of Freedom* (n 11) 18.

[161] A Kavanagh, 'The Constitutional Separation of Powers' (n 1) 235–36.

[162] See the judicial speeches in *R (Jackson) v Attorney General* [2005] UKHL 56, [2006] 1 AC 262, by Lord Steyn at para 102, by Lord Hope of Craighead at paras 104–107, and by Lady Hale at para 159.

[163] In this sense then, the rule of law requires 'protection of the opposition ... between two sides of the law': Palombella, 'The Rule of Law as an Institutional Ideal' (n 152) 22.

[164] This implies that there is not only one, but two sources of legitimation of public powers in a constitutional democracy: the democratic principle on the one hand and the rule of law on the other: J Habermas, 'Law and Morality' in SM McMurrin (ed), *The Tanner Lectures on Human Values*, vol 8 (Salt Lake City, University of Utah Press, 1988); Ferrajoli, *Principia Iuris*, vol 1 (n 41); and see reference to the doctrine of bi-polar sovereignty above at note 147.

ordinary political decision-maker (at least in its fundamental elements) and can be enforced by the courts (if need be).

A constitutional state is effectively characterised, in other words, by the *juridical* limitation of law. This takes place either through the formal entrenchment of constitutional norms above the legislature or through the development (alongside legislated law) of a different type of law, a type of law that has a different source and thus it is not fully disposable by the political authority. Crucially, this understanding of constitutionalism entails not only the existence of a different source of law which limits (at least in some respects) the law created by the political authority (normative requirement). It also entails that this other type of law is administered, in its fundamental elements, by a body that is meaningfully independent from the body wielding ordinary law-making power (institutional requirement). It should be apparent why the normative requirement alone would not 'guarantee' much: if the ordinary legislator could modify the terms of its own constitutional constraints 'at its pleasure',[165] it is doubtful whether those constraints could really be thought to act as such in practice.[166]

The UK constitutional model is routinely used as a rejoinder to this last point. According to defenders of the orthodox theory of parliamentary sovereignty, not only can there be constitutional constraints that are not legally enforceable – so that a statute can be *unconstitutional* and yet still *legal*[167] – but British constitutional history itself proves that judicial enforcement is not necessary for such constraints to be effective. This is misguided, in my view, both as a matter of history and theory. In terms of history, the relationship between Parliament and courts in the UK must be understood within the context of the dualist institutional setting which I have described in this chapter as one of the ways in which the doctrine of constitutionalism can be realised. Against this background, the fact that there are relatively few specific historical instances in which courts have explicitly invalidated acts of Parliament cannot conclusively be used to argue for the absence, from a theoretical perspective, of such power.[168] They rather speak, in my view, to the effectiveness of that shared ideal of inter-institutional comity according to which courts will refrain (and have indeed refrained) from using the power to invalidate statutes unless absolutely necessary – that is, unless Parliament were to go beyond the outer limits of its authority as established by the common law.[169]

This is confirmed, inter alia, by the historical willingness of the courts (and accepted by Parliament) to effectively set aside even the clearest of statutory formulations when these are deemed incompatible with one of the basic tenets of the rule of law. An example is the modern line of cases on legislative attempts

---

[165] Waluchow, 'Constitutionalism' (n 107).
[166] ibid.
[167] See, eg: Goldsworthy, *The Sovereignty of Parliament* (n 155) 190–92.
[168] See G De Q Walker, 'The Unwritten Constitution' (2002) 27 *Australian Journal of Legal Philosophy* 144, 145.
[169] ibid 145–47.

70 *The Distinction between Creation and Application of Law*

to oust the jurisdiction of the courts that starts with *Anisminic* and ends (at the time of writing at least) with *Privacy International*.[170] It is also reflected in the progressive acknowledgement of the principle of legality as a fully fledged *constitutional* principle (rather than as a principle of statutory construction).[171] In other words, what British constitutional history indicates is that the courts have found ways to enforce limits upon the legislative authority of Parliament without formally striking down statutes, but rather through creative construction that often goes beyond the letter of the law (under the pretence of giving effect to the 'intention' of the legislator). And courts will arguably continue to do so, unless pushed into a constitutional corner by the other actors: for instance, on the issue of ouster clauses.

As a matter of (normative) theory, it is of course true that even if one accepts that the power of the ordinary lawmaker should be limited by a set of (constitutional) norms, it does not follow, from a logical point of view, that such constitutional limitations should be enforced by courts.[172] But the need for a separate and independent site for norms enforcement and conflict resolution is not a logical but rather a functional requirement,[173] a requirement that is, in fact, at the core of any account of the rule of law.

Hence, if the objection is deployed to argue that the interpretation and application of the limits upon the law-making power of the political authority should ultimately reside with the very institution that is supposed to be constrained, it is not compelling after all. Especially when it comes to the violation of basic fundamental rights, citizens must have the possibility to seek individual redress from a different body than the one which supposedly infringed (or authorised the infringement) on those rights. And while we must acknowledge that the precise boundaries of some of those rights are legitimately contested (and accordingly require judicial self-restraint in those cases),[174] the conclusion that citizens can only engage in revolutionary mobilisation when their fundamental rights are infringed[175] effectively turns back the clock on more than 200 years of political progress in western civilisation. This would be a rather ironic outcome, as the constitutional protection of most of those rights has been obtained chiefly through (liberal) revolutions.[176]

---

[170] See *Anisminic Ltd v Foreign Compensation Commission* [1969] 2 AC 147; *R (Privacy International) v Investigatory Powers Tribunal and others* [2019] UKSC 22.

[171] A Young, 'Prorogation, Politics and the Principle of Legality' (*UK Constitutional Law Association Blog*, 13 September 2019) http://ukconstitutionallaw.org/2019/09/13/alison-young-prorogation-politics-and-the-principle-of-legality/ accessed 12 March 2021.

[172] See, eg: Goldsworthy, *The Sovereignty of Parliament* (n 155) ch 10; DE Bello Hutt, 'Against Judicial Supremacy in Constitutional Interpretation' (2017) 31 *Revus* 1.

[173] As explained already by Hart in Hart, *The Concept of Law* (n 68) 93–99. A similar point is made by Lord Wilberforce in the seminal *Anisminic* decision: *Anisminic Ltd v Foreign Compensation Commission* [1969] 2 AC 147 at 208B.

[174] See text to n 196 below.

[175] Goldsworthy, *The Sovereignty of Parliament* (n 155) 259–70.

[176] It would be an even more paradoxical outcome, from the perspective of the UK, because it would effectively deny the almost millenary tradition of common law rights protection.

If, instead, what is sought is a forum for 'constitutional dispute resolution' which is an alternative to the courts, this is conceivable from the perspective of constitutionalism defended here, provided that this alternative 'site' is both separate and independent from the ordinary lawmaker.[177] The discussion would then move onto institutional design,[178] and to questions of legitimacy and effectiveness of these alternative systems vis-à-vis constitutional review by courts. Alas, the reality is that no constitutional design can guarantee that a democracy will not turn at some point into an authoritarian or autocratic regime, as shown for instance by the recent Polish constitutional crisis. This example is a grim reminder, more than anything, of the fact that no entrenched constitution can perform a democracy-preserving function if it is not also effica- cious, in the sense that a majority of officials and citizens feel bound by its spirit, terms, and procedures.[179]

VII. THE TWO-FOLD JUSTIFICATORY DEPENDENCE OF CONSTITUTIONAL DEMOCRACY ON THE IDEA OF APPLICATION OF LAW

I have just argued that the existence of a codified, normatively superior consti- tution is not a necessary (nor sufficient) requirement of constitutionalism. Properly conceived of, constitutionalism requires the juridical limitation of the law-making power of the legislature by means of a second type of law that is not disposable by the law-maker via ordinary means, and in some cases not dispos- able at all. Historically, this has been pursued through two alternative models: by the codification of a constitution that is policed by a court as normatively superior to ordinary legislation – the legal model, adopted in most existing constitutional democracies – or by the development of another type of law whose source and administration are not, ultimately, available to the political authority – the common law model. What I can now illustrate is how the distinc- tion between the creation and application of law is constitutive of the legitimacy of our constitutional democracies. In this final section, I will show that this constitutive relationship applies not only to the doctrine of constitutionalism but also to democracy as the ideal of self-rule of the people. Some further impli- cations for the debate between legal and political constitutionalists will then bring the chapter to a close.

---

[177] cf Bello Hutt, 'Against Judicial Supremacy' (n 172) 12.

[178] See, for instance, the proposals in MC Dorf, 'Legal Indeterminacy and Institutional Design' (2003) 78(3) *New York University Law Review* 875.

[179] J Raz, 'On the Authority and Interpretation of Constitutions' in J Raz, *Between Authority and Interpretation: On the Theory of Law and Practical Reason* (Oxford, Oxford University Press, 2009) 154; J Habermas, 'Appendix II: Citizenship and National Identity' in Habermas, *Between Facts and Norms* (n 8) 500; Ferrajoli, *Principia Iuris*, vol 2 (n 127) 55–56; B Bugaric, 'Can Law Protect Democracy? Legal Institutions as "Speed Bumps"' (2019) 11 *Hague Journal on the Rule of Law* 447.

72   The Distinction between Creation and Application of Law

In the common law model of constitutionalism, if it was not possible for a judge to apply the law found in another judicial decision (and, more precisely, the *ratio decidendi*) the doctrine of *stare decisis* could not be ever implemented.[180] This, in turn, would make it very hard to conceive of the decisions of the courts as a *system* of law capable of limiting the power of the political sovereign.[181] Clearly, there is a difference in the degree of interpretive discretion (more on this in chapter four) between the application of a statute and application of a previous judicial decision, given that only in the former might there be an 'official' textual formulation of the norm to be applied.[182] But if it was never possible to apply a previously created norm to a new set of facts, the common law could not be anything more than a set of singular, free-standing decisions by individual courts with little (if any) systemic legitimacy (or efficacy). It would, in short, fail to be a system of *law*.[183] Thus, the common law could not perform the limiting function that is required for a political system to count as constitutional.

In the legal model of constitutionalism, also, denying the theoretical possibility of law-application undercuts the conceptual attainability of the principle of limited government through law. For if law is always indeterminate, then legal norms cannot be applied – but would always be created instead by courts in reaching a decision on any particular case. Thus, not only is it not clear in which sense the constitutional text could constrain the power of the legislature to make laws, it is also unclear how the very existence and jurisdiction of the constitutional court could have come about in the first place. If the norms contained in the constitutional text cannot be applied (or, depending on one's preferred way of putting it, if there are no norms to be applied), on what basis are the individuals sitting on the constitutional court declaring the validity or lack thereof of legislation? How can their decision be considered anything but the mere expression of their personal preferences? And if this is so, how can we say to be living in a democracy (and not in an oligarchy), let alone a constitutional democracy?

These are far from rhetorical questions. An argument dangerously along these lines is deployed by political[184] and (some) popular constitutionalists to attack the legitimacy of judicial supremacy in constitutional interpretation.[185]

---

[180] On the importance of *stare decisis* as a 'bedrock' for the common law tradition, see Gardner, 'Some Types of Law' (n 52) 85; Bellamy, *Political Constitutionalism* (n 25) 85.

[181] For an explicit account of the judicial obligation to apply the law as foundational principle of the common law, see Edlin, *Judges and Unjust Law* (n 157) chs 3–4.

[182] On the difference relevance of the text in statutes and judicial decisions at common law, see J Waldron, *Law and Disagreement* (Oxford, Oxford University Press, 1999) 78–79.

[183] *cf* L Fuller, *The Morality of Law*, rev. edn (New Haven, Yale University Press, 1977).

[184] See M Goldoni, 'Two internal critiques of political constitutionalism' (2012) 10(4) *International Journal of Constitutional Law* 926, 934.

[185] See, eg: MV Tushnet, 'A Note on the Revival of Textualism in Constitutional Theory' (1985) 58(2) *Southern California Law Review* 683; MV Tushnet, 'Critical Legal Studies and Constitutional Law: An Essay in Deconstruction' (1984) 36(1/2) *Stanford Law Review* 623; MV Tushnet, 'Following the Rules Laid Down: A Critique of Interpretivism and Neutral Principles' (1983) 96(4) *Harvard Law Review* 781.

The Two-fold Justificatory Dependence of Constitutional Democracy   73

In substance, because of the general and evaluative language used in any constitutional text, courts reviewing the validity of legislation are left with the utmost degree of discretion in deciding the meaning of constitutional rights and other constitutional norms.[186] In Waldron's words:

> One lesson of American constitutional experience is that the words of each provision in the Bill of Rights tend to take on a life of their own, becoming the obsessive catch-phrase expressing everything one might want to say about the right in question.[187]

As such, critics of judicial supremacy draw a (not always explicit) overall distinction between ordinary and constitutional adjudication, whereby only the former is able to yield determinate outcomes on the basis of the application of norms.[188] Instead, constitutional judges are effectively able to substitute their own view as to the meaning expressed by fundamental clauses (such as 'freedom of speech', 'cruel and unusual punishment', or 'right to health') with that of the democratically elected representative of the people. The problem with such arguments is that constitutional norms and ordinary legislative norms are much more alike than these critics recognise. This is because general and evaluative language is not a unique characteristic of constitutions – and neither is it a necessary characteristic.

On the one hand, ordinary legislation is sometimes affected by the same type of linguistic underdeterminacy (caused by a variable mix of vagueness, polysemy, ambiguity, etc) which is said, by critics of judicial supremacy, to be one of the defining features of constitutional texts.[189] So the difference is, at most, one of degree. On the other hand, there is not just one model of entrenched constitutionalism which is then adopted universally across the world. Historical and existing constitutions vary considerably in almost every aspect, and particularly in the degree of generality or precision of the language they are written in. Versteeg and Zackin have shown that the tendency among

---

[186] While the 'structural' parts of written constitutions are not generally deemed to be affected by the indeterminacy issue in the same vein as the 'Bill of Rights' parts, this has been challenged by A Stone, 'Judicial Review Without Rights: Some Problems for the Democratic Legitimacy of Structural Judicial Review' [2008] *Oxford Journal of Legal Studies* 1, 8–10.

[187] The centrality of this argument in Waldron's attack on judicial review seems confirmed by the fact that this passage is repeated verbatim in three of his most important works on the issue: J Waldron, 'A Right-Based Critique of Constitutional Rights (1993) 13(1) *Oxford Journal of Legal Studies* 18, 26; Waldron, *Law and Disagreement* (n 182) 220; Waldron, 'Core Case' (n 26) 1381. *cf* also Gardbaum, *The New Commonwealth Model of Constitutionalism* (n 143) 75–76.

[188] It should be noted that Kelsen himself – who originally theorised the rigidity of the constitutional order and contributed to the creation of the first centralised constitutional court in 1920 in Austria – harboured similar doubts, to the point that he considered constitutional courts as 'negative legisla-tors': H Kelsen, 'Wesen und Entwicklung der Staatsgerichtsbarkeit' in Lars Vinx (ed and trans), *The Guardian of the Constitution: Hans Kelsen and Carl Schmitt on the Limits of Constitutional Law* (Cambridge, Cambridge University Press, 2015), 47 (1506); see also H Kelsen, 'Judicial Review of Legislation: A Comparative Study of the Austrian and the American Constitution' (1942) 4(2) *The Journal of Politics* 183.

[189] Waldron is explicitly warned to the deeper (and troubling) implications of his 'core case' against judicial review, but chooses not to explore them: Waldron, 'Core Case' (n 26), 1354, fn 21.

74 *The Distinction between Creation and Application of Law*

recently adopted constitutions is to be written in a much more specific language than commonly held in the political theory literature (which makes them more akin to ordinary legislation), while allowing for greater amendability of their provisions (compared to the US Federal Constitution).[190] In this respect, these modern texts usually see a mix of (relatively few) eternity clauses and a majority of constitutional provisions, albeit usually only through some form of parliamentary supermajority vote (and in some cases with the added confirmation of a popular referendum).

Therefore, any general theoretical argument on the legitimacy of judicial supremacy in constitutional interpretation which relies on the characteristics of a particular constitutional system – like Waldron's – will not necessarily be applicable to other and different systems. Such arguments, in other words, effectively lose most of their explanatory and normative bite. To avoid this, political theory should pay attention more systematically to comparative constitutional scholarship.[191] This seems particularly true if we consider that the constitutional framework that has been perhaps most widely debated in the English-speaking literature – the US Federal Constitution and the US Supreme Court – is also in many respects 'exceptional' when compared to other existing constitutional systems across the world.[192] In this regard, a significant strand of the Anglo-American legal and political theoretical debate has failed for a long time to take into account the diversity of constitutional solutions implemented around the world, resulting in a 'one-theory-fits-all' fallacy which returned a distorted theoretical picture of the general scope and limits of a system of constitutional review.[193]

Crucially, the point here is not that constitutional review might be more or less desirable (vis-à-vis parliamentary supremacy) depending on the occurrence, in any particular case, of a number of 'assumptions' that are necessary for a democratic system to be in good working order.[194] Rather, the point is that the very normative legitimacy of constitutional review changes on the basis of different features of constitutional design.

---

[190] M Versteeg and E Zackin, 'Constitutions Unentrenched: Toward an Alternative Theory of Constitutional Design' (2016) 110(4) *American Political Science Review* 657.

[191] *cf* A Stone, 'Putting political constitutionalism in its place?: A reply to Cormac Mac Amhlaigh' (2016) 14(1) *International Journal of Constitutional Law* 198, 203.

[192] See M Versteeg and E Zackin, 'American Constitutionalism Exceptionalism Revisited' (2014) 81(4) *The University of Chicago Law Review* 1641; M Schor, 'Judicial Review and American Constitutional Exceptionalism' (2008) 46(3) *Osgoode Hall Law Journal* 535; A Stone Sweet, 'Why Europe Rejected American Judicial Review – and Why it May Not Matter' (2003) 101(8) *Michigan Law Review* 2744; Bellamy, *Political Constitutionalism* (n 25) 10–11; EJ Segall, *Supreme Myths: Why the Supreme Court is Not a Court and its Justices are Not Judges* (Santa Barbara, Praeger, 2012).

[193] This is evident, for instance, when Goldsworthy claims, on the possibility of British judges being recognised with the legal authority to invalidate statutes, that 'It can reasonably be argued, given their record in the United States, that judges are almost certain to interpret such an authority too broadly': Goldsworthy, *The Sovereignty of Parliament* (n 155) 270.

[194] Waldron, 'Core Case' (n 26).

The Two-fold Justificatory Dependence of Constitutional Democracy   75

This is then perhaps the only observation that can be made at the most general theoretical level on this particular issue: that the legitimacy of judicial supremacy in constitutional interpretation is never fixed, but rather always a function of different elements of constitutional design. These include: 1) the overall precision (or lack thereof) of the language with which the constitutional text is written;[195] 2) the ratio of amendable provisions to unamendable ones, and the complexity of the amendment procedure itself; 3) the nomination process, composition, and tenure of the members of the constitutional court (if there is one), which determine the degree of its independence from the political law-making body; and 4) the extent of institutional self-restraint displayed by judges when equipped with the power to strike down legislation, especially in hard cases (ie those case where there needs to be some form of weighing between two equally protected constitutional rights).

Accordingly, legal constitutionalists should acknowledge more readily the contestable nature of constitutional reasoning when a constitutional provision is made up by general and evaluative clauses (and require, as a result, judicial self-restraint in their normative theories).[196] But political constitutionalists should tread very lightly when doubting, in principle, the extent to which constitutional norms constrain the outcomes of particular cases.[197] For the more they criticise generally – rather than on a case-by-case, constitution-by-constitution basis – the possibility of judicial application of constitutional norms to particular cases, the more they also challenge the legitimacy of ordinary adjudication. This implicitly hollows out the rule of law principles on which their democratic theories are premised explicitly.[198]

Political constitutionalists end up in a conundrum: as long as they maintain an untenable theoretical distinction between the judicial application of constitutional and ordinary norms, they implicitly undermine a fundamental element of their own democratic theories, the rule of law.[199] But if they were instead to acknowledge that the difference between application of constitutional and ordinary legislative norms is not a difference in quality, but at most only in degree,[200] then this key tenet of their arguments against judicial supremacy in constitutional interpretation would lose most of its normative bite.

---

[195] Waldron himself seems to acknowledge this, albeit begrudgingly: ibid 1383.

[196] Even Ferrajoli, perhaps the staunchest supporter of strong constitutional review of legislation in European and Latin-American scholarship, now calls for a reformulation in more precise terms of the constitutional text, and in particular of constitutional rights: L Ferrajoli, 'Costituzionalismo e Giurisdizione' (2012) 23(3) *Questione Giustizia* 7, 19.

[197] *cf* Bellamy, *Political Constitutionalism* (n 25) 35–37.

[198] *cf* L Vinx, 'Republicanism and Judicial Review' (2009) 59(4) *University of Toronto Law Journal* 591.

[199] See specifically Waldron, 'Core Case' (n 26) 1353–1354; Bellamy, *Political Constitutionalism* (n 25) ch 2.

[200] On the presence of 'easy cases' in constitutional adjudication, see A Marmor, *Interpretation and Legal Theory*, rev 2nd edn (London, Hart Publishing, 2005) 144.

76   The Distinction between Creation and Application of Law

The significance of distinguishing between creation and application of law for political constitutionalists does not end here, however. There is a more fundamental sense in which, as I said at the very beginning of this book, the basic political ideal of democratic government is grounded on this juridical distinction.[201] For at its core – especially from a non-instrumental point of view[202] – democracy is always based, in one way or another, on the idea of 'self-determination',[203] or 'self-rule', or 'self-government',[204] *by* the people, *of* the people, *for* the people.[205] This is true whether one places freedom, autonomy, or equality (or a combination of these) as the ultimate value secured by democracy. It is apparent in the case of direct democratic procedures: both in the case of popular assemblies (in systems where size allows collective decision-making), and in the more limited instances of popular referenda. However, the centrality of self-rule is opaquer in the general workings of current mass representative systems, where citizens elect representatives to an assembly or institution tasked with collective decision-making. This implies that, in our current democracies, the people hold most of the time only a supervisory power over law-making – the equally shared control over government[206] – through holding their representatives accountable via regular elections (among other means), rather than direct collective decision-making power itself.

Nevertheless, in both cases, democracy does not hold unless there is the possibility of distinguishing between the activities of law-creation and law-application. For if the law produced by the people, either directly or indirectly through their representatives, is always (or even only mostly) indeterminate – as realists and critical legal scholars affirm[207] – then it cannot be applied to individual cases, and so the decisions reached by judges must always be the product of their creative, jurisgenerative, activity. As a result, there cannot be self-rule, nor 'shared control' over law-making, as relevant judges are not democratically elected. It also prompts the further question: where does the legitimacy of adjudication come from, if this is the case?

In addressing this fundamental issue, Gunther juxtaposes two opposite theories of legitimacy: the 'transmission belt model' and the 'billiard ball model'.[208]

---

[201] This approach is distinctively Kelsenian: A Kalyvas, 'The Basic Norm and Democracy in Kelsen's Legal and Political Theory' (2006) 32(5) *Philosophy and Social Criticism* 573, 575.

[202] For a general overview of contemporary instrumentalist and non-instrumentalist accounts of democracy, see T Christiano, 'Democracy' in EN Zalta (ed), *The Stanford Encyclopedia of Philosophy* (Fall 2018 Edition) http://plato.stanford.edu/entries/democracy/.

[203] H Kelsen, 'Foundations of Democracy' (1955) 66(1) *Ethics* 1.

[204] C Bird, 'The Possibility of Self-Government (2000) 94(3) *American Political Science Review* 563, 563–64.

[205] P Pettit, *On the People's Terms: A Republican Theory and Model of Democracy* (Cambridge, Cambridge University Press, 2012).

[206] ibid.

[207] See, for further discussion, JJ Moreso, *Legal Indeterminacy and Constitutional Interpretation* (Dordrecht, Springer, 1998) ch 5.

[208] K Günther, 'Legal Adjudication and Democracy: Some Remarks on Dworkin and Habermas' (1995) 3(1) *European Journal of Philosophy* 36, 37–38.

The first is clearly presupposed by democratic theory (as exemplified by Rosseau, among many others),[209] in the sense that legal adjudication is justified insofar as it applies the rules created by the people ('for the people, of the people'). The second considers the legitimacy of legal adjudication as independent from democratic legislation, precisely because of the indeterminacy of legislation. However, as Gunther notes, if 'many facts of legal adjudication' point to the truth of the billiard ball model by questioning the determinacy of the 'general law',[210] does it mean that we are only left with acknowledging the illusory character of democratic government?

Gunther sees the solution to this dilemma in his 'discourse theory of application': according to which, in a nutshell, the legitimacy of every judicial act of law-application is not (just) a matter of the features of the law, but of the procedure through which the judge applies it to a case.[211] But the problem of indeterminacy (and resulting 'democratic deficit') remains looming in the background. For if the 'general law' (that is, legislation) is indeed indeterminate, it is not only the legitimacy of adjudication that is at stake, but also that very conduct-guiding function of law, which we have identified (in chapter one) as its most defining feature across time and space.

In other words: how can citizens – law's primary addressees, in most cases – act on the basis of those laws which they have supposedly *given* themselves, if such laws are incapable of being determinate from the start? How can this be understood, even in a minimal sense, as self-rule? Moreover, how can legislation be implemented and constrain administrative action? How could the incredibly complex machinery of government in a modern state work at all, if the application of general norms contained in legislation is not possible?

Pace Gunther then, democracy seemingly requires, at least to a significant extent, that norms created at a previous moment in time can be applied subsequently to a factual situation whose features are intersubjectively determined by those very norms. No procedural legitimacy appears able to supplement this requirement: for if there is nothing to apply in the first place, law becomes a continuous and indistinguishable creative process that is structurally incapable of coordinating the behaviour of large groups.[212] In its ideal form, democracy actually demands that the relevant rule created by the people, either directly or through their representatives, is the rule that is applied in the given individual case by the rule-user.[213] Such rule-user may be a judge, a public official in general, or simply a citizen that wishes to produce the normative effects predetermined by the norm (like the sale of a house). In this regard, too often has legal theory focussed on the question of law-application (or lack thereof) by

---

[209] ibid 38–42.

[210] ibid 38.

[211] K Günther, *The Sense of Appropriateness: Application Discourses in Morality and Law* (Albany, State University of New York Press, 1993).

[212] See Cameron, *Strong Constitutions* (n 1) chs 1–3.

[213] That is, at least in a majority of cases. *cf* Bellamy, *Political Constitutionalism* (n 25) 84–85.

78   *The Distinction between Creation and Application of Law*

courts while pushing to the background the key activities of other officials in the public administration,[214] and law-abidance by laypeople more generally.[215] This is a fundamental mistake, as it means that the vast majority of law-application activity is lost on the theoretical reflection on the juridical practice.

Once we move from the ideal to the actual, this demand of identity must be understood in the context of the possible uncertainties that surround the applicability of any given norm – and sometimes as to the identification of the norm to be applied in the first place. These uncertainties are mainly due to the 'limit, inherent in the nature of language, to the guidance which general language can provide', as memorably put by Hart.[216] As Gunther notes, this is particularly true for legal adjudication (and, I should add, increasingly so for administrative proceedings too), where legal reasons – which are endogenous to the development of law as *ius*[217] – must mediate the application of democratically enacted laws in order to make it 'appropriate' for the particular case at hand.[218] This means that what democracy ultimately demands is, if not always identity 'all the way down', at least that the norm created by the democratic law-maker intersubjectively constrains the range of normative options available to the official in charge of making a decision on the individual case.[219]

To conclude, my main thesis – that constitutional democracy is premised on the possibility of distinguishing the activities of law-creation and law-application – contains a powerful criticism of those political constitutionalist theories which question the legitimacy of judicial review of legislation from a theoretical (rather than pragmatic) point of view. For there is a glaring inconsistency in defending an account of democracy as self-rule (as political constitutionalists clearly do) while denying the distinction between law-creation and law-application when it comes to judicial review of legislation. Not only is there no difference in kind – as opposed to one of degree – between the language used in legislative and constitutional texts, but also empirical analysis indicates that whatever the degree of difference between the two, the extent of such difference has progressively decreased in most constitutional systems around the world.

Therefore, political constitutionalists are faced by an even deeper dilemma than the one about the rule of law. For if they criticise judicial supremacy in constitutional interpretation in general, using even a weak version of the argument from indeterminacy, they end up undermining the fundamental tenet of

---

[214] This tendency in exemplified by Hart's 'relative inattention to the activities of administrators' in his *Concept of Law*: M Kramer, *H.L.A. Hart* (Cambridge, Polity Press, 2018) 76.

[215] P Sandro, 'To whom does the law speak? Canvassing a neglected picture of law's interpretive field' in M Araszkiewicz, P Banas, T Gizbert-Studnicki and K Pleszka (eds), *Problems of Normativity, Rules and Rule-Following* (Cham, Springer, 2015).

[216] Hart, *The Concept of Law* (n 68) 126.

[217] See on the common law obligation to develop the law: Edlin, *Judges and Unjust Law* (n 157) chs 5–6.

[218] Gunther, 'Legal Adjudication and Democracy' (n 208) 52; *cf* also Bellamy, *Political Constitutionalism* (n 25) 83–89.

[219] This will be expanded on in ch 4 when discussing the concept of legal discretion.

their theory of democracy: the possibility of self-rule by the people. But if they instead take seriously their endorsement of the possibility of distinction between law-creation and law-application at the level of ordinary legislation – that law can be, and for the most part is, a collective enterprise capable of inter-subjective determinacy – then they seem forced to limit themselves to empirically driven, case-by-case criticisms of individual systems of constitutional adjudication, and not of the idea of constitutional adjudication per se. Be that as it may, the centrality of the distinction between creation and application of law for constitutional democracy is confirmed.

3

A Critical Evaluation of Moderate Legal Realism

I. INTRODUCTION

ARE WE NOT all realists now? The fact that this question sounds somewhat rhetorical these days indicates clearly the extent to which realist theories of adjudication have become mainstream in legal scholarship.[1] While the origins of legal realism can be traced to the first half of the past century to the concurrent work of two groups of scholars in the US and in Scandinavian countries,[2] its research paradigm and broad agenda have been carried forward, since the second half of the twentieth century, by a wide spectrum of doctrinal movements.[3] These include Critical Legal Studies,[4] so-called race and gender theories,[5] the Italian and French realist schools on the Continent; the Law and Economics[6] and the broader political science approach to US constitutional law.[7]

---

[1] B Leiter, 'American Legal Realism' in D Patterson (ed), *A Companion to Philosophy of Law and Legal Theory, Blackwell Companions to Philosophy*, 2nd edn (Chichester, Wiley-Blackwell, 2010) 261. For the claim that realism is 'omnipresent in American law schools and legal culture': B Leiter, *Naturalizing Jurisprudence: Essays on American Legal Realism and Naturalism in Legal Philosophy* (Oxford, Oxford University Press, 2007) 21.

[2] According to Leiter, American legal realists anticipated, by at least 30 years, the so-called naturalistic turn in the philosophy of science, as originated by the work of Quine: Leiter, *Naturalizing Jurisprudence* (n 1) ch 1.

[3] On the tricky business of identifying schools and movements in legal scholarship, see L Green, 'Law and the Causes of Judicial Decisions' (2009) Oxford Legal Studies Research Paper 14/2009 formerly available at http://papers.ssrn.com/abstract=1374608 accessed 31 March 2012, 5, on file with author.

[4] On the 're-invention' of realists by critical legal scholars: Leiter, *Naturalizing Jurisprudence* (n 1) 18–20; see also, for the claim that realism was 'largely silent on the political influences on decisions', B Leiter, 'Legal Formalism and Legal Realism: What is the Issue?' (2010) 16(2) *Legal Theory* 111, 118–19. On the CLS movement, *cf* eg: G Binder, 'Critical Legal Studies' in D Patterson (ed), *A Companion to Philosophy of Law and Legal Theory, Blackwell Companions to Philosophy*, 2nd edn (Chichester, Wiley-Blackwell, 2010).

[5] See, eg: G Minda, *Postmodern Legal Movements: Law and Jurisprudence at Century's End* (New York, New York University Press, 1995).

[6] See generally: J Hanson, K Hanson and M Hart, 'Law and Economics' in D Patterson (ed), *A Companion to Philosophy of Law and Legal Theory, Blackwell Companions to Philosophy*, 2nd edn (Chichester, Wiley-Blackwell, 2010); more specifically, on the Chicago School as 'founded' by Posner: B Leiter, 'In Praise of Realism (and against Nonsense Jurisprudence)' (2011) 100(3) *Georgetown Law Journal* 865.

[7] See, eg, for an overview, N Sultany, 'The State of Progressive Constitutional Theory: The Paradox of Constitutional Democracy and the Project of Political Justification' (2012) 47(2) *Harvard Civil Rights-Civil Liberties Law Review* 371.

Introduction   81

What all these approaches seem to share is a fundamental rejection of formalist or cognitivist accounts of adjudication as accurate descriptions of our judicial practices. Against these latter theories, in which judges supposedly reach their decision by means of the *cognitive* application of rules to the set of facts before them, realists or sceptics tend to undercut the action-guiding capacity of legal rules in the process of reaching (at least) some decisions.[8] In doing so, some of them purport to demystify adjudication as a more-or-less constraint-free process at the heart of which lie individual hunches or personality.[9] Others primarily claim that, in order to predict judicial outcomes, we need to turn to empirically-sound epistemological paradigms borrowed from psychology, economic analysis, sociology, behavioural sciences, etc. Overall, many of these approaches purport to substitute our normative understanding of legal rules with a more naturalistic understanding, as with the laws of physics or astronomy. But if legal rules bear little or no significance in constraining the decision-making process of judges, then it becomes impossible to distinguish between the activity of creating the law and that of applying it. Law turns into a pervasive creative process and, as a result, the legitimacy and rationality not just of adjudication, but of constitutional democracy more generally (as seen at the end of the last chapter), are completely undermined.

Nowadays radical versions of legal realism seem regressive, to the extent that the current dominant strand of the doctrine in Anglo-American jurisprudence has been termed 'moderate', 'tamed'[10] or 'balanced'.[11] For, unlike radical versions, it purports to undermine the traditional picture of adjudication only for a particular class of legal cases, those that reach the stage of litigation (or even only that before appellate courts).[12] Prima facie, then, the traditional cognitivist account of law and legal reasoning would still hold true for the majority of rule-based phenomena – the so-called 'easy cases' – and this would warrant the traditional idea that the law is, for the most part, an *objective* social practice.

What is wrong then with moderate realism? A first problem lies in the extent to which the indeterminacy of adjudication infringes upon the legitimacy and rationality of law, ie to what extent the indeterminacy of adjudication is deemed compatible with the normative structure of constitutional democracy as we have seen in chapter two.[13] A second objection that will be presented in this chapter

---

[8] See, eg: T Spaak, *Guidance and Constraint: The Action-Guiding Capacity of Theories of Legal Reasoning* (Uppsala, Iustus, 2007).

[9] On the judicial hunch, see generally: F Schauer, *Thinking Like a Lawyer: A New Introduction to Legal Reasoning* (Cambridge, Harvard University Press, 2009) 128.

[10] F Schauer, 'Legal Realism Untamed' (2013) 91(4) *Texas Law Review* 749.

[11] BZ Tamanaha, *Beyond the Formalist-Realist Divide: The Role of Politics in Judging* (Princeton, Princeton University Press, 2009).

[12] Leiter, 'American Legal Realism' (n 1) 267; Schauer, *Thinking Like a Lawyer* (n 9) ch 7.

[13] See, eg: B Leiter, 'Legal Indeterminacy' (1995) 1(4) *Legal Theory* 481, 487.

82 A Critical Evaluation of Moderate Legal Realism

goes to a more fundamental level: how is it possible to separate and distinguish the determinacy of law from that of adjudication? As I will argue, in this respect moderate realism seems ultimately to overcome its self-imposed boundaries and to cover all instances of rule-based reasoning, so that the law as a whole becomes intrinsically indeterminate or subjective.[14] If this is true, then moderate realism is an untenable position, since its central claims are necessarily pervasive in law, and as a result we are faced again with the destructive challenge posed by radical scepticism not only to adjudication, but to the legitimacy and rationality of law and constitutional democracy itself.

I argue in this chapter that while moderate realists correctly warn us about the legitimacy and rationality of judicial adjudication in some (hard) cases,[15] they cannot provide us with the epistemic tools to substantiate satisfactorily the distinction between easy and hard cases. In other words, if moderate realism is to take its premises seriously, every legal case becomes a hard case, and thus its 'moderate' character turns out to be self-defeating. What is left again then is the alternative between cognitivism and radical scepticism,[16] which bears fundamental consequences for our legal and political practices.

II. REALISM VS FORMALISM

From a diachronic point of view, legal realism is a reaction to formalism, also known as 'mechanical jurisprudence' or 'noble dream theory'.[17] In its traditional depiction, formalism is a theory of adjudication which holds that law is always fully determined and that interpretation is a cognitive process, so that there is always one right answer available to decision-makers. In this picture, the practical syllogism governs legal reasoning.[18] The role of the judge is then to retrieve the right answer by means of deductive processes, and there is no space 'left for genuine interpretive discretion'.[19] As a doctrine, formalism is a

---

[14] In this regard, consider the remark that one cannot 'coherently maintain both indeterminacy and subjectivity', for 'indeterminacy presupposes some form of objectivity': J Coleman and B Leiter, 'Determinacy, Objectivity and Authority' (1993) 142(2) *University of Pennsylvania Law Review* 549, 601.

[15] HLA Hart, *The Concept of Law*, 3rd edn (Oxford, Oxford University Press, 2012) 135; HLA Hart, 'Positivism and the Separation of Law and Morals' (1958) 71(4) *Harvard Law Review* 593, 606.

[16] For a first definition of 'legal cognitivism': Coleman and Leiter, 'Determinacy, Objectivity and Authority' (n 14) 627, fn 153.

[17] Leiter, 'American Legal Realism' (n 1) 275–76. Brian Tamanaha vigorously rejects the traditional historical juxtaposition between realism and formalism, and purports to show how both ends of the spectrum were in reality much closer than traditionally deemed: Tamanaha, *Beyond the Formalist-Realist Divide* (n 11); BZ Tamanaha, 'Balanced Realism on Judging' (2010) 44(4) *Valparaiso University Law Review* 1243.

[18] On the traditional structure of the practical syllogism, see, eg: N MacCormick, *Rhetoric and The Rule of Law* (Oxford, Oxford University Press, 2005) ch 3.

[19] R Guastini, 'Rule-Scepticism Restated' in L Green and B Leiter (eds), *Oxford Studies in Philosophy of Law*, vol 1 (Oxford, Oxford University Press, 2011) 150.

product of the Enlightenment and of its moral and political project, as indicated by Montesquieu (whose motto was that the judge should be *bouche de la loi*) and Cesare Beccaria among others.[20] Since then, few (if any) legal and political theorists have actually held a fully fledged formalist position.[21] This is because formalism as a descriptive theory of adjudication is grossly mistaken, and it can be considered more appropriately as an ideology than as an actual theoretical position.[22] The paradigm of formalism, that judges merely apply the law either created by somebody else (civil law) or retrieved in the secular body of the laws of the land (common law), has become embedded into Montesquieu's tripartite model of the separation of powers, and is thus pervasive in the very normative political framework of western democracies. As such, it has been more or less unwillingly carried forward by both positivists, at least before Kelsen and Hart, and natural law theorists alike.[23] This might explain why realism has been conceived of as a critical reaction to it.

Kelsen and Hart, in different ways, sanction the demise of formalism. While Kelsen, as we shall see below, leaves us with (nothing but) the idea that the law is indeed radically indeterminate – as interpretation is a de facto matter in which whoever has the last word gets to establish what the law is,[24] Hart acknowledges the challenge raised by American and Scandinavian realists by offering what has been later called a 'mixed theory'[25] and which I believe can also be

---

[20] ibid.

[21] Leiter ('American Legal Realism' (n 1) 276) identifies Christopher Langdell, Dean of Harvard Law School, as the major exponent of modern formalism in America and thus as the preferred target of many American realists.

[22] This was true already at the time of *l'école de l'exégèse*, and it is in line with Hart's position on the matter: Hart, *Concept of Law* (n 15) 129. The very label 'formalism' is contested, both as to its meaning and as to its applications: for Hart ('Positivism and the Separation of Law and Morals' (n 15) 610) it is a confusing 'misnomer'. Brian Leiter is keen to distinguish between 'formalist' theories that claim the rational determinacy thesis of law and the insularity thesis of legal reasoning (from other domains), and 'Vulgar Formalism' which is tantamount to 'mechanical deduction': Leiter, 'Legal Formalism and Legal Realism' (n 4) 111. For a comprehensive discussion of the several meanings conferred to the label see F Schauer, 'Formalism' (1988) 97(4) *Yale Law Journal* 509. In this article Schauer makes two important points: on the one hand, with the label 'formalism' we can express two opposite attitudes, either the 'denial of choice *by* the judge', or the 'denial of choice *to* the judge' (ibid 521); on the other, that even in hard cases where the 'formalist' or literal application of the rule would produce 'absurd' results – that is results which go against the purpose of the rule – 'formalism is only superficially about rigidity and absurdity. More fundamentally, it is about power and its allocation' (ibid 541). On formalism, see also EJ Weinrib, 'Legal Formalism: On the Immanent Rationality of Law' (1988) 97(6) *Yale Law Journal* 949.

[23] For a discussion of the idea of 'Natural Law Formalism': Leiter, 'Legal Formalism and Legal Realism' (n 4) 115.

[24] Here, I suspect, the 'purity' of the theory plays a key role in Kelsen's attitude towards the theory of interpretation – an attitude we shall find in a similar fashion when considering Guastini's latest restatement of rule-scepticism; *cf* for a cognate remark, B Leiter, 'Legal Realisms, Old and New' (2013) 47(4) *Valparaiso Law Review* 949, 953.

[25] That Hart misread the realist claims has been argued by Brian Leiter multiple times: Leiter, 'American Legal Realism' (n 1) 251; *Naturalizing Jurisprudence* (n 1) 17–18, 59–60.

84 A Critical Evaluation of Moderate Legal Realism

consistently termed as cognitivist.[26] Most legal positivists today subscribe to one version or the other of this cognitivism,[27] and by doing so, the 'indeterminacy threat' is defused, so that legal positivism is paired with a theory of legal reasoning that stems from its theoretical premises.[28] Within this approach the source of the indeterminacy of law resides chiefly in the open-texture of the (natural) language in which the law is expressed and which causes the so-called 'penumbra' cases in the application of legal rules.[29] The indeterminacy of law is confined to a limited number of cases, whereas in the majority of instances the law discharges its function of communicating effectively standards of conduct.[30]

Hart famously distinguishes between clear and unclear cases. The former type of case represents the majority of the rule-following universe, whereas in the latter the law proves to be indeterminate,[31] and hence if judges want to adjudicate, they must exercise discretion. But even more important is the meta-theoretical implication that we can draw from Hart's position: if law is indeterminate in some cases because of the open-texture of the natural languages by means of which normative utterances are expressed, we could then get rid of the indeterminacy of law if we were able to get rid of the open-texture of language itself.[32] This conclusion seems warranted by the fact that Hart himself envisages this possibility and rejects it, given our ignorance of fact and aim which characterises our (fallible) humanity[33] and that creates the need for 'fresh official guidance'.[34] This is also important, says Hart, to avoid both ignoring and exaggerating the indeterminacy of law, which are the vices imputable respectively to formalism on the one hand and to rule-scepticism on the other.[35] We can argue that it is because of Hart's critique that realism stops being generally identified with the (Holmesian) 'predictive theory of law', mutually exclusive with positivism and patently untenable, and starts to be understood progressively as a descriptive theory of adjudication competing

---

[26] The reader should note that for Guastini 'cognitivism' is equivalent to 'formalism', whereas Hartian approaches are termed 'vigil theories': Guastini, 'Rule-Scepticism Restated' (n 19) 150–51.

[27] See, eg: N MacCormick, *Legal Reasoning and Legal Theory*, rev edn, (Oxford, Oxford University Press, 1994); A Marmor, *Interpretation and Legal Theory*, rev 2nd edn (London, Hart Publishing, 2005).

[28] *cf* F Atria, *On Law and Legal Reasoning* (Oxford, Hart Publishing, 2002) ch 7.

[29] Hart, *Concept of Law* (n 15) 126.

[30] ibid 128.

[31] For the remark that Hart seems to confuse open-texture and incompleteness: R Guastini, 'Hart su Indeterminatezza, Incompletezza, e Discrezionalità Giudiziale' (2003) 21(2) *Ragion Pratica* 395.

[32] Of course, it depends on whether we understand open texture properly, as potential vagueness, or as vagueness itself. Only in this latter case my contention seems to hold. Indeed, Hart also recognises the 'indeterminacies of a more complex kind' that a system of precedents, as opposed to statute law, brings: Hart, *Concept of Law* (n 15) 134–136.

[33] ibid 128.

[34] ibid 130.

[35] ibid.

Let Us be Realist about Adjudication. What do Judges Eat for Breakfast? 85

with cognitivist or mixed theories[36] – a descriptive theory of adjudication that, Leiter argues vigorously, in fact is not only not at odds, but indeed entails a positivist theory of law.[37]

III. LET US BE REALIST ABOUT ADJUDICATION. WHAT DO JUDGES EAT FOR BREAKFAST?

Suppose you came across empirical evidence that in a particular legal system judges were deciding cases according to what they ate for breakfast.[38] If, before going to the courtroom in the morning, they had a Continental breakfast with croissants, marmalade, fruits and a good Italian espresso, it appears that they are going to rule consistently in favour of the defendants. If they had instead a much more substantial English breakfast and some juice, you find that they are going to rule more likely in favour of the prosecution. You observe this by means of an empirical survey which clearly shows that, regardless of the rules of the legal system and of the merits of the case, in those sessions in which the judges came from a continental breakfast the probabilities of a ruling in favour of a defendant rises to 89 per cent, whereas in those sessions following an English breakfast the percentage drops to a mere 11 per cent. Clearly judges would seem to decide cases according to their digestion! We could then present a tempting physiological explanation about the interaction between digestion and decision-making processes, showing, for instance, that heavier digestion workloads correspond with a minor blood inflow to the brain and thus reduced cognitive faculties, so that judges have to rely on the prosecution's case without the ability to verify the defendant's response. Or we could simply argue,

---

[36] It is indeed thoroughly debated whether legal realism, and specifically the American strand, can be understood only as a descriptive theory of adjudication. According to Leiter himself, ('American Legal Realism' (n 1) 276–78), many realists (but not Cohen) converged upon a (rather unpretentious) normative theory of adjudication that he terms 'quietism', according to which it would be pointless to give any normative advice to judges as to how they should decide, for how they *should* decide is already how they *actually* decide. There is no widespread agreement on this 'dismissive' reading of the normative ambitions of American realists: see in particular, E Ursin, 'The Missing Normative Dimension in Brian Leiter's Reconstructed Legal Realism' (2012) 49(1) *San Diego Law Review* 1, 4 for the claim that at least in the tort scholarship of Leon Green and Karl Llewellyn one can found an 'ambitious normative agenda', an agenda that brings realists much closer to Dworkin in this regard than ever imagined. For a more detailed critique of Leiter's thesis, and for a restatement of the (non-quietist) realists' theory of law, MS Green, 'Legal Realism as Theory of Law' (2005) 46(6) *William & Mary Law Review* 1915.

[37] Leiter, 'Legal Indeterminacy' (n 13); B Leiter, 'American Legal Realism' in MP Golding and WA Edmundson (eds), *The Blackwell Guide to the Philosophy of Law and Legal Theory* (Malden, Blackwell Publishing, 2005) 63; Leiter, 'American Legal Realism' (n 1); Leiter, *Naturalizing Jurisprudence* (n 1) 60; discussing critically this claim by Leiter: G Tuzet, 'What Is Wrong with Legal Realism?' in D Canale and G Tuzet (eds), *The Planning Theory of Law: a Critical Reading* (Dordrecht, Springer, 2013); D Priel, 'Were the Legal Realists Legal Positivists?' (2008) 27(4) *Law and Philosophy* 309.

[38] A Kozinski, 'What I Ate for Breakfast and Other Mysteries of Judicial Decision Making' (1992) 26(4) *Loyola of Los Angeles Law Review* 993.

86   A Critical Evaluation of Moderate Legal Realism

out of folk psychology,[39] that heavy digestion precludes good decision-making, or that it makes defendants less sympathetic; or even that judges want to deal with cases as quickly as possible in order to 'hit the restroom'.

Now if this was really the case, and you happened to be the lawyer of a defendant scheduled to appear before a court, what would you do in order to best pursue your client's interest?[40] Should you normally try to build up a convincing case for the judge, showing that the law is on your client's side? Or should you rather take into account the results of the empirical survey and therefore try to bring it about that the judge is going to hear your case after having had a Continental breakfast? Let us imagine instead you are a citizen and the empirical survey is brought to the public's attention by the press: how would you react to the news that a judge decides cases according to what she ate for breakfast? What would you think of that judge and how would that make you feel? What would the legislature or the government do about it? But even more importantly, what would we think about the legal system? What would be the point of having a legal system at all, if judges do not decide cases according to the rules of the system, but rather according to their digestion?

Of course, this is nothing but a hypothetical scenario built upon a caricature of legal realism made notorious in the literature.[41] Or at least it was so until recently. An empirical study conducted on a significant (1,000>) number of judicial decisions in parole boards in Israel shows how the probability of denial of the prisoner's parole request increases constantly as judges go through the sequence of cases, only to return to the initial value after each of the two daily food breaks.[42] The implication seems clear: empirical analysis proves one of the realists' core theses that legal rules hardly explain (and thus can hardly cause) judicial decisions, whereas other extraneous factors bear a more incipient causal relation to the outcome of the decision-making process.[43] In this case, the causal explanation would lie in the psychological hypothesis that 'making repeated judgments or decisions depletes individuals' executive function and mental resources, which can, in turn, influence their subsequent decisions'.[44]

---

[39] See generally: I Ravenscroft 'Folk Psychology as a Theory' in EN Zalta (ed), *The Stanford Encyclopedia of Philosophy* (Fall 2010 Edition) http://plato.stanford.edu/archives/fall2010/entries/folkpsych-theory/.

[40] This can be deemed analogous to the famous 'bad man' perspective advocated by Holmes, on which see the meaningful considerations by Green, 'Law and the Causes of Judicial Decisions' (n 3) 11.

[41] Kozinski, 'What I Ate for Breakfast and Other Mysteries of Judicial Decision Making' (n 38).

[42] S Danziger, J Levav and L Avnaim-Pesso, 'Extraneous factors in judicial decisions' (2011) 108(17) *Proceedings of the National Academy of Sciences* 6889. For a critical rejoinder: K Weinshall-Margel and J Shapard, 'Overlooked factors in the analysis of parole decisions' (2011) 108(42) *Proceedings of the National Academy of Sciences* E833. For the reply by the authors of the first piece: S Danziger, J Levav and L Avnaim-Pesso, 'Reply to Weinshall-Margel and Shapard: Extraneous factors in judicial decisions persist' (2011) 108(42) *Proceedings of the National Academy of Sciences* E834.

[43] This is assumed, in the article, against a complex set of logical regressions: Danziger, Levav and Avnaim-Pesso, 'Extraneous factors in judicial decisions' (n 42) 6890.

[44] ibid 6889.

Realism and Realisms in Law: Meta-theory 87

Consequential and repetitive decision-making would, in the long run, 'drain' decision-makers' mental faculties:[45] and as a physiological response, judges would start simplifying their decisions, which in the case-study amounts to 'accept the default, status quo outcome: deny a prisoner's request'.[46] The result is that 'the likelihood of a favourable ruling is greater at the very beginning of the work day or after a food break than later in the sequence of cases'.[47] As such, we would have a striking confirmation of the indeterminacy thesis of law, given that something utterly irrelevant from a legal point of view like having or not having a food break, and not the more-or-less syllogistic connection of law to the facts of the case, would explain how judges decide cases.

IV. REALISM AND REALISMS IN LAW: META-THEORY

To understand which (if any) epistemic and methodological lessons we are entitled to draw from the quantitative study above, we need to have a closer look at legal realism as a doctrine. This is quite challenging, given the variety of approaches currently existing in the literature. Therefore, I will endeavour to retrieve the lowest common philosophical denominator between the many realist strands, using what we might call the 'second-order' or 'new' accounts of legal realism offered by scholars such as Leiter, Guastini and Spaak among others. This project might appear misguided, since different 'schools' labelled 'realist' – such as the American, the Scandinavian and the Continental (Italian and French) – have so little in common that it has actually been stressed how unfortunate and misleading this communal label is.[48] And yet, the question 'is there anything they all share [beyond their name]?' seems worth asking.[49]

Once I have identified what I think is the philosophical common ground of the different strands of legal realism, I will weigh it against the currently predominant version in the literature, the moderate version. To the extent that moderate realism is presented as a descriptive theory of adjudication, it is deemed compatible not only with a positivist theory of law,[50] but more generally with the normative set of foundations of the constitutional democratic model

---

[45] And not just simply as a function of 'elapsed time'; it is worth noticing that the authors' hypothesis is not based on an empirical measurement of judges' mental resources: ibid 6890–92.

[46] ibid 6889.

[47] ibid 6890.

[48] Leiter, 'Legal Realisms, Old and New' (n 24) 950–51.

[49] *cf* T Spaak, 'Naturalism in Scandinavian and American Realism: Similarities and Differences' in P Asp and M Dahlberg (eds), *Uppsala-Minnesota Colloquium: Law, Culture and Values, De Lege 2009* (Uppsala, Iustus 2009); Leiter, 'Legal Realisms, Old and New' (n 24).

[50] For the purposes of this chapter, I will assume a very broad definition of legal positivism as the union of two theses, the social source thesis (law must be posited, that is, it must be determined by some social fact) and the separability thesis (there is no necessary connection between law and morality). Both of these theses are controversial, but for our purposes we need not complicate the discussion here.

88 A Critical Evaluation of Moderate Legal Realism

that we have discussed in chapter two.[51] My ultimate aim is to show how this position is untenable, as moderate realism is eventually self-defeating and hence unable to account for the normativity of law in the great majority of cases.[52] This implies that the only model of adjudication compatible with the structure of democratic constitutionalism, as seen in chapter two, is a (tendentially) cognitive model.

It is very common to find in the literature the terms 'realism' and 'scepticism' used interchangeably. Although there might be historical and philosophical reasons[53] to prefer the latter over the former,[54] the likely cause of the ambiguity lies in the fact that the two labels have been usually meant to represent the same 'attitude' from two opposite viewpoints, one starting from facts (realism) and one from rules (scepticism). In other words, someone is a 'realist' about the facts of law, ie about what is going on in courtrooms, and a 'sceptic' as to the existence, and/or the normativity, and/or causal efficacy of whatsoever is meant by 'legal rules'.[55] It is not entirely clear whether there is any necessary causal

---

[51] This seems to be one of the main assumptions underlying Leiter's project towards a 'naturalized jurisprudence', already embryonically retrievable in its seminal article with Coleman on the determinacy and objectivity of adjudication (Coleman and Leiter, 'Determinacy, Objectivity and Authority' (n 14)).

[52] I conceive of the problem of the normativity of law as the question of how law provides its addresses with reasons for action in order to constrain their decision-making and guide their behaviour; *cf* Tuzet's definition of normativity as 'law as a reason to act and a guide to action': Tuzet, 'What Is Wrong with Legal Realism?' (n 37) 50. For a general overview of the problem, see, eg: T Spaak, 'Legal Positivism, Law's Normativity, and the Normative Force of Legal Justification' (2003) 16(4) *Ratio Juris* 469.

[53] In the history of philosophy, the label 'realism' – as with many others – has been used in several different ways. For an overview, see A Miller, 'Realism' in EN Zalta (ed), *The Stanford Encyclopedia of Philosophy* (Spring 2012 Edition) http://plato.stanford.edu/archives/spr2012/entries/realism/. Thus if we conceive of realism in a platonic idealist sense (M Balaguer, 'Platonism in Metaphysics' in EN Zalta (ed), *The Stanford Encyclopedia of Philosophy* (Summer 2009 Edition) http://plato.stanford.edu/archives/sum2009/entries/platonism/), that is, as the claim of the existence of an ideal object like the prime number 'seven' which is independent of individual beliefs or social practices, it seems utterly doubtful that we can label the kind of claims made by 'legal realists' as such. One can also understand realism through the shift brought by Brian Leiter, with his 'Naturalized Jurisprudence', from 'realism' to 'naturalism' and 'pragmatism' as the key philosophical tenets of realism in law and adjudication. This seems eventually confirmed by the Leiter himself, who argues that while American realists where so 'colloquially', Scandinavians adopted the term 'to signal their opposition to metaphysical idealists': Leiter, 'Legal Realisms, Old and New' (n 24) 951; see also Coleman and Leiter, 'Determinacy, Objectivity and Authority' (n 14) 602, fn 99; Schauer, 'Legal Realism Untamed' (n 10) 749, fn 2.

[54] *cf* M Barberis, 'Separazione dei Poteri e Teoria Giusrealista dell'Interpretazione' in P Comanducci and R Guastini (eds), *Analisi e diritto 2004: Ricerche di giurisprudenza analitica* (Turin, Giappichelli, 2004) 11, fn 30 according to whom 'realism' has to be preferred over 'scepticism'.

[55] The three positions are to be kept conceptually separated, but they can be imagined as three concentric circles: 'scepticism' as to the existence of rules is the most radical, ontological position, that refutes the idea of legal rules as metaphysical entities *tout court*; 'scepticism' about the normativity of legal rules amounts to the thesis that legal rules, despite their ontological status, are unable to provide reasons for action to law's addressees; and lastly 'scepticism' as to rules' causal efficacy, that is, even if legal rules can figure (or act) as reasons for action for its addressees, they are empirically unable to causally constrain (because they always at least underdetermine) the decisions they purport to regulate.

connection between the two claims, and, if any, in which order: is someone a 'realist' about what judges do because she is a sceptic about rules; or, conversely, is someone a sceptic about rules for she is a realist about adjudication, ie from empirical observations she realises that rules do not bear any causal efficacy to judges' decisions? While American legal realism, whose 'members' lacked philosophical training,[56] clearly seems to represent the latter stance, Scandinavian realists, mindful of the 'location problem' in philosophy,[57] were predominantly sceptic because they did not believe that a 'rule' – that is something belonging (if anything) to the world of ought and thus beyond physical reality – could appear in the causal explanation of human behaviour.

A stipulation which seems capable of accommodating terminological ambiguities is that of conceiving of the philosophical doctrine of 'legal realism' as the variable combination of three tenets:[58]

1. (Rule-)scepticism (theoretical tenet): the claim that legal rules do not constrain judges, ie they do not cause them to decide the way they do; or, even more radically, that do not exist at all.[59]
2. Pragmatism (methodological tenet): the idea that a given theory, in order to be worth pursuing, must 'make a difference', which means that a working theory of adjudication must enable us to consistently predict judicial decisions.[60]
3. Naturalism (epistemological tenet): in order to predict what the courts will do, we need to abandon armchair conceptual analysis and to get our hands dirty with scientifically sound – that is, empirical – models of analysis.[61]

---

[56] Felix Cohen actually held a Ph.D. in philosophy from Harvard: MS Green, 'Leiter on the Legal Realists' (2011) 30(4) *Law and Philosophy* 381, 382, fn 6.

[57] Leiter, 'Legal Realisms, Old and New' (n 24) 951.

[58] Riccardo Guastini, in one of his most recent restatements of Italian legal realism, proposes a three-fold framework that is similar to the one put forward here: R Guastini, 'Il Realismo Giuridico Ridefinito' (2013) 19 *Revus* 97.

[59] *cf* Green, 'Law and the Causes of Judicial Decisions' (n 3) 12–13. The latest Leiter claims that Scandinavians' scepticism was not towards 'law, legal systems and legal norms', but rather towards 'the causal efficacy of legal doctrine': Leiter, 'Legal Realisms, Old and New' (n 24) 954.

[60] On legal pragmatism, see, eg: R Warner, 'Legal Pragmatism' in D Patterson (ed), *A Companion to Philosophy of Law and Legal Theory*, *Blackwell Companions to Philosophy*, 2nd edn (Chichester, Wiley-Blackwell, 2010). More specifically on Leiter's characterisation of pragmatism: Priel, 'Were the Legal Realists Legal Positivists?' (n 27) 314, fn 16; Spaak, 'Naturalism in Scandinavian and American Realism' (n 49); Ursin, 'The Missing Normative Dimension in Brian Leiter's Reconstructed Legal Realism' (n 36) 21; E Ursin, 'Clarifying the Normative Dimension of Legal Realism: The Example of Holmes's *The Path of the Law*' (2012) 49(2) *San Diego Law Review* 487.

[61] On naturalism in legal philosophy see, eg: B Leiter, 'Naturalism in Legal Philosophy', The Stanford Encyclopedia of Philosophy (Fall 2012 Edition) http://plato.stanford.edu/archives/fall2012/entries/lawphil-naturalism/. According to Leiter ('American Legal Realism' (n 1) 269), the 'hallmark of the naturalistic impulse is to formulate laws of judicial behaviour', that is causal laws, 'based on actual observation of what it is courts do in particular cases'. *cf* also, from the same author, Leiter, 'American Legal Realism' (n 37) 62. On different conceptions of naturalism: see Priel, 'Were the Legal Realists Legal Positivists?' (n 37) 330–33; Spaak, 'Naturalism in Scandinavian and American Realism' (n 49) 36–39.

90 A Critical Evaluation of Moderate Legal Realism

In what follows, the relationship between these three tenets will be considered in order to highlight what I believe constitutes the very lowest common denominator of realism in law. I will show that the pragmatist and naturalist tenets are parasitic on the theoretical tenet, so that if this latter is untenable, the first two lack a necessary basis and seem uncompelling on their own. This is why the discussion in the rest of this chapter will focus on rule-scepticism.

V. THE LOWEST COMMON DENOMINATOR OF LEGAL REALISM

The essence of legal realism is usually captured by a series of famous 'taunts'.[62] These traditionally refer to the acknowledgement and study of the difference 'between law in books and law in actions', or between 'paper rules and real rules'.[63] The aim is to discover what has been concealed, so realists say, by centuries of formalism. In that difference nests judges' discretion and thus, from the sceptical perspective, realism amounts to the assumption that 'General propositions do not decide concrete cases',[64] or that 'The life of the law has not been logic; it has been experience'.[65]

To be a realist, in other words, means to appreciate what judges really do when they decide cases. And what judges *really* do, is not applying (as formalism holds) predetermined authoritative rules or principles to the facts before them, in a more-or-less mechanical fashion, thus obtaining syllogistically justified outcomes. Judges are not machines, nor do questionable entities called 'rules' hold them at gunpoint. Rather judges decide cases by responding primarily and mostly to the facts of the case and then vesting ex-post the rationalisations of their decisions in 'legal language'.[66] This is, according to Leiter, the 'core claim' of American realism,[67] and this is why the business of the lawyer – and of the theorist, consequently – is to look first and foremost at the facts of the case in order to extract 'the laws of judgment' (similar to the laws of gravity) which can allow us to predict the judges' decisions.[68]

This latter claim is one of the main points of contention among American realists, as illustrated by the differences between the so-called idiosyncrasy and sociological wings,[69] and more generally among realists *tout court*, given that some of them seem to be satisfied, as we shall see with the Genoa school, with

---

[62] Green, 'Law and the Causes of Judicial Decisions' (n 3) 6.

[63] Schauer, 'Legal Realism Untamed' (n 10) 750.

[64] *Lochner v New York* 198 US 45 (1905) (J Holmes dissenting at 76).

[65] OW Holmes, *The Common Law* (Boston, Little, Brown and Co, 1881) 1.

[66] *cf* Leiter, *Naturalizing Jurisprudence* (n 1) 16.

[67] ibid 21; *cf* Green, 'Law and the Causes of Judicial Decisions' (n 3) 23.

[68] Leiter, 'American Legal Realism' (n 1) 261; for a critique of this claim: Schauer, *Thinking Like a Lawyer* (n 9) 132; *cf* Ursin, 'The Missing Normative Dimension Brian Leiter's Reconstructed Legal Realism' (n 36) 8–9.

[69] Leiter, 'American Legal Realism' (n 1).

the critique of the traditional picture of adjudication. In other words, and going back to the three tenets identified above, one can drop pragmatism and still being considered a fully fledged legal realist by retaining rule-scepticism. What about rule-scepticism and naturalism though? Again, it seems that the latter is causally dependent on the former, for only if the former is true, that is if only traditional theories of adjudication fail to carry out their function – ie to predict the decisions of courts adequately – then the need for naturalism as a new paradigm for the science of law arises.[70] So, too, one does not need to be a naturalist in order to be a realist: continental analytical legal realists being a case in point.[71]

What I am pointing at is that rule-scepticism represents the lowest common denominator of realisms in law.[72] I am not claiming that the latter can be reduced to the former: such a remark, if perhaps valid for some individual scholars, would be descriptively mistaken if applied to legal realism overall. Rule-scepticism – ie the claim that the traditional formalist picture of adjudication is descriptively wrong because legal rules (if there is anything like that) prove to be indeterminate and so unable to justify judicial decisions – is the minimum (theoretical) definiens of legal realism, the *conditio sine qua non*.[73] But what kind of rule-scepticism, conceived of as the thesis about 'the causal role of rules in [judicial] decision-making',[74] are we referring to?

Here the point is muddled by the fact that different realist scholars hold different views: a relevant observation when one considers Hart's attack on conceptual (or global) rule-scepticism, as well as Leiter's rejoinder that American realists were empirical and not conceptual sceptics.[75] In this respect, I agree with Leslie Green when he affirms that 'One can deploy concepts defectively without intending to make any conceptual claims',[76] and that, therefore, even if we want

---

[70] For the consideration that the normative and the sociological approaches in the science of law are not opponents, Green, 'Law and the Causes of Judicial Decisions' (n 3) 27–29; L Ferrajoli, *Principia Iuris*, vol 1 (Bari, Laterza, 2007) 8–51; *cf* also Priel, 'Were the Legal Realists Legal Positivists?' (n 37) 319–23. Indeed, even among American realists different kinds of naturalism were upheld: Spaak, 'Naturalism in Scandinavian and American Realism' (n 49) 26.

[71] Pierluigi Chiassoni pointed out to me, in a private conversation, that Genoese analytical legal realists are indeed empiricists when it comes to legal knowledge, and that naturalism is but a variation on it. I welcome the comment, but I think it is ultimately immaterial for the overall point made here, which is that we need to replace theoretical enquiry with a different (naturalised) one only if scepticism is correct.

[72] *cf* Hart, *Concept of Law* (n 15) ch 7.

[73] *cf* Leiter, 'Legal Realisms, Old and New' (n 24) 954. Leiter in this work argues for a 'thin' connection between American and Scandinavian realisms, that of 'skepticism about the causal efficacy of legal doctrine'. As I am about to argue in the body of the text, this thesis seems relevant for legal theory only if coupled with theoretical scepticism, that is, if legal norms are deemed rationally indeterminate and thus unable to 'cause' judicial decisions. If this is true, then I argue that ontological scepticism is the true – and thick – connection between all sorts of realisms in law. *cf* Priel, 'Were the Legal Realists Legal Positivists?' (n 37) 336.

[74] According to which 'rules of law do not make much (causal) difference to how court decide cases': Leiter, 'American Legal Realism' (n 37) 62; Leiter, *Naturalizing Jurisprudence* (n 1) 16.

[75] Leiter, 'American Legal Realism' (n 1) 270–71.

[76] Green, 'Law and the Causes of Judicial Decisions' (n 3) 10.

92 A Critical Evaluation of Moderate Legal Realism

to understand most American legal realists as not making any apparent conceptual claims about rules (as Leiter does), we cannot help but notice that they were all, to a greater or lesser extent, sceptical 'on conceptual grounds about some aspects of *all* legal rules'.[77] As Green continues:

> We should not be misled by the fact that [this type of] sceptic *also* advances an empirical claim ('rules cannot guide decisions'), for what undergirds that claim is his notion of *what it is* for there to be rules or, to put it in another way, his concept of a rule.[78]

This amounts to an internal contradiction in (at least) American realism, where rule-scepticism is embedded in a broader institutional framework that is intelligible only in terms of rules or normativity.[79] Besides, even if by hypothesis we concede to Leiter that American legal realists were empirical and not conceptual rule-sceptics, the point about 'the proper criteria for normative determinacy'[80] comes back at the very centre of the picture nonetheless. For the connection between the indeterminacy thesis and 'scepticism about the causal efficacy of legal doctrine'[81] is merely contingent according to Leiter. Empirical rule-scepticism would be conceptually severable from the indeterminacy thesis of law, as the former is (merely) the empirical observation that in some (or all) cases judges do not decide according to legal rules, but rather they respond to something else.[82] Now, Leiter is evidently right in pointing out that, as a matter of fact, the former can be true even if the latter is not. That which is normative must be violable, and so it is by definition possible that in taking a decision, a judge might not follow the applicable rules, but rather apply her own sense of fairness (or an economic theory, or a biased belief, etc) to the facts of the case.[83]

Is this observation philosophically interesting, other than true? It does not seem so,[84] for if we claim that the law is determinate and that judges reach different outcomes from those prescribed by the rules of the system in the given case, then we might have a problem with the people bound to apply the law, not with law itself (nor with our theory of adjudication).[85] Thus, if we are to take realism as the limited study of the correspondence of historical judicial decisions to the outcomes as (they would have been) prescribed by the system, then realism is

---

[77] ibid 12.

[78] ibid.

[79] See Hart, *Concept of Law* (n 15) 136–137; Green, 'Law and the Causes of Judicial Decisions' (n 3) 35–36. The same remark seems to apply to Scandinavian realism.

[80] As this still seems to imply rule-scepticism: see the examples by Green, 'Law and the Causes of Judicial Decisions' (n 3) 13.

[81] Leiter, 'Legal Realisms, Old and New' (n 24) 954.

[82] Leiter, *Naturalizing Jurisprudence* (n 1) 76.

[83] Or simply she fails to apply correctly the law to the facts of the case: ibid.

[84] To Leiter himself actually: Leiter, 'Legal Indeterminacy' (n 13).

[85] Depending obviously on whether we conceive of a theory of adjudication as a descriptive or (also) prescriptive enterprise: Coleman and Leiter, 'Determinacy, Objectivity and Authority' (n 14) 593.

not only a deserving but also a necessary sociological enterprise, fully compatible with any kind of positivism.[86] De facto unconstrained courts are a puzzle for almost every political system and for their reflexive understanding.[87] They clearly constitute a problem for political science and political philosophy, but not for legal theory. To be philosophically interesting, ie to constitute a problem and thus a subject worth enquiring for legal theory, realism *must* assume that judges are honest, competent and rational epistemic actors,[88] and locate the cause of the indeterminacy of adjudication in the indeterminacy of law, ie in some kind of conceptual rule-scepticism.

VI. THE TWO AXES OF RULE-SCEPTICISM

Let us consider rule-scepticism more closely then. Many distinctions could be mentioned here, as different starting assumptions exist in the literature.[89] Notwithstanding this, a meta-theoretical taxonomy of rule-scepticism can be constructed around two axes: its extension and its source.[90] On the first axis, we have *radical* scepticism, according to which, roughly, it is pointless to talk about rules in legal decision-making at all, for law is globally indeterminate. This has also been termed conceptual rule-scepticism,[91] or the 'Received View' when referring to American legal realism.[92] On the other, we have a *moderate* version of scepticism, which is prevalent today and does not amount to a global claim about the indeterminacy of law, but that rather highlights the indeterminacy – or better, the underdeterminacy[93] – of legal rules in litigated cases, or (more precisely) only in those cases that reach the appellate stage. It presupposes an empirical, and occasionally theoretical, distinction between (the majority of) cases in which the law proves indeed to be determinate, and those cases in which

---

[86] *cf* Schauer, *Thinking Like a Lawyer* (n 9); Schauer, 'Legal Realism Untamed' (n 10); *cf* Green 'Law and the Causes of Judicial Decisions' (n 3) 3–4, 15–16; and see for the claim that in this regard the difference between exclusive and inclusive positivism is irrelevant: Priel, 'Were the Legal Realists Legal Positivists?' (n 37) 335.

[87] In this regard, the Supreme Court of the United States of America represents the most fitting example.

[88] The so-called 'background conditions': Leiter, 'Legal Indeterminacy' (n 13).

[89] *cf* Green, 'Law and the Causes of Judicial Decisions' (n 3) 11–12.

[90] My taxonomy (broadly) follows Leiter's, who distinguishes between *specific* and *general* indeterminacy of reasons, and between *global* and *local* rational indeterminacy: Leiter 'Legal indeterminacy' (n 13) 483.

[91] Leiter, *Naturalizing Jurisprudence* (n 1) 60–68; and *cf* Hart, *Concept of Law* (n 15) 133.

[92] The label 'Received View' purports to highlight the fact that American realists were not global sceptics: Leiter, *Naturalizing Jurisprudence* (n 1) 16; *cf* on this Green 'Law and the Causes of Judicial Decisions' (n 3) 12.

[93] In this regard 'any plausible thesis about the determinacy of law is, strictly speaking, a thesis about the underdeterminacy of law': Leiter, *Naturalizing Jurisprudence* (n 1) 79. There seems to have been a shift in Leiter's position on the issue: *cf* Leiter, 'Legal Indeterminacy' (n 13) 481, when he affirms that to the distinction between indeterminacy and underdeterminacy should not be given too much weight.

94   A Critical Evaluation of Moderate Legal Realism

it does not. In other words, it is a claim about the irrationality and causal inefficacy of legal doctrine in hard cases.[94]

As to the second axis, we can distinguish varieties of scepticism according to the source of the indeterminacy (or underdeterminacy) of law. The reason for distinguishing here might seem less evident than with the first axis, but it is equally important: there are a great deal of consequences depending on whether the indeterminacy of law is 'autonomous' or instead parasitic on other epistemic domains. We have *immanent* indeterminacy when its source is specific to law and legal reasoning, eg from the existence of competing interpretative canons, as some American legal realists have claimed, or from normative defeasibility. We have instead *transcendental* indeterminacy when its source is not located specifically within the juridical universe of discourse, but rather in a broader epistemic domain from which law is somehow dependent.[95] We can of course think of the vagueness and open-texture of natural languages or to the impossibility of metaphysical cognition, as assumed by the Scandinavians.[96]

From the intersection of our two axes we obtain four types of theses about the indeterminacy of law, but I should specify that it might not be possible to square perfectly every strand of scepticism with it. Someone like Alf Ross, whose position on whether judges create law has considerably changed over time,[97] would be probably irreducible to my taxonomy. Still, I believe this classification revolves around – and captures, indeed clarifying – the core of the issue between sceptic and cognitive accounts of law and legal reasoning and the latter's autonomy and rationality. Most of the moderate sceptics defend the rational and legitimate character of judicial adjudication, while most radical sceptics, with some CLS scholars above all, purport to expose adjudication as an ultimately unconstrained, biased and thus illegitimate decision-making process, in which the will of an elite is being imposed on the weakest members of society by coercive means. My assumption is that, by using this classification as a framework for discussion, we can shed further clarity on the sceptical challenge not only to the rationality and legitimacy of adjudication, but to that of law in general.

A. Radical-immanent Indeterminacy Thesis

Radical scepticism obliterates altogether the distinction between easy and hard cases, in the sense that the indeterminacy of law is deemed to be pervasive. As a

---

[94] Leiter, 'Legal Realisms, Old and New' (n 24) 954.

[95] In other words, the indeterminacy of law is parasitic upon the indeterminacy of the broader epistemic domain.

[96] In this regard, Hägerström's philosophical motto was '*Praeterea censeo metaphysicam esse delendam*': A Hägerström, *Philosophy and Religion*, vol 3 (London, Routledge, 2004) 33.

[97] R Guastini, 'Se i Giudici Creino Diritto' in A Vignudelli (ed), *Istituzioni e dinamiche del diritto: I confini mobili della separazione dei poteri* (Milan, Giuffrè, 2009) 391.

prominent example we can think about all those scholars who somehow vindicate 'normative defeasibility' as a necessary feature of law (ie of any possible concept of law). By 'normative defeasibility' I mean the claim that the action-guiding capacity of (positive) law is and can only always be prima facie – that (positive) law can never be a conclusive reason for action if the agent does not take into account further factors. These factors can vary: from the purpose of the rule,[98] to its morality or the agent's sense of what would be the just outcome in the concrete case. This means that all cases are, potentially, hard cases. Source-based rules are systemically unable to constitute ultimate or exclusionary reasons for action or to constrain decision-making.[99]

The thesis of the global normative defeasibility of law is a comprehensive label which encompasses authors that to a large extent disagree in almost every other respect, such as Lon Fuller[100] and other natural law theorists, as well as the late MacCormick and Atria,[101] but also some critical legal scholars (those who do not locate the indeterminacy of law in Wittgenstein's supposed rule-scepticism). To be sure, here 'normative defeasibility' does not amount to the claim that every legal rule contains a variable number of implicit exceptions – this claim, as has been shown, is not that problematic for cognitivist accounts of legal reasoning.[102] Rather the number of implicit exceptions to every legal rule is open and so it can never be specified, not even potentially, in advance, so that it is always the court's task to apply the law 'all things considered'.[103]

B. Radical-transcendental Indeterminacy Thesis

When the source of the indeterminacy of law is located outside law's own universe, we have radical-transcendental indeterminacy. Authors that could not

---

[98] See LL Fuller, 'Positivism and Fidelity to Law: A Reply to Professor Hart' (1958) 71(4) *Harvard Law Review* 630.

[99] J Raz, *Practical Reason and Norms*, 2nd edn (Oxford, Oxford University Press, 1999) ch 1; for a discussion of Raz's exclusionary reasons, see Atria, *On Law and Legal Reasoning* (n 28) 94–100; see also WA Edmundson, 'Rethinking Exclusionary Reasons: A Second Edition of Joseph Raz's "Practical Reason and Norms"' (1993) 12(3) *Law and Philosophy* 329.

[100] On Fuller's remarks on the 'context-sensitivity' of meaning (and rules): Atria, *On Law and Legal Reasoning* (n 28) ch 4.

[101] For Atria, regulative institutions like law are necessarily defeasible: ibid ch 1.

[102] F Schauer, 'On the Open Texture of Law' (2013) 87(1) *Grazer Philosophische Studien* 197.

[103] Schauer, 'Formalism' (n 22) 34–35. We could consider as another example of radical-immanent indeterminacy thesis the reading of the American realist core claim offered by Leslie Green. He seeks to reconcile the fact that, clearly, American realists presuppose social 'boundaries' and 'sources' of law in their accounts with the fact that they believe the law in books does not constrain judges – without collapsing into global rule-scepticism. His way-out is to conceive of their theses as claiming that 'most sources of law are permissive', so that they only exercise a 'weak authority' on judges: 'practice-based "good reasons" for decision': Green, 'Law and the Causes of Judicial Decisions' (n 3) 20; and *cf* Green's reconstruction with Perry's claim that 'On this Holmesian account of the "internal point of view", norms of law are seen by agents as providing – contra Hart – only prudential reasons for action': S Perry, 'Interpretation and Methodology in Legal Theory' in A Marmor (ed), *Law and Interpretation: Essays in Legal Philosophy* (Oxford, Clarendon Press, 1995) 109.

96 A Critical Evaluation of Moderate Legal Realism

be more distant from each other converge on this stance: from Scandinavian realists to those CLS authors who (mistakenly) settle on the sceptical reading of Wittgenstein's rule-following considerations;[104] but also the French school of realism fronted by Troper.[105] All of them, in different ways, locate the pervasive indeterminacy of law outside law itself, either on theoretical grounds (the open-texture of language or Wittgenstein's rule-following paradox which leads to 'anything goes') or meta-theoretical ones (the epistemological anti-idealism or ontological naturalism of the Scandinavians).[106] What is different is the response by these schools to the radical indeterminacy of law: while Scandinavians share with American realists the idea of a legal epistemology borrowed from empirical sciences in order to understand what it is going on when judges say they are applying the law, CLS' main aim is to reveal law and adjudication for what they believe really are, democratically disguised forms of authoritarian social control.

A few more words are due about Scandinavian realism. While it is debated whether Hägerström should be considered as an ordinary member of the movement or rather as its 'founding father',[107] with this label we refer to a group of law professors (Lundstedt, Olivecrona and Ross to name but the most famous) who share a philosophical commitment to naturalism in opposition to the 'distorting influences of metaphysics upon scientific thinking in general and legal thinking in particular'.[108] This notwithstanding, they seem to entertain different versions of naturalism (ontological and semantic for Lundstedt and Olivecrona, methodological for Ross),[109] and Alf Ross' work calls for consideration on his own as he embraces logical positivism.[110] In any case, it seems clear they all share,[111] following Hägerström, a 'legal nihilism',[112] according to which it does not make sense in our natural world to talk about legal rules as binding normative entities because there cannot be anything like that. For Hägerström, Kelsen must

---

[104] On the indeterminacy thesis in critical legal scholarship, see MV Tushnet, 'Critical Legal Theory' in MP Golding and WA Edmundson (eds), *The Blackwell Guide to the Philosophy of Law and Legal Theory* (Malden, Blackwell Publishing, 2005) 81–83. For an illuminating and critical discussion of the reception of the late Wittgenstein in legal theory, see A Halpin, *Reasoning with Law* (Oxford, Hart Publishing, 2001).

[105] See Y Hasebe, 'The Rule of Law and its Predicament' (2004) 17(4) *Ratio Juris* 489, 491.

[106] Leiter, 'American Legal Realism' (n 1) 5; *cf* T Spaak, 'Realism about the Nature of Law' (2017) 30(1) *Ratio Juris* 75.

[107] *cf* J Bjarup, 'The Philosophy of Scandinavian Legal Realism' (2005) 18(1) *Ratio Juris* 1; *cf* Spaak, 'Naturalism in Scandinavian and American Realism' (n 49) 34.

[108] Bjarup, 'The Philosophy of Scandinavian Legal Realism' (n 107) 1.

[109] Spaak, 'Naturalism in Scandinavian and American Realism' (n 49).

[110] This creates a *summa divisio* among Scandinavian realists: Bjarup, 'The Philosophy of Scandinavian Legal Realism' (n 107) 1.

[111] Leiter claims that this is indeed false, as 'None of the Scandinavians, in short, wanted to draw the conclusion that laws and legal system and legal norms did not really exist!': Leiter, 'Realisms, Old and New' (n 24) 952. His position though does not seem warranted by the works of Scandinavian realists, and by their later interpretations.

[112] Bjarup, 'The Philosophy of Scandinavian Legal Realism' (n 107) 7.

The Two Axes of Rule-scepticism 97

believe in magic if he speaks (as he does) of a reality of normative standards which exist alongside the natural world – the only world perceived by our senses, and thus intelligible to us – and in which verbal utterances with no conceptual meaning are transformed in rights and duties.[113] In this view, according to the traditional picture, law is – albeit relevant for social analysis – 'nonsense'.[114] If normative utterances are devoid of any conceptual meaning, they can only work as physical stimuli (or noises)[115] to cause the desired forms of behaviour among people, and this is why Hägerström conceives of the legal order as a 'machine' and of men as its 'cogs'.[116] We can indeed, as Lundstedt does, talk about legal rules, but only in the sense of 'regularities of behaviour'[117] to be analysed either in sociological or psychological terms:[118] 'What Lundstedt calls "laws" are empirical laws stating the causal relations between the legal words and their effects upon human behaviour'.[119] This is also what legal science can and should amount to: observing causal relations in order to extract descriptive patterns of behaviour.[120] For our purposes, the point is that the form of rule-scepticism embraced by Scandinavian realists[121] dispenses altogether with 'the normativity of the law and ... legal knowledge in terms of reasons for belief and action'.[122]

C. Moderate-immanent Indeterminacy Thesis

According to this position, which we can loosely ascribe to many American realists (Llewellyn, Frank, Holmes, and others)[123] and more cogently to Brian Leiter's philosophically mature elaboration of their theses (or 'naturalized jurisprudence' as he calls it) the law is indeterminate and hence it fails to constrain judges only in litigated or appellate cases.[124] As we have said already, moderate realism amounts to the foremost form of realism nowadays. It is shared by

---

[113] *cf* ibid 6–7. Torben Spaak has more recently argued that the realist thesis that 'there are no legal relations' is simply false: Spaak, 'Realism about the Nature of Law' (n 106).

[114] Bjarup, 'The Philosophy of Scandinavian Legal Realism' (n 107) 7; Leiter, 'In Praise of Realism' (n 6).

[115] Bjarup, 'The Philosophy of Scandinavian Legal Realism' (n 107) 7.

[116] A Hägerström, *Inquiries into the Nature of Law and Morals* (Uppsala, Almqvist and Wiksells, 1953) 354.

[117] Bjarup, 'The Philosophy of Scandinavian Legal Realism' (n 107) 11.

[118] Here again the influence of Hägerström's philosophy is manifest, as he proposes a theory of legal rules as 'behavioural patterns that are maintained by the use of force': ibid 9.

[119] ibid 12.

[120] *cf* ibid 9 for a discussion of Hägerström's view of legal science.

[121] Their form of rule-scepticism, differently from the Americans, could be considered as only implied by their more general epistemic position. I owe this pointer, which does not affect my schematisation, to Torben Spaak.

[122] Bjarup, 'The Philosophy of Scandinavian Legal Realism' (n 107) 1.

[123] See Leiter, 'Legal Indeterminacy' (n 13) 486.

[124] According to Leiter (ibid 481) to say that the law is indeterminate 'is equivalent to saying that the legitimate sources of law together with the legitimate interpretive and rational operations are indeterminate'.

98 *A Critical Evaluation of Moderate Legal Realism*

diverse scholars such as Tamanaha and Schauer among others.[125] The assumption is that, in all those law-regulated situations which do not end up before a judge, the law is indeed determinate. Ultimately then this kind of scepticism is not theoretical as much as empirical: it stems from the observation that, in deciding cases, some courts (predominantly in common-law jurisdictions) do not respond primarily to the norms but to facts of the case. This is so for the law, being rationally under-determinate, is causally under-determinate – ie if the law does not point to a unique solution for the case, it cannot explain why the judge took a particular decision (and not another). This rational indeterminacy of law originates mainly in the possibility to extract from the same legal source (statute or precedent) different legal norms and principles which would lead to diverging outcomes in the given case, due to the availability of several and equally legitimate canons of interpretation.[126] Such local indeterminacy is *immanent* to law – it is the result of an unavoidable characteristic of the legal process even when other external sources of indeterminacy are not involved. Most importantly though, this kind of indeterminacy occurs even in face of semantic determinacy – that is when the literal meaning of legal rules would point to a singular result as the correct one in the case.

Another famous example of the immanent indeterminacy thesis can be found in the work of Kelsen, although it is a peculiar example that perhaps straddles our axes. While prima facie it could appear as a moderate thesis, it amounts to a radical one because Kelsen maintains both epistemic and systemic indeterminacy.[127] He clearly identifies the main source of the indeterminacy of law in the 'hierarchical structure of the legal system':[128] given that in the passage from one level to another there is always interpretation, and given that interpretation is for him ultimately a matter of will, indeterminacy is pervasive. Yet he notes how the higher normative levels (the constitutional and the legislative) correspond to higher levels of indeterminacy, whereas the more we go down the *Stufenbau*, the more we should see the law becoming always more and more determinate.[129] This amounts to an intrinsic characteristic of

---

[125] See, Schauer, 'Legal Realism Untamed' (n 10); Tamanaha, *Beyond the Formalist-Realist Divide* (n 11).

[126] See Leiter, 'American Legal Realism' (n 37) 64: 'Indeterminacy, in shorts, resides for the realists not in the rules themselves, but in the ways we have of characterizing what rules statutes and precedents contain'; in this regard, see directly KN Llewellyn, *The Common Law Tradition: Deciding Appeals* (Boston, Little Brown & Co, 1960) 72; but, *cf* with the claim by Leiter 'American Legal Realism' (n 1) 266–67 (echoing Frank and Llewellyn on the point) that indeterminacy comes also from the possibility to *characterise* facts differently.

[127] Flores argues that Kelsen is wrong in assuming systemic indeterminacy, whereas he is correct in assuming epistemic indeterminacy: IB Flores, 'H. L. A. Hart's Moderate Indeterminacy Thesis Reconsidered: In Between Scylla and Charybdis?' (2011) 5 *Problema: Anuario de Filosofía y Teoría del Derecho* 147, 154–55.

[128] H Kelsen, *Introduction to the Problems of Legal Theory: A Translation of the First Edition of the Reine Rechtslehre Or Pure Theory of Law* (BL Paulson and SL Paulson trans, Oxford, Clarendon Press, 1996) 77–89; *cf* Flores (n 127) 152–55.

[129] Kelsen, *Introduction to the Problems of Legal Theory* (n 128) 78.

the nomodynamics of our legal systems in which the higher norms can at most constitute a 'frame' within which a degree of discretion for the lower decision-maker is unavoidable.[130]

For Kelsen, then, there are no single right answers in law, because within the frame of legal decision-making the process is a matter of will and not of cognition. But this form of rule-scepticism, arguably due to the commitment to the purity of his theory, is even more radical. This is because, while the frame should act as a cognitive constraint upon decision-making, even an interpretation completely outside of it is to be accepted as valid by the legal scholar. In other words, he finishes to embrace the radical sceptic thesis that, legally speaking, 'anything goes'. This position greatly influenced the French realist school fronted by Troper, but also the next and last type of indeterminacy thesis resulting from our classification, as put forward by the Genoa School.

D. Moderate-transcendental Indeterminacy Thesis

This is the position assumed by Guastini,[131] whom we can consider (together with Chiassoni) as the most prominent representative of the Genoa realist school in the English-speaking literature.[132] Guastini's latest restatement of rule-scepticism spans our classification (as much as Kelsen's does), for it purports to be (theoretically) moderate but it is (practically) radical. This is an ambiguity which affects Guastini's position and which finds an interesting reflexive expression in his reluctance to be 'cannibalised' from radical or mixed theory positions. Most recently, Guastini claims that 'a plurality of interpretations (of the same text) are *almost* always possible' and this, 'coupled with the thesis that no persuasive criterion of truth exists for interpretive sentences', offers all the necessary ground to rule-scepticism.[133] What does he mean?

To answer this question, we need to dig deeper into the sophistication of his latest restatement of rule-scepticism. Guastini identifies two very different types of indeterminacy of law. On the one hand, we have the so-called 'indeterminacy of the legal system', according to which it 'is not determinate what rules are expressed by legal sources and, in this sense, belong to the legal system'. On the other, we have the 'indeterminacy of rules' which depends 'on the vagueness or open-texture of any predicate in natural languages' and for which 'it is not

---

[130] For a detailed analysis of Kelsen's theory of discretion, see ch 4, section IV.

[131] Guastini, 'Rule-Scepticism Restated' (n 19); *cf* Bjarup, 'The Philosophy of Scandinavian Legal Realism' (n 107).

[132] For some careful considerations as to what extent one can talk of a 'Genoa School': M Barberis, 'Lo scetticismo Immaginario. Nove Obiezioni agli Scettici à la Génoise' in P Comanducci and R Guastini (eds), *Analisi e diritto 2000: Ricerche di giurisprudenza analitica* (Turin, Giappichelli, 2000) 6–7.

[133] Guastini, 'Rule-Scepticism Restated' (n 19) 158–59 (emphasis added).

100 *A Critical Evaluation of Moderate Legal Realism*

determinate what cases fall under the scope of each rule'.[134] These pertain to – better, they are the subjects of – 'text-oriented' and 'fact-oriented' interpretation respectively.[135] He expressly acknowledges that, as to the latter type, 'for any legal text whatsoever, there are easy or clear cases ... as well as borderline hard cases'.[136] This is a surprising statement, for Guastini departs from his earlier position, also shared by radical sceptics like Troper,[137] that no easy or clear cases actually exist due to the 'no-previous-meaning' thesis, according to which meaning is always a product of interpretation and thus cannot precede it.[138] Has he become a moderate sceptic and thus,[139] if we are to follow him ('the vigil theory is but a sophisticated version of cognitivism'),[140] a cognitivist?

The answer is – quite confusingly – no, at least if we are to believe the *latest* Guastini. Precisely the distinction between the indeterminacy of the legal system and that of legal rules, given that the former is pervasive, allows him to maintain that we can find all the 'necessary grounds' for (global) rule-scepticism within it. To put it differently, the fact that he has eventually come to acknowledge, as Hart's theory does, the existence of easy and hard cases in the application of rules to the facts of the case, does not infringe upon his global scepticism. For this kind of application, ie fact-oriented interpretation, always takes place after the very identification of what rules belong to the legal system, or text-oriented interpretation – which is where interpretive discretion truly lies.[141] The problem is: is this move possible? Is there a third position, in between radical scepticism and Hartian (moderate) cognitivism, which Guastini himself calls 'soft scepticism'[142] and to which Leiter aspires with his naturalised jurisprudence?[143]

VII. THE UNBEARABLE LIGHTNESS OF MODERATE SCEPTICISM

The taxonomy of indeterminacy theses proposed in the previous section has the major upshot of highlighting the common characteristics of the different strands of scepticism in legal theory. In particular, while every version of the

---

[134] ibid 144.

[135] ibid 139.

[136] ibid 146–47.

[137] See, eg: M Troper, *La Théorie du Droit, le Droit, l'Etat* (Paris, Presses Universitaires de France, 2001) 69ff; *cf* R Guastini, 'A Sceptical View on Legal Interpretation' in P Comanducci and R Guastini (eds), *Analisi e diritto 2005: Ricerche di giurisprudenza analitica* (Turin, Giappichelli 2005) para 5.

[138] See Barberis, 'Lo scetticismo Immaginario' (n 132) para 2.2.

[139] 'An ambiguous text, first, is not *meaningless* and, second, does not admit *whatever* interpretation. One should take into account this remark when discussing the radical form of interpretive scepticism': Guastini, 'Rule-Scepticism Restated' (n 19) 145, fn 26.

[140] ibid 153.

[141] Guastini, 'A Sceptical View on Legal Interpretation' (n 137) para 7.

[142] ibid 5.

[143] *cf* Barberis, 'Lo scetticismo Immaginario' (n 132) para 3.

radical indeterminacy thesis challenges not only the rationality and legitimacy of adjudication, but that of the law itself in the context of our constitutional democratic theories,[144] moderate (or local) indeterminacy theses are deemed compatible not only with theories of law that uphold the rationality and legitimacy of adjudication, but even with positivist theories. This is the central claim by Leiter that Guastini himself, as a fully-fledged positivist, must agree upon. Moderate scepticism, as a descriptive claim about law-application practices, poses, if anything, a threat only to traditional pictures of adjudication, and not to our theories of law (and consequently of constitutional democracy).[145] Is this really the case?

We can start answering this question by considering radical indeterminacy theses, as we will not have to dwell too long on them. The argument, in broad terms, goes like this: radical scepticism of any kind poses a serious threat not only to adjudication, but also to the very practice of law itself. As seen in chapter two, if law is radically or globally indeterminate, ie if the indeterminacy of law is pervasive, nothing like the rule of law or the principle of democracy can really obtain. As a result, constitutional democracy is completely delegitimised and must be considered a travesty, a rethorical device placed to disguise the exercise of sheer coercive power by elites. This scenario is patently catastrophic: our juridical practices, the very framework of our civic togetherness, would amount to nothing more than a collective self-entrapment within a universe of rules and standards which ultimately *cannot* constrain our institutional decision-making practices.[146] Does law amount to something like the Matrix then?

Surprising as it may sound, it can be argued that radical sceptics' worst enemies have been moderate sceptics, and not formalists. Leiter, more prominently than others, has spent the initial part of his work on realism to redress radical sceptics' mistaken philosophical arguments for law's global indeterminacy (those coming from CLS in particular). In this way, he has contributed to creating a conceptual space for the kind of moderate scepticism to which the majority of American and non-American legal realists nowadays subscribe. The trivial argument against radical scepticism (both immanent and transcendental) can be expressed along these lines: if the law is pervasively indeterminate, that is, if the law bears no rational nor causal influence on any kind of decision-making process, how could we then explain all those countless uncontested activities of rule-following which take place in everyday life? How could we make sense of – ie conceive of as intelligible – all those instances in which agents do follow the (rules of) law when deciding to assume one form of behaviour rather than another? Should we think of them as a matter of pure and astonishing

---

[144] See, eg: Coleman and Leiter, 'Determinacy, Objectivity and Authority' (n 14) passim.

[145] ibid 594; this seems also presupposed by the Genoa school, at least implicitly: Barberis, 'Lo scetticismo Immaginario' (n 132) para 2.9.

[146] *cf* Leiter, 'Legal Indeterminacy' (n 13) 487.

102   A Critical Evaluation of Moderate Legal Realism

coincidence? Should we record them quantitatively as the repetition of singular and yet uncoordinated habits?

Since Hart's argument in chapter seven of his *The Concept of Law*, and subsequent refinements by others, we should no longer worry too much about such positions.[147] Radical or global scepticism has been exposed as an epistemically untenable position, a position that simply fails to account for our legal phenomena satisfactorily.[148] The overall workings of law cannot be explained – which is an activity altogether different from that of describing in a naturalistic sense[149] – by a purely empirical observation of what is going on in courtrooms.[150] Too much is left unexplained and unaccounted for or out of the picture. One could say that radical scepticism altogether misses the essence of law. Additional proof seems to be found in the fact that we have witnessed, throughout the years, many radical sceptics shifting towards moderate positions (Guastini is a case in point, but only prima facie as we shall see), but not vice versa. We must then bring our focus back to moderate versions of scepticism, in particular those of Leiter and Guastini, and ask ourselves, are they feasible? In what way are they 'moderate'? And more importantly, are they really able to challenge our practices of adjudication without encroaching upon the corresponding theories of law?

A couple of preliminary remarks need to be in place before considering these two authors more closely. Both Leiter and Guastini seem to claim that the law is always only partially or locally underdeterminate. They assume, more (Leiter)[151] or less clearly (Guastini),[152] a distinction that has become a *topos* in legal theory, that between easy and hard cases, whereby the underdeterminacy of law roughly coincides with hard cases, which in turn coincide with litigated or appellate cases.[153] Where these theories differ is as to whether and how we can nonetheless establish law's determinacy. American realists, on whose intuitions Leiter draws upon, offered a variety of approaches, from behavioural cognitivism to folk psychology to the more modern and widespread law and economics, which would allow us to explain and ultimately predict judicial decisions. Guastini (and the Genoa School alike) on the contrary does not seem very interested in

---

[147] *cf* Green, 'Law and the Causes of Judicial Decisions' (n 3) 12–14.

[148] Coleman and Leiter, 'Determinacy, Objectivity and Authority' (n 14); Leiter, 'Legal Indeterminacy' (n 13) 486–87; Guastini, 'Rule-Scepticism Restated' (n 19) para 2.4.

[149] *cf* MacCormick, *Legal Reasoning and Legal Theory* (n 27) 275–92.

[150] According to Leiter, *Naturalizing Jurisprudence* (n 1) 66, there are two (minimal) requirements to a satisfactory theory of law: the explanation of legality on the one hand and of normativity on the other.

[151] Leiter, 'Legal Indeterminacy' (n 13) 488.

[152] Barberis, 'Lo scetticismo Immaginario' (n 132) para 2.7.

[153] *cf* M Stone, 'Focusing the Law: What Legal Interpretation is Not' in A Marmor (ed), *Law and Interpretation: Essays in Legal Philosophy* (Oxford, Clarendon Press, 1995) 66–67 for the claim that any version of the indeterminacy thesis only concentrated on adjudication 'blinds us to the law most ubiquitous aspects and occasions' and that 'Moreover, if a plausible version of the determinacy thesis is one thus rooted in "hard cases", we should not expect to support it with considerations about the nature of legal, much less social, rules *as such*'.

The Unbearable Lightness of Moderate Scepticism   103

a predictive theory of adjudication, since this would spill over from the strict analytical paradigm.[154] But they also seem to differ, quite importantly, in the 'moderateness' of their positions. Leiter's scepticism is (spatially) moderate because he recognises the explanatory capacity of traditional doctrine in unlitigated cases, while Guastini 'soft scepticism' seems (qualitatively) so because he rejects the indeterminacy thesis (the no-previous-meaning-thesis, or 'anything goes') and embraces the underdeterminacy one.[155]

Let us weigh the merits of Leiter's 'naturalized jurisprudence' first: is his moderate scepticism feasible? We have seen already that for Leiter, 'any plausible thesis about the determinacy of law is, strictly speaking, a thesis about the underdeterminacy of law':[156] legal rules do constrain judges, even in appellate cases, but, within the range of acceptable decisions, they are ultimately legally free to choose one outcome over the other.[157] It is actually not clear whether this claim is analytical or merely synthetic: it is not clear whether it is always the case that legal rules constrain decision-makers in hard cases or whether this is merely an empirical observation, so that there might still be cases in which the choice by the judge is left completely unconstrained. In any case, the point is that if the law is underdeterminate, something else must cause (and, thus, explain) the judge picking one among the available outcomes. This translates on the meta-theoretical level to the claim that traditional doctrine falls short of explaining what really goes on in courts, particularly in appellate jurisdictions of common law systems, and that therefore we need a different approach – a 'naturalised' approach – if we want to explain and ultimately predict these courts' decisions.[158] Now there is a first but very important aspect to be highlighted, and it pertains to the empiricism of this position: as Schauer puts it,

> because the claims of Realism are empirical, there is no reason to suppose that the empirical conclusions will be the same for all times, for all places, for all judges, and, perhaps most importantly, for all issues and for all courts. At the one extreme of legal indeterminacy, therefore, it is not surprising that we find the Supreme Court of the United States ... It would be a mistake to assume, however, that what is true for the Supreme Court is true for other courts and other issues.[159]

There is indeed little surprise in the fact that the decisions of the US Supreme Court – whose same supervisory jurisdiction had to be established by the

---

[154] Guastini, 'Rule-Scepticism Restated' (n 19) 161.

[155] Guastini, 'Sceptical View on Legal Interpretation' (n 137); Guastini, 'Rule-Scepticism Restated' (n 19) 156–158.

[156] Leiter, *Naturalizing Jurisprudence* (n 1) 79.

[157] ibid 80; *cf* Leiter, 'Legal Indeterminacy' (n 13) 487, fn 20. His thesis here bears striking resemblance with Kelsen's 'frame' theory of discretion, on which see ch 4 of this book.

[158] It is not entirely clear how realists can claim that the norms of commercial cultures are indeed able to constrain courts while legal norms are not: Leiter, 'American Legal Realism' (n 37) 59; *cf* Green, 'Law and the Causes of Judicial Decisions' (n 3) 27.

[159] Schauer, *Thinking Like a Lawyer* (n 9) 139–40. Schauer quotes several empirical studies which show the relevance of rules and principles in lower and other jurisdictions: ibid 140, fn 34.

104   *A Critical Evaluation of Moderate Legal Realism*

court itself with an unprecedented decision, given that the US Constitution did not specify the scope of its jurisdiction[160] – are clearly far less bound by pre-established (legal) rules and principles and can be explained 'only' in terms of either the political preferences of its members (considering also the peculiar process of appointment) or by a vast array of economical or empirical motives of decision-making.[161] Additionally, it is debatable the extent to which supreme court decisions, given the evaluative character of many constitutional provisions, are supposed to be wholly determined by legal rules and principles in the first place.[162] This seems to amount to a first and relevant limitation for the 'naturalised jurisprudence' project, made even more significant by the consideration that, after all, this kind of indeterminacy claim proves to be much more fitting to 'complex, messy common-law systems'[163] than more hierarchically 'neat' civil-law systems – where, for instance, not only the jurisdiction, but even the substantial powers of review of supreme courts are more clearly delimited.[164] Therefore,

> it would be plausible to hypothesize that Realist explanations are more often true for ideologically charged issues than otherwise, more often true in high appellate courts than in trial courts, and more often true for the messier common law than for the interpretation of statutes.[165]

Now, despite these limits stemming from its empirical character, we can still charitably conceive of the 'naturalising' project as a meta-theoretical position, straddling epistemology and methodology, that requires any theory of adjudication to consider primarily the outcomes of the decision-making process, rather than focusing on their inputs. Whether this can be considered a descriptive position at all is unclear, as it is going to be examined when considering Guastini's.[166] In any case, conceived of as a theory of adjudication, it is mutually exclusive from traditional, rule-following explanations of how judges decide cases. There is no conceptual way in which such a position does not imply the assumption that the inputs in the traditional model do not ultimately justify the outputs – or that particular output as chosen by the given court in the given case. Otherwise, if – by means of empirical research – we were to verify that legal inputs and legal outputs coincide, where would the problem lie? The 'replacement step' in Leiter's project, supposedly similar to the one propounded

---

[160] *Marbury v Madison* 5 US 137 (1803).

[161] The US Supreme Court can be understood as a substantively *political* (rather than juridical) institution, and that, together with the limited amount of guidance provided by the text of the Constitution itself, might help to explain why 'legalism', or traditional doctrine, can account for its decision-making activity only to a very limited extent: *cf* Leiter, 'In Praise of Realism' (n 6) 875.

[162] As Leiter himself seems to acknowledge: Leiter, 'Legal Indeterminacy' (n 13) 487, fn 21.

[163] Schauer, *Thinking Like a Lawyer* (n 9) 138.

[164] *cf* Leiter, 'American Legal Realism' (n 1) 278.

[165] Schauer, *Thinking Like a Lawyer* (n 9) 141.

[166] For the claim that realism cannot be a purely descriptive theory of adjudication: Priel, 'Were the Legal Realists Legal Positivists?' (n 37) 338.

The Unbearable Lightness of Moderate Scepticism   105

by Quine in epistemology,[167] seems as such subordinate to the thesis that traditional doctrine falls short in explaining *most* judicial decisions, which in turn as we have seen rests on rule-scepticism.[168] Here the central contradiction in the theoretical foundations of Leiter's project arises: how is this kind of scepticism about adjudication compatible with a positivist theory of law?[169]

Surprisingly (or not) perhaps then, Leiter has recently and explicitly argued that legal positivism – as developed by Hart and Raz among others – is nothing *but* a realistic theory of law.[170] The problem is that he is still not particularly clear about the overall relationship between a theory of law and a theory of adjudication.[171] It seems that, at least from his methodological point of view, the two are patently severable, so that a positivist theory of law could be paired with either a formalist or a realist theory of adjudication. And it is precisely this way of distinguishing between a theory of law and a theory of adjudication, as Priel argues,[172] which leads to the contradiction that plagues his naturalising project. For the kind of positivism discussed by Leiter is premised on the distinction between easy and hard cases.[173] Let us remind ourselves in fact that it is the acknowledgement of 'easy' cases that distinguishes radical and moderate indeterminacy theses. The trouble lies in the fact that in those cases which are easy, or 'regulated' if we want to use Raz's terminology,[174] 'the difference between a theory of law and a theory of adjudication almost vanishes'.[175] In other words, in these cases, despite a number of potential objections,[176] knowing what the law (in books) is – because the 'class' of legal reasons is determinate – means knowing how that case ought to be decided, ie 'the legal component of adjudication is over'.[177] This is also the only way to be able to speak meaningfully of legal mistakes,[178] which is perhaps the main rejoinder used by Hart against Holmes' predictive theory of law. Therefore, as Priel argues,

> if we take the view that only a small number of cases are underdeterminate, then it does not seem to represent the view of the realists, who believed underdeterminacy

---

[167] *cf* Priel, 'Were the Legal Realists Legal Positivists?' (n 37); Green, 'Law and the Causes of Judicial Decisions' (n 3) 28.

[168] Leiter, 'American Legal Realism' (n 1) 264, for whom the reason for adopting 'replacement naturalism' in jurisprudence would lie in the impossibility of the normative foundational project, due to the (general) fact that evidence underdetermines theory. But *cf* on the feasibility of such move, Priel, 'Were the Legal Realists Legal Positivists?' (n 37) 316, 318–19.

[169] Leiter, *Naturalizing Jurisprudence* (n 1) 80.

[170] B Leiter, 'Legal Positivism as a Realistic Theory of Law', in P Mindus and T Spaak (eds), *The Cambridge Companion to Legal Positivism* (Cambridge, Cambridge University Press, 2021).

[171] Priel, 'Were the Legal Realists Legal Positivists?' (n 37) 340.

[172] ibid 341–42.

[173] ibid 341, where he calls it 'positivism of norms'.

[174] J Raz, 'Law and Value in Adjudication' in J Raz, *The Authority of Law: Essays on Law and Morality* (Oxford, Clarendon Press, 1979) 181.

[175] Priel, 'Were the Legal Realists Legal Positivists?' (n 37) 341.

[176] Priel identifies three of them: ibid 341–42.

[177] ibid 342.

[178] ibid 349.

106   A Critical Evaluation of Moderate Legal Realism

is prevalent. If, on the other hand, we believe that the underdeterminacy of law is a common feature of legal systems, then it is not clear that this is something most positivists, at least as the term is currently understood, would happily endorse.[179]

As a result, either one of the two holds: if underdeterminacy is not a pervasive but a merely peripheral phenomenon in law, then the replacement step, which would lead us to the necessity of a naturalised jurisprudence, seems unwarranted, at least if our aim is to give a general account of the legal process as a whole. Conversely, if underdeterminacy is instead a pervasive phenomenon in law, and thus there are few or no easy cases,[180] then it is not clear how a positivist can put forward a theory of law in which the law

> even claims authority, because if this is the case, it is not that the law guides us towards bad actions (which is what happens when it claims to have authority but does not in fact have it), but does not guide us at all.[181]

Is there any way out of this conundrum then? Or was the 'naturalized jurisprudence project' doomed to fail since its inception?

If it yields its descriptiveness as a theory of adjudication and its compatibility, being moderate, with a positivist theory of law[182] – that is, if it purports to be a 'tamed realism' – then it seems indeed doomed to fail, as Schauer has argued. We need to return to Leiter's acknowledgement of easy cases,[183] which in turn rests on the 'plain meaning' theory as put forward by many positivists. Leiter has argued that the so-called 'selection effect' argument – according to which the kind of cases upon which the realists' claims are based is a 'biased sample of all legal events'[184] – is not a stand-alone argument, but rather parasitical on the argument from easy cases, and that in any case it is an efficacious rejoinder only against radical indeterminacy positions, while moderate positions (like his) are left unscathed by it.[185] Schauer's remarks undermine this contention.[186]

---

[179] ibid. Leiter has recently denied this inconsistency, affirming that American legal realists 'did not overstate the irrelevance of rules' (quoting some excerpts from Llewellyn): Leiter, 'Legal Positivism as a Realistic Theory of Law' (n 170) 94.

[180] For the claim that 'Most of the cases that courts of law are called upon to decide are easy ones', SR Lewis, 'Taking Adjudication Seriously' (1980) 58(4) *Australasian Journal of Philosophy* 377.

[181] Priel, 'Were the Legal Realists Legal Positivists?' (n 37) 349. This works also as a rejoinder to the argument that the underdeterminacy thesis does not constitute such a threat to the authority of law (and to the legitimacy of liberal theories) as much as the indeterminacy one, as defended by Coleman and Leiter, 'Determinacy, Objectivity and Authority' (n 14) 587–94.

[182] On the compatibility between realism and positivism, see Green, 'Law and the Causes of Judicial Decisions' (n 3) 15.

[183] In this regard, (some) American realists themselves were aware of the selection effect: Schauer, *Thinking Like a Lawyer* (n 9) 138.

[184] ibid 13, fn 1; see also chs 2, 7 and 8, especially 22–23 and 184–85; on the selection effect, *cf* Green, 'Law and the Causes of Judicial Decisions' (n 3) 34. A good example of how the selection effect is usually neglected by formalism's opponents is in P Leith, 'Fundamental errors in legal logic programming' (1986) 29(6) *Computer Journal* 545.

[185] Leiter, 'Legal Indeterminacy' (n 13).

[186] Schauer, 'Legal Realism Untamed' (n 10) 18–22.

The realist empirical approach shows that, in many if not most cases, the criterion of the selection effect is not that of the plain meaning of paper rules, but rather that the determinant of the easiness or hardness of a case will depend on the content of real rules, namely those internalised by judges; rules that necessarily do not belong to the class of legal reasons.[187]

If this is the case, it implies then that even moderate realism, as a descriptive theory of adjudication, cannot be reconciled with a positivist theory of law, for it assumes that courts apply rules that cannot be traced back to the class of legal reasons, but which can be empirically retrieved only ex-post, and hence become 'law' only for the fact of being so applied by courts. It seems, *pace* Leiter, that even moderate realism ends up undermining legal positivism, thus revealing its ultimate *radical* character. Moreover, the predictive theory of law comes out as the theoretical core of realism: legal norms are not those expressed by paper rules, but by those rules or laws that can predict judicial decisions – and the only rules that can predict judicial decision are those internalised and applied by judges, retrievable by means of naturalised ex-post analysis. In Schauer's words:

> Once we see that the Realist distinction between paper and real rules shifts the ground for selection and deselection even while not eliminating the selection effect, a large part of the Realist claim can no longer be marginalized as peripheral or interstitial. … Realism emerges as a hypothesis about the impotence of paper rules in generating legal outcomes, and, insofar as the hypothesis is borne out as empirically sound, it becomes a description of all of law, and not just the law to be applied when the paper rules are indeterminate. Because this hypothesis challenges the very idea that the written down law is the source of legal determinacy, it can be seen as Realism in its far less interstitial, far less bounded, and thus far less tamed, dimension. Untamed Realism is not the claim that there is no legal determinacy, but is instead the claim that legal determinacy (and thus indeterminacy) is not a product of the plain meaning of paper rules, or is at least much less of a product of the written-down official rules than the traditional picture supposes.[188]

In other words, if we take the methodological and epistemological premises of Leiter's moderate realism seriously, his theory turns out to be, ultimately, self-defeating, for it ends up being 'untamed realism': another form of radical rule-scepticism. As such, it also runs foul of the assumption that there can never be too wide a gap between a theory of law and a theory of adjudication – ie that the two are not only contingently, but necessarily, by and large, connected.

---

[187] In other words, what is the point of having 'paper' rules in the first place, if they do not ever constrain decision-makers? If Schauer's contention is sound, it seems that the realists' thesis does not undermine so much the determinacy, but rather the (criterion of) objectivity of law itself. On the relationship between objectivity and (legitimate) authority: Coleman and Leiter, 'Determinacy, Objectivity and Authority' (n 14) pt 2.

[188] Schauer, 'Legal Realism Untamed' (n 10) 20, 23–24. Schauer's contention seems similar to that by Priel, 'Were the Legal Realists Legal Positivists?' (n 37) 348; *cf* also Leiter, 'American Legal Realism' (n 1) 268–69.

108   *A Critical Evaluation of Moderate Legal Realism*

Does Guastini's 'soft scepticism' escape this conundrum then? Does it amount to a *true* moderate scepticism, in between Hartian mixed theories and radical scepticism? It does not appear so. You will recall that in his latest restatement, Guastini allows for the existence of easy cases in the application of the law to the facts of the case, but argues this is nonetheless 'harmless' for his scepticism, given that the decisive form of indeterminacy lies at the stage of so-called 'text-oriented' interpretation – that is, in the overall identification of which rules belong to the legal system at all – and that these interpretive sentences never bear truth values.[189] His scepticism has gone through some substantial refinement over time, particularly after some very powerful criticism by supporters of Hartian positions.[190] As a result, he has acknowledged the existence of easy cases and of the distinction between interpretation and creation of new rules,[191] and has shifted from the indeterminacy to the under-determinacy thesis. Is it enough though to distance his scepticism from both radical scepticism and Hartian theories and thus cognitivism, as he explictly affirms?[192] Two arguments can be advanced here.

First, it seems that Guastini has simply translated the basic ambiguity of his earlier positions to a different level. If it was the case once that subsumptive statements were *almost* always hard, ie that easy cases were such an insignificant amount that they could be utterly disregarded in the context of a (sceptical) theory of interpretation, now his position seems to be that interpretative statements *almost* never bear truth values.[193] What 'almost' stands for, Guastini – strikingly – does not clarify. It is as if he realises the necessity to keep a 'backdoor' always open to the potentially defeating criticism that empirically admitting of even one easy or determinate case is to theoretically reach Hartian and, at least in the reading proposed in chapter six of this book, Wittgensteinian positions.[194] Second, and perhaps this latter point also helps to explain the former, even his recent restatement of rule-scepticism does not depart from a very specific conception of the theory of meaning, and thus of the theory of interpretation in law. According to his meta-theory, there is a distinction to be

---

[189] Guastini, 'Rule-Scepticism Restated' (n 19) 159. The same claim is made by E Diciotti, *Verità e Certezza nell'Interpretazione della Legge* (Turin, Giappichelli, 1999) 81.

[190] See, eg: Barberis, 'Lo scetticismo Immaginario' (n 132).

[191] Guastini, 'Sceptical View on Legal Interpretation' (n 137) para 4, taking the cue from the criticism, for instance, by Barberis that whoever subscribes to the thesis that meaning is created only with interpretation should bears the burden to distinguish between interpretation and pure creation of law, or *legis-latio*: *cf* Barberis, 'Lo scetticismo Immaginario' (n 132) 22.

[192] Guastini, 'Rule-Scepticism Restated' (n 19) para 2.2.

[193] My claim here is, indeed, elliptic. For Guastini explicitly says that interpretive statements *never* bear truth values and that this, paired with the thesis that two or more interpretations of a given normative statement are *almost* always possible, offers all the necessary ground for radical scepticism – ibid 159. However, in those cases in which only one interpretation of a normative statement is possible, cases that Guastini explicitly admits, are we not allowed then to say that the interpretive statement is indeed truth-apt, viz that that particular interpretation is the only true one (because is the *only* one available)?

[194] Barberis, 'Lo scetticismo Immaginario' (n 132) para 2.7.

The Unbearable Lightness of Moderate Scepticism   109

drawn between descriptive and normative theories of meaning[195] and, within what seems an extreme methodological positivist attitude,[196] only the former are apt for being true or false,[197] whereas the latter 'are of no help for describing what interpretation actually is'.[198]

Thus, Guastini's main claim is that a descriptive theory of legal interpretation does not need any preliminary theory of meaning, either normative or descriptive. It does not need a normative theory of meaning 'since prescribing falls outside its scope'.[199] The consensus between Guastini and Leiter is absolute: naturalism amounts precisely to the methodological and epistemological stance according to which legal theory can and must be descriptive in character, restraining itself to the observation of legal practices eschewing any justifying or evaluative dimension.[200] However, a descriptive theory of interpretation does not need a previous descriptive theory of meaning, 'since a descriptive theory of interpretation *is* but a descriptive theory of meaning in legal contexts (at any rate, the only admissible theory of meaning in legal contexts)'.[201]

Now, this meta-theoretical stance has been already (and convincingly) criticised from several perspectives, all pointing towards the inherent contradictions of such claims.[202] For our purposes, it will suffice to ask how a purely descriptive theory of legal interpretation can uphold the distinction between easy and hard cases which necessarily seems to presuppose a normative framework. Perhaps the biggest point of controversy here is meta-theoretical: whether any theory of meaning, not just in the legal universe, can be purely descriptive, as this seems to be at odds with the shared belief in the philosophy of language that meaning is (at least partially) normative, and therefore that any theory of meaning would be at the same time descriptive and normative (as to the practices of the given community).[203] Bewilderingly, Guastini himself seems to presuppose so, when he argues against the 'no-previous meaning' thesis by saying that

> [i]nterpretation has (conceptual, not factual) limits, in the sense that not every sentence claiming to be interpretive can be reasonably subsumed under the concept of interpretation. Interpreting consists not in ascribing just any meaning, but in ascribing one meaning in the range of meanings admitted by (a) linguistic usage, (b) accepted interpretive methods, and (c) juristic ('dogmatic') constructions ... a limited concept

[195] Guastini, 'Rule-Scepticism Restated' (n 19) para 2.3.
[196] On Bobbio's threefold conception of legal positivism see G Pino, 'The Place of Legal Positivism in Contemporary Constitutional States' (1999) 18(5) *Law and Philosophy* 513, 517–19.
[197] Guastini, 'Rule-Scepticism Restated' (n 19) para 2.3. For a rejoinder to the claim that descriptive theories (only) are apt for truth-values: Barberis, 'Lo scetticismo Immaginario' (n 132) para 2.5.
[198] Guastini, 'Rule-Scepticism Restated' (n 19) 155.
[199] ibid, para 2.3.
[200] ibid. For the clear distinction between descriptive and normative (theories of) jurisprudence, see Leiter, 'American Legal Realism' (n 37) 56–59. It is worth observing that such a position seems indeed normative in itself: *cf* Barberis, 'Lo scetticismo Immaginario' (n 132) para 2.5.
[201] Guastini, 'Rule-Scepticism Restated' (n 19) para 2.3.
[202] See, eg: G Palombella, 'The Cognitive Attitude' (1999) 85(2) *Archiv. für Rechts- und Sozialphilosophie* 151; Barberis, 'Lo scetticismo Immaginario' (n 132).
[203] Barberis, 'Lo scetticismo Immaginario' (n 132) 14, fn 48 (quoting Searle).

110 A Critical Evaluation of Moderate Legal Realism

of interpretation is essential in view of distinguishing between ordinary ascription of meaning to legal texts – i.e., adjudicative interpretation properly understood – and genuine 'interstitial legislation' by jurists and judges.[204]

How can this statement belong to a descriptive theory of interpretation? I believe it cannot.[205] For if a theory purports to be descriptive, it cannot by definition put any (normative) constraint upon its object of study, but it can only 'record' and analyse the available data.[206] Of course, I do not think any theory of meaning can be wholly descriptive, and thus I would rather say that Guastini's position is flawed at its very meta-theoretical core by an inescapable contradiction.[207] Either he drops the non-evaluative requirement of his meta-theory, and in doing so he is able to admit the existence of easy cases while at the same time taking the last step towards a fully fledged cognitivist position; or he is forced to abandon any kind of normative constraint upon the theory of meaning, as in the passage above, reaching in this way the kind of radical scepticism according to which 'anything goes'.[208] I do not see a third possibility, even more generally as to the alternative between cognitivism (Hartian mixed theories) and radical scepticism. There can be no moderate scepticism.

VIII. ON THE NORMATIVITY OF LAW, AND ON THE DIGESTION OF JUDGES

Two considerations, one theoretical and one meta-theoretical, are in place before we can draw together the threads of the argument presented in this chapter and its relevance as to the empirical research we have started with. The first points to the question as to whether, and to what extent, can theories of law and theories of adjudication be detached and considered autonomous from each other. Such extent, if any, seems minimal. For we have seen that in the very moment in which we recognise the existence in law of easy cases which fit the traditional 'syllogistic' model of deductive reasoning, due to their semantic (and pragmatic) clarity, then the gap between a theory of law and a theory of adjudication is null.

---

[204] Guastini, 'Rule-Scepticism Restated' (n 19) 158.

[205] cf MacCormick, Legal Reasoning and Legal Theory (n 27) 277 on the internal and external aspect of rules.

[206] In this sense think about any astronomer before Copernicus who claimed that the sun was rotating around the earth: did such a claim have any normative bearing or pragmatic effect as to its object? In other words, in astronomy the separation between observation and the phenomena to be observed is absolute.

[207] We need only to remind ourselves that we can still describe a normative phenomenon without having to commit ourselves to the source of that normativity: Barberis, 'Lo scetticismo Immaginario' (n 132) (which in turns quotes Hart); cf also Leiter, Naturalizing Jurisprudence (n 1) 268 where he affirms that a 'correct theory of legal interpretation is not a mere matter of philosophical semantics: issues about political legitimacy – about the conditions under which the exercise of coercive power by courts can be justified – must inform theories of legal interpretation, and such considerations may even trump considerations of semantics'.

[208] Guastini, 'Rule-Scepticism Restated' (n 19) para 2.4.

On the Normativity of Law, and On the Digestion of Judges   111

To know what the law is (this is what a theory of law aims at) is equivalent to knowing what a decision-maker ought legally to do in the case (and this is what a theory of adjudication does). It is not at all clear how a naturalised theory, one that purports to displace normative enquiry because it fails to explain judicial decisions, can accommodate for the easiness of most legal phenomena without giving up some of the very premises that support the 'replacement step' in the first place. There seem to be at least two different but related problems. It might be worth stressing that, in any institutional system of law, litigation is a *secondary* means to guide conducts. We have courts, judges, arbitrators and so forth when something in the primary workings of a legal system (the authoritative and general communication of standards of conduct) goes 'wrong', either because the communication ultimately does not fully determine what should be done in a given situation or because somebody is not following the given guidance.

But what if everything 'goes well', as it is the case in most rule-based phenomenology? What is then the point of having a naturalised theory of adjudication which bears no explanatory capacity for the main and physiological part of our universe of discourse?[209] This consideration brings us to the second remark that has to be raised here: if we are to accept realists' empirical claims, and yet not abandon our traditional understanding of law, then we would have at least to assume that the law 'works' in two very different ways, towards judges on the one hand and towards everybody else who is touched upon by law's influence (that is all of us) on the other.[210] The normativity of law would unfold differently between judges and citizens, and we would have to develop two sets of theories in order to accommodate this difference. Does this sound like a rational reconstruction of our juridical practices? Or rather, when we go before a judge, do we not claim that a right of ours has been infringed, or an obligation not fulfilled, and ask the judge to redress this situation: that is, do we not ask the judge to apply those very same rules that were broken?[211]

The explanatory capacity of the theory we adopt is, ultimately, a crucial criterion in appreciating the alternative between cognitivism and scepticism as two different ontological outlooks (and resulting epistemological theories) that compete to explain the same phenomenon. What I have striven to show in this chapter is that there seems to be no middle ground between these two positions. If we agree that mixed theories, to which many scholars subscribe, are but

---

[209] Priel, 'Were the Legal Realists Legal Positivists?' (n 37) 318–19.

[210] I have already rejected this idea in P Sandro, 'To whom does the law speak? Canvassing a neglected picture of law's interpretive field' in M Araszkiewicz, P Banas, T Gizbert-Studnicki and K Pleszka (eds), *Problems of Normativity, Rules and Rule-Following* (Cham, Springer International Publishing, 2015).

[211] This point turns out to be very clear in Ferrajoli's theory of *iurisdictio*, which highlights the relativity of the distinction between primary and secondary rules: Ferrajoli, *Principia Iuris*, vol 1 (n 70) 879–85.

112 A Critical Evaluation of Moderate Legal Realism

disguised versions of cognitivism,[212] and if you agree with my rebuttal of (any version of) moderate scepticism, then we are left with a simple choice: either (moderate) cognitivism or radical scepticism.

But this meta-theoretical choice is not free from the heaviest pragmatic consequences as to its object of study, given its reflexive nature.[213] On the contrary, it is easy to show that the two stances are diametrically opposed. Scepticism takes normativity altogether out of the picture[214] and substitutes it with the naturalistic epistemic position that judicial decisions, and law-abiding phenomena more generally, are to be analysed as physical events of which we need to retrieve the physically-related causes.[215] Cognitivism presupposes instead the normativity (of language and) of law, that is, it conceives of law as constituted by norms that purport to be reasons for actions, and aims to identify not the physical causes of judicial decisions, but to provide us with 'valid reasons for decisions';[216] in other words, with the conditions of correctness of legal reasoning in general.[217] The opposition between the two positions is primarily ontological.[218] To use MacCormick's meaningful words:

> The kind of object which law is or laws are, as Ota Weinberger says, is that of 'thought objects', or 'ideal objects'... In a significant sense, they exist by being believed in, rather than being believed in by virtue of their existence. *Theories therefore do not stand or fall on the issue of their independent existence or nonexistence.* We have to ask: should they then be believed in, and thus brought into existence by our beliefs? This is nothing other than the question whether it makes a difference to practical or political life if we postulate and sustain the ideal of rules and rights, and the surrounding interpretive activities through which we operationalize these ideas both abstractly and concretely.[219]

To the extent that this is true, then, there really cannot be any (pure) naturalistic concept of law,[220] for such a theory would not just obliterate the

---

[212] Guastini, 'Sceptical View on Legal Interpretation' (n 137).

[213] Ferrajoli, *Principia Iuris*, vol 1 (n 70) 32–38.

[214] Tamanaha, 'Balanced Realism on Judging' (n 17) 1265.

[215] Green, 'Law and the Causes of Judicial Decisions' (n 3) 30–31.

[216] ibid 27.

[217] The point of any cognitivist account of law and adjudication is not to deny that judges are human beings with unique personalities – on the contrary, this is the very starting point of any theory that seeks to justify the practice of adjudication in liberal and objective terms. But precisely because judges are human beings with all their singular and unique characteristics, we need a normative theory which justifies adjudication, by way of specification of its intelligibility paradigm, as a tendentially cognitive endeavour: *cf* Leiter, 'American Legal Realism' (n 1) 277.

[218] *cf* Green, 'Law and the Causes of Judicial Decisions' (n 3) 31 for the claim that American realists were perhaps 'pretty timid' naturalists, as they did not revise almost at all the traditional ontology of law, therefore condemning the replacement of traditional jurisprudence with 'a social science of law' to failure.

[219] N MacCormick, 'The Ethics of Legalism' (1989) 2(2) *Ratio Juris* 184, 191, quoting O Weinberger, 'The Norm as Thought and as Reality' in N MacCormick and O Weinberger, *An Institutional Theory of Law: New Approaches to Legal Positivism* (Dordrecht, Springer, 1986) 33–37 (my emphasis).

[220] Green, 'Law and the Causes of Judicial Decisions' (n 3) 35.

On the Normativity of Law, and On the Digestion of Judges 113

normativity of law, but also annihilate law as a distinctive institutional phenomenon altogether.[221] We should rather call this approach a sociological concept of 'regularities in physical conduct in-between social groups', or something similar. But the law, as an object of analysis, would simply no longer exist. This seems to buttress the conclusion that the normativity of law is irreducible to any meta-theoretical stance which purports to fully displace traditional methods of legal analysis with naturalised methods.[222] As Leslie Green aptly puts it:

> What the naturalist will need to produce is an account of norms of decision that are both naturalistic in the favoured sense and yet also *genuine* norms: standards it is possible to violate and violations of which count as a deficit in reason.[223]

To date, no such account has been convincingly put forward, not at least without having to compromise the naturalist stance itself to the extent that eventually one can question the internal consistency of such positions.[224] This is precisely what I have tried to show with my analysis of moderate scepticism. To put it simply, the normativity of law cannot be grasped by any purely descriptive account of adjudication,[225] as much as the normativity of meaning cannot be grasped by any purely descriptive theory of interpretation. As Green, following Kelsen, points out, any descriptive or sociological account of law and adjudication is not only not independent, but necessarily bound to and constrained by its normative understanding, ie jurisprudence.[226] We can and must discuss what the correct relationship between the two is,[227] but

> an explanatory theory of decision-making cannot oust a normative theory of decision-making ... for we need to retain some distinction between how people *actually* decide in a certain domain of judgement, and how they *ought to* decide.[228]

What should we make of our initial empirical survey on parole boards' decisions? Despite some criticisms about 'overlooked factors' in the analysis,[229] the authors of the study maintain that their findings are nonetheless accurate as to the causal role of 'legally irrelevant factors' in the decisions of the parole

---

[221] On the connection between objectivity and normativity see Leiter, *Naturalizing Jurisprudence* (n 1) 271: 'Only a conception of the law as Minimally Objective is, it seems, guaranteed to be compatible with the normativity of law, precisely because (1) communal consensus is constitutive of legal facts, and (2) such consensus is necessarily accessible to that community'.

[222] Green, 'Law and the Causes of Judicial Decisions' (n 3) 27–28.

[223] ibid.

[224] *cf* ibid 31.

[225] ibid 10.

[226] ibid 32–33.

[227] ibid. There is also at least one significant sense in which a normative account is bound 'by' a descriptive account, for a normative theory of decision-making, to the 'extent that ought implies can', must better comply with whatever scientific knowledge we have of human decision-making: ibid 30. On this relationship, *cf* also Barberis, 'Lo scetticismo Immaginario' (n 132).

[228] Green, 'Law and the Causes of Judicial Decisions' (n 3) 25.

[229] Weinshall-Margel and Shapard, 'Overlooked factors in the analysis of parole decisions' (n 42).

114   *A Critical Evaluation of Moderate Legal Realism*

boards examined.[230] Is this really so? First, there is no mention, within the study, either of the relevant laws governing parole hearings in Israel and of their specific attributions to parole boards, or more generally of the extent of discretion entrusted upon parole judges. There is no consideration of the 'normative side of the story' in the survey. How can we then establish the occurrence of those requirements that we must assume, according to Leiter, so that the indeterminacy thesis is not trivial?[231] Not only do we not know what the law governing parole hearings is, we do not know whether the law governs at all these proceedings, or rather whether it leaves an unconstrained discretionary power to parole boards in these situations. This is hardly surprising, as these types of proceedings represent a traditional example of unconstrained judicial discretion in our modern legal systems.[232]

What should we make therefore of the claim that the findings in the survey 'support the view that the law is indeterminate by showing that legally irrelevant situational determinants ... may lead a judge to rule differently in cases with similar legal characteristics',[233] when we do not know what these legal characteristics are, but we know already that the law in these cases is (likely to be) indeterminate as it does not constrain for the most extent the parole judges' decisions? How can such a finding reinforce at all legal realists' core claims? It would do so only if realism's counterpart is formalism, but we have seen from the outset that formalism is an untenable theoretical position and actually more of an ideology of the nineteenth century. It seems that the relevance of this survey is practically close to zero, even for broader reasons. Despite all the theoretical and meta-theoretical rebukes put forward, perhaps it is still too early to evaluate the capacity of naturalised accounts to 'deliver the goods', which in this case would be working theories of adjudication.[234] We are not quite there yet. Rather,

> [w]hat we have in the empirical studies of judicial behaviour are descriptive statistics massaged by variety of data-reduction techniques which are then given causal interpretations. Replication is poor ... Moreover, the predictive power of this work is not much better than that of our ordinary folk psychology: judges are moved by their sense of justice, by what they take to be common sense, by a desire to please those who appoint them, and so on – all this being defeasible, true only by-and-large, and dependent on the jurisdiction and judge in question.[235]

These kinds of studies are utterly silent as to the reasons for the decisions taken. We could offer as many (folk) causal explanations as we want, even less 'noble'

---

[230] Danziger, Levav, and Avnaim-Pesso, 'Reply to Weinshall-Margel and Shapard' (n 42).

[231] Leiter, 'American Legal Realism' (n 37) 51.

[232] See D Dharmapala, N Garoupa and JM Shepherd, 'Legislatures, Judges, and Parole Boards: The Allocations of Discretion under Determinate Sentencing' (2010) 62(4) *Florida Law Review* 1037.

[233] Danziger, Levav and Avnaim-Pesso, 'Extraneous factors in judicial decisions' (n 42) 6892.

[234] Green, 'Law and the Causes of Judicial Decisions' (n 3) 4.

[235] ibid.

On the Normativity of Law, and On the Digestion of Judges   115

than those offered by Green, eg that the judge decided in this way because she is having marriage issues, or because she has just found herself to be seriously ill, or just because she did not sleep well the night before the hearing. They are all potential, and by all means real, causes for a certain judge in a certain case in a certain moment to decide one way or the other, and I do not doubt that sometimes judges might decide a case in this way, unfortunately. But are they *legal* reasons, that is reasons as established by the relevant sources of law? Clearly, they are not. If we are within a theory of legal adjudication, they are indeed irrelevant, at least insofar as that judge can still show that the decision, despite the psychological path that was underwent to decide that way, is still warranted – that is, *justified* – by the class of legal reasons.[236]

This is also why a theory of adjudication cannot be focused exclusively on the outcome of the single case. The Holmesian 'bad man' perspective is quite misleading. In Kelsen's words, 'The prediction of a future court decision might be considered part of the business of a practical lawyer counselling his client. But cognition of the law must not be confounded with legal advice'.[237] There is more to every judicial decision than the outcome of the single case,[238] as much as there is more to legal theory than adjudication: as Green puts it, 'Litigation and adjudication are always the law's Plan B. Plan A is its subjects should be guided by the law without more'.[239]

---

[236] On the distinction between logic of discovery and logic of appraisal, ie between logic of decision and logic of justification, see ibid 24–32; Schauer, *Thinking Like a Lawyer* (n 9) 131, fn 20 where he refers to Wasserstrom's thought; 'Legal Realism Untamed' (n 10) 2–3.

[237] H Kelsen, *Pure Theory of Law*, 2nd edn (M Knight trans, Berkeley, University of California Press, 1967) 89.

[238] *cf* Palombella, 'The Cognitive Attitude' (n 202).

[239] Green, 'Law and the Causes of Judicial Decisions' (n 3) 21.

4

Towards a Unified Account of Discretion in Law

I. INTRODUCTION

I MAGINE A LEGAL rule which established that 'vehicles are not allowed through doughnut holes'. Prima facie it would appear as the silliest rule ever,[1] and yet the shrewd reader might have already started to wonder, what counts as a 'vehicle' for the purposes of the rule? Automobiles clearly do, but what about toy cars? Moreover, are we really sure that even an automobile – surely a core instance of the general term 'vehicle' – cannot pass through the hole of a doughnut? Let us think about a very famous North-American symbol, the giant doughnut that stands out on the top of the buildings of a famous drive-in bakery chain. Does it count as an instance of the word 'doughnut'? Here, a long discussion could arise, as there would be good reasons both for considering it within (it has the shape and the colours of a doughnut!) and for excluding it from (it is not edible!) the field of application of 'doughnut'.[2] Or what about a ride on toy?

These sorts of questions are indeed ubiquitous in legal scholarship, as often the outcome of a single case will depend upon the interpretation of a certain term in a legal act given by a court. The issue is that when a decision-maker finds herself equipped with some degree of choice in the application of a rule like the one above, such application might seem indeterminate – viz it is not clear if the rule applies to the case at hand. Can we still talk about law-application in these situations then? Or is the decision-maker rather creating the law, as Hart famously maintained? As such, a necessary step towards the defence of the possibility of distinction between creation and application of law is a careful analysis of the concept of discretion in law. This is the aim of chapter four.

Now, to those who for professional reasons – unless there is somebody who deliberately takes pleasure in discussing vehicles and doughnuts, instead

---

[1] But *cf* the 'different-speed-limit-according-to-the-car-manufacturer' rule that was enacted some time ago in Italy: N MacCormick, *Rhetoric and The Rule of Law* (Oxford, Oxford University Press, 2005) 191.

[2] In Hart's words, 'there are reasons both for and against our use of a general term': HLA Hart, *The Concept of Law*, 3rd edn (Oxford, Oxford University Press, 2012) 127.

Introduction 117

of simply driving the former and eating the latter – are into Anglo-American jurisprudence, the 'no-vehicles-in-doughnuts-holes' rule should remind them of the well-known debate between Hart and Dworkin about judicial discretion. The first discusses the open-texture of law – as law is communicated by means of open-textured natural language – through the example of the 'no-vehicles-in-the-park' rule. The second pictures discretion as the 'hole in the doughnut', the doughnut being the occurrence of rules and principles in law, and the hole being the space of freedom that remains open for judges when those very rules and principles are exhausted. The Hart-Dworkin debate indicates perhaps why in general jurisprudence (and in Anglo-American jurisprudence in particular) the concept of discretion has been primarily discussed as the degree of choice judges have in adjudicating a case.[3] Yet, the relevance of the concept goes far beyond what judges do in courtrooms, and goes to the core of our constitutional democratic practices.[4]

In this respect, the bearing of discretion on the legal process has dramatically increased as part of the growth of the so-called 'administrative state', which has transformed the institutional frameworks of western democracies since the end of the nineteenth century.[5] Crucial to this development, discretion constitutes the means to delegate law-making power from the legislature onto administrative departments and agencies. This implies a different approach to the concept by administrative law scholarship vis-à-vis the 'jurisprudential' one, from a mainly negative connotation, discretion as an 'undesirable deviation from an ideal government through rules',[6] to a positive connotation, as a 'necessary element of any complex normative system'.[7]

The result is that, at least in Anglo-American scholarship, the idea of discretion appears to be two-pronged, in the sense that we lack a unitary concept which encompasses both general jurisprudence and administrative

---

[3] For a general introduction, see W Lucy, *Understanding and Explaining Adjudication* (Oxford, Oxford University Press, 1999); W Lucy, 'Adjudication' in J Coleman, KE Himma and S Shapiro (eds), *The Oxford Handbook of Jurisprudence and Philosophy of Law* (Oxford, Oxford University Press, 2004) 206.

[4] On the far-reaching implications for political theory: M Klatt, 'Taking Rights less Seriously. A Structural Analysis of Judicial Discretion' (2007) 20(4) *Ratio Juris* 506, 507–08; *cf* also G Christie, 'An Essay on Discretion' (1986) 35(5) *Duke Law Journal* 747, 747, according to whom 'Discretion involves power relationships and the ways that people work out these relationships in an ongoing political system'. For an extended and multifaceted analysis of the relevance of discretion in western democracies: K Hawkins, 'The Use of Legal Discretion: Perspectives from Law and Social Science' in K Hawkins (ed), *The Uses of Discretion* (Oxford, Oxford University Press, 1992).

[5] *cf* B Sordi, 'Rèvolution, Rechtsstaat and the Rule of Law: historical reflections on the emergence of administrative law' in S Rose-Ackerman and PL Lindseth (eds), *Comparative Administrative Law* (Cheltenham, Edward Elgar, 2010); RM Cooper, 'Administrative Justice and the Role of Discretion' (1938) 47(4) *Yale Law Journal* 577, 578–80.

[6] DJ Galligan, *Discretionary Powers: A Legal Study of Official Discretion* (Oxford, Clarendon Press, 1990) ch 1.

[7] W Wade and CF Forsyth, *Administrative Law*, 10th edn (Oxford, Oxford University Press, 2009) 4.

118   *Towards a Unified Account of Discretion in Law*

law. Notably, and contrary to what the author of the most integrated study of discretionary powers in the literature to date maintains explicitly,[8] I will put forward an analytical concept of legal discretion in this chapter. In particular, I will argue that within such a concept, the main distinction must be drawn not between judicial and administrative discretion, but between what I call 'normative' and 'interpretive' discretion. The former amounts to the (intentional) distribution of decision-making power between different agents within a normative system, whereas the latter is the extent of judgment that is present (at least to some degree) in every activity of application of law.

In the first part of the chapter, I will introduce the current state of the literature by highlighting the dual approach to discretion, as offered on the one hand by jurisprudence and on the other by administrative law scholars. From the discussion it will become clear how the two approaches, however close they might appear prima facie, run on parallel lines that rarely intersect. I believe one of the valuable upshots of my inquiry is to bridge that distance, which is why, in the second part of the chapter, I shall propose a unified account of discretion in the legal domain. My approach, as I will show, wields a much greater explanatory potential than existing proposals particularly because the analytical distinction between normative and interpretive discretion clarifies why the latter is sometimes seen as a discrete phenomenon and sometimes as a matter of degree ('a spectrum').[9]

One final introductory remark is in order. While any discussion on the concept of discretion in legal theory cannot but start from considering the 'Hart-Dworkin' debate on the point,[10] an intrinsic risk lies in doing so. For during the second half of the past century Anglo-American jurisprudence has been somewhere between 'obsessed' and 'fixated'[11] on this debate. The risk is that of steering the discussion that follows onto an exhausted path, so to speak. But it seems a risk worth taking considering the degree of uncertainty still surrounding Hart's ideas on the matter, and in light of the recent discovery

---

[8] Galligan, *Discretionary Powers* (n 6) 20. Rubin questions the feasibility of discretion as an analytical concept altogether: in his view, it amounts only to a superfluous re-formulation of two observable phenomena, supervision and policymaking: EL Rubin, 'Discretion and its Discontents' (1996) 72(4) *Chicago-Kent Law Review* 1299. On the importance of an analytical definition of such a concept, see: JH Grey, 'Discretion in Administrative Law' (1979) 17(1) *Osgoode Hall Law Journal* 107, 107–10.

[9] For the latter idea, see G Ganz, 'Allocation of Decision-Making Functions (Part I)' [1972] *Public Law* 215.

[10] See, eg: EP Soper, 'Legal Theory and the Obligation of a Judge: The Hart/Dworkin Dispute' (1977) 75(3) *Michigan Law Review* 473; SJ Shapiro, 'The "Hart-Dworkin" Debate: A Short Guide for the Perplexed' in A Ripstein (ed), *Ronald Dworkin* (New York, Cambridge University Press, 2007); B Leiter, *Naturalizing Jurisprudence: Essays on American Legal Realism and Naturalism in Legal Philosophy* (Oxford, Oxford University Press, 2007) ch 6; F Schauer, 'On the Open Texture of Law' (2013) 87(1) *Grazer Philosophische Studien* 197; RA Shiner, 'Hart on Judicial Discretion' (2011) 5 *Problema: Anuario de Filosofía y Teoría del Derecho* 341.

[11] Shapiro, 'The "Hart-Dworkin" Debate' (n 10) 22–23.

of his 'lost essay' on discretion.[12] The uncertainty is due not only to the inconsistency of Hart's remarks between the *Concept* and the 'Postscript', but also to Dworkin's misleading reconstruction of Hart's position,[13] which has subsequently become a reference in the following debate between positivists and anti-positivists.[14] This, together with the fact that Dworkin's own position has shifted through the years with little or no self-acknowledgement of this shift,[15] has muddled the debate to the extent that it shall take a great amount of theoretical work just to make sense of the position of the two opponents, whilst trying not to move the focus away from the underlying issues at stake.[16]

II. HLA HART AND THE CONCEPT OF DISCRETION.
BACK TO THE FUTURE?

It is not uncommon to find scholars who state Hart's position through Dworkinian lenses.[17] Some of them openly acknowledge that Dworkin misrepresents Hart's position, almost to the point of attributing theses to Hart he never actually maintained.[18] What did Hart really maintain on the concept of legal discretion then? Surprising as it may sound, after more than 50 years from the first publication in 1961 of the *Concept of Law* (hereafter, *Concept*), this is still an unsettled question.[19] To be sure, this is not only due to Dworkin's misrepresentations, as Hart himself has approached the problem of legal discretion in a rather unsystematic fashion.[20] For there seem to be discrepancies between Hart's

---

[12] HLA Hart, 'Discretion' (2013) 127(2) *Harvard Law Review* 652; N Lacey, 'The Path Not Taken: H.L.A. Hart's Harvard Essay on Discretion' (2013) 127(2) *Harvard Law Review* 636; GC Shaw, 'H.L.A. Hart's Lost Essay: Discretion and the Legal Process School' (2013) 127(2) *Harvard Law Review* 666.

[13] Shapiro, 'The "Hart-Dworkin" Debate' (n 10) 24; Leiter, *Naturalizing Jurisprudence* (n 10) 155, fn 10, where he counts up to 'a dozen occasions where Hart has to complain that Dworkin has misstated' his views.

[14] See Leiter, *Naturalizing Jurisprudence* (n 10) 153–154, fn 3, for the remark that Dworkin's 'mischaracterizations' have not stopped with Hart but have indeed carried onto the work of Joseph Raz. This constitutes the main reason for my choice to report the original quotes from the authors discussed hereinafter, rather than paraphrasing them.

[15] See, in this respect, Dworkin's reply to Hart's remarks in the Postscript (and to 'Hartian philosophers' who criticised his theories): R Dworkin, 'Hart's Postscript and the Point of Political Philosophy' in R Dworkin, *Justice in Robes* (Cambridge, Harvard University Press, 2006); R Dworkin, 'Thirty Years On' in R Dworkin, *Justice in Robes* (Cambridge, Harvard University Press, 2006).

[16] Shapiro, 'The "Hart-Dworkin" Debate' (n 10) 25.

[17] See, eg: ibid 28–34.

[18] As Hart himself seems to acknowledge: Hart, *Concept of Law* (n 2) 263. *cf* eg: Leiter, *Naturalizing Jurisprudence* (n 10) 4–5; but *cf* Shapiro, 'The "Hart-Dworkin" Debate' (n 10) 36.

[19] IB Flores, 'H. L. A. Hart's Moderate Indeterminacy Thesis Reconsidered: In Between Scylla and Charybdis?' (2011) 5 *Problema: Anuario de Filosofía y Teoría del Derecho* 147; and see, recently, M Kramer, *H.L.A. Hart* (Cambridge, Polity Press, 2018), ch 4.

[20] Shiner, 'Hart on Judicial Discretion' (n 10).

120 *Towards a Unified Account of Discretion in Law*

accounts of discretion in chapter seven of the *Concept* and in the 'Postscript',[21] which leads one to wonder what are the causes of discretion in his theory. Take the following famous passage from the 'Postscript':

> The sharpest direct conflict between the legal theory of this book and Dworkin's theory arises from my contention that in any legal system there will always be certain legally unregulated cases in which on some point no decision either way is dictated by the law and the law is accordingly partly indeterminate or incomplete. If in such cases the judge is to reach a decision and is not, as Bentham once advocated, to disclaim jurisdiction or to refer the points not regulated by the existing law to the legislature to decide, he must exercise his *discretion* and *make* law for the case instead of merely applying already pre-existing settled law. So in such legally unprovided for or unregulated cases the judge both makes new law and applies the established law which both confers and constrains his law-making powers.[22]

Here, Hart seems to maintain at least three analytical theses on what judicial discretion is:

1) that in any legal system there will always be some unregulated cases, ie cases in which the law is incomplete and does not provide the courts with a clear rule to apply;
2) that it is in these cases, and in these cases alone, that the judge has to exercise her discretion in order (read: if she has) to reach a decision,[23] and in doing so will be making new law; and
3) that such exercise of discretion is not unbridled – that is, that the law's guidance capacity is not wholly exhausted, and thus the judge will make new law and yet apply the established law that 'confers and constrains his law-making powers'.[24]

The first thesis encapsulates Hart's famous moderate position in the debate between rule-sceptics (the Nightmare) and formalists (the Noble Dream), as we have seen in the last chapter. The second thesis follows from that: in these unregulated cases, and in these cases alone, the judge must exercise discretion to reach a decision. This amounts to a first important point, as Hart conceives of a narrow concept of discretion which has been labelled 'strong' by Dworkin.[25]

---

[21] See, eg: M Martin, *The Legal Philosophy of H.L.A. Hart: A Critical Appraisal* (Philadelphia, Temple University Press, 1987) 7ff; A Marmor, *Interpretation and Legal Theory*, rev. 2nd edn (London, Hart Publishing, 2005) 124ff. Shiner (n 10) 355ff concludes that Hart's stance in the Postscript is 'self-contradictory'.

[22] Hart, *Concept of Law* (n 2) 272.

[23] See KE Himma, 'Judicial Discretion and the Concept of Law' (1999) 19(1) *Oxford Journal of Legal Studies* 71, 77–78 for the remark that from the fact that law is necessarily incomplete does not follow that judges necessarily have law-making authority, and thus Hart's view on law indeterminacy or incompleteness does not imply law-making authority upon the judges.

[24] See also Hart, *Concept of Law* (n 2) 274 when he claims that 'It is true that when particular statutes or precedents prove indeterminate, or when the explicit law is silent, judges do not just push away their law books and start to legislate without further guidance from the law'.

[25] See section III below.

HLA Hart and the Concept of Discretion. Back to the Future? 121

For Hart, therefore, discretion does not just arise from every problem of inter-pretation, but only 'where the existing law fails to dictate any decision as the correct one', so that '[the judge] is entitled to follow standards or reasons for decision which are not dictated by the law and may differ from those followed by other judges faced with similar hard cases'.[26]

In the 'Postscript', Hart also clarifies, urged by Dworkin's attacks,[27] that this interstitial law-making power of courts is *limited* in three different senses:[28] first, institutionally, by substantive constraints (arguably legal principles and rules) that narrow the court's choice and make its law-making power altogether differ-ent from the rather 'free' discretionary power of the legislature;[29] second, 'since the judge's powers are exercised only to dispose of particular instant cases he cannot use these to introduce large-scale reforms or new codes';[30] and finally, because the judge 'must not do so arbitrarily,[31] that is the judge must always have some general reasons justifying his decision and he must act as a conscien-tious legislator would by deciding according to his own beliefs and values'.[32] It appears therefore that even if in hard cases the judge has to resort to her 'beliefs and values' to reach a decision,[33] this does not amount to the freedom to reach any decision whatsoever, because some of the requirements of practical reason still apply.

What causes a situation in which 'no decision either way is dictated by the law'?[34] To answer this question, we have to look at chapter seven of the *Concept*, where the issue of discretion is discussed at more length, but with less sharp-ness, than in the Postscript. Hart begins by illustrating how classifications are necessary to communicate standards of conduct to large groups of people.[35] But whether this is done by means of precedents or legislation, we eventually encounter the 'rule-following paradox',[36] according to which a rule cannot control its own application. As he famously put it:

> In all fields of experience, not only that of rules, there is a limit, inherent in the nature of language, to the guidance which general language can provide.[37]

---

[26] Hart, *Concept of Law* (n 2) 273.
[27] See Leiter, *Naturalizing Jurisprudence* (n 10) 157 fn 18.
[28] Hart, *Concept of Law* (n 2) 273.
[29] ibid 274.
[30] ibid 273.
[31] Arbitrarily includes also randomly, ie by tossing a coin: J Raz, 'Legal Principles and the Limits of Law' (1972) 81(5) *Yale Law Journal* 823, 847.
[32] Hart, *Concept of Law* (n 2) 273; but *cf* the above passage with what Hart says already in the first edition of *Concept of Law* (HLA Hart, *The Concept of Law*, 1st edn (Oxford, Clarendon Press, 1961) 204 (205 in the second edition (HLA Hart, *The Concept of Law*, 2nd edn (Oxford, Clarendon Press, 1997)), about the 'characteristic judicial virtues' – impartiality, neutrality, concern for universability – in cases which imply 'a choice between moral values'.
[33] Hart, *Concept of Law* (n 2) 273.
[34] ibid.
[35] ibid 124ff.
[36] L Wittgenstein, *Philosophical Investigations*, rev 4th edn (PMS Hacker and J Schulte eds, Chicester, Wiley-Blackwell, 2009) §§201ff.
[37] Hart, *Concept of Law* (n 2) 126.

122 *Towards a Unified Account of Discretion in Law*

Hart captures this with the by now paradigmatic example of the 'no-vehicles-in-the-park' rule: do ambulances or electric mobility scooters fall under the rule? Due to this 'crisis in communication', a choice must be made between 'open alternatives'[38] – and this is what the exercise of discretion consists in. Thus, discretion depends on what Harts calls the open-texture of rules, which seems prima facie co-extensive with the open-texture of natural languages.[39] This is what I suggest to call the negative understanding of discretion by Hart, to be juxtaposed with a positive understanding that consists in the need for flexibility in the communication of standards of conduct, required by our human nature and its shortcomings: 'our relative ignorance of fact' and 'our relative indeterminacy of aim'.[40] Hart explains how the former (our impossibility to know all the features of the world) implies the latter, for practical situations which we could not envisage in advance will prove unsettled vis-à-vis pre-existing rules.[41] In other words,

> all systems, in different ways, compromise between two social needs: the need for certain rules which can, over great areas of conduct, safely be applied by private individuals to themselves without fresh official guidance or weighing up of social issues, and the need to leave open, for later settlement by an informed, official choice, issues which can only be properly appreciated and settled when they arise in a concrete case.[42]

One straightforward way[43] to do so in modern legal systems, he continues, is when the legislature recognises from the very beginning that in regulating a specific area of social life, the potential features of individual cases play too important a role for the law to be settled rigidly in advance. Thus,

> to regulate such a sphere the legislature sets up very general standards and then delegates to an administrative, rule-making body acquainted with the varying types of case, the task of fashioning rules adapted to their special needs.[44]

Hart is pointing here to the idea of administrative discretion, ie that 'further choice' that is delegated by the legislature to governmental and administrative officials as to the creation of more detailed standards of conduct which take into account the features of particular cases. This kind of law-making activity is ex ante and not adjudicative, as it purports to create standards which are still

---

[38] ibid 127; *cf* M Iglesias Vila, *Facing Judicial Discretion: Legal Knowledge and Right Answers Revisited* (Dordrecht, Springer, 2001) 14.

[39] But see already n 85 below.

[40] Hart, *Concept of Law* (n 2) 128, 251–52.

[41] ibid 129.

[42] ibid 130; *cf* F Schauer, *Thinking Like a Lawyer: A New Introduction to Legal Reasoning* (Cambridge, Harvard University Press, 2009) 190–196; on the reasons for the delegation of law-making power from the legislature to administrative bodies: KC Davis, *Discretionary Justice: a Preliminary Inquiry* (Baton Rouge, Louisiana State University Press, 1969) 20.

[43] Another one is the incorporation of reasonableness (variable) standards into general rules, which will be only ascertained post facto by the courts: Hart, *Concept of Law* (n 2) 132.

[44] ibid 131.

HLA Hart and the Concept of Discretion. Back to the Future? 123

of general application. But just a few lines later he seems to be talking about an altogether different sense of discretion, specific to common law adjudication, ie to the 'communication of general rules by authoritative examples'.[45] The 'acknowledgement of precedent as a criterion of legal validity'[46] creates several epistemic difficulties which eventually result in 'two types of creative or legislative activity'[47] by courts: those of narrowing or widening the rule 'extracted from the precedent'.[48] This leads Hart to conclude that:

> Here at the margin of rules and in the fields left open by the theory of precedents, the courts perform a rule-producing function which administrative bodies perform centrally in the elaboration of variable standards. In a system where *stare decisis* is firmly acknowledged, this function of the courts is very like the exercise of delegated rule-making powers by an administrative body'.[49]

Despite this last remark, it can be argued that for Hart judicial and administrative discretion are two different kinds, the former being the implicit result of the open-texture of law (a necessary characteristic of all legal systems) and of the doctrine of precedent (a contingent characteristic, typical of common law jurisdictions), while the latter is the explicit product of delegated law-making authority in the ex ante specification of general standards of conduct. How do these relate to each other, if at all? And what happens when the courts are confronted by the exercise of administrative discretion? Can they substitute their own view on the matter with the one assumed by the administrative authority? These questions remain without answer in the context of chapter seven of the *Concept*.[50] As such, not only does Hart's treatment of discretion seem incomplete, but by comparing these latter remarks with those in the 'Postscript', a rather confusing overall picture emerges, in the sense that:

1) Hart's language is ambiguous in discussing the causes of discretion in law – to the extent that sometimes by referring to the open-texture of law he refers to the vagueness of the natural language in which rules are expressed, and sometimes he refers to the defeasibility of rules;[51]
2) it is not at all clear whether Hart has one concept of discretion in mind, or whether discretion amounts to a 'family resemblance' concept; and lastly;

---

[45] ibid 134.

[46] ibid.

[47] ibid 135.

[48] ibid; *cf* CE Schneider, 'Discretion and Rules: A Lawyer's View' in K Hawkins (ed), *The Uses of Discretion* (Oxford, Oxford University Press, 1992) 56.

[49] Hart, *Concept of Law* (n 2) 135: *cf* Galligan, *Discretionary Powers* (n 6) 37 for the claim that judicial discretion has a 'special reflexive characteristic' and occurs in three cases: 1) in hard cases; 2) when courts change the existing legal doctrine, and 3) when there is express delegation of powers to the courts by the legislature.

[50] Kramer identifies Hart's 'neglect' of administrators' role in creating and applying the law as one of the main shortcomings of the *Concept*: Kramer, *HLA Hart* (n 19) 206.

[51] And the last quote from Hart, *Concept of Law* (n 2) 135 seems to confirm this: 'here at the margins of rules and in the fields left open by the theory of precedents'.

124   *Towards a Unified Account of Discretion in Law*

3)   depending on the clarification of these points, it is an open question whether discretion is an analytical or rather an empirical feature of legal systems.

As to the first point, discretion originates in the open-texture of law, but it is far from clear what Hart actually understands by open-texture. As Schauer has claimed,[52] although Hart explicitly assumes the idea of the open-texture of language from Waismann's work, they seem to be talking past each other.[53] In Waismann's account, the open-texture of language is not actual vagueness, but 'the *possibility* of vagueness – the *potential* vagueness – of even those terms that appear to have no uncertainties with respect to known or imagined applications'.[54] For Hart, the open-texture of law instead pertains, as the no-vehicles-in-the-park-rule shows, to the actual vagueness 'surrounding the determinate applications of partially non-vague terms'.[55] Schauer highlights the inner ambiguity of Hart's concept of open-texture: what Hart is claiming is not that the law is open-textured because law is expressed by means of language and language is open-textured, but, rather, that the open-texture of law derives from the (normative) defeasibility of legal rules – even in instances of linguistic determinacy.[56] But if this is the case, then discretion is not a product of the actual or potential vagueness of language through which law is communicated, but the result of an a priori conception of legal rules as being *necessarily* defeasible,[57] even in the face of linguistic determinacy.[58] This entails a very different kind of discretion from the one implied by linguistic vagueness, in which interpretative guidance will still constrain the decision-maker's choice among the possible alternatives of meaning.[59] It entails instead the freedom to disregard even what Hart would identify as 'core' cases of application of a rule,[60] like in the 'memorial truck' counter-example offered by Lon Fuller.[61]

---

[52] F Schauer, *Playing by the Rules: A Philosophical Examination of Rule-based Decision-making in Law and in Life* (Oxford, Clarendon Press, 1991) 35, fn 26; Schauer, 'Open Texture' (n 10).

[53] *Contra*, see Shiner, 'Hart on Judicial Discretion' (n 10) 359.

[54] Schauer, 'Open Texture' (n 10) 199.

[55] ibid 200. That the two should not be confused is explicitly stated by Waismann himself: F Waismann, 'Symposium: Verifiability' (1945) 19 *Proceedings of the Aristotelian Society,* Supplementary Volume 119, 123; Hart's overlap is explicit in Hart, *Concept of Law* (n 2) 123.

[56] Schauer, 'Open Texture' (n 10) 206–07. Although in Hart, *Concept of Law* (n 2) 139, the distinction between open texture and defeasibility as different phenomena seems neat. On this point *cf* also Flores, 'H. L. A. Hart's Moderate Indeterminacy Thesis Reconsidered' (n 19) 156.

[57] Schauer correctly stresses how this amounts to a choice by a historical legal system (or reconstruction of it), but it cannot be considered a necessary, conceptual feature of law as such: Schauer, 'Open Texture' (n 10) 212–13.

[58] *cf* with Klatt, 'Taking Rights less Seriously' (n 4).

[59] D Duarte, 'Linguistic Objectivity in Norm Sentences: Alternatives in Literal Meaning' (2011) 24(2) *Ratio Juris* 112, 135–36.

[60] *cf* B Bix, *Law, Language, and Legal Determinacy* (Oxford, Oxford University Press, 1993) 21–22. It is worth noticing that Adolf Merkl, the most prominent of Kelsen's disciples, had already spoken in 1918 of 'core' and 'peripheral' meanings of words: A Jakab, 'Problems of the Stufenbaulehre: Kelsen's Failure to Derive the Validity of a Norm from Another Norm' (2007) 20 *Canadian Journal of Law & Jurisprudence* 35, 39, fn 21.

[61] Schauer, 'Open Texture' (n 10) 209–10, for the remark that Fuller's claim is not empirical but analytical; *cf* also R Kannai, U Schild, and J Zeleznikow, 'Modeling the Evolution of Legal Discretion: An Artificial Intelligence Approach' (2007) 20(4) *Ratio Juris* 530, 533.

HLA Hart and the Concept of Discretion. Back to the Future?   125

As to the second point, if we were to offer a synthesis of Hart's remarks on discretion in chapter seven and in the 'Postscript', his use of the term 'discretion' would stand for at least three different things:

1) the inevitable room for choice in the application of normative statements, caused by the vagueness of natural language in which standards are communicated;
2) the delegation of variable standards to be further specified by administrative authorities;
3) the power of courts in common law jurisdictions to narrow or widen rules from precedents.[62]

What is the connection, if any, between these? Shiner observes that sometimes Hart's remarks fit Dworkin's characterisation of discretion as 'the hole in the doughnut', whereas his central idea of legal rules being provided with a core of certainty surrounded by a penumbra of uncertainty (where discretion would lie) seems to run against it.[63] In turn, the cause of each type of discretion identified above appears different and is certainly contingent with respect to the third type: this makes it problematic to square the idea of discretion with his positivist theory, particularly in light of Hart's claim of applicability to every (municipal) legal system.[64] Overall, it is evident that Hart's remarks on discretion in the *Concept* lack systematicity, almost as if they were part of a wider (but more precise) reflection on the topic which eventually was not thoroughly pursued by Hart in his main work. This is where the recent recovery of his 'lost essay' on discretion comes in.

While elements of the paper – which Hart wrote and circulated (but never published) after his 1956 presentation to the Harvard faculty seminar – have 'resurfaced' in a piecemeal fashion in Hart's later works,[65] when considered on its own we can witness what Lacey aptly called 'the path not taken': a focussed analysis of the concept of discretion which combines Hart's preferred philosophical method (linguistic analysis) with the acknowledgement – arguably prompted by his temporary immersion in the Legal Process school – of the inescapable institutional dimension of the law-making process. Now, the

---

[62] Flores, (see Flores, 'H. L. A. Hart's Moderate Indeterminacy Thesis Reconsidered' (n 19) 167–69) claims that what is even more problematic in Hart's account of discretion is that he 'equates "creative" to "legislative" and "judicial discretion" to "judicial legislation"' (ibid 167). In this sense he denies that such 'creative judicial activity' of common law courts can amount to 'either to the legislative creation of a (new) rule or to the quasi-legislative change of an existing rule' (ibid 168).

[63] Shiner, 'Hart on Judicial Discretion' (n 10) 345–46. For the idea that the use of 'spatial imagery' by Hart runs against a full understanding of his remarks: D Kennedy, 'A Left Phenomenological Alternative to the Hart/Kelsen Theory of Legal Interpretation' in D Kennedy, *Legal Reasoning: Collected Essays* (Aurora, Davies Group Publishers, 2008) 155.

[64] See Hart, *Concept of Law* (n 2) 239; Himma, 'Judicial Discretion and the Concept of Law' (n 23) 76 argues that the discretion thesis as a conceptual necessity of every legal system is inconsistent with the very core of positivism, ie the pedigree thesis; if, instead, it is a contingent thesis, it is not properly part of positivism's theory of law (ibid 80–81).

[65] See Shaw, 'H.L.A. Hart's Lost Essay' (n 12) 675.

126   *Towards a Unified Account of Discretion in Law*

significance of this paper goes beyond the scope of this chapter, as clearly illustrated by the two contributions that accompany it in the *Harvard Law Review*: while Lacey offers an interpretation as to why Hart might have not embraced the more institutionalised view of law displayed in the discretion paper in his following work,[66] Shaw – who is also responsible for the discovery – analyses the paper in great detail and contextualises its intellectual (and causal) roots, reconstructing with historiographical nuance the complex relationship between Hart and his American counterparts of the Legal Process school (including Fuller).[67] For our purposes here, three points must be highlighted.

First, the discretion paper offers a glimpse into what Hart's theory of law could have looked like if it was not for his already mentioned neglect of administrators and administrative law more generally.[68] For the attention to questions of institutional design and their consequences, that we have already identified as characteristic of the Legal Process school, brings about the realisation that a vast – if not the most – amount of official law-creation and law-application happens outside courtrooms. This prompts Hart, in the third section of the paper, to put forward a more analytically neat distinction (vis-à-vis that in the *Concept*) between what he calls 'express' (or 'avowed') and 'tacit' (or 'concealed') discretion.[69] Examples of the former are constituted not only by the diverse range of decision-making powers directly delegated by legislatures to administrative bodies and authorities, but also in the application of specific 'standards' by courts and juries, such as the 'reasonable or proper cause' in malicious prosecution cases or the 'reasonable care' in negligence cases;[70] while the latter is the product of uncertainties in the interpretation of statutes or written rules and in the use of precedent (in the common law).[71] This distinction is fundamental because it clearly indicates that the set of factors that should be considered not just in exercising, but also in reviewing that exercise of discretion, is a 'function of the *type* of discretion at issue'.[72] In my view, the gist of the distinction is not in the commonsensical observation that an administrative decision-maker asked to fix a rate or deciding on a planning permission 'should refer to a set of concerns quite different from that of an appellate judge interpreting a statute',[73] but rather in the observation that whether a discretionary power

[66] See Lacey, 'The Path Not Taken' (n 12) 647–50.

[67] See Shaw, 'H.L.A. Hart's Lost Essay' (n 12).

[68] In this regard, I must confess my surprise when I noticed that Kramer does not engage at all with Hart's lost paper in his (otherwise illuminating) critical reading of Hart's work: Kramer, *HLA Hart* (n 19).

[69] Hart, 'Discretion' (n 12) 655–656. Unfortunately, as noticed by Lacey ('The Path Not Taken' (n 12) 647), Hart neither develops nor explores the significance of the distinction in the paper (nor in later works).

[70] Hart, 'Discretion' (n 12) 655.

[71] ibid, 655–56. A third type or form of discretion is mentioned, 'interference' or 'dispensation' from acknowledge rules, which is however not really developed by Hart.

[72] See Shaw, 'H.L.A. Hart's Lost Essay' (n 12) 708.

[73] ibid.

HLA Hart and the Concept of Discretion. Back to the Future? 127

has been expressly delegated to another decision-maker makes a fundamental difference in how we should understand the exercise, limits, and reviewability of that power (more on this later).

Second, Hart notes that in any case (be it express or tacit), when exercised by administrators or judges, legal discretion cannot be understood as (personal) choice tout court.[74] As he puts it,

> discretion is after all the name of an intellectual virtue: it is a near-synonym for practical wisdom or sagacity or prudence; it is the power of discerning or distinguishing what in various fields is appropriate to be done and etymologically connected with the notion of discerning.[75]

This does not mean that, from a formal point of view, the exercise of discretion in law should not be understood as 'a leeway within a certain framework' [of choice],[76] but that even *within* such a framework (as determined by the legal rules and principles applicable), not every decision should be considered equally acceptable from a legal point of view a priori.[77] More than with the application of determinate rules, in fact, the exercise of a discretionary legal power requires justification, and this for Hart points to at least two features that 'set discretion apart from other forms of decision-making':[78] rationality (not just in the form of 'logical integrity', but also as 'practical wisdom' or phronesis) and the choice of factors on which the discretionary decision is based.[79]

This latter point leads us to the final observation elicited by Hart's lost paper, namely that the ensuing concept of discretion is 'essential' to the rule of law, rather than being 'antithetical' to it:[80] as conceived of in the paper, discretion represents a heavily constrained (also from an institutional point of view)[81] form of decision-making and as such it is a solution to the problem of indeterminacy[82] – not its cause. Hart though decided not to pursue this simple and yet powerful version of his argument in the *Concept*, only to return to it, albeit in an abridged (and not as effective) form,[83] in the 'Postscript' once called upon to deflect Dworkin's attack on the point. In turning now to the latter,

---

[74] Hart, 'Discretion' (n 12) 656–57.

[75] See also Galligan, *Discretionary Powers* (n 6) 8; MR Cohen, 'Rule Versus Discretion' (1914) 11(8) *Journal of Philosophy, Psychology and Scientific Methods* 208, 212.

[76] Klatt, 'Taking Rights less Seriously' (n 4) 1; for Galligan, (*Discretionary Powers* (n 6) 8), discretion amounts to 'autonomy in judgment and decision'.

[77] This is one of the conceptual aspects in which the operationalisation of discretion in the administrative domain gives the edge to administrative law scholarship vis-à-vis general jurisprudence: see, eg: T Endicott, *Administrative Law*, 4th edn (Oxford, Oxford University Press, 2018) 234–36.

[78] Shaw, 'H.L.A. Hart's Lost Essay' (n 12) 706.

[79] ibid, 707.

[80] Lacey notes that, if we were to use Dworkin's later terminology, Hart's conception of discretion in the lost paper should be understood as 'weak' and not 'strong': Lacey, 'The Path Not Taken' (n 12) 644.

[81] ibid.

[82] Shaw, 'H.L.A. Hart's Lost Essay' (n 12) 709.

[83] ibid 723.

128   *Towards a Unified Account of Discretion in Law*

I shall leave open the question of the compatibility of Hart's positivism with the account of discretion defended in the lost paper.[84]

III. DWORKIN AND THE (NORMATIVE) NO-STRONG-DISCRETION THESIS

The consideration of discretion in Dworkin's theory of law seems at first a by-product of his attack on Hartian positivism. Dworkin maintains, in his seminal article 'The Model of Rules I',[85] that positivism (in both Austin's and Hart's fashion) is inevitably committed to the judicial discretion thesis. He argues that there are 'certain confusions about that concept',[86] and moves to dissipate them. To do so, we need to put discretion 'back' in ordinary language, from which positivists allegedly picked it up. In this way, his aim is to demonstrate that even in ordinary language we would never call discretion the ordinary freedom to do or not do something ('to choose a house for my family'), but that rather discretion is

> at home in only one sort of context: when someone is in general charged with making decisions subject to standards set by a particular authority. It makes sense to speak of the discretion of a sergeant who is subject to orders of superiors, or the discretion of a sports official or contest judge who is governed by a rule book or the terms of the contest. Discretion, like the hole in a doughnut, does not exist except as an area left open by a surrounding belt of restriction. It is therefore a relative concept. It always makes sense to ask, 'Discretion under which standards?' or 'Discretion as to which authority?'[87]

Dworkin singles out three different senses – two weak and one strong – in which we can understand the concept. A first weak sense of discretion refers to the (trivial) fact that sometimes an official cannot reach a decision 'mechanically', but he or she needs to use 'judgment' to do so.[88] This can be called 'interpretive discretion'. So the lieutenant ordered by the sergeant to pick the five most experienced men on patrol would have discretion in this weak sense because it is not easy 'to determine which were the most experienced'.[89] The second weak sense of discretion, that we could label 'discretion as finality', refers to

---

[84] See, for discussion, Lacey, 'The Path Not Taken' (n 12) 644–48.

[85] R Dworkin, 'The Model of Rules' (1967) 35(1) *University of Chicago Law Review* 14, reprinted in R Dworkin, *Taking Rights Seriously* (Cambridge, Harvard University Press, 1977) – references are to the original publication.

[86] Dworkin, 'The Model of Rules' (n 85) 31.

[87] ibid 32; *cf* Christie, 'An Essay on Discretion' (n 4) 751–52, who relates discretion to accountability, and not to standards, as the defining framework.

[88] N MacCormick, 'Discretion and Rights' (1989) 8(1) *Law and Philosophy* 23, 28, where he claims that the distinguishing feature of legal discretion is its 'judgement-dependency': in this sense, he draws a distinction between rights and remedies (actions), the former can be judgment-independent while the latter always involve some degree of discretion.

[89] Dworkin, 'Model of Rules' (n 85) 32.

the empirical fact that an official has 'final authority' to make a decision and this decision 'cannot be reviewed and reversed by any other official' within the hierarchy of that particular system.[90] But it is the third and strong sense of discretion that really matters for Dworkin: this is the sense which he assumes positivism is necessarily committed to. An official holds strong discretion when 'he is simply not bound by standards set by the authority in question'. A sergeant who is ordered to pick five men for the patrol, or a judge who in a dog competition can decide which breed to judge first, have discretion in the strong sense. This strong sense, however, 'is not tantamount to license, and does not exclude criticism',[91] for in almost every action are implied 'certain standards of rationality, fairness, and effectiveness'.[92]

Dworkin commits positivism to this third sense of discretion, for commitment to either of the first two would be a rather trivial theoretical fact.[93] I am not going to discuss further Dworkin's attacks on positivism, as this would bring us beyond the scope of this chapter. What is relevant is the fact that the strong discretion thesis is a key tenet of Hartian positivism[94] and Dworkin rejects it thoroughly, but he does not provide us with any further elaboration of the concept.[95] It is perhaps worth noting that 'discretion' is not indexed in *Law's Empire*, *A Matter of Principle*, or *Justice in Robes*. We can therefore conclude that when he is talking about discretion in his theory of 'law as integrity',[96] Dworkin uses it in either of the two weak senses.[97] But how is this so?

His rebuttal of the strong sense of discretion is based upon the notorious one-right-answer thesis.[98] Dworkin argues that judges, even in hard cases, never run out of guidance since law is made up not only of rules but also of principles and these, unlike rules, do not 'run out'. They are not clearly identified within the realm of positive law, but rather they belong to the realm of morality (which is a necessary part of law)[99] and they guide the decision of judges towards the one and *only* right answer, even in the hardest cases. Crucial to this theory are

---

[90] ibid 33.

[91] ibid.

[92] ibid 34; see how Dworkin restates the three senses in Dworkin, *Taking Rights Seriously* (n 85) 69.

[93] Dworkin, *Taking Rights Seriously* (n 85) 69.

[94] Dworkin, 'Model of Rules' (n 85) 17.

[95] For a comprehensive critical evaluation of Dworkin's concept of strong discretion, see WJ Waluchow, 'Strong Discretion' (1983) 33(133) *The Philosophical Quarterly* 321.

[96] R Dworkin, *A Matter of Principle* (Cambridge, Harvard University Press, 1985) pt 2; R Dworkin, *Law's Empire* (London, Fontana, 1986) chs 6–7. For a general discussion of Dworkin's interpretive theory (and its connection with the 'semantic sting' and the 'one right answer thesis'): T Endicott, 'Law and Language' in EN Zalta (ed), *The Stanford Encyclopedia of Philosophy* (Summer 2016 Edition) http://plato.stanford.edu/archives/sum2016/entries/law-language/.

[97] Dworkin, *Law's Empire* (n 96) 350–54.

[98] Dworkin, *Taking Rights Seriously* (n 85) 68–71. According to Galligan (*Discretionary Powers* (n 6) 18), 'the antithesis of the right answer thesis is discretion'.

[99] Up to this point, Dworkin and Alexy's positions seem convergent: G Pino, 'L'Applicabilità delle Norme Giuridiche' (2011) 11 *Diritto & Questioni Pubbliche* 797.

130 *Towards a Unified Account of Discretion in Law*

four ideas:[100] first, that between law and morality there is a necessary connection, and thus in hard cases, when rules run out, a legal argument is a moral argument; second, that in every legal dispute, one party (and exactly one party) has a pre-existing right to win;[101] third, is Dworkin's belief that we can objectively know of values and thus value-laden statements are apt for truth-values;[102] fourth, he upholds the principle of bivalence in law and morality, that for every proposition p, either p or $-p$ is true.[103]

We need not discuss the right answer thesis here. This has been done extensively, to the extent that Dworkin's own version seems to have shifted through the years from a strong to a weak version of it.[104] What matters is that in this shift, due mainly to the argument from vagueness,[105] Dworkin has abandoned his commitment to the bivalence thesis: so that for every legal question there is still the duty for the judge to retrieve the one right answer, but now this right answer is potentially three-fold, for p, $-p$, and also indeterminate – as a substantive and not a default position – can obtain.[106] So, even if not explicitly stated, this constitutes the logical space for the occurrence of discretion in Dworkin's interpretive account of law.

What matters the most for us is Dworkin's original concern with the discretion thesis as (allegedly) upheld by positivism, or better the underlying causes for his original concern. For it seems that the problem of cognitivism, which is logically antecedent to that of discretion, points to the political problem of the authority of law, and of adjudication in particular.[107] In this regard,

---

[100] JR Geller, 'Truth, Objectivity and Dworkin's Right Answer Thesis' [1999] *UCL Jurisprudence Review* 83.

[101] Spaak notes that, at least initially, the right answer thesis applies to cases of rights, but not to cases of interpretation of statutes: T Spaak, *Guidance and Constraint: the Action-Guiding Capacity of Theories of Legal Reasoning* (Uppsala, Iustus, 2007) 127.

[102] This idea progressively strengthened throughout Dworkin's career, so that we now find its strongest defence (together with the rejection of meta-ethics) in his last book on law: R Dworkin, *Justice for Hedgehogs* (Cambridge, Harvard University Press, 2011) pt 1.

[103] *cf* MP Golding, 'The Legal Analog of the Principle of Bivalence' (2003) 16(4) *Ratio Juris* 450.

[104] Geller, 'Truth, Objectivity and Dworkin's Right Answer Thesis' (n 100) 97–98; *cf* Dworkin, *A Matter of Principle* (n 96) ch 5.

[105] Geller, 'Truth, Objectivity and Dworkin's Right Answer Thesis' (n 100) 86–88, where he also argues that the concept of vagueness has to be distinguished from the phenomenon of vagueness, and also that 'vagueness does not entail noncognitivism' but only rebukes bivalence.

[106] For a discussion of how this indeterminacy claim is from an internal, and not an external, position and for the distinction between indeterminacy and uncertainty: ibid 97–98; *cf* Dworkin, *A Matter of Principle* (n 96) 142; R Dworkin, 'Objectivity and Truth: You'd Better Believe It' (1996) 25(2) *Philosophy & Public Affairs* 87, 129ff. In any case, again in Geller's words: 'on the Dworkinian weak Right Answer thesis, this indeterminacy need not worry us; we can still arrive at the right answer, even if that right answer is that there is no right answer': Geller, 'Truth, Objectivity and Dworkin's Right Answer Thesis' (n 100) 99.

[107] 'If ethical noncognitivism and relationism (connection between morality and law) both hold, there would be a problem for legal authority': Geller, 'Truth, Objectivity and Dworkin's Right Answer Thesis' (n 100) 85.

Discretion as a Pervasive Feature of Kelsen's Stufenbaulehre   131

Dworkin's theory purports to lay out positivism's shortcomings not just for the sake of it, but with the broader aim of defending legal adjudication from the challenges brought by American realists and members of the Critical Legal Studies movement.[108] To put it differently, he wants to achieve what (he believes) positivism cannot do, that is meeting the so-called 'sceptical claim' to adjudication.[109] This is because positivism's claim that in hard cases judges hold strong discretion, and thus make *new* law, paves the way for two specific lines of attack against judicial adjudication: on the one hand, for the lack of democratic legitimacy of courts in establishing new law; on the other, for the retroactive character of discretionary adjudication as contrary to the rule of law.

What I am suggesting, in short, is that we should charitably interpret Dworkin's theory of law as integrity, and the (weak) right answer thesis in particular, as normative rather than descriptive:[110] as instructions to judges deciding hard cases to make sense of the legal materials – rules and especially principles – as much as possible, instead of simply stating that the law is either silent or vague and that, as such, they can exercise strong discretion. Dworkin's epistemological claims about law and propositions of law constitute a means for upholding the rationality and legitimacy of adjudication, which seems to be his ultimate aim in his debate with realists and CLS. If this is so, Dworkin's concerns are clearly prima facie justified, for the issue of discretion in adjudication raises fundamental problems when upholding the legitimacy and rationality of the latter. But, at the same time, the one right answer thesis, with its meta-theoretical 'baggage' and untenable consequences, does not seem to be the right answer (pun intended) to ease those worries. Let us then turn to another of the most influential scholars of the twentieth century.

IV. DISCRETION AS A PERVASIVE FEATURE OF KELSEN'S *STUFENBAULEHRE*

Examining Kelsen's work after Hart's requires a significant shift in perspective. If Hart, influenced by the common law structure, predominantly seeks to explain the horizontal dimension of law, Kelsen is utterly focused on the vertical, hierarchical structure of the legal system, the *Stufenbaulehre*.[111] Mutatis mutandis, if Hart conceives of discretion mostly horizontally (as the penumbra surrounding the core of rules), Kelsen locates discretion along the chain of validity of

---

[108] This is why Lucy groups MacCormick, Raz and Dworkin in the same group of 'non-sceptical' accounts against the 'sceptical' claims thrown against judicial adjudication by realist and CLS theorists: Lucy, 'Adjudication' (n 3) 208–09.

[109] ibid.

[110] Himma, 'Judicial Discretion and the Concept of Law' (n 23) 78; Waluchow, 'Strong Discretion' (n 95) 338.

[111] For a critical introduction to the *Stufenbaulehre*: Jakab, 'Problems of the Stufenbaulehre' (n 60).

132 Towards a Unified Account of Discretion in Law

legal norms, from individual norms up to the basic norm (*Grundnorm*) – or vice versa.[112] In his view,

> the legal order is a system of general and individual norms connected with each other according to the principle that law regulates its own creation ...; a norm belongs to this legal order only because it has been created in conformity with the stipulations of another norm of the order.[113]

In other words, 'A norm which represents the reason for the validity of another norm is figuratively spoken of as a higher norm in relation to a lower norm',[114] and this conception of the nomodynamics of the legal system – as opposed to its nomostatics – represents maybe the most distinctive feature of his pure theory of law.[115] However,

> [t]his determination ... is never complete. The higher-level norm cannot be binding with respect to every detail of the act putting it into practice. There must always remain a range of *discretion*, sometimes wider, sometimes narrower, so that the higher-level norm, in relation to the act of applying it (an act of norm creation or of pure implementation), has simply the character of a frame to be filled in by way of the act. Even a meticulously detailed command must leave a number of determinations to those carrying it out. If official A orders official B to arrest subject C, B must use his own discretion to decide when, where, and how he will carry out the warrant to arrest C; and these decisions depend upon external circumstances that A has not foreseen and, for the most part, cannot foresee.[116]

Kelsen's concept of discretion as the internal part of a frame (constituted by the higher norms of the hierarchy)[117] to be filled by the delegated decision-maker

---

[112] In other words, the German original word *Unbestimmtheit* used by Kelsen in the first edition of the Pure Theory must be understood as 'the quality of being not decided' and not as synonymous with vagueness, fuzziness and open-texture (ie 'indeterminacy in a linguistic sense'): C Luzzati, 'Discretion and "Indeterminacy" in Kelsen's Theory of Legal Interpretation' in L Gianformaggio (ed), *Hans Kelsen's Legal Theory: A Diachronic Point of View* (Turin, Giappichelli, 1990) 124–25.

[113] H Kelsen, *General Theory of Law and State* (first published 1945, with a new introduction by A Javier Treviño, New Brunswick, Transaction Publishers, 2005) 132ff.

[114] H Kelsen, *Pure Theory of Law*, 2nd edn (M Knight trans, Berkeley, University of California Press, 1967) 193, 239–40.

[115] On Kelsen's nomodynamics see, eg: L Gianformaggio (ed), *Hans Kelsen's Legal Theory: A Diachronic Point of View* (Turin, Giappichelli 1990); L Gianformaggio (ed), *Sistemi Normativi Statici e Dinamici: Analisi di una tipologia kelseniana* (Turin, Giappichelli, 1991); SL Paulson and BL Paulson (eds), *Normativity and Norms: Critical Perspectives on Kelsenian Themes* (Oxford, Oxford University Press, 1999); B Celano, *La Teoria del Diritto di Hans Kelsen: una Introduzione Critica* (Bologna, Il Mulino, 1999); L Vinx, *Hans Kelsen's Pure Theory of Law: Legality and Legitimacy* (Oxford, Oxford University Press, 2007).

[116] H Kelsen, *Reine Rechtslehre* (Leipzig, Deuticke, 1934), translated in English as H Kelsen, *Introduction to the Problems of Legal Theory: A Translation of the First Edition of the Reine Rechtslehre or Pure Theory of Law* (BL Paulson and SL Paulson trans, Oxford, Clarendon Press, 1997) 77–89, and 78 in particular (my emphasis); H Kelsen (BL Paulson and SL Paulson trans), 'On the Theory of Interpretation' (1990) 10(2) *Legal Studies* 127, 127–28 (English translation of H Kelsen, 'Zur Theorie der Interpretation' (1934) 8 *Internationale Zeitschrift für Theorie des Rechts*).

[117] See Jakab, 'Problems of the Stufenbaulehre' (n 60) 48–49 for the consideration that Kelsen is plainly mistaken in believing that the validity of a norm is conditioned by one single other norm (as opposed to all *relevant* superior norms).

Discretion as a Pervasive Feature of Kelsen's Stufenbaulehre   133

resembles Dworkin's idea of discretion as a doughnut hole. But here this conceptualisation is functional towards the distinction between (aspects of) cognition and (aspects of) will in the law-making process.[118] Furthermore, after stating that the determination between norms of different levels is never complete, Kelsen draws a similar distinction to Hart's lost paper between intended and unintended discretion.[119] The former represents the deliberate delegation of law-creation power from the higher authority to the lower authority, and it can pertain both to the 'why' and the 'what' of the 'prescribed act' – be it another general or individual norm.[120] 'Unintended discretion' instead implies that the lower authority finds itself with a leeway in adopting a norm that was not supposed to be there, and it 'can transcend the intention of the authority issuing the higher level norm'.[121] This can occur in three situations: 1) where there is ambiguity or vagueness in the formulation of the higher norm; 2) when the lower decision-makers finds a discrepancy between the norm formulation and the intention of the norm-issuing authority; and 3) for the existence and (supposed) applicability of two 'valid' and contradictory norms.[122] Therefore,

> [i]n all these cases of intended or unintended indeterminacy of the lower level, various possibilities for applying the higher-level norm suggest themselves. The legal act of applying the legal norm can be made to correspond to one or another of the several possible readings of the norm. Or it can be made to correspond to the norm-issuer's will, however discovered, or to the expression he chooses. Or, in the case of the two norms contradicting each other, the legal act can be made to correspond to one or the other of them, or it can be so fashioned that decisions are taken as if norms abrogated one another. In all these cases the norm to be applied is simply a frame within which various possibilities for application are given, and very act that stays within this frame, in some possible sense filling it in, is in *conformity* with the norm.[123]

This idea of conformity plays a key role here, for in this area – delimited by the frame of higher norms – there is not, and, most importantly, there cannot be one right or 'correct' norm (or decision) to be singled out from all the possible norms. This is because 'traditional jurisprudence' has failed so far in proposing an 'objective' criterion in order to 'settle the conflict between will and expression'.[124] Conformity is, at most, what a higher authority can achieve in

---

[118] On Kelsen's theory of interpretation, see also P Chiassoni, 'Legal Science and Legal Interpretation in the Pure Theory of Law' in L Gianformaggio (ed), *Hans Kelsen's Legal Theory: A Diachronic Point of View* (Turin, Giappichelli, 1990) 63–73.

[119] *cf* Luzzati, 'Discretion and "Indeterminacy" in Kelsen's Theory of Legal Interpretation' (n 112) 134–37.

[120] Kelsen, 'On the Theory of Interpretation' (n 116) 128.

[121] Flores, 'H. L. A. Hart's Moderate Indeterminacy Thesis Reconsidered' (n 19) 153.

[122] Kelsen, *Introduction to the Problems of Legal Theory* (n 116) 78–80; Kelsen, 'On the Theory of Interpretation' (n 116) 128–29.

[123] Kelsen, *Introduction to the Problems of Legal Theory* (n 116) 80; Kelsen, 'On the Theory of Interpretation' (n 116) 129 (my emphasis).

[124] Kelsen, *Introduction to the Problems of Legal Theory* (n 116) 81; Kelsen, 'On the Theory of Interpretation' (n 116) 130; *cf* Chiassoni, 'Legal Science and Legal Interpretation in the Pure Theory of Law' (n 118) 69–71 on the distinction between cognitive and volitional interpretation.

134   *Towards a Unified Account of Discretion in Law*

delegating decision-making power to a lower authority, and this is true at every level of the *Stufenbaulehre*. Inside the frame, or that particular leeway delimited by the set of higher applicable norms, it is no longer a matter of cognition, but rather of will. Thus, in Kelsen's words:

> If 'interpretation' is understood as discovering the sense of the norm to be imple-
> mented, its result can only be the discovery of the frame that the norm to be
> interpreted represents and, within this frame, the cognition of several possibilities
> for implementation. Interpreting a statute, then, does not lead necessarily to a single
> decision as the only correct decision but possibly to several decisions, all of them of
> equal standing measured solely against the norm to be applied, even if only a single
> one of them becomes, in the act of the judicial decision, positive law. That a judicial
> decision is based on a statute means in truth only that the decision stays within the
> frame the statute represents, means only that the decision is one of the individual
> norms possible within the frame of the general norm, not that it is the only individual
> norm possible.[125]

To the extent that the choice among the several possible outcomes reading within the frame established by the general norm(s) is one of 'legal policy' rather than of 'legal theory' – one of will rather than of cognition[126] – Kelsen's position cannot be squared straightforwardly with cognitivism or scepticism. This is even more so since he draws no distinction, here, between the interpretation and application of a constitution by the legislature in enacting a statute, and the interpretation and application of a statute by the courts in adjudicating an individual case. The volitional element in the application of the law is unavoid-able and undermines the traditional picture, according to which, at least in some cases, the law can lead the interpreter to a single correct result solely by means of cognition. And yet:

> In terms of the positive law, there is simply no method according to which only one
> of the several reading of a norm could be distinguished as 'correct' – *assuming, of
> course, that several readings of the meaning of the norm are possible in the context
> of all other norms of the statute or of the legal system* ....[127]

That is, Kelsen seems to allow for the possibility that in some cases only one reading of a given norm formulation might be possible, but does not elaborate further. Rather, he specifies that once inside the frame there might still be some residual 'cognitive activity', but that points to the cognition of norms of morality that make their way into the law-making process through the formulation of norms (with expressions such as 'public interest', 'progress', and such).[128] Kelsen can be then located at the opposite pole from Dworkin: he supports, with the qualification just mentioned, a 'no-right-answer thesis' which leads him to label

---

[125] Kelsen, 'On the Theory of Interpretation' (n 116) 129–30.
[126] ibid 130–31.
[127] ibid 130 (my emphasis).
[128] ibid 131.

Discretion as a Pervasive Feature of Kelsen's Stufenbaulehre   135

the idea of legal certainty as an 'illusion'.[129] As such he also claims not only that 'creation of law is always application of law' – a claim consistent with the framework of a constitutional state in which all law must be traced back to the *Grundnorm* – but also the opposite and much more problematic assertion, that all law-application is also law-creation. As a result, 'every act is, normally, at the same time a law-creating and law-applying act', with the exception of two 'borderline' cases, that of the *Grundnorm* and that of the execution of the sanction (which amounts to the only pure law-application act in which no norm is created).[130]

What needs to be stressed is how his concept of 'legal norm' and his ideas about discretion are linked within the more general distinction between the creation and application of law. The cause lies in Kelsen's inclusion of individual prescriptions into the more general category of 'norms'. As such, he relativises the distinction between general and individual acts, but arguably because he confuses the two couples of general/concrete and general/individual.[131] For while the 'concreteness' of a norm is a matter of degree – so that at the lowest level of the *Stufenbaulehre* one will expect to find always more concrete norms, while the more general norms are usually to be found at the constitutional level – a norm 'is either individual or not'.[132] Hence his inclusion of individual prescriptions into the general category of norms is not a necessary product of the nomodynamic structure of the constitutional state, but rather a theoretical choice which is in need of justification.[133] Why his position is problematic should be clear: if every law-creating act is at least to some extent discretionary, and given that for Kelsen every act of law-application is also an act of norm-creation, then every legal act whatsoever is discretionary, and law in turn is pervasively indeterminate. But would anybody instinctively agree that the administrative officer issuing my birth certificate (or my driving licence) is not just applying, but also *making*, law?

To conclude, a few epistemic problems arise with Kelsen's concept of discretion. For instance, how is one supposed to make sense of his two rather contradictory claims, that until we are dealing with the 'frame' of the legal process, interpretation is cognitive and the law is able to narrow down the range of choices available to the decision-maker; but that once we are inside the frame, interpretation becomes eminently volitional and thus the decision-maker is substantively free to decide among different options? We need to remember that Kelsen is not substantiating this claim – as Hart does, at least in part – upon linguistic vagueness or the open-texture of norms, but rather upon the inability

---

[129] ibid 132.

[130] ibid 128; *cf* Kelsen, *General Theory of Law and State* (n 113) 133ff; Kelsen, *Introduction to the Problems of Legal Theory* (n 116) 77–78.

[131] Jakab, 'Problems of the Stufenbaulehre' (n 60) 46 (citing in particular Robert Walter– ibid, fn 46); *cf* L Ferrajoli, *Principia Iuris*, vol 1 (Bari, Laterza, 2007) 230–32.

[132] Jakab, 'Problems of the Stufenbaulehre' (n 60) 46.

[133] On this, see the extensive discussion in ch six of this book.

136 *Towards a Unified Account of Discretion in Law*

of law to provide constraints upon the appointed decision-maker beyond a certain point. It does not matter whether the law is determinate or not: what counts is that law-application can never be fully cognitive. This is true only in a trivial sense, in that in a modern legal system law is artificial and thus a product of will, before than of cognition. But it is not clear how the law is able to provide guidance only until the interpretive frame (but not 'beyond' it) if Kelsen does not assume an epistemological difference in the degrees of determinacy of legal norms.[134] Lastly, how does he ground the distinction between intended and unintended discretion? It seems that the only possibility is to elect 'intentional interpretation'[135] as the first and only valuable cognitive activity in the legal process, but this is openly denied by Kelsen when he says that once we are inside the frame,

> [f]rom the standpoint of the positive law, it is a matter of complete indifference whether one neglects the text in order to stick to the presumed will of the legislator or strictly observes the text in order to avoid worrying about the usually problematic will of the legislator.[136]

In short, Kelsen's idea of discretion as 'everything that is inside the frame' seems to raise more problems than it settles. We need thus to move forward to the next and last attempt examined here to put forward an analytical concept of discretion in jurisprudence.

V. DISCRETION AS BALANCING IN KLATT (AND ALEXY)

In a recent contribution, Matthias Klatt,[137] explicitly drawing upon the work of Alexy on constitutional rights and legal argumentation,[138] presents a comprehensive and original analysis of judicial discretion. Klatt's model constitutes the best possible way to conclude our survey on the concept of discretion in jurisprudence. This is for two reasons: 1) Klatt's sophisticated analysis sets a more robust path for the elaboration of an analytical concept of discretion, and 2) in doing so, we can also consider Alexy's stance on this issue.

---

[134] Flores, 'H. L. A. Hart's Moderate Indeterminacy Thesis Reconsidered' (n 19) 154–55 supports Kelsen's claim about what he calls 'epistemic indeterminacy', ie our inability to know whether a right answer exists, but argues that he is wrong in assuming 'systemic indeterminacy', 'ie that there is never a single answer following not from the legal statute itself but from the law and the legal system as such'; the same point seems to underpin Waluchow's distinction between having discretion and exercising discretion: Waluchow, 'Strong Discretion' (n 95).

[135] By intentional interpretation, I mean an interpretive stance that purports to find the intentions of the lawmaker as the true meaning of the law.

[136] Kelsen, 'On the Theory of Interpretation' (n 116) 130.

[137] Klatt, 'Taking Rights less Seriously' (n 4).

[138] See R Alexy, *A Theory of Constitutional Rights* (Oxford, Oxford University Press, 2002); R Alexy, 'On Balancing and Subsumption: A Structural Comparison' (2003) 16(4) *Ratio Juris* 433.

The first point to note is that Klatt sets himself on the right methodological track when he affirms that he is pursuing an 'analytical-normative' analysis, one that 'investigates the concept and the argumentation-theoretical construction of judicial discretion'.[139] He begins by considering the Hart-Dworkin debate on the point and by asserting the need, having identified the two positions as extremes on a spectrum, for a 'moderate view and a full picture' of judicial discretion.[140] This is achieved through the original claim that discretion not only 'has to be anchored in the system of weighing and balancing legal principles', but that rather [judicial] discretion is, in itself, a 'formal principle': a principle that 'does not give substantial answers to concrete legal problems, but states who is entitled to establish those answers'. Discretion, in this view, is co-extensive with 'competence'.[141] There are three possible scenarios as to the relationship between the law and legal institutions or officials (legislature, courts, etc), as seen in Figure 1 below:[142]

Figure 1 Klatt's three models of competence

In the first scenario, the purely procedural model, there are only formal and procedural constraints upon the decision-maker, so that she is substantively free – she is not 'commanded or prohibited' – to render any decision. In other words, her 'discretion is unlimited' when it comes to decide what the law is for the case at hand, insofar as he/she respects the procedural requirements prescribed by the law. Klatt assigns this view to radical sceptics, for whom the law is 'completely indeterminate' and adjudication is an arbitrary process disguised as a rational one. The second model, the purely substantive model, is Dworkin's, given that 'the law contains a command or prohibition in respect to every conceivable decision, leaving no room for discretion' upon the decision-maker.[143] Both of these models must be discarded. Only a moderate view like Hart's, in which some things can be commanded, some prohibited and some

---

[139] Rather than a sociological survey of the occurrences of discretion in the class of legal phenomena: Klatt, 'Taking Rights less Seriously' (n 4) 508.
[140] ibid 508–14. It is worth reminding the reader that Klatt writes before the discovery of Hart's lost essay.
[141] ibid 518.
[142] ibid 515–16.
[143] This is another way to depict the 'one-right-answer' thesis: ibid 515.

are neither, is able to fully account for the concept of judicial discretion. As as result (and as illustrated in Figure 2 below), Klatt singles out two different kinds of discretion:[144]

Figure 2 The different kinds of legal discretion in Klatt

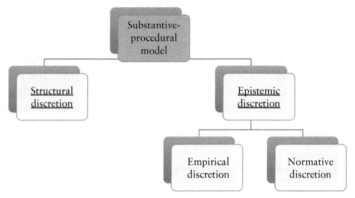

'Structural' discretion – in Alexy's terms[145] – corresponds to Dworkin's strong discretion, as the 'sphere of judicial freedom'[146] delimited by what the law neither commands nor prohibits.[147] 'Epistemic' discretion ensues instead from 'the limits of our capacity to know the limits of the law'.[148] One could call it *meta-discretion*.[149] The epistemological limits of our human nature concern both the realm of facts and the realm of law. Therefore, we have 'epistemic-empirical' discretion when the decision-maker is 'entitled to use uncertain empirical commitments in the internal justification of [her] judgment'. This is nothing but the capacity of any decision-maker to assume a set of historical or empirical facts as the material premise of her decision. More disputed is the idea of 'epistemic-normative' discretion, for decision-makers 'would be entitled to err on what the law, at the structural level, commands, prohibits, and permits, and still make legally correct decisions'.[150]

According to Klatt, the two kinds of epistemic discretion explain (or are explained by, I would say) the hierarchy of courts within any legal system,

---

[144] ibid 516–17.

[145] Alexy, *A Theory of Constitutional Rights* (n 138) 310.

[146] ibid 393.

[147] It also matches Kelsen's idea of the frame to be 'filled' by the decision-maker: Klatt, 'Taking Rights less Seriously' (n 4) 516, 522–23.

[148] This seems to amount to Dworkin's weak sense of discretion: ibid 524.

[149] ibid 524–25, when he defines normative epistemic discretion as a 'competence-competence'.

[150] ibid 517. In this sense the concrete limits on epistemic discretion are variable and set by competing material principles. In other words, there are limits to the competence of some decision-makers within the hierarchy of a certain legal system: ibid 523–24.

for lower courts usually have the final evaluation on matter of facts – and thus empirical discretion – that binds courts of higher instance; whereas the latter are entitled to review lower courts' decision on questions of law and therefore wield normative discretion. Ultimately, it seems that his concept of discretion dissolves into that of competence – both structural and epistemic – and this would 'explain the law-making power of judges'.[151] This is why discretion for Klatt (and Alexy) is a formal principle (like the principle of democracy or the separation of powers)[152] to be weighed against other formal and substantive principles in what he calls the 'balancing model of discretion'.[153] Two scenarios are conceivable of when discretion is at stake in this model.

Figure 3 First scenario of the balancing model of discretion

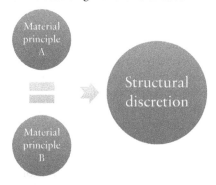

In the first scenario (as illustrated above), when two material principles (ie two substantive constitutional rights) compete with each other but eventually bear the same 'weight', we find what Alexy calls a 'stalemate-case', in other words 'a case in which there is structural discretion because the law neither commands nor prohibits following either of the two conflicting principles'.[154]

In the second scenario, the formal principle of (epistemic) discretion is not the result of the balancing procedure, but rather its object. It is only a prima facie discretion, and two outcomes are foreseeable: if the material principle outweighs epistemic discretion in the concrete case, then the decision-maker has no 'definite' epistemic discretion for limiting that material principle, or vice versa.[155]

---

[151] ibid 518.
[152] Alexy, *A Theory of Constitutional Rights* (n 138) 82.
[153] Klatt, 'Taking Rights less Seriously' (n 4) 518.
[154] ibid 519.
[155] Alexy, *A Theory of Constitutional Rights* (n 138) 313, 414–17.

Figure 4 Second scenario of the balancing model of discretion

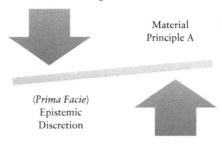

Two observations follow: not only do we have to distinguish between structural and epistemic – both empirical and normative – discretion, but also between prima facie and 'definite' discretion. If this is so, we cannot know the extent of discretion the decision-maker is entitled to until that very process of balancing and weighting has been carried out by the decision-maker herself. Klatt refers to it as a 'procedural or discursive model of discretion':[156] a model that is dynamic in character because it is 'the discourse itself' that 'identifies what is legally permitted and what is forbidden' and therefore 'fixes the scope of judicial discretion';[157] and this would be confirmed by the epistemic 'Law of Balancing' as formulated by Alexy.[158]

Both authors are aware of the most relevant problem with this model, that of the relationship between normative epistemic discretion and structural discretion: for the former seems to dissolve the limits on the latter.[159] To the extent that they have the discretion to decide what the law commands or prohibits, it seems contradictory to affirm that decision-makers are bound by what the law commands or prohibits. Not only would the two different kinds of discretion conflate but, even worse, there would be no such thing as structural discretion in the end, and so law would provide no guidance to decision-makers, confirming the radical indeterminacy thesis. Klatt nonetheless defends this 'discretion-separability' thesis with a three-step argument, which ultimately rests on what he calls the 'thesis of the necessary incorporation of normative-epistemically clear cases';[160] that is, it rests on the claim that we can assume that in each legal system there are such cases.[161]

---

[156] Klatt, 'Taking Rights less Seriously' (n 4) 519.
[157] ibid 522.
[158] 'The more heavily interference in a constitutional right weighs, the greater must be the certainty of its underlying premises': Alexy, *A Theory of Constitutional Rights* (n 138) 418. What Alexy defines as the 'substantive' law of balancing Klatt defines as the 'structural' law of balancing.
[159] ibid 420; Klatt, 'Taking Rights less Seriously' (n 4) 524–26.
[160] Klatt, 'Taking Rights less Seriously' (n 4) 526.
[161] Cases in which it is clear what the law commands or prohibits (or neither), so that the decision-maker discretion is bound by the law: ibid 524.

Overall, Klatt's argument is an elegant and illuminating contribution to our understanding of the concept of discretion in law, particularly as it underscores the important distinction between structural and epistemic discretion. At the same time, it is based upon, and developed through, some assumptions which are theoretically problematic, prompting doubts as to its viability on the whole.[162] Two kinds of criticisms, a theoretical and a meta-theoretical one, can be raised. As to the former, Klatt's defends the possibility – practical and not just theoretical – of the separation between structural and normative epistemic discretion. What strikes me about his argument is that, after having explained the necessity to single out the criteria for this separability, he substantiates these criteria in the 'clear-cases-necessary-incorporation-thesis', according to which, given that we can assume the existence of such clear cases in historical legal systems, then these cases are 'constructively possible'[163] and would prove the possibility of the separation between structural and epistemic discretion. But the existence of such easy cases is precisely what sceptics deny, and so their existence should be demonstrated, rather than assumed.

In other words, his whole argument is premised on the empirical assumption of the existence of those cases – easy cases – which should be theoretically identified as a consequence of his model. This seems to beg the question, and it is even more striking if we consider the high level of theoretical sophistication of Klatt's whole argument and the fact that he acknowledges readily that this step is not an 'analytical ..., but a descriptive one'.[164] Klatt's move here seems circular, and it undermines the whole theoretical construction of the 'discretion-separability' thesis. This means that, as we noted above, normative epistemic discretion appears to phagocytise structural discretion – as it would not make sense to say that courts are bound by what the law commands or prohibits, if the courts have (normative epistemic) discretion to determine what the law commands or prohibits because their decision is final.

To put it differently, Klatt seems to be inadvertently endorsing Dworkin's sense of discretion as finality. This implies that the limits upon discretion could only be identified on an ex post and case-by-case basis: but how can this be considered as an analytical model of discretion?[165] For we could equally say, echoing a realist approach, that discretion is what the higher courts within the system deem it to be, with the result that we could have an idea of what discretion is only through 'empirical or legal-sociological' approaches (which Klatt instead sets aside at the beginning of his contribution).[166]

---

[162] See also Kelsen's critical considerations on the 'principle of the so-called balancing of interest': Kelsen, 'On the Theory of Interpretation' (n 116) 130–31.

[163] Klatt, 'Taking Rights less Seriously' (n 4) 526.

[164] ibid 527.

[165] The very idea of normative epistemic discretion presupposes that there is something out there – objectively identifiable – about what the law says or commands. But this objectivity remains rather presupposed in the context of his argument.

[166] ibid 508.

142 *Towards a Unified Account of Discretion in Law*

Finally, on the meta-theoretical level, this account of discretion is based upon a 'specific legal method',[167] that of the balancing and weighing of principles, which in turn rests on a very contentious jurisprudential position: the thesis of the ontological or strong distinction between rules and principles.[168] Without the space to dwell here on such a debate, one can reasonably wonder about the general relevance of an analytical concept of discretion that is so deeply rooted in a particular and thoroughly challenged theoretical stance. This is why it is even more unfortunate that Klatt does not consider discretion in the domain of the 'interpretation of rules', but apodictically maintains there is a structural similarity between discretion in the balancing of principles and discretion in the interpretation of rules, to the extent that 'the two theories complement and enforce one another, if not culminating into a general and coherent theory of law'.[169] This is all but self-explanatory.[170]

This leads us to the end of the first part of this chapter. Our survey of influential accounts of discretion in jurisprudence presents us with a fuzzy picture in which the concept of discretion in law is far from clear. This might be (partially, at least) explained by pragmatic differences in legal traditions, eg the different role of courts in civil and common law systems. It is also noteworthy that all the accounts examined thus far seem to focus primarily, if not exclusively, on judicial discretion, whereby the empirical fact of the finality of the decisions of some courts 'muddies the waters' even more. Therefore, my suggestion is that we turn to the concept of discretion in the administrative law domain, where those pragmatic differences that seem to affect jurisprudential accounts of (judicial) discretion – as well as the issue of the finality of decisions – might thin out. This should allow us to have a clearer idea of the core of the concept and pave the way towards a unified account of discretion.

VI. THE HISTORY OF DISCRETION IN THE ADMINISTRATIVE DOMAIN

The theoretical elaboration of discretion in the administrative domain lies at the very core of the rise of the 'administrative state', and of administrative law as a discipline, over the last two and a half centuries.[171] This path

---

[167] ibid 520. For an endorsement of Alexy's model of balancing, and for its application in order to provide a formal model of administrative discretion: PLM Lucatuorto, 'Reasonableness in Administrative Discretion: A Formal Model' (2010) 8 *The Journal Jurisprudence* 633.

[168] See, eg: L Ferrajoli, *La Democrazia Attraverso i Diritti: Il Costituzionalismo Garantista come Modello Teorico e come Progetto Politico* (Bari, Laterza, 2013) 110ff.

[169] Klatt, 'Taking Rights less Seriously' (n 4) 521.

[170] F Schauer, 'Balancing, Subsumption, and the Constraining Role of Legal Text' in M Klatt (ed), *Institutionalized Reason: The Jurisprudence of Robert Alexy* (Oxford, Oxford University Press, 2012).

[171] *cf* Sordi, 'Rèvolution, Rechtsstaat and the Rule of Law' (n 5) 23 for the necessary qualification of the relationship between the rise of the administrative state and that of administrative law; see also C Fraenkel-Haeberle, *Giurisdizione sul Silenzio e Discrezionalità Amministrativa: Germania, Austria, Italia* (Trento, Università degli studi di Trento, 2004) 9.

The History of Discretion in the Administrative Domain   143

follows two conflicting trajectories, at least on the continent: an expansive and a contracting one.[172] Initially, the area of discretion represents the necessary extent of power of the public administration in shaping and pursuing the public interest in all those areas in which the 'State island' had progressively taken on the tasks previously held by private corporations and royal bureaucracies.[173] As such, in the passage from the *ancient régime* to the post-revolutionary Europe,

> [t]he State stood over the society. And in that 'State island' which instituted and regulated the entire social fabric, administrative power became the central axis of the government of the territory. ... Modernity henceforth had the unmistakable seal of administration.[174]

This passage was not homogeneous among European nation-states, being of course revolutionary in France and evolutionary in Prussia and Austria[175] – with Italy somewhere in between because of its fragmented institutional structure at the time.[176] What remained constant throughout was the unfolding of discretionary administrative power, already clearly separated from justice,[177] as the means to govern the progressively more and more complex society of the nineteenth and twentieth centuries. This need for regulative freedom was triggered by the industrial revolution, where most aspects of everyday life underwent dramatic changes. The state – identified now with and by that very centralised administrative structure – needed to deal with all of them. At the same time, this centralised accumulation of far-reaching powers, and their insulation from the other functions of the state – legislative and judicial – begins to represent a major cause for concern in political and legal theory. As famously put by Woodrow Wilson: 'liberty depends incomparably more upon administration than upon constitution'.[178] Thus, at the very moment in which administrative power reaches its climax in terms of autonomy and freedom,[179] it also faces the progressive appearance of the *Rechtsstaat* – or *Stato di diritto*, or *État de droit*, or *Estado de derecho* – as theorised first by the German doctrine and soon after in most of western Europe.[180] This doctrine

> sought to reconcile the 'freedom of the State' with that of the citizen; it attempted to make the primacy of the administration compatible with the respect for individual

---

[172] In this sense we can assume that countries such as Germany, Austria, Italy, France, Spain and Portugal are similar to a sensible extent: J Schwarze, *European Administrative Law*, 2nd edn (London, Sweet & Maxwell, 2006) 208.

[173] Sordi, 'Rèvolution, Rechtsstaat and the Rule of Law (n 5) 26.

[174] ibid 27.

[175] So that '*Verwaltungsrecht* in Germany did not appear until well into the nineteenth century': ibid 24.

[176] ibid, *passim.*

[177] ibid *passim.*

[178] W Wilson, 'The Study of Administration' (1887) 2(2) *Political Science Quarterly* 197, 211.

[179] Schwarze, *European Administrative Law* (n 172) 207–08.

[180] On the *Rechtsstaat*, see, eg: ibid 207–11; Sordi 'Rèvolution, Rechtsstaat and the Rule of Law (n 5); P Costa and D Zolo (eds), *The Rule of Law: History, Theory and Criticism* (Dordrecht, Springer, 2007).

144   Towards a Unified Account of Discretion in Law

guarantees. It reflected the broadly accepted idea that power and freedom developed symbiotically.[181]

At the core of this doctrine is the principle of legality,[182] which had already become the paradigm of public law in pre-war Europe.[183] 'Regardless of the name it is given or the form it takes', it requires that 'the powers of the state are limited in ... by law, for the purpose of protecting civil liberties'.[184] It is the product of a specific understanding of the separation of powers doctrine, according to which the government can exercise law-making functions only within those spaces that either the constitutional text, directly, or the legislator, by means of its enactments, have established.[185]

From a functional point of view, the principle is two-fold: on the one hand, it bestows government and administrative authorities with democratic legitimacy, so that every limitation upon people's liberties and rights can be traced back, at least indirectly, to their will.[186] It represents a delegation of law-making powers to the unelected administration while upholding the social contract as the metaphorical foundation of the political institution. On the other, by establishing normative criteria for the exercise of administrative decision-making, the principle of legality becomes the epistemological paradigm of judicial review or 'administrative justice', as it provides courts with a blueprint of how administrative powers ought to be exercised.[187] The principle of legality thus encompasses both kinds of control upon administrative power, the one ex ante by the legislature and the one ex post by the courts, linking them semantically through the text of statutes and secondary legislative instruments.

Interestingly, administrative discretionary power resisted to some extent this process of legalisation: partly because of the still eminently formal or procedural nature of the principle of legality throughout the nineteenth and the first half of the twentieth centuries; and partly for the self-referentiality of the administrative machinery, which had properly blossomed into bureaucracy in the meantime,[188] that was facilitated by the still limited extent of judicial review by administrative courts and tribunals. The weakness, in particular, of a merely formal or procedural principle of legality created the normative space for the exploitation of administrative discretionary power, a phenomenon which contributed to the

---

[181] Sordi 'Rèvolution, Rechtsstaat and the Rule of Law' (n 5) 29.

[182] For an extensive discussion of the principle of legality, see ch 6, section V.

[183] Schwarze, *European Administrative Law* (n 172) 212–32.

[184] ibid 230–31.

[185] Fraenkel-Haeberle, *Giurisdizione sul Silenzio e Discrezionalità Amministrativa* (n 171) 23; Sordi 'Rèvolution, Rechtsstaat and the Rule of Law' (n 5) 32.

[186] Schwarze, *European Administrative Law* (n 172) 215.

[187] It is worth noticing that, if administration and justice had been split into two separate functions, the movement towards 'administrative justice' (*Giustizia nell'amministrazione*, as famously put in Italy by Silvio Spaventa) sought precisely to bridge their normative (and institutional) gap again.

[188] On bureaucracy, see at least M Weber, *Economy and Society: An Outline of Interpretive Sociology*, 4th edn, vol 2 (G Roth and C Wittich eds, Berkeley, University of California Press, 1978) ch 11.

darkest period of modern European history. For one of the recurring characteristics of totalitarian regimes which ruled throughout Europe during the first half of twentieth century was precisely the high degree of discretion with which administrative authorities and officials of the regime were entrusted.[189]

These discretionary decisions involved the most basic rights, from freedom of movement, thought and speech, to property rights, and against them there were no effective legal remedies. It is thus easy to see how the distinction between lawful and unlawful became blurred under these regimes, and why the result of this dramatic historical experience was, at least in continental Europe, a great degree of distrust towards the very concept of 'administrative discretion'.[190] The dangers of broad administrative discretionary powers were still so vivid, for instance, to the Italian constituent mothers and fathers that they specifically provided within the Constitution itself that under no circumstances an administrative decision could not be subjected to judicial review.[191] The combination of these two factors, historically motivated distrust of broad discretionary powers on the one hand, and the establishment of a substantive principle of legality (on the continent) as the paradigm of the modern constitutional state on the other, resulted in the objectification of administrative law that put the administrative decision (or act) at the core of administrative law.

As we shall see, this brief account of the historical evolution of the concept of administrative discretion on the European continent explains some of the differences with how the same concept has been elaborated in England, while at the same time providing the background context that will allows us to highlight the shared theorical elements between the two traditions. Let us now turn to a more detailed consideration of the concept in the relevant specific jurisdictions: Germany, France, Italy and England.

VII. ADMINISTRATIVE DISCRETION IN GERMANY

German administrative law scholarship is paradigmatic in its theoretical consideration of administrative discretion. This is certainly due to the historical reasons mentioned above, but it also reflects the distinguished attitude for analytical sophistication of German legal scholarship as a whole. The result is a marked emphasis on the semantic dimension of administrative discretionary activity, and a rigid formalisation of discretion: for administrative activity

---

[189] cf Schwarze, *European Administrative Law* (n 172) 134, 271; M Forowicz, 'State Discretion as a Paradox of EU Evolution' (2011) EUI Working Paper 11/2011 htpps://cadmus.eui.eu/handle/1814/18835 accessed 14 July 2012, 5.

[190] Y Arai-Takahashi, 'Discretion in German Administrative Law: Doctrinal Discourse Revisited' (2001) 6(1) *European Public Law* 69, 78; Schwarze, *European Administrative Law* (n 172) 271.

[191] Article 113 of the Italian Constitution; cf with the example from Art 35(1) of the South African Constitution as quoted by Schauer, *Thinking Like a Lawyer* (n 42) 192.

is customarily broken down into a tripartite process, whose components are theoretically neatly kept apart (as illustrated in Figure 5 below).[192]

Figure 5 The tripartite formalisation of administrative activity in German scholarship

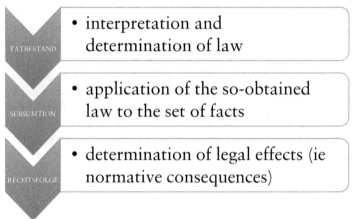

Tatbestand amounts to the determination of the major normative premise of the legal syllogism – once the facts of the case have already been established (*Sachverhaltsfeststellung*). *Subsumtion* pertains to the application of this normative premise to the facts of the case. *Rechtsfolge*, finally, is the moment in which the conclusion of the legal syllogism is drawn, ie in which the decision-maker establishes the legal effects of her decision. According to established doctrine and case law, discretion (*Ermessen*), the power to assume autonomous determinations in the process of the application of a general and abstract norm,[193] can occur only at the last stage of the process, that of *Rechtsfolge*. This is because the first two steps, the determination of the law and the application of the law to the facts, are considered to be 'a cognitive exercise receptive to an objective review', while 'the exercise of discretion is a value-laden action taking into account legal purposes and consequences'.[194]

As such, German courts have two different extents of review of administrative action: unlimited vis-à-vis *Tatbestand* and *Subsumtion*, but not so towards *Rechtsfolge*. The courts will substitute their own decision with the one taken by the administrative decision-maker – if the latter is deemed mistaken – as to the first two steps of the process, while the presence of

---

[192] The following analysis is based upon: Arai-Takahashi, 'Discretion in German Administrative Law' (n 190); Fraenkel-Haeberle, *Giurisdizione sul Silenzio e Discrezionalità Amministrativa* (n 171) ch 1; Schwarze, *European Administrative Law* (n 172).

[193] Fraenkel-Haeberle, *Giurisdizione sul Silenzio e Discrezionalità Amministrativa* (n 171) 14.

[194] Arai-Takahashi, 'Discretion in German Administrative Law' (n 190) 74.

Administrative Discretion in Germany 147

discretion in *Rechtsfolge* implies a margin of appraisal, upon the original decision-maker, vis-à-vis the determination of the actual legal effects of the decision (*Rechtsfolgenbestimmung*). In this last step, all those determinations by the administrative authority which are within the boundaries established by the relevant normative provisions are considered equally legitimate and therefore valid.[195] Yet, the margin of review by the courts is not fixed and varies depending on several factors, which leaves the courts always able to ascertain any wrongful use of discretion (*Ermessensfehler*).[196] This means that discretion can be used in deciding whether to establish a certain normative consequence at all – the *an* of the decision (*Entschließungsermessen*)[197] – or in choosing one among several equally 'lawful decisions suitable for achieving the same legal consequence (*Auswahlermessen*).[198]

A distinctive feature of continental administrative law is the nexus between the recognition of this normative discretion upon the administrative decision-maker and the corresponding position of the individual impacted by the administrative decision. German law is no exception, for where discretion is granted to the administrative authority, the individual has no right to see his or her claim satisfied by the court, but only holds a 'claim to a correct exercise of discretion' (*Anspruch auf ermessensfehlerfreie Verwaltungsentscheidung*).[199] This implies that in this situation the review performed by the courts will be of a negative kind. The courts will look for potential 'vices' of [the use of] discretion – eg if too much or too little discretion has been exercised as opposed to the original delegation of decision-making power by the legislature – and in this case they will quash the decision; but they will not themselves assume that determination, as this would violate the separation of powers doctrine.

Peculiar to German administrative law is instead the fact that 'discretion is allowed to an administrative agency only where this is expressly provided in law'.[200] This express delegation of normative power is semantic through the use

---

[195] This clearly echoes Kelsen's idea of discretion as everything that is inside the normative frame: see Fraenkel-Haeberle, *Giurisdizione sul Silenzio e Discrezionalità Amministrativa* (n 171) 13–14 on the distinction between internal and external barriers (*äußere und innere Schranken*).

[196] Arai-Takahashi, 'Discretion in German Administrative Law' (n 190) 74; Fraenkel-Haeberle, *Giurisdizione sul Silenzio e Discrezionalità Amministrativa* (n 171) 14.

[197] Fraenkel-Haeberle, *Giurisdizione sul Silenzio e Discrezionalità Amministrativa* (n 171) 14.

[198] Arai-Takahashi, 'Discretion in German Administrative Law' (n 190) 74.

[199] This latter claim is defined as 'formal right', whereas when there is no discretion – and thus the extent of review by administrative courts is fullest – the individual has a 'substantial right' to the particular good or utility or (normative) situation she aspires to: Fraenkel-Haeberle, *Giurisdizione sul Silenzio e Discrezionalità Amministrativa* (n 171) 35–38.

[200] Arai-Takahashi, 'Discretion in German Administrative Law' (n 190) 70. Here we witness the historical distrust towards discretionary powers at its apex. In other European countries, 'the courts recognise discretion not only when it is expressly provided for but also where certain general and imprecise norms are at issue whose application requires expert knowledge or demands the assessment of complex sets of facts or the prognosis of future developments': Forowicz, 'State Discretion as a Paradox of EU Evolution' (n 189) 5; see also Fraenkel-Haeberle, *Giurisdizione sul Silenzio e Discrezionalità Amministrativa* (n 171) 14–15.

148 *Towards a Unified Account of Discretion in Law*

in the text of statutes and secondary legislation of operators such as 'can' and 'may';[201] but it is also ascertainable by considering the ratio (and the structure) of the norms itself.[202] The result of such rigidity is two-fold: the enforcement of a strict version of the principle of legality by the courts,[203] which in turn implies a clear responsibility on part of the legislature to

> prescribe requirements and conditions for administrative action in the society as clearly and thoroughly as possible in order to avoid courts nullifying administrative decisions for lack of authorization for their discretion.[204]

This sets a stable semantic criterion to distinguish between discretionary activity and what can be called 'bound activity',[205] and between the different extents of review exercised by courts. Straddling these kinds of review are the so-called 'indefinite legal concepts' (*unbestimmte Rechtsbegriffe*).[206] Examples are general clauses like 'public interest', 'environmentally harmful effect' or 'decency' which, despite their apparent vagueness, are traditionally considered as part of the *Tatbestand* by the courts, and thus apt for cognitive review.

This means that for German courts – both the Federal Administrative Court and the Federal Constitutional Court – there is something like an objective notion of 'public interest' for instance, and it is up to them to enforce this *objective* notion every time an administrative authority departs from it in their determinations.[207] This stance is criticised in the literature, where one can often find a mitigation of the rigidity of the one-right-answer thesis in the *Tatbestand*.[208] I am referring to the doctrine of the margin of appraisal or evaluation in the determination and application of indefinite legal concepts (*Beurteilungsspielraum*),[209] which

---

[201] Schwarze, *European Administrative Law* (n 172) 272–73, where these expressions are defined as 'code-words'.

[202] Fraenkel-Haeberle, *Giurisdizione sul Silenzio e Discrezionalità Amministrativa* (n 171) 14–15.

[203] ibid 22–24.

[204] Arai-Takahashi, 'Discretion in German Administrative Law' (n 190) 70. But see, on the progressive (although ultimately limited) loosening of such rigid requirement towards the legislature: Fraenkel-Haeberle, *Giurisdizione sul Silenzio e Discrezionalità Amministrativa* (n 171) 22–24.

[205] This *bound* activity is what the French would term 'pouvoir lié', translated by Schwarze as 'tied authority': Schwarze, *European Administrative Law* (n 172) 262.

[206] Arai-Takahashi, 'Discretion in German Administrative Law' (n 190) 75–77; Fraenkel-Haeberle, *Giurisdizione sul Silenzio e Discrezionalità Amministrativa* (n 171) 15–22; Schwarze, *European Administrative Law* (n 172) 271–72.

[207] There is a very famous exception – in 1971 – to this consolidated line of case-law, in which the Federal Administrative Court (*Bundesverwaltungsgericht*) 'itself admitted that a concept allowing only one correct decision was a sheer fiction': Arai-Takahashi, 'Discretion in German Administrative Law' (n 190) 76. Some more particular cases in which the Federal Administrative Court has not fully encroached on normative determinations by administrative decision-makers can be found in Fraenkel-Haeberle, *Giurisdizione sul Silenzio e Discrezionalità Amministrativa* (n 171) 25–33.

[208] Fraenkel-Haeberle, *Giurisdizione sul Silenzio e Discrezionalità Amministrativa* (n 171) 19–22.

[209] Arai–Takahashi, 'Discretion in German Administrative Law' (n 190) 75–77.

would prevent, at least to some extent, administrative courts from encroaching on such determinations.[210] In this doctrine, these indefinite legal concepts act as 'delegating concepts', which require 'the administrative authorities to clarify the "normative programme" implicitly intended by the legislature'.[211] As such, they cannot have only one 'right' meaning, as the determination of that very meaning (among the many potentially available) is delegated by the legislature to the administrative authority – and so the court should not interfere with this determination.

VIII. DISCRETION IN THE FRENCH-ITALIAN ADMINISTRATIVE TRADITION

There are good reasons, in this brief *excursus* on the continental conceptualisation of administrative discretion, to put together French and Italian administrative law. The influence of the former on the latter is well-known, to the extent that most of the basic institutions and principles of the two systems are very similar.[212] The Italian *Consiglio di Stato*, the highest administrative court of the land, was explicitly created and modelled after the French *Conseil d'État*, and this reflexively shaped administrative law in both jurisdictions according to their case-law in similar ways.[213] Both courts have played a fundamental role in developing administrative law in their respective legal systems by means of a creative judicial stance which, despite being hard to reconcile with the separation of powers doctrine,[214] has become their distinctive mark.[215] One of the most important ways in which both courts have built their creative judicial role is the review of administrative discretionary powers through the

---

[210] ibid 76. Arai-Takahashi assumes the *Beurteilungsspielraum* to be a necessary feature of the delegation of powers from the legislature to administrative agents, as a way to counterbalance the otherwise excessive rigidity of such delegation which would prevent the delegated decision-maker from pursuing a 'proper balance of interests' in concrete situations. See also Schwarze, *European Administrative Law* (n 172) 273–75, who exposes the limits of the rigid model of review adopted by German administrative courts, arguing that such a system, after all, can run against the objective of securing the utmost degree of legal security and justice to the citizens. However, he continues, the approach is too deep-rooted into the current practice of courts for something to be changing, at least 'in the immediate future'. For an exhaustive list of all the several ramifications of the *Beurteilungsspielraum*: Fraenkel-Haeberle, *Giurisdizione sul Silenzio e Discrezionalità Amministrativa* (n 171) 15–22.

[211] Arai-Takahashi, 'Discretion in German Administrative Law' (n 190) 77.

[212] Schwarze, *European Administrative Law* (n 172) *passim*.

[213] LN Brown and JS Bell, *French Administrative Law*, 4th edn (Oxford, Oxford University Press, 1993) 257.

[214] In point of fact, both courts are not easy reconcilable to the separation of powers doctrine already from the institutional point of view. They were both initially created as 'advice bodies', and only later developed their judicial functions.

[215] Schwarze, *European Administrative Law* (n 172) 100–107.

150 Towards a Unified Account of Discretion in Law

action for abuse of [discretionary] power (*excès de pouvoir/eccesso di potere*). What matters for us is the amount of theoretical work done by administrative scholars in both jurisdictions on the concept of discretion.[216]

In this regard, the core of the concept lies in the modern version of the principle of legality, which represents at the same time the legitimation and the limits of administrative power (as in the German tradition). It has been characterised as 'a functionalised choice since the administration's discretional power has a series of internal limits for the achievement and the satisfaction of social needs'.[217] Thus, we could say that the space of discretion is the space left available by the letter of the law.[218] A distinction is thus drawn between '*competence liée*' ('*attività vincolata*') and '*pouvoir discrétionnaire*' ('*attività discrezionale*').[219] In the former, the public authority has an obligation to perform an action *x* in the presence of some (operative) conditions, and therefore 'the agent cannot but verify the existence of those conditions, and if this is case, her course of action is entirely dictated [by the norm]'.[220]

As a result, 'The competence of the agent is bound: the law does not leave any room to his freedom [of choice]'.[221] The latter constitutes instead a delegation of power to autonomously establish some, but not all, aspects of the decision to be made.[222] Here, the volitional element prevails over the cognitive element: several identifiable and equally legitimate decisions are before the decision-maker, but within this cognitive space she has a protected choice as to what constitutes the 'best' – not the 'right' – decision. This 'space' is that of the *merits* of the administrative act, considered the proper space of administration and therefore unreviewable by the courts.[223] For this space is constituted by standards (political, economical, and such) that are not strictly juridical and which must lie outside the courts' jurisdiction if the separation of powers doctrine and the principle of legality are to be respected.[224]

This space of unreviewable choice is, however, encompassed by constraints and limits established by legislation and by the case law of the administrative

---

[216] *cf* FG Scoca, 'La Discrezionalità nel Pensiero di Giannini e nella Dottrina Successiva' (2000) 50(4) *Rivista Trimestrale di Diritto Pubblico* 1045.

[217] Lucatuorto, 'Reasonableness in Administrative Discretion' (n 167) 634.

[218] Although in both jurisdictions the semantic criterion to distinguish discretionary activity from the rest is looser than in Germany, and thus more debatable even between first-tier and superior courts: Fraenkel-Haeberle, *Giurisdizione sul Silenzio e Discrezionalità Amministrativa* (n 171) 60.

[219] J Waline and J Rivero, *Droit administratif*, 19th edn (Paris, Dalloz, 2002) 81–83.

[220] ibid 81 ('*l'agent ne peut que verifier l'existence de ces conditions: dès qu'il en constate la réunion, son comportement lui est entièrement dicté*').

[221] ibid 82 ('*[l]a competence de l'agent est liée: la loi ne laisse aucune place à sa liberté*').

[222] In other words, a fully discretionary power – as to the *an* and the *quid* of the decision – free from judicial control is not deemed compatible any more with the principle of legality: ibid 82–83; Fraenkel-Haeberle, *Giurisdizione sul Silenzio e Discrezionalità Amministrativa* (n 171) 46.

[223] Schwarze, *European Administrative Law* (n 172) 279–80; see also GE Treves, 'Administrative Discretion and Judicial Control' (1947) 10(3) *Modern Law Review* 276.

[224] Fraenkel-Haeberle, *Giurisdizione sul Silenzio e Discrezionalità Amministrativa* (n 171) 49.

Discretion in the French-Italian Administrative Tradition 151

Figure 6 The legitimacy review in the French-Italian administrative tradition

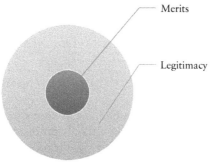

courts, as illustrated in Figure 6 above. These limits constitute the basis for the limited review – termed 'legitimacy review' (*'giudizio di legittimità'*) – of discretionary powers exercised by the courts. Among these constraints, against which the administrative judge weighs the exercise of the discretion by the administrative authority, there are reasonableness, consistency, and coherence standards, plus the thorough ascertainment of the full range of interests entangled in the decision.[225] If these limits are satisfied, then the exercise of administrative discretion – the choice made by the decision-maker among the options available – is legitimate and thus the individual has no remedies against it, even if the decision encroaches negatively upon her rights and interests. But what is this choice about?

Italian scholarship further refines the concept of discretion as the *protected* space of decision-making of the administration:[226] 'the comparative weighting of several secondary interests vis-à-vis [the satisfaction of] a primary interest'.[227] This primary interest is the public interest, as the sum of all the aims and values (health, environment, security, efficiency and such) the enforcement and realisation of which the public administration is committed to. Secondary are all the other (private, collective, etc) interests which happen to intersect with the public interest in a concrete sense.[228] The standards governing this activity of ranking and weighting interests are not fixed, but are established by the decision-maker herself. Therefore, discretion does not belong to the realm of interpretation, but consists in a volitional activity on the part of an authority whose normative outcome possesses an original – or *juris-generative* – character not retrievable

---

[225] ibid.
[226] Scoca, 'La Discrezionalità nel Pensiero di Giannini e nella Dottrina Successiva' (n 216).
[227] MS Giannini, *Diritto Amministrativo*, 3rd edn (Milan, Giuffrè, 1993) 49 (my translation); Lucatuorto, 'Reasonableness in Administrative Discretion' (n 167) 639.
[228] It is worth stressing how this distinction has been progressively relativised: Scoca, 'La Discrezionalità nel Pensiero di Giannini e nella Dottrina Successiva' (n 216) *passim*.

152 *Towards a Unified Account of Discretion in Law*

in a mere interpretive activity.[229] This means that discretionary activity, or better the evaluation processes it is constituted by, cannot be considered a question of law, but rather a question of fact as to the best way to pursue the public interest.[230]

IX. THE CONCEPT OF DISCRETION IN ENGLISH ADMINISTRATIVE LAW

As with many topics in English public law, it seems impossible not to start with a consideration of Dicey's work: not only for historical reasons, but also because Dicey's legacy has undergone a significant process of critical review as to the topic of discretion. The traditional notion is that Dicey distrusted administrative discretionary power, like everything that was deemed to be connected to the continental (and particularly French) idea of public law as a special regime, different from the law of private relationships.[231] Whether this was truly the case is questionable: for if one contextualises Dicey's opposition between the 'personal freedoms enjoyed in the United Kingdom' and the possibility, in countries like the France of the eighteenth century, for people to be deprived of their liberty by means of uncontrolled administrative discretionary decisions, his 'distrust' appears of a more limited scope.[232]

Dicey more likely then only refers to a broad kind of administrative discretionary power which encroaches without limits on people's basic freedoms.[233] Nevertheless, 'the notion that he thought that all discretionary power was bad took root'.[234] But recent historical analysis has found that 'suspicion of administrative discretion is more a contemporary than a Victorian phenomenon',[235] for discretionary powers were consistently delegated to judicial and non-judicial bodies long before Dicey wrote. One must notice, however, how in England an autonomous bureaucratic body we can call 'administration' did not develop as it did on the continent, and thus the problem was not 'discretion' per se. How could it have been, in a system where a 'wide' discretion is a structural characteristic of the judicial function itself?[236] The problem, rather, lay in the

---

[229] MS Giannini, *Il Potere Discrezionale della Pubblica Amministrazione: Concetto e Problemi* (Milan, Giuffrè, 1939) 68–98; *cf* Fraenkel-Haeberle, *Giurisdizione sul Silenzio e Discrezionalità Amministrativa* (n 171) 60.

[230] Scoca, 'La Discrezionalità nel Pensiero di Giannini e nella Dottrina Successiva' (n 216).

[231] Sordi 'Rèvolution, Rechtsstaat and the Rule of Law (n 5) 33.

[232] T Daintith, 'Contractual Discretion and Administrative Discretion: A Unified Analysis' (2005) 68(4) *Modern Law Review* 554, 557–58, quoting AV Dicey, *Introduction to the Study of the Law of the Constitution,* 8th edn (London, Macmillan, 1915) 183–84.

[233] Schauer, *Thinking Like a Lawyer* (n 42) 192.

[234] Daintith, 'Contractual Discretion and Administrative Discretion' (n 232) 558; *cf* Sordi 'Rèvolution, Rechtsstaat and the Rule of Law (n 5) 31–35.

[235] Daintith, 'Contractual Discretion and Administrative Discretion' (n 232) 565.

[236] ibid 559 (and see the citations at fn 28).

The Concept of Discretion in English Administrative Law   153

progressive tendency to delegate increasingly more discretionary powers to non-judicial bodies.[237] This also explains how judicial review of the functions exercised by these bodies soon became the very core of English administrative law.[238] If we look closely at the decisions by the senior judiciary, 'the general tone is one of respect for the honesty and competence of those entrusted by Parliament with discretionary powers'[239] and so 'Overall, the discretion granted to administrative authorities under English law is wider than that granted in other European states'.[240] A two-fold attitude can be observed then:

> On the one hand, where Parliament confers power upon some minister or other authority to be used in discretion, it is obvious that the discretion ought to be that of the designated authority and not that of the court. Whether the discretion is exercised prudently or imprudently, the authority's word is to be law and the remedy is to be political only. On the other hand, Parliament cannot be supposed to have intended that the power should be open to serious abuse.[241]

Here we can see the principles of comity and relativity, as qualifications to the doctrine of parliamentary sovereignty, at work.[242] It is in this rather positive outlook towards the concept of discretion, then, that lies perhaps the greatest difference between English administrative law and its continental counterparts where, as we have seen, the distrust towards administrative discretionary powers has become widespread and rooted in the political and juridical culture.[243] Due also to the lack of a codified constitution, the status of discretion in English administrative law depends on contingent decisions as to the nature of the authority reviewed, so that

> administrative law needs consistent working definitions of the three primary constitutional functions, legislative, administrative and judicial; and also of the hybrid 'quasi-judicial' function which has a part of its own to play.[244]

---

[237] Davis, *Discretionary Justice* (n 42); C Harlow and R Rawlings, *Law and Administration*, 3rd edn (Cambridge, Cambridge University Press, 2012) 200–03.

[238] Endicott, *Administrative Law* (n 77) ch 7; Wade and Forsyth, *Administrative Law* (n 7) 222.

[239] Daintith, 'Contractual Discretion and Administrative Discretion' (n 232) 561.

[240] Forowicz, 'State Discretion as a Paradox of EU Evolution' (n 189) 6.

[241] Wade and Forsyth, *Administrative Law* (n 7) 291. In this sense one needs to remember the *ultima ratio* nature of judicial review – especially where appeals and other redress mechanisms are specifically provided: M Supperstone, J Goudie and P Walker, *Supperstone, Goudie and Walker: Judicial Review*, 4th edn (H Fenwick ed, London, LexisNexis, 2010) 136. The most cited case about the impossibility of an unfettered administrative discretionary power (despite the wording of the empowering statute) is *Roncarelli v Duplessis* [1959] SCR 121, 140 (Rand J).

[242] See Endicott, *Administrative Law* (n 77) ch 7.

[243] For the difference between the American and the British concepts of administrative discretion, due to the different constitutional background in each country: B Schwartz and HWR Wade, *Legal Control of Government: Administrative Law in Britain and the United States* (Oxford, Clarendon Press, 1972) 106.

[244] Wade and Forsyth, *Administrative Law* (n 7) 34; *cf* AW Bradley and KD Ewing, *Constitutional and Administrative Law*, 14th edn (Harlow, Pearson-Longman, 2007) 667–69.

154 *Towards a Unified Account of Discretion in Law*

This contingent character differentiates the English concept of administrative discretion,[245] both in the opinions of courts[246] and in scholarly accounts.[247] In this regard, and perhaps also due the 'generally pragmatic character of English administrative law',[248] the refinement of such a concept has been far from elaborate until recently, to the extent that it has been described as 'inductive'.[249] In Lord Diplock's words:

> The very concept of administrative discretion involves a right to choose between more than one possible course of action upon which there is room for reasonable people to hold differing opinions as to which is to be preferred.[250]

In this respect, the exercise of discretionary powers pertains to the realm of reasonableness, given that

> [a] discretion does not empower a man to do what he likes merely because he is minded to do so – he must in the exercise of his discretion do not what he likes but what he ought. In other words, he must, by use of his reason, ascertain and follow the course which reason directs. He must act reasonably.[251]

---

[245] For the distinction between 'judicial', 'quasi-judicial' and 'administrative discretion': Grey, 'Discretion in Administrative Law' (n 8) 111; Daintith, 'Contractual Discretion and Administrative Discretion' (n 232).

[246] Galligan, *Discretionary Powers* (n 6) 98; on the evolution of the review of discretionary powers: *Greenwich LBC v Secretary of State for the Environment* [1993] Env LR 344.

[247] See, eg: Endicott, *Administrative Law* (n 77) ch 7; Harlow and Rawlings, *Law and Administration* (n 237) ch 5; Supperstone, Goudie and Walker, *Judicial Review* (n 241) ch 7.

[248] Schwarze, *European Administrative Law* (n 172) 281. Such a lack of elaboration by administrative scholarship can perhaps be explained (systemically) also by the theoretical work on discretion done by legal theorists and by its predominance in Anglo-American scholarship – so that, quite often, administrative lawyers refer to the works of Dworkin and others: *cf* Galligan, *Discretionary Powers* (n 6) 14.

[249] Galligan, *Discretionary Powers* (n 6) 21.

[250] *Secretary of State for Education and Science v Tameside MBC* [1977] AC 1014, 1064; doctrinal definitions broadly converge: 'A public officer has discretion whenever the effective limits of his power leave him free to make a choice among possible courses of action and inaction': Davis, *Discretionary Justice* (n 42) 4; 'the room for decisional manoeuvre possessed by a decision-maker': J Jowell, 'The Legal Control of Administrative Discretion' [1973] *Public Law* 178, 179; 'Discretion may best be defined as the power to make a decision that cannot be determined to be right or wrong in any objective way': Grey, 'Discretion in Administrative Law' (n 8) 107; as the freedom of choice between alternative courses of action: Galligan, *Discretionary Powers* (n 6) 7; PP Craig, *Administrative Law*, 6th edn (London, Sweet & Maxwell, 2008) 501, after explicitly avoiding a 'jurisprudential analysis', defines discretion as 'existing where there is power to make choices between courses of action or where, even though the end is specified, a choice exists as to how that end should be reached'; see also Harlow and Rawlings, *Law and Administration* (n 237) 203. Bradley and Ewing, after quoting Lord Diplock's definition, point out that 'power' in administrative law has two meanings not always clearly distinguished: power as 'the capacity to act in a certain way' and power as the 'authority to restrict or take away the rights of others': Bradley and Ewing, *Constitutional and Administrative Law* (n 244) 666. Endicott, *Administrative Law* (n 77) 247–51 identifies five varieties of discretion: 1) express discretion; 2) implied discretion; 3) grants of power in subjective terms; 4) inherent discretion; and 5) resultant discretion.

[251] *Roberts v Hopwood* [1925] AC 578, 613 (Lord Wrenbury): on this case and on its relevance, see DGT Williams, 'Law and Administrative Discretion' (1994) 2(1) *Indiana Journal of Global Legal*

The Concept of Discretion in English Administrative Law   155

Therefore, in English administrative law

> 'unreasonable' as descriptive of the way in which a public authority has purported
> to exercise a discretion vested in it by statute has become a term of legal art. To fall
> within this expression it must be conduct which no sensible authority acting with due
> appreciation of its responsibilities would have decided to adopt.[252]

This constitutes the standard of reasonableness famously crystallised as the 'Wednesbury Test', which still represents the threshold for the review of discretionary powers.[253] The degree of personification of the concept of discretion is striking when compared to the process of objectification of administrative law that we have seen as a persistent feature of continental jurisdictions.[254] It also illustrates what Galligan means when he affirms there are two sides to this concept: one must understand it precisely as the 'scope for personal assessment in the course of a decision',[255] but this assessment is inherently tied to the attitude of other officials – and courts in particular – towards that decision.[256] This 'personal assessment' can pertain to questions of law, questions of facts, and questions of application of the law to the facts, although the central sense of discretion is that of setting one's own standards as the grounds of the decision.[257] While this remark points to the fact that it is possible to distinguish discretionary powers from decisions in which the authority should merely apply the law, Endicott stresses that

> [i]t is popular to divide the law of judicial review into two compartments: control of
> discretionary powers (with *Wednesbury* as the leading case), and control of decisions
> applying the law (with *Anisminic*, as reinterpreted by Lord Diplock, as the leading
> case). It may seem to be an attractive division, because exercising a discretion is a
> matter for the body given the discretion, but applying the law seems to be a matter

---

Studies 191. Such a definition of discretion seems well-rooted in English case-law, for '"Discretion" means when it is said that something is to be done within the discretion of the authorities that that something is to be done according to the rules of reason and justice, not according to private opinion: … according to law and not humour. It is to be, not arbitrary, vague and fanciful, but legal and regular': *Sharp v Wakefield* [1891] AC 173, 179 (Lord Halsbury), which follows *R v Wilkes* (1770) 4 Burr 2527, 2539 (Lord Mansfield). On the reasonableness of administrative discretion, *cf* WA Robson, *Justice and Administrative Law: A Study of the British Constitution* (London, Macmillan, 1928) 229.

[252] *Secretary of State for Education and Science v Tameside MBC* (n 250) 1064 (Lord Diplock); *cf* Grey, 'Discretion in Administrative Law' (n 8) 119.

[253] *Associated Provincial Picture Houses Ltd v Wednesbury Corporation* [1947] EWCA Civ 1, [1947] 2 All ER 680.

[254] While on the continent this objectification of administrative law must be considered as a safeguard against the abuse of power by officials, in England such historical bequest is absent, hence the concept of discretion is still *personal* and *personalised*, as it pertains directly to the faculty of judgment of the person entrusted with it.

[255] Galligan, *Discretionary Powers* (n 6) 9–10.

[256] 'In short, what may be discretionary from an external, legal point of view, may be anything but discretionary from the internal point of view of officials within the system': ibid 13.

[257] ibid 9–10, 33.

156 *Towards a Unified Account of Discretion in Law*

for judges. But that would be a basic mistake. It ought to have become clear ... that *a power to apply the law is a discretionary power.*[258]

To support his conclusion he discusses the case of *R v Gaming Board for Great Britain, ex p Kingsley,*[259] in which the Gaming Board had to decide if Kingsley was a 'fit and proper person' to operate casinos.[260] Endicott argues that the Board, in making this decision, was at the same time applying the law and exercising a discretionary power and thus the distinction does not hold.[261] The Queen's Bench Division established it was the Board's business to decide what considerations would make a person 'fit and proper' for operating casinos, and that its decision could have been quashed only on the basis of unreasonableness. We find here what can be termed a 'permissible field of judgment', which depends on the vagueness of the criterion laid down by the statute:

> [O]nce the court has established its interpretation of the law, the court will interfere with decisions applying that interpretation only on the 'rationality' ground of review that is used in control of discretionary powers. Whether the rationality requirement leaves the administrative decision maker any leeway depends on how vague the 'criterion for a judgement' is.[262]

The problem then lies both in the individuation and construction of the delegation of discretionary power upon the administrative decision-maker. On the systemic level, the individuation of discretion is more complicated than in the continental jurisdictions examined due to the multiple sources from which an authority can derive a decision-making power – such as statutes, prerogative or the common law itself. Distinguishing between these sources becomes then a theoretical priority,[263] particularly if one considers that when a discretionary power is based on prerogative or common law, its delimitation is entirely up to the courts.[264] Things are not simpler on the epistemic level, not even when we are dealing with statutory discretion: for often statutory construction specifies the text of the statute, creating uncertainty as to the ultimate scope of the discretion delegated upon the administrative decision-maker by Parliament.

This issue is particularly relevant when it comes to those 'textual markers' of discretionary powers that play such a relevant role in German administrative

---

[258] Endicott, *Administrative Law* (n 77) 357 (my emphasis); on the last claim, see ibid, ch 5, s 3.1.

[259] *R v Gaming Board for Great Britain, ex p Kingsley* [1996] COD 178; see also *Edward v Bairstow* [1955] UKHL 3, [1956] AC 14; *R v Monopolies and Merger Commission, ex p South Yorkshire Transport* [1993] 1 All ER 289.

[260] For the remark that the use of evaluative words by the legislator results in discretion to the decision-maker: Wade and Forsyth, *Administrative Law* (n 7) 219.

[261] Endicott, *Administrative Law* (n 77) 357.

[262] ibid 354.

[263] Grey, 'Discretion in Administrative Law' (n 8) 110–13; Daintith, 'Contractual Discretion and Administrative Discretion' (n 232) 565.

[264] Although the principles of natural justice always apply: Schwartz and Wade, *Legal Control of Government* (n 243) 222.

The Concept of Discretion in English Administrative Law 157

law, for instance. Prima facie, the function of these markers should be the same in English administrative law too, as, for instance, the Interpretation Act (Northern Ireland) 1954 seems to indicate at section 38:

> In an enactment passed or made after the commencement of this Act, the expression "shall" shall be construed as imperative and the expression "may" as permissive and empowering.[265]

As with Germany, the use of these textual markers in the context of legislation *should* produce a reliable distinction between a duty or 'mandatory provision'[266] on the one hand and a 'discretion'[267] on the other.[268] Instead, and largely due to the interchangeable use of 'shall' and 'may' in English,[269] 'the nature of a power in each case depends heavily on statutory construction'.[270] 'Shall' might mean 'may',[271] while 'may' might mean 'shall',[272] depending on the 'purpose on the conferment of power' or on what the public interest requires in the context of the individual case,[273] and more broadly on the legislative intention supporting the power-conferring statute as a whole.[274] As Lord Reid put it:

> Parliament must have conferred the discretion with the intention that it should be used to promote the policy and objects of the Act; the policy and objects of the Act must be determined by construing the Act as a whole, and construction is always a matter of law for the court.[275]

---

[265] Interpretation Act (Northern Ireland) 1954, s 38; Craig also uses these markers: Craig, *Administrative Law* (n 250) 437.

[266] But see, for a discussion of the difference between 'mandatory' and 'directory' requirements, *London & Clydeside Estates Ltd v Aberdeen DC* [1980] 1 WLR 182.

[267] See, eg: *Holgate-Mohammed v Duke* [1984] AC 437, 443 (Lord Diplock).

[268] Supperstone, Goudie and Walker, *Judicial Review* (n 241) 136.

[269] H Xanthaki, *Drafting Legislation: Art and Technology of Rules for Regulation* (Oxford, Hart Publishing, 2014) 93.

[270] Supperstone, Goudie and Walker, *Judicial Review* (n 241) 137; see also Wade and Forsyth, *Administrative Law* (n 7) 234.

[271] See J Payne, 'The False Imperative' (2010) 26(2) *The Legislative Lawyer*; www.ncsl.org/legislators-staff/legislative-staff/research-editorial-legal-and-committee-staff/volume-xxvi-issue-2-the-false-imperative.aspx accessed 12 October 2020. Think also about cases in which the public 'duty' of an officer is deemed compatible with the broadest degree of discretion (either on the policy or on the operational side), to the point that it can be questioned whether a duty really exists after all: *R v Metropolitan Police Commissioner, ex p Blackburn* [1968] 1 All ER 763; *R v Metropolitan Police Commissioner, ex p Blackburn (Order of Mandamus)* [1973] 1 All ER 324.

[272] *R v Minister of Agriculture and Fisheries ex p Padfield* [1968] UKHL 1, [1968] AC 997, 1033 (Lord Reid). For the remark that 'the case is not authority for the extinction of any distinction between a duty and discretion': Supperstone, Goudie and Walker, *Judicial Review* (n 241) 139. *cf* also *Re Baker, Nichols v Baker* [1890] 44 Ch 262, 270 (Cotton LJ): 'I think that great misconception is caused by saying that in some cases "may" means "must". It never can mean "must", so long as the English language retains its meaning; but it gives a power, and then it may be a question in what cases, where a Judge has a power given him by the word "may", it becomes his duty to exercise it.'

[273] Wade and Forsyth, *Administrative Law* (n 7) 233.

[274] Supperstone, Goudie and Walker, *Judicial Review* (n 241) 137. See also Wade and Forsyth, *Administrative Law* (n 7) 296 for the consideration that whether discretion is wide or narrow depends on the true intent and meaning of the empowering act (see also ibid 304).

[275] *Padfield v Minister of Agriculture, Fisheries and Food* [1968] AC 997, 1030C (Lord Reid).

158 Towards a Unified Account of Discretion in Law

The result of this brief overview is that the concept of discretion in English administrative law (and conversely that of application of law) is substantially amenable by courts and resistant to analytical definitions.[276] For there are several degrees of interaction between duties and discretion[277] and these can be identified only in the context of the particular case.[278] Besides different linguistic practices, the difference with continental jurisdictions can be attributed chiefly to the huge and often unconstrained delegation of discretionary power made by Parliament to non-judicial bodies in the absence (at least until recently) of a clear equivalent to the continental 'principle of legality':[279] a trend that has driven the courts, with time, to assume a progressively more proactive stance in controlling administrative decision-making[280] and which culminated in the ground-breaking *Anisminic* decision.[281]

X. TOWARDS A UNIFIED ACCOUNT OF DISCRETION IN LAW

The analysis in this chapter confirms that discretion is an 'unsettled term' used in multiple ways,[282] in jurisprudence (with the emphasis on the judicial

---

[276] This leads Endicott (*Administrative Law* (n 77) 250) to distinguish between 'a discretion' and 'a discretionary power', and to say that in some cases 'the holder of a discretionary power has not discretion' (because the circumstances of the case mandate only one lawful exercise of such power).

[277] *cf* Grey, 'Discretion in Administrative Law' (n 8) 108 according to whom 'discretion is a power that is almost always or always is attached to some level of duty'. For a review of these potential interactions between duties and discretion: Endicott, *Administrative Law* (n 77) 251; Supperstone, Goudie and Walker, *Judicial Review* (n 241) 136–46.

[278] This seems confirmed by the fact that one of the most common grounds to challenge the exercise of discretionary powers – considered an issue of procedural fairness by H Woolf and others (eds), *De Smith's Judicial Review*, 6th edn (London, Sweet & Maxwell, 2007) ch 11 – is that of an unlawful fettering of one's discretion, that is 'for a body to bind itself or divest itself of any discretion by adopting a blanket policy or adhering over-rigidly to its policy': Supperstone, Goudie and Walker, *Judicial Review* (n 241) 164. In other words, the context of the individual case seems to be apodictically considered more important by the courts than reasonable demands of consistency: Wade and Forsyth, *Administrative Law* (n 7) 271.

[279] 'What is often called 'delegation of lawmaking power' is often not delegation of the power to make rules – which might be undemocratic or politically unwise – but delegation of the authority to give to any decision the force of law, so that, like an act of the legislature, it must be unquestioningly accepted by the courts': FA Hayek, *The Constitution of Liberty* (Chicago, University of Chicago Press, 1978) 212. On the emergence of the principle of legality in English administrative law, see Endicott, *Administrative Law* (n 77) 22–24.

[280] Wade and Forsyth, *Administrative Law* (n 7) 235.

[281] *Anisminic Ltd v Foreign Compensation Commission* [1969] 2 AC 147. In other words, I apply Sir Isaac Newton's third law of motion '*Actioni contrariam semper et æqualem esse reactionem*' (to every action there is always an equal and opposite reaction) to explain the otherwise highly questionable (as to its theoretical consistency) majority verdict in *Anisminic*; and more generally to make sense of the relationship between a Parliament like Westminster that has progressively delegated a growing extent of decision-making power to administrative authorities without providing enough guidance, and the courts which have reflexively and progressively shaped their own powers by statutory construction in the broader common law context. On Newton's law of motion: I Newton, *The Mathematical Principles of Natural Philosophy*, vol 1 (A Motte trans, London, Benjamin Motte, 1729) 20.

[282] Galligan, *Discretionary Powers* (n 6) 54. For Bell, discretion entails three basic elements: a power to determine one's standards in deciding, a unilateral relationship between the decision-maker and

Towards a Unified Account of Discretion in Law 159

function) and administrative law (with the emphasis on the delegation aspect). The account that I propose here seeks to provide a unified basis for the analysis of any exercise of discretionary powers in our modern legal systems. It does so not only by rejecting the functional approach – which would distinguish between administrative and judicial discretion – but also by building upon the most compelling insights of each of the strands of literature considered here. It is therefore 'unified' in this double sense.

The one remark that appears constantly in the several accounts we have examined is that discretion amounts to an always limited power to choose (or to appraise, or to evaluate) certain aspects or elements of a decision – viz it does not amount to a (pure) freedom or liberty.[283] Every discretionary power is a *constituted* juridical power,[284] which is, at least to some extent, normatively limited by higher norms and principles. Obviously, this does not mean that, in reality, there will not be discretionary powers exercised de facto in violation of those limits established by law. But a discretionary power exercised beyond its limits is not normatively tantamount to the exercise of a liberty:[285] the former is unlawful and redress can be sought through the procedures offered by the legal system, whereas the latter is protected by the law. This also explains why the biggest theoretical challenge for many scholars investigating the topic has been that of 'constituting, defining and constraining discretion', with the latter necessarily done through 'legal rules and standards'.[286]

The fundamental distinction defended here between 'normative' and 'interpretive' discretion consolidates Hart's and Kelsen's insights about the difference between intended ('express') and unintended ('tacit') exercises of discretion with Klatt's elegant analytical model, while at the same time embedding in it the more precise features of the exercise of discretionary powers as elaborated by

---

the subject of the decision and the legitimation of that decision-making power by the law: J Bell, 'Discretionary Decision-making: A Jurisprudential View' in K Hawkins (ed), *The Uses of Discretion* (Oxford, Oxford University Press, 1992) 92–97. According to Hayek, over the meaning of the term there is 'confusion'. He singles out three senses in which one can understand the term, first as the 'power of the judge to interpret the law'; second as the 'relation between principal and agent throughout the whole hierarchy of government', and last, and in the sense that matters to him really, as the more general problem of the relationship between government and 'the private citizen and his property', which under the rule of law need to be protected from discretionary powers: Hayek, *The Constitution of Liberty* (n 279) 212–14; *cf* also Christie, 'An Essay on Discretion' (n 4) 747.

[283] Galligan, *Discretionary Powers* (n 6) 6 according to whom there is not 'free' discretion, not even intra-vires; *cf* MacCormick, 'Discretion and Rights' (n 88) 31; Endicott, *Administrative Law* (n 77) 230–34.

[284] MacCormick, 'Discretion and Rights' (n 88) 35; Daintith, 'Contractual Discretion and Administrative Discretion' (n 232) 555; but *cf* T Endicott, 'Lawful Power' (2017) 15(1) *New Zealand Journal of Public and International Law* 1. On the relationship between the causation (of legal effects) of an act and its constitutiveness: Ferrajoli, *Principia Iuris*, vol 1 (n 131) 261–73.

[285] *cf* N MacCormick, 'The Ethics of Legalism' (1989) 2(2) *Ratio Juris* 184. Nor it is tantamount to an authorised exercise of discretion, but see, *contra* the classification by Davis of discretion by (proper) grant of authority and 'self-advocated' discretion by 'street-level bureaucrats': Davis, *Discretionary Justice* (n 42) 215. In this regard an analytical framework like mine (or Klatt's) cannot consider the latter, but only the former – whereas a purely sociological account seems to miss the difference between proper and improper exercises of discretion.

[286] Galligan, *Discretionary Powers* (n 6) 3: *cf* Hayek, *The Constitution of Liberty* (n 279) 212.

160 Towards a Unified Account of Discretion in Law

administrative law scholarship.[287] 'Normative discretion' amounts to the intentional distribution of decision-making power between agents on different levels of an institutional normative system.[288] It involves the power to determine either the normative standard upon which the decision is going to be based,[289] or the normative consequences of the decision. This kind of discretion is normally made linguistically explicit by the use of certain words or expressions in the text of the delegating act and implies the finality of the delegated choice, provided that the latter stays within the authoritatively pre-established procedural and substantive limits. It also entails that the justification of the decision so established lies, at least partially, *outside* the delegating and constraining norms. 'Interpretive discretion' instead indicates the arguable or disputable area of judgment that is present in every applied legal statement,[290] as a result of the general 'discretionary character of knowledge'.[291] It will be broken down into three sub-categories: semantic, factual, and systemic.

The crucial reason to distinguish between normative and interpretive discretion lies in the fact that, while the former is the product of the (deliberate) delegation of decision-making power between different agents in a legal system, the latter captures the intrinsic – and therefore unintended – degree of choice that every decision-maker, to a greater or lesser extent, finds herself equipped with.[292] The fact that, in practice, there might be instances of discretionary powers which straddle the distinction – perhaps because a court recognises a delegation of discretion in the absence of a clear linguistic marker in the relevant statutory norm – does not outweigh the benefits of having an analytical framework against which we can identify the type of discretion at play in the majority of cases.[293] Furthermore, this distinction yields fundamental implications when it comes to the moment in which a discretionary power is subject to review by another authority within the system. For normative discretion implies that the decision of the authority entrusted with discretion should be the last word on the matter, legally speaking (finality) – provided that the authority in question has remained within the normative boundaries of the delegation. Interpretive discretion, on the contrary, does not entail any systemic determination on who has got the last word on the matter at hand, given that this kind of discretion

---

[287] My proposal though not only bears a broader explanatory capacity than Klatt's, due to the fact that I do not assume the strong distinction thesis between rules and principles (and the balancing model) as a theoretical basis, but my characterisation of normative and interpretive discretion also fares better in making sense of the delegation (and intentional) aspect of it: *cf* in this regard Schauer, *Playing by the Rules* (n 52) 227–28.

[288] *cf* Schauer, 'Open Texture' (n 10) 211.

[289] Viz. the normative premise of the legal syllogism.

[290] F Atria, *On Law and Legal Reasoning* (Oxford, Hart Publishing, 2002).

[291] G Palombella, 'The Cognitive Attitude' (1999) 85(2) *Archiv. für Rechts- und Sozialphilosophie* 151.

[292] On the need to recognise interpretive discretion, see M Foy, 'On Judicial Discretion in Statutory Interpretation' (2010) 62(2) *Administrative Law Review* 291.

[293] In other words, it is only by identifying normative and interpretive discretion as ideal types that we are then able to better understand what happens in our practices.

Towards a Unified Account of Discretion in Law   161

is inherent in every act of interpretation and application of law. As such, the review of this latter kind of discretion depends on the combination of institutional rules, judicial conventions, and interpretive canons adopted in a given jurisdiction.

My proposal, while consolidating some key insights as explained above, prompts at least two major overhauls of the current state of the scholarship. First, the distinction between normative and interpretive discretion absorbs and clarifies the distinction between weak and strong discretion as put forward by Dworkin and assumed by a relevant strand of the ensuing discussion,[294] which as a result should be abandoned. This latter distinction is not analytical, but should be understood instead as a function of competing normative theories on the role of the courts within a constitutional democratic system. Indeed, even if we conceive of the debate about discretion as centered around the question of the existence (or lack thereof) of right answers in law and legal reasoning, distinguishing between normative and interpretive discretion seems to fare much better than distinguishing between weak and strong.

For in the case of a decision imbued with normative discretion, the law lacks a right answer by definition, as the decision-maker is entrusted to choose among two or more courses of action. It seems appropriate to say, in this respect, that the acknowledgement of normative discretion and the right answer thesis are mutually exclusive.[295] But even if we are considering a decision that is not imbued with normative discretion, a 'right' answer might still be missing due to the amount of interpretive discretion that is involved in the decision. This second kind of discretion, as we shall see briefly, must be understood as a matter of degree rather than an all-or-nothing feature whose presence (or lack thereof) can be unequivocally ascertained.[296] The most relevant observation, that the 'weak/strong' alternative misses entirely, is that normative and interpretive discretion are asymmetrical and analytically independent from each other.[297] Therefore, one cannot be satisfied with the ascertainment of the former, because the latter is hardly ever entirely reducible, and this helps us to better conceive of the determinacy of legal statements, both theoretically and pragmatically.

As I mentioned already, we should also give up the functional demarcation between administrative and judicial discretion,[298] because there is no difference, on the epistemic level, between the two.[299] Both courts (especially in

---

[294] See, eg: Iglesias Vila, *Facing Judicial Discretion* (n 38) chs 1–3.

[295] *cf* MacCormick, 'Discretion and Rights' (n 88) 36, according to whom 'rights and discretion (albeit discretion can only be weak) are distinct legal techniques, not the same one, as Dworkin, in effect, thinks'; *cf* also Hart, *Concept of Law* (n 2) 205.

[296] MacCormick, 'Discretion and Rights' (n 88) 31.

[297] ibid 32.

[298] *cf* Ganz, 'Allocation of Decision-Making Functions' (n 9); *contra* eg: Kannai, Schild, and Zeleznikow, 'Modeling the Evolution of Legal Discretion' (n 61) 531–32.

[299] *cf*, although starting from what seem to me some different premises: M Taggart, '"Australian Exceptionalism" in Judicial Review' (2008) 36(1) *Federal Law Review* 1, 13; *cf* also J Raz,

162   *Towards a Unified Account of Discretion in Law*

common law systems) and administrative authorities are entrusted with normative discretion: the problem lies instead in the legitimacy of such delegation of decision-making power, especially when too broad, vis-à-vis the democratic principle and doctrine of the separation of powers. Interpretive discretion is instead pervasive in every act of application of law, be it the activity carried out by an administrative authority or that of a court in applying primary or secondary legislation. It will vary according to the degree of syntactical and semantic determinacy of the norms that control the exercise of power, to the complexity of the factual circumstances of the case, and to specific features of a given legal system, such as the presence (and variable interaction) of interpretive canons and conventions.

The point is that this kind of discretion is not ontologically dependent on the level at which it is exercised. This is why the functional distinction is not only meaningless but actually confusing – it suggests the idea that discretion would be different depending on whether it is entrusted to ministers or to judges. But what differs in these cases is not the delegation of decision-making powers or the degree of interpretive leeway, but the political evaluation of how such discretion must be exercised and/or constrained. Finally, departing from this functional characterisation of discretion reduces the analytical gap between civil and common law jurisdictions, and this is yet another sense in which the account of discretion proposed here is 'unified'.

A. Normative Discretion

To say that normative discretion is involved in the 'legislative or policy-making aspect of [discretionary] powers' is correct only to a partial extent, according to the account defended here.[300] It has to do, more generally, with the distribution of decision-making powers across different levels of the *Stufenbaulehre*.[301] For the outcome of this distribution of decision-making can be of two very different types: it can be a new (general) norm or it can be a (individual) determination.[302] Normative discretion can be present in either moment, and this implies not only that the content of the delegated decision is not entirely predetermined by the delegating norms,[303] but also that this delegation purports to prevent – normatively – other agents from encroaching upon the choice

---

'The Institutional Nature of Law' in J Raz, *The Authority of Law: Essays on Law and Morality* (Oxford, Clarendon Press, 1979) 106.

[300] Galligan, *Discretionary Powers* (n 6) 28.

[301] CS Diver, 'Optimal Precision of Administrative Rules' (1983) 93(1) *Yale Law Journal* 65.

[302] This important distinction, overlooked by Kelsen and those following him, will be further discussed in ch 6.

[303] *cf* with the concept of 'meaningful indeterminacy': Palombella, 'The Cognitive Attitude' (n 291) 161.

made by the delegated decision-maker.[304] What differs is that, as we shall see in chapter six, the former situation is one (also) of creation of law, while the latter is one of discretionary application of law.[305]

Normative discretion can pertain to the *an* and/or the *quid* of the decision to be taken.[306] It can amount to the power whether or not to make a decision at all, or it can be about the contents of the decision: for instance, when the decision-maker must pursue a certain aim, it can pertain to how to reach that aim, ie which legal effects are to be implemented in pursuing it. *Pace* Kelsen, this discretion never loses its cognitive aspect despite being volitional. For even if one has discretion to choose among several equally available normative options, once that choice has been made and once she has established her own standards for the decision at stake,[307] those standards become normative together with requirements of practical reason such as rationality, fairness, and so forth – which we have seen are intrinsic to the exercise of discretionary powers.

A good example is that of a civil servant who is given normative discretion to establish the ultimate award criteria for a public procurement. Imagine that she establishes that the public contract will go to the lowest possible price bid, but then offers the contract not to the company that put forward the lowest bid, but to another company, whose offer is markedly higher but according to the administrator guarantees the 'best' overall outcome. The point is that while the public servant has discretion to establish the normative criteria of the award (the decision), she cannot, once having done so, depart from those very criteria in awarding the contract at the conclusion of the public procurement selection.[308] In other words, normative discretion as to the standards of

---

[304] Schauer, *Thinking Like a Lawyer* (n 42) 159–61.

[305] See below ch 6, section X; and *cf* CE Alchourrón and E Bulygin, *Normative Systems* (New York, Springer-Verlag, 1971) 148–51 who distinguish between *declarative* and *normative* decisions, where only the latter but not the former kind contain a norm.

[306] Ferrajoli, *Principia Iuris*, vol 1 (n 131) 593–96. Here 'decision' is used as a sub-type of the more general category of 'legal acts', in the sense that they are manifestations of will not only as to the *an* of the act, but also as to the *quid* (and/or the *quomodo*): ibid 508–09. If the discretion is whether or not to take the decision, it can be characterised as a permission, whereas if the discretion pertains the content of the decision, it amounts to an 'alternative obligation'; see Alchourrón and Bulygin, *Normative Systems* (n 305) 155–58. Whether only two or more options are available to the decision-maker seems not relevant for our purposes here; in any case, see on this the 'Binary-Continuous Axis' by Kannai, Schild and Zeleznikow, 'Modeling the Evolution of Legal Discretion' (n 61) 548–49; see also ibid 551–52, for the consideration that the risk of unjust decisions is greater in binary decisions – ie those decisions in which the decision-maker is to choose between only two outcomes (acquittal or conviction) – than in 'decisions in which' judges 'are given a range of options'. See furthermore on the potential domains of discretion: PLM Lucatuorto, 'Modelli Computazionali della Discrezionalità del Giudice: uno Studio Preliminare' (2006) 7(3) *Ciberspazio e Diritto* 271, 276–77.

[307] Iglesias Vila, *Facing Judicial Discretion* (n 38) 11–12.

[308] In this regard, 'The course of action cannot be separated from the reasons, and therefore the standards on which it is based … To adopt standards that point to action X and then choose action Y is irrational, and therefore illegitimate … discretion pertains not just to final actions but also to standards of decision-making': Galligan, *Discretionary Powers* (n 6) 7; but see the remark (ibid 8) on the fact that the two aspects are usually concealed or ignored in practical decision-making.

164 *Towards a Unified Account of Discretion in Law*

the decision does not necessarily imply the same in relation to the normative effects caused by it.

Another key aspect to highlight is how this kind of discretion can be distributed across different decision-making levels and authorities of a legal system.[309] Our analysis in the first two parts of the chapter showed this is usually done in an explicit linguistic fashion, by using deontic operators of possibility such as 'may', 'can', 'or', etc; or even without using clear deontic operators but rather by means of 'vague' (in a non-technical sense) terms and clauses, such as 'reasonable', 'as it seems appropriate', or 'public interest'. The point is that the distribution (or delegation) of decision-making power is present, and recognisable as such, in an official source (constitution, statutes, secondary legislation, etc). But we have also seen that this can happen without the use of explicit 'markers'. In this case, the distribution or delegation of decision-making power is the product of an interpretive operation that is more opaque than the previous type, given that a higher norm is deemed to equip a decision-maker with a certain leeway either as to the standard, or as to the consequences of it, implicitly.[310] Clearly, this kind of distribution or delegation is inherently more problematic, as there is no clear-cut evidence of it (like in the case of linguistic markers) and a reasonable disagreement among different interpreters might arise as to whether the decision-maker is entrusted with normative discretion or not.[311]

Two observations can be made here: first, and as we shall see in the next section, in this case normative and interpretative discretion can potentially overlap completely.[312] Furthermore, it is worth stressing that every legal system (here in the sense of the established rules of the system together with the relevant conventions within the community of interpreters) can autonomously establish what to recognise as the distribution or delegation of normative discretion. In systems like German administrative law, discretion is recognised by courts and doctrine strictly only when explicitly 'formulated' in the text of an authoritative source; whereas in other continental jurisdictions, as well as in those of the common law, normative discretion is inferred even when implicit. Straddling the divide between these opposite approaches lies the consideration of (technically) vague or imprecise terms or clauses – as the debate over the *unbestimmte Rechtsbegriffe* in Germany indicates. Are they to be considered as expressing the delegation of normative discretion, and thus in principle reviewable only

---

[309] For some considerations as to the extent of discretion that should be delegated across the different levels of any normative framework (from a Law and Economics perspective): S Shavell, 'Optimal Discretion in the Application of Rules' (2007) 9(1) *American Law and Economics Review* 175.

[310] Wade and Forsyth, *Administrative Law* (n 7) 219.

[311] See, on this point, Waluchow's remark that 'It is to the philosopher of law, and not necessarily the practitioner, that we should turn when asking whether judges have, or must have, strong discretion': Waluchow, 'Strong Discretion' (n 95) 336; *cf* Iglesias Vila, *Facing Judicial Discretion* (n 38) 29–31.

[312] It might be easier nonetheless to identify an implicit delegation of normative discretion as to the *an* of a particular act, rather than as to its content.

to a certain extent, or rather as the presence of 'mere' interpretative discretion (of course when there are no other marks to suppose otherwise)? This appears to be a deliberate choice (with pros and cons) that each legal system must make, which resists analytical treatment.[313]

B. Interpretive Discretion

Unlike normative discretion, interpretive discretion is pervasive in legal knowledge. This is not due to a special characteristic of the latter, but rather to its membership in the more general category of scientific knowledge, in which (at least to some extent) there are always present some evaluative moments.[314] This acknowledgment, while prompting the irreversible departure from Kelsen's illusion of a 'pure' theory of law, should not lead to uphold interpretive theories à la Dworkin, nor radical sceptic positions. On the contrary, the peculiarity of law as an object of knowledge – which lies in its administered communicative nature[315] – confers upon interpretive discretion a *relational* paradigm. As it has been put, 'interpretive discretion ... increases as the precision of statutory formulation decreases'.[316] Or, to put it even more precisely:

> Under proper epistemological premises, ... the less vague (or the more semantically determined) the draft of the law, the more easily verifiable the interpretive outcome is likely to be.[317]

While this inversely proportional relation between the degree of semantic determinacy of legal language and the extent of interpretive discretion that lies with a decision-maker is fundamental in conceiving of the possibility itself of objectivity in legal theory and legal reasoning, it should not detract our attention from the fact that there are at least two more sources of interpretive discretion in modern legal systems. That is, in addition to semantic interpretive discretion, we should also identify and distinguish factual and systemic interpretive discretion. Factual interpretive discretion occurs in the process of ascertaining the historical facts or considerations relevant to a decision. In the paradigmatic example of the judicial decision, it pertains to the determination of the factual premise of the legal syllogism, and, despite the inductive nature

---

[313] This seems clear from our survey of administrative law scholarship on the point: in this regard clearly the German solution points to the protection of certainty and foreseeability, but at the price of rigidity and 'overreach' into the policy realm by (unelected) judges: see again Arai-Takahashi, 'Discretion in German Administrative Law' (n 190) 77; and *cf* Luzzati, 'Discretion and "Indeterminacy" in Kelsen's Theory of Legal Interpretation' (n 112) 134–37 who argues for the necessary interpretive character of the discretion implied by vague clauses.

[314] Ferrajoli, *Principia Iuris*, vol 1 (n 131) 21–26.

[315] Discussed in ch 5 below.

[316] Galligan, *Discretionary Powers* (n 6) 109–10.

[317] Palombella, 'The Cognitive Attitude' (n 291) 153ff.

166 Towards a Unified Account of Discretion in Law

of the reasoning involved,[318] it can be heavily constrained by the procedural and substantive rules of evidence in a given legal system. Also, this type of interpretive discretion acquires particular prominence in common law systems, where the technique of distinguishing precedents – either widening or narrowing them – is based on it.[319]

The two sources of interpretive discretion we have mentioned so far, semantic and factual, are not peculiar to law. They are the result of the necessary use of natural languages in legal communication and of the interpretive character of empirical knowledge more generally. The third source of interpretive discretion, which I call systemic, is instead purely a legal phenomenon. It depends on a variety of contingent features of modern legal systems, such as: the accepted defeasibility of legal norms,[320] also in light of the number and scope of general principles accepted in the system; the contradictoriness and fragmentation of the established legal sources; the number of accepted interpretive canons in the system; particular conventions of the officials; and the accepted jurisdiction and structure of courts. The contingent nature of this source of interpretive discretion should not be underestimated:[321] different legal systems (and different areas of law within them) will have different institutional features, and as a result a higher or lower degree of systemic discretion. Thus, for instance, the German system of administrative law seeks to reduce systemic discretion to the lowest possible extent, while English administrative law does not exhibit the same tendency (or at least not until recently, as we have seen above).[322]

The point is to highlight the complex relationship between this type of interpretive discretion, which is peculiar to legal knowledge and dependent on contingent features of historical legal systems, and normative discretion. For the more it is possible for the relevant authorities to depart from (or disregard) the 'letter' of the law as contained in the recognised legal sources because of (some) contingent features of the legal system, the more those authorities will effectively

---

[318] cf N MacCormick, 'Coherence in Legal Justification' in A Peczenik, L Lindahl and B van Roermund (eds), *Theory of Legal Science* (Dordrecht, Springer, 1984) 235.

[319] See, eg: G Lamond, 'Precedent and Analogy in Legal Reasoning' in EN Zalta (ed), *The Stanford Encyclopedia of Philosophy* (Spring 2016 Edition) http://plato.stanford.edu/archives/spr2016/entries/legal-reas-prec/.

[320] That is, (normative) defeasibility pertains not to legal rules as such, but to how a given legal system (or community of interpreters) decides to treat its rules: Schauer, 'Open Texture' (n 10) 205–13. On this point compare Schauer's approach to Imer Flores' ('H. L. A. Hart's Moderate Indeterminacy Thesis Reconsidered (n 19) 155–59), who seems to reach a similar conclusion but from different premises.

[321] For the contrary view that legal adjudication is *necessarily* discretional because of systemic indeterminacy, see SA Reyes Molina, 'Judicial Discretion as a Result of Systemic Indeterminacy' (2020) 33(2) *Canadian Journal of Law and Jurisprudence* 369.

[322] Clearly, historical attitudes towards the evaluation of discretionary powers themselves play a relevant role in the institutional consideration of systemic discretion.

find themselves equipped with some 'unintended' normative discretion, either as to the creation of new norms or of new individual prescriptions (see Figure 7 below). This consideration applies as well to the case in which the discretion is the result of the fragmentation of the system, with a plurality of overlapping and contradictory norms regulating (being applicable to) the same scenario and no established meta-rule resolving the ensuing legal indeterminacy.[323]

Figure 7 Three kinds of discretion

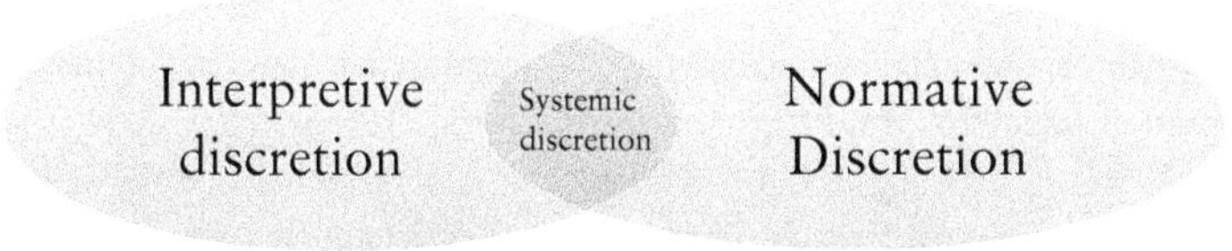

As such, systemic discretion is highly problematic – although perhaps unavoidable, at least to some degree, given the sheer complexity of modern legal systems – for two main reasons. First, due to its 'unintended' character, there is no settled scope for judicial review of the exercise of such discretion, creating therefore the potential for further contradictions and indeterminacies in the legal system. Second, by contributing to reduce the semantic relationship between the universality of the law and the particularity of the individual decision, systemic discretion prevents interpretive discretion from remaining within (intersubjectively) recognisable limits and, as such, undermines the objectivity of the legal system as a whole.

In other words, drawing attention to the indisputable nexus between the degree of semantic and syntactic determinacy of law 'in the books' and the degree of verifiability of (applied) legal statements ('law in action') appears idle if one does not also consider the role played by systemic discretion in a legal system.[324] As we said, this consideration will necessarily be on a case-by-case basis, as different legal systems will 'tolerate' different levels and sources of systemic discretion. But the acknowledgement of the existence and role of systemic discretion allows for a much clearer analytical picture of the way in which our modern legal systems actually work, and to what extent different sources of (interpretive) discretion can be regulated.[325]

---

[323] See J Wróblewski, *The Judicial Application of Law* (Dordrecht, Kluwer, 1992) 319.

[324] *cf* Schauer, 'Open Texture' (n 10) 212–13.

[325] *cf* Galligan, *Discretionary Powers* (n 6) 11, according to whom 'the distinction between applying given standards and having to create one's own is an unsatisfactory basis for precise, analytical distinction'. In his view, rather than as a distinction, this could be characterised as a spectrum, from creating standards, to interpreting and then ranking them – as such discretion becomes a 'function of standards'.

168 *Towards a Unified Account of Discretion in Law*

XI. CONCLUSION

The purpose of this chapter was to shed light upon the concept of legal discretion, the relevance of which is paramount to the theoretical viability of the idea of law-application. Incidentally, in the course of the argument, we have highlighted the asymmetry between the two doctrinal discourses in which discretion is primarily discussed, jurisprudence and administrative law, and brought them back together by means of a novel and unified account of the concept. The latter is based on the distinction between normative and interpretive discretion (and on their potential overlap in some cases). Normative discretion indicates the distribution of decision-making powers across different levels and authorities of a legal system. It can pertain to the creation of general norms or individual determinations. Interpretive discretion is due instead to immanent (semantic and factual) and contingent (systemic) sources of unintended choice(s) with which legal decision-makers can find themselves equipped.[326] The distinction between the two will allow us, in chapter six, to provide an analytical distinction between the creation of law and the discretionary application of law: that is, all those instances in which an agent is equipped with some margin of choice in making a decision, and yet the decision can still be considered meaningfully an act of application (rather than of creation) of law. Central to this idea is the constitutive connection between law and language, which is the theme of the next chapter.

---

[326] Wade and Forsyth, *Administrative Law* (n 7) 292.

5

Law and *Language and* as *Language.*
An Alternative Picture
of a Multifaceted Relationship

I. INTRODUCTION

IN ORDER TO ground the distinction between the activities of law-creation and law-application, it is necessary to illustrate the sense in which, in a great many cases, the law applied by an official is not the product of a jurisgenerative activity on part of the interpreter, but rather consists in the subsumption of a given set of facts, sometimes called 'operative', under a pre-determined (vis-à-vis the case at hand) normative type as expressed by a legal norm.[1] In other words, we need to explain how we can reasonably affirm that in many cases someone is 'merely' applying a legal norm that was created at a moment of time preceding that of its application. How so?

First, if law is, generally speaking, the enterprise of subjecting human conduct to the guidance of rules – as seen in chapter one – then the creation of a normative standard after the relevant conduct has taken place cannot by definition have fulfilled that function, at least vis-à-vis all those forms of behaviour which took place before the (judicial) act of law-creation.[2] This requirement becomes even more relevant if we think that a central feature of modern legal systems is their coerciveness, so that from the lack of conformity to a given standard might ensue the imposition of sanctions or the coercive enforcement of the standard on the individual.[3] And while it is possible for a genuine legal system to be said to exist even if, from time to time, (a degree of) law-creation

---

[1] See N MacCormick, *Legal Reasoning and Legal Theory*, rev edn (Oxford, Oxford University Press, 1994).

[2] RA Duff, *Answering for Crime: Responsibility and Liability in the Criminal Law* (Oxford, Hart Publishing, 2007) ch 2; L Fuller, *The Morality of Law*, rev. edn (New Haven, Yale University Press, 1977) 162–67. There seems to also be an infinite regress problem here, for the normative statement by a court – which establishes what the law is in a particular situation according to sceptics and realists – would need to be interpreted in turn when applied in future cases. Therefore, it is not clear how even judge-made law could perform any guiding function at all.

[3] See A Ripstein, 'Authority and Coercion' (2004) 32(1) *Philosophy & Public Affairs* 2; R Dworkin, *Law's Empire* (Cambridge, Harvard University Press, 1986).

170 An Alternative Picture of a Multifaceted Relationship

takes place after the conduct under examination has taken place, if every act of judicial application of law were to require a corresponding act of law-creation, it would not be clear how such a system could fulfil law's guiding function in the first place. As we have seen already, too wide a difference between the *law on the books* and the *law in action* would raise doubts vis-à-vis their respective qualification as 'law' in the first place.[4]

Second, if every act of law-application were to require a simultaneous and corresponding act of law-creation by the courts, it is not clear how such a system could be defined as 'democratic' even in a minimal sense. As we have seen in chapter two, modern constitutional democracies are premised on the fundamental idea of collective autonomy: but if the law applied to individual cases is *always* the product of the jurisgenerative activity of unelected courts, it is unclear in which sense the people could be said to rule themselves (even indirectly) in such a system.

My contention is that the conceptual significance of both these requirements – which I shall call, respectively, 'action-guidance' and 'collective autonomy' – is often overlooked in the literature,[5] especially following what we could term, after the 'linguistic turn' which ensued from the seminal work of Hart and Bobbio among others,[6] the 'pragmatics turn' that took place in analytical jurisprudence and that is mainly due to the work in philosophy of language by Grice and by those working broadly in his tradition (sometimes referred to as 'neo-' or 'post-' Griceans).[7]

The application of pragmatics to legal communication is said to illuminate several aspects of the practice of law, and of courts in particular,[8] offering new insights into the seemingly endless debate, post-Hart, between mixed (or moderate) and sceptical theories of legal interpretation. These latter theories get the

---

[4] See M Kramer, *Objectivity and the Rule of Law* (Cambridge, Cambridge University Press, 2007) 139–40.

[5] *cf* BH Bix, 'Can Theories of Meaning and Reference Solve the Problem of Legal Determinacy?' (2003) 16(3) *Ratio Juris* 281, 286ff. A version of the 'collective autonomy' requirement might be, among other worries, behind Soames' recent restatement of his theory of legal interpretation: S Soames, 'Deferentialism: A Post–originalist Theory of Legal Interpretation' (2013) 82(2) *Fordham Law Review* 597, 598. For a discussion, see JJ Moreso and S Chilovi, 'Interpretive Arguments and the Application of the Law' in G Bongiovanni et al (eds), *Handbook of Legal Reasoning and Argumentation* (Dordrecht, Springer, 2018). Even Greenberg shares a version of this worry: M Greenberg, 'Legislation as Communication? Legal Interpretation and the Study of Linguistic Communication' in A Marmor and S Soames (eds), *Philosophical Foundations of Language in the Law* (Oxford, Oxford University Press, 2011) 253–54.

[6] See T Endicott, 'Law and Language' in EN Zalta (ed), *The Stanford Encyclopedia of Philosophy* (Summer 2016 Edition) http://plato.stanford.edu/archives/sum2016/entries/law-language/.

[7] For a state-of-the-art overview, see I Skoczeń, *Implicatures within Legal Language* (Cham, Springer International Publishing, 2019); more generally, see W Davis, 'Implicature' in EN Zalta (ed), *The Stanford Encyclopedia of Philosophy* (Fall 2019 Edition) http://plato.stanford.edu/archives/fall2019/entries/implicature.

[8] The best example of this approach to legal meaning and legal interpretation is the work of Pierluigi Chiassoni, on which see, for instance, P Chiassoni, *Interpretation without Truth: A Realistic Inquiry* (Cham, Springer International Publishing 2019) ch 4.

Introduction 171

upper hand from the application of post-Gricean pragmatics to the law-making process, in the sense that the centrality and ubiquitousness of inferential interpretation to legal practice would seem confirmed even from a linguistic point of view, so that we could only talk of the rule-based application of law in a very faint sense, if at all. As a result, not only should we question the possibility of presenting a *theory* of legal interpretation (properly speaking), and not merely an *account* of it,[9] but more importantly we should also reject any claim to legal determinacy in the application of law as defended by the mixed theories, even in so-called easy or clear cases.[10] This in turn would trigger all the troubling consequences of rule-scepticism that we have discussed in chapter three.

In this chapter, I offer a novel argument to resist the kind of scepticism that this 'pragmatics turn' in jurisprudence seems to warrant. The argument presented is novel in that, rather than engaging with pragmatic theories on a case-by-case basis, I plan to question two fundamental assumptions behind the current mainstream understandings of legal practice: that law is a sub-species of ordinary language on the one hand, and that legal communication can be analysed through the same lens of ordinary communication – and particularly speech-act theory – on the other. I shall then introduce an alternative theory of legal meaning based on the semantic minimalism refined, over the course of a decade, by Emma Borg. I will end the chapter by discussing the implications of my approach for a mixed theory of legal interpretation and for the debate as to the contribution of the communicative content of legal texts to the overall content of the law.

Before we continue, an important preliminary observation: the central claims about legal meaning and legal interpretation I put forward in this chapter are neither descriptive nor normative, but rather conceptual. In this regard, I agree with Ramirez Ludena that 'The position one takes up on legal interpretation is connected with which conception of law in general is understood to be most plausible'.[11] If one adopts a 'realist' conception of law according to which law is what courts decide,[12] it is not only intelligible, but fully reasonable, to put forward a purely descriptive theory (or better, account) of legal meaning which collects and analyses the decisions of judges in a given jurisdiction. Mutatis mutandis, if one agrees with Dworkin's concept of law as an

---

[9] Endicott, 'Law and Language' (n 6). Presenting an account – descriptive – of legal interpretation seems the hallmark of legal realism, at least in the Genoese tradition, as we have seen in ch 3.

[10] See, eg: A Marmor, *Interpretation and Legal Theory*, rev. 2nd edn (London, Hart Publishing, 2005) and JJ Moreso, *Legal Indeterminacy and Constitutional Interpretation* (Dordrecht, Kluwer, 1998), for two prominent mixed theories of interpretation post-Hart.

[11] L Ramirez Ludeña, 'The Meaning of "Literal Meaning"' (2018) 18(1) *Analisi e Diritto* 83, 97–8. The same point is made by P Comanducci, 'Conoscere il Diritto' (2008) 38(2) *Materiali per una storia della cultura giuridica* 419, 424–25, quoted by V Velluzzi, 'Interpretazione degli enunciati normativi, linguaggio giuridico, certezza del diritto' (2008) 3 *Criminalia: Annuario di scienze penalistiche* 493, 498–99; see also M Jori, *Del Diritto Inesistente: Saggio di Metagiurisprudenza Descrittiva* (Pisa, ETS, 2010) ch 1.

[12] OW Holmes, 'The Path of the Law' (1897) 10(8) *Harvard Law Review* 457, 461.

172 An Alternative Picture of a Multifaceted Relationship

interpretive practice, it follows that every act of legal interpretation is necessarily an instance of moral reasoning that leads to the one right answer in the instant case, and that a theory of legal interpretation is inherently normative from this point of view.[13] The point is that when we juxtapose different theories of legal interpretation without bringing to the fore their respective underlying conceptions of law, we are risking talking past each other.

This is the sense in which, if the conception of law in a modern democratic system defended in this work appears plausible, the corresponding theory of legal meaning and interpretation must respect rather than frustrate the two requirements, that I already mentioned above, of 'action-guidance' and 'collective autonomy'. And, only a mixed theory of legal interpretation, as resulting from an adequate theory of meaning in legal communication, seems capable of doing so.

II. THE COMMUNICATIVE MODEL OF LAW. A TWO-WAY AFFAIR?

That law is, generally speaking, a communicative enterprise is by no means an original claim,[14] at least from Hart's *Concept* onwards.[15] But what is meant by that?[16] A preliminary observation is that 'communication' is a polysemic term that has no clear and univocal root, as it could derive from any of the following Latin expressions:[17]

- *cum munire*, to tie or to build with;

- *cum munere*, [to act] through deeds or [to give] somebody a present;

- *cum moenia*, to put up walls or to act within the walls [of the city];

- *communis agere*, to act together;

- *communico*, to share or to impart or to make common.

---

[13] *cf* Ramirez Ludeña, 'The Meaning of "Literal Meaning"' (n 11) 97.

[14] For a historical introduction to the application of linguistics and philosophy of language to law, see Endicott, 'Law and Language' (n 6).

[15] HLA Hart, *The Concept of Law*, 3rd edn (Oxford, Oxford University Press, 2012) ch 7. On the law-communication thesis, see at least: M Iglesias Vila, *Facing Judicial Discretion: Legal Knowledge and Right Answers Revisited* (Dordrecht, Springer, 2001) 43ff; M Van Hoecke, *Law as Communication* (London, Hart Publishing, 2002), ch 1; L Ferrajoli, *Principia Iuris*, vol 1 (Bari, Laterza, 2007) *passim*; LM Solan, 'Linguistic Issues in Statutory Interpretation' in LM Solan and PM Tiersma (eds), *The Oxford Handbook of Language and Law* (Oxford, Oxford University Press, 2012); Greenberg, 'Legislation as Communication?' (n 5); S Soames, 'Interpreting Legal Texts: What Is, and What Is Not, Special About the Law' in S Soames, *Philosophical Essays, Volume 1: Natural Language: What It Means and How We Use It* (Princeton, Princeton University Press, 2008); Moreso and Chilovi, 'Interpretive Arguments and the Application of the Law' (n 5); A Marmor, *The Language of Law* (Oxford, Oxford University Press, 2014); H Asgeirsson, *The Nature and Value of Vagueness in the Law* (London, Hart Publishing, 2020).

[16] 'The insight [is] that law cannot exist without it being communicated to the people subject to it. No communication, no law': J Engberg and AL Kjær, 'Approaches to Language and the Law – Some Introductory Notes' [2011] *Hermes – Journal of Language and Communication Studies* 7.

[17] Van Hoecke, *Law as Communication* (n 15) 8; J Derrida, 'Signature Event Context' in J Derrida, *Limited Inc* (Evanston, Northwestern University Press, 1988) 1ff.

The Communicative Model of Law. A Two-way Affair? 173

I am tempted to say that we can find, to some extent, almost all these potential roots in our common and most general understanding of the term, according to which communication is 'the imparting or exchanging of information by speaking, writing, or using some other medium'.[18] Amongst those potential roots, two fundamental characteristics seem to be presupposed. First, that communication is an activity, in the sense that it implies an act – a discernible 'action' or form of behaviour (not necessarily linguistic) – in the external physical world.[19] Second, that this activity is ontologically relational: for it makes sense to talk of communication only because, and insofar as, we are not alone in this world. To communicate means to go beyond the self. Communication, or the ability to communicate, is predicated upon us since the moment in which we come into the world: it does not depend, at least in some sense, upon our rational faculties.[20] As such, it can be considered an objective feature of our mutual being 'together' in the human condition, which can transcend even time and space: 'a conditio sine qua non of human life and social order'.[21]

We communicate even when we do not want to, as long as we are in what has been called an 'interactional situation'.[22] This has led some to speak of the 'impossibility of not communicating'.[23] But, being a predicate of our 'being together' – as communication can also be defined in terms of human interaction[24] – there seems to be indeed one case in which it would be impossible for us to communicate: if what we want to communicate could not go beyond us. In other words, to communicate something, we need at least one actual receiver or recipient. Hence, by definition, every act of communication – and not of merely uttering sounds – involves at least two subjects, a sender and a receiver,[25] and revolves around what is being communicated, ie the communicative content. It is a process in which usually the sender wants the receiver to either think, feel, and/or do something.[26] As Parry puts it:

> To communicate is to transmit a message, but a message, unlike a physical entity, cannot travel in its initial form. Transmission calls for a medium in which selected elements correspond to selected features of the original [object of communication].[27]

---

[18] Lexico, 'Definition of communication' (Oxford University Press- Lexico.com, 30 April 2021) www.lexico.com/definition/communication accessed 30 April 2021.

[19] P Watzlawick, JH Beavin and DD Jackson, Pragmatics of Human Communication: A Study of Interactional Patterns, Pathologies, and Paradoxes (London, Faber, 1968) 48.

[20] cf Van Hoecke, Law as Communication (n 15) 205, and the distinction between spontaneous and rational communication.

[21] Watzlawick, Beavin and Jackson, Pragmatics of Human Communication (n 19) 13.

[22] ibid 48–49.

[23] ibid.

[24] Van Hoecke, Law as Communication (n 15) 7.

[25] E Itkonen, 'The Central Role of Normativity in Language and Linguistics' in J Zlatev, TP Racine, C Sinha and E Itkonen (eds), The Shared Mind: Perspectives on Intersubjectivity (Amsterdam, John Benjamins Publishing, 2008) 284.

[26] cf with the definition of communicative action by F Recanati, Literal Meaning (Cambridge, Cambridge University Press, 2004) 54.

[27] J Parry, The Psychology of Human Communication (London, University of London Press, 1967) 24.

174   An Alternative Picture of a Multifaceted Relationship

This medium or code is usually made of one or more signs, which are the basic units of communication.[28] Semiotics is the discipline that studies signs in general, their nature and their properties, as part of a semiotic system.[29] We have natural and conventional signs, and those that stand somewhere in between.[30] Thunder is a natural sign of a storm; a full stop is a conventional sign to express that a sentence is completed.[31] Overall, the sets of codes available to us for communicative purposes are numerous: besides language, we can think of nonverbal semiotic systems like body language, art, photography, and so forth. The choice of one system over another as the preferred means of communication depends ultimately on the intentions of the author of the communication, both as to what is being communicated and how. For example, if one wants to communicate a precise descriptive statement about the world to an audience, an abstract painting might not constitute the best choice to do so.

This choice is relevant for law as well: for while linguistic signs are arguably the most important category of signs in legal systems, one should not overlook the presence and the fundamental relevance for our shared way of life of other types of signs, like traffic or road signs.[32] Why pictorial signs are preferable to linguistic signs, at least in some cases, to convey content of various kinds should be clear precisely in the case of road or traffic regulations, where it is a key objective of the legal system to transmit relevant (but limited) deontic content and other information to road-users while minimising distractions from the act of driving itself.[33]

With this qualification in mind, the communicative theory of law (the Standard Picture)[34] assumes that the content of law is determined by the linguistic utterances of those agents within the system that are authorised – viz., that have the authority – to create law.[35] To put it in a nutshell, 'the content of the

---

[28] cf W Nöth, *Handbook of Semiotics* (Bloomington, Indiana University Press, 1995) 206.

[29] See M Jori, 'Linguaggio giuridico', in G Pino, A Schiavello and V Villa (eds), *Filosofia del diritto: Introduzione critica al pensiero giuridico e al diritto positivo* (Turin, Giappichelli, 2013), 261, for the claim that no (conventional) sign, taken in isolation, has intrinsic meaning – signs only have meaning as part of systems with at least two or more signs that can be distinguished and thus indicate different 'things' in the world.

[30] D Chandler, *Semiotics: The Basics*, 2nd edn (Oxford, Routledge, 2007) 36.

[31] ibid 36ff.

[32] In this sense, see M Dudek, 'Why are Words not Enough? Or a Few Remarks on Traffic Signs' in M Araszkiewicz, P Banas, T Gizbert-Studnicki and K Pleszka (eds), *Problems of Normativity, Rules and Rule-Following* (Cham, Springer International Publishing, 2015); M Dudek, 'Can Informative Traffic Signs Also Be Obligatory? Polish Constitutional Tribunal and Supreme Court Versus Traffic Signs' (2018) 31(4) *International Journal for the Semiotics of Law* 771.

[33] Admittedly, this could change dramatically with the diffusion of self-driving cars and roadside technologies (which could allow for direct communication of variable standards to the artificial intelligence system driving the car). For discussion, and for the claim that traffic signs should not be considered only as alternatives to written linguistic expressions, see Dudek, 'Why are Words not Enough?' (n 32).

[34] Greenberg, 'Legislation as Communication? (n 5).

[35] Endicott, 'Law and Language' (n 6) – this also means courts (and other officials).

law is what the lawmaker communicates'.[36] More precisely, it implies a form of (metaphysical) relationship between the communicative content, say, of a statute and its legal content.[37] This in turn presupposes the distinction, which we have already mentioned in chapter three, between norm-sentences or norm-formulations (the relevant linguistic clauses of a statute) and norms *tout court* (being the meaning expressed by those norm-sentences). The consequence, from the epistemic point of view, is that we can establish the content of law in the same way in which we can establish the meaning of linguistic utterances in ordinary conversation – hence the proliferation of the use of concepts and tools from linguistics and the philosophy of language, and particularly of speech-act theory, in jurisprudential discourse.[38]

In particular, many existing communication models of law see legal practice as a communicative endeavour between the two main classes of agents that, together, have the authority to determine the content of the law, namely legislatures and courts.[39] The former would be the senders of legal utterances, while the latter would be the receivers tasked with interpreting those utterances and understanding what the legislature meant, thus establishing what the law *is*. Within and around this picture, there seem to be four main areas of discussion in the literature:

1. which level of utterance content is relevant for determining legal content;[40] that is, which theory of meaning should be adopted in legal communication;[41]
2. the exact scope of the contribution of the authoritative linguistic utterance to the overall content of the law;[42]
3. the nature of the communicative exchange (whether cooperative or strategic) between legislatures and courts;[43] and
4. the impact of the interpretive maxims and conventions – the 'interpretive codes' – as practiced by the judiciary in a given legal system.[44]

---

[36] Moreso and Chilovi, 'Interpretive Arguments and the Application of the Law' (n 5) 501.

[37] For discussion, see Asgeirsson, *The Nature and Value of Vagueness in the Law* (n 15) 26–33.

[38] For a general introduction and a rich set of case studies, see CM Hutton, *Word Meaning and Legal Interpretation* (London, Palgrave Macmillan, 2014).

[39] See, eg: D Cao, 'Legal Speech Acts as Intersubjective Communicative Action' in A Wagner, W Werner and D Cao (eds), *Interpretation, Law and the Construction of Meaning* (Dordrecht, Springer, 2007) 76. A notable exception is Marmor, *The Language of Law* (n 15) 1ff.

[40] Moreso and Chilovi, 'Interpretive Arguments and the Application of the Law' (n 5) 501.

[41] For an overview, see Skoczeń, *Implicatures within Legal Language* (n 7) chs 4–5.

[42] Greenberg, 'Legislation as Communication? (n 5); D Smith, 'The practice-based objection to the "standard picture" of how law works' (2019) 10(4) *Jurisprudence* 502; Asgeirsson, *The Nature and Value of Vagueness in the Law* (n 15).

[43] Marmor, *The Language of Law* (n 15); Skoczeń, *Implicatures within Legal Language* (n 7).

[44] See P Sandro, 'To whom does the law speak? Canvassing a neglected picture of law's interpretive field' in M Araszkiewicz, P Banas, T Gizbert-Studnicki and K Pleszka (eds), *Problems of Normativity, Rules and Rule-Following* (Cham, Springer International Publishing, 2015).

176 An Alternative Picture of a Multifaceted Relationship

In what follows, I will not engage with these issues in a systematic way, because my main purpose is instead to cast some doubts on the very premise underlying these debates: namely, the assumption that law is akin to ordinary communicative exchanges. In particular, in section IV, I will offer some grounds to affirm that law is not just a sub-species of natural language, and that from this observation alone important consequences ensue vis-à-vis both our theories of legal meaning and of legal interpretation. Then, in section V, I will resist the conclusion that legal communication is akin to ordinary communication, and that as a consequence we are not epistemically warranted to simply apply theoretical insights from the latter to the former.

For now, my first point of contention with the picture above is that arbitrarily narrowing down the set of parties involved in legal communication to legislatures and courts,[45] as the vast majority of communicative theories do, returns a distorted and ultimately misleading picture of our current legal practices.[46] We should never forget, in this respect, that adjudication is always law's 'plan B'.[47] In other words, if we always needed to go through the adjudicative moment in order to know what the law is for a given situation, it is not clear at all how law – as an institutional normative practice – could ever fulfil that general guiding function that, as we have seen since chapter one, constitutes one of its core and spatio-temporally ubiquitous features. As Hart aptly put it:

> If it were not possible to communicate general standards of conduct, which multitudes of individuals could understand, without further direction, as requiring from them certain conduct when the occasion arose, nothing that we now recognize as law could exist.[48]

Arguably, this 'action-guidance' requirement applies with different degrees of stringency in different areas of law.[49] If we take, for instance, criminal law, which on all accounts is one of the constitutive branches of modern legal systems, this requirement applies in the most cogent way – because of the ensuing potential

---

[45] cf Cao, 'Legal Speech Acts as Intersubjective Communicative Action' (n 39) 76.

[46] I have developed this argument explicitly in Sandro, 'To whom does the law speak?' (n 44). Schauer points to the need 'to understand 'law and not just judging': F Schauer, 'A Critical Guide to Vehicles in the Park' (2008) 83(4) New York University Law Review 1109, 1134. cf also LM Solan, The Language of Statutes: Laws and Their Interpretation (Chicago, University of Chicago Press, 2010) 7, for the claim that the first interpreter of statutes (particularly criminal and administrative) is the police.

[47] L Green, 'Law and the Causes of Judicial Decisions' (2009) Oxford Legal Studies Research Paper 14/2009, formerly available at http://papers.ssrn.com/abstract=1374608 accessed 31 March 2012, 21, on file with author; cf also Fuller, The Morality of Law (n 2) 55; BB Levenbook, 'How a Statute Applies' (2006) 12(1) Legal Theory 71, 74; D Miers, 'Legal Theory and the Interpretation of Statutes' in W Twining (ed), Legal Theory and Common Law (Oxford, Blackwell Publishing, 1986); M Jori, 'Legal Pragmatics' in A Capone and F Poggi (eds), Pragmatics and Law: Philosophical Perspectives (Cham, Springer International Publishing, 2016) 43.

[48] Hart, Concept of Law (n 15) 124.

[49] See discussion in Sandro, 'To whom does the law speak?' (n 44) 213.

The Communicative Model of Law. A Two-way Affair? 177

use of coercive measures from the breach of the law that directly infringe on our most basic liberties.[50] Also, and from a historical perspective, the progressive, more direct, engagement of laypeople with legislation – thanks to spread of general literacy, mass media, and the internet in recent decades – seems to undercut the traditional empirical observation that law would be, ultimately, a technical dialogue between lawyers (those in government and those in the profession).[51]

Thus, considering the general public (and not necessarily the courts) as the main addressee of the legal communication by the legislature seems already to restrict the scope and pragmatic complexity that theories of legal meaning and of legal interpretation can have. As I argued at length elsewhere,[52] this is due to conceptual and not normative considerations: law is the kind of practice whose point is the general guidance of conduct through rules expressed linguistically,[53] and those rules must be able to be followed, by and large, by the public without further intervention by the courts. Otherwise, if the understanding of law by officials were to be noticeably and consistently different from the understanding by laypeople – so that the majority of laypeople in the system would not actually be following the set of standards 'S' as identified by the courts, but a different set 'S*' as autonomously identified – it would not be clear at all whether a legal system could still be said to exist.[54]

Of course, this does not imply the denial of the relevance of the interpretive and technical conventions that characterise the activity of courts in every legal system, especially in the resolution of what are usually called 'hard cases' – cases where the law is only partially determined vis-à-vis the situation under consideration. Rather, what is required is that those interpretive conventions by the courts do not 'license and indeed require' widespread and systematic departure from the understanding of the legal texts – the law in books – by ordinary competent speakers of the language in which statutes themselves are written:[55] that is, the statutes' first and foremost addressees.[56]

---

[50] Duff, *Answering for Crime* (n 2) 166–172; F Stark, 'It's Only Words: On Meaning and Mens Rea' (2013) 72(1) *Cambridge Law Journal* 155, 163; PM Tiersma, 'A Message in a Bottle: Text, Autonomy, and Statutory Interpretation' (2001) 76(2) *Tulane Law Review* 431.

[51] See H Surden, 'The Variable Determinacy Thesis' (2011) 12 *The Columbia Science and Technology Law Review* 1, 66; *contra* D Kurzon, *It is Hereby Performed ...: Explorations in Legal Speech Acts* (Amsterdam, John Benjamins Publishing, 1986) 26–29; *cf* Jori, 'Legal Pragmatics' (n 47).

[52] Sandro, 'To whom does the law speak?' (n 44).

[53] BH Bix, 'Legal Interpretation and the Philosophy of Language' in LM Solan and PM Tiersma (eds), *The Oxford Handbook of Language and Law* (Oxford, Oxford University Press, 2012) 145.

[54] See Kramer, *Objectivity and the Rule of Law* (n 4) 138; Jori, 'Legal Pragmatics' (n 47) 55.

[55] Kramer, *Objectivity and the Rule of Law* (n 4) 139–140. This requirement changes at least in part for specialist legislation (ie legislation that is addressed only to certain special and technical categories of the public).

[56] Sandro, 'To whom does the law speak?' (n 44) 278.

178 *An Alternative Picture of a Multifaceted Relationship*

III. BEYOND 'WHAT IS SAID'. SPEECH-ACT THEORY AND THE RISE OF PRAGMATICS IN LEGAL INTERPRETATION

Let us acritically accept, for the moment, the communicative model of law (and its underlying assumptions) as it is found in the current debate. How does it help us to better conceive of law? At least since John Austin's William James Lectures at Harvard, we know that we can not only say things, but also do things with words.[57] Sometimes we say something about the world around us, for instance providing a piece of information ('the earth rotates around the sun') to somebody. Other times by merely uttering words we order (and promise, pray, etc) somebody to do something. Austin defined these linguistic forms of behaviour as 'speech acts',[58] among which the most straightforward example is the performative (utterance), and the legal performative in particular.[59] According to his by now famous trichotomy, every speech act is actually composed by three different acts:

1. locutionary: the act of saying something;
2. illocutionary: the force of the utterance (promising, ordering, etc); and
3. perlocutionary: the ensuing (intended) effects on the receivers of the illocutionary act.[60]

If we focus on the legislative speech-act,[61] we ought to notice from the outset that a statute must be considered both in its entirety as a singular speech-act with enacting illocutionary force,[62] and as the individual norm-sentences with their different illocutionary forces (of ordering, prohibiting, permitting, and so forth).[63] What we commonly identify as legal rules do not simply state 'things'; they *do* or *bring about* 'things'.[64] These 'things' are (deontic) modalities and (ontic) statuses,[65] which are either the direct product of rule-formulations themselves,[66] or the mediate outcome of further, positive speech-acts, performed by agents imbued with some authority to do so, as individual instances of application of those legal rules.[67]

---

[57] JL Austin, *How to Do Things with Words* (Oxford, Clarendon Press, 1962).

[58] For an introduction to speech-acts, see M Green, 'Speech Acts' in EN Zalta (ed), *The Stanford Encyclopedia of Philosophy* (Winter 2020 Edition) http://plato.stanford.edu/archives/win2020/entries/speech-acts/; and *cf* Kurzon, *It is Hereby Performed* (n 51) 6, on the etymology of 'act'.

[59] Kurzon, *It is Hereby Performed* (n 51) 1.

[60] Austin, *How to Do Things with Words* (n 57) 95–101. Moreover, he divides the locutionary act into phonetic, phatic, and rhetic acts.

[61] On the different speech-acts in law: Cao, 'Legal Speech Acts as Intersubjective Communicative Action' (n 39).

[62] M Matczak, 'Three Kinds of Intention in Lawmaking' (2017) 36(6) *Law and Philosophy* 651.

[63] Kurzon, *It is Hereby Performed* (n 51) 5, 20; clearly, the relationship between the two levels is hierarchical (ibid 16).

[64] Cao, 'Legal Speech Acts as Intersubjective Communicative Action' (n 39) 65–66.

[65] While (ontic) statutes imply the existence of their arguments (eg the capacity to vote) upon the subjects predicated with them, (deontic) modalities only assume the possibility of existence of their arguments (eg any prohibition): see Ferrajoli, *Principia Iuris*, vol 1 (n 15) ch 2.

[66] ibid, ch 8.

[67] See Kurzon, *It is Hereby Performed* (n 51) chs 3–4.

Speech-act Theory and the Rise of Pragmatics in Legal Interpretation   179

Now, the fact that we can do more with words than merely *saying things* points to one of the most significant developments in modern linguistics and philosophy of language: that is, the acknowledgment that in our ordinary conversations we often *mean* more than just what we *say*. As such, what we mean is not fully determined by semantics alone, but it is heavily dependent on the realm of pragmatics.[68] What does this imply? While semantics deals with the 'properties of *types* of expressions'[69] and it purports to analyse the rules and relations occurring on the general level of lexical and grammatical structures, pragmatics concerns the properties that vary from utterance to utterance according to (the different characteristics of) the context of use and the intentions of the speaker.[70] So, if somebody sitting next to me at the table utters 'Do you have the salt?', it is because of the context that what the person actually intends, and what I understand, is not asking me whether I have the salt (which is the literal content of the utterance), but rather requesting me to pass the salt. To be sure, there is a variety of pragmatic factors that might play a role in determining the meaning of an utterance beyond its semantic meaning, and pragmatics is a broad field with rather unclear boundaries.[71] Thus, it is safer to characterise it, quite broadly, as the study of the contribution of context to meaning.[72]

We can imagine an infinite number of conversational exchanges in which the context of an utterance accounts for the divergence between what is *said* and what is *meant*.[73] This seems a rather intuitive distinction, and yet it remained 'under the radar' of philosophical reflection for a considerable amount of time. Then, starting with the seminal work of Grice,[74] philosophers of language have widely come to acquire and develop the fundamental distinction between

---

[68] For a general reference, and for a list of definition of pragmatics (and its distinction from semantics): K Korta and J Perry, 'Pragmatics' in EN Zalta (ed), *The Stanford Encyclopedia of Philosophy* (Spring 2020 Edition) http://plato.stanford.edu/archives/spr2020/entries/pragmatics/; *cf* Kurzon, *It is Hereby Performed* (n 51) 18; K Bach, 'The Semantics/Pragmatics Distinction: What It Is and Why It Matters' in K Turner (ed), *The Semantics/Pragmatics Interface from Different Points of View* (Oxford, Elsevier, 1999); Recanati, *Literal Meaning* (n 26) ch 1; E Borg, 'Meaning and Context: a Survey of a Contemporary Debate' in D Whiting (ed), *The Later Wittgenstein on Language* (London, Palgrave Macmillan, 2009); K Allan and KM Jaszczolt (eds), *The Cambridge Handbook of Pragmatics* (Cambridge, Cambridge University Press, 2012).

[69] Korta and Perry, 'Pragmatics' (n 68).

[70] According to Charles Morris, pragmatics pertains to the 'relation of signs to their interpreters': CW Morris, *Foundations of the Theory of Signs*, International *Encyclopedia of Unified Science*, vol 1, no 2 (Chicago, University of Chicago Press, 1938) 6.

[71] E Borg, 'Semantics without pragmatics?' in K Allan and K Jaszczolt (eds), *The Cambridge Handbook of Pragmatics* (Cambridge, Cambridge University Press, 2012) 513–14; M Ariels, *Defining Pragmatics* (Cambridge, Cambridge University Press, 2010).

[72] Consequently, pragmatics might also be defined as 'dealing with the effects of context': Korta and Perry, 'Pragmatics' (n 68).

[73] For a clear example, see Borg, 'Semantics without pragmatics?' (n 71) 513.

[74] For an introduction, see, eg: RE Grandy and R Warner, 'Paul Grice' in EN Zalta (ed), *The Stanford Encyclopedia of Philosophy*, (Fall 2013 Edition) http://plato.stanford.edu/archives/fall2013/entries/grice/; on the origins of the speaker/literal meaning distinction before Grice, see Bach, 'The Semantics/Pragmatics Distinction' (n 68).

180   An Alternative Picture of a Multifaceted Relationship

two kinds of linguistic content, sentence (or literal) meaning and speaker meaning.[75] Perhaps unsurprisingly then, given what we have said above, the distinction does not have fixed boundaries in the literature.

What we can isolate though are two opposite positions at the respective ends of what Skoczeń has perceptively called the 'Border Wars' in recent philosophy of language:[76] 'formal semantics' on one hand, and 'radical pragmatics' on the other.[77] According to the first, there are good reasons to view semantics as an 'essentially ... *rule-driven*, recursive, context-independent level of [linguistic] content'[78] – and thus maintains 'clear blue water between literal meaning ... as substantially context-independent, and speaker meaning ... as essentially context-dependent'.[79] The second model instead, radical pragmatics, revolves around the idea that

> rich pragmatic processes (that is to say, processes which might look to the whole breadth of a context and which are thus potentially open-ended and non-discrete in nature) must be treated as integral to the determination of literal linguistic meaning.[80]

Viewed in this latter way, pragmatics phagocytises semantics, so that not only speaker meaning, but also literal meaning is pervasively context-dependent.[81]

---

[75] See, eg: K Bach, 'Saying, meaning, and implicating' in K Allan and KM Jaszczolt (eds), *The Cambridge Handbook of Pragmatics* (Cambridge, Cambridge University Press, 2012).

[76] Skoczeń, *Implicatures within Legal Language* (n 7) ch 4. In 'Meaning and Context' (n 68), Emma Borg had put semantic minimalism at one end of the spectrum and occasionalism, as the neo-Wittgenstenian approach advocated by Charles Travis among others, at the other. The middle-ground was filled by positions which always progressively depart from the formal semantics model and move toward an always increased role for context in determining semantic meaning: indexicalism, contextualism and 'added parameters' or 'semantic relativism'. In her later work 'Semantics without pragmatics?' (n 71) 518, Borg groups these latter positions, together with occasionalism, as 'radical pragmatics' as opposed to formal semantics, and in the text here I shall retain this latter approach. This is so because Borg, in 'Meaning and Context' (n 68) persuasively shows how those middle-ground approaches are eventually unstable, so that once we abandon the formal semantics model, it seems theoretically impossible not to slide towards occasionalist, that is the most radical form of contextualist, positions. This conclusion is also explicitly endorsed by H Cappelen and E Lepore, 'Radical and Moderate Pragmatics: Does Meaning Determine Truth Conditions?' in ZG Szabó (ed), *Semantics versus Pragmatics* (Oxford, Oxford University Press, 2005). In this regard, see also E Borg, *Pursuing Meaning* (Oxford, Oxford University Press, 2012) ch 1; and *cf*, on occasionalism, J Haukioja, 'A Middle Position Between Meaning Finitism and Meaning Platonism' (2005) 13(1) *International Journal of Philosophical Studies* 35 (which he calls 'meaning finitism' after Bloor).

[77] Borg, 'Semantics without pragmatics?' (n 71).

[78] ibid 514 (my emphasis). These reasons pertain to what Borg calls 'the constraint of compositionality' (and learnability), that is the need to account for our 'ability to understand sentences we have never encountered before and to manipulate and reconstruct words to form novel yet meaningful arrangements', that is our linguistic competencies called 'productivity' and 'systematicy'. On the compositionality constraint (and for the manifest incapacity of radical contextualism to account for it), see also Schauer, 'A Critical Guide to Vehicles in the Park' (n 46) 1120.

[79] Borg, 'Semantics without pragmatics?' (n 71) 521. A similar distinction is drawn in Ariel, *Defining Pragmatics* (n 71).

[80] Borg, 'Semantics without pragmatics?' (n 71) 516.

[81] H Cappelen and E Lepore, *Insensitive Semantics: A Defense of Semantic Minimalism and Speech Act Pluralism* (Oxford, Blackwell, 2005); and *cf* Recanati, *Literal Meaning* (n 26) ch 9.

Speech-act Theory and the Rise of Pragmatics in Legal Interpretation   181

But if this is so, it is not clear how we can retain any distinction at all between sentence (or literal) and speaker meaning. For instance, in one of its variants (contextualism), radical pragmatics amounts to the explicit claim that 'what is said (the truth-conditional content of the utterance) is nothing but an aspect of speaker meaning'.[82]

Why this is threatening for semantic theories of meaning should be apparent at this point: if we can only and always understand each other by knowing the context 'surrounding' a given utterance, there is no (determinate) meaning and thus no (real) communication before accessing rich contextual resources. In other words, there is no propositional, or truth-apt, content before (accessing) the context of use (by the speaker),[83] and this forces us to recognise the 'semantic underdeterminacy' of our linguistic expressions,[84] to the extent that

> their semantic value varies from occurrence to occurrence, just as the semantic value of indexical do, yet it varies not as a function of some objective feature of the narrow context but as a function of what the speaker means. It follows that semantic interpretation by itself cannot determine what is said by a sentence containing such an expression: for the semantic value of the expression – its own contribution to what is said – is a matter of speaker's meaning, and can only be determined by pragmatic interpretation.[85]

Why is this problematic? Should we not just abandon semantic theories of meaning? The point is that, if it can only be retrieved through 'pragmatic interpretation', meaning seems to involve an utterly different kind of reasoning from semantics, and namely a type of reasoning that goes beyond the application of lexico-grammatical rules and requires instead inferential consideration of each linguistic utterance in its given context.[86] As Recanati puts it,

> The distinguishing characteristic of pragmatic interpretation is its defeasibility. The best explanation we can offer for an action given the available evidence may be revised in the light of new evidence. Even if an *excellent* explanation is available,

---

[82] Recanati, *Literal Meaning* (n 26) 4; or, in other words, that no contrast can be drawn between 'what the speaker means and what she literally says'. We shall see below that occasionalism, the neo-Wittgensteinian approach put forward by Charles Travis among others, is even more radical from this point of view: *cf* Borg, 'Meaning and Context' (n 68); for a strong defence of this position in legal reasoning: L Alexander and E Sherwin, *Demystifying Legal Reasoning* (Cambridge, Cambridge University Press, 2008) 132–37 (and see references there).

[83] This formulation should capture both contextualist and occasionalist positions: *cf* Borg, 'Semantics without pragmatics?' (n 71).

[84] ibid 517. Although there is obviously a difference between claims of indeterminacy and underdeterminacy, for now the distinction does not matter, as both theses ultimately deny (the possibility of) determinacy; *cf* B Leiter, 'Legal Indeterminacy' (1995) 1(4) *Legal Theory* 481, fn 1.

[85] Recanati, *Literal Meaning* (n 26) 56–57; *cf* for another definition of 'semantic underdetermination': Borg, 'Semantics without pragmatics?' (n 71) 517, 527. In passing, it is worth noticing the striking resemblance – Recanati (*Literal Meaning* (n 26) 58) explicitly recalls Waismann – between this position and the claims put forward by realists (as to the only prima facie determinacy of law) we examined in ch 3.

[86] Korta and Perry, 'Pragmatics' (n 68); Chiassoni, *Interpretation without Truth* (n 8) ch 4; S Fish, 'Fish vs Fiss' (1984) 36(6) *Stanford Law Review* 1325.

182 An Alternative Picture of a Multifaceted Relationship

it can always be overridden if enough new evidence is adduced to account for the subject's behaviour. It follows that any piece of evidence may turn out to be relevant for the interpretation of an action. In other words, there is no limit to the amount of contextual information that can affect pragmatic interpretation.[87]

But if this is the case, it seems not only that we lose any possibility to explain some conspicuous features of our linguistic competency like compositionality,[88] but also more generally to treat any kind of (linguistic) content as 'context-invariant' and thus 'theoretically tractable'.[89] The traditional 'mathematical' model of communication,[90] as the result of the two opposite processes of encoding and decoding mental content through a semiotic system,[91] would appear fundamentally misguided. Instead, the contextualists offer us a different model, called 'inferential' (or 'relevance theory'),[92] in which the process to reach the communicative meaning of the utterance consists in inferring the speaker's communicative intentions, necessarily on a case by case basis.[93] What is relevant for us is that within this model, linguistic signs appear to amount to merely defeasible clues – qualitatively similar to all other contextual cues[94] – from which the hearer must infer the communicative intention of the speaker.

Accordingly, as meaning is always about inferring the speaker's intentions and thus it is not (chiefly) a matter of semantic and syntactic rules, it is not clear how any substantial degree of objectivity and determinacy in linguistic communication is attainable – for 'any sign can be used to signify anything'.[95] To avoid being trapped into this (unsustainable) position, some intentionalists concede that words 'might possess some kind of open-ended, holistically

---

[87] Recanati, *Literal Meaning* (n 26) 54.

[88] Borg, 'Semantics without pragmatics?' (n 71). The principle of compositionality roughly says that the meaning of a complex expression is the product of the meanings of its constituent elements and of the rules through which they have been assembled. To be sure, the principle is not globally accepted by linguists and philosophers of language: *cf* ZB Szabó, 'Compositionality' in EN Zalta (ed), *The Stanford Encyclopedia of Philosophy* (Fall 2020 Edition) http://plato.stanford.edu/archives/fall2020/entries/compositionality/.

[89] Borg, 'Semantics without pragmatics?' (n 71) 514.

[90] CE Shannon and W Weaver, *The Mathematical Theory of Communication* (Urbana, University of Illinois Press, 1949); *cf* Recanati, *Literal Meaning* (n 26) ch 1; D Duarte, 'Linguistic Objectivity in Norm Sentences: Alternatives Literal Meaning' (2011) 24(2) *Ratio Juris* 112, 113; and see Korta and Perry, 'Pragmatics' (n 68), for the remark that this model was first put forward by Locke.

[91] For a discussion of the relationship between language and cognitive processes as presupposed by the mathematical model of communication: E Borg, *Minimal Semantics* (Oxford, Oxford University Press, 2004) ch 2. For a general overview on the role of language in cognition: P Carruthers, 'Language in Cognition' in E Margolis, R Samuels and SP Stich (eds), *The Oxford Handbook of Philosophy of Cognitive Science* (Oxford, Oxford University Press, 2012).

[92] D Wilson and D Sperber, 'Relevance Theory' in LR Horn and G Ward (eds), *The Handbook of Pragmatics* (Oxford, Blackwell Publishing, 2004).

[93] Recanati, *Literal Meaning* (n 26) ch 9.

[94] *cf* S Neale, 'Silent Reference' in G Ostertag (ed), *Meanings and Other Things: Themes from the Work of Stephen Schiffer* (Oxford, Oxford University Press, 2016) 275–278, on the 'epistemic determination' role of sentence meaning.

[95] Alexander and Sherwin, *Demystifying Legal Reasoning* (n 82) 136. The authors, somewhat bafflingly, readily accept the charge of 'Humpty Dumptyism' (ibid 137, fn 14).

Speech-act Theory and the Rise of Pragmatics in Legal Interpretation 183

specified meaning', but this 'could at most serve to constrain, rather than determine, the truth conditions of any sentence in which they appear'.[96] Therefore, even with this concession, sentence meaning falls short of propositionality, as it would always underdetermine speaker's meaning.[97] This amounts to one of the reasons why the viability of radical pragmatics has been questioned, for once

> we have given up the idea that what counts for literal content is what can be found at the lexico-syntactic level, it becomes quite unclear how we can isolate just one (or some) of all the possible expansions of a propositional radical as the one(s) that delivers literal meaning.[98]

But if it is always context-dependent in this way, semantic (lexico-syntactic) meaning cannot be used as a general means of transmitting *constantly* any kind of content across different subjects and different contexts,[99] because each and every semantic content is a function of the speaker's meaning and of the individual context of utterance.[100] On this picture then *any* kind of objective relation – even minimal – between signifier and signified is obliterated, despite how one conceives of it.[101] As a result, our words – as semiotic types – seem to lose that potential for 'iterability' (that is, the capacity of signs to be repeatable across contexts) which Derrida considers the only mode of existence of the sign itself.[102]

The consequences for legal theory should be clear: literal or sentence meaning always falls short of propositionality and thus can never constitute the meaning of the legislative utterance before wide contextual resources are accessed and the intention of the legislator is retrieved.[103] And as the content

---

[96] Borg, 'Semantics without pragmatics?' (n 71) 520; also see Recanati, *Literal Meaning* (n 26) 6, according to whom 'what is said' is constrained by 'sentence-meaning' in a way that 'what is implicated' is not. Stephen Neale too rejects the association of intentionalism with 'Humpty Dumptyism' on the basis of the role that sentence meaning plays in constraining what kind of *genuine* communicative intentions a speaker can hold in uttering x (for the clearest presentation of this argument by Neale, see S Neale, 'Stephen Neale on Meaning and Interpretation' in D Edmonds and N Warburton (eds), *Philosophy Bites Again* (Oxford, Oxford University Press, 2014) 254–5, 259–260. For a broader discussion of what Neale has termed 'formatics' – the theory of the 'cognitive processes involved in utterance planning and formation' – see Neale, 'Silent Reference' (n 94) 271ff. This might be, ultimately, the real 'border war' between minimalists and contextualists: they both agree that 'words have meaning independent of the context in which they are produced', but the former claim that this meaning is already truth-apt, whereas the latter strongly deny this possibility: Borg, 'Meaning and Context' (n 68) 111–12.

[97] *cf* for discussion S Chapman, 'In defence of a code: linguistic meaning and propositionality in verbal communication' (2001) 33(10) *Journal of Pragmatics* 1553.

[98] Borg, 'Semantics without pragmatics?' (n 71) 527.

[99] Alexander and Sherwin, *Demystifying Legal Reasoning* (n 82) 153–54.

[100] As to the first, see Recanati, *Literal Meaning* (n 26) ch 2; for the latter, see Borg, 'Semantics without pragmatics?' (n 71) 520 and her considerations on occasionalism.

[101] See, eg: Chandler, *Semiotics* (n 30) ch 1.

[102] Derrida, 'Signature Event Context' (n 17) 9.

[103] This conclusion is explicit in most sceptical accounts of legal interpretation: see, for instance, Chiassoni, *Interpretation without Truth* (n 8) 92–102; F Poggi, 'The Myth of Literal Meaning in Legal Interpretation' (2013) 13 *Analisi e Diritto* 313.

184   *An Alternative Picture of a Multifaceted Relationship*

of legal utterances are the norms themselves – prescribing behaviour, conferring statutes, and so on – this means that we can never know what the law prescribes before a necessarily inferential process of interpretation. Moreover, given that courts often seem to disagree on the meaning of legislative utterances/ provisions – either because of different consideration of the relevant context, or due to the use of different legal canons of interpretation – the pervasive indeterminacy of law seems confirmed also from a linguistic point of view. How can the action-guiding and collective autonomy requirements be satisfied within this picture? What kind of practice would law be then? In the next two sections I purport to address a more fundamental question, however: how accurate is this picture once applied to legal communication?

IV. FIRST OBJECTION: LAW AS LANGUAGE, LAW AND LANGUAGE(S)

To begin, I want to question what is perhaps the most fundamental assumption by current mainstream accounts of legal communication: namely, that law is a 'technical' sub-species (or perhaps a component) of ordinary language, so 'that the pragmatics of legal language is best seen as a deeply integral part of the pragmatics of the use of language in general'.[104] This assumption is mistaken. For once we move from 'micro' to 'macro' pragmatics[105] – that is, to the study of the typical functions and/or effects of the use not of particular instances of language, but of languages (as systems of communication) overall – a much more complex picture emerges. Two interrelated questions must be addressed then: first, what kind of semiotic system is law? Second, what is the relationship between a legal system and the natural language through which the former is expressed? From the answers to these two questions, a very different model of legal communication from that of the current mainstream scholarship will emerge, and this alternative picture will constitute the prelude for a reconsideration of the role of speech-act theory in law in the next section.

In what sense is legal language not just a technical sub-species of natural languages? As an institutional-normative system which purports to guide the conduct of very large numbers of individuals through rules backed up by organised coercive enforcement, what law communicates is first and foremost general standards of behaviour and other normative qualifications, like obligations, statutes, and powers. It does so through, mainly, prescriptive language[106] expressed through the code constituted by the natural language spoken in the

---

[104] *cf* Endicott, 'Law and Language' (n 6).

[105] Jori, 'Legal Pragmatics' (n 47) 40. As it should be clear, my analysis in this section is greatly indebted to the work of Mario Jori in this area.

[106] On the distinction between descriptive and prescriptive language, see Jori, 'Linguaggio giuridico' (n 29) 264–68; Jori, 'Legal Pragmatics' (n 47) 38.

First Objection: Law as Language, Law and Language(s)   185

relevant community.[107] It cannot be denied therefore that to deal with law means to deal – together with the relevant forms of behaviour as prescribed by those norms[108] – with the use, for communicative purposes, of (primarily) linguistic signs in a given community.[109] Hence if one does not speak English, it is doubtful that she will be able to grasp anything at all about the English legal system.[110] At the same time, even a perfectly competent speaker of ordinary language, without legal training, might struggle to grasp fully the workings of the law as a whole. This is because lawyers and officials often talk in ways that are technical and 'difficult' for the ordinary speaker. But is it not the case that one can talk in 'difficult' ways in ordinary conversations as well? What is different when it comes to *legalese*?

The point is that when legislators, lawyers, citizens and judges engage in legal communication, they are using language with an overarching (macro-) pragmatic purpose that differs from ordinary communication.[111] Namely, the creation and maintenance of a separate 'universe of discourse(s)'[112] where group conflicts as to 'what needs to be the case' can be managed, and compromises or authoritative resolutions be reached (as well as peacefully challenged).[113] These discourses are more formalised (in the sense of the precision of their semiotic rules)[114] and less dependent on context than ordinary linguistic conversations,[115] given that a certain degree of impersonality, as to both their producers and their receivers, is a distinctive characteristic of legal discourses (especially statutory and regulatory ones).[116] As a result, these discourses are more intersubjectively verifiable than ordinary linguistic conversations vis-à-vis

---

[107] While this seems self-explanatory in light of the overall guiding function of law that we have already mentioned at several points – so that it is not clear how a group of officials that prescribes using language A within a community that only speaks language B could be considered a viable legal system – there have been some historical cases, like the famous 'Law French': on which see PM Tiersma, 'A History Of The Languages of Law' in LM Solan and PM Tiersma, *The Oxford Handbook of Language and Law* (Oxford, Oxford University Press, 2012).

[108] Ferrajoli, *Principia Iuris*, vol 1 (n 15) 444.

[109] Watzlawick, Beavin and Jackson, *Pragmatics of Human Communication* (n 19) 21. Ferrajoli, *Principia Iuris*, vol 1 (n 15) 3–8, divides the study of law into the study of law's semantics, syntactics and pragmatics; on this, see also Jori, 'Linguaggio giuridico' (n 29) 262–64.

[110] See Schauer, 'A Critical Guide to Vehicles in the Park' (n 46) 1122. An exception perhaps is that of traffic signals, whose function is in fact served by being as universal as possible (so that even visitors can understand them).

[111] Jori, 'Legal Pragmatics' (n 47) 49.

[112] Ferrajoli, *Principia Iuris*, vol 1 (n 15) *passim*.

[113] This is the main thesis of M Croce, *Self-sufficiency of Law: A Critical-institutional Theory of Social Order* (Dordrecht, Springer, 2012); See also Hutton, *Word Meaning and Legal Interpretation* (n 38) 38.

[114] Ferrajoli, *Principia Iuris*, vol 1 (n 15); PM Tiersma, *Legal Language* (Chicago, University of Chicago Press, 1999) ch 5; Tiersma, 'A Message in a Bottle' (n 50).

[115] Neale appears to broadly agree: Neale, 'Stephen Neale on Meaning and Interpretation' (n 96) 263.

[116] Jori, 'Legal Pragmatics' (n 47) 37–38; BG Slocum, *Ordinary Meaning: A Theory of the Most Fundamental Principle of Legal Interpretation* (Chicago, University of Chicago Press, 2015) 52; *Contra*, Endicott, 'Law and Language' (n 6).

186 An Alternative Picture of a Multifaceted Relationship

their application to particular situations, but not as much as the language of natural sciences.[117]

In this regard, and unlike with natural languages, not everything can be said through legal discourses: this artificial nature of legal language – the fact that it is created and maintained in light of a specific purpose[118] – implies that its rules control not only how to say things but, as Jori puts it, their 'aim is to limit and direct the content of what we (legally) say'.[119] For otherwise a legal universe of discourse(s) where anything and its contrary can be *ultimately* maintained[120] – for instance, that φ-ing is permitted and prohibited by the law at the same time – could not serve effectively the institutional aim to guide conduct through the creation and maintenance of a system of rules. The entire workings of a legal system, and particularly the accepted canons of interpretation, are geared to avoid such an outcome. In contrast, the persistence of natural languages as our main semiotic systems is due also to their indifference as to what we say through them.

As such, once 'law is considered as a set of rules to produce correct legal discourses', then 'it seems to consist of both rules about how to speak and rules about what to say'[121] and of the individual products of the use of those rules, viz., the discourse(s) created. That is to say, the practice of law is at the same time a *langue* and a *parole*, a tongue and a discourse.[122] Therefore, the study of law considers – or, as we argued in chapter one, should consider – both the system of rules that are established by authorities, and the forms of behaviour that those rules purport to regulate, especially when those forms of behaviour (like the signing of a well-formed contract, or the redaction of a judicial decision) might produce in turn further normative consequences.[123]

This first cluster of observations leads us to the second question: if law is not merely a technical sub-species of the natural language in which it is 'spoken' (we have not said yet what kind of language law is, just to be sure), what is the relationship between the two? While it is true, as we have seen already, that legal communication can take many forms, at the same time the foremost way in which normative standards are to be communicated to citizens in large societies is through general linguistic acts, for otherwise it would be impossible to reach

---

[117] See Jori, 'Legal Pragmatics' (n 47) 47–53; and *cf* B Jackson, *Making Sense in Law: Linguistic, Psychological, and Semiotic Perspectives* (Liverpool, Deborah Charles, 1995) 86.

[118] This claim of artificiality should not be misunderstood, for natural languages are artificial too – they are a human creation – but only in a weak sense. See Jori, 'Legal Pragmatics' (n 47) 47. See Recanati, *Literal Meaning* (n 26) 1–4, for the opposition between formal (or ideal) languages and natural languages.

[119] Jori, 'Legal Pragmatics' (n 47) 46. On this, see also Ferrajoli, *Principia Iuris*, vol 1 (n 15) ch 4.

[120] Jori, 'Legal Pragmatics' (n 47) 52.

[121] ibid 52.

[122] The distinction between 'langue' and 'parole' (and 'langage', which could be described as the capacity to develop any system of sign) is traditionally attributed to F De Saussure, *Cours de Linguistique Générale* (Lausanne & Paris, Payot, 1916).

[123] Ferrajoli, *Principia Iuris*, vol 1 (n 15) 444–45.

First Objection: Law as Language, Law and Language(s) 187

at the same time such a multitude of recipients.[124] As such, and notwithstanding which theory of law one adopts (be it positivism, natural law, etc), it seems really hard to deny that natural languages represent the basic *code* through which we are able to create deontic content on the one hand and to apply it to particular situations on the other.[125]

By adopting this code, viz the natural language z, a legal system 'subordinates the construction of norm sentences to the rules that are inherent in (or associated with) the adopted language'.[126] These rules are syntactic, 'establishing permitted sequences of words and phrase structure'; semantic, which associate 'expressions of the given language with their meaning through their use in the community of speakers';[127] and, to a lesser extent, pragmatic.[128] In linguistics, this is defined as the process of 'semiotic borrowing' between two natural languages (usually mostly at the semantic level), as for instance when Italian speakers start using English words and expressions (like 'conference call') in their communicative practices.

However, the semiotic borrowing that happens in legal language is different from that between two natural languages. As we just observed, because the natural language z is formally adopted by the legal system, it maintains the autonomy or 'independent pedigree' of its semiotic rules.[129] Yet, while borrowing the natural language as a whole, legal authorities also claim the power to modify ad hoc some of those rules, especially at the semantic level.[130] After all, this is what happens every time a statute (or a supreme court) explicitly redefines the meaning of a natural language term or expression for legal purposes: just think about the expression 'family member' and its more precise meaning(s) in legal discourse vis-à-vis natural language.[131]

Arguably, the main function of the legal (re-)definition of particular terms and expressions from natural languages is to formalise, so to make more intersubjectively ascertainable, the conditions of application of those words and expressions for the purposes of legal practice.[132] Why? Because of the vast array of normative consequences that might ensue when someone is considered

---

[124] Hart, *Concept of Law* (n 15) 124 (barring technological advancements which might make ubiquitous direct communication possible).

[125] Duarte, 'Linguistic Objectivity in Norm Sentences' (n 90) 113.

[126] ibid 114.

[127] ibid 115.

[128] Jori, 'Legal Pragmatics' (n 47).

[129] Duarte, 'Linguistic Objectivity in Norm Sentences' (n 90) 115.

[130] ibid. In this respect, it would make no sense for a legal system to modify syntactic rules as this would defy the very purposes of communicating effectively to laypeople and officials alike the standards of behaviour. If anything, a legal system needs to respect syntactic rules as much as possible so to avoid potential issues of syntactical ambiguity.

[131] ibid. See also Bix, 'Can Theories of Meaning and Reference Solve the Problem of Legal Determinacy?' (n 5) 287–90.

[132] *cf* BG Slocum, 'Introduction' in BG Slocum, *The Nature of Legal Interpretation: What Jurists Can Learn About Legal Interpretation from Linguistics and Philosophy* (Chicago, University of Chicago Press, 2017) 2.

188   *An Alternative Picture of a Multifaceted Relationship*

a 'family member' for the purposes of the law: to name but a few, being able to inherit someone else's estate or to take a decision as to the interruption of someone else's palliative care. This is, in other words, the first way in which the law constraints what can be said (and not merely how to say it) for its purposes; the second being by prescribing what can and cannot form the content of the individual instances of use of those semantic rules, like the prohibition of the infamous contract killing or any substantive constitutional limit (eg freedom of speech) upon the contents of prospective legislation. Hence, when a legislature enacts a statute, when a citizen drafts and signs a contract, or when a judge issues a decision, what these agents are doing is to talk *law* to each other, and not merely *legalese*. They are entertaining a regulated linguistic behaviour in order to produce one or more normative effects or consequences in the legal order.[133]

An inherent tension should become apparent in what we said in this section so far. On the one hand, because of law's overall guiding function and its 'default' semiotic borrowing of the natural language spoken in the given community,[134] if legal normative authorities do not observe, at least to a relevant extent, the syntactic and semantic rules of the adopted natural language z,[135] their 'communicative goal' is bound to fail from the outset.[136] This is relevant for most types of legal communication, but in particular for statutes and all regulatory instruments addressed to the general public.[137] On the other, legal authorities retain the power to modify the rules of legal language (in particular at the semantic level) in their pursuit of a more precise and verifiable intersubjective tool to expose and manage conflicts within the group. To this end, they also establish what can and cannot be said with specific uses of legal language, thus reducing its overall pragmatic scope and underscoring its difference vis-à-vis natural languages. All in all, from the macro-pragmatics point of view, legal language sits somewhere in between natural and artificial languages: it is perhaps the clearest example of the category of 'administered languages', as Jori has put it.[138]

This acknowledgement might explain, at least in part, why some legal scholars have thought of law as a formalised language (like that of arithmetic) and

---

[133] Ferrajoli, *Principia Iuris*, vol 1 (n 15) ch 4. Thus, with these individual acts, the perlocutionary effects are the normative consequences that the law pre-established for a felicitous performance of the given speech-act.

[134] The extent of the semiotic borrowing might explain why many authors consider legal discourse merely as a sub-species of the natural language adopted by it.

[135] This qualification becomes necessary considering the phenomenon of malapropism, that is of semantic (or syntactic) errors and yet successful communication in ordinary conversations, on which *cf* D Davidson, 'A Nice Derangement of Epitaphs' in RE Grandy and R Warner (eds), *Philosophical Grounds of Rationality: Intentions, Categories, Ends* (Oxford, Oxford University Press, 1986).

[136] U Scarpelli, *Contributo alla semantica del linguaggio normativo* (Milan, Giuffrè, 1985) 118; Duarte, 'Linguistic Objectivity in Norm Sentences' (n 90) 115; Bix, 'Legal Interpretation and the Philosophy of Language' (n 53) 145.

[137] Levenbook starts 'with the assumption that statutes that are directives must be capable of guiding the conduct of those they address': Levenbook, 'How a Statute Applies' (n 47) 75.

[138] Jori, 'Legal Pragmatics' (n 47) 56–59.

First Objection: Law as Language, Law and Language(s)   189

some others have readily assumed that legal language is merely a technical sub-species of the natural language through which it is 'spoken'. The point is that legal language cannot be reduced to either, being instead (perhaps fundamentally) characterised by the tension between the necessity to successfully communicate intelligible standards of behaviour (and other deontic contents) to the population at large and the authoritative creation of a (tendentially) verifiable discourse that is separated from ordinary linguistic interactions and which guarantees (as much as possible) intersubjectivity, especially in the administration of the coercive enforcement of legal rules. This does not mean, of course, that legal authorities cannot create inconsistencies and antinomies within a legal system, as for example in the case where two contradictory norms are present at the same time in the system because of an oversight by a parliamentary drafter. The point is rather that a legal system that is not normatively and functionally geared towards the resolution of those potential antinomies – by means for instance of the default rules *lex posterior derogat legi priori* or *lex specialis derogat legi generali* – would be a defective legal system, if at all.[139]

Two final observations can be made. In light of what we just said, another equally complex picture seems to emerge vis-à-vis the relationship between law and natural language as normative practices.[140] For in light of the semiotic borrowing, by which law adopts the linguistic code of the relevant community, the normativity of law can be understood as a second-order normativity premised upon the first-order normativity of language.[141] Obviously, the normativity of language by itself cannot explain 'the role of norms as motives of human behaviour'.[142] Something else is needed in that respect. Nevertheless, norms cannot fulfil their function – constituting reasons for action – if they cannot be successfully intersubjectively communicated in the first place.[143] As I argued

---

[139] One can understand also the ratio of the stare decisis doctrine under this light.

[140] On the role of legal theory in light of this communicative understanding of law, see L Ferrajoli, 'The General Theory of Law: on Its Subject, Its Method and Its Function' (2012) 1(2) *Rivista di Filosofia del Diritto – Journal of Legal Philosophy* 229; Jori, *Del Diritto Inesistente* (n 11) 15–16.

[141] See for a similar remark F Schauer, *Playing by the Rules: A Philosophical Examination of Rule-based Decision-making in Law and in Life* (Oxford, Clarendon Press, 1991) 67; see also Itkonen, 'The Central Role of Normativity in Language and Linguistics' (n 25), and *cf* M Klatt, *Making the Law Explicit: The Normativity of Legal Argumentation* (Oxford, Hart Publishing, 2008).

[142] E Pattaro, *The Law and the Right: A Reappraisal of the Reality that Ought to Be*, A Treatise of Legal Philosophy and General Jurisprudence vol 1 (Dordrecht, Springer, 2005) 188; Pattaro identifies (ibid 189) three fundamental functions of language: 1) indexical-illative; 2) representative-semantic; and 3) directive-conative. The first two are 'strictly linguistic and communicative', and thus are satisfied by any successful communication; the third is not, for it needs non-linguistic factors to succeed. *cf* Kurzon, *It is Hereby Performed* (n 51) 19, for a similar remark in terms of the conditions necessary for the felicitousness of the legal performative; moreover he claims that in legislative texts the conative and the referential functions 'dominate' (ibid 25).

[143] On the ontological necessity of some form of 'external manifestation' for norms, see P Sandro, 'Unlocking Legal Validity: Some Remarks on the Artificial Ontology of Law' in P Westerman, J Hage, S Kirste and AR Mackor (eds), *Legal Validity and Soft Law* (Cham, Springer International Publishing, 2018).

190   *An Alternative Picture of a Multifaceted Relationship*

above, this should caution those theorists of legal meaning and interpretation who focus (explicitly or more often implicitly) on the communicative model of law as being between law-making authorities and courts only, thus excluding laypeople.[144] The latter are relevant not only because they are necessarily the first addressees of law as a communicative enterprise, but also because their linguistic practices – and especially patterns of change and evolution at the semantic level – necessarily yield consequences (in light of the default semiotic borrowing) in those components of legal language that have not been semiotically 'modified' by legal authorities.[145]

Finally, once it is clarified in which sense law cannot be considered merely a sub-species of ordinary languages, it should be apparent why we might not be necessarily warranted – and certainly not uncritically – in applying theories and models derived from ordinary language exchanges to legal communication.[146] As we briefly mentioned already and as we shall discuss in more detail in the next section, a certain degree of impersonality and independence from context seem to be characteristic traits of the authoritative communication of normative standards through statutes and regulations. If this is correct, then it is not the case that Gricean pragmatics – and not just the cooperative principle, as noted in the literature[147] – necessarily apply to legal communication.

V. SECOND OBJECTION: SPEECH-ACT VS TEXT-ACT THEORY

So far, we have discussed two reasons why the predominant application in jurisprudential discourse of linguistics and philosophy of language is unsatisfactory and, ultimately, misleading. First was the fact that, within these approaches, legal communication is understood as a two-subjects exchange between legislatures and courts, thus excluding laypeople (and other important 'middle' categories, like police and other state officials tasked with the implementation of policy) from the picture.[148] The second inaccuracy is the consideration of

---

[144] On the importance of including laypeople more generally in our theories of law, see Jori, *Del Diritto Inesistente* (n 11); Sandro, 'To whom does the law speak?' (n 44).

[145] See Jori, 'Legal Pragmatics' (n 47) 55. This applies, mutatis mutandis, also for terms and expression of other technical languages (like biology) that might be borrowed by legal authorities.

[146] For a very recent attempt to apply Millikan's 'biological' model of language to law, see Matczak, 'Three Kinds of Intention in Lawmaking' (n 62); M Matczak, 'A Theory that Beats the Theory? Lineages, the Growth of Signs, and Dynamic Legal Interpretation' in M Witek and I Witczak-Plisiecka (eds), *Normativity and Variety of Speech Actions* (Leiden, Brill, 2018).

[147] F Poggi, 'Law and Conversational Implicatures' (2011) 24(1) *International Journal for the Semiotics of Law* 21; Marmor, *The Language of Law* (n 15). Defending the relevance of some version of the cooperative principle in law is BG Slocum, 'Pragmatics and legal texts: How best to account for the gaps between literal meaning and communicative meaning' in J Giltrow and D Stein (ed), *The Pragmatic Turn in Law: Inference and Interpretation in Legal Discourse* (Berlin, De Gruyter, 2017).

[148] See once again, as a clear example, the theory of interpretation in Chiassoni, *Interpretation without Truth* (n 8), ch 4.

Second Objection: Speech-act vs Text-act Theory   191

legal language as a mere sub-species of the ordinary language in which each legal system is 'expressed', which conceals the 'administered' nature of legal language geared towards its macro-pragmatic effects.

The resulting and misleading way in which current philosophy of language is applied to law lies in the use of ordinary speech-act theory (as illustrated above) as a basis to argue for the supposed pervasive lack of determinacy of legal utterances before pragmatic enrichment (carried out by interpreters). That is, rather than looking at the macro-pragmatics of legal language as a whole, we are now interested in the micro-pragmatics of individual legal utterances, and in particular of norm-formulations as contained in statutes and general regulatory instruments (by-laws, delegated legislation, administrative regulations, and so forth). Is legal communication akin to ordinary verbal communicative exchanges from this perspective, as readily assumed by most scholars working in the field?[149]

That this might not be exactly the case was perhaps already entertained by Hart in the Concept, in particular when he discusses the misleading potential of talking of 'addressees' of laws, as if statutes of a legal system were the orders of a sovereign to the public at large (like Austin thinks).[150] What Hart noted is that, by saying that laws are 'addressed' to (classes of) people, what is meant is that those laws apply to those people, viz. that those people are required to act as the law demands. This is a result of the two levels of generality of normative guidance through statutes, the generality of subjects and of the forms of behaviour required. As a result, in conceptualising law as communication, we should be wary of presupposing a 'parallel to face-to-face' situations.[151]

As with many things, Hart was on the right track.[152] After some sporadic interventions in the literature of the last few decades,[153] there seems to be a new and more systematic theoretical awareness emerging in legal theory that rejects the straightforward application of 'ordinary' speech-act theory – that is, speech-act theory modelled on face-to-face or conversational communicative instances – to legal utterances.[154] Interestingly, there seems to be also a resulting

---

[149] A clear example is R Ekins, *The Nature of Legislative Intent* (Oxford, Oxford University Press, 2012). In general, on the relevance acquired by speech-act theory in legal theory, see, eg: P Amselek, 'Philosophy of Law and the Theory of Speech Acts' (1988) 1(3) *Ratio Juris* 187.

[150] Hart, *Concept of Law* (n 15) 22–23.

[151] ibid 22.

[152] See M Kramer, *H.L.A. Hart* (Cambridge, Polity Press, 2018) 131–32, for a discussion of Hart's neglect of pragmatics in his *Concept of Law*.

[153] On which see Slocum, *Ordinary Meaning* (n 116) ch 2.

[154] See the contributions by M Matczak ('Why Legal Rules Are Not Speech Acts and What Follows from That?'), BG Slocum ('The Ordinary Meaning of Rules') and myself (Sandro, 'To whom does the law speak?' (n 44)) in M Araszkiewicz, P Banas, T Gizbert-Studnicki and K Pleszka (eds), *Problems of Normativity, Rules and Rule-Following* (Cham, Springer International Publishing, 2015); Cao, 'Legal Speech Acts as Intersubjective Communicative Action' (n 39); Duarte, 'Linguistic Objectivity in Norm Sentences' (n 90); V Villa, 'Le Tre Concezioni dell'interpretazione Giuridica' in G Pino, A Schiavello and V Villa (eds), *Filosofia del Diritto: Introduzione critica al pensiero giuridico e al diritto positivo* (Turin, Giappichelli, 2013) 302, for the acknowledgment that our theories of

192 *An Alternative Picture of a Multifaceted Relationship*

positive feedback loop vis-à-vis philosophy of language, where this new awareness in jurisprudential discourse reveals the limitations of the predominant pragmatics-dominated models of ordinary communication.[155] Where does the difference between ordinary conversation and legal communication lie then? We can isolate, for analytical purposes, two levels where such differences lie: a general level, that is related to legal communication being eminently written, and a particular level, that relates instead to the particular functions pursued – and thus to the particular locutionary, illocutionary and perlocutionary intentions involved – by legal authorities.

At the most general level, the first obstacle towards the application of traditional speech-act theory to legal communication is that the latter happens through the use of complex texts. It is in fact all too easy to note how Gricean and neo-Gricean accounts of communication are clearly premised on the verbal, face-to-face model of communication.[156] As such, they make a number of assumptions about the cooperative nature of the exchange,[157] the intentions of the speaker, the constitutive role and epistemic accessibility of what has been called conversational or physical context (that is the context shared by the speakers at the time of the production and reception of the utterance),[158] and about the cognitive mechanisms involved in the communicative act. But it is not clear at all that these assumptions may be straightforwardly applied to written communication of the kind entertained in legal practice.[159]

In the first place, written communication eliminates the possibility of paralinguistic cues (for instance, body movements accompanying an utterance, like the pointing in one direction when asking for something to be passed) as well as prosody (changes in the intonation, rhythm or other features of speech that might constitute evidential cues to the illocutionary intention of an utterance). As Slocum puts it:

> With a text, the entire message must be expressed in [written] words. ... The writer's audience is, in a sense, a fiction, and the writer must set up a role in which absent and often unknown readers can cast themselves. The situation calls for much greater

---

meaning are exclusively based upon our 'conversational language'. *cf* also A Marmor, *Philosophy of Law* (Princeton, Princeton University Press, 2011) ch 6.

[155] A recent example is E Borg, 'Explanatory Roles for Minimal Content' (2019) 53(3) *Noûs* 513. As we have already mentioned, even an intentionalist like Neale seems to concede the point ('written law is quite different from ordinary speech': Neale, 'Stephen Neale on Meaning and Interpretation' (n 96) 263).

[156] *cf* C Bianchi, 'How to do things with (recorded) words' (2014) 167(2) *Philosophical Studies* 485.

[157] *cf* T Endicott, 'Interpretation and Indeterminacy: Comments on Andrei Marmor's *Philosophy of Law*' (2014) 10(1) *Jerusalem Review of Legal Studies* 46, 52–56; Skoczeń, *Implicatures within Legal Language* (n 7) ch 2.

[158] On which, see D Canale and F Poggi, 'Pragmatic Aspects of Legislative Intent' (2019) 64(1) *The American Journal of Jurisprudence* 125, 132, for the remark that the context of legal communication is 'constitutively opaque'.

[159] See F Poggi, *Il Modello Conversazionale: Sulla differenza tra comprensione ordinaria e interpretazione giuridica* (Pisa, ETS, 2020).

Second Objection: Speech-act vs Text-act Theory   193

precision in verbalization where the individual words, and their combination, are called on to do more than in an oral conversion.[160]

In other words, only on this 'negative' basis, the epistemic contribution of pragmatic elements towards utterance meaning in written communication seems reduced vis-à-vis that in 'face-to-face' verbal communication. But there is more to written communication than the lack of availability of paralinguistic or other cues in communicational contexts. At least since Saussure – who contributed to the dismissal of an archaic mistrust vis-à-vis written communication that originates possibly in Plato's Phaedrus[161] – we should understand that writing developed not as a substitute for oral communication, but as an altogether different semiotic system. For the 'artificiality and technologically driven nature of writing'[162] has enabled the storing of information and the consequent progressive accrual (and criticism) of knowledge across time and space.[163] As we discussed already in chapter one, this seems to represent a condition sine qua non for the emergence of centralised political (and religious) authority.[164]

By allowing for far greater degrees of precision and objectivity (in the sense of intersubjectivity) than oral conversations,[165] writing has been said to have enabled ways of thinking previously held simply impossible.[166] The most important characteristic of writing, qua social tool, is its capacity to allow successful communication across time and space. It lies in the detachment of the author of a text and of the text itself, and in the creation of what has been termed the 'autoglottic space' in which the text 'speaks for itself', so that 'writing may be interpreted by those who have no idea of the identity of the author'.[167] Or, as it has also been put, writing can be considered the paradigmatic form of 'autonomous',[168] or 'unsponsored',[169] or 'context-free' communication.[170]

---

[160] Slocum, *Ordinary Meaning* (n 116) 46–48. See also Tiersma, 'A Message in a Bottle' (n 50); D Biber and B Gray, 'Challenging stereotypes about academic writing: Complexity, elaboration, explicitness' (2010) 9(1) *Journal of English for Academic Purposes* 2, 11.

[161] Slocum, *Ordinary Meaning* (n 116) 46.

[162] ibid.

[163] Matczak has explicitly talked of the 'diachronic nature of written communication': Matczak, 'Why Legal Rules Are Not Speech Acts and What Follows from That?' (n 154) 334.

[164] See ch 1, n 106.

[165] Jackson, *Making Sense in Law* (n 117) 86.

[166] R Harris, 'How does writing restructure thought?' (1989) 9(2/3) *Language & Communication* 99, 103. Both this and the previous citation are quoted in Slocum, *Ordinary Meaning* (n 116) 51.

[167] Slocum, *Ordinary Meaning* (n 116) 51.

[168] P Kay, 'Language Evolution and Speech Style' in BG Bloun and M Sanches (eds), *Sociocultural Dimensions of Language Change* (New York, Academic Press, 1977).

[169] Slocum, *Ordinary Meaning* (n 116) 51–54, and see the references there.

[170] W Ong, *Orality and Literacy: The Technologizing of the Word* (London, Routledge, 2002), as discussed in Slocum, *Ordinary Meaning* (n 116) 49–51. See also V Iturralde Sesma, *Interpretación literal y significado convencional: una reflexión sobre los límites de la interpretación jurídica* (Madrid, Marcial Pons, 2014) 77.

194   An Alternative Picture of a Multifaceted Relationship

This, of course, does not mean to do away with the intentionality of meaning from a systemic point of view.[171] Meanings arise out of the practices of beings capable of intentions (like us): collective practices in which signs are routinely used to refer to other beings, things, or features of the world (and beyond). This is undeniable, and applies to written communication as well.[172] But with texts, more than with verbal natural languages, the meaning of one's utterance must be encoded in lexico-grammatical structures (sentence or literal meaning), as the context of interpretation of the token text/utterance will not typically correspond to the context of its creation.[173] This is utterly different than typical face-to-face communication, upon which mainstream speech-act theory is based. The failure to address this difference between typical speech-acts and text-acts[174] has been called by Matczak the 'fallacy of synchronicity',[175] and can also be stated as the typical lack of a shared 'conversational'[176] or 'situational' context between the producer and the receiver(s) of a text-act.[177]

As a result, complex text-acts are also 'closed' and 'unilateral',[178] in the sense that they do not typically presuppose the possibility of interaction between author and receiver – and thus explicit clarification does not seem an available resource to overcome semantic ambiguity and indeterminacy more generally. It seems then reasonable to speak of a general 'multi-contextual' or 'a-contextual'[179] nature of written communication – that is, the fact that text-acts will be interpreted in a potentially infinite number of contexts where there might also be no direct epistemic access to the context of creation (with the exception of the relevant co-text, as we are about to see). But if there is no level of utterance content that is at the same time context-invariant

---

[171] See N Duxbury, *Elements of Legislation* (Cambridge, Cambridge University Press, 2012) 1 23–24, for the point that meaning and intention are 'distinguishable' concepts; see also Asgeirsson, *The Nature and Value of Vagueness in the Law* (n 15) 41.

[172] For example, in understanding a series of marks on the sand as meaningful and expressing the word 'help', we must presuppose an author to those marks and her communicative intentions: Alexander and Sherwin, *Demystifying Legal Reasoning* (n 82) 197.

[173] Clearly, the discussion in this chapter does not apply to those instances in which textual communication is used with the same function as verbal communication (as in the case of a secret social media chat exchange between two siblings in a room with their parents).

[174] WB Horner, 'Speech-Act and Text-Act Theory: "Theme-ing" in Freshman Composition' (1979) 30(2) *College Composition and Communication* 165.

[175] Matczak, 'Why Legal Rules Are Not Speech Acts and What Follows from That?' (n 154).

[176] See Biber and Gray, 'Challenging stereotypes about academic writing' (n 160) 11. See also Sandro, 'To whom does the law speak?' (n 44) 269, for the distinction between 'situational' and 'lifeworld' context.

[177] Slocum, *Ordinary Meaning* (n 116) 45–46; Sandro, 'To whom does the law speak?' (n 44) 269–70.

[178] Duarte, 'Linguistic Objectivity in Norm Sentences' (n 90) 113 (he only refers to legal utterances, but the point is generalisable).

[179] F Poggi, 'Grice, the Law, and the Linguistic Special Case Thesis' in A Capone and F Poggi (eds), *Pragmatics and Law: Philosophical Perspectives* (Cham, Springer International Publishing, 2016) 245 (she only refers to legislation, but the point, again, is generalisable).

Legal Texts as 'Autonomous' Text-acts   195

and 'applicable'[180] – as radical contextualists claim – and therefore stable across multiple contexts in time and space, how can these types of written communication ever be (even minimally) successful? What would be the point of writing in the first place?

VI. LEGAL TEXTS AS 'AUTONOMOUS' TEXT-ACTS

Let us then consider in more detail why legislative utterances should not be conceived of through ordinary speech-act theory. First, as complex autonomous or 'unsponsored' text-acts,[181] legislative utterances are a-contextual or multi-contextual,[182] both in the sense that there is no shared 'situational' context between producers and receivers, and in that, by definition, legal utterances are created to be applied over multiple contexts across time and space. We also just said that typical text-acts in general are 'closed' and 'unilateral', in that there is no possibility for interaction between senders and receivers as in normal conversational exchanges. Legislative text-acts are perhaps the clearest example, as they do not require an answer by their recipients but rather they purport, together with other factors,[183] to elicit a form of behaviour that is not even 'oriented towards the normative authority' itself.[184] These two features combined – the 'autonomy' and the closed and unilateral nature of legislative text-acts – point to an additional relevant observation, that

> norm sentences are a kind of speech act where the connection speaker→hearer (reader) is played out on both sides by indeterminate actors. ... Even though it is possible to connect a norm sentence with the person or group of persons that at a certain time act as the normative authority, from the speaker's point of view, the fact is that the speaker is, precisely, the normative authority and not that person or group of persons.[185]

As I argued elsewhere,[186] this observation is central to understanding which sense we can properly (ever) talk of the 'rule of law' (as opposed to a 'rule of men') in a given normative system. For the lack of relevance of the actual people on both sides of law's communicative endeavour guarantees not only that laws

---

[180] In the sense of being either 'truth–apt' or 'abiding-apt': Chiassoni, *Interpretation without Truth* (n 8) 88.

[181] For Waldron, legislation is 'unintentional': J Waldron, *Law and Disagreement* (Oxford, Oxford University Press, 1999) 119, 124 and 145; *cf* also Iturralde Sesma, *Interpretación literal y significado convencional* (n 170) 78.

[182] See I Skoczeń, 'Implicatures Within the Legal Context: A Rule-Based Analysis of the Possible Content of Conversational Maxims in Law' in M Araszkiewicz, P Banas, T Gizbert-Studnicki and K Pleszka (eds), *Problems of Normativity, Rules and Rule-Following* (Cham, Springer International Publishing, 2015) 360.

[183] Pattaro, *The Law and the Right* (n 142); Marmor, *The Language of Law* (n 15).

[184] Duarte, 'Linguistic Objectivity in Norm Sentences' (n 90) 116.

[185] ibid 117.

[186] Sandro, 'To whom does the law speak?' (n 44) 271.

196 An Alternative Picture of a Multifaceted Relationship

apply – in principle – irrespectively of the personal identity and characteristics of its addressees (formal equality), but also that those laws are created by the institution and not by the people who temporarily make up the latter.[187] This is the sense then in which we can meaningfully affirm that the British Parliament has been passing law uninterruptedly for hundreds of years, rather than different sets of MPs in each legislature – even though, of course, those different laws have been physically approved by those different sets of MPs in each legislature.[188]

As such, the actual locutionary intentions of the members of Parliament – as opposed to their illocutionary intentions[189] – cannot be relevant, constitutively, towards the determination of the meaning of the legislative utterance. For otherwise that 'veil' of individual indeterminacy that (minimally) instantiates the rule of law would be pierced through. This constitutes an additional (to the impossibility of aggregating single locutionary intentions in order to retrieve a group-intention)[190] and neglected reason why we can only always talk about the 'reconstructed' intention – viz., the 'objective' intention that a reasonable 'hearer' would understand – of the legislator.[191] In this regard, the single locutionary (and perhaps perlocutionary) intentions of the members of Parliament who voted for a bill, as retrievable in Hansard or in preparatory works, can only at best represent (pro tanto) evidence.

An even more problematic shortcoming produced by the application of ordinary speech-act theory to legislative utterances has been termed by Matczak 'the fallacy of a-discursivity'. It involves

> treating a legal rule as if it were a relatively short, single statement, similar to an oral order and able to be interpreted in isolation from other statements.[192]

Once again, we can perhaps identify the root of this fallacy in the historical association of the legislative utterances by the political authority (especially in the paradigmatic idea of the 'sovereign') with the individual commands (eg 'close the window!') that we routinely come across in ordinary, face-to-face, communication.[193] And while – as I shall illustrate in a moment – there are good reasons from a conceptual point of view to demand that there should be as

---

[187] cf Waldron, *Law and Disagreement* (n 181) 144, and Duxbury, *Elements of Legislation* (n 171) 99–100, for how this consideration solves an apparent puzzle in Waldron's theory.

[188] This is another way of putting Hart's criticism of Austin's command theory based on the continuity of laws.

[189] Matczak, 'Three Kinds of Intention in Lawmaking' (n 62).

[190] ibid.

[191] cf Poggi, 'Grice, the Law, and the Linguistic Special Case Thesis' (n 179); Slocum, *Ordinary Meaning* (n 116) 52 (and the further discussion there); Asgeirsson, *The Nature and Value of Vagueness in the Law* (n 15); Moreso and Chilovi, 'Interpretive Arguments and the Application of the Law' (n 5). For an epistemic, and not normative reconstruction of legislative intent: R Poscher, 'The Normative Construction of Legislative Intent' in Institut Michel Villey (eds), *Le droit et la philosophie analytique*, Droit & Philosophie vol 9 (Paris, Dalloz, 2018).

[192] Matczak, 'Why Legal Rules Are Not Speech Acts and What Follows from That?' (n 154) 336.

[193] cf Greenberg, 'Legislation as Communication? (n 5) 43.

much univocal *correspondence* as possible between individual legislative provisions (the individual norm-sentences making up the legislative text) and the norms so produced, from the descriptive point of view it is easy to show that there is no such *necessary* correspondence. On the one hand, from one (semantically or sintactically ambiguous) norm-sentence we might obtain two or more norm-meanings, like with the norm-sentence 'No person with a mole can enter restaurants in the city of Rome.' Who is being prohibited from entry, people with the animal mole, or people with the skin spot? Or both?

On the other hand, often several norm-sentences interact with each other – in what is (somewhat poorly) called in Italian '*combinato disposto*' and rendered in English as 'combined provisions' – to yield only one, complex, norm-meaning. In this sense, individual norms are obtained starting from so-called 'base clauses' and then integrated with 'supplementing clauses' that are expressed by other norm-sentences, possibly even contained in different statutes than the one where the base clause is.[194] To be sure, this interaction between different provisions can not only result in a complex norm(-meaning), but also in the specifications of substantive and procedural requirements vis-à-vis the judicial ascription of responsibility for the violation of the original duty-imposing norm. The *mens rea* requirement in criminal law, and its interaction with substantive duty-imposing norms, comes to mind here.[195] A perhaps even more telling example, for our purposes, relates to the famous 'no vehicles in the park' rule, which since the Hart-Fuller debate has generated an incredible wealth of literature.[196] For one of the counter-examples that are supposed to show the indeterminacy (or underdeterminacy) of the rule before contextual or teleological interpretation is that of an ambulance that is entering the park in order to assist a person who has fallen from a tree and is gravely injured. Does the rule apply to the ambulance or not?

One possibility that has not seemingly gained traction in the literature is that, as a matter of fact, the 'no vehicles in the park' norm-sentence might need to be integrated, while being applied by a court to a specific case, by another normative fragment as expressed by a different norm-sentence in the relevant legal system.[197] This would certainly be the case in Italy, for instance, where

---

[194] Matczak, 'Why Legal Rules Are Not Speech Acts and What Follows from That?' (n 154) 336. See also Duxbury, *Elements of Legislation* (n 171) 143–44. This acknowledgement seems also implicit in Asgeirsson's 'Pro Tanto View' about legal content: Asgeirsson, *The Nature and Value of Vagueness in the Law* (n 15) 13–20.

[195] In this regard, it seems utterly counterintuitive (and ultimately misleading) to consider the *mens rea* presumption as generating instead a 'limitation on the scope of the obligation' created by the primary criminal law provisions: Smith, 'The practice-based objection to the "standard picture" of how law works' (n 42) 511–512. The form of behaviour prohibited by the primary norm does not become lawful because of the *mens rea* presumption: for example, the legal system might still require compensation to be paid to those who have been affected by the wrong.

[196] On which, see, eg: Schauer, 'A Critical Guide to Vehicles in the Park' (n 46).

[197] T Endicott, 'Legal Interpretation' in A Marmor (ed), *The Routledge Companion to Philosophy of Law* (New York, Routledge, 2012) 118, seems to hint at this possibility.

198 An Alternative Picture of a Multifaceted Relationship

Article 4 of law 689/1981 states a number of exceptions that prevent the ascription of responsibility to an agent for violation of an administrative norm (like the no vehicle in the park rule). In this case, the rule is *determined* after all, in that it applies to ambulances entering the park – as an ambulance clearly falls under the linguistic meaning of the rule – but, if the driver of the ambulance is entering the park to rescue someone gravely injured, she will not be held responsible for the violation of the rule.[198]

This fallacy of a-discursivity, and its many ramifications, points to the important pragmatic observation that with legal text-acts the relevant co-text – that is, the relevant context as constituted by other legal provisions – can go beyond the immediate norm-sentence and even beyond the statute in which the given norm-sentence is contained. In this respect, Poggi has isolated four potential levels of co-text identifiable in modern legal systems: 1) the other paragraphs of the same section of a statute as the given norm-sentence; 2) the other sections of the same statute; 3) different statutes in the legal system; or 4) the general principles of the system.[199] She argues that the lack of accepted rules as to which level should be considered in establishing the content of each legal utterance confirms the pervasive underdeterminacy of their literal meanings.

I have two kinds of replies to Poggi's remarks. First, as I just said, my impression is that this co-textual integration of a provision happens often at the level of the substantive and procedural requirements of its official application to individual cases, and not at the level of the semantic content of the provision itself. That is, the integration of the 'no vehicles in the park' rule with the administrative provision that excuses officials who breach that rule in performing their functions does not change the content of the former. There is still a violation of the no-vehicle rule, but this violation will not attract liability – the same applies in the criminal case of *mens rea* requirements, and with other instances of these so-called 'modifier laws'.

Second, when it comes to the contribution of the co-text to the literal meaning of an individual legislative provision, not all levels as identified by Poggi seem relevant. For while the first three she identifies can indeed (and by default) contribute to the saturation of indexical and semantic connotations of specific words or expressions of the given (textual) utterance, the fourth level – the general principles of the system – comes into play as co-text only if contained in legislation in the first place. If instead these general principles are customary, they should be properly considered outside the 'frame' of the co-text and within the wider category of the accepted interpretive criteria of the system.[200]

---

[198] Conversely, if the driver of the ambulance enters the park to enjoy his lunch break in the sunshine and quiet, the fact that he is driving an ambulance will not matter and he will be held responsible for violation of the rule.

[199] Poggi, 'The Myth of Literal Meaning in Legal Interpretation' (n 103) 320–21.

[200] In other words, we cannot consider these general principles (*qua* norms) as linguistically relevant for the co-text. I owe this observation to David Duarte.

Overall, the always potential interplay between individual (textual) utterances and these levels of co-text clarifies the sense in which legislative utterances should be considered as 'complex' text-acts. But while I disagree with Poggi about the possibility of theoretical determination of these levels of co-text, I do accept that current law-making and interpretive practices in many legal systems identify the relevant levels of co-text in unsystematic and sometimes contradictory ways. The problem is also that, the *further* the relevant level of co-text is from the legislative utterance in question, the more likely a court might depart from the literal meaning of the individual utterance, particularly with the third level (and, bearing in mind what we just said, to the fourth level as well).

In other words, this potential 'distance' between utterance and (levels of) co-text produces an additional source of interpretive discretion for courts, which in turn can make the content of the law *opaque* to its addressees in the first place. For even a zealous layperson, who looks for the content of the law in the statute that is supposed to regulate the activity she is interested in, will likely miss a 'supplementing clause' that bears on the legal effect of the first provision but is contained in a different statute (or in one of the general principles of the system). And how could anyone blame her? In the current context of over-inflation and fragmentation of legislative activity – or 'hyper-regulation' – this source of interpretive discretion represents, in my view, one of the biggest (but perhaps less politically significant) threats to the rule of law in our constitutional democracies.

To be sure, the dangers for the rule of law associated with this source of interpretive discretion already constituted the drive behind the idea of codifying entire parts of large, all-encompassing modern legal systems. The point of an 'enclosed' codex is precisely that of collecting, in one place, all the norms that are relevant in a given area of social life, so as to minimise the extent of interpretive discretion due to the gap between individual provisions and their potential interaction with other provisions (that is, their co-text). Alas, this tendency has arguably only got worse in recent decades, to the point that the inflation and fragmentation of legislation – particularly delegated legislation – has prompted in many countries the call for a constitutional 'codex reservation', at least for criminal norms: that is, the obligation for the legislator who wants to modify a certain area of the law to do so only through the modification of the codex itself.[201] This prompts two remarks in concluding this section.

First, the possibility of codification of entire areas of a legal system marks another fundamental difference between legal and ordinary communication: the boundaries of the relevant co-text of the legislative utterance can be artificially fixed *ex-ante*,[202] unlike in ordinary communicative exchanges. This diminishes

---

[201] See, eg: L Ferrajoli, *Il paradigma garantista. Filosofia e critica del diritto penale* (Naples, Editoriale scientifica, 2016) 215ff.
[202] Poggi, 'The Myth of Literal Meaning in Legal Interpretation' (n 103) 317 correctly notes that the co-text of legal utterances is, in this sense, 'fixed'.

200 An Alternative Picture of a Multifaceted Relationship

the overall scope for pragmatic enrichment in supplementing the literal meaning of individual legislative utterances and the resulting degree of interpretive discretion courts will find themselves equipped with. More precisely, this source of indeterminacy could be, if not fully avoided, drastically reduced by codifications that clearly exhaust the relevant co-text of a given sub-system of norms (possibly also by stating the principles that are applicable *ratione materiae*).

Second, and more generally, the discussion of legal meaning developed here should caution against the idea that normative theories of interpretation (à la Dworkin) might ever succeed by themselves in constraining the discretionary powers of courts in modern legal systems.[203] This is not just the Hartian remark that a degree of judicial discretionary decision-making is actually desirable, given the human incapacity to predict all possible contexts of application of a legal rule.[204] Rather, the point is that legal theory should focus on the enterprise of modelling a science of *good* legislation, reverting to the lessons of an important strand of the Enlightenment.[205] This science of legislation is preoccupied with facilitating the fulfilment of the action-guidance requirement, especially in those areas of the law in which, from the lack of compliance, the use of coercion and punishment against the individual might ensue. Ultimately, what I am saying is that the pursuit of the values embodied by fundamental doctrines such as the rule of law and the separation of powers is, from a meta-theoretical point of view, significantly more dependent on a rigorous model (and process) of law-creation than on sophisticated theories of interpretation of law.

VII. AN ALTERNATIVE THEORY OF LEGAL MEANING: SEMANTIC MINIMALISM

My aim so far in this chapter has been to question, and ultimately to reject, the idea that we are entitled to straightforwardly apply Gricean and post-Gricean pragmatic theories to law.[206] *Pace* Poggi, there *is* a 'fracture' between ordinary conversation and legal communication – which is not 'difficult to explain'

---

[203] *cf* Duxbury, *Elements of Legislation* (n 171) 131.

[204] In this sense, it seems reasonable to observe that the communication of legal standards by means of general rules addressed to the public at large is necessarily primarily aimed at those contexts of application where the agent is faced with prototypical instances of a given word or expression as picked out by the rule itself.

[205] G Filangieri, *La scienza della legislazione* (first published 1780–1785, Naples, Grimaldi, 2003); J Bentham, *Introduction to the Principles of Morals and Legislation* (JH Burns and HLA Hart eds, London, Athlone Press, 1970); and see, more recently, LJ Wintgens, *Legisprudence: Practical Reason in Legislation* (Farnham, Ashgate, 2012).

[206] These also include the original theory of legal implicatures advanced by Skoczeń, *Implicatures within Legal Language* (n 7).

An Alternative Theory of Legal Meaning: Semantic Minimalism   201

after all.[207] It is due to the written, administered, multi-contextual, autonomous, closed, and unilateral nature of legal communication. This different nature of legal language and communication does not mean that pragmatic enrichment of sentence meaning is not relevant in legal interpretation. On the contrary, I argue this is exactly how to draw the boundary between the two most famous existing methods of legal interpretation, the literal and the purposive method. What the different nature of legal communication seems to indicate, instead, is that radical contextualism is not a theory 'for all seasons' (if at all), and that we can only intelligibly account for instances of multi-contextual, text-based communication if we adopt some form of semantic minimalism as the theory of legal meaning, especially in the form defended by Emma Borg for instance.[208]

Thus, far from being ideological,[209] the preference for literal or sentence meaning in legal interpretation is a conceptual necessity,[210] also vis-à-vis the action-guidance and collective autonomy requirements that we have discussed at the beginning of this chapter.[211] If law is the enterprise of guiding conduct through rules, the communication of such rules must generally suffice for law's addressees – in their different categories, from the larger (laypeople) to the smaller (for example, doctors) – to understand what is required of them. That is to say, the legal system needs to successfully communicate standards of behaviour (at least in a majority of cases) to incredibly vast audiences in a stable manner across time and space and through multiple contexts. But if these contents were to be, in the vast majority of cases, a function of the *opaque* context of creation and potentially infinite wide contexts of reception, then it is not clear how the law could communicate in a stable manner anything at all.

This is the key respect, I submit, in which legal and ordinary communication are nothing alike. Ordinary, face-to-face communication relies heavily on

---

[207] Poggi, 'The Myth of Literal Meaning in Legal Interpretation' (n 103). It is worth noting that Poggi's own contextualism, in subsequent writings, appears to have become more 'moderate': *cf*, for instance, Poggi, *Il Modello Conversazionale* (n 159) 315–19.

[208] I originally argued for the application of Borg's semantic minimalism to legal interpretation in my doctoral dissertation at Edinburgh. See P Sandro, 'Creation and Application of Law: A Neglected Distinction' (PhD thesis, University of Edinburgh, 2014). Skoczeń has expanded on the application of Borgian 'liberal truth conditions' to legal interpretation in I Skoczeń, 'Minimal Semantics and Legal Interpretation' (2016) 29(3) *International Journal for the Semiotics of Law* 615. Borg has now explicitly acknowledged the scope for application of her minimalism in legal theory: Borg, 'Explanatory Roles for Minimal Content' (n 155). For a rejection of the application of semantic minimalism to law (albeit from within a defence of the ordinary meaning doctrine): Slocum, *Ordinary Meaning* (n 116) 152–53; instead, for a contextualism-based rejection, see, eg: Chiassoni, *Interpretation without Truth* (n 8) ch 4.

[209] Chiassoni, *Interpretation without Truth* (n 8) 75.

[210] See Slocum, 'Pragmatics and legal texts' (n 147) 142; V Velluzzi, *Le Preleggi e L'interpretazione: Un'Introduzione Critica* (Pisa, Edizioni ETS, 2013) 30; Neale, 'Stephen Neale on Meaning and Interpretation' (n 96) 263 ('if we don't treat legislation as drafted literally and carefully, then we're essentially undermining the very idea of law').

[211] *cf* Ekins, *The Nature of Legislative Intent* (n 149) 126.

202   *An Alternative Picture of a Multifaceted Relationship*

pragmatic features of the context of utterance (which is normally shared by speaker and hearer), as this enables lexico-syntactical structures to be kept at a minimum, maximising the immediacy and efficiency of the speech-act. Legal communication instead, given its different macro-pragmatic functions, must rely as little as possible on the context of utterance (besides the co-text) and instead encode as far as possible a given deontic content in the lexico-syntactical 'vehicles' making up the text.

Of course, this does not deny that in some contexts of application what is communicated by the law might turn out to be underdetermined or might generate consequences that were not foreseen by the legislator. As we shall see in a moment, rich pragmatic enrichment plays a role especially in cases that are mostly discussed by scholars in the literature. But if this lack of determinacy were to happen in each and every context of application – because of the default impossibility of reaching truth-evaluable communicative meaning before accessing rich contextual resources[212] – then law, as a normative practice, could never reach any coordinative or cooperative function in the first place. This is without even considering the fact that, if a legal system is also democratic, the 'collective autonomy' requirement bites too, thus demanding even more strictly that the normative standards that govern the community are directly or indirectly created by 'the people' themselves (and not by unelected and unaccountable courts).

What does this semantic minimalism look like? Borg offers a concise definition of it as the 'conjunction' of four main claims:

(i)   Semantic content for sentences is truth-evaluable content.
(ii) Semantic content for sentences is fully determined by syntactic structure and lexical content: the meaning of a sentence is exhausted by the meaning of its parts and their mode of composition.
(iii) There are only a limited number of context-sensitive expressions in natural language.
(iv) Recovery of semantic content is possible without access to current speaker intentions (crudely, grasp of semantic content involves 'word reading' not 'mind reading').[213]

It should be noted immediately how this view does not depart completely from pragmatics, for it acknowledges the role of the latter but within the 'structure' as given to it by lexico-syntactic elements, so that it has also been defined as 'formal pragmatics'.[214] That is, in order to yield propositional or truth-evaluable content, the content generated by (well-formed) lexico-syntactic sequences

---

[212] Chiassoni, *Interpretation without Truth* (n 8) 97.

[213] Borg, 'Semantics without pragmatics?' (n 71) 521–22; and for the difference between her semantic minimalism and that of Cappelen and Lepore, see ibid 522's endnote 16 (672–73); and *cf* Borg, *Pursuing Meaning* (n 76) ch 1.

[214] Borg, 'Semantics without pragmatics?' (n 71) 522.

An Alternative Theory of Legal Meaning: Semantic Minimalism 203

must be 'relativized to a context of utterance in order to allow for reference assignment for indexicals, demonstratives, and tense markers'.[215] And while (iii) distinguishes minimalism from 'indexicalist' positions like Stanley's,[216] where the majority (if not all) linguistic expressions are considered to have indexical elements, it is (iv) that should readily indicate why semantic minimalism can account neatly for what we usually call, in legal practice, sentence (or literal) meaning.[217] Once again, radical contextualist theories (à la Recanati) applied to legal communication reinforce certain strands of scepticism, and are used to disprove the notion of sentence (or literal) meaning as a valid candidate for the meaning of legal utterances.[218]

My argument instead shows how, once the differences between the ordinary, face-to-face model of communication – after which Gricean and post-Gricean pragmatics are modelled – and some types of communication through complex written texts are properly identified, it is precisely only a minimalist approach to sentence meaning that can account for our capacity to communicate complex sets of information about the world that remain stable despite the potentially infinite context of reception of those acts of communication. This amounts to the grain of truth captured since time immemorial by traditional semantic theories of legal interpretation (and their 'quasi-cognitivism') despite their philosophical coarseness. But once supplemented by the semantic minimalism à la Borg, these theories acquire renewed strength against their contextualist counterparts.[219] I should also note how, interestingly, the semantic theories I have in mind here have been recently clarified – as part of their defences of contextualism – by authors like Chiassoni or Poggi.[220]

To be sure, the key dispute as explicitly acknowledged by some on both sides of the theoretical divide in the relevant literature,[221] is about the notion of 'what is said'. In this regard, both approaches – minimalists and contextualists – recognise the existence of a level of a-contextual meaning (which for contextualists corresponds to the meaning of the sentence-type, the sentence before contextual enrichment) and of a level of pragmatic meaning that instead tracks the intended meaning of the speaker. The fundamental difference is as to whether the notion of 'what is said' by a speaker in uttering a certain sentence is already

---

[215] Borg, 'Explanatory Roles for Minimal Content' (n 155) 515.

[216] See, eg: J Stanley, 'Making it Articulated' (2002) 17(1–2) Mind & Language 149.

[217] Borg herself has explicitly acknowledged this explanatory role for minimalism in Borg, 'Explanatory Roles for Minimal Content' (n 155).

[218] Chiassoni, Interpretation without Truth (n 8) ch 4.

[219] This can be explicitly seen in Skoczeń, 'Minimal Semantics and Legal Interpretation' (n 208).

[220] See Poggi, 'The Myth of Literal Meaning in Legal Interpretation' (n 103) 319–21, with her notion of 'legal textual meaning', and Chiassoni, Interpretation without Truth (n 8) 87–92, with his illustration of 'literalism'.

[221] See, eg: E Borg, 'Minimalism versus Contextualism in Semantics' in G Preyer and G Peter (eds), Context-Sensitivity and Semantic Minimalism: New Essays on Semantics and Pragmatics (Oxford, Oxford University Press, 2007).

204 *An Alternative Picture of a Multifaceted Relationship*

a fully pragmatic notion or whether instead it is determined by lexico-semantic components prior to *rich* contextual enrichment.[222]

But as Borg has recently noted, the notion of 'what is said' seems to be shifting depending on the 'social aims and purposes' of the different linguistic acts that we perform.[223] This implies that, while in the case of ordinary conversational exchanges 'what is said' by someone in uttering a certain sentence will normally amount to something different than the literal meaning of the sentence uttered, in some written communicative endeavours – and certainly in legal communication – 'what is said' is determined by the semantic (or literal) content of the utterance prior to wide (or rich) pragmatic enrichment. This is because, in these situations, written language is a means to communicate standards of behaviour and other normative contents to a multitude of recipients across different – both in time and space – contexts of application. It is also a consequence of the fact that, in the case of typical text-acts, the context of creation of the utterance that is fully accessible to the recipients of the communication is limited to the co-text.[224] And as we said already, there seems to be a fundamental difference between the notion of co-text of a text-act and that of the context surrounding a speech-act, in that the former – but not the latter – can be purposely *fixed* by the author of the text-act itself.[225]

This means, in other words, that the author of a text-act can make the co-text of an utterance as informative as she considers necessary for the successful outcome of the communicative act, keeping in mind that, unlike in a face-to-face conversation, the receiver of the text will not be able to ask for clarification if in doubt about the intended meaning of the utterance. As such, in these communicative text-acts the author, if she wants to successfully transmit exactly the *same* message to any number of different recipients across a variety of contexts, must seek a higher degree of 'accuracy and precision of meaning' than in ordinary, face-to-face conversation.[226] This means not just reducing as far as possible syntactical ambiguity, but also, for instance, making the co-text as informative as possible – so that the saturation and/or connotation of lexical-grammatical elements are exhausted by said co-text and, in this sense, determined by it.[227]

---

[222] Chiassoni distinguishes between three levels of meaning: what is proffered (conventional), what is said (pragmatic explicit), and what is implied (pragmatic implicit): Chiassoni, *Interpretation without Truth* (n 8) 97.

[223] Borg, 'Explanatory Roles for Minimal Content' (n 155) 517.

[224] See, for discussion, Poggi, 'The Myth of Literal Meaning in Legal Interpretation' (n 103) 319–21; this is roughly what I understand Chiassoni as identifying as 'semantic context': Chiassoni, *Interpretation without Truth* (n 8) 90.

[225] Skoczeń, 'Minimal Semantics and Legal Interpretation' (n 208) 617, 628.

[226] Borg, 'Explanatory Roles for Minimal Content' (n 155) 522; see also Tiersma, 'A Message in a Bottle' (n 50). In this sense one can distinguish legal communication from poetry, for instance, where instead the intention of the author of the poem might be – and typically is – much looser as to the 'sameness' of the message elicited in the audience of the poem.

[227] Poggi correctly argues that as long as this saturation is a function of the limited co-text of a certain legislative clause, the fact that literal meaning might need this saturation does not amount

Prolegomena to a Theory of Legal Interpretation 205

The overall point is that, in order to communicate content consistently across time and space, the author must 'settle' for the only stable and context-invariant level of meaning that even some contextualists acknowledge:[228] again, sentence meaning (as relativised to the context of utterance, which in case of text-acts amounts to the relevant co-text). In a nutshell, she must *make* 'what is said' into a conventional, rather than pragmatic, notion.[229]

Therefore, in the case of complex text-acts, what is said is not a direct function of the intention of the speaker, as contextualists claim for ordinary communication, but of what we can call 'objective' determinants:[230] lexico-grammatical structures and their interrelations as part of a complex text. As such, when we seek the 'authorial intention' in legal communication, what we are actually doing is to reconstruct the *hypothetical* intention of a collective body like a legislature. In this regard I agree with all those authors, like Raz or Matczak, who argue that the only illocutionary intention that members of a legislature might share – and that is epistemically accessible, and aggregable – is the illocutionary intention of enacting a given text as law.[231] The locutionary intentions of the members of the legislature might even be absent, as in the extreme but not unlikely scenario of a member of a legislative assembly who votes on a bill without having even read it. One could imagine the case in which members of a parliamentary majority are whipped by the party to vote and approve a bill no one among them has read. Yet the text-act will nonetheless have a meaning which is a function of the objective determinants of the text-act – lexico-grammatical structures and their interrelations as part of the co-text. Of course, a number of factors – and particularly the finite nature and informative richness of the co-text – will influence the degree of determinacy of the utterances that make up the text-act. But it is precisely in the cases in which the content of the single utterance is not determinate – that is, in those cases of application in which lexico-grammatical structure underdetermine the meaning of the utterance (for instance because of ambiguity, like in the example of the mole above) – that we must seek the 'intention' of the author of the text-act.

VIII. PROLEGOMENA TO A THEORY OF LEGAL INTERPRETATION

What are the consequences of the theory of meaning proposed here for legal interpretation? While I cannot put forward a comprehensive theory in the context

---

to a problem for the supporter of traditional semantic theories: Poggi, 'The Myth of Literal Meaning in Legal Interpretation' (n 103).

[228] Borg, 'Explanatory Roles for Minimal Content' (n 155) 522. This contention is even more noteworthy in the legal case, as there is not any single actual (locutionary) intention behind the adoption of a given text as law. *cf* also Ong, *Orality and Literacy* (n 170) 110.

[229] Borg, 'Explanatory Roles for Minimal Content' (n 155) 522.

[230] Slocum, 'Introduction' (n 132) 7; Skoczeń, 'Minimal Semantics and Legal Interpretation' (n 208) 622.

[231] Matczak, 'Three Kinds of Intention in Lawmaking' (n 62).

206 *An Alternative Picture of a Multifaceted Relationship*

of this book, I would like to highlight the most noteworthy clarifications that the theory of semantic minimalism defended here yields. To be sure, we should begin by pointing out that interpretation is used in legal discourse with a variety of meanings, the result being that we face an inherently polysemic concept.[232] Properly speaking, with interpretation we refer either to the activity of ascribing meaning to an object (which could be an utterance, a text, a painting, or any sign in general), or to the result itself of that activity. Moreover, in legal discourse, by interpretation is often meant the whole of the operations carried out by judges and jurists.[233] This is problematic, as we often end up calling certain activities 'interpretation' which are not, properly speaking, interpretive at all.[234]

In particular, two basic distinctions remain often implicit when discussing different types of legal interpretation: that between text-oriented and fact-oriented interpretation, and that between cognitive and adjudicative interpretation.[235] Text-oriented interpretation is the (mental) activity that brings us from a legal text to the norm(s) as expressed by the norm-sentences contained in the text. In this sense, it presupposes the distinction we have already encountered between norm-sentences (or provisions) and norms *tout court*. It can also be called interpretation *in abstracto*, as it does not refer to any particular case, unlike fact-oriented interpretation which instead refers to the activity of subsuming a given set of facts, sometimes called operative, under a previously identified norm.[236] It is worth noting how both state officials (including courts) and laypeople (and in particular lawyers and law professors) can, and routinely do, perform both types of interpretive activities, with the difference that only those carried out by the former category will be directly (as opposed to indirectly) authoritative for the legal system.[237]

The second distinction, between cognitive and adjudicative interpretation, appears to straddle the previous distinction. For Guastini, explicitly following Kelsen on this point, cognitive interpretation

> consists in identifying the various possible meanings of a legal text – the meanings *admissible* on the basis of *shared* linguistic (syntactic, semantic, and pragmatic)

---

[232] Riccardo Guastini, for one, has dedicated a great deal of his work to unpack the concept of legal interpretation: see, for instance, in English: R Guastini, 'Rule-Scepticism Restated' in L Green and B Leiter (eds), *Oxford Studies in Philosophy of Law*, vol 1 (Oxford, Oxford University Press, 2011) 138–44.

[233] ibid 142.

[234] Endicott, 'Legal Interpretation' (n 197).

[235] See Guastini, 'Rule-Scepticism Restated' (n 232), 138–44.

[236] Guastini (ibid, 140) clarifies that while text-oriented interpretation deals with the sense ('*Sinn*') of an utterance, fact-oriented interpretation has to do with its extension or reference ('*Bedeutung*').

[237] This does not imply that the importance of text-oriented and fact-oriented interpretation by lawyers and law professors (among others) should be underestimated: the former, because very often the decision by a court in a specific legal proceeding will be based on the interpretation carried out by counsel for one of the two parties; the latter, because law-professors train the future generations of lawyers and judges, critically shaping their interpretive outlook since the beginning of their law careers (and potentially influencing departures from existing interpretive canons in the given legal community). *cf* P Chiassoni, *Tecnica dell'interpretazione giuridica* (Bologna, Il Mulino, 2007) 2.

rules, accepted methods of legal interpretation, and existing juristic theories – without choosing any one of them.[238]

Adjudicative interpretation amounts instead to selecting one of the meanings so identified (or identifiable) as *the* correct legal meaning of a text. Both of these activities should be instead contrasted with so-called 'creative interpretation', that is with the ascription of meaning to a legal sentence that is not amongst the meanings identified through cognitive interpretation (ie, that is outside the proverbial Kelsenian 'frame' as established through the cognitive interpretation of the text). Guastini correctly notes that when a meaning outside the 'admissible' meanings is assigned to a given norm-sentence, we should not be talking anymore of interpretation, but rather of 'interstitial legislation' or '[juristic] construction'.[239]

This, by one of the most famous legal realists from the Genoa school, amounts to an absolutely crucial observation: even if one were to concede that all interpretation can be said to have a discretionary element, the ascription of meaning outside the 'frame' identified by cognitive interpretation appears to be an altogether different endeavour from it.[240] The problem is that we seem warranted in making a distinction between interpretation (properly speaking) and interstitial legislation or construction only if legal interpretation is a rule-governed activity in the first place, and therefore we can discriminate between those interpretive results that are permissible under the established rules (in Kelsenian terms, that are within the frame) and those which fall outside of them.[241]

For otherwise, if legal interpretation is the ascription of potentially *any* meaning to an object – that is, if legal interpretation is ultimately subjective – then it is not clear on which basis we could (and should) distinguish between admissible and 'inadmissible' interpretations of the same linguistic object. This might be the case perhaps with abstract forms of art where the ascription of meaning is left entirely to the subjectivity of the beholder. But could anything that we currently (or in the past) identify as law exist, if legal interpretation were to be a subjective practice like abstract art? As I have discussed in chapter one and argued at length in another work,[242] this does not seem to be the case: for law is an institutional normative practice precisely because it is not subjective, otherwise no cooperation nor coordination (and neither the other further social aims that can be pursued through these two) could ever be achieved through it.

---

[238] Guastini, 'Rule-Scepticism Restated' (n 232) 141 (my emphasis).

[239] ibid 142.

[240] See Klatt, *Making the Law Explicit* (n 141). The distinction between interpretation and construction is used in a slightly different way in Anglo-American scholarship: see, eg: L Solum, 'The Interpretation-Construction Distinction' (2010) 27(1) *Constitutional Commentary* 95.

[241] As we argued in ch 3, this undermines the internal consistency of Guastini's position: see ch 3, n 203.

[242] Sandro, 'Unlocking Legal Validity' (n 143).

208 An Alternative Picture of a Multifaceted Relationship

Instead, law is a specific instrument of social control precisely because the 'no vehicles in the park' rule can be applied to cars and possibly electric scooters, but a person walking with a dog on a leash cannot be stopped from entering the park on this basis – and if she is, we can readily criticise that decision as being *arbitrary*.[243] It would be an inadmissible interpretation and application of the legal utterance in question. But this is in turn only possible if we have some inter-subjective criteria to distinguish between interpretations and 'constructions' of a given legal text. It is here that we can appreciate the difference between the minimalist approach to legal meaning defended here and contextualist approaches. The latter, if they take their contextualism seriously, cannot provide any such criteria without undermining the internal consistency of their position according to which meaning is, for any given context of utterance, a function of speaker's intention and not of lexico-syntactical elements.[244] Accordingly, Poggi admits (with a bit of an understatement) that once we accept contextualism

> the boundary between interpretation and creation of law (or between application and interpretation) must be drawn in a different way (and appears more uncertain).[245]

But undercutting the distinction between the creation and application of law, as we said at the beginning of this chapter, yields the impossibility to fulfil the two fundamental requirements – action-guidance and collective autonomy – that are presupposed by modern legal systems. On the one hand, if there was no tenden-tially intersubjective criteria to establish, in most occasions, what a given legal text means (or at least the range of linguistic permissible meanings),[246] it is not clear how the normative practice we identify as law could ever succeed in secur-ing coordination and cooperation in a large and differentiated social group. On the other, how could we ever affirm that the people, even indirectly, govern themselves if unelected judges were always able to ascribe whatever meaning to a legislative text as enacted by the people themselves (through a referendum) or by their representative? This is the sense in which, then, Guastini correctly affirms that 'Constructing unexpressed rules amounts to disguised legislation by interpreters.'[247]

As such, within the theory of meaning and legal interpretation defended here, there is no contrast between the interpretation and the application of law. Interpretation – which, as we shall clarify in the next chapter, does not always involve a creative or discretionary activity – is what bring us from a legal text (a source of law) to the meaning(s) *expressed* by that text (a legal norm). Application is instead, in a first approximate sense, the activity of using a legal

---

[243] See Slocum, 'Introduction' (n 132).

[244] To put it differently, under the radical contextualist picture, there is no limit to the pragmatic enrichment brought by context to the literal meaning of the utterance.

[245] Poggi, 'The Myth of Literal Meaning in Legal Interpretation' (n 103).

[246] Slocum, 'Introduction' (n 132) 3.

[247] Guastini, 'Rule-Scepticism Restated' (n 232) 144.

Conclusion   209

norm as a reason for action and thus for deciding to act in a certain way rather than another *because* of the norm. This means that someone could apply a norm that is the product of interpretation (or understanding), as well as a legal norm that is not the result of interpretation, but of construction or interstitial legislation. In one sense, then, all judicial decision are acts of law-application. The real question is whether 'the law', as identified by the judge and which is the basis for the decision in the instant case, is the product of understanding or interpretation, or of construction by the judge. Once again, if we apply a radical contextualist picture of meaning to legal communication, this latter distinction disappears, for there are no (conventional) limits to the potential meanings expressed by each individual utterance.

IX. CONCLUSION

In summary, the text-act theory of legal meaning sketched in this chapter explains in which sense we should properly understand claims, such as Slocum's, that communicative meaning and literal (or sentence) meaning in law 'often correspond', unlike in ordinary conversations.[248] In explaining why this is the case, I have endeavoured to reject the applicability of radical contextual positions to explain how legal communication works. 'What is said' by a legislative text-act is, in my account, a function of the literal level of meaning, allowing only for relativisation to the context of utterance, which is in turn exhausted by the co-text of the utterance and thus conceptually more determinate vis-à-vis the context of ordinary face-to-face conversations.

This has two key theoretical advantages over contextualist models: it can straightforwardly explain the multi-contextuality of legislative text-acts – that is, the expression of a meaning that is stable across multiple contexts of interpretation, while also coherently making sense of the possibility of interaction between the literal meanings of different norms in the legal system, as part of said co-text. As to the former, a convincing explanation of the communication of meaning across contexts is even more relevant in such cases, like legislative texts, where there is typically no single locutionary intention that ultimately determines the linguistic content of such acts. Contextualists instead seem only able to affirm that, in these types of communicative scenarios, there is a *striking* convergence of (pragmatic) interpretations, despite multiple contexts of interpretation and lack of a shared conversational context between author and readers. But what is this convergence due to, if not precisely to the conventionality of (the level of) meaning deployed by the author(s) of a text?

The second explanatory advantage should not be underestimated either: the minimalist theory of legal meaning defended here appears to be the only one

---

[248] Slocum, 'Introduction' (n 132) 2; Skoczeń, 'Minimal Semantics and Legal Interpretation' (n 208) 629; *cf* Schauer, *Playing by the Rules* (n 141) 54–56.

210   *An Alternative Picture of a Multifaceted Relationship*

that allows us to distinguish in a principled way between not only (linguistically) clear and unclear cases in law, but also between judicial interpretations of a given text that can be considered properly so, and operations by courts which instead are inherently *creative*, in the sense that they assign a meaning to a legal text outside the frame of 'valid' or acceptable meanings expressed by the text itself (including also those derived through the methods of interpretation accepted in the given jurisdiction). In this regard, it clarifies that the potential source of indeterminacy is not in the interaction of two or more legislative utterances per se – or between a legislative utterance and a principle of the system – but in how *salient* that interaction is made by the legal system itself. For the more the different levels of co-text to any legislative utterance are fixed by means of systematisation (and ultimately codification) of an entire area of law, the more determinate the literal meaning of those individual utterances will be.

To conclude, I cannot explore here all the implications that the novel approach to legal meaning defended in this chapter has vis-à-vis the debate as to the contribution of the communicative meaning of legal utterances to the content of the law. I have to leave that for another occasion. In the rest of this book, I assume that the content of the law is typically determined by what the authorities communicate, as most legal theorists do anyway. If anything, I believe that the text-act theory presented here gives new support to this position, especially in light of some very recent objections that have been brought against it.[249] It does so while questioning the epistemic assumptions of the Standard Picture (the mainstream conception of legal communication), and by claiming that we should adopt a different understanding of how the communicative content of legal utterances comes about: namely as part of a text-based discourse in which the linguistic content of individual norm-sentences interact with each other to produce the overall content of the law.[250]

This understanding, I submit, fits much better with how legal practice works, and in particular with what drafters, lawyers, and judges do. It also allows us not only to make sense in a principled way of the different types of interaction between individual provisions (and canons of interpretation) as contained in different parts of the legal system (like in the *mens rea* example mentioned above), but also to highlight what causes the potential gap (and how to tackle it) between the individual norm-sentences as contained in legislation and other sources, and the overall content of the law.

---

[249] See Smith, 'The practice-based objection to the "standard picture" of how law works' (n 42).
[250] See also Asgeirsson, *The Nature and Value of Vagueness in the Law* (n 15) ch 1.

6

Creation and Application of Law.
An Analytical Distinction

I. INTRODUCTION

A S WE HAVE seen in chapter two, the key structural characteristic of modern constitutional democracies lies in the normative-institutional tension between the principle of collective autonomy and the protection of individual rights (as heteronomous limits to the former).[1] On the paradigmatic level, this idea has been expressed – by both Habermas and Ferrajoli – through the image of constitutional democracy being the union of the two spheres of 'what is' and 'what is not' *decidable* (in their constant interaction).[2] In the common vocabulary of political philosophy, these two spheres correspond, respectively, to the two basic principles of democracy and of constitutionalism. According to Ferrajoli, this dyadic structure is mirrored on the institutional level by two (and not three, as we shall clarify in the next chapter) different kinds of state functions, 'government' and 'guarantee' (as illustrated in Table 1 below).[3] Finally, at the most basic level of this structure, the juridical level, we find the distinction between creation and application of law.

Table 1 The dyadic structure of modern constitutional democracy

LEVELS	AUTONOMY	HETERONOMY
Paradigmatic	Sphere of what is decidable	Sphere of what is not decidable
Political Philosophy	Democracy	Constitutionalism
Institutional	Functions of government	Functions of guarantee
Juridical	Creation of law	Application of law

One of the overall objectives in chapter two was precisely to show how this 'bottom' level is the one upon which all the higher levels are premised. For if

---

[1] *cf* Hart and Sacks' 'principle of institutional settlement' in HM Hart, Jr and AM Sacks, *The Legal Process: Basic Problems in the Making and Application of Law* (WN Eskridge and PP Frickey eds, New York, Foundations Press, 1994) 4–5.

[2] See ch 2, sections V and VI.

[3] L Ferrajoli, *Principia Iuris*, vol 1 (Bari, Laterza, 2007) 873–75.

212 *Creation and Application of Law. An Analytical Distinction*

there cannot be anything like a distinction between the activities of creation and application of law, those very principles (democracy and constitutionalism) and institutional structures (government and guarantee functions), which lie at the core of our modern constitutional democracies, appear indefensible,[4] even from the normative point of view.[5] It is in this sense that the possibility to distinguish between law-creation and law-application transcends the jurisprudential debate and appears crucial for political theory too.

To be sure, even if one is not convinced by this reconstruction, there seems to be compelling (and exclusively) juridical reasons to resist sceptical attempts to dismiss the distinction in question. The most important of them has to do with the concept of law – as the enterprise of subjecting human conduct to the guidance of rules (and rulings) – that, as discussed in chapter one, seems to be shared by many different modern scholars and which appears at least compatible with pre-theoretical understandings of the legal phenomenon across time and space (as argued in legal anthropology scholarship). For if there is nothing that can be applied, once created by a given institution, by other agents or institutions within that normative system, then it is not clear how law could ever achieve that general action-guiding function that seems to characterise it as the kind of 'thing' it is.

My claim here then is conceptual and not normative: it does not make any sense to understand law, at the most general level, as the enterprise of subjecting human conduct to the guidance of rules, if we at the same time deny the possibility of distinguishing between the activities of law-creation and law-application.[6] Two notable consequences ensue: on the one hand, my argument does not hold vis-à-vis those theories of law that appear to presuppose an altogether different concept of law, like realist or interpretivist theories.[7] On the other, unlike normative accounts of the separation of powers that presuppose the distinction (without grounding it), the account defended here cannot be charged with being ideological.[8]

---

[4] See, for similar remarks: M Klatt, 'Semantic Normativity and the Objectivity of Legal Argumentation' (2004) 90 *Archiv für Rechts- und Sozialphilosophie* 51, 61; M Klatt, *Making the Law Explicit: The Normativity of Legal Argumentation* (Oxford, Hart Publishing, 2008) 1–2.

[5] J Coleman and B Leiter, 'Determinacy, Objectivity and Authority' (1993) 142(2) *University of Pennsylvania Law Review* 549, 558.

[6] See, for a similar approach, V Velluzzi, *Le Preleggi e L'interpretazione: Un'Introduzione Critica* (Pisa, Edizioni ETS, 2013) 30.

[7] Clearly, at this point the question becomes which concept of law, among the ones put forward by different jurisprudential schools, is to be preferred from an explanatory point of view. I have discussed in ch 1 the epistemic reasons that favour the concept of law adopted in this book, and in ch 3 the reasons to reject the realist conception of law. For a critique of Dworkin's interpretivism, see, eg: J Raz, 'Dworkin: A New Link in the Chain' (1986) 74 *California Law Review* 1103; J Mackie, 'The Third Theory of Law' (1977) 1(1) *Philosophy and Public Affairs* 3; J Gardner, 'Law's Aims in Law's Empire' in S Hershovitz (ed), *Exploring Law's Empire: The Jurisprudence of Ronald Dworkin* (Oxford, Oxford University Press, 2006); A Marmor, *Social Conventions: From Language to Law* (Princeton, Princeton University Press, 2009) ch 7.

[8] *cf* J Wróblewski, *The Judicial Application of Law* (Z Bankowski and N MacCormick eds, Dordrecht, Springer, 1992).

The Two Extremes: Rejecting vs Assuming the Distinction 213

Among other things, I will not bolster the naïve picture according to which legislatures always (and only) create the law and courts always (and only) apply the law. Such a claim would be simply untenable from a descriptive point of view, and it is doubtful whether any modern scholar has ever entertained something even remotely close to it. As a matter of fact, legislatures also do things other than making law – for instance when they adjudicate on internal disputes – and courts not always (and not only) apply the law created by other authorities. This is true not only for common law systems, where the courts' authority to create new law is undisputed, but also, in some cases, for high courts in civil law systems too. And it is precisely the capacity to distinguish between cases in which a court can be said to have (only) applied existing law, and cases instead where they have created (and applied) new law, which should be considered one of the most important theoretical upshots of the analytical distinction between creation and application that I am about to put forward.[9]

The starting point of our discussion will be a critical reading of Kelsen's idea of 'creation of law', which for him encompasses the individual rulings of judicial decisions. After having illustrated the reasons which run against such an understanding of 'creation of law', we will begin unpacking the stratified idea of law-application. This will involve discussing the notion of rule-following in general and the different normative structures of duty-imposing and power-conferring norms in law. The upshot of this discussion will be the clarification of the subjects of law-application: I will argue, against the prevalent position in the literature, how it is not only officials who (can be said to) apply the law. This will allow me to put forward the analytical account of creation and application of law I have developed around the key distinctions between formal and substantive (or material) application and bound and discretionary application. Finally, I will tackle one important objection – that goes beyond legal theory, and which originates in a sceptical reading of Wittgenstein's rule-following considerations – as to the very idea of the application of rules *tout court*.

II. THE TWO EXTREMES: REJECTING VS ASSUMING THE DISTINCTION

In the previous chapters of this book, we have already discussed some individual scholars or even entire legal schools that, for philosophical or political reasons, deny the idea that we can meaningfully (or even 'at all') talk of 'law-application' when referring to the activities of courts, particularly in modern constitutional democracies.[10] As Wróblewski notes in his (still unparalleled) study on the

---

[9] *cf* Klatt, *Making the Law Explicit* (n 4), which shares a very similar goal (albeit pursued through a different argumentative strategy).

[10] See also Klatt, 'Semantic Normativity' (n 4) 19–22. The possibility of maintaining a clear distinction between the two is deemed by Hutton 'very hard': CM Hutton, *Word Meaning and Legal Interpretation* (London, Palgrave Macmillan, 2014) 26, 37.

214   *Creation and Application of Law. An Analytical Distinction*

judicial application of law, this denial must be understood historically in the context of the rejection of the ideology of legal reasoning known as formalism.[11] The latter, particularly after its theoretical entrenchment as part of the tripartite doctrine of the separation of powers made famous by Montesquieieu, became effectively the dominant paradigm of legal reasoning especially in civil law countries.[12]

Clearly, the rejection of the ideological position that courts always (and only) apply the law does not also logically imply subscribing to the idea we can never talk meaningfully of the 'application of law'.[13] Yet it is this kind of scepticism, as we have discussed in chapter three, that is nowadays predominant in legal theory, especially after the assault on legal positivism that we have witnessed in the last few decades. Most modern positivists, indeed, do not seem too bothered by the sceptical challenge, due to the assumption that a clear distinction between creation and application can be maintained without really arguing for it.[14] Ordinary legal discourse and practice side with them: in our common legal parlance, we – judges, lawyers, law professors, law students, regulators, and so forth – routinely (and unproblematically) talk of legislatures and governments having *created* some laws and of courts having *applied* some legal rule. Are we fooling ourselves?

One prominent positivist who instead accepts and explicitly defends the distinction is Joseph Raz.[15] While, as we shall see in the next section, his account has the significant merit of avoiding a major shortcoming of Kelsen's influential discussion of the distinction, it still does not provide us with clear analytical grounds to substantiate this distinction (but rather takes it as dogmatically asserted).[16] Taking the cue from Hart's concept of the rule of recognition,[17] Raz argues that the distinction between the creation and application of law is necessary to address correctly the so-called problem of identity of legal systems. What matters for us is that he strongly advocates the theoretical feasibility and necessity of the distinction, while at the same time acknowledging that:

> One should remember that clear conceptual distinctions do not entail the existence of clear instances of the concepts involved. Therefore, the absence of clear instances

---

[11] Wróblewski, *The Judicial Application of Law* (n 8) ch 12.

[12] Cesare Beccaria arguably also played an influential role in this respect: see C Beccaria, *On Crimes and Punishments and Other Writings* (first published 1764, R Bellamy ed, R Davies trans, Cambridge, Cambridge University Press, 1995) 14.

[13] See, eg: Hart and Sacks, *The Legal Process* (n 1) 1372; T Spaak, 'Principled and Pragmatic Theories of Legal Reasoning', in A Fogelklou and T Spaak (eds), *Festskrift till Åke Frändberg* (Uppsala, Iustus Forlag 2003), 236–37.

[14] This applies to the prominent positivist theories of both Hart and Marmor, for example. See HLA Hart, *The Concept of Law*, 3rd edn (Oxford, Oxford University Press, 2012); A Marmor, *Interpretation and Legal Theory*, rev. 2nd ed (London, Hart Publishing, 2005) 122.

[15] J Raz, 'The Identity of Legal Systems' in J Raz, *The Authority of Law: Essays on Law and Morality* (Oxford, Clarendon Press, 1979) 90ff; and *cf* Hart, *Concept of Law* (n 14) 282.

[16] Klatt, *Making the Law Explicit* (n 4) 11.

[17] Raz, 'The Identity of Legal Systems' (n 15) 90–93.

The Two Extremes: Rejecting vs Assuming the Distinction   215

should not deter one from striving to formulate clear conceptual distinctions. The courts, in most cases brought before them, probably neither merely apply an existing law nor do they merely initiate a new law. They may be doing a little of both. But this does not detract from the ability of a clear distinction between applying existing law and creating a new one to shed light on legal processes.[18]

Now, Raz's analysis is clearly grounded in the context of Anglo-American legal theory and practice. Indeed, it can be argued that the distinction between creation and application is more blurred here than in civil law systems,[19] due to the theory of precedents and to the inherent power of courts to distinguish from previous decisions.[20] It must also be understood against the background of the default position in jurisprudential discourse which considers the judicial moment as the only moment in which the application of law takes place (or at least the only one that is worth discussing).[21] Raz is aware of the shortcomings of this 'default position' (especially from the institutional point of view) and strives to broaden it via the identification of a class of 'norm-applying institutions' that is not just restricted to courts. In this regard he distinguishes between institutions that 'apply norms by making other norms', like courts, and those 'which apply norms by not making other norms but by physically implementing them' (such as police forces, the prison services, etc) – he calls the latter 'norm-enforcing institutions'.[22]

In this respect, Raz correctly suggests that the majority of official law-application might be carried out by bodies and state personnel other than judges and courts, as part of the administrative process (both at the central and local levels) which constitutes without doubt the regulatory core of the modern state. He also correctly understands that most of these administrative decision-makers (government departments, local officials, independent agencies, and so forth) apply the law in the same way as courts, in the sense that the result of the law-applying activity is a further (individual) decision that regulates a given situation (think about a planning decision).[23]

But the main merit of his resulting definition of 'primary law-applying organs'[24] is, as it will become clear in the course of this chapter, to clearly depart

---

[18] ibid 93–94. See also ibid 97, where he affirms that the distinction 'is seen to be more a difference of degree than of kind. This fact, together with the fact that in practice it is often difficult to decide whether in a particular case a new law was created or an old law applied, does not mean that the distinction cannot be drawn or that it is unimportant'.

[19] J Raz, 'Law and Value in Adjudication' in J Raz, *The Authority of Law: Essays on Law and Morality* (Oxford, Clarendon Press, 1979) 206–09.

[20] For a discussion of the common law's evolution in this respect see Klatt, *Making the Law Explicit* (n 4) 7–11.

[21] A notable exception is constituted by Hart and Sacks, who describe as 'self-application' the fact that laypeople (as the primary 'addressees') can follow regulations without further official guidance. See Hart and Sacks, *The Legal Process* (n 1) 120.

[22] J Raz, 'The Institutional Nature of Law' in J Raz, *The Authority of Law: Essays on Law and Morality* (Oxford, Clarendon Press, 1979) 107.

[23] ibid 108–111.

[24] ibid 109–110.

216   *Creation and Application of Law. An Analytical Distinction*

from Kelsen's idea that the creation of 'individual norms', like those produced by courts when individualising statutory norms, are to be considered as instances of law-creation: with the result that courts are always at the same time law-creating and law-applying institutions. Raz instead correctly warns that we should clearly keep separate the 'power to make binding applicative determinations' from those 'to create precedent and lay down general rules' and 'to issue orders to individuals to perform certain actions'.[25] Let us then consider why this is relevant by contrasting it with Kelsen's discussion of the distinction.

III. KELSEN ON THE RELATIVITY OF THE DISTINCTION BETWEEN CREATION AND APPLICATION OF LAW

Like Raz, Kelsen offers an explicit discussion of the distinction between creation and application of law, albeit with a (prima facie) surprising critical outcome.[26] For, contrary to the traditional or ideological picture we have outlined above,[27] he affirms the distinction is 'relative' in character, given that 'creation of law is always application of law'.[28] With this he means that we should not consider the two concepts, as the traditional theory (supposedly) does, like 'absolute opposites', with the result that:

> It is not quite correct to classify legal acts as law-creating and law-applying acts; for, setting aside two borderline cases ..., every act is, normally, at the same time a law-creating and law-applying act.[29]

How come? It is reasonable to assume that Kelsen's 'relativity' thesis is conditional upon the particular nomodynamic structure of modern legal systems:[30] it is 'an immediate consequence of the fact that every law-creating act must be determined by the legal order'.[31] In this regard, it is a necessary consequence of the (institutionalised) ideal of legality, according to which every law-making power within the system needs itself to be regulated by the law and so to involve an application of existing law (at least to a minimum extent).[32] There would be nothing objectionable up to this point, but Kelsen goes on to observe that the determination of the law-creating act by the legal system

> may be of different degrees. It can never be so weak that the act ceases to be an application of law. Nor it can be so strong that the act ceases to be a creation of law.

---

[25] ibid 110.

[26] H Kelsen, *General Theory of Law and State* (first published 1945, with a new introduction by A Javier Treviño, New Brunswick, Transaction Publishers, 2005) 133–35; H Kelsen, *Pure Theory of Law*, 2nd edn (M Knight trans, Berkeley, University of California Press, 1967) 234ff.

[27] *cf* N MacCormick, *Rhetoric and the Rule of Law* (Oxford, Oxford University Press, 2005) 5.

[28] Kelsen, *General Theory of Law and State* (n 26) 133.

[29] ibid.

[30] See G Tarello, *L'interpretazione della legge* (Milan, Giuffrè, 1980) 45.

[31] Kelsen, *General Theory of Law and State* (n 26) 134.

[32] G Palombella, 'The Rule of Law as an Institutional Ideal' in L Morlino and G Palombella (eds), *Rule of Law and Democracy: Inquiries into Internal and External Issues* (Leiden, Brill, 2010);

As long as a norm is established through the act, it is a law-creation act, even if the function of the law-creating organ is in a high degree determined by the higher norm.[33]

Are there no 'mere' acts of application of law in a legal system then? For a start, even if, by definition, the creation of law was always to involve some degree of application of law (as it does),[34] this would not (logically) imply in turn that the application of law always involves creation. Where does the issue really lie? Kelsen affirms that 'Only acts by which no norm is established may be merely application of law', and the only (and 'extreme') case he can think of is 'the execution of a sanction in a concrete case'.[35] But is not Kelsen himself too 'extreme' here? Could we not readily think of some legal acts in our legal systems in which there is no execution of 'sanctions' involved, and that yet are nonetheless considered to be law-applying acts? The first type of act that comes to mind is that of issuing or granting administrative licences such as drivers' licences. That these acts are not to be considered 'legal' acts – acts issued by state officials in their legal capacity which yield their effects only if produced in compliance with the superior norms – is a claim that, I suppose, nobody would entertain. But, by the same token, would anyone easily grant that these are acts of law-creation? What would be norm-creating about the act of issuing a driving licence to a lay-man who is entitled, by law, to it?

As already mentioned in chapter four, the overall problem does not seem to be with Kelsen's understanding of 'creation of law' per se, but with his definition of 'norm' which encompasses individual prescriptions like commands or the individual rulings of judicial decisions.[36] Thus, for Kelsen, even a judicial decision that merely applies a pre-existing norm to a concrete situation without any discretion involved – that is, what we could call a linguistically and legally clear case – is creating law. In his own words, 'The judicial function is thus, like legislation, both creation and application of law'.[37] This claim, taken at face value, is striking,[38] considering that it does not come from a jurist trained in common law (where it could have been more easily conceived of, perhaps).[39] One can make

---

cf J Raz, 'The Rule of Law and its Virtue' in J Raz, *The Authority of Law: Essays on Law and Morality* (Oxford, Clarendon Press, 1979) 212; L Ferrajoli, *La Democrazia Attraverso i Diritti: Il Costituzionalismo Garantista come Modello Teorico e come Progetto Politico* (Bari, Laterza 2013) 204.

[33] Kelsen, *General Theory of Law and State* (n 26) 134 (my emphasis).

[34] As illustrated in ch 1, we can meaningfully talk of 'creation' only in the case of formal norms, whereas with social or customary (informal) norms we should be talking of their 'emergence'.

[35] Kelsen, *General Theory of Law and State* (n 26) 134.

[36] See ch 4, n 131. See also E Bulygin, 'Judicial Decisions and the Creation of Law (1966)', in E Bulygin, *Essays in Legal Philosophy* (C Bernal, C Huerta, T Mazzarese, JJ Moreso, PE Navarro, and SL Paulson eds, Oxford, Oxford University Press, 2015).

[37] So that between the two there 'is a difference in degree only': Kelsen, *General Theory of Law and State* (n 26) 134.

[38] HLA Hart, 'Kelsen's Doctrine of the Unity of Law' in HLA Hart, *Essays in Jurisprudence and Philosophy* (Oxford, Oxford University Press, 1983) 340.

[39] Kelsen seems to be aware of this: Kelsen, *General Theory of Law and State* (n 26) 135.

218   *Creation and Application of Law. An Analytical Distinction*

sense of it, perhaps, only by contextualising it again within his broader account of the nomodynamics of the legal system. As he puts it:

> Statutes and customary laws are, so to speak, only semi-manufactured products which are finished only through the judicial decision and its execution ... The general norm which, to certain abstractly determined conditions, attaches certain abstractly determined consequences, has to be individualized and concretized in order to come in contact with social life, to be applied to reality. ... The individual norm of the judicial decision is the necessary individualization and concretization of the general and abstract norm.[40]

If we were to take these remarks at face value, it would not be clear how the law could ever possibly constitute a means of guidance for the behaviour of its addressees, ie both laypeople and legal officials.[41] In what sense are statutes 'only semi-manufactured products'? If Kelsen is conveying here the idea that statutes – or better, the norm-sentences as contained within them – are not able by themselves to guide the conduct of their addressees without a mediating act of interpretation, the objection would be strong but, as we shall see, rebuttable, at least in a majority cases. If instead Kelsen is saying that statutory norms, due to their (necessary) generality and/or abstractness, are never able to express deontic content fit for law's action-guiding purposes (so that action-guiding norms come into being exclusively by means of judicial interpretation), then his attack against the determinacy and objectivity of law would cut much deeper. It would openly contradict the concept of law and the intuitive model of the functioning of a legal system that most of us – Kelsen included – share.[42]

Perhaps Kelsen's peculiar position can be explained by the fact that, being predominantly focused on the nomodynamics of the constitutional order, he does not fully realise the consequences that the entrenched constitutionality of modern legal systems brings about vis-à-vis the systems' nomostatics.[43] In his theory, only one kind of hierarchical relationship seem to exist between norms belonging to different levels of the *Stufenbau*:[44] a formal hierarchy, in the sense that any substantive infringement of the lower act vis-à-vis the higher norm regulating its creation is to be conceived of as a violation of their formal (and not substantive) relationship.[45] It is precisely this wanting acknowledgement of the consequences of the nomostatic relationship between different levels of a constitutional legal order that can explain Kelsen's belief that adjudication is always law-creation – ie, that the judicial function is never purely declaratory

---

[40] ibid.

[41] For a similar criticism see A Marmor, 'The Rule of Law and its Limits' (2004) 23 *Law and Philosophy* 1, 35.

[42] *cf* M Jori, *Del Diritto Inesistente: Saggio di Metagiurisprudenza Descrittiva* (Pisa, ETS, 2010).

[43] Ferrajoli, *Principia Iuris*, vol 1 (n 3) 114–115, 454–58.

[44] Kelsen, *General Theory of Law and State* (n 26) 132ff.

[45] R Guastini, 'Garantismo e Dottrina Pura a Confronto' in P Di Lucia (ed), *Assiomatica del Normativo: Filosofia Critica del Diritto in Luigi Ferrajoli* (Milan, LED, 2011) 218–20.

Creation of Law: Of the Typicality of Legal Rules 219

but always constitutive.[46] Of course, many judicial decisions are constitutive of the *further* legal effects they establish: viz of those legal effects which are not predetermined by a higher substantive norm, but rather established by the decision-maker herself.[47]

IV. CREATION OF LAW: OF THE TYPICALITY OF LEGAL RULES

The question to be addressed then is this: what counts as 'creation of law'? We have seen that, for Kelsen, the traditional view according to which courts are always merely applying the law is false. In his view, courts are also always at the same time creating

> an individual norm providing that a definite sanction shall be executed against a definite individual. *This individual norm is related to the general norms as a statute is related to the constitution.* The judicial function is thus, like legislation, both creation and application of law.[48]

The difference between a judicial decision, which is 'ordinarily determined by the general norms both as to procedure and as to the contents of the norm to be created', and a legislative act, which is 'usually determined by the constitution only in the former respect',[49] is for Kelsen in degree only. While this might be true in a sense, the broad understanding of 'creation of law' by Kelsen has been criticised in the literature:[50] in this regard, to hold that a judge who is applying a general norm to an individual case is always also creating the law is, at best, 'misleading'.[51] Why? For Kelsen, law 'includes individual norms', that is

> norms which determine the behaviour of one individual in one non-recurring situation and which therefore are valid only for one particular case and may be obeyed or applied only once.[52]

Now, while it would be fanciful to deny that individual provisions in judicial rulings are to be considered a key part of any legal system,[53] there seem to be valid theoretical reasons to restrict the notion of 'creation of law' vis-à-vis Kelsen's. As it has been noted famously by Bulygin among others,[54] unless we are dealing with an arbitrary decision, the conclusion – that is, Kelsen's individual norm – will amount to the 'logical consequence' of the premises of the reasoning. As such, the individual norm (or statement) is 'deduced' from the

---

[46] Kelsen, *General Theory of Law and State* (n 26) 135.
[47] Ferrajoli, *Principia Iuris*, vol 1 (n 3) 419–28.
[48] Kelsen, *General Theory of Law and State* (n 26) 134 (my emphasis).
[49] ibid.
[50] See, eg: Ferrajoli, *Principia Iuris*, vol 1 (n 3) 229–32; 471 fn 1.
[51] CE Alchourrón and E Bulygin, *Normative Systems* (New York, Springer-Verlag, 1971) 154, fn 2.
[52] Kelsen, *General Theory of Law and State* (n 26) 38.
[53] See ch 1, section III.
[54] Bulygin, 'Judicial Decisions' (n 36) 78–81.

220   *Creation and Application of Law. An Analytical Distinction*

general normative, factual and qualificatory premises, but not 'created'.[55] What really matters, in order to understand whether or not the decision by the court has innovated the legal system in question, is having a viable criterion to distinguish between decisions which are based on pre-existing norms, and those which are not. This is precluded if we accept Kelsen's thesis that courts' decisions are *always* applying and creating the law.

In addition, the idea of an 'individual norm' contrasts with the thesis of the typicality of rules/norms that we have already discussed in previous chapters.[56] According to the latter, a norm needs to constitute a type, either as to the class of its subjects (generality), and/or as to the class of the forms of behaviour governed (abstractness).[57] Kelsen's individual 'norms' cannot constitute any type then, being instead more correctly identified as individual commands or orders (or rulings). In this regard, one can speak of the necessary universalisable character of norms (and of law-creation consequently):[58] a feature that fundamentally distinguishes norms from the adoption of individual prescriptions.[59]

This feature of law-creation seems inherently tied to the ideal of formal rationality or justice.[60] The generality of norms guarantees the equality of deontic qualification of the same form of behaviour no matter *who* adopts it, while their abstractness guarantees the same equality no matter *when* and *where* a form of behaviour takes place.[61] Hence it is the same structure of norms (and law) which conveys the idea that 'like cases should be treated alike': law-creation is by definition a matter of formal rationality, and this explains another sense in which the rule of law is to be starkly contrasted with the rule of men (which needs not be universalisable).[62] If we were instead to accept Kelsen's definition of 'norm', encompassing also individual prescriptions, each legal system would

---

[55] ibid 80. The only sense of 'creation' which seems at play here is in the (very weak) sense that, obviously, such an individual prescription (as the whole decision) is a product of an act of will. But this seems to be too broad a criterion to determine the concept of norm-creation, as it would give it 'excessive reach': ibid 79.

[56] For the claim that the typicality of modern law is the main vehicle of law's normativity see E Pattaro, *The Law and the Right: A Reappraisal of the Reality that Ought to Be, A Treatise of Legal Philosophy and General Jurisprudence,* vol 1 (Dordrecht, Springer, 2005) 22–23; and *cf* Alchourrón and Bulygin, *Normative Systems* (n 51) 30; see also Bulygin, 'Judicial Decisions' (n 36) fn 7 (quoting Von Wright).

[57] Ferrajoli, *Principia Iuris*, vol 1 (n 3) 229–232; see also Hart, *Concept of Law* (n 14) 21, and *cf* Marmor, 'The Rule of Law and its Limits' (n 41) 9–14 (he calls it generality of norm-subjects and of norm-acts).

[58] Ferrajoli, *Principia Iuris*, vol 1 (n 3) 229.

[59] On universalisability as a normative requirement for good judicial decision-making see, eg: MacCormick, *Rhetoric* (n 27) ch 5.

[60] See also LJ Wintgens, 'Legisprudence as a New Theory of Legislation' (2006) 19 *Ratio Juris* 1, 17: 'It is because we care for equality that law as rules is preferred to law as a command' – noting also (correctly) that 'Formal justice as a rule of decision-making is not absolute, since decision-making is subject to time'.

[61] Ferrajoli, *Principia Iuris*, vol 1 (n 3) 232; *cf* FA Hayek, *The Constitution of Liberty* (Chicago, University of Chicago Press, 1978) 153ff.

[62] Ferrajoli, *Principia Iuris*, vol 1 (n 3) 232; but *cf* Raz, 'The Rule of Law and its Virtue' (n 32) 211.

Creation of Law: Of the Typicality of Legal Rules   221

contain billions of norms that are different from each other to a relevant extent and not universalisable. As a result, the very concept of norm (or rule) would lose much of its explanatory fruitfulness.

There seems to be then, *pace* Kelsen, good reasons to adopt a narrow definition of norm and thus of 'creation of law' as all and only those acts that establish a new norm, ie a new normative type. This norm can be new either because it was not present altogether in the given normative system before, or because it innovates in one of its relevant features (generality and/or abstractness) a pre-existing norm.[63] In either case, this norm must constitute a type, so that individual prescriptions, like the ones addressed exclusively to the parties by a court, are not to be considered 'creation of law'.[64] In this way, where the individual prescription put forward by a court is not the application of a pre-existing general norm (as obtained through the process of cognitive interpretation, discussed in the last chapter), but rather of another norm which is the product of 'construction' or 'invention' by the court itself,[65] then the decision could be indeed considered as an act of law-creation. Clearly, while the court's decision can be considered as an act of law-creation overall, the 'created' norm will not be the individual ruling addressing the parties. Rather, the newly created norm will be expressed by the ratio decidendi, the general statement of law that represents the (legal) reason for the decision in the actual case.[66]

One of the upshots of the narrow definition of norms adopted here is that of making it easier to clarify the status of judicial decision-making across both civil and common law jurisdictions. In what sense is adjudication an activity of application of law? And is this characterisation appropriate? In a general but important sense it is, because the outputs of adjudication are individual prescriptions which apply (are based on) one or more general norms and whose bindingness is usually between the parties only.[67] And yet it is possible for judges, at the same time, to create law, as clearly recognised in common law systems: they do so every time they adopt as a ground for their individual ruling (that is, every time they apply) a general norm that is not retrievable in – viz. not statically derivable from – the existing sources of the legal system in question.[68]

---

[63] See Bulygin, 'Judicial Decisions' (n 36) fn 8.

[64] In other words, it is confirmed the general character of *jus dicere* of the judicial moment; see Raz, 'The Institutional Nature of Law' (n 22) 111 for the claim that 'applicative determinations are most closely related to declaratory judgments'.

[65] See T Endicott, *Vagueness in Law* (Oxford, Oxford University Press, 2000) 181–82 for the distinction between application and invention.

[66] See Bulygin, 'Judicial Decisions' (n 36). Hence if the judge is deciding according to a vague standard and picks one among the many potential norms expressed by such a standard, she is still *applying* the given standard; whereas if she fills a normative gap, or if she invents a new norm (for whatever reason), then we can say that she is *creating* the law.

[67] Litigation is driven by the interest of the parties, and this holds even in the common law: what matters indeed systemically is the ratio decidendi, not the individual ruling.

[68] *cf* Raz, 'Law and Value in Adjudication' (n 19). To be sure, the orthodox common law doctrine presents the decision-making of judges as an act of retrieval of existing norms (as established by the

222 *Creation and Application of Law. An Analytical Distinction*

Why is this 'general' sense of application important? Because if a court were to decide a case without applying any general norm or principle – not even a norm created *ex novo* by the court and that could be applied to similar cases in the future – then such a decision could hardly be defined as juridical at all.[69]

Now, by considering the universalisable character of legal norms, we have begun to answer the question 'what is being created?' when we are referring to the activity of law-creation. Let us remind ourselves that we adopted a broad understanding of law, an understanding according to which law amounts, in its different historical forms, to the enterprise of subjecting human conduct to the governance of rules (and rulings). The stress in this definition must be laid on the latter component, 'guidance of rules', and not on the former, 'subjecting'. For if we were to emphasise the 'subjection' element from our understanding of law, then whatever means to achieve subjection could turn out to be acceptable. For example, inculcation by subliminal messages hidden in TV adverts could then be a perfectly legitimate means to achieve the subjection of individuals to law's 'guidance'. On this account though, as Marmor correctly notes, rather than the law guiding conducts, it would be the law-makers themselves doing so directly: as such, 'Not every conceivable mode of affecting human conduct is legalistic'.[70]

The 'guidance of rules' element then must be given priority in elaborating our understanding of law, and it must be conceived of as guidance through the provision of norms as (authoritative) reasons for action.[71] This is, once again, perhaps the clearest sense in which law, and not men, *rules*.[72] This also implies that the 'what is being created' question is necessarily connected to the 'how is it being created' question. If law-creation amounts to the creation of normative types that purport to provide reasons for action that can guide individual decision-making, not only must these reasons for action be of a certain kind to reach their goal (I call these the conditions of deontic intelligibility), but they must also be created in a way that does not frustrate that very goal. Both these requirements are addressed by the principle of legality.

V. THE PRINCIPLE OF LEGALITY AS A (SEMANTIC) META-NORM ON LAW-CREATION AND LAW-APPLICATION

As we have discussed at length in the previous chapters of this book, for a certain social practice to be considered as law it needs (at least) to provide its

---

'immemorial' customs of the land), rather than as an act of creation of new norms. On the historical origin of what is now considered a 'fictio', see ch 2, n 62.

[69] Bulygin, 'Judicial Decisions' (n 36).

[70] Marmor, 'The Rule of Law and its Limits' (n 41) 15.

[71] ibid 16.

[72] Palombella, 'The Rule of Law as an Institutional Ideal' (n 32). For an account of the qualities required in legal decision-making see C Michelon, 'Practical Wisdom in Legal Decision-Making' in A Amaya and HL Ho (eds), *Law, Virtue and Justice* (Oxford, Hart Publishing, 2013).

Principle of Legality as a (Semantic) Meta-norm on Law-creation 223

recipients with 'guidance', that is with the possibility to take law into consideration as an authoritative source of reasons for action.[73] This implies, in modern legal systems where large societies are to be regulated, 'linguistic intelligibility' and the possibility of 'empirical knowability':[74] in short, that what the law requires must be knowable in advance by its addressees. Thus, one can say that the creation of law must be first of all manifest, or to put it differently, positive or formal[75] – the creation of law must consist of an activity in the world which is in principle recognisable as such by its addressees.[76]

If this was not the case, it is not clear how the practice of law could ever attain its guidance function vis-à-vis its first addressees, that is, laypeople.[77] This seems to amount, then, to a first and prima facie difference between law-creation and law-application: for while the former must always be, in a (legal) system whose ultimate aim is the guidance of behaviour through the provision of reasons for action, a positive (or formal) activity, the latter need not necessarily be so. Due to law's formality then,[78] we cannot conceive of an act of law-creation that is not, at least to a minimal extent, constituted by its form and empirically recognisable as such. According to Ferrajoli, this is precisely one of the great revolutions of modern law – its facticity[79] – according to which *auctoritas non veritas facit legem.*[80]

It is through the principle of legality, conceived of within the specific communicative theory adopted in this book,[81] that law's facticity is connected to its certainty. This constitutes one of the connections between the stages of creation and of application of law, and perhaps the most relevant one. For while the generality of legal norms guarantees in itself (formal) equality under the law, their abstractness undergirds the pre-determination of the forms of behaviour relevant for the law and thus the extent of the latter's certainty.[82]

---

[73] *cf* BB Levenbook, 'How a Statute Applies' (2006) 12 *Legal Theory* 71.

[74] The latter amounts to the requirement of 'promulgation': *cf* Marmor, 'The Rule of Law and its Limits' (n 41) 15–19.

[75] Guastini, 'Garantismo e Dottrina Pura a Confronto' (n 45); P Sandro, 'Unlocking Legal Validity: Some Remarks on the Artificial Ontology of Law' in P Westerman, J Hage, S Kirste and AR Mackor (eds), *Legal Validity and Soft Law* (Cham, Springer International Publishing, 2018).

[76] As I shall discuss in more detail below, there is a fundamental difference between 'following' a rule and 'acting in accordance' with it. This distinction is crucial because, if the overall aim of law as an institutional practice were to be the latter and not the former, we could reach it by means of subliminal messages transmitted through TV commercials: *cf* Marmor, 'The Rule of Law and its Limits' (n 41) 10–12.

[77] *cf* M Kramer, *Objectivity and the Rule of Law* (Cambridge, Cambridge University Press, 2007) 113–118; L Alexander and E Sherwin, *Demystifying Legal Reasoning* (Cambridge, Cambridge University Press, 2008) 130.

[78] On law's necessary formal character see Ferrajoli, *Principia Iuris*, vol 1 (n 3); Jori, *Del Diritto Inesistente* (n 42).

[79] See J Habermas, *Between Facts and Norms: Contributions to a Discourse Theory of Law and Democracy* (W Rehg trans, Cambridge, MIT Press, 1996).

[80] Ferrajoli, *Principia Iuris*, vol 1 (n 3) 16 (echoing Hobbes on the point).

[81] ibid 444–49; *cf* L Fuller, *The Morality of Law*, rev. edn (New Haven, Yale University Press, 1977) ch 2.

[82] Ferrajoli, *Principia Iuris*, vol 1 (n 3) 232.

224   *Creation and Application of Law. An Analytical Distinction*

The idea of certainty pertains to the degree of determinacy that can be reached in a legal system.[83] If the positive character of legal norms, together with their abstractness, guarantees in a first sense the pre-determination of the law vis-à-vis the forms of behaviour it purports to guide, the principle of legality makes provisions for law's determinacy, that is, for the necessary action-guiding capacity of law. The principle of legality is thus a meta-rule on the creation of norms that establishes the conditions for the latter to be meaningful *qua* law.[84]

These conditions pertain to law's deontic intelligibility: not only in the sense of the possibility of law being understood by its addressees, but also in the sense of the capacity to successfully refer to the world in such a way that allows law (as a reason for action) to be considered in our decision-making. As we shall see in a moment, application is, in this regard, always a matter of degree: not because of some particular structural feature of law, but rather for the inherent and inescapable transience of our capacity to know of the world around us. This need not frighten us: instead of finding shelter in scepticism's comforting epistemology, at the price of undermining the very justification of our juridical practices, we can seek to unpack the relationship between creation and application of law, in order to show under which conditions of the former we can reasonably talk of the latter as a legitimate category and not as a 'doctrinal' fig-leaf. Understood as such, the principle of legality is what inversely connects law-creation and law-application: the more the former process departs from the requirements of legality, the less we will be authorised to speak in terms of the latter, for there would be indeed nothing to apply.[85] In Ferrajoli's words:

> The nexus between [the principle of] legality and [the principle of] certainty, that is between (the degree of) semantic definiteness of normative definitions and (the degree of) legal verifiability of propositions that use such normative definitions, depends precisely on the relationship of *langue* to *parole* that exists between norms and acts which constitute norms' argument. Only if the words of the legal *langue* with which norms denote their arguments are aptly defined by those very norms with sufficient clarity and exactness, their use in legal *parole* can take place with sufficient certainty. ... In this sense the principle of strict legality can be deemed as a semantic rule on the requirements to use the predicate 'true' in legal language.[86]

---

[83] On the relevance of law's certainty: H Surden, 'The Variable Determinacy Thesis' (2011) 12 *The Columbia Science and Technology Law Review* 1; *cf* G Pino, 'La certezza del diritto e lo Stato costituzionale' (2018) 2 *Diritto Pubblico* 517; and S Bertea, 'Remarks on a Legal Positivist Misuse of Wittgenstein's Later Philosophy' (2003) 22(6) *Law and Philosophy* 513. According to Bertea, it is precisely the problem of certainty that troubles legal positivists into a contradictory reading of Wittgenstein.

[84] See also Surden, 'The Variable Determinacy Thesis' (n 83) 8.

[85] See D Priel, 'Reconstructing Fuller's Argument Against Legal Positivism' (2013) 26(2) *Canadian Journal of Law & Jurisprudence* 399, for the claim that according to Fuller a total failure in one of the eight desiderata means no legal system at all.

[86] Ferrajoli, *Principia Iuris*, vol 1 (n 3) 445 (my translation).

Principle of Legality as a (Semantic) Meta-norm on Law-creation   225

As such, it is true that 'John Black is guilty of theft' according to the Italian penal code if we can apply the relevant norm on theft[87] to the facts of the matter with (relative) certainty, and this in turn depends on the precision of the connotation of the empirical characteristics of the form of behaviour to be taken into account and to the (resulting) determinacy of the field of denotation of the type (of behaviour) *in abstracto* regulated.[88] The principle of legality amounts to a 'meta-normative rule'[89] that requires law-creation, as much as possible, to conform to precision and determinacy. For only if these two features are appropriate for law to constitute intelligible reasons for action, we can then qualify, within legal propositions whose truth or falsity can be ascertained with (always relative) certainty, the historical form of behaviour considered under the abstract type established by the norm.[90]

To summarise, the communicative understanding of law adopted in this book clarifies that the principle of legality purports to constrain not only the form (or procedure) of law-creation, but also its contents – in a way that has nothing to do with the moral evaluation of the law.[91] What the principle of legality tells us is that if legal language is utterly vague, ambiguous, ridded with inconsistencies or gaps, such language will not be able to refer meaningfully to any (empirical) state of the world and hence to constrain any kind of decision-making power;[92] with the result that every decision-maker empowered with 'legal' authority will be substantially free to decide whatever they like.

On the contrary, the more precise, the more adequate and the more determinate the language adopted by acts of law-creation is, the more the law will be able to refer to empirical states of the world and thus to provide intelligible reasons for action to its addressees. This, of course, does not (because it cannot) mean that in reality legal language will always be precise and determinate, and thus always adequate. Legality is an aspiration,[93] a juridical ought on law-creation itself – one that can only, and always, be attainable only to a certain extent: either because of the presence of meaningful indeterminacies, as with the discretionary

---

[87] In the Italian criminal code, Art 624 provides for the offence of theft, establishing – in its first part – that 'anyone who takes possession of the movable object of another person, by taking it away from the actual holder, with the aim of gaining profit from it for himself or for others, is punishable with a term of imprisonment in between six months and three years and with a fine of between 154 and 516€' (my translation).

[88] Ferrajoli, *Principia Iuris*, vol 1 (n 3) 445.

[89] ibid.

[90] ibid 446, recalling explicitly Hobbes on the same point. See T Hobbes, *De Cive* (first published 1651, London, Anodos Books, 2017) ch 18. See also J Rawls, *A Theory of Justice* (rev ed, Cambridge MA, Belknap Press, 1999) 209–11.

[91] See Raz, 'The Rule of Law and its Virtue' (n 32): 'Like other instruments, the law has a specific virtue which is morally neutral in being neutral as to the end to which the instrument is put. It is the virtue of efficiency; the virtue of the instrument as an instrument. For the law this virtue is the rule of law. Thus the rule of law is an inherent virtue of the law, but not a moral virtue as such'; *cf* Fuller, *The Morality of Law* (n 81) 162.

[92] *cf* Raz, 'The Rule of Law and its Virtue' (n 32) 214.

[93] Fuller, *The Morality of Law* (n 81) ch 1.

226 *Creation and Application of Law. An Analytical Distinction*

delegation of powers from one agent to another, or because of the unavoidable degree of fallibility of every human interaction, including linguistic interactions. What legality tells us is that, if such an ideal is not respected at least to a minimum degree (whose threshold cannot be theoretically established, being instead an empirical matter that changes from legal system to legal system) then legal communication between those who make the law and those who are supposed to apply it breaks down and, as a consequence, law as an institutional practice loses even the *potential* to guide (and constrain) behaviour.

Significantly, in this latter scenario the 'rule of law' – while maintaining its appearance – deteriorates into the 'rule of men': for in these cases, far from being anymore a power-constraining device, law becomes a 'sheer instrument' of domination.[94] But then what is the relationship between the principle of legality, presented here as a meta-rule on law-creation, and the rule of law? Many of the features that I have listed as required by legality are usually and widely deemed part of the rule of law requirements, in particular after the influential work of Lon Fuller.[95] The rule of law is nonetheless always a thicker institutional ideal than the principle of legality I have just illustrated.[96] This latter pertains (only)[97] to the very possibility of authoritative rule-following in a broad social group, where guidance can only be reasonably attained by means of general communication. As we shall discuss in more detail below, rules can only be truly said to be followed if they are known to the agent, for only in this case can a norm constitute a source of reasons for action that purports to guide the agent's behaviour.

The rule of law, instead, asks for more than 'just' a dimension of 'communicative adequacy' from the law, and at times might even run foul of the idea of legality.[98] Unlike the latter, the rule of law is a multifaceted ideal, an ideal that purports to achieve an institutional balance through different and sometimes competing objectives, like the protection of legitimate expectations and the principle of non-retroactivity of laws.[99] For example, while a retroactive statute cannot but represent an absolute violation of the principle of legality – because a retroactive norm cannot by definition constitute a reason for action knowable

---

[94] Palombella, 'The Rule of Law as an Institutional Ideal' (n 32) 8; and see Raz, 'The Rule of Law and its Virtue' (n 32) 224 for the contention that 'The rule of law is essentially a negative value. The law inevitably creates a great danger of arbitrary power – the rule of law is designed to minimize the danger created by the law itself'.

[95] Fuller, *The Morality of Law* (n 81) ch 2; *cf* Marmor, 'Rule of Law' (n 20).

[96] See Palombella, 'The Rule of Law as an Institutional Ideal' (n 32) 4: 'As an ideal, Rule of law is not just a set of statements reflecting what is needed for law merely to be law'.

[97] In other words, it is not even rule *by* law; for it has to do only with the *ruleness* quality of law.

[98] Marmor, 'The Rule of Law and its Limits' (n 41) (n 21); *cf* Raz, 'The Rule of Law and its Virtue' (n 32) 225, for the relationship between the rule of law, its principles and the 'direct' (as opposed to the indirect) purposes of the law.

[99] So that, for instance, non-retroactivity might be violated in order to guarantee the protection of legitimate expectations. This, of course, calls for a balancing assessment between the two competing principles, something that is absent from legality: see Palombella, 'The Rule of Law as an Institutional Ideal' (n 32) 26; Raz, 'The Rule of Law and its Virtue' (n 32) 228.

Unpacking the Idea of 'Application of Law' 227

to the agents before the action is to take place[100] – in some cases, it can nonetheless be considered as implementing the rule of law ideal.[101]

Dynamically, this means that while there cannot be the rule of law without a minimum, or basic, degree of legality, once above that threshold, legality and the rule of law can, in some cases, diverge and thus pull in opposite directions. In these cases, how can we make sense of the contrast between the two? By precisely conceiving of the different normative dimension of the two ideals: legality being a semantic meta-norm about law's capacity to guide conduct, while the rule of law is chiefly an institutional ideal.[102] In every mature and functioning legal system, an equilibrium is reached at some point between the two, an equilibrium that, of course, is never absolutely 'fixed' but rather evolves according to the particular historical moment and needs of that society.

VI. UNPACKING THE IDEA OF 'APPLICATION OF LAW'

We have mentioned already that the idea of 'application of law' has a long and stratified intellectual history, during which it has become inextricably interwoven, for better or worse, with the tripartite version of the separation of powers doctrine. Kelsen was the first to note, prominently, that law-creation and law-application are not 'absolute opposites', but he went too far by claiming that every legal act (barring two extreme cases) is both an act of creation and application of law. Legal realists, critical legal scholars, and interpretivists instead hold that the idea of the application of law is misleading (at best). More recently, Raz and most current post-Hartian positivists affirm the distinction but fail to substantiate it convincingly.

The result of this 'journey' is that we – judges, lawyers, academics, journalists, laypeople – talk routinely of acts of application of law in our modern legal systems, but no one so far has explained how, in doing so, we are not fooling ourselves (as the realists, implicitly, hold). Therefore, in what follows I endeavour to unpack the idea of 'application of law' and provide the first analytical account of it. In particular, I will illustrate under which conditions we are reasonably warranted to conceive of a certain form of behaviour as 'an act of application of law'.[103]

Why do we need to unpack the notion of law-application? Simply put, because we often refer to different 'things' – activities, products, objects – by it.

---

[100] *cf* Raz, 'The Rule of Law and its Virtue' (n 32) 214.

[101] Marmor, 'The Rule of Law and its Limits' (n 41) 20–26.

[102] Palombella, 'The Rule of Law as an Institutional Ideal' (n 32) 28. Rawls, while correctly identifying the possibility of a contrast between the demands of the principle of legality and of the rule of law, fails to adequately distinguish between the two (especially as to their different normative dimension). See Rawls, *A Theory of Justice* (n 90) 212–13.

[103] Such an endeavour, to be sure, cannot but be stipulative in character, and its success (or lack thereof) has to be evaluated against two main criteria: the coherence of the proposed account of law-application with the concept of law defended in this work, and their combined and overall explanatory fruitfulness vis-à-vis our existing legal practices.

228 *Creation and Application of Law. An Analytical Distinction*

And while these different 'things' are, intuitively, interconnected, it is only through disambiguation that we are able to offer a more precise account of the conditions necessary to define law-application in this context. In this regard it is important to distinguish from the outset between:[104]

1. the application of norms from their applicability (both internal and external);
2. the application of norms (and other deontic requirements) from the application of norm-sentences (norm-statements, norm-formulations, or provisions);
3. law-application as a process (the mental activity of applying the law to something, of reasoning) from law-application as the product of that process (for instance, the decision to perform action A in situation B or to issue judgment X in circumstances Y).

These three distinctions are widely accepted in the legal-analytical literature, particularly in Romance languages-speaking countries. First, it has been noted that the concept of law-application suffers from the same 'process or product' ambiguity as was seen with that of interpretation.[105] In other words, by referring to law-application we might indicate the (mental) activity – the reasoning – through which one applies law to a certain object (a case, a situation, a scenario, etc) as well as the result (mental or external) of that process of reasoning. For instance, the individual prescription – ordering one party to the proceedings to do X because norm Y requires so in the circumstances in question – of a judicial ruling. Clearly, while there cannot be product-application without process-application, the latter is self-standing, in the sense that there might be (mental) processes of application of law which never culminate in a (external) decision (think about a law professor explaining to students how a certain norm should have been applied by a court in a case).

In addition, this first distinction bears explanatory fruitfulness vis-à-vis the second distinction between application and applicability. For it is one thing to say that a certain provision or norm has been applied – *in* or *to* a case – and another to say that a norm or provision is applicable to it. The former is a statement about something that was done, which does not necessarily contain any evaluative consideration as to the correctness of the process of application itself. The latter statement instead could be purely theoretical, and in any case evaluative: to affirm that a norm or provision is applicable to a case is to say that there are (good) reasons which justify the application of that norm or provision to the case or situation at hand.[106] But what kind of claims? And which reasons justify the application of a norm or provision to a given case?

---

[104] The remarks in this section are clearly indebted to the discussion in G Pino, 'L'Applicabilità delle Norme Giuridiche' (2011) 11 *Diritto & Questioni Pubbliche* 797.

[105] See JJ Moreso and JM Vilajosana, *Introducción a la teoria del derecho* (Madrid, Marcial Pons, 2004) ch 7.

[106] Pino, 'L'Applicabilità delle Norme Giuridiche' (n 104) 812.

Unpacking the Idea of 'Application of Law' 229

Applicability claims can be divided into internal and external claims.[107] Internal applicability refers to the semantic relationship between the type-situation usually described in the antecedent of a conditional norm, and the real-world scenario in question. For a norm to be (internally) applicable, the real-world scenario must constitute a token-situation that is subsumable under the type(-situation) as specified by the antecedent of the formulated norm.[108] This requires the determination of the meaning of the norm, by means of inter-pretation (or understanding, as we shall see below).[109] External applicability has to do with the reasons that justify the use of that norm in the case at hand: it implies, although it cannot always be 'reduced' to,[110] the existence of a second-order norm (a power-conferring norm) which prescribes or authorises the use of the first-order norm (the norm that is semantically applicable).[111] In short, for a norm to be applicable to a case, it must be both internally and externally so.[112] And yet, clearly, the applicability of a norm to a case does not necessarily imply its (actual) application: application is an external act (of will) of a certain type, whereas a claim of applicability is a mental act.[113]

At this point, the third fundamental distinction has already been introduced – almost seamlessly – in our analysis. It pertains to the widespread equivalence, in current legal discourse, between the application of provisions and the applications of norms (or rules) when we talk of law-application. As we have said multiple times already in this book, provisions (norm-sentences, norm-formulations) and norms are not the same kind of object and thus ought to be distinguished. A provision (norm-sentence) is a linguistic utterance, as contained

---

[107] The distinction between internal and external applicability has been developed by Moreso and Navarro, from an intuition by Bulygin: P Navarro and JJ Moreso, 'Applicability and Effectiveness of Legal Norms' (2005) 16 *Law and Philosophy* 201. The distinction between internal and external justification of the legal syllogism can be traced back to J Wróblewski, 'Legal Decision and Its Justification' (1971) 14(53–54) *Logique et Analyse* 409. See, for discussion, P Chiassoni, *Tecnica dell'interpretazione giuridica* (Bologna, Il Mulino, 2007) ch 1.

[108] See Pino, L'Applicabilità delle Norme Giuridiche' (n 104) 819–21.

[109] This semantic relationship can be problematised in a number of important ways, but for our purposes here we do not have to go beyond its more general characterisation.

[110] In this respect, 'criteria of applicability' can also consist in secondary norms that are not power-conferring (as with the Italian Art 12 of 'preleggi' which ranks the interpretive criteria available to the judge). I owe this remark to Giorgio Pino.

[111] P Comanducci, 'Alcuni problemi concettuali relativi alla applicazione del diritto' (2010) 10 *Diritto & Questioni Pubbliche* 121, 125. This idea is compatible with the legal syllogism as recon-structed by both Wróbleski and Alexy: see Chiassoni, *Tecnica dell'interpretazione giuridica* (n 107) ch 1.

[112] Pino, L'Applicabilità delle Norme Giuridiche' (n 104) 821. An example might help illustrate the difference: imagine a religious norm, existing in a given culture, according to which any person who cheats on his or her spouse must receive a corporal punishment publicly. Now, even if a spouse were to bring a case before a judicial court proving that her spouse had cheated on her and asking for the punishment to be imposed, the judge should apply the religious norm only in the case in which there is another legal norm that obliges or authorises her to do so. This is in spite of the fact that the religious norm clearly would be internally applicable to the alleged factual situation.

[113] In this respect, one should not confuse an applicability claim as a mental act (the product of an act of reasoning) and a statement of applicability given as part of the motivation for a certain judicial decision, for instance (which is instead the external expression of that mental act).

230 *Creation and Application of Law. An Analytical Distinction*

in a text (typically a statute) which constitutes the source of a potential norm. A norm is the meaning of that linguistic utterance, which is said to be the product of the interpretation of the latter.

Judges typically talk of application of norms and provisions interchangeably, but this practice can be misleading: a single provision might be ambiguous and express (linguistically) more than one norm, or the judge might actually be applying a norm that is outside the linguistic frame as expressed by the provision explicitly cited.[114] In the former case, the equivalence of the application of norm and provision obscures the fact that the meaning of the norm assumed by the decision-maker is not the only one available, but the one chosen by her after performing what Guastini calls adjudicative interpretation.[115] As we shall see briefly, while this can still be properly considered a case of law-application (albeit discretionary), the same might not necessarily hold vis-à-vis the second scenario, where the judge is assigning a meaning to the provision which is not among the meanings expressed linguistically by it (and thus, in this way, creating *new* law).

Now, while we can certainly talk meaningfully of the application of legal provisions, in the sense of the mental activity of interpreting those peculiar linguistic utterances that are found in authoritative legal texts with the aim of obtaining a norm(-meaning),[116] it is on the application of the latter that we must focus in what follows. For it is the relationship between a norm and a form of behaviour which is constitutive of the possible 'applicative' character of the former.[117] To say instead that a provision has been applied in deciding a case is at best an elliptical statement, and at worst a strategic (or naïve) one.[118] In part, as a result of this observation, not everything that is routinely called – especially by judges – 'application' of law can and *should* be considered as law-application (properly speaking). A purely descriptive account of the application of law – an account that purports to track what judges ordinarily say is 'application of law' – could not get off the ground for a number of reasons, the most important being that it is part and parcel (in other words, a pre-requisite) of the concept of application in any normative practice that some applications might be mistaken.

As such, judges (or other decision-makers) might call 'application of law' something that is actually not so. Also, it seems worth noting again that under

---

[114] Or, to put it differently, the norm used is not (statically) derivable from the authoritative linguistic utterance (or provision).

[115] See ch 5, n 239.

[116] In other words, the 'application of a provision' forms part of what we have called interpretation 'as process'.

[117] Pino, L'Applicabilità delle Norme Giuridiche' (n 104) 816 fn 34, while noticing that strictly speaking a norm-sentence can only be interpreted and not applied, broadens the language of applicability to also include provisions ('disposizioni' in Italian).

[118] The only scenario in which we seem warranted to speak of the application of a provision directly is the case in which the provision expresses one and only one norm (the so-called 'isomorphic' norm case): Wróblewski, *The Judicial Application of Law* (n 8) 33, 93–95.

Potential Asymmetry between Norm-following and Norm-application 231

a purely descriptive account every judicial decision would be a decision of application of law in a sense, given that courts' decisions are normally based on *a* norm (no matter how or from where it was obtained)[119] and that, in most systems, courts themselves can authoritatively declare what the law *is* (so that any norm figuring at the basis of a judicial decision would be, in light of this fact alone, a legal norm).[120] Thus, in this (purely descriptive) sense, it would be true that judges always 'apply' the law. But is this really the sense of 'application of law' that we have in mind, when we say, for instance, that courts *should* apply the law – in light of the guidance and collective autonomy requirements we discussed at various points in this book? It does not seem so. The question is, then, under which conditions (if any) are we reasonably allowed to talk of a certain act as an act of application of law, given the concept of law defended here?

VII. THE POTENTIAL ASYMMETRY BETWEEN NORM-FOLLOWING AND NORM-APPLICATION

We have just discussed the following claims, still somehow underdeveloped in Anglo-American scholarship: that we must unpack the idea of law-application and distinguish the application of provisions (norm-sentences) and the application of norms (as the meanings of those provisions); that the application of a provision is the (mental) activity of interpreting that provision in order to obtain one or more norms; and that it is only the application of norms, strictly speaking, that determines whether a certain act can be deemed an act of application of law (in the fuller sense we are trying to capture here). How so?

Because it is norms – all kinds of (epistemic and practical) norms, rules, principles, and so forth – that, in different degrees, 'set apart a subset of possible actions, judgements … as correct or as otherwise more appropriate'.[121] Norms, and not norm-formulations, 'require things of agents'.[122] This is what

---

[119] This is then how the identification and application of provisions (rather than of norms) is relevant for the qualification of something as an activity of application *of law*: for the application of a religious norm that is not part of the legal system in question could not, in itself, constitute an application of (a source of) law.

[120] In this sense, the only case in which a judicial decision cannot be said to be an application of law is the case in which there is no norm at the basis of the decision (that is, a purely *ad hoc* decision).

[121] J Haukioja, 'Is Solitary Rule-Following Possible?' (2005) 32 *Philosophia* 131, 132; *cf* P Pettit, 'The Reality of Rule-Following' (1990) 99(393) *Mind* 1, 2–3; S Bertea, 'Obligation: A Legal-Theoretical Perspective' in M Araszkiewicz, P Banas, T Gizbert-Studnicki and K Pleszka (eds), *Problems of Normativity, Rules and Rule-Following* (Cham, Springer International Publishing, 2015) 157; M Alvarez, 'Reasons for Action: Justification, Motivation, Explanation', in EN Zalta (ed), *The Stanford Encyclopedia of Philosophy* (Winter 2017 Edition), https://plato.stanford.edu/archives/win2017/entries/reasons-just-vs-expl/.

[122] G Brennan, L Eriksson, R Goodin, and N Southwood, *Explaining Norms* (Oxford, Oxford University Press, 2013) 3.

232   *Creation and Application of Law. An Analytical Distinction*

constitutes the very possibility of following or applying them: the fact that, *because* of the norm, a subset of potential actions or beliefs has been identified as something the agent must (or must not) do or think. Clearly, an agent could do what a norm requires without being aware of it, which is why we have come to routinely distinguish the activity of merely complying with a norm from the activity of (intentionally) applying or following it.[123] It is to the intentionality of norm-application that we must now turn.

What is the relevant intention in following or applying a norm? At the most general level, the relevant intention seems to be that of acting in order to satisfy whatever the norm requires of us.[124] It is not enough to do φ in the circumstances in which the norm requires to φ: one must φ because the norm requires φ-ing. Or, to put it differently, our act of φ-ing must be *explained* by the fact that the norm requires us to φ (or does not prohibit us from φ-ing).[125] This implies that, for our purposes, any 'norm-responsive way' of acting in accordance with the norm constitutes following or applying it, regardless of the possibility of distinguishing between treating the norm as an instrumental or non-instrumental reason for action.[126]

Two important observations are in order here: first, while following and applying a norm can be (and routinely are) used interchangeably, an act of norm-application seems to require something more than just having *followed* the relevant norm, namely that the act itself is actually warranted or justified by the norm. In other words, there can always be an important asymmetry between the intention that must be displayed by the agent in applying a norm and the content of the relevant act which is the result of the intentional state. That a norm figures – qua instrumental or non-instrumental reason for action – as part of the motivation to act does not necessarily mean that the resulting action will be justified by the norm. This is precisely what happens every time we are faced with the (genuine) *mistaken* application of a norm by an agent. The application might be mistaken for two main reasons: either because the agent misunderstood the content of – what is required by – the norm, or because there might

---

[123] See, eg: Hart, *Concept of Law* (n 14) 140. Raz distinguishes between conformity to and compliance with a reason: see J Raz, *Practical Reasons and Norms*, 2nd edn (Oxford, Oxford University Press 1999) 178–81. Outside legal philosophy terminology is not consistent – see, eg: Brennan et al, *Explaining Norms* (n 122) 195, for whom complying with a norm is an intentional activity (unlike 'acting in accordance' with the norm, which corresponds to the Razian 'conformity').

[124] Haukioja, 'Is Solitary Rule-Following Possible?' (n 121) 132; GP Baker and PMS Hacker, *Wittgenstein: Rules, Grammar, and Necessity. An Analytical Commentary on the Philosophical Investigations: Essays and Exegesis of 185–242*, vol. 2, 2nd edn extensively revised by PMS Hacker (Hoboken, Wiley-Blackwell, 2009) 129.

[125] As such, the norm acts both as a motivating as well as an explanatory reason.

[126] Hart, *Concept of Law* (n 14) 197, 231–32; Brennan et al, *Explaining Norms* (n 122) chs 9–10, where the authors claim that in the case of formal norms, it is more likely that norms are treated instrumentally (because treating formal norms non-instrumentally would involve some degree of irrationality on part of the agent). As we shall see, this observation seems immaterial when considering the case of legal norms.

Potential Asymmetry between Norm-following and Norm-application   233

be a performance error and/or problem.[127] But the (perhaps obvious) point is, once again, that to have the intention to apply or follow the norm is not enough to qualify the resulting act as an act of norm-application, if the act itself is not (objectively) warranted or justified by the norm.

Second, do norms always require following, or merely compliance? Or do different types of norms require different things? While the analysis so far in this section has been about the phenomenon of norm-following in the general, at this juncture we must start focussing on legal norms in particular. For while it is vigorously debated (at least since Kant) whether or not morality always requires not just doing the 'right' thing, but also doing the right thing for the 'right' reasons,[128] there is instead a standard and uncontroversial position in legal philosophy according to which legal norms, in general, require only 'unthinking'[129] compliance, and not the (more demanding) intentional application (or following).

This seems intuitive enough: for a legal norm to be satisfied – say, the prohibition of smoking in public spaces – all that is required is that its addressees actually refrain from smoking in public spaces, independently of why they (decide to) do so. Granted, and as we have said already in the first chapter, this still implies treating law's addressees as agents, thus allowing the possibility for them to act on the reasons that the law provides and so respecting, at least in theory, their autonomy. But law, as we have come to understand it, is not concerned in general with the internal motivation of its addressees: what it seeks is, ultimately, the production of a certain state of affairs.[130]

Why 'in general' though? Because, in part possibly due to Hart's underdeveloped treatment of the normativity of power-conferring norms in the Concept,[131] the fundamentally different way in which duty-imposing and power-conferring

---

[127] P Boghossian, 'Rules, Norms and Principles: A Conceptual Framework' in M Araszkiewicz, P Banas, T Gizbert-Studnicki and K Pleszka (eds), *Problems of Normativity, Rules and Rule-Following* (Cham, Springer International Publishing, 2015) 7.

[128] See for discussion G Pavlakos, 'The Relation Between Moral and Legal Obligation: An Alternative Kantian Reading' in G Pavlakos and V Rodriguez-Blanco (eds), *Reasons and Intentions in Law and Practical Agency* (Oxford, Hart Publishing, 2015).

[129] See Hart, *Concept of Law* (n 14) 110–117, 140; L Green, 'Introduction', in Hart, *Concept of Law* (n 14); J Waldron, 'All We Like Sheep' (1999) 12(1) *Canadian Journal of Law & Jurisprudence* 169.

[130] See C Redondo, 'El Ideal de las Acciones Basadas en Normas Jurídicas' in P Comanducci and R Guastini (eds), *Analisi e diritto 2008: Ricerche di giurisprudenza analitica* (Turin, Giappichelli, 2008). In an unpublished manuscript, I argue that this characterisation of law's normativity must be understood in the context of the creation and protection (sometimes indeed at the expenses of the autonomy of the individual agent) of accountability in a legal system. On the functional understanding of norms – in general – as accountability-creating devices, see Brennan et al, *Explaining Norms* (n 122).

[131] See M Kramer, *H.L.A. Hart* (Cambridge, Polity Press, 2018) 46–52. In this respect, Hart only hints, at the beginning of ch 3 of *The Concept of Law*, at this fundamental difference between duty-imposing norms, which require some course of action 'irrespective of [the] wishes' of their addressees, and power-conferring norms, that instead 'do not require persons to act in certain ways whether they wish or not'. See Hart, *Concept of Law* (n 14) 27.

234 *Creation and Application of Law. An Analytical Distinction*

norms purport to guide conduct has not acquired prominence in the literature.[132] When it comes to power-conferring norms, in fact, it is not enough that a certain state of affairs – uttering 'I do' when the officiating official asks me if I want to marry my partner – obtains for the function of the norm to be satisfied. Unlike duty-imposing rules, power-conferring norms require also the relevant intentionality: that is, that the agent is following the norm in doing what the norm requires (or authorises) when exercising the power conferred. Or, to put it differently, power-conferring norms can be said to guide conduct mediately, by requiring that the relevant norm figures – as a reason – in the process of practical reasoning of the power-holder and thus determines (justifying) the decision.[133] Let us unpack this.

VIII. ON THE (DIFFERENT) NORMATIVITY OF POWER-CONFERRING NORMS

As clarified already by Hohfeld, a legal power is nothing but the ability to bring about some form of change in a normative, or legal, relationship.[134] The existence of a power logically entails the existence of a corresponding 'liability' to it. As such, power-conferring norms of a legal system – what Hart calls 'rules of change' and 'rules of adjudication'[135] – constitute the most important type of 'secondary' norms. These are the norms that, as Hart correctly underscored, allow the existence of complex, far-reaching, and durable modern legal systems, in that they introduce the possibility of *deliberate* change of the existing norms and of adjudication of disputes over the contents of the latter.

It should be clear why, then, a legal system (*qua* normative *system*) requires the intentional application of – and not just the mere compliance with – power-conferring norms: because their exercise will determine a change in the legal situation of someone or even everyone, as in the case of norms that confer legislating powers on a given institution. That any change of this kind could happen 'unreflectively' – that is, without any intention by the power-holder to bring about such change – would not only be problematic vis-à-vis those subjects who 'hold' the liabilities corresponding to the power, but would also defy the very purpose of allowing avenues for *deliberate*, and not random, change in the normative system.[136]

---

[132] For Hart, the main difference between the two types of norms lies in their different functions: see Hart, *Concept of Law* (n 14) 27. *cf* T Spaak, 'Norms that Confer Competences' (2003) 16(1) *Ratio Juris* 89, for an outright rejection of the thesis that power-conferring norms give reasons for action.

[133] Redondo, 'El Ideal de las Acciones' (n 130) (even though she refers it to principles).

[134] See also A Halpin, 'The Concept of a Legal Power' (1996) 16(1) *Oxford Journal of Legal Studies* 129, 140.

[135] See Kramer, *H.L.A. Hart* (n 131) 76.

[136] Thus, to be even more precise, the relevant intentionality for the valid exercise of power-conferring norms pertains to the production of the legal consequences as pre-established by the norm. See also: Halpin, 'The Concept of a Legal Power' (n 134); Ferrajoli, *Principia Iuris*,

On the (Different) Normativity of Power-conferring Norms   235

That this is the case seems confirmed by a number of key elements.[137] The most relevant is, in my opinion, that if a legal power is exercised by an agent that is subsequently found not to have had the relevant intention(s), the corresponding act or decision will be either void (*ex tunc*) or voidable (*ex nunc*). Such a principle cuts across different families and traditions of legal thought and it is shared, in different forms, by most modern legal systems (and certainly those which are at least partially derived from Roman law). It also applies to the exercise of both public and private powers (contracts, marriages, wills, etc).[138] The point is that the existence (or lack thereof) of the relevant intention by the power-holder is considered to be so relevant by the legal system, that in some cases it might even be given priority over the legal positions of (innocent) third parties which have consolidated in the meantime between the (vitiated) exercise of the power and the authoritative decision to annul it.

Now, the avid reader will immediately reply: surely it is not the presence of the relevant intention, but how someone acts, that determines whether the conditions of a power-conferring norm have been satisfied or not. And as we do not have reliable epistemic access to other people's mental states,[139] this rejoinder to the thesis I have defended here must be sound, must it not? The clearest example is that of the making of an objective contract, in which one or more parties might not have the relevant intention – and yet the law draws a 'reasonable inference'[140] from the parties' behaviour to conclude that they must have had the intention to enter into the contract. This example, on closer inspection, can actually ground another independent line of criticism vis-à-vis the position defended here.[141] For, rather than claiming that some powers do not require the relevant intention to be exercised, the criticism could be that it would be 'awkward' to consider cases like objective contracts as examples of the exercise of a power, given that the relevant intention is actually absent.[142] Again, must not this be intuitively right?

---

vol 1 (n 3); G Klass, 'Three Pictures of Contract: Duty, Power and Compound Rule' (2008) 83 *New York University Law Review* 1726.

[137] For instance, most modern legal systems limit the capacity of certain categories of subjects (children, adults with certain mental disorders, etc) to exercise legal powers, precisely because it is held that individuals belonging to these categories are not able to *form* the relevant intentions.

[138] Notably, the fact that the invalid exercise of a legal power might determine its annullability has been used as a potential counterargument to Hart's rejoinder of Austin's famous view of norms – all norms – as general orders backed by threats. See, eg, for discussion: Kramer, *H.L.A. Hart* (n 131) 37–46). But the annullability of a decision – for instance, to marry someone – which lacked the relevant intention is not a sanction: rather, it indicates that while a decision has been made prima facie, this decision should not produce those normative effects as pre-established by the relevant power-conferring norm.

[139] On the 'epistemic access problem', see, eg: MJ Shaffer, *Counterfactuals and Scientific Realism* (London, Palgrave Macmillan, 2012) ch 3.

[140] Halpin, 'The Concept of a Legal Power' (n 134) 144.

[141] The position defended here, revolving around the volitional element of the exercise of legal powers, is in this respect Hohfeldian, and compatible with Raz's position: see J Raz, 'Voluntary Obligations and Normative Powers (Part II)' (1972) 46 *Aristotelian Society Supplementary Volume* 79, 81; Raz, *Practical Reason and Norms* (n 123) 104.

[142] This is one of the main criticisms of Raz's definition of legal powers by Halpin, who calls it a 'conceptual contortion': Halpin, 'The Concept of a Legal Power' (n 134) 144. For an excellent

236   *Creation and Application of Law. An Analytical Distinction*

Interestingly, the answer to both objections is the same, and relies on the acknowledgement that the 'epistemic access' problem (that is, not being able to reliably know of other people's mental states) is not confined only to some scenarios, but is ubiquitous in law, as well as in other aspects of social life. In other words, it is not only in some cases that we must draw a 'reasonable inference' from someone's behaviour to the relevant intention – it is *always* the case. For someone could always utter 'I do' in response to the wedding official's question not because she has the relevant intention (to get married and modify the legal sphere of both herself and her spouse), but because she had been hypnotised before the ceremony and instructed to answer positively to any question she is asked. Or, perhaps less sinisterly, one could simply be drunk and not realise that the ceremony officiated by an Elvis Presley lookalike in a small kitsch chapel in Las Vegas could be a valid, binding wedding for the law.

The point is that, precisely because of the epistemic impossibility to access someone else's mental state, we are *always* inferring the presence of the required intention to apply the relevant power-conferring norm from external behaviour. To make that intention epistemically more accessible – or better, to make the inference easier and more intersubjectively reliable – we create formalities (or rituals) through which we are deemed to express (to signal) our intention to get married, or to be bound by the terms of the contract, or to issue a given text as law.[143] This is one the functions performed by law's formality since (at least) the Roman *stipulatio* – that of giving substance in the external world to the agent's will or mental state.[144] But this should never trick us into thinking that when someone says 'I do' before the wedding official, we are indeed directly accessing the intention behind the utterance. We are not, and this is also confirmed by the fact that the prima facie validity of the external act which constitutes exercise of the power-conferring norm can always be questioned before a court.

Therefore, it is not the case that, in holding an involuntary contractor bound by a contract which she did not necessarily have the intention to be bound by, we are committing a 'conceptual contortion' – as Halpin holds.[145] What happens in this type of case is, instead, that there might be policy reasons to deem the external behaviour sufficient to infer (objectively) the relevant intention to be bound by the contract even less *conspicuous* than what is typically recognised as expressing that intention (like a handshake after an offer has been made).[146]

---

discussion of the 'objective contract' case vis-à-vis the distinction between duty-imposing and power-conferring norms see Klass, 'Three Pictures of Contract' (n 136) 1750–56.

[143] Klass, 'Three Pictures of Contract' (n 136) 1743ff.

[144] *cf* LL Fuller, 'Consideration and Form' (1941) 41(5) *Columbia Law Review* 799, 801.

[145] My point is, in other words, that if we take Halpin's argument at face value, we are always committing a 'conceptual contortion', even when we assign to someone that replies 'I do' to the official's question the relevant intention to get married.

[146] Klass resolves the tension between the structure and function of power-conferring norms and the progressive 'objectivisation' of contract law by adding a third type of norm alongside power-conferring and duty-imposing norms: 'compound' norms, that is, norms whose function is to impose a duty and to create powers at the same time. As the argument in the main text should

Can only Officials Apply the Law? 237

This also implies, finally, and in response to the first line of criticism, that in a certain sense it is *always* how someone acts – what someone says, or does, or even a mere acquiescence in some cases[147] – which will determine whether a legal power has been exercised or not.[148] But this should not lead us astray from the fundamental observation that, when it comes to power-conferring norms, and unlike the case with duty-imposing norms, external behaviour is to be understood as a proxy for the presence – or lack thereof – of the relevant intention.

IX. CAN ONLY OFFICIALS APPLY THE LAW?

Why did we have to go through what some readers might feel was a digression on the distinction between power-conferring norms and duty-imposing norms? I contend that by clarifying the different institutional function of the two types of norm, we are able to make better sense of the dominant position in the literature according to which law-application, properly speaking, is an activity which can be carried out only by the officials in a legal system, and not by laypeople as well (who instead *comply* with the law).[149] Otherwise why would it sound 'incongruous' to say that a driver applies the highway code when stopping at the red traffic light, whereas 'it makes sense' to say a police officer applies it when issuing a ticket to a driver for running the light?[150]

The reason, I believe, lies in the fact that only in the second case does the law necessarily require the norm to appear in the decision-making process of the agent: that is to say, only in the second case does the norm becomes relevant as a power-conferring norm, and thus the law requires its *application* to the case

---

make apparent, there is no such theoretical need for a third type of rule (rather than, perhaps, for something called 'compound institutions').

[147] Thanks to Martin Kelly and Visa Kurki for reminding me of this latter possibility.

[148] I think this is what Raz was pointing to when he wrote that 'An action is the exercise of a legal power only if one of the law's reasons for acknowledging that it effects a legal change is that it is of a type such that it is reasonable to expect that actions of that type will, if they are recognized to have certain legal consequences, standardly be performed only if the person concerned wants to secure these legal consequences' and that, at the same time, 'it is possible to exercise power and to make a contract or some other legal transaction with no intention to do so, if one does not correctly appreciate the legal consequences of one's action'. See Raz, 'Voluntary Obligations and Normative Powers' (n 141) 81.

[149] See, eg: Pino, L'Applicabilità delle Norme Giuridiche' (n 104) 802–09, where he lists three principal reasons supporting this position: 1) current linguistic practices among lawyers and academics; 2) the fact that 'application' seems to refer to a norm as a reason to take an authoritative decision and not just as a reason for action; and 3) that 'application' seems to imply an intentional or volitional activity, for it is not possible to 'apply' a legal norm without being aware of it – whereas this is perfectly possible with the (mere) compliance by private citizens. He also further distinguishes between application in a strong sense (by legal officials) and application in a weak sense (by legal academics): ibid 808–09. See also R Guastini, *Interpretare e Argomentare* (Milan, Giuffré, 2011) 253 fn 2, who considers only legal officials capable of applying the law, while citizens can only 'interpret' it.

[150] Pino, L'Applicabilità delle Norme Giuridiche' (n 104) 803.

238   *Creation and Application of Law. An Analytical Distinction*

at hand. We only need drivers to comply with the highway code, and as such we do not have to presuppose an intentional action aimed at the satisfaction of the normative requirement; whereas this is necessary to identify the decision by the police officer to issue the fine (which clearly changes the legal sphere of its recipient) as the exercise of a legal power. As this observation can be extended to cover every duty-imposing and power-conferring norm in a legal system, it prompts two remarks.

First, and contrary then to the dominant position in the literature, there seem to be no good theoretical reasons to restrict the use of 'law-application' only to the activities of officials in a legal system. Indeed, the reason why we routinely and intuitively say that officials – civil servants, police officers, judges, and so forth – apply the law is because these categories of individuals (or the institutions they embody) are normally the recipients of the two main types of power-conferring norms as identified by Hart: (public) rules of change and adjudication. These power-conferring norms, as we argued in the last section, must figure in and determine the decision-making process of the agent. Therefore, when private individuals are also the recipients of power-conferring norms (as in the case of contracts, for instance), it makes perfect sense to say that they must apply the law if they want to produce the legal consequences pre-established by the norms themselves. In fact, I contend that there is nothing counter-intuitive in saying that someone has to apply (or follow) the relevant norm(s) in signing a written contract when buying a new house: this is exactly what someone has to do (among other things) in order to modify her legal sphere and acquire the ownership of the house. When it comes to law-application, in other words, there is no qualitative difference between officials of a system and non-officials: what matters is instead whether the norm in question is a duty-imposing or power-conferring norm.

Second, and relatedly, the example of the driver and the police officer above allows us to bring to the fore and clarify another underdeveloped aspect of the concept of law-application. While we have just affirmed that in our modern legal systems only power-conferring norms require application (and not mere compliance), one should always be alert to the relative character of the distinction between power-conferring and duty-imposing norms. For any duty-imposing norm, when it comes to the ascertainment of its violation, will become normative, as a power-conferring norm, on the part of the decision-maker who is authorised (by a different power-conferring norm) to consider, decide, or adjudicate on it.[151] Take the following formulation of the traffic light offence (fixed penalty) in the UK:[152]

> Any motorist has the obligation to stop behind the (white) stop line when the red light is showing. Anyone who fails to comply with a red traffic signal will be fined £100.

---

[151] *cf* Ferrajoli, *Principia Iuris*, vol 1 (n 3) 427–428, 516; see also, for what is possibly an inchoate expression of this point, Raz, 'The Institutional Nature' (22) 112.

[152] In the formulation above, I am not considering explicit exceptions to the rules (when a police officer's instructions are different from the light showing, the police officer's instruction should be

The norm, which we shall call N₁, can be reconstructed under the standard conditional structure (if someone fails to stop at a red light, they will be fined £100)[153] and is clearly duty-imposing upon all ordinary motorists on British streets. It is duty-imposing also towards police officers (when they are not on duty) and towards magistrates and judges. But when these officials are instead performing their institutional roles in light of a power-conferring norm (which we shall call N₂) that gives them the competence to ascertain the violation of the norms of the highway code,[154] our duty-imposing norm N₁ will then become relevant as power-conferring, and will be applied (substantively) in the exercise of the relevant power, that is, in issuing a motorist with a £100 fine for having failed to stop at the red light (the decision). This is illustrated in Figure 1 below.

Figure 1 The relative character of the distinction between duty-imposing and power-conferring norms in the application of law

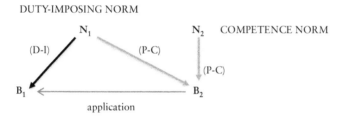

This is the sense, I believe, in which the legal syllogism, for instance as put forward by Alexy's 'Subsumption Formula',[155] captures the idea of the application of law: by showing how duty-imposing norms become (substantively)

---

followed) and other so-called 'special reasons' under which no prosecution would be enforced (for instance, if someone went beyond the stop line to allow an ambulance to drive through).

[153] Chiassoni, *Tecnica dell'interpretazione giuridica* (n 107) 31; G Pino, *Teoria Analitica del Diritto I: La Norma Giuridica* (Pisa, Edizioni ETS 2016) ch 2.

[154] To illustrate the point as clearly as possible, I am assuming here that there is only one power-conferring norm which establishes the different competences of police officers and magistrates – the reality, of course, will be more complex and one will likely see a number of different power-conferring norms for each of these categories of officials.

[155] R Alexy, 'On Balancing and Subsumption. A Structural Comparison' (2003) 16(4) *Ratio Juris* 433, 433–435. Alexy's syllogism can be reconstructed with the following logical notation (Chiassoni, *Tecnica dell'interpretazione giuridica* (n 107) 30–35):

N: $(x)\ (Dx \rightarrow VRx)$
F: Da

DEC: VRa

Other important authors (Wróbleksi, MacCormick, and Alchurron among others) adopt schemes of reconstruction of the legal syllogism similar to this. For an overview, see Chiassoni, *Tecnica dell'interpretazione giuridica* (n 107) ch 1.

240   *Creation and Application of Law. An Analytical Distinction*

power-conferring in the authoritative ascertainment of their violation and implementation of their juridical consequences.[156] In this regard, if the police officer issues a £1,000 rather than £100 fine as authorised by the norm (N_1), the motorist will be able to bring an action in judicial review to annul the decision of the police officer, precisely because the police officer will have gone beyond the boundaries of the power that was *conferred* upon her. Duty-imposing rules, in this respect, will be relevant as substantive power-conferring norms, in that they limit what can actually be decided by the relevant authority, whereas the power-conferring norms that assign the competence (or jurisdiction) to take the decision in the first place will usually also establish formal or procedural requirements on the decision-making power – such as the need for the decision to be written (in a given form), filled out and signed by the decision-maker, and so forth.[157]

X. FORM AND SUBSTANCE. TOWARDS AN ANALYTICAL ACCOUNT OF LAW-APPLICATION

What we have just illustrated points to the first fundamental element of the analytical account of law-application defended here. It pertains to the fact that law-application can always be divided into formal and substantive law-application, depending on the number and type of constraints that are imposed by hierarchically superior norms on the exercise of the relevant power. So the written form of a contract or a statute is a formal or procedural constraint imposed by superior norms, whereas the specification of the exact amount of the fine which can be imposed by a police officer for a certain type of driving offence is a substantive constraint.

While both types of requirements perform the general function of limiting the exercise of the power by the designated decision-maker, we have already seen that formal requirements (or at least a subset of them) carry out at the same time the fundamental function of making the relevant intentionality – the intention to apply the norm in order to produce the normative effects predisposed by it – *external*, in the sense of knowable to others and recognisable as such. For this reason, at least one formal norm (but normally several of them) must be applied for a certain behaviour to be recognised as a prima facie power-exercising *act*; while for the same act to be considered valid, all of the relevant formal and procedural norms must be applied.[158] An example of

---

[156] For a critical discussion of the idea that the traditional legal syllogism 'models' law-applying decisions see L Duarte D'Almeida, 'On the Legal Syllogism' in D Plunkett, SJ Shapiro, K Toh (eds), *Dimensions of Normativity: New Essays on Metaethics and Jurisprudence* (Oxford, Oxford University Press 2019).

[157] Sometimes there might be, next to the power-conferring norm, a duty imposing one: *cf* Kramer, *Objectivity and the Rule of Law* (n 77) 38.

[158] On the significance of the difference between existence and validity of law see Sandro, 'Unlocking Legal Validity' (n 75).

Form and Substance. Towards an Analytical Account of Law-application 241

this (always potential) asymmetry between existence and validity can be seen in the case of a will which looks prima facie formally valid (that is, produced in accordance with all the necessary procedural requirements) but whose signature turns out to be a forgery. The fact that the will might exist for the legal system – that is, being recognised for what it is and potentially produce its typical effects *rebus sic stantibus* – does not also imply its validity, which might be ultimately ascertained by a judge if an action is brought before her.

Therefore, every behaviour that is recognised at least prima facie as a juridical act – a token-act, as specified by the type-act in the relevant power-conferring norm – is in this respect applicative of at least some of the formal norms on its production.[159] Or, to put it differently, if a certain form of behaviour is not even minimally applicative of the relevant formal norms on its production, it cannot exist as a juridical act (of the type in question) in the first place.[160] This means that every existing legal act which is the exercise of a power-conferring norm is, in a sense, already an act of (formal) application of law – albeit partial – irrespective of its contents. Full formal application (and validity) will obtain instead only when all the formal (or procedural) norms on the production of the act are satisfied.

Perhaps the most important reason to distinguish between formal and substantive application of law lies in the following: the former always requires conformity with the norms establishing formal or procedural requirements for the exercise of a power-conferring norm, so that the decision-maker is *bound* to do exactly (and all) what the formal norms require in order to produce a valid token-act of the type established by the power-conferring norm. The written form of a contract, the specific parliamentary procedure for adopting a constitutional statute in Italy, the requirement of a signature by the judge who writes the judicial ruling: all of these formal requirements are obligatory if the decision-maker wants to exercise her power correctly.

Through substantive or material requirements – that is, requirements that pertain to the contents of the decision rather than to its form – a decision can be regulated in two alternative ways instead.[161] In addition to the modality of obligation, in which the contents of the decision are pre-established by the relevant power-conferring norm (as happens with formal norms), a norm might permit a decision-maker to establish the contents (or part thereof) of the decision herself, provided that she does not decide something that is prohibited by other superior norms. This is the modality of permission, that is the leeway which occurs for the decision-maker each time the contents of the decision (which is the expression of the power conferred) are not entirely predetermined by the relevant power-conferring norms.[162]

---

[159] Ferrajoli, *Principia Iuris*, vol 1 (n 3) 527–29.
[160] See Sandro, 'Unlocking Legal Validity' (n 75).
[161] Ferrajoli, *Principia Iuris*, vol 1 (n 3) 556–560.
[162] If constraints are only formal and/or procedural, the decision-maker will have, as a result, an absolute legal discretion to establish the contents of the decision: this is, for instance, what happens with the traditional understanding of the principle of parliamentary sovereignty in the UK.

242 *Creation and Application of Law. An Analytical Distinction*

The resulting distinction between *bound* and *discretionary* (substantive) law-application is long established in, as we have seen, continental administrative law scholarship,[163] but it should actually be considered as part of the general theory of law. For it is not only in administrative law that there are two different possibilities of (substantive) compliance between norms and acts that purport to apply them: discretionary powers are also those of a legislature in making new laws (which must not violate the substantive limits imposed by constitutional norms),[164] as well as those of private citizens in pursuing their own interests and aims through the freedom of contract (again, without going beyond the established limits of that contractual autonomy). Bound application is instead traditionally predicated on adjudication, particularly in civil law jurisdictions and in criminal law matters where the principle of legality applies strictly.

Still, the clearest examples to illustrate the difference between bound and discretionary application are to be found in administrative law. Think about the decision by the Driver and Vehicle Licensing Agency (DVLA) to grant a driving licence, and the decision by a local authority to regulate the planning of a new factory within a metropolitan area. In the former case, upon the acknowledgement of the possession of the legal requirements by the applicant, the DVLA is bound to take the decision of granting the driving licence. In the latter case, the local authority has discretion to regulate the planning of the new factory: what ought to be the minimum distance between the first residential building and the factory, what ought to be the factory's opening hours, and so forth. In the former case, the contents of the decision have been established already by the power-conferring norm, thus the administrative authority has merely a decision-*taking* power; while in the latter the administrative body has the decision-*making* power to determine the actual contents of the decision to be taken, provided that the latter are consistent with – ie, they do not contradict – the substantive requirements on the exercise of the power. In the former case, the substantive norms must be fully applied, while in the latter (merely) respected.[165]

Finally, it is important to stress that the fact that a decision is bound, as to its contents, by higher norms, does not necessarily imply that it is also determinate. A major upshot of the analytical distinctions we have engaged with in this book is that legal determinacy is the product not of one, but of two concurrent axes: that of the deontic modality (obligatory or permitted) and that of 'interpretive discretion' (as discussed in chapter four). In this regard, if a decision is non-obligatory it is also, necessarily, discretionary. But a decision could be obligatory and yet there could still be margins of choice available to the decision-maker, for instance because the norm-formulation is ambiguous or vague ('Go to the

---

[163] See ch 4, section VIII.

[164] According to Wintgens, 'Legisprudence as a New Theory of Legislation' (n 60) 23, the 'rule-following behaviour' of legislators 'is then confined to not violating the rules they are supposed to follow'.

[165] *cf* MacCormick, *Rhetoric* (n 27) 203.

Form and Substance. Towards an Analytical Account of Law-application 243

supermarket and buy about half a dozen bananas!').[166] As a result, we seem warranted in talking of bound law-application – what sometimes goes under the name, not entirely satisfactory of subsumption[167] – only when the decision is obligatory *and* the extent of interpretive discretion present (semantic, factual, and systemic) is negligible.[168] These are what Raz would called 'clear' cases,[169] and are those that constitute the basis for the increasing degree of computability of (administrative) law-application.[170]

Table 2 The square of law-application

	OBLIGATORY	NON-OBLIGATORY
DETERMINATE	Bound application of law	Discretionary application of law
NON-DETERMINATE	Discretionary application of law	Autonomous application of law

All the other cases of application, both when the decision is obligatory but non-determinate or non-obligatory but determinate, are discretionary in the sense that the decision-maker yields some power to choose vis-à-vis the exercise of the relevant power (see Table 2 above). When the exercise of the relevant power-conferring norm is both (substantively) non-obligatory and non-determinate – as in the case of the law-making powers of legislatures, or of the contractual capacity of physical and legal persons – it is constrained in such a way that Ferrajoli calls these powers 'autonomous'.[171] For in these cases the law chiefly demands conformity with formal norms in pursuing aims which, albeit authorised by the legal system, are autonomously established. Clearly, such neat distinctions are not always going to be capable of being straightforwardly used when analysing historical administrative and judicial decisions, where the axes of the deontic modality and of the degree of interpretive discretion – and particularly systemic discretion, as we argued in chapter four – might be blurred. But having them as analytical tools allows for a more rigorous scrutiny of the exercise of power-conferring norms and identification of the sources of their discretion (normative and/or interpretive).

---

[166] The example is from Endicott, *Vagueness in Law* (n 166) 48–49.

[167] See Ferrajoli, *Principia Iuris*, vol 1 (n 3) 560ff.

[168] *cf* Marmor, *Interpretation and Legal Theory* (n 14) 95.

[169] Raz, 'Law and Value in Adjudication' (n 19) 181–182.

[170] Surden, 'The Variable Determinacy Thesis' (n 83) 80. For one of the first examples of formalisation of the application of a particular statute see MJ Sergot, F Sadri, RA Kowalski, F Kriwaczek, P Hammond and HT Cory, 'The British Nationality Act as a Logic Program' (1986) 29(5) *Communications of the ACM* 370. Since then, the astonishing advancements (thanks to machine learning) of artificial intelligence systems raise a plethora of important ethical tradeoffs vis-à-vis their use in automated legal decision-making. See, eg, the recent collection of essays in S Deakin and C Markou (eds), *Is Law Computable?: Critical Perspectives on Law and Artificial Intelligence* (Oxford, Hart Publishing, 2020).

[171] Ferrajoli, *Principia Iuris*, vol 1 (n 3) 609.

244 *Creation and Application of Law. An Analytical Distinction*

XI. CONCLUSION

The analytical account of the distinction between creation and application defended in this book can be summarised, by way of conclusion, in the following manner. Against sceptical stances towards the distinction, I have explained (in chapters one and two) why its possibility remains fundamental for both legal and political theory. At the same time, I have argued against those simplistic or ideological views which neatly divide creation and application between two different type of institutions, legislatures and courts. Thanks to the distinction between formal and substantive application, we have seen that even legislatures generally apply the law, in the sense of the formal and procedural norms on the production of statutes normally found in the constitution of the system. At the same time, courts can be said to be always applying the law, in the sense of deriving the individual decision in the case from *a* general norm. While this explains why courts are normally (and, in this sense, correctly) identified as law-applying institutions, we have then pushed to identify a *stricter* sense of law-application.

In particular, we need a different criterion to distinguish between cases in which courts are indeed applying, even with some discretion, law which pre-exists their decision, and cases in which instead they are applying law that they have themselves created – ie a general norm which was not *part* of the legal system before the decision. This has required three separate but related argumentative lines: first, the analysis of the concept of legal discretion in chapter four; second, the defence of the conventionality of law's communicative meaning (at least in a majority of cases) in chapter five; and finally, the clarification of the notions of creation and application of law in this chapter. The result is a more complex – but with greater explanatory potential – picture of the distinction between creation and application of law than existing accounts in the literature, thanks to the two (independent) axes of deontic modality and interpretive discretion and the resulting fundamental distinction between bound and discretionary application of law.

We have seen in chapter five that even prominent legal realists like Guastini agree on the necessity to distinguish between interpretation (properly speaking) of a legal source and the ascription of a meaning to it which cannot be considered as expressed by the text in question (also in light of the co-text). This latter and jurisgenerative operation is variously called (juristic) construction, interstitial legislation,[172] or even judicial development of the law.[173] The point is that, while we are warranted in describing an act as 'law-application' when the norm being applied to a case is within the communicative frame expressed by the relevant text (within the theory of legal meaning defended in this work), the decision to consider as 'law-application' any ascription of meaning that is

---

[172] See ch 5, n 240.
[173] Klatt, *Making the Law Explicit* (n 4).

outside the communicative frame is a contingent decision, which will vary not just across time and space, but also between different parts of the same legal system.[174] This possibility is premised on the existence (and extent) of what we have called in chapter four 'systemic' discretion – the contingent (and more or less) recognised leeway to depart from the communicative meaning of a legal source, depending on the different interpretive canons (teleological, analogical, and so forth) and 'juristic theories' existing in each legal system. Evidently, the more 'systemic' discretion the courts have in a given system to depart from the communicative meaning of the legislative text, the less clear the overall boundary between legal interpretation and interstitial legislation will appear.

Furthermore, while it would be fanciful to deny that, at least in some cases (and particularly those that reach the appellate stages of litigation), the communicative and the judicial meaning of a legal provision can part ways, it is crucial to highlight that the more the judicial meaning of a provision is distant from its communicative one, the more the justificatory strength of the concept of law-application is undermined. That is, the more the decision by a court in the instant case cannot be said to be based exclusively on the application of a pre-existing norm as put forward by the authority with the power to do so, the more the decision of the court will need to be supplemented through a different type of legitimacy (and will be open to contestation).

This is where, arguably, the duality between *lex* and *ius* that we have discussed in chapter two comes back to the fore: the more the decision of a court is not based on the application of *lex* but on the exercise of *ius*, the more the decision by the court will have to be justified on the grounds of its merits and other systemic considerations, rather than on being (linguistically) warranted by the general norm at its basis. This might be, in the end, the most important upshot of the distinction between creation and application put forward in this work: not the (descriptively untenable) rejection of the law-creation power of courts, but the clarification that in such cases the decision cannot be fully justified by the idea of application of law.

XII. PS ONE FINAL OBJECTION: INTERPRETATION, INTERPRETATION, INTERPRETATION!

There seems to be a looming threat vis-à-vis the account just defended. It pertains to the concept of following or applying a rule and, more basically, to that of 'rule' (or 'norm') itself. The problem is, as concisely put by Hart, that a rule does not seem able to 'step forward to claim its own instances'.[175] But if this is so, in what sense can rules be said to be normative? That is, why do we

---

[174] This can be seen, for instance, in the prohibition (in many legal systems) of analogical legal reasoning only in criminal law (and unless the result would favour the defendant).

[175] Hart, *Concept of Law* (n 14) 126; *cf* with P Pettit, 'The Reality of Rule-Following' (n 121) 9.

246 *Creation and Application of Law. An Analytical Distinction*

think in terms of correct and incorrect applications?[176] What makes them so, if not the rule itself?

We came across this problem in previous chapters already, and it is time now to examine it more thoroughly. Stated broadly, the objection is that every application of a rule is actually an interpretation of it.[177] This picture returns us to the idea of a gap between a rule and its applications. As such, 'rules are *never* simply applied; [they are] never clear',[178] so that it 'is interpretation that gives us the rule, not the other way around'[179] or, as Duarte puts it, so that 'all norms are unknown before interpretation'.[180] This position has been called the 'current interpretive orthodoxy'[181] and it is variously held by a 'striking range of theorists',[182] notably Dworkin, Fish and Schauer.[183]

As Endicott correctly notes, this orthodoxy, in itself, would 'not compel any particular view on indeterminacy'.[184] The 'critical predicament'[185] ensues from the acknowledgment that, in ordinary discourse, the term 'interpretation' is used to express the activity of 'making choices as to the meaning of an expression or a text'.[186] Interpretation makes us think, intuitively, of a creative process,[187] a process – by definition undetermined to a greater or lesser extent – in which is up to the interpreter to imbue an object with meaning.

In fact, this intuitive juxtaposition of 'understanding' and 'interpreting' as different activities seems tracked in ordinary legal discourse by the maxim *interpretatio cessat in claris*.[188] Here lies the problem then: if everything in law is interpretation,[189] that is if between every rule and its application to a particular case there is a gap to be filled by such interpretive activity, and 'if you … simultaneously hold in your head the idea that interpretation is a matter of

---

[176] In other words, there is an (intuitive) sense in which normativity appears to be intrinsically embedded within the very notions or concepts of 'rules' and 'rule-following': Haukioja, 'Is Solitary Rule-Following Possible?' (n 121) 132.

[177] T Endicott, 'Linguistic Indeterminacy' (1996) 16(4) *Oxford Journal of Legal Studies* 667, 671.

[178] M Stone, 'Focusing the Law: What Legal Interpretation is Not' in A Marmor (ed), *Law and Interpretation: Essays in Legal Philosophy* (Oxford, Oxford University Press, 1995) 32.

[179] D Cornell, *The Philosophy of the Limit* (New York, Routledge, 1992) 101.

[180] D Duarte, 'Linguistic Objectivity in Norm Sentences: Alternatives Literal Meaning' (2011) 24(2) *Ratio Juris* 112, 114.

[181] Endicott, 'Linguistic Indeterminacy' (n 177) 671 fn 14.

[182] ibid 671.

[183] See ibid 671–72, for an extended list of authors and quotes. Endicott notes at 672 that this is 'a bizarre consensus among people who agree on nothing else', but that eventually 'They all think that no legal question can be answered except by an interpretation'.

[184] ibid 672.

[185] ibid 671–74.

[186] ibid 673.

[187] Rather than a process (at least in some cases) of discovery.

[188] Stone, 'Focusing the Law' (n 178) 35. A similar maxim is 'in *claris non fit interpretatio*': JJ Moreso, *Lógica, Argumentación e Interpretación en el Derecho* (Barcelona, Editorial UOC, 2006) 113.

[189] 'So interpretation has become like a pair of glasses that colours everything we see': Stone, 'Focusing the Law' (n 178) 43.

PS One Final Objection: Interpretation, Interpretation, Interpretation! 247

making choices among open alternatives',[190] what does it mean *to follow* a rule? There seems to be no such thing, for before interpretation there is nothing to be followed, and therefore what we call 'application of law' is revealed as an inherently subjective and, at least in one potential sense, political activity.[191]

This clearly threatens law's autonomy:[192] as Stone puts it, 'according to this thesis, the presence of plain meaning testifies to the hegemony, so to speak, of a particular interpretation, not to the absence or superfluousness of interpretation as such'.[193] As such, the problem seems to be with the determinacy as much as with the objectivity of legal rules:[194] it is not only about whether law is pervasively indeterminate or not, but also about what makes an application of law *correct* and another one *incorrect*. Is there any meaningful sense of 'objective' in legal discourse? Or are we but forced to uncover the true nature of law as a pervasive and subjective interpretive process?

If the need for interpretation arises at all, it is because, as we have said, rules cannot 'jump out' and claim their own applications – rules in this sense are inert as to their relationship with the world. This is nothing but the sceptical interpretation of the problem of rule-following, which is among the most debated puzzles in modern analytical philosophy, at least since the late Wittgenstein. To begin with, one can (and should) distinguish three levels on which this problem can be discussed:

1) philosophically, in which it asks a constitutive question on the dynamics of rule-following *tout court*;
2) linguistically, in which it pertains to the relationship between the words we use and their meaning; and
3) juridically, in which the issue is with legal rules and their application in particular cases.

The relationship between these three levels is complex, for although someone can be a sceptic on the legal level without being so on the first two, in the great majority of cases one is sceptical 'all the way up'. But how does the philosophical problem of rule-following bear on what we mean by our words and concepts? According to Vila Iglesias,

> understanding the meaning of a linguistic formulation seems to be very closely related to following a rule or acting in accordance with it. Given that rules are expressed by

---

[190] Endicott, 'Linguistic Indeterminacy' (n 177) 673.

[191] CM Yablon, 'Law and Metaphysics' (1987) 96 *Yale Law Journal* 613.

[192] Stone, 'Focusing the Law' (n 178) 33. He claims (ibid 36) that this form of scepticism arises from what he terms 'the illusion of determinacy', ie the claim that 'if there is to be law, it must be possible to follow it to the particular case'.

[193] ibid 43.

[194] On their relationship in law, see, eg: Coleman and Leiter, 'Determinacy, Objectivity and Authority' (n 5); Kramer, *Objectivity and the Rule of Law* (n 77); Sandro 'Unlocking Legal Validity' (n 75).

248   *Creation and Application of Law. An Analytical Distinction*

means of language, the range of conducts that constitute acts of rule-following will be specified insofar as the meaning of normative formulations is determined.[195]

It is in this sense that 'meanings are rules', for 'to apply words and concepts with the aim of complying with these correctness conditions is to follow rules'.[196] But if rules in the first place cannot claim their own applications, how could we mean anything by our words? This might explain why Wittgenstein was drawn to the problem of rule-following in the first place, given his more general conception of philosophy as a critique of language.[197] The point is that any attempt to derive sceptical conclusions from his discussion of the problem is questionable. I shall proceed as follows: first, I will briefly recall some of Wittgenstein's own remarks. Second, I will explain how the sceptical challenge arises. Third, the non-sceptical reading of Wittgenstein will be contrasted. Fourth, the objections against the latter will be mentioned. Lastly, I shall briefly try to dissolve these objections. My ultimate aim is to defend a sense of 'applying a rule' which is objectively determinate and that allows for the existence of clear cases of linguistic meaning.

The object of Wittgenstein's criticism is the 'classic realist picture' of meaning in which the latter is explained in terms of truth-conditions, a model he himself had defended in the *Tractatus Logico-Philosophicus*.[198] Undergirding this conception is 'meaning platonism', according to which 'the correct applicability of a term in new cases is determined by virtue of its being associated with an intermediate object such as an idea or a universal'.[199] The point is that the rules of meaning are seen as laying down in advance, mechanically,[200] their applications to an infinite series of cases.[201] In Wittgenstein's words:

> Whence the idea that the beginning of a series is a visible section of rails invisibly laid to infinity? Well, we might imagine rails instead of a rule. And infinitely long rails correspond to the unlimited application of a rule.[202]

What Wittgenstein realises is that this picture of meaning is unsatisfactory, in particular when it comes to the application of words to new cases that we (as

---

[195] M Iglesias Vila, *Facing Judicial Discretion: Legal Knowledge and Right Answers Revisited* (Dordrecht, Springer, 2001) 58 fn 79.

[196] Endicott, 'Linguistic Indeterminacy' (n 177) 690; J Haukioja, 'A Middle Position Between Meaning Finitism and Meaning Platonism' (2005) 13(1) *International Journal of Philosophical Studies* 35, 36.

[197] Baker and Hacker, *Wittgenstein: Rules, Grammar, and Necessity* (n 124) 41.

[198] SA Kripke, *Wittgenstein on Rules and Private Language* (Cambridge, Harvard University Press, 1982) 72–74.

[199] Haukioja, 'Middle Position' (n 196) 39.

[200] Stone, 'Focusing the Law' (n 178) 44–45.

[201] For the remark that meaning determinism is not necessarily linked to meaning Platonism: Haukioja, 'Middle Position' (n 196).

[202] L Wittgenstein, *Philosophical Investigations*, rev. 4th edn (PMS Hacker and J Schulte eds, Chichester, Wiley-Blackwell, 2009) §217.

PS One Final Objection: Interpretation, Interpretation, Interpretation! 249

competent language-users) have never encountered before. He puts forward then the so-called 'paradox' of rule-following which, taken at face value, seems indeed puzzling. The example in the *Philosophical Investigations* is that of the 'plus two' rule that a pupil is being asked to continue by his teacher. According to a great variety of scholars who believe they are correctly following Wittgenstein on the point,[203] the example purports to show that whatever (act of) application of the rule – even the series '1000, 1002, 1004, 1008' – could be brought in accordance with the 'add two' rule by means of interpretation.[204] As he puts it,

> no course of action could be determined by a rule, because every course of action can be brought into accord with the rule. ... If every course of action can be brought into accord with the rule, then it can also be brought into conflict with it. And so there would be neither accord nor conflict here.[205]

It is precisely the idea that 'interpretation ... determine[s] the correct application of rules' that leads to the paradox, because each interpretation can be in turn further interpreted, and as such we slide into an endless regress.[206] There is not a fact or 'set of facts which determines that a speaker is following one rule rather than another'.[207] The result is that, where there used to be once the 'platonistic rail' connecting a rule with its applications, now there is a gap.[208] Now, that semantic Platonism is to be abandoned seems almost a platitude today.[209] Yet what happens to meaning once we abandon Platonism? According to Kripke:

> There can be no such thing as meaning anything by any word. Each new application we make is a leap in the dark; any present intention could be interpreted so as to accord with anything we may choose to do.[210]

If this is so, it is not only that objectivity and determinacy when it comes to rule-following seem an illusion;[211] rather, is there anything we ought to call 'rule-following' at all?[212] Kripke has famously proposed a 'sceptical' solution

---

[203] Kripke, *Wittgenstein on Rules and Private Language* (n 198); see also F Schauer, *Playing by the Rules: A Philosophical Examination of Rule-based Decision-making in Law and in Life* (Oxford, Clarendon Press, 1991) 207; Duarte, 'Linguistic Objectivity in Norm Sentences' (n 180) 114; Iglesias Vila, *Facing Judicial Discretion* (n 195)58ff.

[204] This way of posing the paradox is convergent with the thesis of the underdetermination of meaning in radical pragmatics: see ch 5, n 97.

[205] Wittgenstein, *Philosophical Investigations* (n 202) §201.

[206] Baker and Hacker, *Wittgenstein: Rules, Grammar, and Necessity* (n 124) 129.

[207] R Holton, 'Meaning and Rule-following: Philosophical Aspects' in N Smelser and P Baltes (eds), *International Encyclopedia of the Social & Behavioral Sciences* (Amsterdam, Elsevier, 2001).

[208] Stone, 'Focusing the Law' (n 178).

[209] Coleman and Leiter, 'Determinacy, Objectivity and Authority' (n 5) 601ff.

[210] Kripke, *Wittgenstein on Rules and Private Language* (n 198) 55; Haukioja, 'Middle Position' (n 196) 47 defines Kripke an 'irrealist' about meaning.

[211] Stone, 'Focusing the Law' (n 178) 36, argues that this form of scepticism 'arises from the illusion that we have understood this demand for determinacy "as the *impossibility* of doubt"'.

[212] On why reductionism is misplaced, see Baker and Hacker, *Wittgenstein: Rules, Grammar, and Necessity* (n 124) 228.

250   *Creation and Application of Law. An Analytical Distinction*

to the paradox.[213] In his view, all we can aim to, and achieve, is a surrogate of objectivity and determinacy in rule-following. As he puts it:

> There is no objective fact – that we all mean addition by '+', or even that a given individual does – that explains our agreement in particular cases. Rather our license to say of each other that we mean addition by '+' is part of a 'language game' that sustains itself only because of the brute fact that we generally agree.[214]

On this reading, 'rule following is essentially social',[215] and so must be language. Thus, according to Kripke, Wittgenstein's solution to the sceptical paradox brings to light, as a 'corollary',[216] the so-called 'private language argument'.[217] It is this 'community-view'[218] that allows us to speak *as if* there were rules: in this sense, 'following a rule' is another way of saying 'doing what other members of the community say is following a rule'.[219] This implies that, when we speak of a clear case of the application of a word, what we are actually speaking about is a social fact, a matter of agreement.[220] For our purposes, it is not the case then that there are not clear cases, rather the point is that there is nothing objective out there that makes them so. In this way, the 'critical predicament' we have started our analysis with comes to the fore, for

> the distinction between easy and hard cases is too innocently won and should be re-described as a distinction between cases in which the interpretive assumptions conditioning the judgement are uncontroversial and those in which they are not.[221]

Kripke's account has been criticised in two relevant ways: having been deemed 'unfaithful' to Wittgenstein's remarks, it has been attributed to a fictional 'Kripkenstein' in order to distinguish it more clearly from the discussion of rule-following by the Austrian-British philosopher. More importantly, Kripke's solution is troubled and does not fare particularly well when it comes to account for our rule-following practices.[222] Hence Kripkenstein has been contrasted with

---

[213] Kripke, *Wittgenstein on Rules and Private Language* (n 198) 4.

[214] ibid 92.

[215] Endicott, 'Linguistic Indeterminacy' (n 177) 691.

[216] Kripke, *Wittgenstein on Rules and Private Language* (n 198) 68.

[217] Haukioja ('Is Solitary Rule-Following Possible?' (n 121) 132) notes that there is no consensus as to exact location of the Private Language Argument (PLA) in the *Philosophical Investigations*. According to Kripke, the PLA starts with the discussion on rule-following and culminates in §202. Baker and Hacker vigorously contend this interpretation, putting forward (convincing) arguments as to why the locus of the PLA is the more traditional §§243 ff. See Baker and Hacker, *Wittgenstein: Rules, Grammar, and Necessity* (n 124) 158.

[218] Kripke, *Wittgenstein on Rules and Private Language* (n 198) 89ff.

[219] Endicott, 'Linguistic Indeterminacy' (n 177) 690.

[220] Kripke, *Wittgenstein on Rules and Private Language* (n 198) 96.

[221] Stone, 'Focusing the Law' (n 178) 43; see S Fish, *Doing What Comes Naturally: Change, Rhetoric, and the Practice of Theory in Literary & Legal Studies* (Durham, Duke University Press, 1989) 122ff.

[222] See, eg: Baker and Hacker, *Wittgenstein: Rules, Grammar, and Necessity* (n 124) 145; S Soames, 'Facts, Truth Conditions, and the Skeptical Solution to the Rule-Following Paradox' (1998) 32 *Nous* 313.

PS One Final Objection: Interpretation, Interpretation, Interpretation! 251

the 'non-sceptical' reading of the rule-following remarks in the *Investigations*, the reading considered more faithful to Wittgenstein's broader philosophical outlook. On this latter reading, the rule-following paradox is only illusory, and Wittgenstein's philosophical aim is to dispel it. For it is not that there is no answer to the question 'what connects a rule with its applications?', but rather that the question should not be asked at all.[223]

In this regard, the metaphor of the rule as a 'platonistic' rail and the idea of interpretation as the only possible gap between a rule and its applications are the two sides of the same, *forged*, coin:[224] that of trying to understand how rules work outside their context of use – so that the rule, *qua* sign, 'seems dead'.[225] What Wittgenstein purports to do instead is to clear this philosophical muddle,[226] created by the tendency of a certain philosophical tradition to question some phenomena that should be only looked at.[227] In other words, once things are put in the right perspective, we are left with a picture of rule-following in which there is no necessary gap which always needs to be bridged, because a rule is *internally* connected to (at least some of) its applications.[228]

This is why Wittgenstein's famous remark that 'there is a way of grasping a rule which is not an interpretation'[229] constitutes an insuperable obstacle for any sceptical reading of his analysis.[230] This form of understanding is shown – together with the relevant intentions – by *simply* following a rule, that is by acting in accordance with it within the broader context of a practice.[231] In the way Wittgenstein puts it, obeying a rule *is* a practice,[232] and as Stone notes there is a striking convergence between him and Kant on the point.[233]

---

[223] Endicott, 'Linguistic Indeterminacy' (n 177) 691; Stone, 'Focusing the Law' (n 178) 65–66.

[224] Stone, 'Focusing the Law' (n 178) 53; for how can interpretation in the first place fill that gap without giving rise to an infinite regress? (ibid, 54). See also Baker and Hacker, *Wittgenstein: Rules, Grammar, and Necessity* (n 124) 129.

[225] Stone, 'Focusing the Law' (n 178) 53; *cf* Endicott, 'Linguistic Indeterminacy' (n 177) 690.

[226] Baker and Hacker, *Wittgenstein: Rules, Grammar, and Necessity* (n 124) 155.

[227] ibid.

[228] On the internal relation thesis see also Stone, 'Focusing the Law' (n 178) 50; Iglesias Vila, *Facing Judicial Discretion* (n 195) ch 2; and *cf* Baker and Hacker, *Wittgenstein: Rules, Grammar, and Necessity* (n 124) 130, 165.

[229] Wittgenstein, *Philosophical Investigations* (n 202) §201; see also Stone, 'Focusing the Law' (n 178) 35; Endicott, 'Linguistic Indeterminacy' (n 177) 673; Baker and Hacker, *Wittgenstein: Rules, Grammar, and Necessity* (n 124) 126, 129.

[230] Endicott, 'Linguistic Indeterminacy' (n 177) 690. This is confirmed by another famous remark in L Wittgenstein, *On Certainty* (GEM Anscombe and GH von Wright eds, Oxford, Basil Blackwell, 1969) §370, where Wittgenstein claims that 'The fact that I use the word "hand" and all the other words in my sentence without a second thought, indeed that I should stand before the abyss if I wanted so much as to try doubting their meanings – shews that absence of doubt belongs to the essence of the language-game, that the question "How do I know ..." drags out the language-game, or else does away with it'.

[231] Holton 'Meaning and Rule-following' (n 207).

[232] Wittgenstein, *Philosophical Investigations* (n 202) §202.

[233] Stone, 'Focusing the Law' (n 178) 40, 57; Baker and Hacker, *Wittgenstein: Rules, Grammar, and Necessity* (n 124) 156; *cf* Haukioja, 'Is Solitary Rule-Following Possible?' (n 121) 149.

252 *Creation and Application of Law. An Analytical Distinction*

The community view meanwhile falls short of representing a viable model of our normative practices. Whether Kripke's account is faithful to Wittgenstein's or not, taken on its own merits it appears inherently flawed.[234] To assess this, it is worth fleshing out the requirements that any theory must possess if it purports to account for the intuitive notion of rule-following we have considered at the beginning of this section.[235] Three requirements in particular stand out.

First, a theory must allow not just for the possibility of mistakes,[236] but for the additional requirement of 'making sense' of them:[237] it is definitional of the activity of rule-following that an agent might err in following the rule or in applying the rule to her judgements or actions.[238] The possibility of making mistakes, viz. to go against the rule, is logically co-extensive with that of following it in the first place. Second, this 'erring-condition' bears a double dimension, for it must also allow for the possibility of 'community-mistakes':[239] it must account for the possibility of the community at large to be in error about the application of a particular rule. In other words, it must differentiate between *consensus* and *correctness*.[240] Clearly this standard of correctness, against which such instances of rule-following are to be weighed, cannot be what seems right to the agent or to the community, for otherwise we would not be able to distinguish between correct and incorrect applications of a rule. As Hacker and Baker put it:

> 'To think one is following a rule is not to follow a rule' prefigures PI §258. The rule is the yardstick against which the act is measured. But a yardstick that expands or contracts according to what one thinks is its length is no yardstick at all. Likewise, merely believing that one is following a rule does not suffice for following a rule.[241]

Rule-following requires then some form of objectivity, conceived of (at least) as the '*possibility* of genuine testing'.[242] Lastly, if an agent is to follow a rule, and

---

[234] See, eg: Alexander and Sherwin, *Demystifying Legal Reasoning* (n 77) 162 (and further references there).

[235] Having already presupposed the distinction between (merely) acting in accord with a rule and following a rule. See Iglesias Vila, *Facing Judicial Discretion* (n 195) 192; Baker and Hacker, *Wittgenstein: Rules, Grammar, and Necessity* (n 124) 131, 137, 145.

[236] E Itkonen, 'The Central Role of Normativity in Language and Linguistics' in J Zlatev, TP Racine, C Sinha and E Itkonen (eds), *The Shared Mind: Perspectives on Intersubjectivity* (Amsterdam, John Benjamins Publishing, 2008) 280–281; this has been termed 'the condition of semantic errors': Klatt, 'Semantic Normativity' (n 4) 52–53. *cf* Baker and Hacker, *Wittgenstein: Rules, Grammar, and Necessity* (n 124) 165.

[237] Haukioja, 'Is Solitary Rule-Following Possible?' (n 121) 133.

[238] Itkonen, 'The Central Role of Normativity' (n 236) 280.

[239] Holton 'Meaning and Rule-following' (n 207); Haukioja, 'Is Solitary Rule-Following Possible?' (n 121) 138.

[240] Haukioja, 'Is Solitary Rule-Following Possible?' (n 121) 133; he notes that it is this awareness of the standard that makes rule-followers different from machines.

[241] Baker and Hacker, *Wittgenstein: Rules, Grammar, and Necessity* (n 124) 131. See also Klatt, 'Semantic Normativity' (n 4) 51; Iglesias Vila, *Facing Judicial Discretion* (n 195) 193.

[242] Itkonen, 'The Central Role of Normativity' (n 236) 281; Iglesias Vila, *Facing Judicial Discretion* (n 195) 193.

PS One Final Objection: Interpretation, Interpretation, Interpretation! 253

if this is possible only by being aware of it, the rule must exist in advance of the agent's acts, and so must be the criterion of correctness. At least some instances of correct application of the rule must be determined in advance of anyone's judgements about it,[243] ie it is necessary that 'the rule somehow guides its own instances of use'.[244] This is the third constitutive requirement, that of (advance) *determination*. Otherwise, the existence of a gap between the rule and its applications would appear again, and so would the sceptical challenge.

Against this framework, it should be apparent why Kripke's solution does not work: replacing truth-conditions with assertibility conditions based on the 'degree of general consensus generated by every alleged rule-following act' implies that 'the correct applications of terms is not governed by rules available to the agent when attempting to use the language', so that to 'the sceptic, the interpreter's act will be no more than a leap in the dark based on her interpretation of the contents of the rule';[245] moreover, as correctness and consensus are co-extensive, it does not seem possible for the community at large to err about the application of a rule.[246] The sceptical 'solution' does not get off the ground, for there is no viable notion of normativity that can be defended by embracing it.[247] So must we admit that rule-following is nothing but an illusion? What about the non-sceptical reading of Wittgenstein then?

This question is paramount for our purposes because the most prominent defenders of partial determinacy (or cognitivist) approaches in Anglo-American jurisprudence seem to rely exclusively on the 'internal-relation' thesis. This position would seem warranted only prima facie: according to Vila Iglesias, there is an inner contradiction that plagues it. This would lie in accepting the internal relation thesis between a rule and (some of) its application, while at the same time maintaining that agreement in a given language-community is what (a-priori) determines linguistic meaning. But we have seen already that it is doubtful whether agreement can fulfil such a role, for

> this is precisely the problem that scepticism points out to: that taking a past event as a semantic criterion does not in any determine the meaning of a text, because we can reconstruct past events in a multiplicity of ways.[248]

In other words, 'to take the behaviour of the majority to be the criterion of correctness in applying rules would be to abrogate the internal relation of a

---

[243] Haukioja, 'Middle Position' (n 196); see also Pettit, 'The Reality of Rule-Following' (n 121) 3.
[244] Iglesias Vila, *Facing Judicial Discretion* (n 195) 191.
[245] ibid 59.
[246] Also, scepticism seems unable to account for language change: Haukioja, 'Middle Position' (n 196); Holton 'Meaning and Rule-following' (n 207).
[247] See, eg: S Soames, 'Skepticism About Meaning: Indeterminacy, Normativity, and the Rule-Following Paradox' (1998) 23 *Canadian Journal of Philosophy* 211; see also Haukioja ('Middle Position' (n 196) 47) for an interpretation of Kripke that leads to a form of 'middle position' between Platonism and finitism akin to the position defended here.
[248] Iglesias Vila, *Facing Judicial Discretion* (n 195) 61.

254   *Creation and Application of Law. An Analytical Distinction*

rule to acts that accord with it'.[249] The two theses appear then to be clearly in conflict with one another. Those who defend the (partial) 'determinacy thesis' in law 'need to tender a different relationship between meaning and consensus'.[250] Some of them (Bix, Marmor, Schauer), argues Vila Iglesias, try basically to rely on Hacker and Baker's interpretation of Wittgenstein's remarks that 'agreement on definitions and judgments, as a sign of a shared form of life, is what makes possible the existence of rules, and the very idea of following rules' – although in this way 'their starting point seems to be their ending point too'.[251] Once again:

> Consensus on the form of life as the criterion for meaning invalidates the thesis of an internal relationship between the rule and its instances of use [and] leads [back] to the sceptical problem.[252]

Is this really so? There is some unpacking to do here, both as to Iglesias Vila's criticisms, as well as more generally to the internal relation thesis and its relationship with agreement. As to the former, there seems to be two related sets of problems for partial determinacy theses in law according to Iglesias Vila. The first problem is that reliance on any sort of agreement, even if (only) at the very primordial level of the 'form of life', as the determinant for the criterion of correctness invalidates the internal relation thesis.[253] If this is true, then it is yet to be established how the thesis of the internal relationship could warrant both the second and third requirements of a successful theory of rule-following: objectivity and (advance) determination.

In other words, 'we are urged to show that there is a way to predetermine without resort to facts, metaphysical entities, or collective conventions, which acts embody a correct application of the rule' – and without collapsing into subjectivism at the same time.[254] Iglesias Vila seems to acknowledge that Pettit's 'response-dependence' theory,[255] according to which the 'fixers' of the references of (at least some of) our concepts are our responses in 'favourable' conditions,[256]

---

[249] Baker and Hacker, *Wittgenstein: Rules, Grammar, and Necessity* (n 124) 150.

[250] Iglesias Vila, *Facing Judicial Discretion* (n 195) 61. Here, agreement and consensus are synonyms and this might be part of the problem, as agreement needs not be conscious, whereas consensus cannot but be volitional. Thus, we could *happen* to agree on something simply because we do, and not because we willingly reached or achieved such agreement. This is how, I submit, we must understand agreement in Wittgenstein's account. I owe this very important point to Felipe Oliveira de Sousa.

[251] Iglesias Vila, *Facing Judicial Discretion* (n 195) 61.

[252] ibid 64, fn 108; but *cf* Baker and Hacker, *Wittgenstein: Rules, Grammar, and Necessity* (n 124) 223.

[253] If understood as a reference to rule-following *tout court*, that is to the *grammatical* notion of it, Baker and Hacker agree. See Baker and Hacker, *Wittgenstein: Rules, Grammar, and Necessity* (n 124) 227.

[254] Iglesias Vila, *Facing Judicial Discretion* (n 195) 193.

[255] Pettit, 'The Reality of Rule-Following' (n 121).

[256] For an illuminating discussion of Pettit's and other accounts of response-dependence, see J Haukioja, 'Different Notions of Response-Dependence' in M Hoeltje, B Schnieder and A Steinberg (eds), *Varieties of Dependence: Ontological Dependence, Grounding, Supervenience, Response-Dependence* (Munich, Philosophia Verlag, 2003).

PS One Final Objection: Interpretation, Interpretation, Interpretation! 255

represents the most promising attempt to explain how a normative practice can arise without relying on any external mediator between a rule and its applications.[257] Yet she departs from it when it comes to *public* rule-following, as she argues that Pettit puts too strict a constraint on our collective normative practices, namely that 'a collective inclination to perceive a sequence of cases as exemplifications of the rule is required'.[258]

This requirement, in her opinion, could lead once again to the argument that an external mediator between rules and instance of use is required – the thesis that Pettit purports to avoid committing to in the first place.[259] On these grounds, Iglesias Vila eventually arrives at the conclusion that Dworkin's interpretivism offers us the (only) viable solution to this conundrum, as it allows us to claim (some version of) determinacy in rule-following without 'falling into scepticism or realist semantics'.[260] I will not engage here with the merits (or lack thereof) of Dworkin's interpretivism. Rather, I shall instead assess and refute Iglesias Vila's belief that resorting to Dworkin is necessitated by the lack of alternatives. This involves clarifying the relationship, both grammatical and non-grammatical, between agreement and correctness in public as opposed to 'non-public' rules. If this argument succeeds, we should then be able to distinguish between an objective and determinate core of meaning of our words and consequently to talk of linguistically clear cases of application – as opposed to interpretation – of a rule.

We must begin by pointing to what seems an unwarranted conflation in Iglesias Vila's argument: that between the *grammatical* question of what connects a rule with its applications and the *empirical* question of what connects words with their meaning in natural languages.[261] These questions should be kept separated, not only because one is theoretical whereas the other pertains to an empirical phenomenon,[262] but also because there might already be a degree of asymmetry between the grammatical question of rule-following and the question of linguistic meaning: to the extent that there could 'well be additional considerations having to do with linguistic meaning which make speaking a language a more demanding task than rule-following in general'.[263] If this is true, it would seem to allow precisely what Iglesias Vila rejects about partial determinacy theses held by the legal scholars mentioned above: namely upholding at the same time the 'internal relation' thesis about rule-following and some version of 'community view' about linguistic meaning. Is this option available?

---

[257] Itkonen, 'The Central Role of Normativity' (n 236) 283.
[258] Iglesias Vila, *Facing Judicial Discretion* (n 195) 195.
[259] ibid.
[260] ibid 196.
[261] *cf* Endicott, 'Linguistic Indeterminacy' (n 177) 691.
[262] See Baker and Hacker, *Wittgenstein: Rules, Grammar, and Necessity* (n 124) 168; Haukioja, 'Is Solitary Rule-Following Possible?' (n 121) 150.
[263] Haukioja, 'Is Solitary Rule-Following Possible?' (n 121) 131; *cf* Baker and Hacker, *Wittgenstein: Rules, Grammar, and Necessity* (n 124) 151, 223.

256   *Creation and Application of Law. An Analytical Distinction*

Let us begin by considering *solitary* (or private) and public rule-following. We said that for Wittgenstein rule-following is a practice and there are several reasons to believe that it need not be *grammatically* a social practice.[264] There seems to be then one sense in which solitary rule-following could be possible,[265] for there would be nothing conceptually wrong in the notion of an unshared rule.[266] Kripkenstein, with his understanding of the 'private language argument', would contest this claim but this quarrel need not concern us here.[267] What we are eminently interested in is the case of *public* rule-following, of shared rules, and in particular those of linguistic meaning. What then does it take for a rule to be shared? What are the consequences, in terms of the relationship between the internal thesis and consensus?

According to Pettit, a public or shared rule is a rule 'which another person can know you follow'.[268] A shared rule must be logically opposed not to an unshared rule, but rather to an *unshareable* rule.[269] What makes a rule *unshareable*? We know by now that social rules, while not being practices in themselves, stand in some necessary relation to the practice of following them;[270] therefore, in order to find out whether a rule is being followed, we need to know the criterion of correctness applied in the practice. The criterion of correctness must be behaviourally expressed for us to be able to grasp it. If this criterion of correctness is unknowable to others, how could we ever find out whether this rule or another is being followed?[271]

> That's why 'following a rule' is a practice. And to think one is following a rule is not to follow a rule. And that's why it's not possible to follow a rule 'privately'; otherwise, thinking one was following a rule.[272]

This additional requirement on public rule-following is expressed by Pettit as that of being 'interpersonally interactive'. That is, the inclination according to which we act, in following one and the same rule, must be 'interpersonally standardized' – and not merely inter-temporally so as with solitary rule-following.[273] The proper relationship between correctness and consensus is not qualitatively different between private and public rules, rather it is quantitatively so.

---

[264] Baker and Hacker, *Wittgenstein: Rules, Grammar, and Necessity* (n 124) 143.

[265] Haukioja, 'Is Solitary Rule-Following Possible?' (n 121).

[266] Baker and Hacker, *Wittgenstein: Rules, Grammar, and Necessity* (n 124) 223.

[267] See Itkonen, 'The Central Role of Normativity' (n 236) 280–83.

[268] Pettit, 'The Reality of Rule-Following' (n 121) 21.

[269] Baker and Hacker, *Wittgenstein: Rules, Grammar, and Necessity* (n 124) 223. Therefore, Wittgenstein's PLA must be understood as arguing against these latter kind of rules, rather than against merely 'unshared' rules (ibid 133).

[270] *cf* Brennan et al, *Explaining Norms* (n 122) ch 2.

[271] Pettit, 'The Reality of Rule-Following' (n 121) 19 defines this a 'weak condition of knowledge'.

[272] Wittgenstein, *Philosophical Investigations* (n 202) §202; *cf* Baker and Hacker, *Wittgenstein: Rules, Grammar, and Necessity* (n 124) 131.

[273] Pettit, 'The Reality of Rule-Following' (n 121) 19–20.

PS One Final Objection: Interpretation, Interpretation, Interpretation! 257

For agreement does not suddenly become the criterion of correctness,[274] but it is empirically (rather than grammatically) required to be *inter*-personal for rules to be shared. In Baker and Hacker's words:

> There are no such things as shared rules independently of agreement over what accords with the rules, for *understanding* a rule is knowing what accords with it. ... Furthermore, there are no shared rules without shared patterns of normative activities, and so shared judgements about justification, criticism, explanation, description, etc. This general (*but not uniform*) consensus is part of the peaceful working of a *common* form of representation. Again, there are no shared techniques without general agreement on the results of employing the techniques, for in certain kinds of case, for example in calculating, the results are part of the technique, and in other kinds of case, for example counting or measuring objects, constant disagreement in results would rob the technique of its point and so too of its sense, and the technique would not exist. These forms of agreement or consensus are immediate consequences of explaining what *shared* rules are, given the previous explanation of what rules are.[275]

In grammatical terms, this means that while a private standard need only to be shareable, rather than be necessarily shared, to be considered properly speaking a *rule* – ie its criterion of correctness must be potentially inter-personally accessible[276] – a *public* rule cannot just be shareable. Rather, it needs to be *shared*, since there must be 'agreement in its application: these are not two distinct things, but two sides of the same coin'.[277] Agreement in behaviour constitutes the framework presupposed by every public rule, 'but this does not "annul logic" or soften the "hardness of the logical 'must'", since logic belongs to the rules of the language-games we play, and the framework conditions in general and agreement in particular are not included in those rules'.[278] Therefore

> [i]t is crucial that we do not have to explain to a child how to take our gesture of pointing at a sample and that we do not have to explain why he takes it as he does.[279]

This seems to be then the ultimate *locus* from which this kind of normativity arises: as such it is inevitably pre-theoretical – that is inapt for scientific explanation – while its 'philosophical (or metascientific) significance is enormous'.[280] And if this is true of public rule-following in general, it is even more so of language, where if communication is to be possible, (some degree of)

---

[274] Baker and Hacker, *Wittgenstein: Rules, Grammar, and Necessity* (n 124) 229: 'Our agreement does not determine truth – that is up to the world'.

[275] ibid 224 (my emphasis, except the last one).

[276] ibid 168.

[277] 'Of course, this principle holds only for such cases where the truth of a judgement is not readily separable from the correct application of expressions': ibid 228.

[278] ibid 227.

[279] ibid.

[280] Itkonen, 'The Central Role of Normativity' (n 236) 293.

258 *Creation and Application of Law. An Analytical Distinction*

agreement is necessary. As Wittgenstein put it, 'It is not only agreement in definitions, but also (odd as it may sound) agreement in judgements that is required for communication by means of language'.[281] For

> to agree in a rule (other things being equal) is to agree over what counts as its correct applications. So it follows that we must also agree in judgements about the world or at least in a *core* of judgements about the world.[282]

This in turn depends initially on – but is not *constituted by* – our sharing a common form of life. Thus, we can argue that language is primarily, albeit not necessarily, social[283] or shared.[284] A private language used as a 'private toolbox' for one's own purposes could indeed be envisaged;[285] but if 'language is to be a means of communication we must agree on the application of our rules of grammar and laws of logic, otherwise we could not agree on the rules at all, ie nothing would be shared'.[286] Undeniably then, agreement plays a pivotal role in our shared linguistic practices, a role through which we can try to rescue the communitarian view: perhaps in a slightly altered form, as proposed, for instance, by Haukioja.[287]

This version is based on a generalisation of the distinction of three kinds of linguistic errors, and in particular between 'rule-requirement' and 'rule-application' errors.[288] In this way, 'a more plausible version of the community view might hold that, as far as rule-applications are concerned, consensus and correctness may come apart, but that they cannot come apart for rule-requirements';[289] so that when it comes to language the community at large might be temporarily wrong as to the application of a word to a specific case, but not generally 'about what their words mean'.[290] Hence, Iglesias Vila's criticism against determinacy theses is misplaced, for there seems to be nothing contradictory – given the asymmetry between rule-following and language-speaking – in holding at the same time the internal-relation thesis for the former and the modified community view for the latter. The modified community view can make sense of disagreements in a promising way.[291] Iglesias Vila's proposal

---

[281] 'This seems to abolish logic, but does not do so': Wittgenstein, *Philosophical Investigations* (n 202) § 242.

[282] Baker and Hacker, *Wittgenstein: Rules, Grammar, and Necessity* (n 124) (my emphasis).

[283] Itkonen, 'The Central Role of Normativity' (n 236) 283.

[284] Baker and Hacker, *Wittgenstein: Rules, Grammar, and Necessity* (n 124) 165.

[285] ibid 166.

[286] ibid 224.

[287] Haukioja, 'Is Solitary Rule-Following Possible?' (n 121); *cf* Bertea, 'Remarks' (n 83), 530ff.

[288] Haukioja, 'Is Solitary Rule-Following Possible?' (n 121) 133–34.

[289] ibid 136.

[290] ibid; *cf* again Bertea, 'Remarks' (n 83) 532–33.

[291] In particular using the distinction between terms we learn by 'ostension' (like that of 'redness'), and terms we stipulate: see Itkonen, 'The Central Role of Normativity' (n 236); Haukioja, 'Middle Position' (n 196) 46ff; Baker and Hacker, *Wittgenstein: Rules, Grammar, and Necessity* (n 124) 229–30.

PS One Final Objection: Interpretation, Interpretation, Interpretation! 259

to get out of the conundrum, based on Dworkin' interpretivism, is also inherently flawed in that it requires mere shareability and not actual sharedness for the contents of public rules:[292] but we have just seen that communication requires agreement (sharedness) in definitions and judgements, and not the mere possibility of it.

Hence there appear to be good reasons to uphold some version of the moderate determinacy thesis in language. There is a middle ground, which Haukioja calls 'meaning determinism',[293] between the two extreme positions in the philosophy of language, Platonism and occasionalism, or finitism. This position allows us to retain linguistic determinacy in core cases[294] without the need to resort to Dworkin's interpretivism. In these core or easy cases, it is confirmed that 'the correct application of a term to a new instance is something we *discover* rather than *invent*',[295] and this normativity is not based on some untenable form of Platonism, but rather on the kind of beings we are and on the 'scaffolding of facts'.[296] In these cases, application 'is not *correct* because it is natural'; rather, 'It is because we find it natural that we *make it correct*'.[297]

Not only does there not seem to be anything philosophically odd in this claim,[298] but Wittgenstein himself, I believe, would agree with it. As he put it:

> It is only in normal cases that the use of a word is clearly laid out in advance for us; we know, are in no doubt, what we have to say in this or that case. The more abnormal the case, the more doubtful it becomes what we are to say. And if things were quite different from what they actually are – if there were, for instance, no characteristic expression of pain, of fear, of joy; if rule became exception, and exception rule; or if both became phenomena of roughly equal frequency – our normal language-games would thereby lose their point.[299]

---

[292] Iglesias Vila, *Facing Judicial Discretion* (n 195) 199–200.

[293] Haukioja, 'Middle Position' (n 196); this account is only for 'semantically basic terms', that is, terms we learn by ostension. *cf* Baker and Hacker, *Wittgenstein: Rules, Grammar, and Necessity* (n 124) 213; and see also Stone, 'Focusing the Law' (n 178) 50, according to whom this position is compatible with Wittgenstein's account of rule-following.

[294] In other words, 'the content of the rule is predetermined for all the standard applications of the rule in the future': Bertea, 'Remarks' (n 83) 526.

[295] Haukioja, 'Middle Position' (n 196) 47.

[296] Baker and Hacker, *Wittgenstein: Rules, Grammar, and Necessity* (n 124) 211ff.

[297] ibid 217 (my emphasis). See also Haukioja, 'Middle Position' (n 196) 46, who seems to accommodate Bertea's critique of the classical positivist use of Wittgenstein (Bertea, 'Remarks' (n 83) 529).

[298] Stone, 'Focusing the Law' (n 178) 63–64.

[299] Wittgenstein, *Philosophical Investigations* (n 202) §142.

7

The Separation of Powers.
A Meta-theoretical Reassessment

I. INTRODUCTION

A S DISCUSSED AT several points in this book, a naïve picture of the distinction between creation and application of law has become conceptually interwoven, for better or worse, with the doctrine of the separation of powers (hereinafter 'separation of powers'). In this respect, the historical conflation of a normative claim (legislatures should only create the law and courts should only apply it) and of a descriptive claim (legislatures only create the law and courts only apply it) has resulted in a diffuse scepticism over the theoretical validity of both assertions. And yet 'separation of powers' is not only still a working term in the vocabulary of both political and constitutional theorists, but a rather crucial one – as it can have very tangible implications for the lives of people in a political system depending on whether or not (and to what extent) it is implemented.

For example, in October 1939 – shortly after Hitler's invasion of Poland – the Italian dictator Benito Mussolini told the Italian magistrates:

> In my conception, there does not exist a separation of powers within the State. To conceive of it we need to go back in time to a century and a half ago, and perhaps then it was more justified from a practical rather than doctrinal point of view. But in our conception power is unitary: there is no separation of powers, but only of functions.[1]

This speech sounds remarkably eerie these days, as we have begun to witness the (democratically legitimated) unfolding of European constitutional democracies like Hungary or Poland.[2] Particularly in the case of the latter, the first significant sign of democratic decay has been indeed the extraordinary attack by the government and the ruling majority party (the Law and Justice party) against

---

[1] The speech is reported in S Foderaro, 'La teorica della divisione dei poteri nel diritto pubblico fascista' (1939) 31(1) *Rivista di diritto pubblico e della pubblica amministrazione in Italia* 745, 745 (my translation).

[2] For a more general discussion of the current processes of democratic decay worldwide see, eg: T Ginsburg and AZ Huq, *How to Save a Constitutional Democracy* (Chicago, University of Chicago Press, 2019).

Introduction 261

the entire Polish judiciary, whose independence from the government has been dismantled piece by piece (or better, court after court).[3] Is the attack on the independence of the Polish judiciary a clear sign that Poland is sliding towards the kind of totalitarianism Mussolini was able to realise in Italy during the fascist *ventennio*?

Even if we cannot answer this question, these recent events can be considered as the latest evidence of the connection between the health of democratic systems and the degree of instantiation of the separation of powers in those systems. In other words, far from being merely a theoretical debate, the separation of powers constitutes one of the most important elements of constitutional design: for it can help to keep the democratic game in check and, as such, lies at the core of our modern constitutional democracies.[4] This is why it is all the more surprising to acknowledge that, in spite of the essential role the separation of powers appears to be playing in our lives, it 'represents an area of political thought in which there has been an extraordinary confusion in the definition and the use of terms'.[5]

In recent times, the separation of powers in its traditional or 'received' account – a tripartite separation of legislature, executive, and judiciary within the state – has been deemed obsolete in the literature, from both a descriptive and a normative point of view:[6] descriptively, as it cannot account consistently anymore for the plurality and/or fragmentation of *loci* of exercise of public powers; normatively, either because it is deemed unable after all to constrain the exercise of those powers, or because it is considered as an obstacle vis-à-vis the efficient policy-making that seems necessary in our globalised world.

In this closing chapter, my aim is two-fold. First, I purport to 'restore' the meaning and usefulness of the separation of powers, both as an analytical tool and as a normative doctrine. In this regard, in the first part of the chapter I will offer a reconstruction of the current debate around the separation of powers by identifying a number of genealogical, meta-theoretical, and theoretical issues that often overlap and are sometimes even conflated. My hope is that the reconstruction offered will constitute a worthwhile addition to the literature in itself, contributing to dissolve pragmatic ambiguities surrounding the doctrine and its historical instantiations.[7] Once I have carried out this exercise in 'conceptual housekeeping', in the second part of the chapter, I will argue that we should keep clearly separate the use of the separation of powers as an analytical tool

---

[3] See W Sadurski, *Poland's Constitutional Breakdown* (Oxford, Oxford University Press, 2019).

[4] See C Möllers, 'The Separation of Powers', in R Masterman and R Schultze (eds), *The Cambridge Companion to Comparative Constitutional Law* (Cambridge, Cambridge University Press, 2019).

[5] MJC Vile, *Constitutionalism and the Separation of Powers*, 2nd edn (first published 1967, Carmel, Liberty Fund, 1998) 2.

[6] *cf* Möllers, 'The Separation of Powers' (n 4) 233–34.

[7] This part of the chapter builds on and departs from the already excellent discussion in A Vignudelli, 'Sulla Separazione dei Poteri nel Diritto Vigente' (2007) 7 *Diritto & Questioni Pubbliche* 201, and in Möllers, 'The Separation of Powers' (n 4).

262   The Separation of Powers. A Meta-theoretical Reassessment

to describe existing political systems and as a normative doctrine to guide the choices of constitutional and regulatory design. The two are independent and are clearly grounded in a different set of considerations. This dual approach, in my view, enhances the explanatory fruitfulness of the former while at the same time clarifying the justificatory premises of the latter.

I will conclude by presenting (in its main elements) a theory of the separation of powers based on a clear analytical distinction between an understanding of separation as independence (or non-usurpation) between different powers or functions, and as division (or sharing, or distribution, or articulation) of powers and/or functions. I will also sketch a normative model of the separation of powers that abandons its traditional tripartite structure and is instead based on the distinction between law-creation and law-application, as defended in this book.

II. GENEALOGICAL ISSUES. WHEN WAS THE SEPARATION OF POWERS 'INVENTED'?

It is conventional wisdom, at least in many constitutional law classrooms, to simplify and teach students that the separation of powers was put forward by Locke in the *Two Treaties of Government* and made famous, in its tripartite version, by Montesquieu in the eighteenth century. I am myself guilty, at least in part, of this 'sin'. In reality, the intellectual origin of the doctrine has been for quite some time now the subject of heated debate between historians, political theorists, and constitutional lawyers.[8] To whom should we attribute the 'invention' of the doctrine then?[9]

My impression is that a question like this is conducive to theoretical confusion, as it arguably exacerbates the tendency to pre-empt the doctrine through the decontextualisation of whatever author is in question. Indeed, it has been affirmed that the first historical elaboration of the separation of powers is to be found in classical times, for instance in Plato's *Republic*,[10] Aristotle's *Politics*[11] or in Polybius's *The Histories*.[12] And while there are indeed considerations by each of the aforementioned authors that, taken in isolation, can be used in conceptualising our modern idea of separation of the branches of the state,

---

[8] Möllers, 'The Separation of Powers' (n 4) 232–35.

[9] Vignudelli, 'Sulla Separazione dei Poteri' (n 7) fn 3 associates (among others) the following authors with the development of the separation of powers doctrine: Plato, Aristotle, Polybius, Cicero, Henry de Bracton, Marsilius of Padua, Locke, Rousseau, Kant, Constant, Hegel, Laband, Jellinek, Kelsen and Carré de Malberg.

[10] Plato, *Republic* (C Rowe trans, London, Penguin Books, 2012) Bk VIII.

[11] Aristotle, 'Politics' in C Lord (ed), *Aristotle's Politics*, 2nd edn (Chicago, Chicago University Press, 2013) Bk IV, ch XIV.

[12] See BC McGing, *Polybius' Histories* (Oxford, Oxford University Press, 2010) ch 5 (and also 216–17).

Genealogical Issues. When was the Separation of Powers 'Invented'? 263

we commit an intellectual mistake if we do not stress that in those authors' works the distribution of political power is predicated across the different social components of the *polis*, rather than upon different branches of the state. For it was exactly this distribution that would lead to the best form of government attainable, the famous 'mixed constitution' which represents 'the forerunner of modern republican regimes'.[13]

This 'classical' conceptual genealogy appears then ultimately based on a historiographical stretch.[14] For it is only perhaps with Marsilius of Padua and his *Defensor Pacis* that we find an articulation of the power(s) of the state where sovereignty belongs to the people, the law-making process is conceived of in positivist terms,[15] and the power of the 'ruler' is not unlimited and must be kept in check[16] – in other words, an inchoate form of separation of functions and institutions that squarely fits the fundamental coordinates of political modernity. Overall, while certainly relevant for the sake of historical accuracy vis-à-vis the political thought of the authors discussed, I argue that pinpointing the precise origin of the separation of powers – as for several other basic concepts of political theory – is, in many respects, a non-problem. More relevant is, instead, the tracing of its development through history.

Is there in fact a historical root to the enduring ambiguity surrounding the separation of powers? Has the expression 'separation' or 'division' of powers been used (roughly) consistently by different political theorists, or has its meaning shifted so much throughout history that it is by now inherently ambiguous?[17] And if this has happened, why? Answering these questions requires a diachronic viewpoint which seeks to identify and isolate the changes in the use of the doctrine, sometimes beyond the explicit assertions in the canonical texts.

In this sense then, the revived interest of legal theory scholarship in the conceptual history of the doctrine is particularly praiseworthy. This can be seen on two parallel fronts: the first which begins by critically analysing the 'received account' of the separation of powers in its Montesquieian tripartite version and questions its historical and conceptual soundness. The second analyses the impact that the 'received account', understood normatively, has had on historical constitutions – the post-independence constitutions in North America and the post-revolutionary ones in Europe – to uncover whether, beyond the more or less explicit ceremonial appeals to it, it has indeed been ever implemented and to what success (if any).

---

[13] F Miller, 'Aristotle's Political Theory', in EN Zalta (ed), *The Stanford Encyclopedia of Philosophy* (Winter 2017 Edition) http://plato.stanford.edu/entries/aristotle-politics/.

[14] See A Blau, 'How (Not) to Use the History of Political Thought for Contemporary Purposes' (2021) 65(2) *American Journal of Political Science* 359.

[15] Vignudelli, 'Sulla Separazione dei Poteri' (n 7) fn 3.

[16] Marsilius of Padua, *Defensor Pacis*, 2nd edn (first published 1324, A Gewirth trans, CJ Nederman ed, New York, Columbia University Press, 2001) 87–89.

[17] ME Magill, 'The Real Separation in Separation of Powers Law' (2000) 86(6) *Virginia Law Review* 1127.

264 *The Separation of Powers. A Meta-theoretical Reassessment*

The 'received account', to be sure, is the one in which the separation of powers is functionally organised around the *trias politica* – the qualitative distinction between legislature, executive, and judiciary, and which famously sees the judge as mere *bouche de la loi*: which is, as seen in previous chapters, perhaps the most famous theoretical instantiation of the formalist idea(l) of 'mechanical jurisprudence' – according to which the judges never make the law, but always apply it.

Regarding the first directive of scholarship, while Vile already questioned the novelty of Montesquieu's doctrine vis-à-vis 'contemporary English writers' (and Locke in particular),[18] it is only very recently that the 'received account' has been scrutinised in a number of respects: 1) as to the supposed inner failings of Montesquieu's analysis, based among other things on his inability to appreciate the law-making role of English courts;[19] 2) as to the potential spuriousness of the 'received account' as a result of the confusion of different models of distribution of power in Montesquieu's own thinking;[20] 3) as to the failings of both formalist (the 'received account') and non-formalist (like the realist critiques of Montesquieu's idea of the judge as *bouche de la loi*) receptions of Montesquieu, which equally betray his 'relational view of law and justice' that is based, rather than on a functional separation of powers, on a model of 'moderate government' in which the three actors of the *trias politica* should recognise their 'entangledness in a precarious equilibrium that constantly needs recalibration in light of specific circumstances'.[21] On the other hand, the critical analysis of the 'received account' of the separation of powers has been prominent in continental literature (and in particular in French, German, and Italian) for some time already, and it is only recently that this wealth of separation of powers studies has begun to find its way into the English-speaking literature through translations.[22]

The second line of scholarship questions instead the actual implementation of the received account – granted, notwithstanding its uncertain boundaries (as we shall see, between functional separation and institutional check and balances) – into historical constitutional orders.[23] Overall, it can be noted that while on

---

[18] Vile, 'Constitutionalism' (n 5) 94–99.

[19] L Claus, 'Montesquieu's Mistakes and the True Meaning of Separation' (2005) 25(3) *Oxford Journal of Legal Studies* 419.

[20] M Goldoni, 'Montesquieu and the French Model of Separation of Powers' (2013) 4(1) *Jurisprudence* 20.

[21] L van der Berge, 'Montesquieu and Judicial Review of Proportionality in Administrative Law: Rethinking the Separation of Powers in the Neoliberal Era' (2017) 10 *European Journal of Legal Studies* 203, 213.

[22] See, eg: C Möllers, *The Three Branches: A Comparative Model of Separation of Powers* (Oxford, Oxford University Press, 2013); G Bognetti, *Dividing powers: A theory of the separation of powers* (A Baraggia and LP Vanoni eds, Milan, Wolters Kluwer Cedam, 2017).

[23] See, eg: Vile, 'Constitutionalism' (n 5); G Conway, 'Recovering a Separation of Powers in the European Union' (2011) 17(3) *European Law Journal* 304; EA Posner and A Vermeule, *The Executive Unbound: After the Madisonian Republic* (Oxford, Oxford University Press, 2011); AZ Huq and JD Michaels, 'The Cycles of Separation-of-Powers Jurisprudence' (2016) 126(2) *Yale Law Journal* 346; R Masterman and S Wheatle, 'Unpacking Separation of Powers: Judicial Independence, Sovereignty and Conceptual Flexibility in the UK Constitution' [2017] *Public Law* 469.

A Twofold Meta-theoretical Ambiguity Plaguing the Discussion 265

the European continent the major factor influencing the 'pure' implementation of the separation of powers was the idea of popular sovereignty (which grants an inherent superiority to one of the three branches over the other two), in the US instead there was indeed an early attempt (in some state Constitutions like Virginia or Maryland)[24] to implement the 'pure' version of the separation between legislature, executive, and judiciary, only to awake soon thereafter to the (practical) impossibility of 'avoiding any mixture of those departments'.[25] This is the most likely cause – together with the original federalist structure of the newly independent United States of America – which brought about the normative model of separation of powers as checks and balances that is, in fact, commonly associated with the North-American experience.[26]

Still, despite such scholarly efforts to critically analyse the doctrine, the meaning of the separation of powers remains inherently ambiguous, oscillating between several distinct – and sometimes logically irreconcilable – uses. And it is precisely to this ambiguity that we now turn.

III. A TWOFOLD META-THEORETICAL AMBIGUITY PLAGUING THE DISCUSSION

In my view, there is in fact a twofold meta-theoretical ambiguity that seems at play every time the separation of powers is being discussed, either on its own or as a part of a wider theoretical project. This two-fold ambiguity constitutes one (if not the main) source of confusion around the doctrine.

First, is the separation of powers a descriptive theory or a normative doctrine? Certain textual passages could indicate that the separation of powers is actually a descriptive theory aimed at the classification of governmental functions into three distinctive types (legislative, executive, and judicial). Barberis points out that, at least in Montesquieu, the tripartite theory is to be understood indeed as a 'cognitive' theory, but in an analytical rather than empirical sense:[27] it is not borne out of data, so to speak, but it is rather true by definition of every possible governmental framework (that is, even if a given constitution does not explicitly mention the three functions). As such, this understanding of the separation of powers can be contrasted with other theories that identify either more[28] or fewer functions,[29] but cannot be criticised from a teleological point of view.

---

[24] See the excellent discussion in E Carolan, *The New Separation of Powers: A Theory for the Modern State* (Oxford, Oxford University Press, 2009) ch 2.

[25] J Madison, 'The Federalist No. 47' in A Hamilton, J Madison and J Jay, *The Federalist Papers* (first published 1787–88, L Goldman ed, Oxford, Oxford University Press, 2008).

[26] For a critical discussion see J Waldron, 'Separation of Powers in Thought and Practice' (2013) 54 *Boston College Law Review* 433.

[27] M Barberis, 'Separazione dei Poteri e Teoria Giusrealista dell'Interpretazione' in P Comanducci and R Guastini (eds), *Analisi e diritto 2004: Ricerche di giurisprudenza analitica* (Turin, Giappichelli, 2004) 3.

[28] See, eg: B Ackerman, 'The New Separation of Powers' (2000) 113(3) *Harvard Law Review* 633.

[29] See, eg: H Kelsen, *General Theory of Law and State* (first published 1949, New Brunswick, Transaction Publishers, 2005).

266 *The Separation of Powers. A Meta-theoretical Reassessment*

There are, however, other passages in Montesquieu's *L'Esprit des Lois* that indicate an altogether different understanding of the separation of powers, namely as a normative doctrine.[30] In this sense it would amount to an ideal (or blueprint) of good institutional design or good government, whose normative bite has however changed constantly throughout history. There seem to be cycles in terms of its relevance, as suggested by empirical research vis-à-vis its use as a basis for constitutional decisions in the US and in the UK.[31] Contemporary scholarship can be divided in two broad camps: those who dismiss its relevance altogether,[32] either on the basis of the rejection of formalist theories of law and of the related idea of law-application,[33] or on the loss of centrality of the nation-state and its law-making powers;[34] and those who strive to defend its re-acquired crucial role in light of post-modern phenomena like globalisation[35] and neoliberalism.[36]

The second meta-theoretical issue emerges once we conceive of the doctrine in normative terms: is it a political or a legal doctrine? This problem can be attributed, at least partially, to the historical disconnection between political philosophy and constitutional law.[37] In this regard, the separation of powers would have evolved along two parallel universes of discourse – the political and the legal/constitutional discourse – that would rarely intersect. This is perhaps clearer if we think that, as a legal doctrine, the separation of powers would have more determinate empirical references in the text of the constitution and in the decisions by the apex court in the given country, with the downside that a doctrine of separation of powers so understood would be necessarily jurisdiction-bound and so hardly universalisable.[38]

When understood instead as a *pure* political normative doctrine that can prescind, to an extent, from references to existing institutional designs, two further issues arise. On the one hand, such an approach is often undermined by too wide a gap between the blueprint and existing institutional realities, underscoring the relative little interest that political theory sometimes has for the conditions of institutionalisation of its own standards,[39] which in turn

---

[30] Charles de Secondat, Baron de Montesquieu, *The Spirit of the Laws* (AM Cohler, BC Miller and HS Stone eds, first published 1748, Cambridge, Cambridge University Press, 1989) Bk XI, ch IV, 155–156; ch VI, 156–166. Chs 4, 6.

[31] See, respectively, Huq and Michaels, 'The Cycles of Separation-of-Powers Jurisprudence' (n 23); Masterman and Wheatle, 'Unpacking Separation of Powers' (n 23).

[32] See, eg: Posner and Vermeule, *The Executive Unbound* (n 23).

[33] Claus, 'Montesquieu's Mistakes' (n 19).

[34] J Mendes and I Venzke, 'Introducing the Idea of Relative Authority', in J Mendes and I Venzke (eds), *Allocating Authority: Who Should Do What in European and International Law?* (Oxford, Hart Publishing, 2018).

[35] Möllers, *The Three Branches* (n 22).

[36] van der Berge, 'Montesquieu and Judicial Review of Proportionality in Administrative Law' (n 21).

[37] In addition to the discussion on this point in ch 2 of this book, see also Möllers, *The Three Branches* (n 22) 6–7.

[38] Möllers, 'The Separation of Powers' (n 4).

[39] Möllers, *The Three Branches* (n 22) 6.

A Twofold Meta-theoretical Ambiguity Plaguing the Discussion   267

increases the risk of being irrelevant to actual politics.[40] On the other, as we shall see in section IV below, there is considerable variance – and disagreement – in terms of the ultimate justification of a doctrine of separation of powers. As a consequence, it has also been asserted how it might be impossible to establish a monistic justificatory strategy for the doctrine, and that we should rather acknowledge a normative pluralistic landscape in which the separation of powers is 'intended to simultaneously advance and harmonize diverse and conflicting normative ends'.[41]

What is the result of this two-fold ambiguity? My claim is that, in combination with the shift in meaning of the doctrine between different authors and against the background of different historical contexts, we still lack at present a settled meaning when we refer, in our debates, to the 'separation' or 'division' of power(s). Waldron, in what has quickly become an influential contribution, distinguishes for instance between:[42]

A. *separation of powers*, which 'counsels a qualitative separation of the different functions of government – legislation, adjudication, and executive administration';
B. *division of power*, 'counseling us to avoid excessive concentrations of political power in the hands of any one person, group, or agency'; and
C. *checks and balances*, 'holding that the exercise of power by any one power-holder needs to be balanced and checked by the exercise of power by other power-holders'.

It is worth noting that, after distinguishing between the different meanings of the separation of powers and agreeing with Vile that the confusion around 'the definition and the use of the terms' is paramount, Waldron goes on to charge the analytical philosopher with 'futility' for stressing the importance of clarifying between the different uses of the expression, because 'People use a phrase as they use it'.[43] We will come back to this in a moment. For now, let us note that Möllers published his English monograph on the separation of powers in the same year as Waldron's article and converges, at least nominally, on the three meanings ('manifestations' or 'concepts') of the doctrine. A more careful analysis though reveals immediately substantial differences between the two accounts. For while Waldron and Möllers converge on the principle of checks and balances, they diverge on the meaning of separation of powers – given that for Möllers it requires an 'organisational division of different parts of the polity'[44] – and

---

[40] N Barber, 'Prelude to the Separation of Powers' (2001) 60(1) *Cambridge Law Journal* 59, 62–63.
[41] Huq and Michaels, 'The Cycles of Separation-of-Powers Jurisprudence' (n 23) 378.
[42] Waldron, 'Separation of Powers in Thought and Practice' (n 26) 434–444. He identifies two more 'meanings' of the doctrine, namely the Bicameralism and Federalism principles, which seem specific to the US constitutional system.
[43] ibid 439.
[44] Möllers, *The Three Branches* (n 22) 43.

268 The Separation of Powers. A Meta-theoretical Reassessment

on that of division, which Möllers describes as 'a ban on any functional usurpation of power'.[45]

In stark contrast to Waldron's suggestion then, one of the main theses defended in this chapter is not only that terminological ambiguity is at the very root of the contestation around the separation of powers, but that a stricter analytical approach can help shed light on the boundaries of the doctrine and its *potential* and *actual* uses.[46] In this regard, a few preliminary observations can be made from the juxtaposition of the two accounts.

First, for Waldron the difference between separation and division is between a qualitative and quantitative articulation of powers, so that what the latter 'cares about is that power be dispersed; it does not care particularly what the dispersed powers are';[47] while the former requires 'articulated governance' exercised by the three powers of the state (legislative, executive, and judiciary) on the basis of their respective integrity.[48]

For Möllers, the difference between separation and division is instead between an organisational and a functional division of powers, where 'powers' in the former indicate the different branches of government, while in the latter they indicate the functions or 'duties' that are allocated to each of them. And while he correctly stresses the importance of clearly differentiating between these two senses of 'power',[49] in both senses the separation or division requires the same institutional design: the independence of the given branch or function from the others. As to the former, '[a]ll institutions or departments that are named in the constitution must be put in a position to independently carry out the duties assigned to them';[50] while as to the latter, what is imposed is 'a prohibition against the exercise of a particular power by an institution to which this power has not been allocated'.[51]

At any rate, both accounts seem still to presuppose the classical *trias politica*, albeit seemingly for different reasons: Waldron, normatively, due to the different and respective 'integrity' of each branch of government; Möllers, empirically, because almost all systems examined in his comparative study bear the tripartite distinction between legislature, executive, and judiciary.[52] And both accounts point to the acknowledgment of an inherent contradiction which is rarely made fully explicit in the debate: that while they are often used interchangeably in legal and political discourse, separation and checks and balances are – in their pure forms – mutually exclusive. For if the powers and branches are fully separated

---

[45] ibid 48.
[46] See also Möllers, 'The Separation of Powers' (n 4) 235–236.
[47] Waldron, 'Separation of Powers in Thought and Practice' (n 26) 442.
[48] ibid 434–35.
[49] Möllers, *The Three Branches* (n 22) 47; see also section VI below.
[50] ibid 44.
[51] ibid 48.
[52] ibid 50; see also Möllers, 'The Separation of Powers' (n 4) 239. This observation might also be prompted by Möllers' methodological belief, noted above, that political theory cannot allow itself to abstract too much from the actual institutionalisation of its own normative requirements.

A Twofold Meta-theoretical Ambiguity Plaguing the Discussion   269

from each other, there cannot be, logically, any mutual checks going on *between* them. Conversely, a relative degree of division (or sharing) of powers seems to be a necessary condition for checks and balances to be at least minimally implemented in a given political system.[53]

Finally, and notwithstanding the different approaches and understandings, we can observe empirically that in almost every current political system which purports to adhere to some version of the separation of powers, there is always some degree of separation between legislatures (including executives) and courts.[54] But it is a separation between institutions or functions – or both?

The polysemy of the concept-word 'power' (or *pouvoir, potere, Gewalt*), discussed already in chapter one, is even more relevant when it comes to the separation of powers discussion, given that it is used to denote both the *function* and the *body* that performs it. In this respect, this polysemy has contributed certainly to the confusion about the meaning(s) of the doctrine. For 'separation' of powers as independence (or non-usurpation) could alternatively mean 'separation of state functions' or 'separations of branches' (or institutions); likewise, 'division' (in the sense of 'sharing') could stand for either the division of a function across multiple subjects, or the division of a branch in multiple institutions.[55] And as if this was not enough, when we say that the aim of the separation of powers is the distribution or limitation of *power*, we are referring to *political* or *state* power as a whole, which needs to be distributed to protect the liberties of everyone who is subject to it.

Through this remark alone, it is possible to account for many of the confusing – and sometimes openly conflicting – uses of the doctrine. For at times the 'separation' and/or the 'division' is predicated of the branches, and sometimes of the functions, and sometimes of both at the same time. Thus, for instance, limiting our consideration to the two theories examined earlier, we can appreciate how Möllers is clearer in accounting for the possibility of separating branches and functions (which in Waldron's theory appears to be left implicit), while Waldron explicitly refers to the need to avoid the concentration of 'too much political power onto any given body or institution' (while this necessity does not appear to be at the fore of Möllers' normative account).

Of course, we would not be interested in separating or dividing the functions or the institutions of the state if at stake was not the organisation and limitation of political power – given how, at least since the rise of the nation-state (but arguably much earlier than that), political power necessarily finds its form or expression through the state. And if we think of the main way in which political

---

[53] *cf* Möllers, *The Three Branches* (n 22) 46.

[54] This is perhaps best exemplified by the debate surrounding the separation of powers in the UK which resulted in the adoption of the Constitutional Reform Act 2005, establishing the UK Supreme Court.

[55] Here, I am already anticipating that we should understand 'separation' and 'division' not as synonyms, but rather as opposite techniques of distribution of political power.

270   *The Separation of Powers. A Meta-theoretical Reassessment*

power manifests itself, we are bound to conclude, it seems to me, that what the separation of powers is ultimately about is law-making power(s). Möllers reaches the same conclusion,[56] although, as we shall see, he rejects the fundamental distinction between law-creation and law-application and thus defends a model of the separation of powers in which the three branches are continuously *creating* the law.

As with most things regarding the separation of powers, the claim that the main focus of the doctrine is law-making power does not come unchallenged. On the one hand, you have several other types of powers – that might be loosely termed 'formal' – which are not exclusively wielded by the state, such as economic powers. On the other, you have informal or 'soft' powers,[57] that is, those powers that lack a coercive dimension (usually associated with 'hard' law) and yet are still deployed to induce and co-opt the desired form of behaviour of their addressees. The kind of libertarian paternalism advocated by Thaler and Sunstein is a very apt example in this respect,[58] as well as the recent flurry of soft law instruments which have been vehemently occupying central stage in international law scholarship in the last few decades.[59] Why should not a theory of separation of powers deal with these *manifestations* of power as well?

The answer to this question will likely depend on the justification(s) or aim(s) that one assigns to the separation of powers. If we take the two most common normative rationales associated with the doctrine,[60] namely the limitation of political power and the protection of autonomy or liberty, it is easy to see that law-making power is relevant because its exercise is usually (if not intrinsically)[61] backed by the use of force or coercion. As the use of coercion fundamentally negates the (moral) agency of the addressee of the relevant norm,[62] it always potentially and directly infringes on the liberty or autonomy of those who are subjects to the law.[63]

This is why informal or soft powers, while sharing law's principal aim – the guidance of behaviour – are not necessarily relevant for a theory of the separation of powers, given that they lack the coercive element and so do not restrict,

---

[56] Möllers, *The Three Branches* (n 22) 80–84.

[57] JS Nye Jr, *Soft Power: The Means To Success In World Politics* (New York, PublicAffairs, 2004).

[58] R Thaler and CR Sunstein, *Nudge: Improving Decisions About Health, Wealth, and Happiness* (New Haven, Yale University Press, 2008).

[59] See, eg: J D'Aspremont and T Aalberts, 'Which Future for the Scholarly Concept of Soft International Law? Editors' Introductory Remarks' (2012) 25(2) *Leiden Journal of International Law* 309.

[60] *cf* Möllers, 'The Separation of Powers' (n 4) 244–246.

[61] I am referring here to the possibility that coercion might, after all, be a much more central element to our 'concept' of law than most other legal theorists have held since Hart's refutation of Bentham's and Austin's accounts: F Schauer, *The Force of Law* (Cambridge, Harvard University Press, 2015).

[62] J van der Rijt, 'Coercive Interference and Moral Judgment' (2011) 14(5) *Ethical Theory and Moral Practice* 549.

[63] See also Mendes and Venzke ('Introducing the Idea of Relative Authority' (n 34) 3) who conceive of public authority 'as a law-based capacity to influence the freedom of others'.

The Justificatory Debate. Monism vs Pluralism   271

in an important sense, the individual's freedom of choice.[64] This consideration seems to also apply to economic powers: for while it would be impossible
to deny the relevance that economic decisions by private actors can have for
people's lives – imagine the decision of a manufacturing firm to delocalise to
another country where the job regulations are more 'favourable' – the exercise of
these private powers cannot usually bring about the unilateral modification of
someone's else basic freedoms (that is, without that person's consent).[65]

IV. THE JUSTIFICATORY DEBATE. MONISM vs PLURALISM

Understood as a normative doctrine, the separation of powers is in need of
normative justification, and in this respect the scope for (reasonable) disagreement is wide. Different authors see the separation of powers as fulfilling different
objectives, sometimes in conflict with each other.[66] There is even a growing
strand of scholarship according to which, far from the limitation of power, the
real function served by the doctrine would be the *facilitation* of the exercise
of political power in a constitutional state.[67] Is it then possible to establish, at
all, a single convincing justification for the separation of powers? Or should we
embrace pluralistic theories of legitimacy?

To be sure, for the Montesquian 'received account', the aim of the separation of powers is the limitation of despotic power or, as it is often put, 'the
protection from arbitrary rule'.[68] This seems also to encompass Waldron's
idea of 'articulated governance' as opposed to 'undifferentiated modes of
governance',[69] with the former better protecting the liberties of the subjects
impacted by the exercised power(s). However, according to Möllers, what actually lies at the basis of modern conceptions of the separation of powers doctrine
is the attempt to *compose* the conflicting claims of individual and collective
autonomy *within* the political order. In other words, the fundamental justification of the doctrine would reside in the guarantee of autonomy, both in its

---

[64] This does not mean that the use of soft law, especially by governments, might not occasionally become relevant for the separation of powers. For a very recent example in the context of the
Covid-19 pandemic in the UK, see T Hickman, 'The Use and Misuse of Guidance during the UK's
Coronavirus Lockdown' (September 4, 2020). Available at SSRN: http://papers.ssrn.com/sol3/
papers.cfm?abstract_id=3686857 accessed 10/03/2021.

[65] What I just said implies, conversely, that if a private body wields indeed the power to unilaterally
modify the basic freedoms of other subjects, then that body would fall within the purview of the
separation of powers doctrine.

[66] Huq and Michaels, 'The Cycles of Separation-of-Powers Jurisprudence' (n 23).

[67] See, eg: Barber, 'Prelude to the Separation of Powers' (n 40); C Thornhill, *A Sociology of
Constitutions: Constitutions and State Legitimacy in Historical-Sociological Perspective* (Cambridge,
Cambridge University Press, 2011); MA Cameron, *Strong Constitutions: Social-Cognitive Origins
of the Separation of Powers* (Oxford, Oxford University Press, 2013). Möllers ('The Separation of
Powers' (n 4) 243–44) calls these the 'cognitive rationales' for the doctrine.

[68] Möllers, *The Three Branches* (n 22) 18.

[69] Waldron, 'Separation of Powers in Thought and Practice' (n 26) 434.

272 The Separation of Powers. A Meta-theoretical Reassessment

individual (through rights) and collective (through democratic procedures) exercise.[70] As such, a legal system will have two – always potentially conflicting – sources of legitimacy: the protection of individual rights and democratic decision-making.[71] This 'guarantee' is only procedural, though: the doctrine in fact 'does not provide any material standards for statutory interpretation',[72] so that the difference between 'legislating and adjudicating is a procedural one'.[73]

As we have already mentioned, attempts to conceptualise the separation of powers under a 'monistic' theory of legitimacy, be it that of the facilitation or limitation of political power or the guarantee of autonomy, have been criticised in the literature.[74] This is because choices of institutional design 'implicate many conflicting normative goals simultaneously' among which 'liberty (of diverse forms, against diverse threats), accountability, integrity, welfare-maximizing government, deliberation as an intrinsic good, and likely others too'.[75]

This last remark elicits two general comments. On the one hand, it is hard to deny that in every choice of institutional design there might be an underlying potential alternative or even conflict between different values or goals. The most important point, methodologically, would be to make that alternative or conflict explicit rather than obfuscating it behind thick assertions of principle. At the same time, it cannot be excluded that some or all of those values or goals might be evaluated against each other, in order to carve out a normative ranking that allows one to speak of a certain institutional choice to protect, say, liberty – in the first instance – and other values consequently (as by-products).[76]

On the other, clarification of the scope of the doctrine of separation of powers might shed light on its justificatory premises. The empirically observable stable separation of the legislative and executive branches from the judiciary across several jurisdictions that we have already mentioned seems to point to a fundamental difference between those powers of the state that structure collective decision-making, and those which instead preside over the protection of individual rights. This fact, while not necessarily exhaustive of the justificatory argument, cannot be easily set aside if we want the normative doctrine of the separation of powers to be relevant for our existing political practices. But the

---

[70] Möllers, *The Three Branches* (n 22) 109.

[71] ibid 66. In this sense, Möllers' approach confirms (from a different angle) the fundamental duality of constitutional democracy we have illustrated in this book, on which see ch 2, sections V and VI, and ch 6, section I.

[72] ibid 95.

[73] ibid.

[74] Huq and Michaels, 'The Cycles of Separation-of-Powers Jurisprudence' (n 23).

[75] A Huq, 'A Distinctively American Doctrine: Review of The Three Branches: A Comparative Model of Separation of Powers, by Christoph Möllers' (*The New Rambler*, 25 November 2015) http://newramblerreview.com/book-reviews/law/a-distinctively-american-doctrine accessed 12/10/2020.

[76] See, for instance, the interesting discussion by Möllers (*The Three Branches* (n 22) 64–65) about the contested 'justificatory asymmetry' between individual and collective will (following Habermas on the point).

The Justificatory Debate. Monism vs Pluralism   273

inherent danger in this argumentative strategy lies in the circular regress between the ascertainment of the scope of the doctrine and of its justification – which comes first, that is, which one determines the other?

Complicating the picture even more is the acknowledgment of the always potential gap between the doctrine in its normative form and the actual workings of any historical legal or political system. This is one of the reasons why Möllers argues emphatically that we must look at the distinction between political theory and positive law 'as something necessary but only relative', in the sense that 'political theory must be interested in the conditions of institutionalizing its own standards'.[77] For otherwise those normative standards, once operationalised, might fall fundamentally short of their objective, therefore relegating the doctrine to practical irrelevance. We could call this the problem of 'permeability' of the separation of powers. It has been recently brought to the fore in constitutional theory by a strand of scholarship which began with a seminal article by Levinson and Pildes[78] and that has been recently picked up and developed, among others,[79] by Gardbaum.[80] What this discussion shows, for instance, is how historical changes in the political party and electoral systems can affect a given formal separation of powers arrangement and hinder its concrete workings, and therefore the actual attainment of its normative objectives.

This recognition of the permeability of the separation of powers to institutional variables,[81] other than the formal relationship between the branches themselves, can be addressed, in its current understanding, in two ways: either we argue that the formal normative doctrine of separation of powers must expand to include other institutional variables (such as the structure of political parties and of the electoral system in general, but also likely the regulation of the legal profession and of the judiciary, and so forth), or we have to concede that any model of separation of powers, to be relevant and potentially able to fulfil its function(s), must already take into account – that is, must be *tailored to* – the empirical circumstances of the given political system.

The first scenario has two theoretical drawbacks: on the one hand it is not clear, at least to me, where we should draw the line as to the 'institutional variables' that might be relevant for the 'expanded' theory of separation of powers (for instance, inclusion of the regulation of the legal profession would likely also include regulation of law schools in the system); on the other, the more

---

[77] Möllers, *The Three Branches* (n 22) 6. It is thus not readily clear why Huq, in his critical review of Möllers' book, claims that the author 'understates the degree to which the effect of institutional arrangements depends on extrinsic social and political circumstances': see Huq, 'A Distinctively American Doctrine' (n 75).

[78] DJ Levinson and RH Pildes, 'Separation of Parties, Not Powers' (2006) 119(8) *Harvard Law Review* 2311.

[79] See, eg: Huq and Michaels, 'The Cycles of Separation-of-Powers Jurisprudence' (n 23).

[80] S Gardbaum, 'Political Parties, Voting Systems, and the Separation of Powers' (2017) 65(2) *American Journal of Comparative Law* 229.

[81] ibid.

274   *The Separation of Powers. A Meta-theoretical Reassessment*

'expanded' the theory of separation of powers, the less distance there would be, arguably, between a theory of separation of powers and the (corresponding) theory of democracy. And while most people would readily agree that the separation of powers is part of the theory of democracy, I suspect far fewer would be willing to consider the separation of powers as almost co-extensive with it. The second scenario would lead instead, once again, to the fragmentation of the separation of powers, in the sense that it would be very hard to conceive of a theory of separation of powers that is at the same time universalisable (ie applicable across jurisdiction) as well as fine-grained enough to be *relevant* (rather than a mere general statement, for instance, that the power of the state must be vaguely divided into three, or four, or five branches).

V. CRITICAL APPROACHES

As we have already mentioned, the separation of powers has been, as of late, the subject of more intensive critical scrutiny.[82] The result is that it has been considered, for instance, 'obsolete' vis-à-vis the 'exigencies of modern government',[83] or problematic 'when analysing supra- and international exercises of authority'.[84]

At this point of our discussion, it should be clear though that most analyses of the separation of powers in the literature are a mix of descriptive and normative claims which are not always easy to keep apart – and the critical discussion about its fruitfulness does not escape this issue. Thus, descriptively, the widespread narrative is that national parliaments – and their principal normative output, statutory law – have progressively lost their law-making centrality along two directives. Vertically, to supranational organisations of various nature and functions, such as supranational courts, private transnational networks, and even multinational companies. Horizontally, national parliaments themselves have been empowering for decades with unprecedented law-making powers (for non-elected bodies) a number of ad hoc institutions that are commonly referred to as 'independent authorities'.[85] This phenomenon, together with the always more prominent role played by the executive in law-making, especially through the use of delegated legislation, has reinforced (perhaps inadvertently) the idea that we have transitioned from the 'legislative state' into the 'administrative state'.[86]

---

[82] See, eg: Posner and Vermeule, *The Executive Unbound* (n 23); see also the contributions in J Mendes and I Venzke (eds), *Allocating Authority: Who Should Do What in European and International Law?* (Oxford, Hart Publishing, 2018).

[83] Waldron, 'Separation of Powers in Thought and Practice' (n 26) 434.

[84] Mendes and Venzke, 'Introducing the Idea of Relative Authority' (n 34) 14.

[85] See, eg: R Caranta, M Andenas, D Fairgrieve (eds), *Independent Administrative Authorities* (London, British Institute of International and Comparative Law, 2004).

[86] *cf* Möllers, 'The Separation of Powers' (n 4) 252.

Critical Approaches   275

This is particularly problematic for the classic threefold separation doctrine for two reasons:

1) because of the lack of separation (as independence) between governments and parliaments in exercising the legislative function;
2) because the executive 'moment' – between legislative law-making (*legislatio*) and judicial decision (*iurisdictio*) – has never fit seamlessly within legal doctrines of the separation of powers.[87]

And while there would be at least one immediate reason to resist this (by now) commonplace narrative, in the sense that there was never a neat separation of three functions to begin with,[88] it seems undisputable that in the last few decades we have witnessed a fragmentation of law-making powers both within and outside the traditional 'boundaries' of the nation-state, at least in the way we had grown accustomed to think of them. As a result, two related questions are constantly asked now of the separation of powers from a descriptive point of view: is the separation of powers indissolubly tied to the classical nation-state structure that developed in the West over the last two centuries? And if not, how can it still be explanatory relevant in the regulatorily fragmented, post-national world order?

From a normative point of view, some critiques of the traditional doctrine of the separation of powers point to the idea that separating the power of the state might represent an obstacle to its efficient exercise, especially when it comes to the regulation of the economy. In other words, if 'modern government' or *governance* consists of collective decision-making procedures based on rationalities different from autonomy – such as economic efficiency – and run by experts or 'systemic necessities',[89] then indeed traditional versions of the separation of powers should be considered a hindrance toward the maximisation of 'effective government'. Should we resist these claims and defend some version of the separation of powers, today more than ever? Van der Berge for one affirms that 'the neoliberal state invests its agents with discretionary powers that even tend to exceed those of the social state' and that, for this reason, there must be a 'mutual balance' between powers, in what he affirms being the true Montesquian spirit at the basis of the doctrine.[90]

The 'received account' of the separation of powers has also been recently the object of criticism from a narrower legal-theoretical perspective, particularly in the continental literature.[91] The issue is the theoretical compatibility of

---

[87] Möllers, *The Three Branches* (n 22) 96.
[88] ibid 8.
[89] ibid 232.
[90] van der Berge, 'Montesquieu and Judicial Review of Proportionality in Administrative Law' (n 21) 233.
[91] See, in addition to the works by Claus and Möllers already discussed: R Guastini, *Lezioni di teoria costituzionale* (Turin, Giappichelli, 2001); M Barberis, 'Divisione dei Poteri e Libertà da Montesquieu a Constant' (2001) 31(1) *Materiali per una storia della cultura giuridica* 83; Vignudelli, 'Sulla Separazione dei Poteri' (n 7).

276   The Separation of Powers. A Meta-theoretical Reassessment

the received account of the separation of powers with current dominant legal doctrines. The best-known example is that the thesis according to which courts in a given system should only apply the law is directly contradicted by the legal realist thesis that there is no such thing as *pure* application of law (or, in its most extreme version, application of law *tout court*). This issue affects the traditional account of the separation of powers in both its descriptive and normative versions: descriptively, because it would be clearly inaccurate to claim that courts apply the law if that is not possible from a theoretical point of view to begin with; normatively, for the doctrine would then lay an impossible requirement over its own institutionalisation and be, as a result, self-contradictory.

This seems to raise, once again, what is at stake from the theoretical point of view in any version of the separation of powers, which will now also necessarily have to include a corresponding theory of adjudication and of legal interpretation. It seems an unavoidable conclusion if we agree that law-making powers are the main reference of any version of the separation of powers – as we have seen above, in fact, the question is if the separation of powers should include other powers, and not whether law-making powers should be excluded from its scope.

A similar problem of compatibility arises, in constitutional law, between the received account and the traditional, state-centred legal doctrine of sovereignty, with the clearest illustration of the issue being perhaps the case of the UK 'political constitution' and its *unruly* relationship with the separation of powers. For the most famous scholar of British constitutional law, in fact, the separation of powers was 'the offspring of a double misconception' and was not to be included among its fundamental constitutional principles.[92] And how could it be, given that sovereignty is indivisible and belongs to the Queen-in-Parliament?[93]

Famously, one of the central tenets of the Diceyan orthodoxy is that 'no person or body is recognised by the law of England as having a right to override or set aside the legislation of Parliament',[94] and this explains why, according to the orthodoxy, the validity of legislation is situated wholly outside the jurisdiction of the courts. More generally, the normative status of any type of constitutional judicial review – and in particular of strong versions of it – is another aspect of constitutional design that is particularly complicated for traditional theories of the separation of powers to account for coherently.[95]

---

[92] AV Dicey, *Introduction to the Study of the Law of the Constitution*, 8th edn (London, Macmillan, 1915) 13.

[93] It is worth noting already here the theoretical elegance of the solution to this quandary found by the Italian constitutional fathers: in the first article of the Italian republican Constitution, after stating that Italy is a Republic founded on labour, they go on to say that 'Sovereignty belongs to the people and is exercised by the people in the forms and within the limits of the Constitution'. The point is not as much about the idea of limited sovereignty (this needs to be understood in the context of the liberation from the Fascist state), as it is about the formal solution according to which, while belonging to the people, sovereignty must be exercised in the forms prescribed by the Constitution, subject to, for instance, (strong) constitutional judicial review.

[94] AV Dicey, *Introduction* (n 92) 3–4.

[95] *cf* Möllers, 'The Separation of Powers' (n 4) 249–250.

VI. THE SEPARATION OF POWERS AS A FORMAL THEORY AND AS A NORMATIVE DOCTRINE. ON THE ADVANTAGES OF MAINTAINING A STRICT DISTINCTION

The range of issues we have surveyed in the first part of this chapter should suggest, among other things, that pursuing analytical clarity is a necessary endeavour (*pace* Waldron) in order to dispel many (if not most) of the ambiguities surrounding the separation of powers and its uses.[96] In other words, before either lamenting that the 'received account' of the separation of powers is obsolete and lacks explanatory and normative bite vis-à-vis the new models of 'governance' in nation-states[97] or delineating 'emerging' frameworks of 'relative authority' for the international and supra-national spheres,[98] our task is to question whether the 'received account' does capture effectively the essence of the doctrine. As I am about to show, a different analytical approach is available, one which allows us to elucidate the core elements of the separation of powers, free from historical and pragmatic distortions.

The most important meta-theoretical move in this respect is to retain, whilst clearly separating, discourses in which the separation of powers is used as an analytical tool to describe historical political arrangements, and discourses in which instead the separation of powers is used as a normative doctrine to influence, or criticise, choices of constitutional design.[99] In the former, the separation of powers works as an analytical tool that does not demand any particular institutional setting (being a descriptive scheme) and does not seem open to normative contestation. In the latter, it is instead deployed as a blueprint which requires powers to be separated or divided in a variety of ways – depending on the normative objectives pursued. In this respect, I believe there are a number of meta-theoretical advantages in retaining (while making explicit) this two-fold nature of the separation of powers, rather than combining its descriptive and normative dimensions into a 'reconstructive' approach:[100]

1) the elucidation of the different and opposing strategies that can be used to organise and limit political power as analytical categories rather than as normative standards;
2) the explanation of the relationships between the three 'meanings' more commonly associated with the doctrine: separation of powers, division of power, and checks and balances; and

---

[96] The importance for legal and political discourse of analytical clarity was already prominent in Marsilius of Padua's *Defensor Pacis*: see C Vasoli, 'Introduzione', in Marsilio da Padova, *Il Difensore della pace* (C Vasoli ed, Turin, UTET, 1960) 25.

[97] Posner and Vermeule, *The Executive Unbound* (n 23); but *cf* Möllers, 'The Separation of Powers' (n 4) 233–5.

[98] Mendes and Venzke, 'Introducing the Idea of Relative Authority' (n 34).

[99] Barberis, 'Separazione dei Poteri' (n 27) 2–7.

[100] Mendes and Venzke, 'Introducing the Idea of Relative Authority' (n 34) 5.

278   *The Separation of Powers. A Meta-theoretical Reassessment*

3)   the possibility to adopt the formal theory without having to commit to any normative doctrine: for the former is compatible with the widest range of normative models as to the *which* and *how* powers should be separated or divided.

In the last part of the chapter, I will pursue two, parallel, endeavours. I will first illustrate a model of the separation of powers, as a formal theory, that is not based on any set tripartite framework and the resulting theoretical advantages for its use in constitutional and political theory. Second, whilst acknowledging that on the normative plane there is indeed an open number of justifications and criteria that might ground a certain model of the separation of powers, I will sketch a legal-theoretical justification that is based on the – non-naïve – distinction between creation and application of law defended in this book. Among other things, I will argue that such a justification of the separation of powers has the advantage of being less open to normative contestation than self-standing political justifications.

A. The Formal Theory of the Separation or Division of Powers

In this section I will present a formal theory of the organisation of powers in a political system. Following Ferrajoli,[101] I submit that, underneath the thick layer of historical confusion and pragmatic ambiguities that we have endeavoured to unveil, there are only two – and opposite, in their absolute form – institutional techniques to *organise* the political power of a state:

1)   the separation of powers, that is, one or more competence norms that establish the *independence* of the exercise of one given normative function from the others (non-usurpation); and

2)   the division of powers, in the sense of the participation of more than one institutional subject in the performance of a function: in other words, the distribution or articulation of the *same* power amongst a plurality of decision-makers, so that the exercise of that power is *shared* and there is interdependence between them.[102]

This first clarification needs to be supplemented with the disambiguation of the concept of 'power', which as we have seen above is often used to indicate both the power exercised (the 'function', understood as an activity or a class of acts) as well as the power-holder and/or the office (which could be a single official

---

[101] L Ferrajoli, *Principia Iuris: Teoria del Diritto e Della Democrazia*, vol 1 (Bari, Laterza, 2007) 864ff.

[102] I decided to keep the English noun 'division' (over the perhaps intuitively clearer 'sharing') because this allows us to map the formal model proposed here onto the traditional uses of the separation of powers doctrine, hopefully clarifying them.

On the Advantages of Maintaning a Strict Distinction   279

as well as an institutional body).[103] If we keep those two uses of power clearly separated, we then obtain four potential strategies for the organisation of public powers:[104]

1a) *Institutional division*: it occurs when the official or body entrusted with a certain function can be discretionally appointed or removed by another official within the same branch (*intra-institutional* division) or from another branch (*inter-institutional* division). An example of the former is when a minister can be removed by the prime minister, while an example of the latter is, for instance, when a parliament can appoint or remove the prime minister.

1b) *Functional division*: indicates that the decision or formal act with which a function is expressed is the product of a process in which different officials contribute, with different responsibilities, towards the final act; it is *internal* division if the officials taking part in the decision-making process are from the same institution or branch, and it is *external* division if the officials taking part are from different institutions (or branches). The former is exemplified by any decision in which a court is composed of more than one judge, and on a larger scale by the fact that on the same issue multiple courts, at different stages, might make an authoritative decision; while the latter is depicted by any law-making process in which more than one institution or branch is involved before a given bill can become law.

2a) *Institutional separation*: it is the norm of competence that excludes the *inter-institutional* division of power, that is, it prohibits the official or body holding a certain function to be discretionally appointed or removed by officials from other branches entrusted with different functions. This is clearly illustrated by the degree of judicial independence (at all levels) that is guaranteed by many constitutions, in the sense that judges' careers (appointment, progression, dismissal, and so forth) cannot be decided by members of the executive or legislature.

2b) *Functional separation*: the norm of competence that excludes *external* functional division, ie that the decision or the formal act with which a certain function is expressed is the product of a process in which officials from other branches do not take part. Again, judicial independence is the clearest example – the fact that members of the other branches cannot take part in the determination of the outcome of individual cases.

The greater explanatory potential of this model vis-à-vis the tripartite, 'received' model of the separation of powers should be apparent. Between two powers (as institutions) there is separation only if there is no division, and vice-versa. If there is (external) functional division between them, there is no functional separation; and if there is [inter-]institutional division, there is no institutional

---

[103] See also Möllers, 'The Separation of Powers' (n 4) 240–241.
[104] Ferrajoli, *Principia Iuris* (n 101) 866–867.

280 The Separation of Powers. A Meta-theoretical Reassessment

separation. But simple (intra) institutional division is logically compatible with functional separation, and so is institutional separation with (internal) functional division.

Thus, as we have just seen, the judicial branch is usually the one more strictly separated from the others (functionally as well as institutionally) but also the most functionally divided branch within itself. Why is this (almost) always the case? Evidently, if judicial power is shared by the different courts and the different judges within those courts, no single judge wields too much power overall. In other words, the model defended here allows us to see clearly that, while the judicial power is kept separate from the legislative and executive powers (more on this below), it is also internally divided across different judges and different courts, so as to limit the possibility that individual judges might abuse that independence with which they are equipped.

Another key clarification that Ferrajoli's model yields is about the 'proximity' between the legislature and executive in many constitutional systems, as for instance in the UK's case. For, far from a 'clear violation' of the separation of powers, it is instead within this model a wholly consistent example of a variable mix of inter-institutional and external functional division of power, where legislature and government share the legislative function. Our model also clarifies the relationship, again fairly stable in many modern constitutional democracies, between the politically appointed (and legitimated) cabinet and the a-political civil service: while between the two there is functional division vis-à-vis the executive function (that is, the function to 'give effect' to the laws passed by the legislature), there is also usually a degree of institutional separation between the two, in the sense that politically appointed ministers cannot exert undue influence on civil service personnel by having formal decision-making power on their appointment, progression, or dismissal.

From a pragmatic point of view, and for reasons of clarity, the model proposed here eschews the third meaning usually associated with the separation of powers – checks and balances – as theoretically redundant. More trivially, in fact, checks and balances are just the variable combinations of the arrangements of separation and division of powers (in both their institutional and functional dimensions) historically implemented in different jurisdictions. In this way, the apparent paradox of the relationship between separation of powers and checks and balances, where the pure version of the former would preclude the latter,[105] is dissolved. We can certainly retain the expression of checks and balances as an 'umbrella' term of our political vocabulary,[106] but only with the awareness that there is not a *third* institutional strategy to distribute political powers beyond separation and division. This conclusion might be particularly striking given that we have seen above how checks and balances appears to be the only meaning

---

[105] Möllers, *The Three Branches* (n 22) 46.
[106] If anything, for reasons of consistency with previous scholarship.

On the Advantaging of Maintaning a Strict Distinction   281

associated with the traditional account of the separation of powers largely agreed upon. But what Montesquieu, Waldron, Möllers and many others agree upon seems to be the telos of the separation of powers, that is, the limitation through distribution of political power, as a result of the variable combination of different and combined strategies of separation and division.

This model – as a formal theory of the organisation of power – carries also other advantages vis-à-vis some of the problems about the separation of powers identified above. First, it does not necessarily presuppose the traditional *trias politica* of legislature, executive, and judiciary (and corresponding functions). As a formal theory that identifies two opposing techniques (but four potential resulting arrangements) to organise political power, it can be applied to the most diverse governmental structures, independently from the number of branches or functions recognised in the system.[107] It does not tell us which branches or functions should be separated (or divided), and why – that is the theoretical job of a normative doctrine. It is also, in this sense, neutral vis-à-vis other parts of legal theory. As argued above though, it has distinctive explanatory advantages over the 'received', tripartite model, in that it is able to make sense consistently of many existing institutional arrangements in modern constitutional democracies. At the same time, it is not connected to the historical structure of the nation-state, so that it can be fruitfully deployed to analyse past arrangements, complex federal or quasi-federal structures (like the European Union) and also in a variety of international and transnational arrangements.

B. A Normative Doctrine of the Organisation of Political Power Based on the Distinction between Law-creation and Law-application

Things are different once we move on to the normative plane. We have already seen that, in relation to any version of the separation of powers – that is, any theory that tells us which powers *should* be separated or divided and *why* – the most relevant issue is arguably that of its justification, in light of different and potentially competing aims. Whilst, as we have seen, several authors seem to converge on the idea that the doctrine of the separation of powers is based on the need to balance democracy and liberalism or, to put it more accurately, to protect and guarantee at the same time individual and collective autonomy (or freedom), there is still indeed a number of scholars who disagree on the ultimate *rationale* of the doctrine and who sometimes even question whether a single *rationale* – rather than a variable combination of them – can be identified at all.[108] As such, within a rather pluralistic normative world in which different

---

[107] As such, the theory does not suffer from the 'executive sting': that is, it can accommodate without issue the position of a branch called 'executive' or 'administration' within a wider governmental structure. See Möllers, 'The Separation of Powers' (n 4) 241, 247.

[108] Huq and Michaels, 'The Cycles of Separation-of-Powers Jurisprudence' (n 23); *cf* Möllers, 'The Separation of Powers' (n 4) 244–6.

282   *The Separation of Powers. A Meta-theoretical Reassessment*

people will tap into different political objectives with space for reasonable disagreement as to which one is the most valuable, a claim to state *the* doctrine of the separation of powers might sound indeed rather fanciful.

With this in mind, I want to conclude this chapter by defending a specific doctrine of the organisation of power that is premised upon the distinction between the creation and application of law. This distinction is assumed, as we have seen at various points in this book, by a number of influential authors, including Locke, Rousseau, Kant, Kelsen, Gunther, Alexy, Ferrajoli, Raz and Habermas. However, due a combination of being rarely (if ever) explicitly defended and having become, in the last few decades, one of the main targets of some critical legal movements (legal realism and critical legal studies, to name but two), the distinction between law-creation and law-application is now widely considered to be a naïve assumption that (among other things) cannot ground any doctrine of the separation of powers.[109]

In this book, I have gone beyond mere assumptions and instead explicitly defended an analytical distinction between creation and application of law that is grounded in a minimalist theory of legal meaning and within the context of what I have called text-act theory. This model, I have argued, is the only one compatible with the predominant understanding of law as a social technique that purports to guide the conduct of very large groups of individuals through the use of rules (and rulings). In this sense, it is the only model capable of accounting coherently for both the majority of instances of juridical rule-following and rule-application that do not end up being litigated before a court (the so-called 'easy' or 'clear' cases),[110] and for those cases that instead require some form of official settlement.[111]

What I want to do in what follows is to illustrate not only what a normative doctrine of the organisation of power based on such distinction looks like (at least in its main elements), but also why such a model can be considered normatively preferable, as it is more persuasive and less open to contestation than other models. A preliminary observation is that the model of the separation of powers grounded in the distinction between creation and application of law is much more complex and nuanced than the attention it has received so far in the literature.[112]

A common line of criticism against the early writers (eg Marsilius, Locke, Montesquieu, Madison) who first postulated the principle of separation of law-making and law-applying functions is the following.[113] Besides the need to put

---

[109] Kelsen's theory is a rare example of a theory of separation of powers that is explicitly premised on the distinction between creation and application of law: see Kelsen, *General Theory of Law and State* (n 29) Part III, A.

[110] See for discussion W Lucy, 'Adjudication', J Coleman and S Shapiro (eds), *The Oxford Handbook of Jurisprudence and Philosophy of Law* (Oxford, Oxford University Press, 2004).

[111] HLA Hart, *The Concept of Law*, 3rd edn (Oxford, Oxford University Press, 2012) 130.

[112] See for an overview Möllers, *The Three Branches* (n 22) 82–84.

[113] See, eg: Waldron, 'Separation of Powers in Thought and Practice' (n 26) 447.

On the Advantages of Maintaning a Strict Distinction   283

a check on the 'human frailty' of those in power from abusing their authority by bending the application of the very rules they created 'to their own private advantage',[114] is the separation of law-creation and law-application enough to prevent tyranny?[115] And if not, how else can it be justified when it comes to the institutional design of our law-making processes?

In its more modern elaborations (eg Kelsen, Ferrajoli), such a doctrine is premised upon the need to account for the co-existence of individual and collective autonomy – as different sources of legitimation of public powers in constitutional democracy – and for their (always potential) conflict.[116] In this sense, the application of law by certain institutions (including courts) would protect individuals not just by reducing the possibility of the arbitrary exercise of power by law-making authorities, but also by enforcing limits vis-à-vis the overall of the democratic majority (in the form of fundamental rights). The criticism against these modern versions is that, as we have seen, law is pervasively indeterminate before interpretation by courts. This is in particular when it comes to constitutional adjudication, where the content of rights cannot be objectively pre-established on the basis of language alone. Thus, when the courts are 'applying' those rights as limits to the democratic power of collective self-determination, they are indeed taking political decisions without possessing the necessary legitimation (both formal and procedural), even if those right are enshrined in a constitutional document.[117]

As we have addressed the argument from indeterminacy in the previous chapters of this book, let us here consider instead the criticism against the early writers, about the effective extent of limitation of political power that can be achieved by separating those officials who make and those who apply the law. To put it concisely: the criticism is sound, but it does not apply only to the theory of the separation of powers we are currently considering. In fact, it highlights the inherent danger in overstating the relevance of *any* theory of the separation of powers *qua* technique for the limitation (rather than organisation) of political power. As Constant had already warned in his *Principles of Politics*:[118]

> When political authority is not limited, the organization of government becomes a very secondary question. The mutual supervision of the diverse sections of the government is useful only in preventing one of them from aggrandizing itself at the expense of the others. But if the total sum of their powers is unbounded, if when they band together these government sections are permitted to invade everything, who is to stop them forming coalitions to engage in oppression at will?

---

[114] J Locke, 'The Second Treatise' in P Laslett (ed), *Locke: Two Treatises of Government* (first published 1689, rev. edn, Cambridge, Cambridge University Press, 1988) 364.

[115] Montesquieu, *The Spirit of the Laws* (n 30) Bk XI, ch VI, 157.

[116] Möllers' theory, as we have seen, is also concerned at its core with this tension.

[117] Möllers, *The Three Branches* (n 22) 76; 'The Separation of Powers' (n 4) 249–250.

[118] B Constant, *Principles of Politics Applicable to all Governments* (first published 1815, E Hoffman ed, D O'Keeffe trans, N Capaldi introduction, Indianapolis, Liberty Fund, 2003) Bk II, ch III, 35–36.

284   *The Separation of Powers. A Meta-theoretical Reassessment*

> What matters to me is not that my personal rights shall not be violated by one such power-group, without the approval of another such, but that this violation be forbidden to all sections of government. It is not enough that the executive's agents have to invoke the authorization of the legislature. Rather, it is that the legislature shall not authorize their actions except in a specified jurisdiction. It is not worth much that the executive power has no right to act without the assent of a law, if no limits are placed on this assent, if no one declares that there are things about which the legislature has no right to make laws, or, in other words, that there are areas of individual existence in relation to which society is not entitled to have any will.

In other words, no theory of the separation and/or division of powers can, in itself, ultimately prevent arbitrary rule or tyranny. This result can only be achieved, normatively, by establishing absolute limits on *every* law-making power in a given system.[119] Going back again to our discussion in chapter two, what we just said confirms that while the separation of powers should be considered as a central tenet of the modern doctrine of constitutionalism, it cannot be deemed co-extensive with it. For while both aim at the limitation of political power (at least in their respective most common understandings), constitutionalism requires a substantive – and not just procedural – limitation.

At the same time, this last remark does not mean that the separation of creation and application of law is not already a first (and crucial) guarantee of individual freedom. First, and as Locke and Montesquieu had already illustrated, the more these two powers are from the external perspective functionally and institutionally separated (while being internally divided), the harder it will be for tyrannical rule to obtain, for it will likely take more far-reaching coordinated efforts to overcome this fragmentation (*qua* organisation) of political power. But there is another and, I argue, more relevant sense in which this model of the separation of powers protects individual freedom. For in this case the underlying public expectation is that the application of law will not be based on the whims of the decision-maker, but rather on an *intersubjectively discernible* application of the normative standards as created by the law-making authorities.

As such, this model of the separation of powers protects individual freedom in a double sense: first, as it demands different forms of public, regulated (and not whimsical) decision-making,[120] in the sense that the grounds of the decisions by officials in the system must be intersubjectively accessible and thus rationally comprehensible. Second, this model operationalises the understanding of law as a social technique to guide conduct through the provision of reasons for action to its addressees, as illustrated throughout this book. In this way, law respects the agency, and thus the individual freedom, of those subject to it. These remarks are valid not only for civil law jurisdictions – where the idea of a

---

[119] Clearly, the fact that there are absolute normative limits on every law-making power in the system does not guarantee that violations of those limits will not, de facto, take place.

[120] J Raz, 'Law and Value in Adjudication' in J Raz, *The Authority of Law: Essays on Law and Morality* (Oxford, Clarendon Press, 1979) 181ff.

On the Advantages of Maintaning a Strict Distinction   285

clear functional distinction between law-makers and law-appliers is accepted as a basic element of the legal order – but also for common law jurisdictions, given that the difference between the two, when it comes to the use of law as a social technique to guide conducts (and to the idea of application of intersubjectively available rules), appears less substantial than what was traditionally deemed by many scholars.[121]

It is also important to stress that this normative doctrine of the organisation of power is normatively *thin*, in the sense of being compatible with those accounts which deem the separation of powers as also enabling, rather than just limiting, political power. Nor is it fundamentally premised on disputable political values, and in particular on counter-majoritarian approaches, which makes it compatible with a pluralistic normative landscape. It is a legal normative doctrine of the separation of powers based exclusively on the understanding of law as a social technique to guide conduct by providing reasons for action through public rules (and rulings).

Once again, this implies that before those moments of institutional application of law, there are already standards (as least in a majority of cases) that can effectively guide the conduct of the addressees of the legal system, and as such these standards will be used – and recognised – as part of the basis of the decision on their institutional enforcement. This is the way in which separating the functions of creation and application of law already protects individual autonomy without having to be based on thicker, more contestable normative considerations. It also allows this doctrine to be relevant vis-a-vis most (if not all) modern legal systems, independently of the democratic character of their political practices. In other words, it is in principle compatible with both political and legal constitutional architectures,[122] given that it does not require a particular hierarchy between institutions, nor does it exclude the possibility that there might be two or more institutions dividing (co-exercising) the power to make law.[123]

Even more importantly, this approach to the separation of powers does not presuppose any tripartite structure (or any other type of institution), nor a state-based institutional framework (and so it is equally applicable to the supranational and global context). While Möllers might consider this as a downside,[124] it is in my view one of its greatest advantages, as it avoids the need to identify at all costs an 'executive' or 'administrative' function that is somewhat awkwardly 'in between' the creation and application of legal rules. Strictly speaking, even if we routinely identify a branch called the 'executive' or 'public administration', that branch is just a diverse mix of bodies and institutions that should be analysed and evaluated depending on whether they perform, taken individually,

---

[121] *cf* Hart, *The Concept of Law* (n 111) ch 7.
[122] *cf* Möllers, 'The Separation of Powers' (n 4) 246.
[123] On the compatibility of strong constitutional review with this model, see ibid 249–250.
[124] ibid 239–40.

286 *The Separation of Powers. A Meta-theoretical Reassessment*

a (chiefly) law-creating or a law-applying function. This also allows to account neatly, in this model, for a whole host of law-applying institutions (like electoral or fiscal commissions) which are neither straightforwardly administrative or judicial in character, and thus hard to reconcile with the traditional tripartite structure of the branches of the state.

While more work needs to be done in order to flesh out all the consequences of this approach, allow me to briefly mention only one: a clearer distinction between administrative bodies (or officials) that perform law-creating and law-applying functions has the potential to dispel, at least in part, the common objection according to which substantive judicial review of administrative action is incompatible with the separation of powers.[125] This is only true, in our model, vis-à-vis those administrative bodies that perform a law-making function (for instance, because they adopt delegated legislative instruments under the authority of a primary act) and only insofar as the protection of constitutional rights is not involved. But the objection falls in relation to all those administrative functions (and related decisions) that are essentially law-applying in character, such as the obligatory granting of a licence. Here, there is no violation of the separation of powers if a court reviews substantially the decision taken by the administrative official, but rather a fully intelligible, under the model presented here, functional external division (sharing) of that particular legal power.

Finally, the doctrine presented here is also open to a thicker, more normatively demanding, justification. For until now nothing has explicitly hinged on whether the creation of law – as the necessary primary expression of political power – is the product of democratic procedures or not. That is, the thin normative doctrine of the separation of powers illustrated so far is open to monarchical systems too, and to any system in which the law-making power is not in the hands of elected representatives or of the people themselves (or in a variable combination of both). This is what makes it normatively attractive, as it can be agreed upon by people with very different political values and institutional conceptions. But nothing prevents it from being supplemented with a thicker normative layer in which are recognised, within liberal constitutional democracies, the different and tendentially opposite spheres of legitimation of two activities: democratic decision-making for the creation of law, and the protection of everyone's basic rights (and thus on an inviolable sphere of individual autonomy) for the application of law. In this case, the doctrine would assume a more stringent normative bite, because it would now also tell us which institutions should be separated (either institutionally or functionally) and which institutions can instead share the same powers (as part of a division), depending on their respective spheres of legitimation. It would also strengthen the democratic legitimacy of law-applying functions: given that now the product of the

---

[125] See, eg: R Cotterell, 'Judicial Review and Legal Theory' in G Richardson and H Genn (eds), *Administrative Law and Government Action: The Courts and Alternative Mechanisms of Review* (Oxford, Clarendon Press, 1994).

law-making activity would be imbued with democratic legitimacy, and so would be its application to particular cases (within the constitutional limits of what is *decidable* by the law-maker).

VII. CONCLUSION

In this final chapter I have endeavoured, having identified a number of relevant issues around the 'received', tripartite account of the separation of powers, to clarify the meaning and the scope of the doctrine. I started by out noticing how current events have shown that the doctrine, far from being an academic 'fetish' from a long and obsolete past (as Mussolini would have us believe already in 1939), is at the very core of our liberal democracies and a key indicator of their institutional state of 'health'.

However, the result of my discussion pointed to what could perhaps be considered three counterintuitive conclusions. First, I argued that only two techniques to organise political power exist, separation as independence and division as sharing, and that we should consider the traditional 'checks and balances' as a term of political discourse that is not analytically helpful. Second, I have stressed the importance – and the meta-theoretical advantages – of keeping clearly differentiated the understandings and uses of the separation of powers as a descriptive theory and as a normative doctrine.

Finally, I have argued that, before abandoning the idea of the separation of powers due to its inability to account for recent trends of institutional and regulatory transformation, both at the nation-state and supra-national levels, we should consider looking back at the intuitive version of the separation of powers that is grounded in the distinction between law-creation and law-application. This version in fact carries a number of advantages over the traditional, tripartite models and can successfully constitute a theoretical canvas for further and much needed work on the organisation and limitation of public powers at the national and supra-national levels.

Bibliography

Ackerman, B, 'The New Separation of Powers' (2000) 113(3) *Harvard Law Review* 633.

Alchourrón, CE and Bulygin, E, *Normative Systems* (New York, Springer-Verlag, 1971).

Alexander, L and Sherwin, E, *Demystifying Legal Reasoning* (Cambridge, Cambridge University Press, 2008).

Alexy, R, *A Theory of Constitutional Rights* (Oxford, Oxford University Press, 2002).

—— 'On Balancing and Subsumption: A Structural Comparison' (2003) 16(4) *Ratio Juris* 433.

Allan K and Jaszczolt KM (eds), *The Cambridge Handbook of Pragmatics* (Cambridge, Cambridge University Press, 2012).

Allan, TRS, *Law, Liberty, and Justice: The Legal Foundations of British Constitutionalism* (Oxford, Oxford University Press, 1993).

—— *Constitutional Justice: A Liberal Theory of the Rule of Law* (Oxford, Oxford University Press, 2001).

Amselek, P, 'Philosophy of Law and the Theory of Speech Acts' (1988) 1(3) *Ratio Juris* 187.

Arai-Takahashi, Y, 'Discretion in German Administrative Law: Doctrinal Discourse Revisited' (2001) 6(1) *European Public Law* 69.

Arendt, H, *On Revolution* (London, Penguin Books, 1963).

—— *On Violence* (New York, Harcourt, 1970).

—— *The Human Condition*, 2nd edn (Chicago, University of Chicago Press, 1998).

Ariels, M, *Defining Pragmatics* (Cambridge, Cambridge University Press, 2010).

Aristotle, 'Politics' in C Lord (ed), *Aristotle's Politics*, 2nd edn (Chicago, Chicago University Press, 2013) Bk IV, ch XIV.

Asgeirsson, H, *The Nature and Value of Vagueness in the Law* (London, Hart Publishing, 2020).

Atria, F, *On Law and Legal Reasoning* (Oxford, Hart Publishing, 2002).

Austin, JL, *How to Do Things with Words* (Oxford, Clarendon Press, 1962).

Bach, K, 'The Semantics/Pragmatics Distinction: What It Is and Why It Matters' in K Turner (ed), *The Semantics/Pragmatics Interface from Different Points of View* (Oxford, Elsevier, 1999) 65–84.

Baker, GP and Hacker, PMS, *Wittgenstein: Rules, Grammar, and Necessity. An Analytical Commentary on the Philosophical Investigations: Essays and Exegesis of 185–242*, vol. 2, 2nd edn extensively revised by PMS Hacker (Hoboken, Wiley-Blackwell, 2009).

Barber, NW, 'Prelude to the Separation of Powers' (2001) 60(1) *Cambridge Law Journal* 59.

—— *The Principles of Constitutionalism* (Oxford, Oxford University Press, 2018).

Barberis, M, 'Lo scetticismo Immaginario. Nove Obiezioni agli Scettici à la Génoise' in P Comanducci and R Guastini (eds), *Analisi e diritto 2000: Ricerche di giurisprudenza analitica* (Turin, Giappichelli, 2000) 1–36.

—— 'Divisione dei Poteri e Libertà da Montesquieu a Constant' (2001) 31(1) *Materiali per una storia della cultura giuridica* 83.

—— 'Separazione dei Poteri e Teoria Giusrealista dell'Interpretazione' in P Comanducci and R Guastini (eds), *Analisi e diritto 2004: Ricerche di giurisprudenza analitica* (Turin, Giappichelli, 2004) 1–21.

Beccaria, C, *On Crimes and Punishments and Other Writings* (first published 1764, R Bellamy ed, R Davies trans, Cambridge, Cambridge University Press, 1995).

Bell, J, 'Discretionary Decision-making: A Jurisprudential View' in K Hawkins (ed), *The Uses of Discretion* (Oxford, Oxford University Press, 1992).

Bellamy, R, *Political Constitutionalism: A Republican Defence of the Constitutionality of Democracy* (Cambridge, Cambridge University Press, 2007).

Bibliography 289

Bello Hutt, DE, 'Against Judicial Supremacy in Constitutional Interpretation' (2017) 31 *Revus* 1.

Bentham, J, *Introduction to the Principles of Morals and Legislation* (JH Burns and HLA Hart eds, London, Athlone Press, 1970).

Bertea, S, 'Remarks on a Legal Positivist Misuse of Wittgenstein's Later Philosophy' (2003) 22(6) *Law and Philosophy* 513.

—— *The Normative Claim of Law* (Oxford, Hart Publishing, 2009).

—— 'Obligation: A Legal-Theoretical Perspective' in M Araszkiewicz, P Banas, T Gizbert-Studnicki and K Pleszka (eds), *Problems of Normativity, Rules and Rule-Following* (Cham, Springer International Publishing, 2015) 147–63.

—— *A Theory of Legal Obligation* (Cambridge, Cambridge University Press, 2019).

Bianchi, C, 'How to do things with (recorded) words' (2014) 167(2) *Philosophical Studies* 485.

Biber, D and Gray, B, 'Challenging stereotypes about academic writing: Complexity, elaboration, explicitness' (2010) 9(1) *Journal of English for Academic Purposes* 2.

Binder, G, 'Critical Legal Studies' in D Patterson (ed), *A Companion to Philosophy of Law and Legal Theory*, *Blackwell Companions to Philosophy*, 2nd edn (Chichester, Wiley-Blackwell, 2010) 267–78.

Bird, C, 'The Possibility of Self-Government (2000) 94(3) *American Political Science Review* 563.

Bix, BH, *Law, Language, and Legal Determinacy* (Oxford, Oxford University Press, 1993).

—— 'Can Theories of Meaning and Reference Solve the Problem of Legal Determinacy?' (2003) 16(3) *Ratio Juris* 281.

—— 'Legal Interpretation and the Philosophy of Language' in LM Solan and PM Tiersma (eds), *The Oxford Handbook of Language and Law* (Oxford, Oxford University Press, 2012).

Bjarup, J, 'The Philosophy of Scandinavian Legal Realism' (2005) 18(1) *Ratio Juris* 1.

Blau, A, 'How (Not) to Use the History of Political Thought for Contemporary Purposes' (2021) 65(2) *American Journal of Political Science* 359.

Bobbio, N, *Democracy and Dictatorship: The Nature and Limits of State Power* (Oxford, Polity Press, 1989).

Boghossian, P, 'Rules, Norms and Principles: A Conceptual Framework' in M Araszkiewicz, P Banas, T Gizbert-Studnicki and K Pleszka (eds), *Problems of Normativity, Rules and Rule-Following* (Cham, Springer International Publishing, 2015) 3–11.

Bognetti, G, *Dividing powers: A theory of the separation of powers* (A Baraggia and LP Vanoni eds, Milan, Wolters Kluwer Cedam, 2017).

Borg, E, *Minimal Semantics* (Oxford, Oxford University Press, 2004).

—— 'Minimalism versus Contextualism in Semantics' in G Preyer and G Peter (eds), *Context-Sensitivity and Semantic Minimalism: New Essays on Semantics and Pragmatics* (Oxford, Oxford University Press, 2007) 339–359.

—— 'Meaning and Context: a Survey of a Contemporary Debate' in D Whiting (ed), *The Later Wittgenstein on Language* (London, Palgrave Macmillan, 2009) 96–113.

—— *Pursuing Meaning* (Oxford, Oxford University Press, 2012).

—— 'Semantics without pragmatics?' in K Allan and K Jaszczolt (eds), *The Cambridge Handbook of Pragmatics* (Cambridge, Cambridge University Press, 2012) 513–28.

—— 'Explanatory Roles for Minimal Content' (2019) 53(3) *Noûs* 513.

Bracton H, *On the Law and Customs of England* (vol 4) (available at https://amesfoundation.law.harvard.edu/Bracton/Unframed/English/v4/159.htm).

Bradley, AW and Ewing KD, *Constitutional and Administrative Law*, 14th edn (Harlow, Pearson-Longman, 2007).

Braudel, F, *The Mediterranean in the Ancient World* (S Reynolds trans, London, Penguin Books, 2002).

Brennan, G, Eriksson, L, Goodin, R and Southwood, N, *Explaining Norms* (Oxford, Oxford University Press, 2013).

Brown, LN and Bell, JS, *French Administrative Law*, 4th edn (Oxford, Oxford University Press, 1993).

290 Bibliography

Bryce, J, 'Flexible and Rigid Constitutions' in J Bryce, *Studies in History and Jurisprudence*, vol 1 (Oxford, Oxford University Press, 1901).

Bugaric, B, 'Can Law Protect Democracy? Legal Institutions as "Speed Bumps"' (2019) 11 *Hague Journal on the Rule of Law* 447.

Bulygin, E, 'Judicial Decisions and the Creation of Law (1966)', in E Bulygin, *Essays in Legal Philosophy* (C Bernal, C Huerta, T Mazzarese, JJ Moreso, PE Navarro, and SL Paulson eds, Oxford, Oxford University Press, 2015) 75–87.

Burazin, L, Himma, KE and Roversi, C, (eds), *Law as an Artifact* (Oxford, Oxford University Press, 2018).

Calamandrei, P, 'Prefazione' in C Beccaria, *Dei Delitti e delle Pene*, 1st edn (P Calamandrei ed, Florence, Le Monnier, 1945) 7–129.

Caldeira, GA, Kelemen, RD and Whittington KE (eds), *The Oxford Handbook of Law and Politics* (Oxford, Oxford University Press, 2008).

Cameron, MA, *Strong Constitutions: Social-Cognitive Origins of the Separation of Powers* (Oxford, Oxford University Press, 2013).

Canale, D and Poggi F, 'Pragmatic Aspects of Legislative Intent' (2019) 64(1) *The American Journal of Jurisprudence* 125.

Canevaro, M, 'Athenian Constitutionalism: Nomothesia and Graphe Nomon Me Epitedeion Theinai', in G Thür, U Yiftach and R Zelnick-Abramovitz (eds), *Symposion 2017. Vorträge zur griechischen und hellenistischen Rechtsgeschichte (Tel Aviv, 20–23. August 2017)* (Vienna, Australian Academy of Sciences Press, 2019) 65–98.

Cao, D, 'Legal Speech Acts as Intersubjective Communicative Action' in A Wagner, W Werner and D Cao (eds), *Interpretation, Law and the Construction of Meaning* (Dordrecht, Springer, 2007) 65–82.

Cappelen. H and Lepore, E, *Insensitive Semantics: A Defense of Semantic Minimalism and Speech Act Pluralism* (Oxford, Blackwell, 2005).

—— and Lepore, E, 'Radical and Moderate Pragmatics: Does Meaning Determine Truth Conditions?' in ZG Szabó (ed), *Semantics versus Pragmatics* (Oxford, Oxford University Press, 2005) 45–71.

Caranta, R, Andenas M and Fairgrieve D (eds), *Independent Administrative Authorities* (London, British Institute of International and Comparative Law, 2004).

Carolan, E, *The New Separation of Powers: A Theory for the Modern State* (Oxford, Oxford University Press, 2009).

Carruthers, P, 'Language in Cognition' in E Margolis, R Samuels and SP Stich (eds), *The Oxford Handbook of Philosophy of Cognitive Science* (Oxford, Oxford University Press, 2012).

Castillo-Ortiz, P, 'The Dilemmas of Constitutional Courts and the Case for a New Design of Kelsenian Institutions' (2020) 39(6) *Law and Philosophy* 617.

Celano, B, *La Teoria del Diritto di Hans Kelsen: una Introduzione Critica* (Bologna, Il Mulino, 1999) 129–49.

—— 'Law as Power: Two Rule of Law Requirements', in W Waluchow and S Sciaraffa (eds), *Philosophical Foundations of the Nature of Law* (Oxford, Oxford University Press, 2013).

Chandler, D, *Semiotics: The Basics*, 2nd edn (Oxford, Routledge, 2007).

Chapman, S, 'In defence of a code: linguistic meaning and propositionality in verbal communication' (2001) 33(10) *Journal of Pragmatics* 1553.

Chiassoni, P, 'Legal Science and Legal Interpretation in the Pure Theory of Law' in L Gianformaggio (ed), *Hans Kelsen's Legal Theory: A Diachronic Point of View* (Turin, Giappichelli, 1990).

—— *Tecnica dell'interpretazione giuridica* (Bologna, Il Mulino, 2007).

—— 'Constitutionalism Out of a Positivist Mind Cast: The Garantismo Way' (2011) 17(4) *Res Publica* 327.

—— *Interpretation without Truth: A Realistic Inquiry* (Cham, Springer International Publishing 2019).

Christie, G, 'An Essay on Discretion' (1986) 35(5) *Duke Law Journal* 747.

Bibliography   291

Claus, L, 'Montesquieu's Mistakes and the True Meaning of Separation' (2005) 25(3) *Oxford Journal of Legal Studies* 419.

Cohen, MR, 'Rule Versus Discretion' (1914) 11(8) *Journal of Philosophy, Psychology and Scientific Methods* 208.

Coleman, J and Leiter, B, 'Determinacy, Objectivity and Authority' (1993) 142(2) *University of Pennsylvania Law Review* 549.

Comanducci, P, 'Conoscere il Diritto' (2008) 38(2) *Materiali per una storia della cultura giuridica* 419.

—— 'Alcuni problemi concettuali relativi alla applicazione del diritto' (2010) 10 *Diritto & Questioni Pubbliche* 121.

Constant, B, *Principles of Politics Applicable to all Governments* (first published 1815, E Hoffman ed, D O'Keeffe trans, N Capaldi introduction, Indianapolis, Liberty Fund, 2003).

Conway, G, 'Recovering a Separation of Powers in the European Union' (2011) 17(3) *European Law Journal* 304.

Cooper, RM, 'Administrative Justice and the Role of Discretion' (1938) 47(4) *Yale Law Journal* 577.

Cornell, D, *The Philosophy of the Limit* (New York, Routledge, 1992).

Costa, P and Zolo, D (eds), *The Rule of Law: History, Theory and Criticism* (Dordrecht, Springer, 2007).

Costa, V, 'Osservazioni sul Concetto di Isonomia' in A D'Atena and E Lanzilotta (eds), *Da Omero alla Costituzione Europea. Costituzionalismo Antico e Moderno* (Tivoli, Tored, 2003) 33–56.

Cotterell, R, 'Judicial Review and Legal Theory' in G Richardson and H Genn (eds), *Administrative Law and Government Action: The Courts and Alternative Mechanisms of Review* (Oxford, Clarendon Press, 1994).

Craig, PP *Administrative Law*, 6th edn (London, Sweet & Maxwell, 2008).

Croce, M, *Self-sufficiency of Law: A Critical-institutional Theory of Social Order* (Dordrecht, Springer, 2012).

D'Aspremont, J and Aalberts, T, 'Which Future for the Scholarly Concept of Soft International Law? Editors' Introductory Remarks' (2012) 25(2) *Leiden Journal of International Law* 309.

Daintith, T, 'Contractual Discretion and Administrative Discretion: A Unified Analysis' (2005) 68(4) *Modern Law Review* 554.

Danziger, S, Avnaim-Pesso, L and Levav, J, 'Extraneous factors in judicial decisions' (2011) 108(17) *Proceedings of the National Academy of Sciences* 6889.

—— Avnaim-Pesso, L and Levav, J, 'Reply to Weinshall-Margel and Shapard: Extraneous factors in judicial decisions persist' (2011) 108(42) *Proceedings of the National Academy of Sciences* E834.

Davidson, D, 'A Nice Derangement of Epitaphs' in RE Grandy and R Warner (eds), *Philosophical Grounds of Rationality: Intentions, Categories, Ends* (Oxford, Oxford University Press, 1986) 157–74.

Davis, KC, *Discretionary Justice: a Preliminary Inquiry* (Baton Rouge, Louisiana State University Press, 1969).

De Saussure F, *Cours de Linguistique Générale* (Lausanne & Paris, Payot, 1916).

Deakin S and Markou C (eds), *Is Law Computable?: Critical Perspectives on Law and Artificial Intelligence* (Oxford, Hart Publishing, 2020).

Del Mar, M, 'Beyond the State in and of Legal Theory', in SP Dolan and L Heckendorn Urscheler (eds), *Concepts of Law: Comparative, Jurisprudential, and Social Science Perspectives* (Burlington, Ashgate, 2012) 19–42.

Derrida, J, 'Signature Event Context' in J Derrida, *Limited Inc* (Evanston, Northwestern University Press, 1988) 1–23.

Dharmapala, D, Garoupa, N and Shepherd, JM, 'Legislatures, Judges, and Parole Boards: The Allocations of Discretion under Determinate Sentencing' (2010) 62(4) *Florida Law Review* 1037.

Dicey, AV, *Introduction to the Study of the Law of the Constitution*, 8th edn (London, Macmillan, 1915).

Diciotti, E, *Verità e Certezza nell'Interpretazione della Legge* (Turin, Giappichelli, 1999).

292 Bibliography

Dickson, J, *Evaluation and Legal Theory* (Oxford, Hart Publishing, 2001).

Diver, CS, 'Optimal Precision of Administrative Rules' (1983) 93(1) *Yale Law Journal* 65.

Dolan, SP and Heckendorn Urscheler, L, 'Concepts of Law: An Introduction', in SP Dolan and L Heckendorn Urscheler (eds), *Concepts of Law: Comparative, Jurisprudential, and Social Science Perspectives* (Surrey, Ashgate, 2012).

Dorf, MC, 'Legal Indeterminacy and Institutional Design' (2003) 78(3) *New York University Law Review* 875.

Dowding, K, 'Why should we care about the definition of power?' (2012) 5(1) *Journal of Political Power* 119.

Duarte D'Almeida, L, 'On the Legal Syllogism' in D Plunkett, SJ Shapiro, K Toh (eds), *Dimensions of Normativity: New Essays on Metaethics and Jurisprudence* (Oxford, Oxford University Press 2019) 335–64.

Duarte, D, 'Linguistic Objectivity in Norm Sentences: Alternatives in Literal Meaning' (2011) 24(2) *Ratio Juris* 112.

Dudek, M, 'Why are Words not Enough? Or a Few Remarks on Traffic Signs' in M Araszkiewicz, P Banas, T Gizbert-Studnicki and K Pleszka (eds), *Problems of Normativity, Rules and Rule-Following* (Cham, Springer International Publishing, 2015) 363–72.

—— 'Can Informative Traffic Signs Also Be Obligatory? Polish Constitutional Tribunal and Supreme Court Versus Traffic Signs' (2018) 31(4) *International Journal for the Semiotics of Law* 771.

Duff, RA, *Answering for Crime: Responsibility and Liability in the Criminal Law* (Oxford, Hart Publishing, 2007).

Duxbury, N, *Elements of Legislation* (Cambridge, Cambridge University Press, 2012).

Dworkin, R, 'The Model of Rules' (1967) 35(1) *University of Chicago Law Review* 14.

—— *Taking Rights Seriously* (Cambridge, Harvard University Press, 1977).

—— *A Matter of Principle* (Cambridge, Harvard University Press, 1985).

—— *Law's Empire* (London, Fontana, 1986).

—— *Freedom's Law: The Moral Reading of the American Constitution* (Cambridge, Harvard University Press, 1996).

—— 'Objectivity and Truth: You'd Better Believe It' (1996) 25(2) *Philosophy & Public Affairs* 87.

—— 'Hart's Postscript and the Point of Political Philosophy' in R Dworkin, *Justice in Robes* (Cambridge, Harvard University Press, 2006) 140–86.

—— Thirty Years On' in R Dworkin, *Justice in Robes* (Cambridge, Harvard University Press, 2006) 187–222.

—— *Justice for Hedgehogs* (Cambridge, Harvard University Press, 2011).

Edelstein, D, 'The ancient constitution and the Roman law: on Benjamin Straumann's Crisis and Constitutionalism' (2019) 4(3) *Global Intellectual History* 261.

Edlin, D, *Judges and Unjust Law: Common Law Constitutionalism and the Foundations of Judicial Review* (Ann Arbor, University of Michigan Press, 2008).

Edmundson, WA, 'Rethinking Exclusionary Reasons: A Second Edition of Joseph Raz's "Practical Reason and Norms"' (1993) 12(3) *Law and Philosophy* 329.

Ehrenberg, K, *The Functions of Law* (Oxford, Oxford University Press, 2016).

Ekins, R, *The Nature of Legislative Intent* (Oxford, Oxford University Press, 2012).

Eleftheriadis, P, 'Law and Sovereignty' (2010) 29(5) *Law and Philosophy* 535.

Elster, J 'Introduction' in J Elster and R Slagstad (eds), *Constitutionalism and Democracy* (Cambridge, Cambridge University Press, 1988) 1–18.

Endicott, T, 'Linguistic Indeterminacy' (1996) 16(4) *Oxford Journal of Legal Studies* 667.

—— *Vagueness in Law* (Oxford, Oxford University Press, 2000).

—— 'Legal Interpretation' in A Marmor (ed), *The Routledge Companion to Philosophy of Law* (New York, Routledge, 2012) 109–22.

—— 'Interpretation and Indeterminacy: Comments on Andrei Marmor's *Philosophy of Law*' (2014) 10(1) *Jerusalem Review of Legal Studies* 46.

—— 'Lawful Power' (2017) 15(1) *New Zealand Journal of Public and International Law* 1.

Bibliography 293

—— *Administrative Law*, 4th edn (Oxford, Oxford University Press, 2018).

Engberg J and Kjær, AL, 'Approaches to Language and the Law – Some Introductory Notes' [2011] *Hermes – Journal of Language and Communication Studies* 7.

Feldman, D, (ed), *Law in Politics, Politics in Law* (Oxford, Hart Publishing, 2013).

Ferrajoli, L, *La sovranita' nel mondo moderno*, 2nd edn (Rome, Laterza, 2004).

—— *Principia Iuris: Teoria del Diritto e Della Democrazia*, vol I (Bari, Laterza, 2007).

—— *Principia Iuris: Teoria del Diritto e Della Democrazia*, vol 2 (Bari, Laterza, 2007).

—— 'Costituzionalismo e Giurisdizione' (2012) 23(3) *Questione Giustizia* 7.

—— 'The General Theory of Law: on Its Subject, Its Method and Its Function' (2012) 1(2) *Rivista di Filosofia del Diritto – Journal of Legal Philosophy* 229.

—— *La Democrazia Attraverso i Diritti: Il Costituzionalismo Garantista come Modello Teorico e come Progetto Politico* (Bari, Laterza, 2013).

—— *Il paradigma garantista. Filosofia e critica del diritto penale* (Naples, Editoriale scientifica, 2016).

—— *La Democrazia Costituzionale* (Bologna, Il Mulino, 2016).

—— 'Il pensiero innovatore di Giovanni Tarello' (2018) 18(1) *Diritto & Questioni Pubbliche* 205.

Filangieri, G, *La scienza della legislazione* (first published 1780–1785, Naples, Grimaldi, 2003).

Finnis, J, *Natural Law and Natural Rights*, 2nd edn (Oxford, Oxford University Press, 2011).

Fish, S, 'Fish vs Fiss' (1984) 36(6) *Stanford Law Review* 1325.

—— *Doing What Comes Naturally: Change, Rhetoric, and the Practice of Theory in Literary & Legal Studies* (Durham, Duke University Press, 1989).

Flores, IB, 'H. L. A. Hart's Moderate Indeterminacy Thesis Reconsidered: In Between Scylla and Charybdis?' (2011) 5 *Problema: Anuario de Filosofia y Teoria del Derecho* 147.

Foderaro, S, 'La teorica della divisione dei poteri nel diritto pubblico fascista' (1939) 31(1) *Rivista di diritto pubblico e della pubblica amministrazione in Italia* 745.

Foy, M 'On Judicial Discretion in Statutory Interpretation' (2010) 62(2) *Administrative Law Review* 291.

Fraenkel-Haeberle, C, *Giurisdizione sul Silenzio e Discrezionalità Amministrativa: Germania, Austria, Italia* (Trento, Università degli studi di Trento, 2004).

Frank, J, *Law and the Modern Mind* (originally published 1930, Gloucester, P. Smith, 1970).

Freeman, S, 'Constitutional Democracy and the Legitimacy of Judicial Review' (1990) 9(4) *Law and Philosophy* 327.

Friedman, B, 'The Birth of an Academic Obsession: The History of the Countermajoritarian Difficulty, Part Five' (2002) 112(2) *Yale Law Journal* 153.

Fukuyama, F, *The End of History and the Last Man* (New York, Free Press, 1992).

Fuller, LL, 'Consideration and Form' (1941) 41(5) *Columbia Law Review* 799.

—— *The Morality of Law*, rev. edn, (New Haven, Yale University Press, 1977).

—— 'Positivism and Fidelity to Law: A Reply to Professor Hart' (1958) 71(4) *Harvard Law Review* 630.

Galligan, DJ, *Discretionary Powers: A Legal Study of Official Discretion* (Oxford, Clarendon Press, 1990).

Ganz, G, 'Allocation of Decision-Making Functions (Part I)' [1972] *Public Law* 215.

Gardbaum, S, 'How Successful and Distinctive is the Human Rights Act? An Expatriate Comparatist's Assessment' (2011) 74(2) *Modern Law Review* 195.

—— *The New Commonwealth Model of Constitutionalism: Theory and Practice* (Cambridge, Cambridge University Press, 2013).

—— 'What's so weak about "weak-form review"? A reply to Aileen Kavanagh' (2015) 13(4) *International Journal of Constitutional Law* 1040.

—— 'Political Parties, Voting Systems, and the Separation of Powers' (2017) 65(2) *American Journal of Comparative Law* 229.

Gardner, J, 'Law's Aims in Law's Empire' in S Hershovitz (ed), *Exploring Law's Empire: The Jurisprudence of Ronald Dworkin* (Oxford, Oxford University Press, 2006) 207–24.

294   Bibliography

—— 'Some Types of Law' in J Gardner, *Law as a Leap of Faith: Essays on Law in General* (Oxford, Oxford University Press, 2012) 54–88.

—— 'The Legality of Law' in J Gardner, *Law as a Leap of Faith: Essays on Law in General* (Oxford, Oxford University Press, 2012) 177–94.

—— 'The Supposed Formality of the Rule of Law' in J Gardner, *Law as a Leap of Faith: Essays on Law in General* (Oxford, Oxford University Press, 2012) 195–220.

Gee G and Webber, GCN, 'What is a Political Constitution' (2010) 30(2) *Oxford Journal of Legal Studies* 273.

Geller, JR, 'Truth, Objectivity and Dworkin's Right Answer Thesis' [1999] *UCL Jurisprudence Review* 83.

Gianformaggio, L (ed), *Hans Kelsen's Legal Theory: A Diachronic Point of View* (Turin, Giappichelli 1990).

—— (ed), *Sistemi Normativi Statici e Dinamici: Analisi di una tipologia kelseniana* (Turin, Giappichelli, 1991).

Giannini, MS, *Il Potere Discrezionale della Pubblica Amministrazione: Concetto e Problemi* (Milan, Giuffrè, 1939).

—— *Diritto Amministrativo*, 3rd edn (Milan, Giuffrè, 1993).

Giddens, A, *A Contemporary Critique of Historical Materialism*, vol 2 (Berkeley, University of California Press, 1985).

Ginsburg, T, 'The Global Spread of Constitutional Review' in GA Caldeira, RD Kelemen and KE Whittington (eds), *The Oxford Handbook of Law and Politics* (Oxford, Oxford University Press, 2008) 81–95.

—— and Versteeg M, 'Why do Countries Adopt Constitutional Review?' (2014) 30(3) *Journal of Law, Economics and Organization* 587.

—— and Huq, AZ, *How to Save a Constitutional Democracy* (Chicago, University of Chicago Press, 2019).

Golding, MP, 'The Legal Analog of the Principle of Bivalence' (2003) 16(4) *Ratio Juris* 450.

Goldoni, M, 'Two internal critiques of political constitutionalism' (2012) 10(4) *International Journal of Constitutional Law* 926.

—— 'Montesquieu and the French Model of Separation of Powers' (2013) 4(1) *Jurisprudence* 20.

Goldsworthy, J, *The Sovereignty of Parliament: History and Philosophy* (Oxford, Clarendon Press, 1999).

Green, L, *The Authority of the State* (Oxford, Oxford University Press, 1988).

—— 'Gender and the Analytical Jurisprudential Mind' (2020) 83(4) *Modern Law Review* 893.

Green, MS, 'Legal Realism as Theory of Law' (2005) 46(6) *William & Mary Law Review* 1915.

—— 'Leiter on the Legal Realists' (2011) 30(4) *Law and Philosophy* 381.

Greenberg, M, 'Legislation as Communication? Legal Interpretation and the Study of Linguistic Communication' in A Marmor and S Soames (eds), *Philosophical Foundations of Language in the Law* (Oxford, Oxford University Press, 2011).

Grey, JH, 'Discretion in Administrative Law' (1979) 17(1) *Osgoode Hall Law Journal* 107.

Grey, TC, 'Constitutionalism: An Analytical Framework' in JR Pennock and JW Chapman (eds), *Constitutionalism: Nomos XX* (New York, New York University Press, 1979) 189–209.

Griffith, JAG, 'The Political Constitution' (1979) 42(1) *Modern Law Review* 1.

Grimm, D, 'Types of Constitutions', in M Rosenfeld and A Sajó (eds), *The Oxford Handbook of Comparative Constitutional Law* (Oxford, Oxford University Press, 2012) 98–132.

—— *Constitutionalism: Past, Present, and Future* (Oxford, Oxford University Press, 2016).

Guarneri, C and Pederzoli, P, *The Power of Judges: A Comparative Study of Courts and Democracy* (Oxford, Oxford University Press, 2002).

Guastini, R, *Lezioni di teoria costituzionale* (Turin, Giappichelli, 2001).

—— 'Hart su Indeterminatezza, Incompletezza, e Discrezionalità Giudiziale' (2003) 21(2) *Ragion Pratica* 395.

—— 'A Sceptical View on Legal Interpretation' in P Comanducci and R Guastini (eds), *Analisi e diritto 2005: Ricerche di giurisprudenza analitica* (Turin, Giappichelli 2005) 139–44.

Bibliography 295

—— 'Se i Giudici Creino Diritto' in A Vignudelli (ed), *Istituzioni e dinamiche del diritto: I confini mobili della separazione dei poteri* (Milan, Giuffrè, 2009) 389–400.

—— 'Garantismo e Dottrina Pura a Confronto' in P Di Lucia (ed), *Assiomatica del Normativo: Filosofia Critica del Diritto in Luigi Ferrajoli* (Milan, LED, 2011) 113–24.

—— *Interpretare e Argomentare* (Milan, Giuffré, 2011).

—— 'Rule-Scepticism Restated' in L Green and B Leiter (eds), *Oxford Studies in Philosophy of Law*, vol 1 (Oxford, Oxford University Press, 2011) 138–61.

—— 'Il Realismo Giuridico Ridefinito' (2013) 19 *Revus* 97.

Günther, K, *The Sense of Appropriateness: Application Discourses in Morality and Law* (Albany, State University of New York Press, 1993).

—— 'Legal Adjudication and Democracy: Some Remarks on Dworkin and Habermas' (1995) 3(1) *European Journal of Philosophy* 36.

—— 'Law and Morality' in SM McMurrin (ed), *The Tanner Lectures on Human Values*, vol 8 (Salt Lake City, University of Utah Press, 1988) 219–79.

Habermas, J, *Between Facts and Norms: Contributions to a Discourse Theory of Law and Democracy* (W Rehg trans, Cambridge, MIT Press, 1996).

—— 'Constitutional Democracy: a Paradoxical Union of Contradictory Principles' (2001) 29(6) *Political Theory* 766.

Hägerström, A, *Inquiries into the Nature of Law and Morals* (Uppsala, Almqvist and Wiksells, 1953).

—— *Philosophy and Religion*, vol 3 (London, Routledge, 2004).

Halperin, JL, 'Law in Books and Law in Action: The Problem of Legal Change' (2011) 64(4) *Maine Law Review* 45.

Halpin, A, 'The Concept of a Legal Power' (1996) 16(1) *Oxford Journal of Legal Studies* 129.

—— *Reasoning with Law* (Oxford, Hart Publishing, 2001).

—— 'The Search for Law: A review of Mariano Croce, *Self-Sufficiency of Law: A Critical-Institutional Theory of Social Order*' (2014) 5(2) *Jurisprudence* 409.

Hanson, J, Hanson, K and Hart, M, 'Law and Economics' in D Patterson (ed), *A Companion to Philosophy of Law and Legal Theory, Blackwell Companions to Philosophy*, 2nd edn (Chichester, Wiley-Blackwell, 2010) 299–326.

Hardt, M, 'Translator's Forward: The Anatomy of Power' in A Negri, *The Savage Anomaly: The Power of Spinoza's Metaphysics and Politics*, 3rd edn, (M Hardt trans, Minneapolis, University of Minnesota Press, 2003).

Harlow, C and Rawlings, R, *Law and Administration*, 3rd edn (Cambridge, Cambridge University Press, 2012).

Harris, R 'How does writing restructure thought?' (1989) 9(2/3) *Language & Communication* 99.

Hart, HLA, 'Positivism and the Separation of Law and Morals' (1958) 71(4) *Harvard Law Review* 593.

—— *The Concept of Law*, 1st edn (Oxford, Clarendon Press, 1961).

—— 'Kelsen's Doctrine of the Unity of Law' in HLA Hart, *Essays in Jurisprudence and Philosophy* (Oxford, Oxford University Press, 1983).

—— *The Concept of Law*, 2nd edn (Oxford, Clarendon Press, 1997).

—— *The Concept of Law*, 3rd edn (Oxford, Oxford University Press, 2012).

—— 'Discretion' (2013) 127(2) *Harvard Law Review* 652.

Hart, HM and Sacks, SM, *The Legal Process: Basic Problems in the Making and Application of Law* (Westbury, Foundation Press, 1994).

Hasebe, Y, 'The Rule of Law and its Predicament' (2004) 17(4) *Ratio Juris* 489.

Haugaard M (ed), *Power: A Reader* (Manchester, Manchester University Press, 2012).

—— 'Introduction', in M Haugaard, *Power: A Reader* (Manchester, Manchester University Press, 2012).

Haukioja, J, 'Different Notions of Response-Dependence' in M Hoeltje, B Schnieder and A Steinberg (eds), *Varieties of Dependence: Ontological Dependence, Grounding, Supervenience, Response-Dependence* (Munich, Philosophia Verlag, 2003) 167–92.

296   Bibliography

—— 'A Middle Position Between Meaning Finitism and Meaning Platonism' (2005) 13(1) *International Journal of Philosophical Studies* 35.

—— 'Is Solitary Rule-Following Possible?' (2005) 32 *Philosophia* 131.

Hawkins, K, 'The Use of Legal Discretion: Perspectives from Law and Social Science' in K Hawkins (ed), The Uses of Discretion (Oxford, Oxford University Press, 1992) 11–46.

Hayek, FA, *The Constitution of Liberty* (Chicago, University of Chicago Press, 1978).

Henninger M and Negri A, 'From Sociological to Ontological Inquiry: An Interview with Antonio Negri' (2005) 23(1) *Italian Culture* 153.

Hickman, TR, 'In Defence of the Legal Constitution: Review Article' (2005) 55(4) *University of Toronto Law Journal* 981.

Himma, KE, 'Judicial Discretion and the Concept of Law' (1999) 19(1) *Oxford Journal of Legal Studies* 71.

—— 'Do Philosophy and Sociology Mix? A Non-Essentialist Socio-Legal Positivist Analysis of the Concept of Law' (2004) 24(4) *Oxford Journal of Legal Studies* 717.

—— 'A Comprehensive Hartian Theory of Legal Obligation: Social Pressure, Coercive Enforcement, and the Legal Obligations of Citizens' in W Waluchow and S Sciaraffa (eds), *Philosophical Foundations of the Nature of Law* (Oxford, Oxford University Press, 2013) 152–82.

—— 'Conceptual Jurisprudence. An Introduction to Conceptual Analysis and Methodology in Legal Theory' (2015) 26 *Revus* 65.

Hirschl, R, *Towards Juristocracy: The Origins and Consequences of the New Constitutionalism* (Cambridge, Harvard University Press, 2004).

Hobbes, T, *A dialogue between a philosopher and a student of the common laws of England* (first published 1681, J Cropsey ed, Chicago, University of Chicago Press, 1971).

—— *De Cive* (first published 1651, London, Anodos Books, 2017).

Holmes, OW, *The Common Law* (Boston, Little, Brown and Co, 1881).

—— 'The Path of the Law' (1897) 10(8) *Harvard Law Review* 457.

Holmes, S, 'Precommitment and the Paradox of Democracy' in J Elter and R Slagstad (eds), *Constitutionalism and Democracy* (Cambridge, Cambridge University Press, 1988) 195–240.

Holton, R 'Meaning and Rule-following: Philosophical Aspects' in N Smelser and P Baltes (eds), *International Encyclopedia of the Social & Behavioral Sciences* (Amsterdam, Elsevier, 2001).

Horner, WB, 'Speech-Act and Text-Act Theory: "Theme-ing" in Freshman Composition' (1979) 30(2) *College Composition and Communication* 165.

Huq, AZ and Michaels, JD, 'The Cycles of Separation-of-Powers Jurisprudence' (2016) 126(2) *Yale Law Journal* 346.

Hutton, CM, *Word Meaning and Legal Interpretation* (London, Palgrave Macmillan, 2014).

Iglesias Vila, M, *Facing Judicial Discretion: Legal Knowledge and Right Answers Revisited* (Dordrecht, Springer, 2001).

Issacharoff, S, *Fragile Democracies: Contested Power in the Era of Constitutional Courts* (Cambridge, Cambridge University Press, 2015).

—— 'Judicial Review in Troubled Times: Stabilizing Democracy in a Second-Best World' (2019) 98(1) *North Carolina Law Review* 1.

Itkonen, E, 'The Central Role of Normativity in Language and Linguistics' in J Zlatev, TP Racine, C Sinha and E Itkonen (eds), *The Shared Mind: Perspectives on Intersubjectivity* (Amsterdam, John Benjamins Publishing, 2008) 279–305.

Iturralde Sesma, V, *Interpretación literal y significado convencional: una reflexión sobre los límites de la interpretación jurídica* (Madrid, Marcial Pons, 2014).

Jackson, B, *Making Sense in Law: Linguistic, Psychological, and Semiotic Perspectives* (Liverpool, Deborah Charles, 1995).

Jackson, F, *From Metaphysics to Ethics: A Defence of Conceptual Analysis* (Oxford, Oxford University Press, 1998).

Jakab, A, 'Problems of the Stufenbaulehre: Kelsen's Failure to Derive the Validity of a Norm from Another Norm' (2007) 20 *Canadian Journal of Law & Jurisprudence* 35.

Jori, M, *Del Diritto Inesistente: Saggio di Metagiurisprudenza Descrittiva* (Pisa, ETS, 2010).
—— 'Legal Pragmatics' in A Capone and F Poggi (eds), *Pragmatics and Law: Philosophical Perspectives* (Cham, Springer International Publishing, 2016) 33–60.
—— 'Linguaggio giuridico', in in G Pino, A Schiavello and V Villa (eds), *Filosofia del diritto: Introduzione critica al pensiero giuridico e al diritto positivo* (Turin, Giappichelli, 2013) 257–87.
Jowell, J, 'The Legal Control of Administrative Discretion' [1973] *Public Law* 178.
Kalyvas, A, 'The Basic Norm and Democracy in Kelsen's Legal and Political Theory' (2006) 32(5) *Philosophy and Social Criticism* 573.
Kannai, R, Schild U and Zeleznikow J, 'Modeling the Evolution of Legal Discretion: An Artificial Intelligence Approach' (2007) 20(4) *Ratio Juris* 530.
Kant, I, 'Über den Gemeinspruch: Das mag in der Theorie richtig sein, taugt aber nicht für die Praxis' (originally published 1793) in I Kant, *Gesammelte Schriften, hrsg Konigliche Preussische Akademie der Wissenschaften*, vol 8 (H Maier, M Frischeisen-Köhler and P Menzer eds, Berlin and Leipzig: Walter de Gruyter, 1912).
—— *Perpetual Peace and Other Essays* (T Humphrey trans, Indianapolis, Hackett, 1983).
Katarani, K, *Isonomia and the Origins of Philosophy* (J Murphy trans, Durham, Duke University Press, 2017).
Kavanagh, A, 'What's So Weak about "Weak-Form Review? The Case of the UK Human Rights Act 1998' (2015) 13(4) *International Journal of Constitutional Law* 1008.
—— 'The Constitutional Separation of Powers', in D Dyzenhaus and M Thorburn (eds), *Philosophical Foundations of Constitutional Law* (Oxford, Oxford University Press, 2016) 221–40.
Kay, P, 'Language Evolution and Speech Style' in BG Bloun and M Sanches (eds), *Sociocultural Dimensions of Language Change* (New York, Academic Press, 1977) 21–33.
Kelman, M, *A Guide to Critical Legal Studies* (Cambridge, Harvard University Press, 1987).
Kelsen, H, 'The Law as a Specific Social Technique' (1941) 9(1) *University of Chicago Law Review* 75.
—— 'Judicial Review of Legislation: A Comparative Study of the Austrian and the American Constitution' (1942) 4(2) *The Journal of Politics* 183.
—— 'Foundations of Democracy' (1955) 66(1) *Ethics* 1.
—— *Pure Theory of Law*, 2nd edn (M Knight trans, Berkeley, University of California Press 1967).
—— (Paulson BL and Paulson SL trans), 'On the Theory of Interpretation' (1990) 10(2) *Legal Studies* 127 (English translation of Kelsen, H, 'Zur Theorie der Interpretation' (1934) 8 *Internationale Zeitschrift für Theorie des Rechts* 9).
—— *Introduction to the Problems of Legal Theory: A Translation of the First Edition of the Reine Rechtslehre Or Pure Theory of Law* (BL Paulson and SL Paulson trans, Oxford, Clarendon Press 1996) [English translation of Kelsen, H, *Reine Rechtslehre* (Leipzig, Deuticke, 1934)].
—— *General Theory of Law and State* (first published 1945, with a new introduction by A Javier Treviño, New Brunswick, Transaction Publishers, 2005).
—— 'Wesen und Entwicklung der Staatsgerichtsbarkeit' in Lars Vinx (ed and trans), *The Guardian of the Constitution: Hans Kelsen and Carl Schmitt on the Limits of Constitutional Law* (Cambridge, Cambridge University Press, 2015).
Kennedy, D, *A Critique of Adjudication: Fin de Siècle* (Cambridge, Harvard University Press, 1997).
—— 'A Left Phenomenological Alternative to the Hart/Kelsen Theory of Legal Interpretation' in D Kennedy, *Legal Reasoning: Collected Essays* (Aurora, Davies Group Publishers, 2008) 153–73.
King, J, 'The Democratic Case for a Written Constitution' (2019) 72(1) *Current Legal Problems* 1.
Klass, G, 'Three Pictures of Contract: Duty, Power and Compound Rule' (2008) 83 *New York University Law Review* 1726.
Klatt, M, 'Semantic Normativity and the Objectivity of Legal Argumentation' (2004) 90 *Archiv für Rechts- und Sozialphilosophie* 51.
—— 'Taking Rights less Seriously. A Structural Analysis of Judicial Discretion' (2007) 20(4) *Ratio Juris* 506.

298 Bibliography

—— *Making the Law Explicit: The Normativity of Legal Argumentation* (Oxford, Hart Publishing, 2008).

Knight, CJS, 'Bi-Polar Sovereignty Restated' (2009) 68(2) *Cambridge Law Journal* 361.

Kozinski, A, 'What I Ate for Breakfast and Other Mysteries of Judicial Decision Making' (1992) 26(4) *Loyola of Los Angeles Law Review* 993.

Kramer, M, *Objectivity and the Rule of Law* (Cambridge, Cambridge University Press, 2007).

—— *H.L.A. Hart* (Cambridge, Polity Press, 2018).

Kripke, SA, *Wittgenstein on Rules and Private Language* (Cambridge, Harvard University Press, 1982).

Kurzon, D, *It is Hereby Performed ...: Explorations in Legal Speech Acts* (Amsterdam, John Benjamins Publishing, 1986).

Kyritsis, D, *Shared Authority: Courts and Legislatures in Legal Theory* (Oxford, Hart Publishing, 2017).

Lacey, N, 'The Path Not Taken: H.L.A. Hart's Harvard Essay on Discretion' (2013) 127(2) *Harvard Law Review* 636.

Lakin, S, 'Debunking the Idea of Parliamentary Sovereignty: The Controlling Factor of Legality in the British Constitution' (2008) 28(4) *Oxford Journal of Legal Studies* 709.

Lanni, A, *Law and Order in Ancient Athens* (Cambridge, Cambridge University Press, 2016).

Leiter, B, 'Legal Indeterminacy' (1995) 1(4) *Legal Theory* 481.

—— 'American Legal Realism' in MP Golding and WA Edmundson (eds), *The Blackwell Guide to the Philosophy of Law and Legal Theory* (Malden, Blackwell Publishing, 2005).

—— 'American Legal Realism' in D Patterson (ed), *A Companion to Philosophy of Law and Legal Theory, Blackwell Companions to Philosophy*, 2nd edn (Chichester, Wiley-Blackwell, 2010) 249–66.

—— 'Legal Formalism and Legal Realism: What is the Issue?' (2010) 16(2) *Legal Theory* 111.

—— 'In Praise of Realism (and against Nonsense Jurisprudence)' (2011) 100(3) *Georgetown Law Journal* 865.

—— 'Legal Realisms, Old and New' (2013) 47(4) *Valparaiso Law Review* 949.

—— *Naturalizing Jurisprudence: Essays on American Legal Realism and Naturalism in Legal Philosophy* (Oxford, Oxford University Press, 2007).

—— 'Legal Positivism as a Realistic Theory of Law', in P Mindus and T Spaak (eds), *The Cambridge Companion to Legal Positivism* (Cambridge, Cambridge University Press, 2021).

Leith, P, 'Fundamental errors in legal logic programming' (1986) 29(6) *Computer Journal* 545.

Levenbook, BB, 'How a Statute Applies' (2006) 12(1) *Legal Theory* 71.

Levinson, DJ and Pildes, RH, 'Separation of Parties, Not Powers' (2006) 119(8) *Harvard Law Review* 2311.

Lewis, SR, 'Taking Adjudication Seriously' (1980) 58(4) *Australasian Journal of Philosophy* 377.

Llewellyn, KN, *The Common Law Tradition: Deciding Appeals* (Boston, Little Brown & Co, 1960).

Locke, J, 'The Second Treatise' in P Laslett (ed), *Locke: Two Treatises of Government* (first published 1689, rev edn, Cambridge, Cambridge University Press, 1988).

Loughlin, M, *Sword and Scales: An Examination of the Relationship between Law and Politics* (Oxford, Hart Publishing, 2000).

—— *Foundations of Public Law* (Oxford, Oxford University Press, 2010).

—— and Tierney S, 'The Shibboleth of Sovereignty' (2018) 81(6) *Modern Law Review* 989.

Lucatuorto, PLM, 'Modelli Computazionali della Discrezionalità del Giudice: uno Studio Preliminare' (2006) 7(3) *Ciberspazio e Diritto* 271.

—— 'Reasonableness in Administrative Discretion: A Formal Model' (2010) 8 *The Journal Jurisprudence* 633.

Lucy, W, *Understanding and Explaining Adjudication* (Oxford, Oxford University Press, 1999).

—— 'Adjudication' in J Coleman, and S Shapiro (eds), *The Oxford Handbook of Jurisprudence and Philosophy of Law* (Oxford, Oxford University Press, 2004) 206–67.

Luzzati, C, 'Discretion and "Indeterminacy" in Kelsen's Theory of Legal Interpretation' in L Gianformaggio (ed), *Hans Kelsen's Legal Theory: A Diachronic Point of View* (Turin, Giappichelli, 1990) 123–77.

Bibliography 299

Mac Amhlaigh, C, 'Does Legal Theory Have a Pluralism Problem?', in S Berman (ed), *The Oxford Handbook of Legal Pluralism* (Oxford, Oxford University Press 2020).
—— 'Putting political constitutionalism in its place' (2016) 14(1) *International Journal of Constitutional Law* 175.
MacCormick, N 'Coherence in Legal Justification' in A Peczenik, L Lindahl and B van Roermund (eds), *Theory of Legal Science* (Dordrecht, Springer, 1984) 235–51.
—— 'Discretion and Rights' (1989) 8(1) *Law and Philosophy* 23.
—— 'The Ethics of Legalism' (1989) 2(2) *Ratio Juris* 184.
—— *Legal Reasoning and Legal Theory*, rev. edn (Oxford, Oxford University Press, 1994).
—— *Rhetoric and The Rule of Law* (Oxford, Oxford University Press, 2005).
Machiavelli, N, *Il Principe* (first published 1532, Milan, Garzanti, 2008).
Mackie, J, 'The Third Theory of Law' (1977) 1(1) *Philosophy and Public Affairs* 3.
Madison, J, 'The Federalist No. 47' in A Hamilton, J Madison and J Jay, *The Federalist Papers* (first published 1787–88, L Goldman ed, Oxford, Oxford University Press, 2008).
Magill, ME, 'The Real Separation in Separation of Powers Law' (2000) 86(6) *Virginia Law Review* 1127.
Marmor, A, 'An Institutional Conception of Authority' (2011) 39(3) *Philosophy & Public Affairs* 238.
—— 'The Rule of Law and its Limits' (2004) 23 *Law and Philosophy* 1.
—— *Interpretation and Legal Theory*, rev. 2nd edn (London, Hart Publishing, 2005).
—— *Social Conventions: From Language to Law* (Princeton, Princeton University Press, 2009).
—— 'An Institutional Conception of Authority' (2011) 39(3) *Philosophy & Public Affairs* 238.
—— *Philosophy of Law* (Princeton, Princeton University Press, 2011).
—— *The Language of Law* (Oxford, Oxford University Press, 2014).
Marsilius of Padua, *Defensor Pacis*, 2nd edn (first published 1324, A Gewirth trans, CJ Nederman ed, New York, Columbia University Press, 2001).
Martin, M, *The Legal Philosophy of H.L.A. Hart: A Critical Appraisal* (Philadelphia, Temple University Press, 1987).
Matczak, M, 'Why Legal Rules Are Not Speech Acts and What Follows from That?' in M Araszkiewicz, P Banas, T Gizbert-Studnicki and K Pleszka (eds), *Problems of Normativity, Rules and Rule-Following* (Cham, Springer International Publishing, 2015) 331–39.
—— 'Three Kinds of Intention in Lawmaking' (2017) 36(6) *Law and Philosophy* 651.
—— 'A Theory that Beats the Theory? Lineages, the Growth of Signs, and Dynamic Legal Interpretation' in M Witek and I Witczak-Plisiecka (eds), *Normativity and Variety of Speech Actions* (Leiden, Brill, 2018) 180–205.
McGing, BC, *Polybius' Histories* (Oxford, Oxford University Press, 2010).
McIlwain, CH, *Constitutionalism, Ancient and Modern* (Ithaca, Cornell University Press, 1940).
McSweeney, TJ, *Priests of the Law. Roman Law and the Making of the Common Law's First Professionals* (Oxford, Oxford University Press, 2019).
Mendes J and Venzke I (eds), *Allocating Authority: Who Should Do What in European and International Law?* (Oxford, Hart Publishing, 2018).
—— 'Introducing the Idea of Relative Authority', in J Mendes and I Venzke (eds), *Allocating Authority: Who Should Do What in European and International Law?* (Oxford, Hart Publishing, 2018) 1–26.
Michelon, C, 'Practical Wisdom in Legal Decision-Making' in A Amaya and HL Ho (eds), *Law, Virtue and Justice* (Oxford, Hart Publishing, 2013) 29–50.
Miers, D, 'Legal Theory and the Interpretation of Statutes' in W Twining (ed), *Legal Theory and Common Law* (Oxford, Blackwell Publishing, 1986) 115ff.
Miller, D, *Political Philosophy: A Very Short Introduction* (Oxford, Oxford University Press, 2003).
Minda, G, *Postmodern Legal Movements: Law and Jurisprudence at Century's End* (New York, New York University Press, 1995).
Möllers, C, *The Three Branches: A Comparative Model of Separation of Powers* (Oxford, Oxford University Press, 2013).
—— 'The Separation of Powers', in R Masterman and R Schultze (eds), *The Cambridge Companion to Comparative Constitutional Law* (Cambridge, Cambridge University Press, 2019) 230–57.

300 Bibliography

Montesquieu, CL de Secondat, Baron de, *The Spirit of the Laws* (first published 1748, AM Cohler, BC Miller and HS Stone eds, Cambridge, Cambridge University Press, 1989).

Moreso, JJ, *Legal Indeterminacy and Constitutional Interpretation* (Dordrecht, Kluwer, 1998).

—— and JM Vilajosana, *Introducción a la teoria del derecho* (Madrid, Marcial Pons, 2004).

—— *Lógica, Argumentación e Interpretación en el Derecho* (Barcelona, Editorial UOC, 2006).

—— and Chilovi S, 'Interpretive Arguments and the Application of the Law' in G Bongiovanni et al (eds), *Handbook of Legal Reasoning and Argumentation* (Dordrecht, Springer, 2018) 495–517.

Morris, CW, *Foundations of the Theory of Signs*, International Encyclopedia of Unified Science, vol 1, no 2 (Chicago, University of Chicago Press, 1938).

Murphy, JB, *The Philosophy of Positive Law: Foundations of Jurisprudence* (New Haven, Yale University Press, 2005).

Navarro, P and Moreso, JJ, 'Applicability and Effectiveness of Legal Norms' (2005) 16 *Law and Philosophy* 201.

Neale, S, 'Stephen Neale on Meaning and Interpretation' in D Edmonds and N Warburton (eds), *Philosophy Bites Again* (Oxford, Oxford University Press, 2014) 240–64.

—— 'Silent Reference' in G Ostertag (ed), *Meanings and Other Things: Themes from the Work of Stephen Schiffer* (Oxford, Oxford University Press, 2016) 229–322.

Negri, A, *L'anomalia selvaggia. Saggio su potere e Potenza in Baruch Spinoza* (Milan, Feltrinelli, 1981).

Newton, I, *The Mathematical Principles of Natural Philosophy*, vol 1 (A Motte trans, London, Benjamin Motte, 1729).

Nöth, W, *Handbook of Semiotics* (Bloomington, Indiana University Press, 1995).

Nye Jr, JS, *Soft Power: The Means To Success In World Politics* (New York, PublicAffairs, 2004).

Okoth-Ogendo, HWO, 'Constitutions without Constitutionalism. Reflections on an African Political Paradox' in D Greenberg, SN Katz, MB Oliviero and SC Wheatley (eds), *Constitutionalism and Democracy. Transitions in the Contemporary World* (New York/Oxford, Oxford University Press, 1993).

Oliveira de Sousa, F, 'A Realistic Theory of Law' (2018) 9(2) *Jurisprudence* 438.

Ong, W, *Orality and Literacy: The Technologizing of the Word* (London, Routledge, 2002).

Ostwald, M, *Nomos and the Beginnings of the Athenian Democracy* (Oxford, Clarendon Press, 1969).

Palombella, G, 'The Cognitive Attitude' (1999) 85(2) *Archiv. für Rechts- und Sozialphilosophie* 151.

—— 'The Rule of Law as an Institutional Ideal' in L Morlino and G Palombella (eds), *Rule of Law and Democracy: Inquiries into Internal and External Issues* (Leiden, Brill, 2010) 3–37.

Pansardi, P, 'Power to and power over: two distinct concepts of power?' (2012) 5(1) *Journal of Political Power* 73.

Parry, J, *The Psychology of Human Communication* (London, University of London Press, 1967).

Pattaro, E, *The Law and The Right: A Reappraisal of the Reality that Ought to Be, A Treatise of Legal Philosophy and General Jurisprudence*, vol 1 (Dordrecht, Springer, 2007).

Paulson SL and Paulson BL (eds), *Normativity and Norms: Critical Perspectives on Kelsenian Themes* (Oxford, Oxford University Press, 1999).

Pavlakos, G, 'The Relation Between Moral and Legal Obligation: An Alternative Kantian Reading' in G Pavlakos and V Rodriguez-Blanco (eds), *Reasons and Intentions in Law and Practical Agency* (Oxford, Hart Publishing, 2015).

Payne, J, 'The False Imperative' (2010) 26(2) *The Legislative Lawyer* www.ncsl.org/legislators-staff/legislative-staff/research-editorial-legal-and-committee-staff/volume-xxvi-issue-2-the-false-imperative.aspx accessed 12 October 2020.

Perry, S, 'Interpretation and Methodology in Legal Theory' in A Marmor (ed), *Law and Interpretation: Essays in Legal Philosophy* (Oxford, Clarendon Press, 1995) 97–136.

Pettit, P, 'The Reality of Rule-Following' (1990) 99(393) *Mind* 1.

—— *On the People's Terms: A Republican Theory and Model of Democracy* (Cambridge, Cambridge University Press, 2012).

Pino, G, 'The Place of Legal Positivism in Contemporary Constitutional States' (1999) 18(5) *Law and Philosophy* 513.
—— 'L'Applicabilità delle Norme Giuridiche' (2011) 11 *Diritto & Questioni Pubbliche* 797.
—— *Teoria Analitica del Diritto I: La Norma Giuridica* (Pisa, Edizioni ETS 2016).
—— 'La certezza del diritto e lo Stato costituzionale' (2018) 2 *Diritto Pubblico* 517.
Pirie, F, 'Law Before Government: Ideology and Aspiration' (2010) 30(2) *Oxford Journal of Legal Studies* 207.
—— *The Anthropology of Law* (Oxford, Oxford University Press, 2013).
Plato, *Republic* (C Rowe trans, London, Penguin Books, 2012).
Poggi, F, 'Law and Conversational Implicatures' (2011) 24(1) *International Journal for the Semiotics of Law* 21.
—— 'The Myth of Literal Meaning in Legal Interpretation' (2013) 13 *Analisi e Diritto* 313.
—— 'Grice, the Law, and the Linguistic Special Case Thesis' in A Capone and F Poggi (eds), *Pragmatics and Law: Philosophical Perspectives* (Cham, Springer International Publishing, 2016) 231–48.
—— *Il Modello Conversazionale: Sulla differenza tra comprensione ordinaria e interpretazione giuridica* (Pisa, ETS, 2020).
Poscher, R, 'The Normative Construction of Legislative Intent' in Institut Michel Villey (eds), *Le droit et la philosophie analytique, Droit & Philosophie* vol 9 (Paris, Dalloz, 2018) 121–50.
Posner, EA and Vermeule, A, *The Executive Unbound: After the Madisonian Republic* (Oxford, Oxford University Press, 2011).
Posner, R, *Law and Legal Theory in England and America* (Oxford, Clarendon Press, 1996).
Postema, GJ, 'Philosophy of the Common Law', in J Coleman and S Shapiro (eds), *The Oxford Handbook of Jurisprudence and Philosophy of Law* (Oxford, Oxford University Press, 2002) 588–622.
—— *Legal Philosophy in the Twentieth Century: The Common Law World*, A Treatise of Legal Philosophy and General Jurisprudence, vol 11 (Dordrecht, Springer, 2011).
Pound, R, 'Law in Books and Law in Action' (1910) 44(1) *American Law Review* 12.
Priel, D, 'Were the Legal Realists Legal Positivists?' (2008) 27(4) *Law and Philosophy* 309.
—— 'Reconstructing Fuller's Argument Against Legal Positivism' (2013) 26(2) *Canadian Journal of Law & Jurisprudence* 399.
Ramirez Ludeña, L, 'The Meaning of "Literal Meaning"' (2018) 18(1) *Analisi e Diritto* 83.
Rawls, J, *A Theory of Justice*, rev. edn (Cambridge, Belknap Press, 1999).
Raz, J, 'Legal Principles and the Limits of Law' (1972) 81(5) *Yale Law Journal* 823.
—— 'Voluntary Obligations and Normative Powers (Part II)' (1972) 46 *Aristotelian Society Supplementary Volume* 79.
—— 'The Identity of Legal Systems' in J Raz, *The Authority of Law: Essays on Law and Morality* (Oxford, Clarendon Press, 1979) 78–102.
—— 'Law and Value in Adjudication' in J Raz, *The Authority of Law: Essays on Law and Morality* (Oxford, Clarendon Press, 1979) 180–209.
—— 'The Institutional Nature of Law' in J Raz, *The Authority of Law: Essays on Law and Morality* (Oxford, Clarendon Press, 1979) 103–21.
—— 'The Rule of Law and its Virtue' in J Raz, *The Authority of Law: Essays on Law and Morality* (Oxford, Clarendon Press, 1979) 210–29.
—— 'Dworkin: A New Link in the Chain' (1986) 74(3) *California Law Review* 1103.
—— 'Introduction', in J Raz (ed), *Authority* (New York, New York University Press, 1990) 1–19.
—— *Ethics in the Public Domain* (Oxford. Oxford University Press 1994).
—— *Practical Reason and Norms*, 2nd edn (Oxford, Oxford University Press, 1999).
—— 'On the Authority and Interpretation of Constitutions' in J Raz, *Between Authority and Interpretation: On the Theory of Law and Practical Reason* (Oxford, Oxford University Press, 2009) 323–70.
—— 'Why the State?' in N Roughan and A Halpin (eds), *In Pursuit of Pluralist Jurisprudence* (Cambridge, Cambridge University Press, 2017) 136–162.

302   *Bibliography*

Recanati, F, *Literal Meaning* (Cambridge, Cambridge University Press, 2004).

Redondo, C, 'El Ideal de las Acciones Basadas en Normas Jurídicas' in P Comanducci and R Guastini (eds), *Analisi e diritto 2008: Ricerche di giurisprudenza analitica* (Turin, Giappichelli 2008) 99–118.

Rescigno, GU, 'Ripensando le convenzioni costituzionali' (1997) 28(4) *Politica del Diritto* 499.

Reyes Molina, SA, 'Judicial Discretion as a Result of Systemic Indeterminacy' (2020) 33(2) *Canadian Journal of Law and Jurisprudence* 369.

Ripstein, A, 'Authority and Coercion' (2004) 32(1) *Philosophy & Public Affairs* 2.

Roberts, S, 'After Government? On Representing Law Without the State' (2005) 68(1) *Modern Law Review* 1.

Robson, WA, *Justice and Administrative Law: A Study of the British Constitution* (London, Macmillan, 1928).

Romeo G, 'The Conceptualization of Constitutional Supremacy: Global Discourse and Legal Tradition' (2020) 21(5) *German Law Journal* 904.

Roughan, N, *Authorities: Conflicts, Cooperation, and Transnational Legal Theory* (Oxford, Oxford University Press, 2013).

—— and Halpin, A (eds), *In Pursuit of Pluralist Jurisprudence*, (Cambridge, Cambridge University Press, 2017).

Rousseau, JJ, *The Social Contract; and Discourses* (GDH Cole trans, London, Dent, 1973).

Roux, T, 'In Defence of Empirical Entanglement: The Methodological Flaw in Waldron's Case against Judicial Review' in R Levy, H Kong, G Orr and J King (eds), *The Cambridge Handbook of Deliberative Constitutionalism* (Cambridge, Cambridge University Press, 2018) 203–19.

Rubin, EL, 'Discretion and its Discontents' (1996) 72(4) *Chicago-Kent Law Review* 1299.

Rushworth, J, 'Historical Collections: 1628 (part 3 of 7)' in J Rushworth, *Historical Collections of Private Passages of State, Volume I 1618–29* (London, 1721) available at British History Online www.british-history.ac.uk/rushworth-papers/vol1/pp549-588 accessed 17 March 2021).

Sacco, R, *Antropologia Giuridica. Contributo ad una Macrostoria del Diritto* (Bologna, il Mulino, 2007).

Sadurski, W, *Poland's Constitutional Breakdown* (Oxford, Oxford University Press, 2019).

Sajó, A and Uitz, R, *The Constitution of Freedom: An introduction to Legal Constitutionalism* (Oxford, Oxford University Press, 2017).

Sandel, MJ, 'Political Liberalism' (1994) 107(7) Harvard Law Review 1765.

Sandro, P, 'Creation and Application of Law: A Neglected Distinction' (PhD thesis, University of Edinburgh, 2014).

—— 'To whom does the law speak? Canvassing a neglected picture of law's interpretive field' in M Araszkiewicz, P Banas, T Gizbert-Studnicki and K Pleszka (eds), *Problems of Normativity, Rules and Rule-Following* (Cham, Springer International Publishing, 2015) 265–80.

—— 'Unlocking Legal Validity: Some Remarks on the Artificial Ontology of Law' in P Westerman, J Hage, S Kirste and AR Mackor (eds), *Legal Validity and Soft Law* (Cham, Springer International Publishing, 2018) 99–123.

Sartori, G, 'Constitutionalism: A Preliminary Discussion' (1962) 56(4) *The American Political Science Review* 853.

Scarpelli, U, *Contributo alla semantica del linguaggio normativo* (Milan, Giuffrè, 1985).

Schauer, F, 'Formalism' (1988) 97(4) *Yale Law Journal* 509.

—— *Playing by the Rules: A Philosophical Examination of Rule-based Decision-making in Law and in Life* (Oxford, Clarendon Press, 1991).

—— '(Re)taking Hart' (2006) 119(3) *Harvard Law Review* 852.

'A Critical Guide to Vehicles in the Park' (2008) 83(4) *New York University Law Review* 1109.

—— *Thinking Like a Lawyer: A New Introduction to Legal Reasoning* (Cambridge, Harvard University Press, 2009).

—— 'Balancing, Subsumption, and the Constraining Role of Legal Text' in M Klatt (ed), *Institutionalized Reason: The Jurisprudence of Robert Alexy* (Oxford, Oxford University Press, 2012) 307–16.

—— 'Legal Realism Untamed' (2013) 91(4) *Texas Law Review* 749.

—— 'On the Open Texture of Law' (2013) 87(1) *Grazer Philosophische Studien* 197.

—— *The Force of Law* (Cambridge, Harvard University Press, 2015).

Schiavone, A, *The Invention of Law in the West* (J Carden and A Shugaar trans, Cambridge, Harvard University Press, 2012) (originally published as Schiavone, A, *Ius. L'invenzione del Diritto in Occidente* (Turin, Einaudi, 2005)).

Schneider, CE, 'Discretion and Rules: A Lawyer's View' in K Hawkins (ed), *The Uses of Discretion* (Oxford, Oxford University Press, 1992) 47–88.

Schor, M, 'Judicial Review and American Constitutional Exceptionalism' (2008) 46(3) *Osgoode Hall Law Journal* 535.

Schwartz, B and Wade, HWR, *Legal Control of Government: Administrative Law in Britain and the United States* (Oxford, Clarendon Press, 1972).

Schwarze, J, *European Administrative Law*, 2nd edn (London, Sweet & Maxwell, 2006).

Scoca, FG, 'La Discrezionalità nel Pensiero di Giannini e nella Dottrina Successiva' (2000) 50(4) *Rivista Trimestrale di Diritto Pubblico* 1045.

Scott, JC, *Against the Grain: A Deep History of the Earliest States* (New Haven, Yale University Press, 2017).

Segall, EJ, *Supreme Myths: Why the Supreme Court is Not a Court and its Justices are Not Judges* (Santa Barbara, Praeger, 2012).

Sergot, MJ, Cory, HT, Hammond, P, Kowalski, RA and Kriwaczek, F, 'The British Nationality Act as a Logic Program' (1986) 29(5) *Communications of the ACM* 370.

Shaffer, MJ, *Counterfactuals and Scientific Realism* (London, Palgrave Macmillan, 2012).

Shannon, CE and Weaver, W, *The Mathematical Theory of Communication* (Urbana, University of Illinois Press, 1949).

Shapiro, S, 'Authority', in J Coleman and S Shapiro (eds), *The Oxford Handbook of Jurisprudence and Philosophy of Law* (Oxford, Oxford University Press, 2004).

—— 'The "Hart-Dworkin" Debate: A Short Guide for the Perplexed' in A Ripstein (ed), *Ronald Dworkin* (New York, Cambridge University Press, 2007).

—— *Legality* (Cambridge, Harvard University Press, 2011).

Shavell, S, 'Optimal Discretion in the Application of Rules' (2007) 9(1) *American Law and Economics Review* 175.

Shaw, GC, 'H.L.A. Hart's Lost Essay: Discretion and the Legal Process School' (2013) 127(2) *Harvard Law Review* 666.

Shiner, RA 'Hart on Judicial Discretion' (2011) 5 *Problema: Anuario de Filosofia y Teoria del Derecho* 341.

Skoczeń, I, 'Implicatures Within the Legal Context: A Rule-Based Analysis of the Possible Content of Conversational Maxims in Law' in M Araszkiewicz, P Banas, T Gizbert-Studnicki and K Pleszka (eds), *Problems of Normativity, Rules and Rule-Following* (Cham, Springer International Publishing, 2015) 351–62.

—— 'Minimal Semantics and Legal Interpretation' (2016) 29(3) *International Journal for the Semiotics of Law* 615.

—— *Implicatures within Legal Language* (Cham, Springer International Publishing, 2019).

Slocum, BG, *Ordinary Meaning: A Theory of the Most Fundamental Principle of Legal Interpretation* (Chicago, University of Chicago Press, 2015).

—— 'The Ordinary Meaning of Rules' in M Araszkiewicz, P Banas, T Gizbert-Studnicki and K Pleszka (eds), *Problems of Normativity, Rules and Rule-Following* (Cham, Springer International Publishing, 2015) 295–317.

—— 'Introduction' in BG Slocum, *The Nature of Legal Interpretation: What Jurists Can Learn About Legal Interpretation from Linguistics and Philosophy* (Chicago, University of Chicago Press, 2017).

—— 'Pragmatics and legal texts: How best to account for the gaps between literal meaning and communicative meaning' in J Giltrow and D Stein (ed), *The Pragmatic Turn in Law: Inference and Interpretation in Legal Discourse* (Berlin, De Gruyter, 2017) 119–44.

304   Bibliography

Smith, D, 'The practice-based objection to the "standard picture" of how law works' (2019) 10(4) *Jurisprudence* 502.

Soames, S, 'Facts, Truth Conditions, and the Skeptical Solution to the Rule-Following Paradox' (1998) 32 *Nous* 313.

—— 'Skepticism About Meaning: Indeterminacy, Normativity, and the Rule-Following Paradox' (1998) 23 *Canadian Journal of Philosophy* 211.

—— 'Interpreting Legal Texts: What Is, and What Is Not, Special About the Law' in S Soames, *Philosophical Essays, Volume 1: Natural Language: What It Means and How We Use It* (Princeton, Princeton University Press, 2008).

—— 'Deferentialism: A Post–originalist Theory of Legal Interpretation' (2013) 82(2) *Fordham Law Review* 597.

Solan, LM, *The Language of Statutes: Laws and Their Interpretation* (Chicago, University of Chicago Press, 2010).

—— 'Linguistic Issues in Statutory Interpretation' in LM Solan and PM Tiersma (eds), *The Oxford Handbook of Language and Law* (Oxford, Oxford University Press, 2012) 87–99.

Solum, L, 'The Interpretation-Construction Distinction' (2010 27(1) *Constitutional Commentary* 95.

Solvason, BTR, 'Institutional evolution in the Icelandic Commonwealth' (1993) 4(1) *Constitutional Political Economy* 97.

Somek, A, *The Legal Relation: Legal Theory After Legal Positivism* (Cambridge, Cambridge University Press, 2017).

Sommerville, J, *Thomas Hobbes: Political Ideas in Historical Context* (New York, St Martin's Press, 1992).

Soper, EP, 'Legal Theory and the Obligation of a Judge: The Hart/Dworkin Dispute' (1977) 75(3) *Michigan Law Review* 473.

Sordi, B, 'Rèvolution, Rechtsstaat and the Rule of Law: historical reflections on the emergence of administrative law' in S Rose-Ackerman and PL Lindseth (eds), *Comparative Administrative Law* (Cheltenham, Edward Elgar, 2010) 23–37.

Spaak, T, 'Norms that Confer Competences' (2003) 16(1) *Ratio Juris* 89.

—— 'Legal Positivism, Law's Normativity, and the Normative Force of Legal Justification' (2003) 16(4) *Ratio Juris* 469.

—— 'Principled and Pragmatic Theories of Legal Reasoning', in A Fogelklou and T Spaak (eds), *Festskrift till Åke Frändberg* (Uppsala, Iustus Forlag 2003) 235–62.

—— *Guidance and Constraint: The Action-Guiding Capacity of Theories of Legal Reasoning* (Uppsala, Iustus, 2007).

—— 'Book Review: Brian Leiter, Naturalizing Jurisprudence' (2008) 74(4) *Theoria* 352.

—— 'Naturalism in Scandinavian and American Realism: Similarities and Differences' in P Asp and M Dahlberg (eds), *Uppsala-Minnesota Colloquium: Law, Culture and Values, De Lege 2009* (Uppsala, Iustus 2009) 33–83.

—— 'Realism about the Nature of Law' (2017) 30(1) *Ratio Juris* 75.

Stanley, J, 'Making it Articulated' (2002) 17(1–2) *Mind & Language* 149.

Stark, F, 'It's Only Words: On Meaning and Mens Rea' (2013) 72(1) *Cambridge Law Journal* 155.

Stein, PG, 'The Roman Jurists' Conception of Law', in A Padovani and PG Stein (eds), *The Jurists' Philosophy of Law from Rome to the Seventeenth Century, A Treatise of Legal Philosophy and General Jurisprudence*, vol 7 (Dordrecht, Springer, 2007) 1–30.

Stone Sweet, A, *Governing with Judges: Constitutional Politics in Europe* (Oxford, Oxford University Press, 2000).

—— 'Why Europe Rejected American Judicial Review – and Why it May Not Matter' (2003) 101(8) *Michigan Law Review* 2744.

Stone, M, 'Focusing the Law: What Legal Interpretation is Not' in A Marmor (ed), *Law and Interpretation: Essays in Legal Philosophy* (Oxford, Clarendon Press, 1995) 31–94.

—— 'Judicial Review Without Rights: Some Problems for the Democratic Legitimacy of Structural Judicial Review' [2008] *Oxford Journal of Legal Studies* 1.

—— 'Putting political constitutionalism in its place?: A reply to Cormac Mac Amhlaigh' (2016) 14(1) *International Journal of Constitutional Law* 198.

Bibliography   305

Straumann, B, *Crisis and Constitutionalism: Roman Political Thought from the Fall of the Republic to the Age of Revolution* (Oxford, Oxford University Press, 2016).

Sultany, N, 'The State of Progressive Constitutional Theory: The Paradox of Constitutional Democracy and the Project of Political Justification' (2012) 47(2) *Harvard Civil Rights-Civil Liberties Law Review* 371.

Supperstone, M, Goudie, J and Walker P, *Supperstone, Goudie and Walker: Judicial Review*, 4th edn (H Fenwick ed, London, LexisNexis, 2010).

Surden, H, 'The Variable Determinacy Thesis' (2011) 12 *The Columbia Science and Technology Law Review* 1.

Taggart, M, '"Australian Exceptionalism" in Judicial Review' (2008) 36(1) *Federal Law Review* 1.

Tamanaha, BZ, *A General Jurisprudence of Law and Society* (Oxford, Oxford University Press, 2001).

—— *Beyond the Formalist-Realist Divide: The Role of Politics in Judging* (Princeton, Princeton University Press, 2009).

—— 'Balanced Realism on Judging' (2010) 44(4) *Valparaiso University Law Review* 1243.

—— *A Realistic Theory of Law* (Cambridge, Cambridge University Press, 2017).

Tarello, G, *L'interpretazione della legge* (Milan, Giuffrè, 1980).

Taylor, RB, 'The Contested Constitution: An Analysis of the Competing Models of British Constitutionalism' [2018] *Public Law* 500.

Thaler, R and Sunstein, CR, *Nudge: Improving Decisions About Health, Wealth, and Happiness* (New Haven, Yale University Press, 2008).

Thornhill, C, *A Sociology of Constitutions: Constitutions and State Legitimacy in Historical-Sociological Perspective* (Cambridge, Cambridge University Press, 2011).

Tiersma, PM, *Legal Language* (Chicago, University of Chicago Press, 1999).

—— 'A Message in a Bottle: Text, Autonomy, and Statutory Interpretation' (2001) 76(2) *Tulane Law Review* 431.

—— 'A History Of The Languages of Law' in LM Solan and PM Tiersma (ed), *The Oxford Handbook of Language and Law* (Oxford, Oxford University Press, 2012) 13–26.

Tocqueville, A, *Democracy in America* (G Bevan trans, Penguin Classic, 2003).

Tomasello, M, *A Natural History of Human Morality* (Cambridge, Harvard University Press, 2016).

Tomkins, A, 'Review: In Defence of the Political Constitution' (2002) 22(1) *Oxford Journal of Legal Studies* 157.

—— *Our Republican Constitution* (London, Hart Publishing, 2005).

Treves, GE, 'Administrative Discretion and Judicial Control' (1947) 10(3) *Modern Law Review* 276.

Troper, M, *La Théorie du Droit, le Droit, l'Etat* (Paris, Presses Universitaires de France, 2001).

Tushnet, MV, 'Following the Rules Laid Down: A Critique of Interpretivism and Neutral Principles' (1983) 96(4) *Harvard Law Review* 781.

—— 'Critical Legal Studies and Constitutional Law: An Essay in Deconstruction' (1984) 36(1/2) *Stanford Law Review* 623.

—— 'A Note on the Revival of Textualism in Constitutional Theory' (1985) 58(2) *Southern California Law Review* 683.

—— 'Critical Legal Theory' in MP Golding and WA Edmundson (eds), *The Blackwell Guide to the Philosophy of Law and Legal Theory* (Malden, Blackwell Publishing, 2005) 80–89.

Tuzet, G, 'What Is Wrong with Legal Realism?' in D Canale and G Tuzet (eds), *The Planning Theory of Law: A Critical Reading* (Dordrecht, Springer, 2013) 47–63.

Twining, W, 'A Post-Westphalian Concept of Law' (2003) 37(1) *Law and Society Review* 199.

Ursin, E, 'The Missing Normative Dimension in Brian Leiter's Reconstructed Legal Realism' (2012) 49(1) *San Diego Law Review* 1.

—— 'Clarifying the Normative Dimension of Legal Realism: The Example of Holmes's The Path of the Law' (2012) 49(2) *San Diego Law Review* 487.

Valentini, L, 'Ideal vs. Non-ideal Theory: A Conceptual Map' (2012) 7(9) *Philosophy Compass* 654.

306   Bibliography

van der Berge L, 'Montesquieu and Judicial Review of Proportionality in Administrative Law: Rethinking the Separation of Powers in the Neoliberal Era' (2017) 10(1) *European Journal of Legal Studies* 203.

van der Rijt, J, 'Coercive Interference and Moral Judgment' (2011) 14(5) *Ethical Theory and Moral Practice* 549.

Van Hoecke, M, *Law as Communication* (London, Hart Publishing, 2002).

Vasoli, C, 'Introduzione', in Marsilio da Padova, *Il Difensore della pace* (C Vasoli ed, Turin, UTET, 1960).

Velluzzi, V, 'Interpretazione degli enunciati normativi linguaggio giuridico, certezza del diritto' (2008) 3 *Criminalia: Annuario di scienze penalistiche* 493.

—— *Le Preleggi e L'interpretazione: Un'Introduzione Critica* (Pisa, Edizioni ETS, 2013).

Versteeg, M and Zackin, E, 'American Constitutionalism Exceptionalism Revisited' (2014) 81(4) *The University of Chicago Law Review* 1641.

—— and Zackin, E, 'Constitutions Unentrenched: Toward an Alternative Theory of Constitutional Design' (2016) 110(4) *American Political Science Review* 657.

Vignudelli A, 'Sulla Separazione dei Poteri nel Diritto Vigente' (2007) 7 *Diritto & Questioni Pubbliche* 201.

Vile, MJC, *Constitutionalism and the Separation of Powers*, 2nd edn (first published 1967, Carmel, Liberty Fund, 1998).

Villa, V 'Le Tre Concezioni dell'interpretazione Giuridica' in G Pino, A Schiavello and V Villa (eds), *Filosofia del Diritto: Introduzione critica al pensiero giuridico e al diritto positivo* (Turin, Giappichelli, 2013) 289–315.

Vinx, L, *Hans Kelsen's Pure Theory of Law: Legality and Legitimacy* (Oxford, Oxford University Press, 2007).

—— 'Republicanism and Judicial Review' (2009) 59(4) *University of Toronto Law Journal* 591.

Vlastos, G, 'Isonomia' (1953) 74(4) *The American Journal of Philology* 337.

Wade W, and Forsyth, CF, *Administrative Law*, 10th edn (Oxford, Oxford University Press, 2009).

Waismann, F, 'Symposium: Verifiability' (1945) 19 *Proceedings of the Aristotelian Society, Supplementary Volume* 119.

Waldron, J, 'A Right-Based Critique of Constitutional Rights (1993) 13(1) *Oxford Journal of Legal Studies* 18.

—— 'All We Like Sheep' (1999) 12(1) *Canadian Journal of Law & Jurisprudence* 169.

—— *Law and Disagreement* (Oxford, Oxford University Press, 1999).

—— 'The Core of the Case Against Judicial Review' (2006) 115(6) *Yale Law Journal* 1346.

—— 'Separation of Powers in Thought and Practice' (2013) 54 *Boston College Law Review* 433.

Waline J, and Rivero, J, *Droit administratif*, 19th edn (Paris, Dalloz, 2002).

Walker, G De Q, 'The Unwritten Constitution' (2002) 27 *Australian Journal of Legal Philosophy* 144.

Walker, N, 'Review: Sword and Scales: An Examination of the Relationship between Law and Politics' [2001] *Public Law* 644.

—— 'Constitutionalism and the Incompleteness of Democracy' (2010) 39(3) *Rechtsfilosofie & Rechtstheorie* 206.

Walther, M, 'Natural Law, Civil Law, and International Law in Spinoza' (2003) 25(2) Cardozo Law Review 657.

Waluchow, WJ, 'Strong Discretion' (1983) 33(133) *The Philosophical Quarterly* 321.

Warner, R, 'Legal Pragmatism' in D Patterson (ed), *A Companion to Philosophy of Law and Legal Theory, Blackwell Companions to Philosophy*, 2nd edn (Chichester, Wiley-Blackwell, 2010) 406–14.

Watzlawick, P, Beavin, JH and Jackson, DD, *Pragmatics of Human Communication: A Study of Interactional Patterns, Pathologies, and Paradoxes* (London, Faber, 1968).

Weber, M, *Economy and Society: An Outline of Interpretive Sociology*, 4th edn, vol 2 (G Roth and C Wittich eds, Berkeley, University of California Press, 1978).

Weinberger, O, 'The Norm as Thought and as Reality' in N MacCormick and O Weinberger, *An Institutional Theory of Law: New Approaches to Legal Positivism* (Dordrecht, Springer, 1986).

Bibliography 307

Weinrib, EJ, 'Legal Formalism: On the Immanent Rationality of Law' (1988) 97(6) *Yale Law Journal* 949.

Weinshall-Margel, K and Shapard J, 'Overlooked factors in the analysis of parole decisions' (2011) 108(42) *Proceedings of the National Academy of Sciences* E833.

Westerman, P, 'Validity: The Reputation of Rules' in P Westerman, J Hage, S Kirste and AR Mackor (eds), *Legal Validity and Soft Law* (Cham, Springer International Publishing, 2018) 165–82.

Wheare, KC *Modern Constitutions*, 2nd edn (London, Oxford University Press 1966).

White, MJ, *Political Philosophy: An Historical Introduction*, 2nd edn (Oxford, Oxford University Press, 2012).

Whittington, KE, Kelemen, RD and Caldeira, GA, 'The Study of Law and Politics' in GA Caldeira, RD Kelemen and KE Whittington (eds), *The Oxford Handbook of Law and Politics* (Oxford, Oxford University Press, 2008).

Wilkinson, MA, 'Between Freedom and Law: Hannah Arendt on the Promise of Modern Revolution and the Burden of 'The Tradition', in M Goldoni and C McCorkindale (eds), Hannah Arendt and the Law (Oxford, Hart Publishing, 2012) 35–62.

Williams, DGT, 'Law and Administrative Discretion' (1994) 2(1) *Indiana Journal of Global Legal Studies* 191.

Wilson D and Sperber, D, 'Relevance Theory' in LR Horn and G Ward (eds), *The Handbook of Pragmatics* (Oxford, Blackwell Publishing, 2004) 607–32.

Wilson, W, 'The Study of Administration' (1887) 2(2) *Political Science Quarterly* 197.

Wintgens, LJ, 'Legisprudence as a New Theory of Legislation' (2006) 19(1) *Ratio Juris* 1.

—— *Legisprudence: Practical Reason in Legislation* (Farnham, Ashgate, 2012).

Wittgenstein, L, *On Certainty* (GEM Anscombe and GH von Wright eds, Oxford, Basil Blackwell, 1969).

—— *Philosophical Investigations*, rev. 4th edn (PMS Hacker and J Schulte eds, Chichester, Wiley-Blackwell, 2009).

Wolff, J *An Introduction to Political Philosophy*, 3rd edn (Oxford, Oxford University Press, 2015).

Woolf H and others (eds), *De Smith's Judicial Review*, 6th edn (London, Sweet & Maxwell, 2007).

Wróblewski, J, 'Legal Decision and Its Justification' (1971) 14(53–54) *Logique et Analyse* 409.

—— *The Judicial Application of Law* (Z Bankowski and N MacCormick eds, Dordrecht, Springer, 1992).

Xanthaki, H, *Drafting Legislation: Art and Technology of Rules for Regulation* (Oxford, Hart Publishing, 2014).

Yablon, CM, 'Law and Metaphysics' (1987) 96 *Yale Law Journal* 613.

Yoffee, N, *Myths of the Archaic State: Evolution of the Earliest Cities, States, and Civilizations* (Cambridge, Cambridge University Press, 2005).

Zamboni, M, *Law and Politics: A Dilemma for Contemporary Legal Theory* (Berlin/Heidelberg, Springer, 2007).

—— *The Policy of Law, A Legal Theoretical Framework* (London, Hart Publishing, 2007).

Zimmerman, A, 'Constitutions Without Constitutionalism: The Failure of Constitutionalism in Brazil' in M Sellers (ed), *The Rule of Law in Comparative Perspective* (Dordrecht, Springer, 2010).

ONLINE SOURCES

Alvarez, M, 'Reasons for Action: Justification, Motivation, Explanation' in EN Zalta (ed) *The Stanford Encyclopedia of Philosophy* (Winter 2017 Edition), http://plato.stanford.edu/archives/win2017/entries/reasons-just-vs-expl/.

Balaguer, M, 'Platonism in Metaphysics' in EN Zalta (ed), *The Stanford Encyclopedia of Philosophy* (Summer 2009 Edition) http://plato.stanford.edu/archives/sum2009/entries/platonism/.

Christiano, T, 'Authority' in EN Zalta (ed) *The Stanford Encyclopedia of Philosophy* (Summer 2020 Edition) http://plato.stanford.edu/archives/sum2020/entries/authority/.

308   *Bibliography*

—— 'Democracy' in EN Zalta (ed), *The Stanford Encyclopedia of Philosophy* (Fall 2018 Edition) http://plato.stanford.edu/entries/democracy/.

Davis, W, 'Implicature' in EN Zalta (ed), *The Stanford Encyclopedia of Philosophy* (Fall 2019 Edition) http://plato.stanford.edu/archives/fall2019/entries/implicature.

Endicott, T 'Law and Language' in EN Zalta (ed), *The Stanford Encyclopedia of Philosophy* (Summer 2016 Edition) http://plato.stanford.edu/archives/sum2016/entries/law-language/.

Forowicz, M, 'State Discretion as a Paradox of EU Evolution' (2011) EUI Working Paper 11/2011 http://cadmus.eui.eu/handle/1814/18835 accessed 14 July 2012.

Grandy, RE and Warner, R, 'Paul Grice' in EN Zalta (ed), *The Stanford Encyclopedia of Philosophy* (Fall 2013 Edition) plato.stanford.edu/archives/fall2013/entries/grice/.

Green, L, 'Law and the Causes of Judicial Decisions' (2009) Oxford Legal Studies Research Paper 14/2009, formerly available at http://papers.ssrn.com/abstract=1374608 accessed 31 March 2012, on file with author.

Green, M, 'Speech Acts' in EN Zalta (ed), *The Stanford Encyclopedia of Philosophy* (Winter 2020 Edition) http://plato.stanford.edu/archives/win2020/entries/speech-acts/.

Hickman, T, 'The Use and Misuse of Guidance during the UK's Coronavirus Lockdown' (September 4, 2020). Available at SSRN: http://papers.ssrn.com/sol3/papers.cfm?abstract_id=3686857 accessed 10 March 2021.

Huq, A, 'A Distinctively American Doctrine: Review of The Three Branches: A Comparative Model of Separation of Powers, by Christoph Möllers' (*The New Rambler*, 25 November 2015) http://newramblerreview.com/book-reviews/law/a-distinctively-american-doctrine accessed 12 November 2020.

Korta, K and Perry, J, 'Pragmatics' in EN Zalta (ed), *The Stanford Encyclopedia of Philosophy* (Spring 2020 Edition) http://plato.stanford.edu/archives/spr2020/entries/pragmatics/.

Lamond, G, 'Precedent and Analogy in Legal Reasoning' in EN Zalta (ed), *The Stanford Encyclopedia of Philosophy* (Spring 2016 Edition) http://plato.stanford.edu/archives/spr2016/entries/legal-reas-prec/.

Leiter, B, 'Naturalism in Legal Philosophy', *The Stanford Encyclopedia of Philosophy* (Fall 2012 Edition) http://plato.stanford.edu/archives/fall2012/entries/lawphil-naturalism/.

Lexico, 'Definition of communication' (Oxford University Press- Lexico.com, 30 April 2021) www.lexico.com/definition/communication accessed 30 April 2021.

Lord Neuberger, 'The British and Europe' (Cambridge Freshfields Annual Law Lecture, Cambridge, 12 February 2014) http://resources.law.cam.ac.uk/privatelaw/Cambridge_Freshfields_Annual_Law_Lecture_2014_Lord_Neuberger_The_British_and_Europe.pdf.

Miller, A, 'Realism' in EN Zalta (ed), The Stanford Encyclopedia of Philosophy (Spring 2012 Edition) http://plato.stanford.edu/archives/spr2012/entries/realism/.

Miller, F, 'Aristotle's Political Theory' in EN Zalta (ed), *The Stanford Encyclopedia of Philosophy* (Winter 2017 Edition) http://plato.stanford.edu/entries/aristotle-politics/.

Peter, F, 'Political Legitimacy' in EN Zalta (ed), *The Stanford Encyclopedia of Philosophy* (Summer 2017 Edition) http://plato.stanford.edu/archives/sum2017/entries/legitimacy/.

Ravenscroft, I, 'Folk Psychology as a Theory' in EN Zalta (ed), *The Stanford Encyclopedia of Philosophy* (Fall 2010 Edition) http://plato.stanford.edu/archives/fall2010/entries/folkpsych-theory/.

Steinberg, J, 'Spinoza's Political Philosophy' in EN Zalta (ed), *The Stanford Encyclopedia of Philosophy* (Spring 2009 Edition) http://plato.stanford.edu/archives/spr2009/entries/spinoza-political/.

Szabó, ZB, 'Compositionality' in EN Zalta (ed), *The Stanford Encyclopedia of Philosophy* (Fall 2020 Edition) http://plato.stanford.edu/archives/fall2020/entries/compositionality/.

Waldron, J, 'The Rule of Law', in EN Zalta (ed), *The Stanford Encyclopedia of Philosophy* (Summer 2020 Edition) http://plato.stanford.edu/archives/sum2020/entries/rule-of-law/.

Waluchow, W, 'Constitutionalism' in EN Zalta (ed), *The Stanford Encyclopedia of Philosophy* (Spring 2018 Edition) http://plato.stanford.edu/entries/constitutionalism/.

Young, A, 'Prorogation, Politics and the Principle of Legality' (*UK Constitutional Law Association Blog*, 13 September 2019) http://ukconstitutionallaw.org/2019/09/13/alison-young-prorogation-politics-and-the-principle-of-legality/ accessed 12 March 2021.

Index

A

Action-guidance
see also **Political autonomy**
  application in different areas of law 176
  indeterminacy of law 184
  law in a modern democratic system 172
  preference for literal meaning as a
      conceptual necessity 201
  science of legislation 200
  theory of legal interpretation 170
Administration
  accommodation within the separation of
      powers doctrine 281 fn 107
  and the growth of discretionary
      powers 143
Administrative decisions
  see also **Judicial review**
  delimiting the scope of law creation 3–4
  judicial discretion
    decisions involving basic rights 145
    English administrative law 152–158
    French-Italian tradition 149–152
    German administrative law 145–149
    principle of legality 144–145
  legitimacy of judicial review 45
  scope of judicial review 8–9
  unified approach to judicial
      discretion 161–162
Application of law
  asymmetry between norm-following and
      norm-application 231–234
  creation of law distinction
    'action-guiding' requirement of
      constitutional democracies 17–18
    crucial component of political
      theory 2–3
    formal and substantive
      requirements 6–7
    tension in legal discourse 1
    theoretical perspectives 1–2
  dependence of constitutional democracy on
      application of law
    common law model of
      constitutionalism 72
    comparative constitutional
      scholarship 74

    contestable nature of constitutional
      reasoning 74
    dilemma facing political
      constitutionalists 78–79
    distinction between the creation and
      application of law constitutive of
      legitimacy 71
    importance of 'self-determination' 76
    legal constitutionalism 72
    legitimacy of judicial supremacy 74
    ordinary and constitutional
      adjudication 72–74
    theories of legitimacy 76–78
  discretionary application of law 8
  dominant position of officials in a legal
      system 237–240
  dyadic structure of modern constitutional
      democracy 211
  English administrative law 158
  importance of distinguishing from creation
      of law
    legitimacy of courts in performing
      judicial review 45
    misrepresentations of existing
      arrangements in legal and political
      analysis 46
  Kelsen's *Stufenbaulehre* 134–135
  meaning of
    bound and discretionary
      (substantive) law application
      distinguished 242–243
    courts as law-applying institutions 244
    equivalence of application of
      provisions and the application of
      norms 229–230
    formal and substantive law 240–241
    internal and external applicability 229
    judicial decisions 230–231
    Kelsen's 'relativity' thesis 216–219
    language and interpretation 244–245
    legality as a meta-norm 222–227
    positivist defence of distinction from
      law-creation 214–216
    rejection of legal formalism 213–214
    substantive or material
      requirements 241

310 *Index*

modern constitutional democracies 170
no contrast with legal
    interpretation 208–209
normative doctrine of the organisation of
    political power 278–281
power conferring norms 234–237
square of law-application 243
theories of law and adjudication 110–115

Authority
see also **Political power**
and text-acts 195
as source of law instead of reason 48
conditions of existence 36–42
different from isonomia 33
law's claims to 106
problems of legitimation and
    limitation 60–61
relationship with constitutions 56
relationship with law 24, 26–30, 51–55
relationship with writing 44

B
'Billiard ball model' of legitimacy 76–78
Bound law-application 7–8, 243

C
Checks and balances
as a theoretically redundant
    expression 280–81
Waldron's definition 267

Coercion
as negation of the agency of the
    individual 270

Collective autonomy
application of law 231
conflicting claims within political
    order 271
creation of normative standards 202
effect of distinguishing creation and
    application of law 208
indeterminacy of law 184
law in a modern democratic system 172
legal interpretation as a conceptual
    necessity 201
legitimation of public powers 283
normative-institutional tension 211
separation of powers 281
square of law-application 243
theory of legal interpretation 170

Constitutional democracy
application of law 170
and connection with separation of
    powers 260–261

creation and application of law 2–3
dependence on application of law
  common law model of
    constitutionalism 72
  comparative constitutional
    scholarship 74
  contestable nature of constitutional
    reasoning 74
  demand of identity 78
  dilemma facing political
    constitutionalists 78–79
  importance of 'self-determination' 76
  legal constitutionalism 72
  legitimacy of judicial supremacy 74
  ordinary and constitutional
    adjudication 72–74
  theories of legitimacy 76–78
dyadic structure of modern constitutional
    democracy 211

Constitutional review
and alternative systems 71
distinction from judicial supremacy
    66 fn 146
global spread 45
normative legitimacy 74–75

Constitutionalism
duality of law as *lex* and *ius*
  development and practice of the English
    common law 52–53
  emergence of second type of law in the
    Roman Republic 51–52, 245
  necessity of separating constitutions
    from constitutionalism 55
  paradigmatic shift in Schiavone's
    account 53–54
  relationship between law and political
    power 50–51, 245
  search for a Roman
    'constitution' 54–55
dyadic structure of modern constitutional
    democracy 211
'government limited by law' 59–60
as 'legal otherness'
  common law and Commonwealth models
    of constitutionalism 65–68
  entrenchment of a constitutional
    document 68–69
  juridical limitation of law 69
  legal constitutionalism 64–65
  normative theory 70–71
tension with democracy
  identifying the social contract 62–63
  legitimation problem 60–61

Index 311

multi-levelled relationship 63–64
reconciliation of majority rule with
autonomy of minorities 61–62
Constitutions
'doubly normative character' 55
duality of law as *lex* and *ius*
necessity of separating constitutions
from constitutionalism 55
search for a Roman 'constitution' 54–55
Grey's classification of constitutional
norms 57–58
historical constitutions and state
'blueprints' distinguished 56
stratified history of the term
'constitution' 56
three common ways of distinguishing
constitutions 56–58
Cooperation
ultimate function of formal rules 2, 35–40
Creation of law
and application of law distinguished
'action-guiding' requirement of
constitutional democracies 17–18
formal and substantive requirement 6–7
creation of normative standards 169–170
delimiting the scope of law creation
approach to discretion 3–4
judicial decisions 3
theories in philosophy of language 4
dyadic structure of modern constitutional
democracy 211
Kelsen's *Stufenbaulehre* 133–135
meaning of
courts as law-creating institutions 244
creation recognisable as such by its
addressees 222–223
Kelsen's 'relativity' thesis 216–219
legality as a meta-norm 222–227
only those acts that establish a new
norm 219–222
positivist defence of law-application
distinction 214–216
recognisable as such by its
addressees 222–223
rejection of the ideology of
legal reasoning known as
formalism 213–214
normative doctrine of the organisation of
political power 278–281
separation of powers 270
Critical legal scholarship (CLS)
adjudication as illegitimate decision-making
process 94

contested relationship between law and
politics 49–50
dependence of constitutional democracy on
application of law 74
distinction between creation and
application of law 1–2
history and development of legal
realism 80
radical-transcendental indeterminacy
thesis 95–97

D
Democracy
see also **Constitutional democracy; Collective
autonomy**
as self-rule 76
incompleteness 63
isonomia distinguished 32–34
procedural and substantive
conceptions 2–3
tension with constitutionalism
identifying the social contract 62–63
legitimation problem 60–61
multi-levelled relationship 63–64
reconciliation of majority rule with
autonomy of minorities 61–62
Determinacy
as result of the evolution of normative
systems 41
of language 124, 182
of law and of adjudication
and certainty 224–225
as the product of two concurrent
axes 242–3
relationship 82–83, 92–108
and rule-following paradox 245–259
Discretion
administrative decisions
decisions involving basic rights 145
English administrative law 152–158
French-Italian tradition 149–152
German administrative law 145–149
principle of legality 144–145
two conflicting trajectories 142–144
Dworkin's no-strong discretion
thesis 128–131
formal and substantive requirement 7–8
Hart/Dworkin debate 116–119
Hart's account of discretion
discretion is 'essential' to the rule of
law 127–128
discretion originates in open-texture of
law 124

312 Index

idea of administrative
  discretion 122–123
inescapable institutional dimension of
  the law-making process 125–126
judicial and administrative
  discretion 123
neglect of administrators and
  administrative law 126–127
as (personal) choice tout court 127
'rule-following paradox' 121–122
three different meanings of
  'discretion' 125
identification and evaluation of systemic
  discretion 9
importance 117, 168
Kelsen's *Stufenbaulehre*
  discretion as penumbra 131–133
  distinction between the creation and
    application of law 134–135
  epistemic problems 135–136
  importance of conformity 133–134
  intended and unintended discretion 133
Klatt's model
  'analytical-normative' analysis 137
  balancing and weighing of
    principles 142
  'clear-cases-necessary-incorporation-
    thesis' 141
  balancing models of discretion 136–140
  structural and epistemic discretion 141
  three models of competence 137–138
'normative' and 'interpretive'
  discretion 159–165

E
English administrative law 152–158

F
Formal requirements
application of law 240–241
distinction between creation and
  application of law 6–7
Klatt's model of judicial discretion
  different kinds of legal
    discretion 138–139
  first scenario of the balancing model of
    discretion 139
  second scenario of the balancing model
    of discretion 140
  three models of competence 137–138
Formalism
German administrative law 146
'mechanical jurisprudence' 82–83, 264

'noble dream theory' 120
overview 12–13
rejection by legal realism
  Hart's contribution 84–85
  Kelsen's contribution 83–84
  'noble dream theory' 82–83
rule-scepticism 91
separation of powers 266
theories of law and adjudication
  distinguished 114
untenable theoretical position 114
French administrative law 149–152

G
German administrative law 145–149

I
Indeterminacy thesis of law
confirmation of the indeterminacy thesis of
  law 85–87
legal realism 92–93
variants of modern scepticism 100–110
meta-theoretical taxonomy of
  rule-scepticism 94–100
Interpretation
see also **Language; Legal communication**
application of a rule is actually an
  interpretation of it 246
cognitive and adjudicative
  interpretation 206–207
descriptive theory of legal
  interpretation 171–172
juxtaposition of 'understanding' and
  'interpreting' 246–247
'rule-following paradox' 121–122, 245–259
text-oriented and fact-oriented 206–207
theory of 205–209
Isonomia
democracy distinguished 32–34
equality in a normative order 34–35
'living reality' in city-states of Ionia 33–34
reconciliation of freedom and equality 34
rules but no rule 34
Italian administrative law 149–152
Intention
in following versus applying a
  norm 232–237
of the legislator
  guiding principle in reviewing the
    exercise of discretion
  as objective intention 196
  rhetorical device in UK public law 70
  in UK administrative law 157

Index   313

of the speaker
  contribution to meaning
    of text-acts   205
  determinative of meaning in ordinary
    speech-act theory   179–184

J
Judicial decisions
  application of law   230–231
  courts as law-applying institutions   244
  deeper juridical core of
    constitutionalism   59
  delimiting the scope of law creation   3
  square of law-application   243
Judicial review
  see also **Administrative decisions**
  adjudication as illegitimate decision-making
    process   94
  confirmation of the indeterminacy thesis of
    law   85–87
  English administrative law   153
  legal realism   80–82
  legitimacy of judicial review   45
  ordinary and constitutional
    adjudication   72–74
  scope for judicial review   8–9
  theories of law and adjudication   110–115

L
Language
  see also **Interpretation; Legal
    communication**
  application of law   244–245
  artificial nature of legal language   186
  category of 'administered
    languages'   188–189
  conceptual analysis of law   19
  intentionality of meaning   194
  judicial discretion   168
  law as a component of ordinary
    language   184–185
  law as instrument of social control   208
  legal communication versus ordinary
    communication   185–186
  ordinary and constitutional
    adjudication   72–74
  polysemy of 'power'   28–29
  problem of rule-following   247–259
  relationship between law and
    language   186–190
  rules about how to speak and rules about
    what to say   186
  scope of law creation   4

semantic minimalism   200–205
speech-act theory   190–193
text-act theory   194–200
Law
  application of *see* **Application of law**
  as a communicative enterprise   172–177
  conceptual analysis   19–20
  constitutionalism as 'legal otherness'
    common law and Commonwealth models
      of constitutionalism   65–68
    entrenchment of a constitutional
      document   68–69
    juridical limitation of law   69
    legal model of constitutionalism   64–65
    normative theory   70–71
    progressive acknowledgement of the
      principle of legality   69–70
  contested relationship with politics
    'autonomous' model   47–50
    diachronic and a meta-theoretical
      perspective distinguished   48–49
    embedded model   49–50
    intersecting model   50
    Loughlin's sword and scales   48–49
    major strands of modern jurisprudential
      scholarship   49–50
  creation of law *see* **Creation of law**
  duality of law as *lex* and *ius*
    development and practice of the English
      common law   52–53
    emergence of second type of law in the
      Roman Republic   51–52
    institutionalised setting   68–69
    necessity of separating constitutions
      from constitutionalism   55
    paradigmatic shift in Schiavone's
      account   53–54
    relationship between law and political
      power   50–51, 245
    search for a Roman 'constitution'   54–55
  relationship with political power   27–30,
    50–51, 245
  relationship with politics   23–25, 46–47
  rules about how to speak and rules about
    what to say   186
  theories of law and adjudication   110–115
Legal communication
  see also **Interpretation; Language**
  analysis
    'text-act' theory   5–6
    speech-act theory   4–5
  application of law   245
  pragmatics   170–171

314 Index

category of 'administered
languages' 188–189
law as a communicative
enterprise 172–177
rigid and fixed nature of textual
communication 44
speech-act theory 178–184
text-act theory 209–210
versus ordinary communication 185–186
Legal constructivism 1–2
Legal pluralism
attention to customary orders 40
conceptual analysis of law 19–20
general jurisprudence 10, 23
separation of powers 267, 271–274, 281,
285
Legal realism
contested relationship between law and
politics 49–50
continuity between legal theory and
empirical sciences 21–22
current 'moderate' strand 80
distinction between creation and
application of law 1–2
as a doctrine 87–90
essence of 90–92
history and development 80
mainstream approach to adjudication 80
reaction to formalism
Hart's contribution 84–85
Kelsen's contribution 83–84
'noble dream theory' 82–83
rejection of formalist or cognitivist accounts
of adjudication 81
Legal texts
as 'autonomous' text-acts 195–200
ordinary and constitutional
adjudication 72–74
rigid and fixed nature of textual
communication 44
'text-act' theory 6
Legality (principle of)
dependence on rigorous model of
law-creation 200
formal conception 25–26
French-Italian administrative law
tradition 150
judicial discretion 127–128, 144–145
legal texts as 'autonomous' text-acts
195–196, 199
as a meta-norm for creation and application
of law 222–227
principle of constitutionalism 55

Legitimacy
dependence of constitutional democracy on
application of law 71
French-Italian administrative law
tradition 151
judicial review 45
judicial supremacy 74
nature of any political structure 35–36
political authority 36–37
political power 18
separation of powers 272
tension between democracy and
constitutionalism 60–61
theoretical perspectives 76–78

M
'Mechanical jurisprudence' 82–83, 264
Moderate indeterminacy theses
lightness of modern scepticism 106–110
moderate-immanent indeterminacy
thesis 97–99
moderate-transcendental indeterminacy
thesis 99–100

N
Natural law
contested relationship between law and
politics 49–50
global normative defeasibility of law 95
legal communication 187
realism as a critical reaction to
formalism 49–50
Naturalism
American legal realists 21, 80
judicial decisions 103–107, 109, 111–113
notion of 'power over' 31
Scandinavian realism 96
theories of law and adjudication 113
understanding of legal rules 81
'Noble dream theory' 82–83, 120
Normativity
application of law
asymmetry between norm-following and
norm-application 231–234
dominant position of officials in a legal
system 237–240
equivalence of application of
provisions and the applications of
norms 229–230
power conferring norms 234–237
three key distinctions 228
conditions of existence for political
authority

Index 315

accountability 37–38
customary rules 38–40
generated by certain kinds of rules 37
institutionalisation of secondary
norms 41
primary and secondary norms
distinguished 38
constitutionalism as 'legal
otherness' 70–71
constitutions 55
core of political and legal theory 30–31
creation of law 219–222
creation of normative standards 169–170
duality of law as *lex* and *ius* 53
Dworkin's no-strong discretion thesis 131
German administrative law 146–148
global normative defeasibility of law 95
Grey's classification of constitutional
norms 56–58
interpretation 246–259
legality as a meta-norm for creation and
application of law 222–227
political power 29–30
separation of powers 265–287
text-act theory 195–197
theories of law and
adjudication 110–115
unified approach to judicial
discretion 159–165
Norms
duty-imposing and
power-conferring 234–237
formal
as norms on the production 241
and substantive norms 240–245
practice-independence 39–41

O
Objectivity
of law and legal reasoning
legitimacy of constitutional
democracies 9
and principle of legality 223
relationship with interpretive
discretion 165–67
and rule-scepticism 88–107
and sceptical reading of
Wittgenstein rule-following
considerations 247–254
of linguistic communication
and 'humpty dumptyism' 182
and writing 193
One-right-answer thesis 129–130

P
Political authority
capacity to rule over a certain
population 24
conditions of existence 36–41
duality of law as *lex* and *ius* 50–51
historical constitutions and state
'blueprints' distinguished 56
'ineluctability' of the state 35
mixed blessings 42
non-normative and normative senses of
'power over' 30–31
tension between democracy and
constitutionalism 60–64
Political autonomy
see also **Collective autonomy**
requiring the possibility of
law-application 2
as self-rule 61
ultimate value of democracy 62
Political power
capacity to rule over a certain
population 24
collective decision-making 31–32
importance of distinguishing
between creation and application of
law 18
isonomia 32–35
limitation and legitimation 18
non-normative and normative senses of
'power over' 30–31
relationship with law 27–30, 50–51, 245
separation of powers 271–287
Politics
contested relationship with law 47–50
separation of powers as political
doctrine 266–267
Positivism
contested relationship between law and
politics 49–50
creation and application of law
distinguished 214–216
judicial discretion 128–131
legal communication 187
as a realistic theory of law 105–106
Power *see* **Political power; Separation of
powers**
Pragmatics
legal communication 170–171
semantic minimalism 200–203
speech-act theory 179–193
Procedural requirements *see* **Formal
requirements**

316 *Index*

R

Radical indeterminacy theses
lightness of modern
  scepticism 100–106
radical-immanent indeterminacy
  thesis 94–95
radical-transcendental indeterminacy
  thesis 95–97

Realism *see* **Legal realism**

Reasons for action
and action-guidance 222–26
function of norms 189
and indeterminacy of law 2, 95

Rule of law
common-law development 66–68
and legality distinguished 226–227
premised on law's determinacy 195–196
principle of constitutionalism 55
relationship with concept of law 26
relationship with political constitutionalist
  theories 75–78

Rule-scepticism
essence of legal realism 91
judicial discretion 120–121
meta-theoretical taxonomy of
  rule-scepticism 93–100

Rules *see* **Normativity**

Rule-scepticism
ambiguity with realism 88–89
and cognitivism 111–112
lowest common denominator of legal
  realism 91–100, 120–121
moderate indeterminacy theses 106–110
radical indeterminacy theses 100–106

S

Semantic minimalism
'authorial intention' 205
capacity to communicate complex sets of
  information 203
literal or sentence meaning in legal
  interpretation as a conceptual
  necessity 201–202
need to settle for stable and
  context-invariant level of
  meaning 205
rejection of pragmatic theories to
  law 200–201
role of pragmatic enrichment 202–203
theoretical divide about 'what is
  said' 203–204

Semantics
relationship with pragmatics 179–84

Separation of powers
application of law 214
and constitutional democracy 260–261,
  287
critical scrutiny of doctrine 274–276
delegation of decision-making power 162
dependence on rigorous model of
  law-creation 200
and division of powers 15
Ferrajoli's formal theory 278–81
French-Italian administrative law
  tradition 149–150
Italian administrative law 149
meaning and usefulness as a normative
  doctrine 261–262
origins and development 262–265
paradigm of formalism 83
principle of constitutionalism 55
principle of legality 144
reconstruction of current
  debate 263–287
relation between law and politics 46
twofold meta-theoretical
  ambiguity 265–270

Speech-act theory
alternative contextualist
  model 182–184
analysis of legal communication 4–5
emergence of more systematic theoretical
  awareness 191–193
'formal semantics' and 'radical
  pragmatics' 180–182
legislative speech-acts 178
meaning more than just what is
  said 179–180
pervasive lack of determinacy 190–191

State
and concept of law 24–25
constitutional 69
and customary legal orders 40
expansion 143
pre- or early states 35–36, 44
rejection of Hobbesian theory of its
  ineluctability 30–36
relationship with general
  jurisprudence 10, 19–20

T

'Text-act' theory
analysis of legal communication 5–6
'closed' and 'unilateral' 194–195
correspondence of communicative and
  literal meaning 209–210

legal texts as 'autonomous' text acts
  co-texts   198–199
  codification of entire areas of a legal
        system   199–200
  'combined provisions'   197
  dangers for the rule of law   199
  fallacy of a-discursivity   196–198
  judicial discretion   200
  no shared 'situational' context
        between producers and
        receivers   195

norm sentences   195
rule of law   195–196
semantic minimalism as alternative
      theory   204–205
Texts *see* **Legal texts**
**'Transmission belt model' of
      legitimacy**   76–78

V
Vagueness
  and open-texture distinguished   124

Printed in the USA
CPSIA information can be obtained
at www.ICGtesting.com
LVHW010454170224
772058LV00001B/60